THE MELLON FAMILY

A FORTUNE
IN HISTORY

By Burton Hersh

THE MELLON FAMILY

THE EDUCATION OF EDWARD KENNEDY

THE SKI PEOPLE

THE
MELLON

ANDREW W. MELLON

FAMILY

A FORTUNE IN HISTORY

By BURTON HERSH

WILLIAM MORROW AND COMPANY, INC.

NEW YORK   1978

Library of Congress Cataloging in Publication Data

Hersh, Burton.
    The Mellon family.

    Bibliography: p.
    Includes index.
    1. Mellon family.   I. Title.
HC102.5.M38H47   338′.092′2 [B]   77-18797
ISBN 0-688-03297-4

BOOK DESIGN   CARL WEISS

Printed in the United States of America.

2 3 4 5 6 7 8 9 10

IN MEMORY OF

MARGERY EISEMAN,

WHO MIGHT

HAVE APPRECIATED THIS

PREFACE

FERDINAND LUNDBERG once insisted sixty families rule America. This was in 1936, when conspiracy theories abounded. Lundberg's documentation influenced policy-makers, and thirty years afterward he projected in a systematic way the circles of plutocracy in *The Rich and the Super-Rich*. He'd isolated, Lundberg felt, an elite among these: four constellated ducal families —fixed, yet ubiquitous and permeating, their combined mandate alone sufficient to drag the drift of civilization.

Three names people recognized. Rockefeller. Du Pont. Ford. As concerned the other? The Mellons survived someplace, informed Americans knew that, but—except for one tough, muckraking biography of Andrew Mellon culled from the records early in the Thirties, and now and then a spate of publicity whenever one wayward member had marital problems or another saw fit to expose his French collection—the family's anonymity held. They themselves remained invisible, a kind of clustered White Dwarf, and this was particularly enticing, since after the Second World War most analysts would agree that, among the surviving megafortunes, theirs now was supreme. By 1957 a chart in *Fortune* would identify the richest of the rich. Within the uppermost two categories—people whose estimated estates ran certifiably between four hundred million and a billion dollars—*Fortune* pinpointed eight individuals. Four entries were Mellons; a fifth, Arthur Vining Davis, Mellon banking developed. No other American family was represented twice.

Could these people truly remain this inaccessible? The spring of 1973, fortified by a publisher's advance, I reconnoitered their defenses. I'd attempted something similar throughout the turn of the Sixties, while compiling what became *The Education of Edward Kennedy*. The Kennedys operated politically, there were publicity mechanisms, yet here, too, I found out quickly enough, nobody on the inside was eager at all to permit anybody unfamiliar to glimpse what genuinely mattered. I kept moving around, months passed, and ultimately it developed, in the enlarging confusion, that everybody lost track of what I was aware of and what I wasn't; and whatever I needed, I got.

This is no place to go into detail about how I insinuated myself finally among the purlieus of the Mellons, beyond noting that congeniality played some part, as well as gall. "What are you asking for *now*, Burton, a copy of my will?" Paul Mellon broke out one morning quite recently. By then I was.

There is a paradigmatic little theater piece by Max Frisch, *The Firebugs*, which concerns the materialization of two self-possessed and implacable young thugs within the attic of the apprehensive bourgeois Biedermann. It is arson season. Soon, despite Biedermann's torturous misgivings, he finds himself supporting these busy, inexorable striplings, lugging food up there, then tinder, soon gasoline, and in the end he supplies his intruders their necessary match. There have been times, as the surviving Mellons, their friends, their critical employees gave in and agreed to talk with me, submitted photographs, found documents, when I increasingly sensed that the pent-up silence of a century had gradually become insupportable. The fortune was musty now, heavy against the conscience. Out came the scandals, the hatreds, the infatuations, the absurdities, the manipulations— they piled up quickly, all combustibles, with much in each situation I couldn't—wouldn't—use. I merely happened along. Each had his match all ready.

Still, again and again, following this history through, I bumped against suspicions that I was recapitulating not merely the cycle of a fortune but increasingly—more importantly—the confessions of a *caste*, of one generation upon another of largely unconscious seekers after mystical possibilities in America. In its paradoxical way, materialism too represents an era's struggle to transcend the mundane, the hidebound. Ours is a religious age—the end of a religious age—and for a century now people like the Mellons have borne with the worries and privileges each culture traditionally accords its priests. Their fatigues are ours.

BURTON HERSH

Bradford, New Hampshire
August, 1977

CONTENTS

BOOK II

INTRODUCTION

THE SUMMER OF 1932 was undoubtedly our worst. Banks failed; grocery store proprietors and automobile manufacturers stumbled together into bankruptcy; the unending prairie soil appeared to give the country up, parched out, blew off like talcum powder and left even flourishing counties hardpan. All elements somehow reversed.

Agony was universal. In Chicago, the winter just past, authorities permitted the jobless to burn the wooden paving blocks to keep from freezing. The aghastness and confusion of all the previous months now coalesced as grievance. The President in Washington, digging in both heels, was keeping his convictions as firm as that flat solar plexus against which he was forever encouraging his surviving Cabinet members to heave a medicine ball. Uncomplicated people, who had their difficulties comprehending Mr. Hoover's exceptional integrity, tended to blame *him* for all the anxiety and helplessness. The President appeared peevish but forbearing.

Insiders laid blame elsewhere. Hoover took things over, according to the emerging rationale, but that ubiquitous poltergeist who set them up for so much punishment had already stolen away. Stolen what they had away—depressions demand plain speaking. Mellon. Whatever develops, fault Mellon.

Mellon hadn't seemed historical. He'd seemed an accident, a worn-looking little old gentleman from Pittsburgh his valet dressed neatly every morning and released to join the double-breasted Wall Street diplomacy amateurs and the obesity victims from Ohio who Warren Harding imagined might comprise a Government. Mellon lasted. Before Coolidge accepted control, the narrow, long, closely molded Scottish skull of Andrew W. Mellon was everywhere familiar; millions could already identify the aged Treasurer with such a sculpted droop about the eyelids it made him look at you with a kind of sleepy dazzle, confounding, observing less and more than anybody anticipated.

He became an archetype. Legendary—rumor had it, the world's wealthiest individual, and mantled under whatever *that* implied throughout furtively Protestant America. He brought treasure—he could generate treasure, he bestowed of grace. William Allen White, bitter in the aftermath, would label the Treasurer an unmitigated "bad angel. Under his halo he smiled a wan, detached, other-worldly fishy-eyed benediction on the raging bulls in the pit. . . ." White subsequently observed.

That was years afterward. Later everything seemed unfair. Children of the Okies gnawed tumbleweed roots to assuage dry fever. The unemployed wore sacks for trousers and jostled municipality breadlines. Brokers splashed across pavements.

From the embassy residence, Morgan's donation off Prince's Gate, the newly designated United States Ambassador to the English, Andrew Mellon, never saw any bulletins about that. The elusive old gentleman was fitfully observed, calm, passing the time at royal luncheon parties and unhurried perusals of the great British art collections. The inestimable Mellon holdings too, muckrakers shrilled, bypassed the general disaster. "By some magic the keystone of the Mellon financial structure was unaffected by the catastrophic wave of failures which closed 5,096 banks between January 1, 1930, and December 31, 1932," maintains Harvey O'Connor, not pleased at all.

The financier languished. In Pittsburgh, where doors stayed closed, that handful of industrial retainers genuinely intimate with the Mellons' affairs were attempting each in his way to contain utter panic. They were misleading O'Connor; that wasn't much compensation as they stood around, increasingly upset, while wave after wave of disastrous market quotations rolled over the Alleghenies. Hadn't they anticipated this? Assets of the Aluminum Company were huge. Capital funds quietly earmarked for Gulf were likely to see the oil company through even this wild cycle no matter which trend carried. Even their utilities pyramid, Koppers, still manifested every likelihood of stabilizing upon its engineering reputation. Their banks had prepared.

Yet throughout that sticky depression summer of 1932 the expectation of ruin, the extinction of everything they had, was constantly so close it seemed to members of the family a presence they might at any time touch—waiting, hot, specific enough to fondle. And such an absurdity—who expected it there? Such risks, routinely taken, and suddenly the overlooked Gulf bond offering they'd collateralized with family securities affected whatever they'd developed, exercised its automatic lien upon virtually every cell of their unblemished gigantic corporate body.

In exile in London, musing, the genius who engendered it all was indulging his characteristically longer view. Ruin really seemed inconceivable. They'd simply carried Nature out; they certainly hadn't deviated—fundamentally. Richard, his brother, who looked after day-to-day matters as things came up in Pittsburgh, would keep him informed. They invariably came through. Whenever things weren't self-evident they'd always simply asked each other, "Well, what do you think Father would have done?" which very often eased things. They could comfortably guess—the Judge was remorselessly consistent—yet mentioning the old fellow's name could calm the nerves like stroking a rabbit's foot. Familiar touch, hidden bone—everything became more legitimate.

Pittsburgh seemed so far.

BOOK

The normal condition of man is hard work, self-denial,
acquisition and accumulation; and as soon as his descendants are freed from the necessity of such exertion
they begin to degenerate sooner or later in both body
and mind.

—THOMAS MELLON, 1885

The rich don't need to kill to eat. They give employment
to people, as the saying goes.

—LOUIS-FERDINAND CÉLINE, 1932
Journey to the End of the Night

1 | THE JUDGE

1

WHAT *Father* WOULD have done. Right! Father, their Founder, the *Judge,* as the old rectitudinarian liked to be called decades after he abandoned the Allegheny County Court of Common Pleas. How Father reasoned, the direction Father would have selected for all of them to stumble in hopes of averting this financial mudslide . . .

Except that—Andrew knew, of course. He would have been peckish about where all this was likely to leave the country but pleased with himself that events had inevitably borne out even his long-range worries. "I fear that if degeneracy progresses at the same rate a catastrophe will be reached before the end of another half century," Father prophesied in 1885. "I am not alone in these views of the situation, and can scarcely hope to be mistaken."

How like Father. Scrawny little thing, hobbling into the bank mornings to dictate those pestilential memoirs of his, the Judge was still so sure of himself it saddened him that whatever he anticipated must occur. Busy, nobody in the family had really been paying enough attention to what the old party was up to in that back office he retained behind the banking rooms. Even when his privately issued remembrance appeared in 1885, a formidable tome bound handsomely in dried-blood-colored pebble-grained Leatherette. *Thomas Mellon and His Times,* "Printed for his family and descendants exclusively." Its author bustled around Pittsburgh distributing copies to surviving friends. So there had been something of a delay before it happened that somebody in the immediate family, nonchalantly, took time to peruse whatever *this* was.

Nobody read far. There was an immediate conference; members of the family rushed out to saddle up buckboards and scour Pittsburgh in hopes of overtaking whichever copies of the book had already escaped the Negley Avenue compound.

Father's testament. Like Father, like riffling through Father. Too much like Father perhaps, starting with the old man's intimidating likeness. That unforgettable intent long face bristling out of the frontispiece phototype, analytical around the luminous hollowed eyes. Meaty farmer's ears, flat cheeks, that faintly malicious primness about the mouth, shored up by all those decades of programmatic self-denial. Complete to the old patriarch's hand-stitched swallowtail coat and vest, which already looked bulky around Father's shoulders because his onsetting dotage was starting to shrink him inside his dependable 'lifetime wardrobe. Just underneath the gleaming rim of the over-starched high shirt collar that flanged the gullies of his neck, Thomas Mellon's omnipresent narrow black silk bow tie imparted a priestly gravity to offset the touch of boyishness where a hank of pewter hair refused to quite lie flat.

This was a face full of hints, some kindly. City-bred, very possibly his preoccupied sons deluded themselves into believing that the stormy integrity their farm-boy father had once devoted to splitting rails and plowing stony topsoil might somehow be suspended when he got around to splitting and plowing the years. It wasn't. *Thomas Mellon and His Times* comes out of our undiscovered literature tight-corked and fermenting still, rich, acid, every bit the shocker today as when his boys attempted to suppress it because they recognized at once that their father's masterpiece lay across the palate of the age like vinegar.

2

Virtually every family that came to importance in America, Thomas Mellon observes near the start of his opus, began as "hard working, careful, industrious common people, distinguished from others chiefly in having the faculties of industry, self-denial and accumulation more fully developed—the mud-sills on which fortunes were constructed which required a subsequent generation or two to scatter." The elderly banker certainly did not except his own. The thatch-roofed cottage around which Thomas Mellon pottered his earliest childhood definitely wasn't anything to catch a gentleman's eye. Another Irish hovel, something his father and his uncle Archy had plastered up in a hurry to keep

The Bible
THOMAS MELLON

the rain off the cow. A corner of the ancestral farm, reduced to twenty-three acres for which only the intrusive tax collector claimed a great deal of value. Poor soil, pebble-riddled clay, not good for much besides raising oats. Family geese waddled under the few scrubby trees; from time to time the dog bounded among them and sent them squawking.

Early memories. Other impressions survive, the harvest table weighted all around its edges with the elbows of aunts and uncles, animated in the lamplight, parceling out what little was left before the first among themselves started on to America.

The Mellons were pulling up. The awe of changing everything churned inside even this baby of the clan as he scampered across the braes, sneaked up on river rats among the tufted broom, accompanied by the dog. A century and a half of suffocation among the "wild Catholic natives" was close to ending; they were selling out, giving up the gore-encrusted bargain their primary Scottish ancestor Archibald had crossed the cold North Channel to grab off after 1641. The implacable Puritan Cromwell had brought to judgment impudent County Tyrone; after his ecstatic Roundheads finished he opened the remains to Protestants. Blood-soaked peat sold attractively.

The two hundred acres that constituted Archibald's Lower Castleton holding was arable largely, if patchy in places with bog and heather. Settling down directly to tillage, the original Mellons hadn't worried particularly as to what it might feel like to be involved in a Protestant "plantation" effort that followed a "Catholic depopulation" campaign. By 1800 they knew. Archibald's acquisition had been subdivided into scraps and corners so many times his descendants were themselves scarcely better off than cotters.

Genocide works a hardship on neighborhood associations. Along with Archibald's totemic cane, "rather a plain looking article," Thomas Mellon inherited a distaste for the enveloping Catholic "savages," whom he persistently judged "blindly ignorant and superstitious," sinking of an inherent foulness into "a state of degradation approaching the nature of the predatory animal," cherishing "the gall and bitterness of malice, nursed in the heart from generation to generation."

Swish, grunt—that swallowtail waistcoat is off already, along with the inhibitions of the vest, and so far as the Judge is concerned the heel of his ax is more than sharp enough to lay open the Irishmen in Ulster, not bothering to mention any encountered throughout the decades in Pennsylvania. Bandy-legged Hibernian hoodlums—Thomas Mellon can still remember the way they stood around in mobs, staring wormholes into the necks of his upright old-country uncles every market day. Spiteful indigents, with their frowzy women plucking at their sleeves. Good for laying crossties and slopping down the booze, with one of the males competent possibly to trim up the autumn orchard.

Triumphant snobbery plays powerfully into this, of course, and perhaps the bruise of guilt, but more of it than Thomas Mellon presumably would care to admit—his became a secular age—derives from stolid Presbyterian origins. "Mass-mongers," John Knox had labeled the encroaching Catholics, bringing down his blacksmith's hammer of a tongue with a definitive clang. Altarboys at their pernicious "Synagogue of Satan." Thomas Mellon, crowded with his kin into the self-sufficient Synod meetinghouse, reverberated. Work hard, prosper, demonstrate your eligibility among the Lord's elect. Dignity would be recognized. Suppliant, deacon perhaps, *elder* for the truly deserving—even you, small Thomas, might very well one day wag your mighty pow in God's own pulpit.

Theology passes; fear abides. But smugness too? Well, probably the pastor himself would have to admit that *smug* serves cosmic purposes. It must; it's there, quiet, patient upon its own broad bottom.

Important background, all this; but still, what pinched the Mellons out of County Tyrone was straightforward country economics. Because just after the eighteenth century petered out, and Thomas Mellon's father, Andrew, prepared to marry and accept his portion, the twenty-three acres he was to receive amounted to just about the smallest serviceable plot out of which it would be possible to scrabble even a meager living. This was foreseen. There was already a kind of flexible resettlement scenario. Several of Father Andrew's brothers would buy their passage to the United States and look the country over. Once they had selected an area choice enough for a primary homestead, *their* father, the patriarchal droop-nosed Archibald and his subservient Elizabeth, would book passage along with the two unmarried daughters. The grandparents would purchase a farm. With this new and hopefully much enlarged Mellon holding properly established as a rallying point, the rest of the children, leaving back only Andrew, could proceed to the United States to prosecute their fortunes. Anything in which they cared to involve themselves, so long as it was honest farming.

Except that—already, even as the Mellons' middle generation began to dribble across the Atlantic, there were . . . other possibilities being considered. The family's long post-Reformation agricultural slumber was uneasy. Deeper than intention, than resolution, at molecular levels, they were becoming precommercial. That too they muted. "Our ancestors," Thomas Mellon later boasted, "as far as known, and all the modern branches of the family, avoided soldiering, except as a necessary duty, confining their energies to the industrial pursuits of private life; and were notable only for good habits and paying their debts." He specifically excepted Harriet, the actress from the Fairy Water branch of the family who tempted into marriage the City of London's most prominent banker and so bewitched the man "that he left his whole immense fortune to her absolutely. This was the more remarkable," sniffed Thomas, "as he had no children by her, but had numerous relatives; and to me it only manifests weakness in the great banker."

In 1808 uncles Armour and Thomas, the advance guard, put out of Londonderry. The wars against Napoleon had used up manpower, and vessels of the British navy were overhauling foreign ships and seizing unmarried men. Armour's bride was aboard; when a cruiser loomed, she produced something ladylike into which her brother-in-law might squeeze. As the English press-gang picked over the manpower, Uncle Thomas, his complexion set off by a "jaunty" cap, tended his unaccustomed knitting.

They landed in Philadelphia. One of the grandfather's relatives had written the family about the choice and easily cleared farming country of western Pennsylvania. Armour roamed Westmoreland County and bought the inheritance of an Ulster-born maiden lady just beyond New Alexandria.

Uncles Archy and William arrived in August of 1816. In November that year the grandparental party, including Annie and Margaret, and one of the older boys, John, pushed on to Unity township to connect with Armour. Winter was settling in. Grandfather Archibald acquired what seemed to him the comeliest farm around, adjacent to Crabtree, and kinsmen would celebrate November 9 as the date on which "the Mellon family crossed the Chestnut Ridge on their way to the crab-tree."

The uncles moved around. Samuel joined Archie and bid in several turnpike building contracts. By then Brother Thomas was already doing nicely, dealing in sugar and cotton around New Orleans. He'd arrived in time to join Jackson's regulars in the defense of the city;

atop one cotton-bale rampart he'd torn a gun from an oncoming British trooper and bayoneted him upon his assault ladder.

Thomas civilized himself. When his delicate wife discovered that the miasmal delta climate was ruining her health, Thomas sold his share of the commodities business for a quarter of a million dollars and reestablished in Philadelphia and wound up a director of the Pennsylvania Railroad.

His influence exceeded financial importance. Even as a child he'd shown such precocity the family had sacrificed to send him to study alongside the Gaelic *Domine*. Once everybody was settled, and the Philadelphian discovered that his farm-boy namesake had begun to show an inclination for letters, he started dispatching books by the crateful. This presented the alternative.

3

The ritual of seeing off relatives to America—faces tear-stained, carts toppling with household goods—was called a living wake. Nobody returned. It had been Grandfather Archibald's intention to bequeath the Camp Hill homestead to his natural firstborn, Armour, but Armour's bride didn't please his father. This left the privilege of remaining to Archibald's next in line, young Thomas's father, Andrew.

That seemed all right as long as the family was around. Once Uncle Samuel sailed, even little Thomas noticed the way his father was mooning about, perusing gazetteers and geography books. Andrew's young wife, Rebecca, came from realistic Dutch stock; she knew that must not continue. It required two years to sell the farm and dispose of the animals. Rebecca stitched their two hundred guineas, worth a thousand dollars, into a money belt she wore until they might reinvest in land.

She lugged it longer than anybody had expected. Just as the family goods were being loaded on their vessel in Derry, Andrew suddenly felt feverish; his ears rang constantly. Rebecca nursed him stubbornly in harborside back rooms. The fever got worse. Rebecca wrote old Archibald in Pennsylvania to ask whether, should she be widowed, he wanted her to come ahead or take little Thomas and return to her people at Kinkitt.

The fever slowly broke. Over eighty years afterward the boy would hush his great-grandchildren with tales of a crossing so miserable the

Father Andrew
PAUL MELLON

Mother Rebecca
PAUL MELLON

Camp Hill
MATTHEW MELLON

crapulous immigrant families were reduced to sitting in a circle be-
lowdecks, each eying all others, the allotment of potatoes for the day
boiling in the common pot in sacks on tightly clutched strings. Most
envied were members of the Galey family, accompanied by a milkable
goat.

They arrived in Baltimore in October of 1818 and chartered a
Conestoga wagon to haul their goods to Greensburg. Little Thomas
was five. The months of travel had remained a frolic for the child—
the chance to smuggle a ha'penny now and again to the crone near
the wharf in return for a sweet, climbing among battlements in Derry
to gawk down Roarin' Meg. America itself was serious. This was a
dangerous paradise. Sixty-five years later his memory could savor the
radiating perfumed lushness of his initial peach, selected at the owner's
behest from windfalls strewed across autumn grass underneath the
trees. The weather was fine; yet when the weather darkened, the convulsions of thunder, the glare of sharp unceasing lightning seemed
actually to burst through uncurtained windows, strike into those bleak
rough rooms—this terrified, nothing like the soft wet storms among
the glens and brae. Thomas became a boy.

Near Youngstown they approached the camp of uncles Samuel and
Archy, still completing their piece of the Greensburg and Stoystown
turnpike. They spotted their grandmother first, milking a cow while
jocular Grandfather Archibald watched, perched on a log, puffing on
his pipe. The elders were dumbfounded. They'd just gotten Rebecca's
letter informing them that Andrew was probably doomed.

The arrivals wintered over at the farm near Crabtree; by April
Andrew had committed his two hundred guineas as down payment on
a tract along one of the tributaries of Turtle Creek in Franklin township. They started with a dilapidated cabin, meadows and a sufficient
woodlot, and apple trees just about to blossom. Everything waited to
do, yet somehow the worst seemed overcome.

The primitive log structure with which they began was so uncouth
it took handfuls of clay mortar slapped in around the chimney to
keep the roof from starting into flames. Grandfather Archibald stayed
over to whittle wooden door hinges and latches to keep the livestock
secure. Even after the down payment there still remained a worrisome
indebtedness, but the place was free for the most part of the old
country's ruinous taxes and rents. At that, the farm was seven times
the size of the Irish property.

Then, just as the family was under way, had carted back from the village their fine new moldboard with its hand-forged plowshare, and negotiated for seed, and put in their first spring crop—a panic struck. The Crash of 1819—the first of a great series of financial spasms that were to disfigure the Mellon family history the way unbearably cold winters craze particular rings across the core of a tree.

Everything went. Overexpanded as that economy was, with every furnace maker and turnpike builder issuing his own "shinplaster" currencies, only greenhorns like the Mellons were completely surprised. "The vitals of trade were destroyed by the canker worm of credit," Thomas Mellon summed up, "bloated inflation spread and increased until the decayed carcass dropped dead." That first summer's corn and oats, good money crops when they went into the ground, were harvested at prices that made it sensible to put them to sweetening the dunghill.

Payments on the farm fell due nevertheless. By luck, Father Andrew's contract permitted him to pay off his obligation with cash, oats, or bags "at market prices." There was no money, oats were selling at nothing, but bags had held up as high as fifty cents each, and so the Mellon family, hastily planting a crop of flax, spent much of the next four years hand-spinning and looming the tow of the flax into the coarse material out of which to produce homespun commodity sacks. Along with several measures of oats so as to observe the letter of his contract, Andrew sent two packhorses loaded with bags into town every April.

It saved the farm. Impending bankruptcy had brought the family together, inclined the adults to make a confidant out of little Thomas, and out of it all he was to derive a principle of his own. "As a general rule parents, especially such as are in easy circumstances or engaged in extensive enterprises, hold their children at too great a distance from them. They underrate their capacity for comprehension and judgement, and do not admit them close enough in their confidence. . . . Make your child a partner in your joys and sorrows, your hopes and fears. . . . It produces a bond of affection between you that is not easily broken, and affords you an opportunity of insight into your child's nature which is not otherwise obtainable."

The depression wore off. "My parents," Thomas Mellon observes, "were of a class who never wearied in well doing. . . ." As the country stabilized there were abundant opportunities. The roads were bad

enough to make whiskey the easiest medium by which to convey fruit and grain; Andrew Mellon began to distill his leftover apple and peach crop into brandy for sale. In 1826 he had the money to buy another large farm. Then a couple of nearby houses and lots; then another farm. Mother Rebecca produced Brother Samuel and the three sisters, Margaret, Elinor and Eliza.

Then, one day while Thomas was still fourteen, out plowing a neighbor's field for part of the buckwheat crop, he turned up a badly dilapidated copy of Benjamin Franklin's autobiography. With puberty we uncover saints. From then on Franklin meant so much to Thomas Mellon that forty-three years later, when Mellon was finally building the bank that enshrined his ambitions, he posted an iron statue of Franklin squarely above the pediment.

". . . here was Franklin, poorer than myself, who by industry, thrift, and frugality had become learned and wise, and elevated to wealth and fame." The hook snagged deeper. Along with the cheerful materialism that makes his very inflections lean, Franklin offered tableau after tableau that delineated men in the streets, cultivated and rational, crisp with the day's affairs. Even Father Andrew was something of a reader, with a bias toward the rationalism of the day. The sophisticated Franklin carried young Thomas another step. "I had been religiously educated as a Presbyterian," Franklin wrote, "and tho some of the dogmas of that persuasion, such as *the eternal decrees of God, election, reprobation, etc.* appeared to me unintelligible, others doubtful, and I early absented myself from the public assemblies of the sect, Sunday being my studying day."

By the 1880s, grappling with the great religious questions of the century without quite permitting skepticism, Mellon makes it clear that studies of Darwin and Huxley and Herbert Spencer have forced his thinking. The "unreasoning masses . . . do not perceive that if hell and the devil, and punishment in a future state of existence, are eliminated from religion, it does not follow that the consequences of good or evil are abolished. They do not perceive that all experience, whether scientific or unscientific, goes to prove that every act and thought is attended with its good or bad consequences to the party concerned in this life and to his posterity after him." When death comes, he presumes elsewhere, "we drop out again without alarm into that unconsciousness from which we were awakened on coming in." Only this world matters.

4

There is a subversive excitement to so much of this, a dryness that embitters with longing the cords of this eager farm boy's tongue, and the secret reason for *that,* he realizes well enough, is that what Franklin is now tempting him to contemplate is the abandonment of the land. This stirs profound misgivings. He anticipates only too accurately the contempt father Andrew is going to feel. Some of the father's resistance is simple disappointment: the younger brother, Samuel, is obviously never going to turn into any kind of a manager, and who besides Tom is left to take over this bountiful place?

Only—everything goes deeper than that. There is the legendary dread that almost the instant this industrious youngster wipes away the cow manure and rattles the last of the field pebbles out of his boots his life in Nature will really be over. This desertion is mixed up somehow with the way in which God is already thinning out for the boy. That unshakable deity who stared after everything one did, compressing a brow line even denser with bristle than John Knox's own, has demonstrated since Biblical days His regular displeasure with city types—the false priests and moneylenders and puffed-up hubris-fattened pontificatios clever enough to attach themselves, painless as creek leeches, to honest working farmers.

This is the father's view; the son, however he now marshals his arguments, feels identical lifelong pulls. A distrust for the neighbors has moderated in this New World from fear of retaliation to fear of contamination, and tinctures caution into the most casual of relationships. Even that preponderance of their neighbors of German origin, the "Pennsylvania Dutch," turned out, sexually speaking, "rather loose, and organized religious worship could hardly be said to exist." More, they were somewhat uncritical, full of comical superstitions, and not nearly as tireless as the Scotch-Irish about "well doing" for themselves.

And these were the most virtuous among the outsiders. When he had finally found words in which to suggest to his father that he would very much like to further his education, Thomas got back exactly what he expected. "For me to abandon the honest and noble profession of an independent farmer, and become a doctor or a teacher or miserably dependent preacher; or what was in his eyes worst of all, to enter the tricky, dishonest profession of the law, was a proposition which seemed to him too preposterous to contemplate."

Thomas was already contemplating. Furtively, encouraged during early adolescence by books from that namesake uncle in Philadelphia. With Mother Rebecca wheedling, the boy was finally permitted to board out and attend the nearby Greensburg Academy during the midwinter lulls. By now the dense, clumsy, genial children of the neighborhood bored him; he invested free moments in reading.

The seam ripped when Thomas was seventeen. With a familial cunning about immiring the young, Father Andrew had arranged to take over a sizable adjacent homestead which Thomas might work while paying off its big deferred mortgage. Biting his lip, Thomas seemed agreeable to the whole transaction the morning his father and the farmer next door rode into town to attend the closing. The boy was cutting rail timbers. Brooding, edge-walking despair at the prospects of a lifetime devoted to an "honest, frugal living by hard labor," Thomas suddenly hurled the ax in his hand over the fence into the yard and ran ten miles, up and down a succession of muddy, hilly roads, to intercept his destiny. He overtook the two farmers barely dismounted. The two could agree to anything they liked, the lad gasped, but without him. Father Andrew understood.

Squinting through last light of the summer evenings, before and after church, the boy now struggled to perfect his English grammar, did sums, gave himself a start in Latin. Then, the spring of 1832, Thomas began to board weeks with the Reverend Jonathan Gill, a Covenanter minister who resided near Monroeville. By 1834 Mellon felt he was ready for college. After a false start in Jefferson College, near Canonsburg, which he discovered too frivolous for his ambitions, Thomas Mellon transferred to Western University in Pittsburgh. With this the dynasty seeded.

5

The city of Pittsburgh was just becoming recognizable to the un-aided historical eye. Earliest to emerge behind the Appalachian wall among those titanic Middle Western glands of the industrial future, Pittsburgh was to remain, relatively speaking, both choice and small —the pancreas of Empire.

The town had started its existence as a trading center—the delta of the Alleghenies beyond which the unimpeded Ohio River fed barge traffic all the way to the Mississippi. Early in that bloodthirsty slow grappling in the dark throughout which the French and the English contested for the wilderness heartland, both recognized the strategic necessity of controlling the critical fork. The leatherstocking skirmishes that marked these forays, usually after the enlistment of one or another tribe of the fickle Indians, left evidences of a true renegade barbarism characteristic of Europeans so deep in the forests of the alien continent that they really did not have any idea where they were, let alone what in hell they were supposed to be doing there. One adventurer in the employ of the French collected a crowd of Ottawas and Ojibway and descended on the Miami Indian outpost at backwoods Pickawillany, an English trading center. Aroused, they decimated the Miami and reportedly boiled to taste and consumed their portly but flavorsome chief. This was enough to chill even an Englishman's blood, and the creative Britishers ultimately retaliated with strategies like distributing among the redskins wool blankets freshly contaminated by the leakage of expiring smallpox victims. It was an enterprising interlude.

They all knew Pittsburgh was out there. In 1747 some Virginia gentlemen formed the Ohio Company and petitioned the English Privy Council for title to the several hundred thousand acres that comprised the fork of the Ohio. Nothing important was on the point quite yet—a woebedraggled Delaware settlement called Shannopin's Town, shanties underneath the bluffs—but the Virginia traders and land speculators who formed the Company understood that here was the important confluence. So did the French.

From 1752 on it was like a noble French elkhound fighting off a horde of greedy English terriers for possession of a rabbit. Goaded by that cast-iron boy surveyor George Washington, who was an investor along with his brother Lawrence in the Ohio Company, the English set about the construction of Fort Prince George. The installation was partially completed when the French appeared and drove the English out and erected the eccentric six-pointed Fort Duquesne. Washington, smelling profits, kept after both Parliament and the Virginia legislature to help him raise militia forces enough to take the Company's grant back. In despair after himself guiding units of British regulars to the wilderness juncture, Washington, late in 1758, finally watched the British army under the ailing General Forbes file into the crumbling ashes the Indian mercenaries had deserted. The brickwork ramparts of Fort Pitt rose.

By 1834, when Thomas Mellon took rooms near Western University, the forest Indians who regarded your skull as something with

Settlement Pittsburgh
CARNEGIE LIBRARY

Post-Colonial Pittsburgh
CARNEGIE LIBRARY

The Forge of the West
CARNEGIE LIBRARY

which to cap a pike pole were items in medicine shows. The predominantly Anglo-Saxon townspeople hadn't changed much. There
was rather a raucous middling moment when the community made
a name for itself primarily as a place to water the packhorses or run
off the fatigues of the river trade along with a dollar or two into the
care of some sticky barmaid who maintained a flea-ridden bear pelt
on the back-room floor of one of the dockside gin houses. But as early
as 1791 a bypassing army officer described the town as "the muddiest
place I ever was in; and by reason of using so much coal, being a
great manufacturing place and kept in so much smoke and dust, as to
affect the skin of the inhabitants." Pittsburgh then numbered no more
than 376 people; that legendary pall of soot was already starting to
bury the community; overwork had already replaced copulation as
the besetting time killer.

By the 1830s Pittsburgh was long since a city, with an environing
population of upward of 25,000 people and a reputation that was
beginning to attract European laborers to the Forge of the West.
There were veins enough of iron ore in the surrounding counties, and
plenty of coal, and raw iron production had mounted to just under
five million tons. Textile production was next. Breweries and blowers
of heavy green glass and the descendants of early families such as
Jeffrey Scaife, who started his tinplate business in 1802, spotted factories out along the Monongahela and Allegheny. Public buildings
demanded masonry fronts, and the families of successful commercial
people such as Jacob Negley, whose steam-operated gristmill had
fascinated Thomas Mellon on an earlier visit, now lived in Georgian
mansions. That imprimatur of plutocracy anywhere, class snobbism,
squeezed down to reface town proportions. "We have our castes of
society, graduated and divided with as much regard to rank and
dignity as the most scrupulous Hindoos maintain," the 1826 *Pittsburgh
Directory* tripped happily over its tongue to assert.

6

Thomas Mellon (lately of that outlying meadowland it pained him
to overhear townspeople label Poverty Point) recognized himself for
Untouchable. "Litigants will pass by friends and relatives and retain
whoever will serve them to the best advantage," Mellon was to write
of his early lawyering. "Caste or class and relationship have little
influence. Although I was comparatively poor and obscure, yet I

soon had a fair share of clients of wealth and position in society, even among those who had nephews or other relatives in the profession."

The lumpkin of 1834 had already finished both Western University and his overlapping legal studies and secured his admission to the local bar by late in 1838. The years had involved the usual poor-boy's patchwork of part-time jobs—organizing a day school, a flyer in Ohio at bookselling, the periodic eleven-mile tramp back to the family farm to give a hand with the harvesting, a fill-in post as the university's Latin professor. A contact he had developed as a member of the university's literary group, the Tilghman Society, helped get him the post of assistant deputy prothonotary in the Allegheny County Court of Common Pleas—one of two clerks. The day-to-day bustle of cases passing through the court gave the law student points of jurisprudence around which to bunch his studies.

Cordial to his fellows, remote, the flicker of underdog contempt that tempered his stolid expression hinted at opinions acute enough to shave with. Father Andrew's distrust of city things could start Thomas's feelings aching unexpectedly like an inherited ague. After repeatedly conferring the snort of the newly graduated on the questions of his fellow clerk, Mr. MacConnell, Mellon found himself being even further annoyed that "I found it very difficult to answer some of his questions satisfactorily; and being a college graduate I could not plead ignorance on any point of knowledge. I was occasionally even put to the necessity of skirmishing for time to secretly consult my books at home for an answer. Although he had neither been to an academy or college and I had a regular diploma, he would not take it for granted that I knew everything, which I thought courtesy at least demanded of him, but like the locksmith in Dickens, he was continually 'wanting to know.' But it was not a great while until I discovered the unpleasant fact that he really *did* know far more about the Greek, at least, and algebra and some other branches of mathematics than I did myself; and that his questions were only prompted through an earnest and honest desire to be informed rather than to display his own knowledge or chaff me. I was greatly surprised to find him a really self-educated man. . . ."

A sip of cabinet liqueur from the Mellon family stock. So far as he was himself concerned—he, Thomas Mellon, churl—the bona fides of an academic parchment offered the only available stropping surface against which to sharpen practical abilities. But for his posterity?

The practice of the law, too, soon came to amount to well-remunerated donkey labor. Piecework for the powerful, an institution grown self-important profiteering from their squabbles. As to the poor? Almost fifty years later Mellon remembered a painting of two countrymen at issue before an English barrister. The judge was just in the process of forking the succulent meat out of an oyster; the shell was divided between the ignorant adversaries at law. The subscript ran:

> A pearly shell for you and me,
> The oyster is the lawyer's fee.

Viciousness showed. Out of a lifetime of colleagues the old man distinguished "a lower grade . . . whom nature never intended for the profession, who were unqualified either in mind or morals—guerrillas—a kind of floating class who eke out a living by pettifogging until something occurs to slough them off."

Unpleasant company; the spleen of Presbyterian pessimism was already enlarged enough by middle life to give almost *everything* something of an aftertaste. Politics is corrupt; the greater the theft from the public, the louder the popular acclaim. "It is only the small fry of criminals that are caught in the net of justice. . . ." As for society overall: "Apart from the 'real hardened wicked' class you must bear in mind that your fellow men for the most part have in them a taint of insanity, or mental or moral obliquity, and you may as well regard them accordingly," the Judge assures his grandchildren. "In a community of crooks, cranks, imbeciles, and weaklings of all degrees, the stream of human affairs cannot be expected to flow smoothly all the time without obstruction and conflict. Instead therefore of crimination and resentment, or vain regrets at your troubles, or disappointments, or losses, my advice in every case is to blame yourself in the first place: you will be surprised at the benefit derived from this habit of introspection."

Chaos threatens continually: another of those bits of doggerel touches at the refuge:

> To gather gear by every wile
> That's justified by honor.

"I take it," the Judge concludes, "this is the pith of the whole matter and the true course supported by philosophy, morality and common sense. Accordingly when I obtained money I used it to the best advantage, in the safest and most profitable investments I could find;

and thus by my earnings and investments and reinvestments, my accumulations have increased ever since."

A-men.

Ownership. In property *pax*. Yet that insistent suspicion that, tantalized by greed, he had already fallen out of Nature clearly tormented the young lawyer's dreams. His book and many of his surviving letters grow glum with reminders to his heirs that wealth and position can do no more than extend the range of disappointments. Yet even here, between the philosophizings, the mood is close to hysterical that this investment was entrusted into the wrong hands, that speculation was treacherously advised.

Because underneath everything the frantic belief has taken hold that if ever he or these descendants of his are to clamber back to sanctity their access is somehow via property. There are way stations. He considers the ministry, except: "I could not give up the hope of bettering my condition by the acquisition of wealth, nor could I submit to become a pliant tool of any church organization. . . ." In 1859, prevailed upon by friends and tempted because his practice had grown so large his health was endangered by chronic dyspepsia, Thomas Mellon stood successfully as a candidate for Allegheny County judge in the Court of Common Pleas.

Ten years of "wagging his pow" impartially at wrongdoers and lawyers seemed to confirm Mellon in his dignity enough to ease his restlessness. He appreciated the overview. Whereas, as an attorney pleading, he had discovered himself at times unsure as to the right and wrong of an issue, or reduced to choking down vehement feelings, as a judge he was surprised at how clearly the justice of each situation presented itself. Nothing else was left most of the time except help load up the arguments and direct the testimony so as to ensure that ignorant juries brought in the verdict properly. Practical always, he discriminates between the "manly criminals," who, "stricken with repentance and remorse," are public-spirited enough to "manfully rid the world of their presence, and society of the expense and trouble of their trial and punishment. It is only the mean spirited and cowardly, for the most part, who occupy the time and attention of our courts through long trials under trumped up pleas of insanity and other excuses and invoke public sympathy to screen them from their just deserts."

This middle-aged man who promotes suicide as decency to the

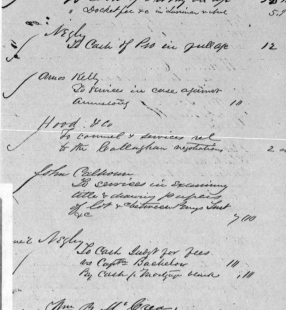

Attorney Thomas Mellon
PAUL MELLON

taxpayers is hard to remember around Poverty Point. Amiable folk,
which of them—easing down a manure fork to watch this starched
figure in the frock coat treading off house lots—could identify that
personage as Andrew Mellon's bookish boy? While he was still in
school Thomas Mellon had followed his idol Franklin by reinvesting
the few dollars he was able to scrimp together in such casual paper
as mechanics' liens and discounted personal loans. Once into his practice he found capital accumulating a good deal faster than he had
expected. Some he put out at the prevailing 10 to 15 percent. His
expectations were rigorous; court records soon suggested a widening
torrent of foreclosures. When the Great Fire of 1845 gutted the central city Thomas Mellon took advantage of the rebuilding boom and
put his money into offices and homes. In 1846 alone he had constructed eighteen rental dwellings.

Mellon's holdings were widespread enough by 1849 for him to have
to seize by foreclosure sixty acres of coal-bearing land alongside the
Pennsylvania Canal. Irregularities in the seam ultimately forced
Thomas Mellon and his operating partner out of the business—at a
profit. By 1859 he had invested in the coal business on a much larger

scale. Later, functioning unnoticed as the "capitalist" behind J. B. Corey & Company, Mellon slipped out of the shadows to try to collect on the forty thousand dollars' worth of Corey coal which had been trapped in barges in New Orleans throughout the middle years of the Civil War before being sold to the corrupt Union commandant of the occupied city, General Benjamin Butler. Butler's brother, the treasurer of the expedition, had tried to extort a bribe from the Corey agent in the city before paying off the company's vouchers. The Judge divested himself of the official robes for long enough to travel to Washington to pay a call on his fellow Pittsburgh attorney and "intimate," Secretary of War Edwin Stanton. Stanton, plugging Mellon hard, sent the Judge over to his commissary general, Meigs, who recognized that this was too influential a personality to keep waiting for his payment and helped Mellon establish his position vis-à-vis the claims court. Buttresses of the Mellons' future, reputation and fortune, could support each other.

7

For perhaps twenty years the Judge's association with Corey undertunneled his investments; it is undoubtedly worthwhile to back up momentarily and attempt some analysis. They made contact early, around 1859, just as the Judge had decided to announce for the Court of Common Pleas. Friends drew Mellon aside to warn the freshly gowned Judge that Corey had already been elbowed decisively out of his own family coal enterprises. Mellon waved everybody off: he liked this go-getter; with railroads coming through, coal mining was clearly the likeliest place possible to invest gathering capital; Corey's eagerness to operate a major property "in his name exclusively" played harmoniously into Mellon's own urge to corner big profits without besmirching his aspirant family name. The two became partners.

Corey ran the works; Mellon found the cash. Corey directed Mellon's capital into mines at Braddock and Sandy Creek. Then, typically, Corey signed enormous long-term contracts to supply a pair of nearby iron mills at what proved catastrophically low prices. Making good on either would ruin them both; the Judge looked elsewhere to let his resourceful partner slither out of one of the contracts by providing such shoddy coal, so unreliably, that his customer finally quit.

Corey's other customer resisted. Corey approached his partner and declared himself so seized by patriotic fervor he'd decided to raise a Company and fight the Rebels. Mellon stiffened. That other contract first. Corey located a buyer and dumped the Sandy Creek property. Mellon took the down payment; Corey embezzled subsequent proceeds. Their bookkeeper grumbled. "I was never a very good judge of private character," Mellon would admit freely. Corey "had that particular tact, which some men have, of ingratiating themselves into your good will by manifesting friendship and dependence. They will constitute themselves your friend whether or no."

Their legal partnership dissolved in 1864. The association still smoldered. Corey snooped the berm banks and unattended hollows of backcountry Pennsylvania in search of temptingly underpriced coal property. He reported his discoveries to his august ex-partner, motivated, so far as the Judge could make it out, by "a constant itching to negotiate purchases either on his own or other people's account." The Judge might sigh—after all, in this industrially damned century, coal was the devil's topsoil—but he provided capital. Corey struck his bargain; in time the title passed along to join Mellon's other real properties.

Quid inevitably involved *quo*. Mellon loaned Corey money, endorsed Corey's unsecured notes, received discounted paper Corey took over from other bankrupts, and accepted security over which others—unsuspected by the Judge—exerted primary claims.

Why—how had the prudent banker intruded *himself* into such financial lunacy? "I knew he was very shrewd and cunning," Mellon attempts to explain, "and had great ability in scheming and contriving, but I had not yet discovered the full extent of his ability at concocting schemes of so dangerous a nature as he finally developed in this case." In 1873, just when the Judge's new little T. Mellon and Sons banking venture was deepest into financial upheaval, and bad loans and weak mortgages and unanticipated fiduciary masonry of every description half buried the lot of them—Corey sued! Mellon dumped what equities Corey left with the bank, and things were getting down to sheriff's sales, when . . . the thing *was incredible* . . . Mellon's beneficiary now took it upon himself to file a voluminous affidavit in which he asserted that *throughout*, long after they abrogated their legal partnership, he and Judge Mellon had functioned by oral agreement as equals and partners.

The notion was shocking. Worse, Corey demanded fully half the profits Mellon made on the Braddock works, as well as half the returns from whatever parcels Corey scavenged out of the hills—one of which

alone, the Judge would admit, was good for ten thousand annually. The Judge got half Corey's business losses; the differential was
$150,000. Corey awaited a check.

The retired Judge fumed; Corey pressed into equity. With this
he'd blundered. The banker easily "succeeded in having a highly respectable and competent member of the bar appointed as master."
Testimony consumed three years; the court dismissed Corey's complaint.

Archaic stuff, the old gentleman's dotage fulminations. Still, looking the facts over, certain of the details . . . Because the entire
business with Corey seems a . . . an embryonic prototype, floating
in its jar of provincial court history.

Primitive, God knows. Adumbrations. But wouldn't there always
turn out to be one Corey or another, once things got rolling? Some
self-inflated backslapper, eager, pacing back and forth and muttering
until the Judge disrobed?

One required such intermediaries. Colonel Guffey, sniffing oil,
hawking that tobacco quid into Andrew Mellon's tidy little office
fireplace. Boss Magee, pleased enough to let the Mellon boys in on
the City's development schedules. Warren Harding. Obsessive Henry
Rust, half palsied, piling his utility pyramid. Cresting Richard Nixon.
Whiteford allocating systematic bribes.

Inspired ruffians. Clumsy, on occasion; hardhanded country go-
betweens so ambitious and barefaced as to leave even *Pittsburgh*
businessmen sucking eyeteeth thoughtfully. Determined—*here* was
the crucial quality—activated by that "constant itching" which so
recommended Corey. Corey was merely first.

8

In 1856 Thomas Mellon uncovered, consequent to foreclosure, a
1,700-acre property in West Virginia that included a blast furnace
and a tremendous stock of ore. The milling of pig iron was barely
into its adolescence. Mellon investigated the business thoroughly and
sold the assets off. He craved something sizable.

The need became virulent. "I write this," the stultified jurist remarks
in a letter to his wandering son James, "and wrote the last on the
bench whilst the lawyers are making speeches to the jury. I sit from
nine till five and am so closely engaged all day as to make me very
tired in the evening." His health had improved, he caught his reading

up, but no such compensation could overshadow the fact that "General business became so active that such opportunities for making money had never before existed in all my former experience; and for some two years before the end of my term, although the judicial office was entirely to my taste, I discovered that in holding it I was making too great a pecuniary sacrifice. . . ."

So that in 1869 Thomas Mellon's penance to status ended with the expiration of his term. He did not choose to stand for reelection. ". . . two bright boys just out of school, the idols of my heart, merging on manhood, and with fine business capacities, whom I was eager to launch on this flood tide of business prosperity, and to pilot them in the channel for some part of their way," provided justification enough. Talk around the Judge's big residence at 401 North Negley Avenue was about a bank.

Why *bank*? Banking seemed rather an undemanding thing to the self-assured Judge. "There is nothing in banking but what you ought to be able to learn in a week or two . . ." he writes Son James, although "I have a great conceit in banking business myself. . . ." Commerce or manufacturing directly: these were the swine pens inside which capitalists like Carnegie, visible from courtroom windows, were already lolling comfortably.

This approach was productive. Mellon comprehended his age. Except . . . except that . . .

Mellon couldn't. Not that way.

Because how is one to justify a lifetime of shaping and imparting tone to this very demeanor—jowls of a military firmness underneath the big bumpy cheekbones, glinty reproachful eyes—by besmirching those last few decades with industrial plunging? Standing over Irishmen, tongue-lashing teamsters who think they deserve another dollar a week? Once prices got high Mellon relinquished his block of rentals, unloaded Corey coal.

Irritable as he so easily becomes—Pittsburgh's rooster of rectitude, pecking up opportunities—his is the queasiest of stomachs. When James, eager to demonstrate his eye, recommends a play in tobacco the aging man clutches: "Indeed, the way currency is thrown loose by Mr. Chase's resignation, it is hard to predict whether prices will go up or down. This kind of speculation is the way merchants deal. They make the best guess they can and then run the risk. I never dealt any that way; I always bought things I was sure I would get my own money out of, at least."

Only sure things. Although when tobacco took a jump the Judge admitted that he had recently considered flyers in wheat and pig iron, but ". . . I am not in a position that I could attend to it, nor would it look well."

Banking would look well. Somewhere at the bottom of those judicial entrails he still feels, from time to time, a twinge of uncertainty about whether the soil he deserted might yet be biding its time. Good for a righteous shudder, ideas like that. Even if—even if the crapulous Luther was correct, even if this phobic universal moneymaking has already enveloped the human experience in the devil's own Empire of Dung, who avoids his moment? Better to wind up Archbishop of the Anti-Christ.

Because the modern consciousness insists that not only is Nature fertile: Capital is fertile too. The subtle Judge acknowledges in himself at least an inkling of the medieval abhorrence at the notion of *interest*. In some paradoxical way, interest has estranged everybody who attempts to live from it, ejected its closest dependents from *time*. The condition in which each moment was at hand to savor because it partook immediately of eternity has become modernity's unhappy recollection.

Time—the time which is money, the time within whose syncopated grinding molars we are implacably reduced to incompetence and ugliness and senility and the exhaustions of every mortal bankrupty—time owns what God and Nature have forsaken. So that the anxiety of our abandoned lives is somehow to outdistance time. Remain productive. Hold on to those negotiable good looks. Invest with shrewdness enough so that one's interest laps inflations.

Somehow, between projects and projections, we have inadvertently heaved ourselves out of the irreplaceable human moment. By now—it is the Presidency of Grant—we kowtow without remission toward horizons of future before which the unstable nervous present must sacrifice itself unwhimpering. One's identity—its eternal self-respecting part— one's trust funds, one's corporations, the blood of one's precious lineal descendants: nothing has a chance unless it hurtles intact into some cosmos of atoms whirling (of which his readings recently informed the Judge), where it can snap together finally into that unrushed substance our intuitions remember whole.

Until this happens, until existential Resurrection Day, wealth consecrates our reality.

Therefore—banking. Like priests, moneylenders have historically dealt with the unclean multitude from an acceptable elevation. Among more subtle civilizations the leadership understood the potency of wealth well enough to require that only holy men might lend. Long generations before Jesus, temples sheltered the moneylenders; astute bankers ever since have insisted on both the hushed reverential tones and the architectural reinforcement otherwise characteristic of churches. And received it: who except the priest could damn so many people to helplessness and poverty or absolve them and let them prosper? For Thomas Mellon, banking permitted the closest thing to a recovered sanctity his acquisitiveness permitted. Henceforth—till capital.

9

So that the storefront off Smithfield Street the Judge rented was more than merely a business for the boys. This became the alternative Mellon homestead—a place to repose that ghostly substance Thomas Mellon had been wringing his liver to amass for more than thirty years: their overstrained capital.

Accumulation was one preoccupation; the other was offspring, heirs to this struggle of a lifetime. Homelife, even more than business life, had been a matter of deliberation.

Here, too, Thomas Mellon could imagine no reason to scrimp his habits. One mated ultimately; practicality told one when. For almost a decade, beginning with his semesters of bad cooking at the Western University Sumptuary Society, Mellon had been shifting among a succession of hotels and boarding situations. Discouraged with that, he induced his parents to move to town. But old Farmer Andrew was ill at ease, mistrustful of the townspeople. Anyway, Thomas confessed to himself, he was forever assailed by "daydreams of . . . a happy home with loving wife and bright children. . . ."

This might retard accumulation, Thomas faced up, but as he rounded thirty he regarded his circumstances. He was completely eligible, a man of "settled habits," although not quite yet hardened over into "the crusty disposition of a bachelor." Appraising himself as "clear of the fog arising from the *veally* conditions of the emotions at an earlier date," Mellon sought a female equally unsentimental. The lead turned up while Mellon was hearing out the complaints of a friend about to marry one of Jacob Negley's daughters. Another of the Negley sisters, Sarah Jane, was "rather too independent, had no elasticity in her composition, and did not seem to appreciate gentlemen's attentions." Rigid, aloof, indifferent—Thomas Mellon was attracted.

He finagled an introduction. Mellon accompanies his rendition with that bruising pizzicato of asides he favors whenever he is telling a story on himself. The aspirant lawyer hoodwinks another marriageable acquaintance—herself "the right type of womanhood for a wife, and of a good family and very wealthy; but I feared hereditary consumption"—into presenting him around the old Negley mansion. There in "the sunlight which was struggling through the window curtains," he encountered his potential "one of destiny. . . . quiet, pleasant, and self-possessed," the "person" of whom "would do if all right otherwise."

Calculation at first glance; the attorney attempted siege. Courtship visits quickly settled into a regular, frustrating pattern. Sarah Jane was "pleasant, cheerful, polite," but, for all the lessons in "flora culture" and interminable readings from her scrapbook, she was quite artful about never "affording the slightest opening toward intimacy." "But to her credit," Mellon sighs in fairness, "I must say she never inflicted any music upon me. . . ."

This dragged; one warm June day, rebelling at such waste of valuable evening hours, Mellon seized the pretext of visiting some farming relatives to look up a pretty little daughter of one of his boyhood schoolteachers. Object of Mellon's undeclared calf love, "afterwards throughout all my tedious years of study and bachelor life, Mary would occasionally appear to my fancy in all her early beauty."

He uncovered "my Mary" settled with her mother in a squalid cabin. A lank, frowzy-haired creature, slovenly among the chicks peeping around the cabin floor, Mary pulled up a stool behind the cooking stove from which to eye the stranger and puffed, all suspicious, upon a crockery pipe; Mellon fled.

He couldn't go back; Mellon resumed those dogged visits to the Negleys. Others understood his intentions—the Negley brothers were around town, checking—but Sarah remained remote. Then, one "interview," the two were left alone a moment in the moonlight of a

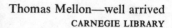

Thomas Mellon—well arrived
CARNEGIE LIBRARY

401 Negley—"solid, classical
. . . harmonious to the eye."
WESTERN PENNSYLVANNIA
HISTORICAL SOCIETY

Sarah Jane
CARNEGIE LIBRARY

dusky evening; Mellon "drew her to me and took a kiss unresisted and said that would do, I was satisfied; and left her abruptly, feeling unnerved for conversation."

". . . the transaction was consummated on the 22d of August, 1843," Mellon notes. "It was a marriage of judgement and discretion in the first place, ripening into a love afterwards, and for over forty years has been a happy one."

One studio portrait, mounted cameo-style, survives of this Mellon dowager as a younger woman. Protuberant large round eyes seem more emphatic underneath the marble brows, the severe tight bun. One spit curl is permitted to modify a cheekbone; Sarah has a hand drawn up alongside her jaw, forefinger outstretched to ensure control. The mouth seems no more than a quizzical mistrustful line, emphasizes the soulfulness of the eyes, approaches *sad*. Pleats of her formal gown pinch around her waist like armor.

The study was posed in 1849; Sarah Jane was thirty-one. Then—always—things had been arduous, demanded self-possession. Her father's family descended directly from the Swiss-Rhenish immigrant Alexander Negley, who migrated to Allegheny County and settled a sizable farm there in 1778. He was the ancestor who built the gristmill. Jacob Negley, Sarah Jane's father, was among the scions of the community by the time Thomas Mellon, nine, stood astonished before the Negley mill, contemplated the beautifully kept pastures and the palatial houses of the 1,500-acre Negley estate.

A surveyor and mechanical engineer, Jacob had invested heavily in a steam-powered flouring mill, erected most of the buildings that formed the basis of suburban East Liberty, served as a director on the local turnpike boards, collected books, contributed the village's first Presbyterian brick church—operated grandly, the local laird. His children, walking home from school on a special raised roadbed, often stopped off to share the late-afternoon picnic victuals sent out on horseback from the manor house to refresh the "men."

Caught by the collapse of 1819, everything caved in. A sympathetic friend, Senator James Ross, bought up the property after Jacob died in 1827 to give Sarah Jane's brothers a chance to redeem the farms. Jacob's widow herself ran the remaining thousand acres as well as healing the neighbors with roots and herbs from her medicinal gardens. Always a "leader among the young ladies of her set," Sarah Jane brought into marriage with rising Tom Mellon, along with much bountiful Negley acreage, the familial orthodoxy, the crimp of obligation that kept Sarah Jane active in her stubborn pursy-mouthed way, looking after the local old, the indigent homeless.

By marrying one of the heiresses of "Negleytown," Thomas Mellon took on more than Sarah's corner of the recovered farmland. Marriage tempered him; children made him vulnerable. The summer of 1844 brought Thomas Alexander, first of the babies; eighteen months afterward James Ross Mellon arrived. The couple was started into "the fond anxiety of parenthood." Emma, born with a congenital heart defect, died as a three-year-old; the next in line, Rebecca, succumbed to dysentery in 1852. The losses obviously wrenched the parents, but Thomas, at least, was consoled to reflect that they were spared the pain of maternity or the chance of a drunkard for a husband, "consequences so tremendous, that daughters who die young need not be greatly lamented. . . ."

After attempting life downtown, Thomas Mellon conceded that "the contracted space and sulphurous atmosphere produced by the coal smoke of the lower part of the city seemed to me to have a depressing effect on my wife's health and spirits. . . ." The family took over a cottage on the Negley property; in 1850, Thomas Mellon looked after the construction of the house at 401—solid, classical, barely ornamented but "harmonious to the eye" while eschewing that "spirit of shoddyocracy common among those grown suddenly rich."

Invigorated by country air, the Mellons produced four successive boys. Selwyn was born in 1853, Andrew in 1855, Richard in 1858, finally George, the baby, in 1860. While he himself rode horseback into town almost every day to confer with clients or preside over court, the Judge so arranged matters to keep his large family isolated. He ran the homestead as a farm. The twenty-five or thirty adjacent acres went without delay into tillage, hogs passed from sucklings to smokehouse without leaving the premises. Experimental orchards engrossed him; his grandson William Larimer Mellon remembers of the aging Judge "a passionate interest in horticulture that transcended kindred feelings to be encountered on the average farm. A concern for all the processes of Nature, of Life, was burning incessantly in his strong mind."

The atmosphere was practical. The peeling schoolboy diaries of James Ross, the second son, washed into historical archives, convey the plainest of existences: waking up in chilly dark rooms to carry down the ashes and feed the chickens, make beds or run errands for "ma" before dinner, help older brother Thomas hammer out broad-headed nails and pour lead into bullet molds. James was just eleven: he records his responsibility that two-year-old Andrew not toddle into the flames. The treat of the day was an interlude stolen to read in *Swiss Family Robinson.*

Fearful of public rabble, "coarse and low by nature" and of a "class of schoolboy [that] rejoices in vulgarity, disobedience, and contempt for study," the Judge had his own schoolhouse constructed and directed the pedagogy. Thoroughness was critical: the teacher was to leave the child alone until he was able to apply what he had learned to each fresh problem. Appropriate skills, enough college preparation were fitted into each life "until all my children had obtained such a degree of education in the arts and sciences as fitted them fairly for the pursuits they were to follow."

Which pursuits, all knew. "For business men it is unnecessary to waste much time on the classics. . . ." Judge Mellon counsels his eighteen-year-old son James, in Milwaukee, to consider merchandising: "This I had determined once or twice and if I had stuck to it, I have no doubt I would be as well off now as I am for I could have done well at dealing. But I had no capital and no one to start me, so the best thing I could do was to go to the learning."

So far as the Judge could tell, raising boys was largely a matter of whetting commercial appetites while suppressing all else. When the older pair announced that they had selected the same profession, blacksmithing, their wily father fitted out a forge and some bellows and an anvil in one of the shanties in the back and let them compile enough grime. But "Like most parents . . . I had heard so much about the necessity of coercion and chastisement in the proper training of children . . . that at the outset I was in danger of overdoing the business in that line. . . ."

This rarely meant strappings. The jurist was subtler. "I made it a rule, therefore, even in their childhood, to give them a pecuniary interest in the performance of whatever work they chose to engage in. In this way the earning of pocket money was made a pleasure; and the labor of earning it afforded them an idea of its value and a disposition to economize its expenditure."

Push became pull. Cajoled, directed, tested, even praised when necessary—inactivity must never pad those dainty Mellon bones.

Young Thomas, the namesake, liked to throw his weight around more than the Judge approved, but he was good-natured, and didn't cause problems. He alarmed both parents by impulsively signing himself into an emergency regiment that defended the Maryland frontier in 1862. After that he returned home without fuss, puttered with the orchard, and occupied himself with turning over successfully the nursery business of one of the mother's relatives, General Negley. His father lent capital—at 12½ percent.

James Ross was mavericky. He had his own ideas, a weakness his vigilant father suspected. By 1862, mail from the Judge, urgent with good advice, would keep the worried boy, off at Jefferson College, wriggling.

Stop showing off. Make of trustee Judge Sterrett your "particular friend." No backwardness about that; otherwise you will lose "a great deal of advantage." Be glad you only had to pay three dollars to the townspeople for joining in the Halloween "scrape": an excellent lesson, better than anything else you are likely to learn around that place. Gymnastic lessons? Humbug!

Finally, rallying, James denies comporting himself like a "fop," defends his right to be "in society a little," and maintains that "I am sure I have not got my notions elevated as you said by coming here, but if a fellow is not pretty bold, he cannot get along well here."

To improve uneven health, the boy tries Milwaukee. Paternal letters batter in. "It is hard for a boy away from home influences to resist the allurements of fashionable (and as he would suppose good) company," the Judge forever reminds the boy. "Indeed, I have never warned you enough against female company keeping. I know nothing which so unfits a young man for manly serious studies or business and it is worse than useless. No man but a fool will think of marrying till he is over twenty-five years of age and in proper situation to keep a family and for any other use in the way of company, female society is injurious. It is mostly excused on the plea of refining the manners but this is all bosh." James must be reminded of a note he wrote a girl while in college, thus "making a fool of yourself and being talked about. . . ." The sap of youth is reserved for commerce.

Most reprehensible, so far as the Mellons are concerned, is service in the military. When James writes asking permission to enlist in one of the Wisconsin "hundreds," both parents reply. "I had hoped my boy was going to make a smart, intelligent business man and was not such a goose as to be seduced from his duty by the declamations of buncombed speeches," the father explodes. "I had thought you were a boy of stronger mind and better sense or I never would have allowed you to go from home," Sarah Jane returns. Deflated, James

Ross settles back into legal chores and daydreams of tobacco-market killings.

The years pass slowly; the 1860s are dragging the family back. The bench is frustrating; the war stretches on under the lugubrious Lincoln; around Allegheny County the indigent have taken over and are taxing the provident into penury. Mellon is privately uneasy about Corey. Heartsickeningly, several among the children who are his worry and delight show susceptibilities. James's health is touchy; Thomas has a close brush with typhoid fever. Both little girls died; then—the sharpest blow—Selwyn contracted diphtheria and expired after terrible sessions, gagging horribly on medicine his desperate father attempted to drive down his throat.

"The recollection of every little unkindness I subjected him to affects me with remorse," the Judge wrote over twenty years afterward. "When I review in memory his short life in sickness or in health, I discover nothing to justify the slightest harshness of treatment." Selwyn's death—like George's later—mitigated the paternal arrogance. "Andrew was the first to experience the change wrought in the old man by the loss of Selwyn," Grandson William Larimer notes. "Every stern and reproving word the father uttered to his older boys, and especially the lost one, he now tried to redeem by gentle words spoken to little Andy."

2 | THE ANOINTED SON

1

B Y THE TUMULTUOUS SIXTIES, Victorian America—like counterpart Western Europe—was deep into the secular mythology of the age. Its heroes and monsters were Aging Great Men; it was a generation of Distinguished Gaffer worshipers. Goethe, Carlyle, Longfellow, Bismarck, Gladstone, Renoir, Gerhart Hauptmann—the archetype is familiar enough, lion-maned hyperopinionated old things, clotted with a lifetime of pomposities to choke any journalist's notebooks.

Usually a secondary figure surfaced sometime during the interview. Faded, trained to a discreetness, edging across one corner of the room so as not to interrupt anything. A belated wife—so often a nurse raised almost at the end to pre-mortem glory. The widowed younger sister. The devoted spinster daughter.

So far as the eminent Judge Mellon went, the figure clearly marked as retainer and protégé as early as those years on the bench was, of course, his third-born surviving son, Andrew.

Of course? Bucking and pawing, throwing sand and opinions and keys to the human experience around in every direction throughout these senescent writings of his, the Judge refers rarely to the omnipresent Andrew. Andy is simply . . . there, looking after things, forever at the father's elbow.

What . . . distinguished Andrew, exactly? The Judge's lips approximate a line, his matted visage tips to frame some glitter of recollection. Across the writing table the amanuensis's upright pen casts an oblique, narrow shadow. Andrew. "Fitted for the business of the bank," perhaps? But that was evident. Why otherwise, before thirty, would anybody have presented the boy with title to the place?

Judgment? That sounded commonplace too. It touched on something, nevertheless. Andrew . . . took in so much. That composed look—even as a child, his drawn little mouth unwilling to commit itself much of the time. One learned the subtleties of the face. A moue of contempt, that disconcertingly prolonged blankness. Had that been characteristic?

He often appeared remote—devoted, but solitary. Too young to interest the bustling eldest brothers, yet already hanging back, not given to tumbling and exchanging catcalls with Richard and George —chasing through the orchards and arbors, hiding in the springhouse, dawdling behind the gangs of rascally Irish teamsters who harnessed their foul-tempered army mules for turning the gardens.

Occasionally Andrew got involved. He followed the younger ones in imploring the sinewy Mrs. Cox, Sarah's termagant of a housekeeper, to steep a reward of tangy spruce beer. The three would run off expectantly behind a potting shed wheelbarrow to fetch a cake of iceworks ice on which to set the beloved crock. Later Willie tagged along —James's firstborn, a spunky little thing who immediately clambered up into the bed of the wheelbarrow to demand a ride. After ice was loaded Willie had to walk. The return was taxing. Sometimes, Andrew would relent and swing Willie up and bear him silently, all squirmy and proud, wavering above Andrew's scanty hollow shoulder blades. Before the final effort up Black Horse Hill, Willie would wriggle free, while all three uncles dug in to heave their enormous waddling block up over the crest and across the dooryard to the protective dank inside the great house's subcellar.

Such breakouts were memorable. What playmates Andrew attracted would remember an ashen little creature, gelid to the touch. His neat, close-fitted child's features betrayed very little expressiveness.

Andrew's leanings were practical; even wrathful Mrs. Cox managed differently with him. "With the exception of my grandfather," young Will would write, "every man in the family during his boyhood had come under the sway of her dual power which was equally capable of delighting him with goodies or of whipping him within an inch of his life. I know that she thrashed me and my father before me." James had been incorrigible, a prankster who cleaned out the henhouse for months and sold his loot throughout the neighborhood; an East Liberty grocer finally told the troubled Sarah Jane what made her chickens barren.

Andrew measured from childhood that shadowy distinction between thievery and enterprise. After months of noticing the wagons of farmers straining past the property, the lad started tying up bundles of fresh Mellon grass to peddle to passersby at five cents each. His produce business flourished. The highly amused Judge contributed a cart and donkey, which roamed the precinct delivering the Mellons' celebrated asparagus and cherries and peaches and Indian corn. It wasn't very long before Richard and George were actually plucking the fruit and lashing the unhappy donkey—Andrew waited at home, general manager and bookkeeper. Sarah was again replenishing her larder around neighborhood markets.

This child respected property. When Confederate outriders started threatening western Pennsylvania, the municipality sent out a horde of drifters to throw up earthworks along the perimeter of the Judge's estate. The troop of ne'er-do-wells upset the muscular Mrs. Cox much more than marauding soldiers. She summoned her pinched, wan Andrew and posted the eight-year-old—dutiful, keeping track of everything from behind those dreamy, hooded Negley eyes, cradling in his skimpy arms an unloaded shotgun very nearly as long as himself with which to ward workmen away from the ripening cherries.

That would have been . . . into the war, the summer before Gettysburg. Reflex crimps a muscle beside the old Judge's mouth. When all the fighting looked serious Andy was rarely around. The extinction, at ten, "in the morning of life," of winsome little Selwyn so humbled and depressed the Judge that day-to-day existence in the big square house on Mellon Lane turned into an ordeal of silence. This the parents regretted. Andrew had been closest in age to Selwyn, his inevitable sidekick, and Thomas and Sarah Jane decided to send the boy to winter over for several years about five miles away, at a village farm, with Thomas's sister the widow Stottler. There was a grammar school nearby. The Judge now reconsidered. Quite possibly one mustn't contrive everything. Andrew could attend there.

This child was lucid; obviously they ought to encourage preparation. After Andrew came back the Judge decided to enroll him in the Grant Street School in downtown Pittsburgh. They would commute together.

The apprenticeship took hold. Every morning except Sunday the Pennsylvania Railroad coach hissed to a halt at the East Liberty siding to take the couple aboard. Regulars greeted the pair—the compact judicial presence, quietly seating itself bolt upright alongside an available window, hiking at a knee before crossing his legs, tugging free of wrinkles the azure doeskin broadcloth waistcoat. By then the grave but attentive eleven-year-old had settled silently into the contour of the bench, that narrow bony face alert. From time to time the mature man spoke.

The boy volunteered little. Much passed. "The Judge," Cousin Willie would write, "talked to his son not as a little boy but as to one with a mature intellect and thereby challenged the youngster to think as a man. Indeed, I sometimes think that this companionship shortened A.W.'s boyhood."

Perhaps *absorbed* is closer. Researchers identify the sensitive if delicately integrated personality which, badly devastated in childhood, thereafter curtails human involvement while brooding on strategies which assure subsequent mastery of others and events. "But eventually this drive," observes the perceptive Karen Horney, "with the insatiable pride that accompanies it, becomes a monster, more and more swallowing all feelings. Love, compassion, considerateness—all human ties—are felt as restraints on the path to a sinister glory. This type should remain aloof and detached." The sufferer is "in actual fact afraid of people," assailed intermittently by the compulsion to vindicate himself, "restore his pride and to protect himself from lurking self-contempt. . . ." Such people are usually "hard," self-righteous and ascetic.

This fell across Andrew, inexorable as Father's shadow. One looks to Selwyn's traumatic end—the child gaping up, beseeching, entreating, that precious little swollen gray throat still straining to gag out words, death blackening his vitals. It reproached the Judge. He had been stiff-necked, too cocksure of himself to respond early enough, prepared unthinkingly to punish, and now this quiet surviving playmate whose existence was linked to Selwyn's must come to terms with Father's excoriating guilt.

Redemption as strategy hadn't changed—work, proved acceptable by increase of property. The war was dragging, but across the dinner table the older boys talked excitedly about the profits piling up between lumber and subdividing. Schoolmates discovered the new boy from East Liberty a courteous fellow, bland, not very much interested in romping with the others. He tended to disappear after classes ended and make his way to his father's chambers, where he became apt at helping sort through cases.

The Judge looked on. Waiting beside his father, the child stared fixedly as the train bearing the recently reelected Lincoln paused at the Pittsburgh depot. "When the train stopped I was very near the rear platform, and as Mr. Lincoln stood up I remember how astonished I was. He seemed to unspiral himself and rise to a great height." Like an enormous blacksnake, he told his children. An ungainly thing, just as the Judge anticipated, although the boy retained a "memory of his voice" as "gentle and well modulated."

One might interpret history by understanding Father's gestures. The day Lee capitulated the boy had concealed himself in the knee-hole of his father's bench. Eavesdropping on the pleading, his still, crouched body was hidden from the courtroom by the judicial folds. When news broke through, the place was pandemonium. "My father pounded his gavel in an attempt to restore order. By this time, though, the lawyers had climbed up on the tables, so my father crashed the gavel down and said: 'Court's adjourned.' We left the courtroom together, but he stopped on the way to wind the clock."

To wind the clock. Let politicians get excited. Prudent citizens had obligations.

The semesters on Grant Street provided the undemonstrative boy a following of lifelong acquaintances. They took their places, this handful of familiars like Pennock Hart, refugees from expiring childhood. After that the watchful Judge enrolled his offspring in one of the preparatory sections of Western University, as dilapidated a building as when he himself had pursued "the learning." Andrew soon passed unnoticed into one of the undergraduate departments, an inobtrusive adolescent with something on his mind.

Fragments from a packet of schoolboy compositions suggest the stripling's nervous sententiousness, a puberty of tensions reabsorbed. He justifies public art galleries as worthy, overall, insofar as they "refine the minds and characters of men, and divert them from selfish and sordid enjoyments." Several papers about "Wimen" speak boldly for admission of "the weaker sex" into higher education, where they "are as well qualified to master the higher studies and practice professions as men, and in some professions excel them by their quickness and foresight. It is, moreover, a remarkable fact that when a woman does take hold of a business she generally manages better than most men would in the same position." As for women's suffrage, "I think women should be allowed to vote and to hold office the same as men, if they wish it, which I think a majority of them do. . . . It would not make any material difference on the great questions at stake, but only increase the number of votes on each side." This anticipates the man—doctrine watery with afterthought.

Such are the observations of a reliable plain mind. Iconoclasms of the father crop out, unexpected "progressive" notions he culls from incessant reading. By nightfall those overworked eyes ache; he turns to Andrew usually when he prefers to listen. Uncomplaining, this silent middle son would appear in Father's gloomy library, settle himself beside the flickering of a lamp, take up the volume of Adam Smith or Fourier or Karl Marx or Dickens or Horace Greeley or Thomas Huxley, and attempt the evening's extended portion. Against Andrew's light intonations the Mellon Saint Bernard, Rover, wheezed in its slumber somewhere beyond the knots of the carpet.

Just before the Christmas interruption of 1869 the increasingly restless Common Pleas Judge laid his gavel aside, looked after the clock beside the courtroom door and folded his robes away permanently. "I did not care," he himself records, "to return to the legal profession as I had now too many pecuniary and other interests of my own to make it profitable to attend to the affairs of other people; and in view of the condition of the times, and the position it might afford for some of my younger sons, I concluded to open a banking house."

Interest alone wasn't tempting. Throughout the uncertain Sixties the jurist felt nettled each time he remembered how completely the years were frittering away his most important asset since abandoning Poverty Point—his reputation, his appreciable private credit. It must be put to account.

He need not stoop to testimonials. Pittsburgh recognized his integrity—silent, thorough, roaming the fusty storefront at 145 Smithfield Street, making certain the clerk and the inexperienced cashier didn't befuddle the ledgers. Before he started classes, Andrew invariably stopped off. Besides the conventional tumblers, the Judge had insisted that the imposing iron safe be secured at nightfall by heavy woven cable, dragged around its face, padlocked. Andrew supplied the key. Mornings produced a shuttered Pittsburgher *Laocoön* —the Judge himself presiding over his designated son and one rugged assistant, lugging open the coils of workaday capital.

His astute familiars anticipated that, at fifty-six, Thomas Mellon hadn't disrobed to dedicate his maturity to nodding at depositors and facing down loan applicants. He required this stronghold. "T. Mellon and Sons," financial clearinghouse. He distrusted the postwar economy—the easy prevailing credit was inflating a "mania" of speculation he expected to "explode at the first spark of distrust." Foreclosures would assure bargains.

The landmark he commissioned in 1871 incarnated the format. Upon a choice midtown lot up Smithfield Street he raised a four-story iron-fronted commercial building, its low, lapping marble steps overhung by the stout cast effigy of Benjamin Franklin, who bore his legendary bun bag like tablets to practical men's laws. The cast and arched facade rose three blank floors to a topping crest, a see-through balustrade centered with a floral French spike anchored at the corners against the mizzling Pittsburgh sky by molded vitrines.

The first-floor banking lobby contained the building's barest occupant. Tenants at 512–514 Smithfield included a barbershop and a saloon, a tailor shop, a hall fitted out for concerts and religious revivals. Off the entrance (north) a bullpen of clerks soon looked after the repairs and tax obligations, the rents due and conditions of maintenance of the Judge's real estate, the rumored million dollars' worth of "Mellon interests." Off the entrance (south) the banking lobby remained uninviting—long counter, the familiar safe, a varnished pine desk, the potbellied stove, a couple of chairs.

Furnishings of greater dignity were supplied the private office in the rear Thomas called the "banking parlor." After classes, idling along the carpet, young Andrew listened thoughtfully to terms on a promissory note the Judge was exacting—evenly enough, that tough farmer's back braced against the rolltop to confront the last of the afternoon's callers, who gaped up uneasily out of the high-backed Windsor. Interest rates, discounting, the evaluation of collateral— financial variations were mesmerizing. What combinations were possible! Andrew drifted in Saturdays, volunteered at the bank each morning throughout vacations.

The Judge took pains to familiarize the boy with the necessary elements. Each situation was different. Think each one through. However a situation went, one must be watchful to take back value, to secure the *substance*. Learn to assess character. Pursue only "sure things." There are indeed circumstances in which an unfortunate may find himself strapped for reasons truly beyond anticipation. Illness, natural disaster—both self-interest and charity occasionally require

A storefront on
Smithfield Street
ONE HUNDRED YEARS
OF BANKING—
MELLON NATIONAL BANK

The youthful Andrew Mellon
PAUL MELLON

The iron front behind Franklin
ONE HUNDRED YEARS OF BANKING—
MELLON NATIONAL BANK

a banker to delay a repayment schedule, shave interest rates retro-actively. Then—demand something on account.

But overall, Thomas himself noted, "By outsiders, throughout the business period of my life, I was regarded as a hard practical man, disposed to acquire wealth by every fair means. This is true to a certain extent and I have never discovered its wrong!" Standing be-side the Judge, at sheriff's auctions, stealing a look at that resolute, impassive profile above the wing collars—the black, long-skirted frock coat scarcely registering a flutter as Thomas's oaken mouth put for-ward its dispossessingly low bid to take mortgagee's farm—the hollow-cheeked middle son acknowledged Father's sincerity.

Andrew couldn't stay away. Overworked just then, the father couldn't help entrusting heavy responsibility to this surefooted col-lege boy. Agents for the Judge were identifying properties far from western Pennsylvania. The farsighted banker acquired townships along the route of the Northern Pacific, tucking away key tracts all across the newly opened Dakota territories, in Colorado and Kansas and Idaho and Wisconsin and Missouri. Let Andrew appraise these. Once, visiting Thomas Alexander's Kansas in-laws, the Caldwells, Andrew surveyed the West while representing the make of wagon the Cald-wells manufactured.

Things kept coming up. The summer after Andrew's junior year a mortgage he held on the Chestnut Street Theater went sour, and so the Judge delegated Andrew to proceed to Philadelphia and select a replacement competent to manage the playhouse. The seventeen-year-old put up with relatives and made it a point to attend the performance every evening, allegedly to count the house. Later on that year Thomas sent the boy to analyze eighty acres of land he'd accumulated between Baltimore and Washington. Most went into house lots. Andrew recommended holding back one parcel—a strip which bordered several promising local streets, ideal for future trackage. The price the railroad ultimately met startled the Judge himself.

Prodigious. Nevertheless. Was all this well-advised? At unguarded moments the Judge now surprised his lean, watchful shadow—Andy's neat ears pricking, those tense noncommittal lips hedged against the onslaught of heavy and premature responsibilities. His understudy's pale eyes responded with a look the Judge felt linger upon himself with unintended reproachfulness. Run-down, increasingly haggard, the boy was apprehensive about finding the time to catch up on his neglected studies before final examinations, jittery at the prospect of addressing a graduation audience.

Why gamble with that? Let Andy drop out. The concerned father worried "lest the confinement and close attention to the banking business at so early an age might be injurious to Andrew's health." There were diabolical risks; something threatened to denature this peaked middle boy.

The older two had accomplished such wonders with that East Liberty lumberyard. The Judge started thinking. James particularly appeared astute. He demonstrated his mettle first by leasing the Judge's slow-moving Osceola Coal Works and pushing that off. Between building-lot sales and coal and lumber the Judge couldn't wait to record that the older pair were worth in excess of $100,000 before James reached twenty-one. The subsidiary joint stock company the brothers had formed in 1867 solidified into the East End Bank.

The Judge now powerfully suggested that the younger two look into something similar. Unless Andrew raised objections he intended to pick up property about eight miles out of town, in Mansfield, along the Pan Handle railroad, surrounded by subdivisible lots. Andrew said very little.

Forthwith, reports the satisfied Judge, "On these properties Andrew and Dick went to work with a will." The office went up, along with sheds and a warehouse. "They surveyed and divided their other grounds into building lots themselves, as they were competent civil engineers for all ordinary practical purposes."

Those months play jerkily. The dervish was Andrew—everywhere, simultaneously, conveyancing an eighth-acre house lot one minute, scrambling up the wood-barn stairs a half hour afterward to feed an order of molding strips and lath and walnut quarter-round out into a delivery wagon. Pushing, making good the hard way with his silken shirt sleeves up beyond the knobs of his elbows as sawdust powders his vest and cakes the perspiration below his noble hairline. One distracted eye twitches each time he passes the snarl of the blade.

Eighteen, finished with higher education. Out back, most enthusiastic, fourteen-year-old brother Richard is busy bumping fresh-ripped planks onto an eye-high pile.

The Judge produced guffaws each time he suggested how Andy unloaded the place. The panic of 1873 was in the offing: Jay Cooke had failed. The boy now expeditiously resold the adjoining twenty-five-acre tract to the regretful farmer. One night shortly afterward a lumber conflagration burned flat Andrew's main local competitor. The embers hadn't settled before Andrew himself appeared, muttering condolences. Softly, he proposed a long-term lease too tempting to refuse.

It required ten years before Thomas Mellon fully recovered his forty-thousand-dollar investment, along with accumulated interest. But payments arrived reliably, their capital was protected. Andrew proved his willingness; now he returned quietly, reclaimed that unornamented pine desk, off to one side, which dominated the counting room.

2

After the Civil War the panic of 1873 turned into the cataclysm of the century. Transcontinental railroads had inaugurated the boom; when Jay Cooke defaulted it was a train wreck. The pileup included everybody from riggers of the Crédit Mobilier to wary Thomas Mellon. Vexed at having been bypassed by so many lucrative speculations, the Judge got in just before everything toppled: his available cash went heavily into Pennsylvania Railroad paper, which now became non-negotiable. The T. Mellon and Sons deposits on hand in New York and Philadelphia banks passed into oblivion along with their repositories.

By October the list of T. Mellon and Sons collateral diminished radically to sixty thousand dollars of jealously protected capital, the iron-front building at 512 Smithfield Street, devalued mortgages and unsalable house lots.

Mellon was considered "impregnable." October 15 the cash on hand was down to fifteen thousand dollars. The boys scrambled all around Pittsburgh to call in loans, and the disconcerted Judge informed depositors that there would be no drawing out except in hardship cases. The door never closed; a month after suspension enough cash was recovered to resume as before.

The Judge came close to writing off banking. The $4,500 or so a year the effort was netting the family seemed paltry against risks like these. They closed the East End Bank out completely. Fifty-seven years afterward Andrew himself summed up: "The effects of the panic were felt for years, and in 1877 long bread lines formed in the cities. There were serious labor troubles, due to unemployment and reduction in wages, which caused riots, especially among workers on the railroad. . . . I remember the excitement caused by the burning of Union Station and the grain elevator here by rioters. It was followed by looting of the cars in the yards and also attempts to sack the city, which were finally stopped by the police and the militia."

Andrew drew lifelong conclusions: "Many of the troubles which business men faced during the period could be traced to the inadequacy of the country's banking structure." Overall control was missing. He'd seen for himself the effects of true free enterprise. Ravaging competition meant 1873—bankruptcies, mobs in the streets, the plasm of capital blasted beyond recovery. Terrifying risks became unavoidable. The entrepreneur should anticipate the conditions his capital might expect. One must dictate events.

3

With Andrew back permanently, the Judge started prospecting for something appropriate to Dick. Richard wasn't particularly bookish. He still seemed puppylike, a heavy-bodied jug-eared enthusiast beneath whose bulge of forehead the closely set eyes could assume rather a lugubrious cast. Richard dressed the rich man's son. His moods were spontaneous, even emotional at moments; the boy remained tempted to blurt his feelings. He met people warmly, and after the two got back from Mansfield the father kept Dick running around looking after his "outside affairs and property."

It was with Richard in mind the Judge ultimately consented to finish the Ligonier Valley Railroad. Dick needed a pick-me-up. The panic had overtaken the syndicate which earlier planned trackage along that critical ten-and-a-half-mile series of cuts and gulches which formed the Loyalhanna Gap between the Pennsylvania Railroad's juncture at Latrobe and bountiful Ligonier Valley. Rough grading was in before the project's ruined sponsors gave up its charter in order to salvage a last few thousand by permitting a sheriff's sale. Ligonier natives were stunned; they acquired the franchise and approached the Judge in hopes that he might underwrite a $100,000 railroad mortgage in return for four-fifths of the stock and a ten-thousand-dollar bonus.

Thomas Mellon stewed. What this really involved was building that headache. Construction made him uneasy—his earlier dabblings had left him "averse to outside enterprises of any kind." But Tom and Dickie never let it rest. Ligonier Valley stirred memories. These were the farmlands on which Alexander Negley, Sarah's grandfather, lived among the savages of Fort Duquesne. The Judge's uncles Samuel and Archy got started by paving a section of the Greensburg and Stoystown turnpike into good cracked stone. To the susceptible boys railroading carried real glamour. They pressed their case, and early in 1877 James started checking land titles against surviving rights-of-way while Willie, already an impish eight-year-old, stood posted beside the turnpike shoulder, writing down how many bypassing loads of tanner's bark and lumber and cartfuls of produce a hauler might expect.

The numbers weren't promising. Nevertheless, "I was induced to consent," Thomas records, and by mid-September the boys were already rounding up men by offering a dime a day more than the Pennsylvania Railroad and weeding out shirkers. James backed things up as purchasing agent; Dick bossed the gangs out grading and bridging and spiking down track. Andy watched the books from Smithfield Street.

President Tom represented management. He appeared each morning just as the sun was hottest, stately behind tremendous moustaches, to drive slowly alongside their toiling Irish laborers, a keg of beer on ice lashed conspicuously behind the perch of his buckboard. Up ahead, farther than anybody anticipated, Tom tethered his horse and directed the burial of the keg. If tracks got that far the beer was theirs. In peewee Will's opinion these roustabouts were "a rude and reckless lot, terrifying when they teased me," yet somehow the sight of all that beer made sore muscles heave. The brothers rarely needed to elevate their voices.

Two months after starting, with the undemonstrative old Judge propped into the reupholstered royal blue plush which Sarah had selected, the Mellons' reconditioned locomotive puffed its inaugural circuit between Latrobe and Ligonier. The cynosure was Richard. He kept his cap cocked low enough so none of the others could miss the gold-embroidered letters CONDUCTOR stitched above his thick leather visor. "From that day forward," Will later wrote, "the railroad line and the region it served became the charge of Dick, who was as devoted as a mahout to his elephant. . . ."

The Judge was quietly gratified. "My boys," he wrote his surviving uncle Archibald in December, "have got through with their little Rail Road project and are highly pleased with the prospects." For five lively years Dick punched tickets snappily and heaved travelers' luggage into racks. Wherever coal turned up, the railroad ran spurs to accommodate the mouths of the pits. Just off the ridge, three miles from Latrobe, a subsidiary of Booth and Flinn started quarrying the inimitable "Belgian" blocks with which it ultimately paved Pittsburgh. To lure out city people the Mellons founded Idlewild amusement park.

Then events leaned hard. In 1880, while looking after some house-building contracts for the Judge, George, the family baby, developed a bronchial inflammation that seized both lungs. Doctors quickly diagnosed George's lassitude and midday fevers as tuberculosis. The patriarch agonized: he proceeded from text to text, from specialist to specialist, determined somehow to save the boy. As George's health vacillated, the Judge sat restlessly through rooming-house life in Aiken, South Carolina, and strenuous tours with the despairing semi-invalid around the British Isles. In 1883 the old man decided that George and the faithful Richard should proceed "out West" to another community in which the climate might give their consumptive a chance.

The two wound up in Bismarck, North Dakota. Bismarck, the end of the Northern Pacific track, was on the verge of a land boom. Dick sniffed the bracing northern wind. He took a job tending bar in a local hotel and bought himself a fringed buckskin jacket. Within months the boys opened Mellon Brothers Bank. Richard directed the bank; George looked over real estate operations.

When James's boy Willie, fifteen now, showed up to spend one summer in Bismarck he found himself constrained with "poor George" to a tent four miles outside town. The real estate consisted primarily of busting a thousand acres of prairie sod with oxen in hopes of a crop of valuable northern wheat. Will was to remember a succession of blistering treeless days appended to a hayrake, working the mosquito-infested bottomland. Evenings, alone with George in a tent that contained nothing except two cots and a locked box to protect their whiskey, Will appreciated Dick's devotion.

In 1887 Richard's long sacrifice ended. The land boom petered out; overproduction collapsed wheat prices; George took a side trip to Denver, where he contracted spinal meningitis and died. While George was living the Judge had hedged his worry with philosophy—"It is easy for an old person to die when he has gone through and knows how little happiness compared with its troubles life affords. . . ." Gradually the practical impinged: "Should his health not be so fully

Sarah with her boys—(left to right) Richard, James, Andrew, George, Thomas Alexander

The Bismarck branch
ONE HUNDRED YEARS
OF BANKING—MELLON
NATIONAL BANK

Out West: George, Richard B., James Jameson (1883)

CONSTANCE MELLON BURRELL

restored, I rely upon his good common sense to restrain him at all times within the bounds of his income." Death itself proved devastating.

Richard Mellon had returned from western exile alive, his imagination singed permanently with memories of hunting trips across the dusk prairies in an elegant canvas-topped spring wagon driven by a "wire-thin colored man named Crawford." A compass was mounted, fitted in leather to the dashboard; guns waited on racks inside. There had been tuxedoed soirées in company with the elegant émigré Marquis de Mores, publisher of *The Badlands Cowboy*; evenings of splendid tale-swapping with the hulking, controversial Sheriff Alex MacKenzie; a venture in mule breeding. Dick got himself appointed Deputy Sheriff of the Dakotas. Pried open, his packing cases yielded treasures like the mastodonic hatrack, all mirrors and buffalo horns, and the bisected buffalo head, one glass eye glaring, which he insisted on hanging prominently in the reception hall of the mansion he built a few years later for red-haired Jennie.

Out West—the infinite horizon, the badlands, the outward-bleeding frontier. Prairie sod, virgin muck—the amiable Richard had made some kind of an existence for himself out there, stomped through several seasons alternately enjoying the wildness and pulling back disgusted by the foul exchanges between the oxen handlers, the choking cyclones, the stench of the panhandling Indians who hung around the slaughterhouse all afternoon to wolf down entrails white butchers would heave at them through gore-encrusted drapes. Even this most warm-blooded of the Mellons now found himself glad to see Pittsburgh. Domesticated for good now, the voluble R.B. was grateful for Andy's offer of equal shares in T. Mellon and Sons. "I just said to come in," Andrew Mellon would recollect, "and he came in. . . ."

4

The A. W. Mellon who took in Richard in 1887 never specified how workaday affairs would proceed. Dick Mellon knew that. " 'Now, Father would have told us that we would be wise to do thus and so,' " Willie quoted A.W. The patriarch lived on; A.W. meant Father during an earlier period. ". . . Andrew had a way of incorporating an older judgement into our councils." Meaningful leadership had passed.

By now Andrew's erratic fringy neophyte's moustache had lost its frizz completely, masked off his corners of expression solid as poultices. Gray threaded his careful smooth hair. The judge acknowledged completely his capacity to direct "my banking business with eminent ability and success," and had, in fact, simplified his own restless existence by flatly turning over the bank to Andrew five years earlier. His bequest was specific:

Pittsburgh, January 5, 1882

Proposition to son Andrew for services past and future.

He is to have the entire net profits of the bank from January 1, 1881, including my salary, the books to be readjusted accordingly, from 1st January instant. He is to have entire net profits of bank and pay me an annual salary of two thousand dollars as its attorney and fifteen hundred per annum rent for the banking room; and I to allow him forty-five hundred per annum for attending to my private affairs and estate—selling lots, collecting rents, etc., as done heretofore.

This arrangement to last till superseded by another or annulled by either party.

THOMAS MELLON

Old Thomas still appeared once in a while. Scratched around his banking parlor, left off the papers on workhorses he'd bought in Kentucky to supplement the teams of the Pittsburgh, Oakland and East Liberty Company, a horse-drawn railway he'd taken in bankruptcy. But visits were rarer, although when something important needed doing he still took up that roll-brimmed white flat-topped Quaker hat and investigated personally. His solemn, lined face still stood for ruthlessness and integrity all over western Pennsylvania. By now his eyesight was extremely poor. "A long life is like an ear of corn with the grains shrivelled at both ends," he wrote in 1885.

Andrew carried affairs forward. His arrival was punctual; he entered the banking room mornings with his wing collar garnished modestly by the four-in-hand above the buttons of his vest, still wearing his low-crowned derby. "Natural shyness," Will submits, "caused him to walk as if all he met and passed were cloaked in invisibility." His gauntlet of clerks and tellers run, the bank's young owner now centered the derby upon the mantel of his unencumbered pine desk and bent his lean back emphatically toward surrounding distractions. There was a half-panel behind which Andrew sat stiffly now, annotating away without relief. It had a small inset window. From time to time somebody might peer through to ask about something. The banker would rise, whatever was in question was dispatched in hushed definite tones, and then the proprietor went back to whatever he was writing until it was time to proceed to luncheon at the Duquesne Club or interview a caller.

He left the help alone. One surviving anecdote features the banker coming upon a messenger as he experimented with flourishes upon the bank's choice rag paper. "Joe," the proprietor warned, "you shouldn't scribble on such expensive stationery." Otherwise Mellon seemed detached. Underlings surprised him occasionally with one of those rank little rattail cigars he'd taken to smoking forgotten between his teeth, his concentration so intense that perspiration in fine grave beads shone across his temples.

He existed very quietly. There was a period when Andrew ventured "into society a good deal," noted the Judge passingly, and even contemplated marriage. But that passed off. Society meant very little. The family provided enough, although Andy did appear to enjoy getting together with some of the Grant Street holdovers once in a while, and nobody outguessed him twice during an evening of poker. Overall, Andrew kept to himself. Except for one individual. Except for Henry Frick.

5

He'd also inherited Frick. Frick was Father's customer, one of the first to appear soon after the Judge had taken the original storefront. Father often reminisced keenly about the closemouthed little coke speculator—his scoop of a jawbone still hollow and beardless, barely started his twenties, an electric mane of crinkly brown Swiss hair tickling into relief the urn-handle ears. Smoldering self-confidence, underlining to the Judge how little the bank would risk in backing up Frick and his cousins with fifty beehive cooking ovens.

The Judge lent ten thousand dollars. The money came back on schedule; the firm continued to expand; young Henry Clayton Frick's carriage horse, which supposedly knew enough to traipse without a flicker of the reins from one Pittsburgh moneylender to the next, paused first at Smithfield Street. The panic of 1873 caught all of them desperately strapped for capital. Frick proved an inspired conniver— shuddering off personal bankruptcy, he scurried to buy up farmers' right-of-way options between Broadford and Mount Pleasant before surrendering his packet to the Baltimore and Ohio Railroad for a fifty-thousand-dollar commission. As competing coke producers went under all across the rich Connellsville fields, Frick ignored their pleas for consolidation and, taking on for backing the aging Pittsburgh businessman E. M. Ferguson, digested their financial carcasses.

Frick had an approach the Mellons could understand. Hearing rumors that their persistent client was living in a shack, working as a storekeeper for the Youghiogheny Overholts and sleeping on a counter, the Judge promptly shipped his henchman J. B. Corey east to assess their borrower. "Lands good," Corey reported, "ovens well built; manager on job all day, keeps books evenings, may be a little too enthusiastic about pictures but not enough to hurt. . . ."

Fine, close enough to what the Judge had anticipated—he ventured his opinion to Andrew that old Abraham Overholt's grandson was evidently a careful enough boy, energetic and industrious if inclined to be impetuous and "daring on his own account," although "so cautious in his dealings with others disposed to take chances that I doubt if he would make a successful banker." The boy looked certain to make a success of things "unless he overreaches."

Five decades of involvement would bear the old man out. Andrew was congenitally evasive, but Frick could peer up level and distrusting at just about anybody. There were rarely exceptions: throughout all the years they knew each other Frick called Andrew Mellon *Andrew*; Andrew addressed the coke baron modestly as *Mister Frick*.

Their personal association began in 1876. Frick had been around the bank to draw on what ultimately became his $100,000 line of credit; as he concluded negotiations the Judge made it a point to lead Frick over to the window to meet his apostle, Andrew. The two stood chatting; Frick wondered whether Mellon might enjoy spending "Saturday and Sunday" with him down in the little place he maintained alongside the coking ovens near Broadford.

Young Mellon had looked over coal properties enough for his father to anticipate the landscape. He recognized the coking ovens—cinder igloos, glowing through every aperture, pluming fly ash. The shanties, the streams of miners too exhausted to grunt hauling themselves up out of the shafts underneath sheens of coal dust thick enough to crack wherever their bellies wobbled.

Frick was the surprise. Mellon entered his shack; the entrepreneur was steeping himself in Lord Chesterfield's letters to his son. Volumes of Addison and Macaulay attended the reading table. Frick's ambitions went considerably beyond fortune-building. He was re-creating himself.

Not that he ignored many opportunities to corner a dollar. By 1880, when affairs around the bank had largely straightened out and Henry Frick's relentless land shuffle left him the master of the Connellsville bituminous coal beds, the taciturn associates decided to undertake the popular "Grand Tour" of the European continent. Both felt there ought to be somebody in the party to "do the talking"; they retained a featherweight from Pittsburgh society to think up ditties and volunteer little anecdotal turns. To make a fourth, Frick announced one day, he had already invited a stultifying older businessman. Andrew complained; Frick informed him curtly that there was a "special reason" for including the slow-witted fellow. Mellon let it go.

Despite their obtuse fourth man the vacation was spirited. They ran up an American flag beside the Blarney Stone, pondered the exquisite Wallace collection in London, surfeited themselves with Paris. Their "dash across the Continent" cost more than their phlegmatic acquaintance had thought, but he was having the devil's own time, and considerate Henry Frick was doing whatever was imaginable to keep his exuberance building.

In Venice, Frick drew his middle-aged friend aside. Pretty soon the rest of them must get along back. He shouldn't give up. Why not push farther, look over the remaining world? *That* would impress Pittsburgh.

It was a tempting notion. The trouble was, the duffer grumped confidentially, there wasn't enough . . . he didn't have cash along for anything like that.

Frick understood completely. It happened—Frick mentioned this hesitantly—his senior friend held title to important coal-bearing property in the Connellsville area? Well, then—he, Frick, had plenty of currency. Perhaps they might work a swap, and with the proceeds the friend might finance his adventure.

Andrew watched all this more enlivened than surprised. The banker understood Henry well enough by then. In 1880, approaching thirty-two, Frick bruited it about that his own financial worth, his personal third of H. C. Frick and Company, now placed him in the . . . he was a millionaire, dammit! He'd steamed it together: just over a thousand first-quality coking ovens, plenty of reserves, 80 percent of

Pittsburgh's—which meant the country's—coke business just as the price of a ton of coal was hopping from ninety cents to five round dollars. Three-fifths represented profit.

The Grand Tour: Henry Frick (*left*), Andrew Mellon (*seated*)
CARNEGIE LIBRARY—
STEFAN LORANT

A photograph survives of the quartet that looked over Europe in 1880. Significantly out of focus, the entertainer and the dupe are included largely to compose the frame. The two in foreground seem sharper, more revealing. Mellon peers out fleshlessly, a sallow male mannequin now going on twenty-six. Frick is more interesting. At thirty-one his big disproportionate skull cants ominously to size up the photographer, an inverted glowering teardrop whose look of appraisal augments strangely the floppy and unbuttoned vest, across which Frick's knob-headed walking cane is hung like a bandolier from a gleaming leather strap. He sports the clipped full Vandyke one associates with Beelzebub.

By 1880 the intimacy between Henry Frick and Andrew Mellon depended on much besides friendship. They were accomplished confederates. Both accorded this collaboration the utmost in privacy—it patches the unwritten industrial and political history of the next forty years at unexpected junctures, along hollows and creases, like documentary psoriasis.

Frick first steps in once 1873 is starting to float its corpses. Badly shaken still, the unremitting Judge Mellon is nonetheless soliciting his trustworthy banking contacts to line up backers to help young Andrew and himself into control of the pathetically floundering Pittsburgh National Bank of Commerce. A centrally chartered bank could legitimately issue currency on its own. Frick awaits no follow-up invitation. There might be dividends, eventually; right then, Frick wanted no more than opportunity to hear those board meetings, sucking on premium cigars, his country opinions left to himself while bluebloods like Philander Knox offered statesmanlike presentations. There would be recompense in time for all the scrimping, for wheedling those humiliating advances against the Overholt inheritance. Getting inside promises everything. Who else from Connellsville was accumulating mental notes each time the methodical treasurer ran over his loan portfolio, emphasizing the vulnerability of empires like those of elderly, failing James Kelly, the seigneur of Wilkinsburg? Moving in alongside Andrew, pocketing failures pleasantly cheap?

After 1882 Pittsburgh quickened. Thomas Mellon had retired; the silent young man who took his place would decide for himself what served everybody's interests. With Father getting older certain . . . crotchets appeared. As prices began rising the bill for the midday meal in the nearby Henry Hotel lunchroom now exceeded a total the Judge would accept. He attempted strong action: once he had eaten he brushed himself off, rose, and clapped down the quarter he regarded as more than appropriate to cover the fare. The proprietor quietly noted the difference and presented Andrew a statement monthly to cover the arrears. This Andrew paid, bemusedly.

In 1890 the Judge suddenly resolved to divest himself utterly. He presented his possessions, an inventory his grandson William would assess at "a little more than $2,450,000" according to the most conservative of appraisals, to Andrew for dispersal among the designated heirs. He estimated the holdings of his four sons together at something like his own, with Andrew's personal worth well known to have risen by then to perhaps a million dollars. ". . . I never desired wealth on its own account but for the accomplishment of some ulterior purpose," Thomas Mellon later wrote. "Possession and ownership involve cares and responsibilities inconsistent with the entire freedom I had enjoyed in my youth when I was impecunious and my main care and desire was centered in the acquisition of wealth to make me independent. After the necessary wealth was acquired, I voluntarily parted with wealth to promote my freedom from the care and re- sponsibility requisite for retaining it, until nature should grant me the final divorce."

With that, at seventy-seven, the fiery ex-jurist removed to Kansas City, Missouri. Sarah watched over things at 401 Negley. There was, people claimed, a medium in Kansas City with powers to resurrect both voice and appearance of the beloved dead. Old wounds throbbed remorselessly. Andrew confirmed one episode in a séance parlor during which a little boy materialized pushing a wheelbarrow, all ringlets and wearing a frilly collar like toddler Selwyn's best, to traverse the ghostly light beyond the portieres and whimper, heart- breakingly: "Father! Father!"

How credulously the skeptical Judge actually regarded the per- formance is debated among relatives. He lingered out West five years. In time he joined a syndicate of businessmen in proposing a system of ramps much like the Mount Washington inclined planes he'd pro- vided his own street railway. "Boodlers" prevented that; the incensed Judge mounted a campaign of editorials in the Kansas City *Leader* which brought down indictments.

6

Pittsburgh ached and erupted, feverish with industrial transforma- tion. Tree trunks became telephone poles; the dilatory horsecars gave way to snappy little trolleys, which trailed their sparks up every exploitable thoroughfare. Ironmaking loaded the riverbanks with communities of furnaces, and titanic pear-shaped Bessemer con- verters gushed steel like divine wombs.

Wherever "rock oil" surfaced the specter of Rockefeller now tended to materialize. Arid as his legend, he exuded a need for information so acute it seemed his eyes canted sideways, ranging like a sand shark's. From high enough ground to avoid all danger of spattering his puttees he attended the mobs of laborers in bowlers, squatting beneath the "walking arm" of one of their homemade drilling con- traptions, sniffing mud in wads. It filled his soul with regrets.

The bankers on Smithfield Street succumbed to reverberations.

William Larimer Mellon as schoolboy (briefly)
JAMES R. MELLON II

Another world was rising. Enormous figures, delineated industries to come—at times their legacy could seem so cold and unpromising. The antiquated arched iron-front, unimportant directorships, the yellow pine desk, Father's carefully invested money, useful political arrangements, building lots—dead eggs, stale pods, forsaken by their spider. Mightn't everything be dormant? Wasn't Pittsburgh their precinct? They must append themselves.

Yet . . . how, exactly? Where? They started looking around, and then in 1889, just as the winter receded, J.R.'s unsettled Willie wandered into the bank in hopes his uncles might offer something livelier, less frustrating than putting through shipping orders. Nothing exactly . . . recommended itself. James's ungainly twenty-year-old was serious, yet there was still something phlegmatic about the boy, perhaps merely the way those sloe eyes dawdled over whatever was happening. Willie's hangdog look, accentuated by the drooping face and long, leafy ears.

He'd been so restless. Will's inclinations were practical, countrified even—he drifted, off balance, around that neo-Grecian residence J.R. laid up alongside the Judge's property. Formal palms in urns, a colonnade of fluted Ionic pillars to accent the loggia. Pretension left Will uncertain. It seemed from childhood he'd trailed his younger Mellon uncles, inherited Andrew's pony cart, tended booths at Idlewild Park, ambled over to read to the Judge when nobody was around.

Confinement left him antsy. Neighbors marked the lad as suspiciously "harum-scarum," the type who evened old scores at Halloween. Classroom attendance was erratic, although nobody need worry. He'd invariably turn up—throwing out a line, crouched in the dapples of a willow or stalking a cornfield in hopes of flushing up grouse. Perturbed, James Ross and Rachel sent away their hooligan to profit from regimentation at a military academy in Chester, Pennsylvania. Will fidgeted worse there. When one of his irritable masters objected each time he lit his pipe in class the boy grew disgusted with education and repaired to Pittsburgh to try the lumberyard. The Judge supposedly chipped in twenty thousand dollars to get Will going.

Plainspoken older relatives were fond of attributing the wildness to Willie's Larimer blood. Larimers wouldn't settle down. Rachel's father, General William Larimer, had been an intimate of the Judge since both were youngsters. An errant speculator's instincts had left the general with holdings in banking, coal mining, a Conestoga wagon freight service, random "gold mining enterprises" and assorted questionable railroads. A recession in 1854 had caught him overextended. Bankrupt, he carted his sizable family west; they roamed the grasslands for years, through floods and sandstorms and repugnant Indian migrations, and staked their claims to real estate from LaPlatte to Denver. The middle-aged promoter had barely reestablished himself in merchandising and farming around Fort Leavenworth, Kansas, before he was reactivated in 1863 and, at fifty-four, he fought the war's terminal battles.

The stolid Pittsburgh Judge never quite lost touch with the mercurial general. When young James Ross stopped over to examine Thomas Mellon's Fort Leavenworth properties he found those roving Pittsburgh Larimers. Their black-haired Rachel caught James's vagrant eye. The two were compliant about delaying their engagement a year; Judge Mellon regarded both as impetuous and immature.

Their firstborn, William, appeared in 1868. Perhaps Will did harbor certain fugitive Larimer impulses. The lumberyard closed in; he attempted house contracting. He liked that better, certainly. His father and Thomas Alexander had long since resumed their lending operations as the East Liberty City Deposit. That too seemed . . . lifeless, in its way. Sedentary. Andy was pushing out. He'd better ask downtown.

The best post A.W. could recommend was agent to a gas plant the bank now owned in Connellsville. Willie packed his trunk. Then, barely a day afterward, a rumor swept Pittsburgh about a tremendous oil find in neighboring Economy. Will hovered, fascinated, whenever wildcatters like ponderous John Galey dropped in to yarn his grandfather about gushers they'd struck throughout Clarion County farms. The Judge himself dabbled sometimes in Galey's secondary leases. The uproar outside Economy now stirred Will powerfully; he abandoned his trunk to join the excitement.

He smelled the overflow even before he located the greenish-orange geyser of crude oil erupting, exploding, spattering the far-flung meadow. Pastures in every direction were "carpeted" with men and horses, rigs already being hoisted to tap surrounding tracts. Lease buyers, duded out in high silk hats and square-brimmed derbies to impress the country people. Willy dogged the field representative of the Bridgewater Gas Company, a Mellon-controlled utility.

The uncles listened sympathetically and financed the boy. He hired a Hookstown driller; excitement kept him sleeping on the ground underneath the great stroking rocker arm of the derrick throughout its long second "tower." After weeks a disappointing twenty-five-barrel-a-day producer purled up; the uncles on Smithfield Street rushed out with congratulations.

Oil made his blood itch. He devoted the next several years to tramping the creek beds and browsing the graveyards of western Pennsylvania's oil terrain. Milking farmers discovered Willie lolling patiently beside the stable lantern, documents ready for signature. Even Galey got disgusted with encountering the boy on the predawn road, spruce, leaseholder around yesterday's bonanza.

Gushers and dry wells tended to average out. The "W. L. Mellon Special," as A.W. tagged the arrangement, joined other risky investments. Western Pennsylvania still dominated the "rock oil" business, and tank cars and pipeline networks owned by the Standard companies moved production to market. A medley of thugs, bribes, lawyers, ruinous price cutting, and dynamite had disburdened the Rockefellers of competitors like Tidewater.

Suddenly Will got lucky. His leases girdling Coraopolis and the McCurdy farm boosted Mellon reserves; W.L. corroborated rumors that the huge French refiner Fenaille & Despeaux needed petroleum acutely but abhorred John Rockefeller. By 1891 the W. L. Mellon Special owned four hundred tank cars.

They understood all along that Rockefeller was positioning himself. Then—once the pendragon established that the Mellons were locked into delivery contracts—Rockefeller selected the means. The

Pennsylvania Railroad, footling to the Standard, published a revised schedule, which jacked the rates over Pennsylvania trackage to ruinous new levels.

Willy remembered the day they got the rate revisions. He admitted being stunned at the time, if tickled a little to think how earnestly the Oil Trust regarded his incessant barnyard efforts. Richard B. reddened furiously, his powerful nostrils dilated. Andrew stared into space.

They recouped momentarily by rerouting deliveries via tracks of the Reading, which happily was feuding just then with the mighty Pennsylvania. That couldn't last either. To protect their outlays they'd need a carrier of their own, from well to seacoast. Whatever chance they had depended on utilizing their resources, as W.L. wrote, "without going out of the state of Pennsylvania. This was common sense because we had friends all over Pennsylvania."

By 1891 the bank enjoyed a plethora of involvements west of the Alleghenies. Andrew Mellon's wily enzyme showed up in everybody's saliva. The statesmen around Harrisburg were especially susceptible. The bankers remained informed. A.W. was aware, for example, how keenly Pennsylvania's legislative czar, Matt Quay (while still gorging insouciantly off kickbacks from the Pennsylvania Railroad), had come to resent the extent to which Mark Hanna and other Rockefeller flunkies openly manipulated the lawmakers. Alerted, the Mellons made sure to feed the irritable Quay a diet of alarming rumors through Pittsburgh go-between Philander Knox. Within the Iron City —where municipal money and municipal influence now washed in a ceaseless fertilizing tide between City Hall and Mellon depositories— Christopher Magee felt cross-tows while supplementing his responsibilities as mayor by moonlighting as purveyor of Pennsylvania Railroad trackage.

Staving the Standard off, the Mellons got active. A Reading Railroad official found W.L. the North Chester butcher from whom he secretly bought fifty acres of Marcus Hook shoreline with draft enough for tankers. Now came the pipeline. Pipe itself was costly. On A.W.'s orders Will bought on time. The links and pumping stations were approaching the Reading's terminal at Carlisle when a Rockefeller maneuver pushed out the Reading's president and installed a Rockefeller puppet, who lost no time in abrogating the Mellon contracts.

They continued laying pipe. Just behind their cadre of seasoned lease buyers, Mellon lawyers exacted rights-of-way by eminent domain. Predictable havoc broke loose whenever the pipeline passed beneath the roadbed of the Pennsylvania. Crews ripped up pipe; the Mellons obtained court orders and pressed for the incarceration of railroad employees.

Along the Marcus Hook shore, W.L. now pushed his roustabouts through completion of the dockside storage tanks, the tiny transfer railroad, the primitive refinery. By now—late 1892—the Mellons were alleged to be shipping a tenth of the continent's exported crude. The W. L. Mellon Special—which now included Crescent Pipeline and Bear Creek Refinery—had cost the family two and a half million dollars. They'd fended off Standard, but oil was draining their risk capital ominously.

Money tightened. Western fields were opening—glut threatened the industry. The crisis passed; hysteria abated; A.W. initiated meetings. There was a Pennsylvania state regulation which prohibited the merger of competitive pipelines. In 1895, managed around the legislature by Pittsburgh representative Thomas Marshall, the repealer went through.

This made the agreements legal; Standard bought their oil business. The Mellons pocketed four and a half million dollars from Rockefeller subsidiary National Transit. W.L. kept 30 percent; the pair on Smithfield Street divided up the rest.

Abraded loyalties soon healed. A Pennsylvania Railroad representative came in to join the board of directors of Mellon-dominated Union Trust Company; the jocular Richard B. began his decades of commuting to directors' meetings of the Pennsylvania Railroad in Philadelphia. The Mellons had blooded themselves—they'd whipped the Standard.

Was this all above board? Nobody asked the Judge. It never took much to sully that finicky moralist's mouth. Politics blighted his life. Even during the Grant Administration he'd stomped around berating the "outrageous system of swindling and theft under the pretext of government." He harangued public gatherings in Horace Greeley's behalf. When personable Christopher Magee organized Pittsburgh in 1883, Thomas Mellon launched tirades before the reform-minded Select Council. Magee must be deposed. The boss was venal—from what the Judge could tell his talents were devoted mostly to fattening his co-conspirator, William Flinn, by ramming through brainless civic "improvements," while he himself grabbed traction franchises.

Nobody listened. A decently "high standard of character" had "nearly disappeared" from public life, the Judge concluded sourly, and "even the desire for fame, which came next to it, is now in a measure subordinated to a grovelling desire for office and its emoluments. . . . In a corrupt democracy the tendency is always to give power to the worst."

Andrew remained more flexible. Hadn't they experienced chaos? He tended toward Rockefeller's judgment—new modes of integration were inevitable. "The day of combination is here to stay," as the pendragon observed. "Individualism has gone never to return."

Magee merely epitomized progress. Mellon enjoyed Magee personally: a dressy plump easygoing drummer, very adept at parting his downy layered hair spang up the middle. He surveyed all petitioners with crafty, indulgent eyes. A sabbatical in Manhattan had convinced the Pittsburgher that it was possible to construct a political ring "safe as a bank." His prescriptions were simple. Determine one's own preferences, then rework the constitution to allow a captive mayor's council to surrender prizes completely within the law. Cut in unremitting opponents; even Democrats appreciate concessions from time to time. Abet commerce. Remain agreeable, but keep on hand somebody hardheaded enough to bump around incorrigibles.

Magee's co-conspirator William Flinn looked molded for the part. Dour, graceless, with one of those intimidating prowlike stomachs which meant that success had arrived and quickly proved digestible. Flinn served as paymaster while maintaining his monopoly on municipal building contracts.

What helped Magee last was his unbelievable penetration. Everything wound up institutionalized. A necessary civic entrepreneur—say, madam of a whorehouse—must placate not merely the policemen loitering outside; Mayor Magee's knowledgeable representative exacted his unwavering percentage from the moment the proprietress attempted to sublet premises, through ward syndication, and into the procurement of overpriced liquor and shoes and dresses from the "official liquor commissioner" and the "official wrapper maker."

Intercourse with the facility the Mellon brothers ran wasn't nearly so one-sided. "Neither," wrote the edgy Lincoln Steffens in 1903, "can I stop for the details of the system by which public funds were left at no interest with favored depositories from which the city borrowed at a high rate, or the removal of funds to a bank in which

Boss Magee
CARNEGIE LIBRARY

The undimmed eye—Judge
Mellon in maturity
WESTERN PENNSYLVANIA
HISTORICAL SOCIETY

Boss Flinn
CARNEGIE LIBRARY

the ringsters were share-holders." By 1931, apropos of William Flinn, Steffens calmed down enough to risk an identification: "Yes, there were big business men back of him; and they knew what their names were—well known names, Andrew W. Mellon, for example."

By then the Mellon-Flinn relationship had become a cliché of second-generation muckraker journalism. Exhumed records bear witness to the regularity with which the Mellon-Frick "interest" bought into crucial downtown corners or took over alleyways just as Mayor Magee's dunking-bird city council was voting to pull an artery across exactly that thoroughfare, start boulevard widening *there*; values took a leap. Flinn hauled those bluish "Ligonier blocks" most municipal contracts required on Mellon's little railroad. When Mellon and Frick threw up their Union Steel flanking action against Carnegie, Flinn volunteered Sharon Steel. He completed his business career dignified by the Mellons, solidly Pittsburgh Upper House—a director at Gulf.

Sociologists of the epoch later concluded that Bill Flinn idolized money, whereas Magee adored power. Wealth retained its utility even for Magee. This was the era of kickbacks to political leaders in return for traction franchises. Philadelphia's Elkins and Widener was famously generous with these, and Magee was famously receptive. The farsighted young mayor was scrupulous about forestalling for himself the sort of grand-jury blanket-rolling sessions which chafed other eastern metropolitan officials: he publicly designated himself manager for Elkins and Widener's sprawling Consolidated Traction Company. His responsibilities seemed endless: he wound up agent statewide to the Pennsylvania Railroad, proprietor of the Pittsburgh *Times*, owner of Duquesne Traction. He imported natural gas; he lent his expertise to board deliberations of numerous banks and insurance companies. The Mellon bank supported Magee's underlying mortgages. Magee countenanced no payoffs; why should anybody challenge his well-earned fees?

Nobody doubted Magee's worth. Cherubic tyrant—who else could breast this flood of foreigners the mills kept encouraging? Numbers were spurting crazily. Mightn't the Mellons contribute? The public wanted transportation. A.W. summoned W.L.

They began in 1895 by commissioning a bridge. The listless, polluted Monongahela opened wide and inconvenient between the Carnegie Brothers' Braddock sprawl, the Edgar Thompson works and all those finishing mills near Homestead. The river separated families —A.W. now predicted a heavy, regular flow the moment some span was up. Will retained a civil engineer, George Davison, and conveyed his uncle's desire for "a toll bridge strong enough to carry a street car line."

Commerce slackened; labor was available, cheap, and steel was off. A.W. inconspicuously exchanged an issue of neglected Waverly Coal Company bonds for control of the Homestead and Highland Street Railway, which ran between Homestead and Pittsburgh's Schenley Park. They pushed into Braddock, and picked up property along the Rankin side of their West Braddock bridge, and built an imposing coal-fired power plant.

Christopher Magee peered up; Mellon utilities were clamping the downtown triangle. What could he do—they underwrote his bonds, they retained his mortgages. He accepted their offer of two and a half cents per customer so that their powerful yellow Westinghouse-designed streetcars might utilize Consolidated tracks.

The Mellon system ramified—East Pittsburgh, Pitcairn, outlying towns like Vernon. Their Monongahela Light and Power Company tied into secondary grids. Then A.W. covertly picked up an established midtown carrier, the Pittsburgh and Birmingham Street Railway; this left the traditional operators, Consolidated and Brown Brothers, simultaneously penetrated and contained. W.L. invaded Charleroi. The overwhelmed carriers merged; they sold in panic to the much larger Philadelphia Company.

The managers in Philadelphia soon recognized what choice they actually had. Mellon named his price. In 1902 the bankers worked out a deal with the Philadelphia Company that relieved them of operating responsibility by way of a nine-hundred-year lease. Payments ascended with earnings; young William L. Mellon subsequently assumed his place upon the Philadelphia Company's board.

Much later Will recalled their underfunded modus operandi. "As Eliza had to cross the river on ice cakes," he admitted, "so a traction company has to move from payroll to payroll." Not that his practical uncle balked at . . . unannounced expenditures. "Practically every bit of franchise hunting had to be done at night for the reason that the suburban towns from which we were soliciting franchises never had any town meeting except at night," Will explained, prose dancing. Councilmen ranged from saloonkeepers to muckers in the works.

"There were all kind of influences making hidden currents in these turbulent little political areas around Pittsburgh. I had my back in this thing and there was only one way to hold my own and that was to go out and live among the people." With understanding—and openhandedness.

A.W. could tell when public opinion shifted. "I feel that I would not care to invest in any public service corporation," he replied to one tempting inquiry in 1910. "There seems to have developed in legislative bodies and municipalities such an attitude unfavorable to individual ownership and property rights that such investments do not appeal to me." Even generosity had limits.

7

Notice. Throughout. Like gusts of fly ash to marble those immaculate Mellon sauces—reminders of Henry Frick. That gas plant around Connellsville W.L. never managed. The leverage they needed to wangle into Homestead. Shared tips on real estate. Help in the legislature from Philander C. Knox, the urbane Pittsburgh attorney who served the Mellons long after he surfaced as Frick's fluent toady. Everything redolent of Henry.

Frick remains an anomaly. As befitted overnight millionaires, both Mellon and Frick had astonished the elite of Pittsburgh in 1880 with thousand-dollar canvases and Bond Street toppers, "beavers," the cut of stovepipe Carnegie himself flaunted. Both hats quickly disappeared. Mellon's increased his awkwardness; in Frick's situation, commercial leaders still felt he hadn't any business with such a talisman.

As industrial prospects widened, Frick's chokehold on metallurgical bituminous slipped month after month. Interests from the coast founded competitive properties. Tonnage prices quickly collapsed while debts required servicing.

Retrenchment endangered Frick's digestion. He now acknowledged limits: the reputation he'd nurtured as "the most successful industrialist of his years" couldn't service fresh tale-bearing about skulls distorted professionally, about feet turned around.

Besides that, he'd married. In 1881, hanging back with Andrew at a ball reception, he'd wondered, suddenly, transfixed: "There is the handsomest girl in the room. Do you know who she is?"

Andrew recognized Adelaide Childs.

"Daughter of Asa P.?"

The Childses were New Englanders. In shirt-sleeved Pittsburgh company they represented real cultivation.

"I want you to introduce me."

Andrew hesitated. Shouldn't this be managed by somebody . . . closer to the father? Somebody . . . better connected? Mellon selected an intermediary.

Frick obviously needed refinancing. He initiated inquiries; the proposals he liked he heard from straightforward Thomas Carnegie, in Pittsburgh to supervise the Edgar Thompson complex. Tom's older brother, Andrew, now lived with their elderly mother in a Manhattan hotel. The winter of 1882 Carnegie invited the honeymooning Fricks to dinner.

Carnegie was typically hilarious; Frick's manners were studied. The meal was ending when Carnegie sprang to his feet to toast their "partnership."

Carnegie's mother was shocked. "Surely, Andrew," the old woman expostulated, "that will be a fine thing for Mr. Frick, but what will be the gain to us?"

Frick bit his lip quite often after that. Their 1882 agreement traded the Carnegies into H. C. Frick and Company with just over a seventh of the shares in return for considerable assumption of indebtedness and $325,000 in capital. The disadvantages appeared afterwards. As early as 1883—when Frick routinely purchased the encroaching Hutchinson properties—Carnegie evidenced such disapproval that Frick quickly sent his associate an analysis which specified, "I am free to say, I do not like the tone of your letter." He then offered Carnegie forthrightly what Carnegie was already conspiring to procure from Frick's aging backers, the Fergusons—control of H. C. Frick and Company. The transfer was accomplished, but shortly after that, when Carnegie placated wildcat strikers in Frick's own mines to save the expense of banking Carnegie blast furnaces, Frick resigned in disgust.

. Carnegie wooed him back. When strikes swept coal mining again Carnegie let Frick be. "Gradually, under the compelling force of public opinion, the County authorities intervened sternly on behalf of law and order," Frick's idolatrous biographer George Harvey records, "shooting to kill and actually killing, until at the end of three months the rioters had been driven out of the region, and mining was resumed peaceably, without recognition of the union, upon the company's own

Andrew Carnegie considers
CARNEGIE LIBRARY

terms, which incidentally proved to be eminently satisfactory to the miners."

In 1889 Carnegie acknowledged the coke baron's "positive genius" for management and installed him at Carnegie Brothers itself as chairman and chief operating officer. Frick preserved his distance; "Mr. Carnegie" inveterately labeled his works manager "Old Pard" and breathed fresh plaudits and familiarities into Frick's impassiveness like garlic.

Fourteen years Frick's elder, Andrew Carnegie still pranced through life on lovely little size five feet, exuded charm and Shakespeare, and spent the preponderance of his time fly-fishing the tarns around his Scottish castle and composing such exuberant egalitarianisms as "He who dies rich dies disgraced." Throughout Pittsburgh, where pig iron counted, the Carnegie mills reverted immediately under Frick from the experimental eight- to the traditional twelve-hour shift. "I drank two buckets of water in twelve hours, the sweat drips through my sleeves and runs down my legs and fills my shoes," as one veteran testified.

The quote is drawn from Andrew Carnegie's authorized biography.

Old Thomas Mellon also distrusted the results of converting the yeomanry into machine-tending digits within "the system of aggregated capital invested in extensive mines and mills and factories." Where was this likely to take their already corrupted democracy?

Frick wasn't that uncomfortable. If progress meant importing enough Slavs and Polacks to feed those networks of aboveground catacombs, that stream of agonized foreigners forever roasting and withdrawing the clinkers of bituminous from underneath the viaduct-like stoneways along which donkeys dodged flaming gases—Frick accepted his responsibilities. Deaths arrived unsurprisingly early: the coke industry contributed a disproportionate number of cadavers to local medical schools, although students were disinclined to muddle over-long among such revoltingly carbonized lungs.

Frick took the larger view. Contemptuous of Carnegie's dictum that "Pioneering don't pay," he realigned the company's motley holdings into a vertical monopoly. To the titanic installation at Homestead and the Edgar Thompson, Frick added the great rail maker at Duquesne: his longstanding Mellon involvement helped out with special-issue Carnegie bonds, virtuoso financing just then. Frick inaugurated the Bessemer furnace, cold rolling of rails, company limestone mines and ore boats and railroad hookups and—plowing against Carnegie's doubts—set up the acquisition of the massive Oliver iron deposits of the limitless Mesabi. The company owned everything—steam shovel, ladle, billet.

Frick expected labor controlled. When the company extended the shift at the Edgar Thompson, the Knights of Labor struck. "The usual disorders took place," Frick's literary associate James Bridge reports, "resulting in a slight loss of life; but eventually the contest was won by the company."

Andrew Carnegie had observed all this from secure Jersey City, wagging his great ox face mournfully, ruminating on his well-advertised industrial slogan, "Thou shalt not take thy neighbor's job." Frick himself felt otherwise; by 1892 representatives of the Amalgamated Association were booming their homemade cannons at scows of Pinkertons which Frick ordered assembled up the Monongahela to reoccupy the Homestead. Then Alexander Berkman intervened. For Sunday-supplement purposes Berkman was ideally typecast, a kind of anarchist eel in a tight-fitting salt-and-pepper suit, "half-crossed eyes," a musky Russian accent he had brought with him a few years before when he fled Vilna ahead of the Czar's secret police, a handgun, nicotine-stained fingers, and a "dirk" he made for himself by grinding down a file. Frick had returned to his office just after his usual heavy lunch at the Duquesne Club and was going over a few minor matters with Vice Chairman Leishman when Berkman pushed in and punctuated their afternoon. One bullet struck Frick from above, passed through his left ear lobe and lodged finally in his shoulder; another creased his neck. Leishman fell on Berkman; Berkman occupied these last few moments with stippling Frick's ribs and hip with his homemade dagger.

What caught the imagination of the turn-of-the-century business community was Frick's characteristic self-possession once he and Berkman came unstuck. Supporting himself one-handed on his desk, he prevented a company maintenance man from staving Berkman's head in with a hammer. Berkman appeared to be mumbling; Frick directed that his jaws be pried apart and the capsule of fulminate of mercury underneath his tongue, enough "to blow everyone in the room to bits," be extracted cautiously. Once Berkman was led away, gasping that he had done this thing "to free the earth of the oppressors of the workingman," Frick summoned Philander Knox and remodeled his will while the doctor probed, without anesthetic, and extracted several bullets. Somebody then helped Frick into his desk chair so he could sign the afternoon's correspondence, arrange for a line of company credit, and wire the unwelcome Carnegie: "There is no need for you to come home. I am still in shape to fight the battle out."

Unexpectedly, Frick lived. A wave of sympathy undercut the Iron Workers. The strike petered out just before the holidays, leaving the labor union movement in the United States retarded by forty years. Frick emerged a hero to his class.

He was forty-three. Famous now, unfailingly dressed in public "as if the minute in which you saw him was the most important occasion of his life," Frick's widely respected judgment and that restful impersonality awakened confidence among virtually all the lions just emerging from the nineteenth century.

Frick's sideline became politics. As early as 1893 he assisted a syndicate of businessmen in rescuing William McKinley from bankruptcy; when McKinley became President, Frick boosted Philander Knox into the Attorney Generalship. Knox alternated as U. S. Senator from Pennsylvania and (under Frick's Prides Crossing golfing companion, William Howard Taft) Secretary of State; in that post he came under fire for "dollar diplomacy." Knox retained his position

Young Frick
CARNEGIE LIBRARY

Frick the Industrialist
CARNEGIE LIBRARY

The adviser to Presidents
CARNEGIE LIBRARY

on boards of the Mellon enterprises. It is no accident that Andrew
Mellon first involved himself in western Pennsylvania politics after
Frick moved away, or accepted a U.S. Cabinet post only after Frick
died. The involvement of *both* of them would represent a waste.

Gradually Pittsburgh caught on. It seemed at times as if both as-
pirants cast one intercommunicating shadow. They filtered common
light. Neither commanded venture capital, but Mellon was particularly
compelling. He laid on hands, his touch could fluff into generosity
such skeptics as button-eyed William Thaw, the transportation magnate. Businessmen endowed his promotions. In 1883, peevish about
those premiums going out, the banker took control of Union Insurance Company. Opportunities came to him. Three years after that
he joined the combine that bankrolled Fidelity Title and Trust.

Frick had also participated. He was characteristically overobligated
—another year wouldn't pass before the scourge of Connellsville was
reduced to bartering the third of the Overholt distillery he inherited
to Mellon for $25,000. But Mellon made clear that Fidelity was
important.

Fidelity emphasized estate management. When Pennsylvania banking laws prohibited the manager of an estate from representing underage beneficiaries or pocketing transfer agent's fees, Fidelity's president
John Jackson rounded up his backers and capitalized a paper affiliate: The Union Transfer and Trust Company. To dignify this
convenience, Jackson routinely listed A. W. Mellon as Union Transfer's president.

Their appendage remained dormant, several forgotten rooms somewhere upstairs around the Fidelity building. When townspeople in
search of help lugging pianos kept interrupting the clerks, the company dropped "Transfer."

One afternoon in 1893, when money was tight, A.W. himself
showed up. The truth was, he indicated to Jackson, the businessmen
who provided Union Trust its $100,000 of capitalization were getting
somewhat . . . restive, perhaps. Awkward remarks were overheard
during Duquesne Club lunches. Union Trust wasn't profitable.
Shouldn't Fidelity consider liquidating Union Trust and refunding
the backers?

Money was awfully close. A thing like that meant sacrificing assets.

Mellon didn't look surprised. Why shouldn't Union Trust open up
a street floor lobby?

Jackson seemed even warier. Couldn't that involve . . . competition with Fidelity? Mellon's smile was ambiguous.

Mellon convened his Union Trust directors. What the rejuvenated company needed was an activist president. He proposed a salary high enough to attract somebody competent. Alarmed, Fidelity representatives on Union's board objected. Mellon let them talk; after everything was out he volunteered to buy the stock of anybody too uncomfortable to endorse his action. Soon Mellon and H. C. Frick had cornered four thousand of the five thousand shares available.

So they were interchangeable. By 1900 Pittsburgh's ruling *nouveaux riches* gathered expectantly at midday in a palatial third floor dining room within the Duquesne Club. There, W.L. remembers fondly, "in the mood of boys," the ascendant steelmakers and attorneys and railroad men ate, gossiped, guessed stock market futures, shook poker dice to see who paid for lunch. "But the one A.W. looked for almost wistfully any time he wasn't there was Henry Clay Frick. The two would talk about coke or banking, or Rembrandts, Whistlers, El Grecos and Raphaels, or mutual friends abroad and at home."

"Wistfully." Pittsburgh was in upheaval, owned overnight by iron puddlers whose shareholdings in Carnegie Associates eventually made them rich enough to pass out cigars banded with heraldic seals and gild their grand pianos and demand of their groundkeepers full Florentine gardens to receive the ever-thickening drizzle of blast-furnace soot.

Frick had evolved delicacy. Close-cropped now, everything below those sensitive pinched nostrils a pattern of dark wire whiskers, Frick was received wherever he went as the plenipotentiary of the age, Industry's killer courtier. Andrew Mellon understood more. He remembered the young man who had been willing to risk the gibes of his backcountry Tinstman cousins by giving a thousand dollars for a *painting* during their exploratory European sally. Pittsburgh knew the iron negotiator; Andrew Mellon had watched the exhausted Chairman march through the entry of his baronial mansion, Clayton, and sink to his knees to accomplish those last few feet to a settee on which he might sprawl to recover himself; the inflammatory rheumatism that had sapped his strength from boyhood was ravaging him again.

Malevolence incarnate to leftists, Frick was a fond teasing husband and father behind closed doors. The strike at Homestead had left Frick critically wounded: the shock of it endangered the life of gentle

Adelaide. Their newborn son, Frick's namesake, died in the aftermath. Loathing Carnegie's public generosity, Frick was a considerable secret contributor to working-class charities; through blinds he underwrote the care of agitators at Homestead.

Frick brooded. Carnegie sensed Frick's appetites, made available to Henry 2 percent of the company's stock, which he might purchase as he liked. "I should like to feel I was out of debt for once," Frick wrote to Carnegie in 1892, his tone extraordinarily plaintive, tempered perhaps by Berkman. Carnegie soft-shoed away—"Remember that you are not really *in debt*"—but Frick persisted, and there were rearrangements that left Frick 16 percent of Carnegie Brothers stock, and Carnegie almost all the H. C. Frick Coke Company.

They'd drawn too close. Carnegie saw no reason to spare the coke company now, and imposed a president of his own, who signed a five-year contract with Carnegie that generated massive losses while assuring the steelmaker a competitive edge. When Frick and Andrew Mellon privately acquired a Peter's Creek tract along the Monongahela and resold it lucratively to Carnegie Brothers, old Carnegie stormed back to rescind the purchase.

The two complementary "pony-built" titans had marched each other straight to the brink: in 1899 Carnegie forced Frick out as Chairman of the steel company. Frick went without ado. He retained his Chairmanship of the coke company (in which both Mellons also maintained important percentages), and with the Spanish-American War business Carnegie stock was valuable.

Carnegie hadn't quite finished. In 1900 he visited Frick's offices to inform his onetime manager he intended to take back Frick's stock in Carnegie Brothers according to the reduced evaluation stipulated in the company's notorious "ironclad" clause. Frick understood the arrangement—he himself stripped out four earlier Carnegie Associates—but at the very suggestion that Carnegie might apply the formula to *himself* Frick's celebrated composure shattered. Employees around the company offices rushed from their desks to observe their Chairman pursuing Andrew Carnegie through doors, down corridors. . . .

It was an outburst Frick immediately regretted. Better than anybody else, Frick recognized the depth of Carnegie's fatigue with commerce, his need for relief before he trapped himself completely outside his century. Before Frick was ousted he'd acted as broker for a prospective syndicate: he, Carnegie's other major shareholder, Henry Phipps, and the speculative Moore brothers from Chicago came up with the $1,170,000 to bind a deal for ninety days until the members got together $250,000,000 to buy the steel company. The money market tightened; the syndicate members requested a short-term extension; enraged at the report that Frick would split a five-million-dollar brokerage fee with Phipps, Carnegie dumped the negotiation and confiscated the down payment, which included Frick's $85,000. Carnegie's recall proved uncertain—"When the option was not executed, I lost all interest in it, and things that came to me bearing on it I never read," he sighed before a Congressional committee—then, with the offhandedness Frick hated, the old Scotsman tossed away his partners' option money to the handiest charity.

Andrew Mellon had followed these negotiations very closely. All along Frick kept A.W. well informed of bookkeeping details not only around the coke company, but also inside the Carnegie works. The Mellons lent working capital, upper six-figure amounts, to Andrew Carnegie personally for many, many years. Now, tired out, Carnegie distrusted quite openly whoever was supporting Frick, "your friends," as he would call them sometimes.

Here Carnegie had grounds. Mellon had been bitterly disappointed when Judge Moore refused him participation in the syndicate that had approached Carnegie in 1899. Through Frick, the banker once offered Moore twice the per-share amount the Chicago speculator committed. After that fell through Mellon approached Carnegie directly and negotiated what he had believed was a mutually binding purchase agreement. This transaction was pending—Carnegie granted Mellon time to scare up supplementary backing—when Carnegie suddenly unloaded. "Carnegie double-crossed me," A.W. once wheezed to young Frank Denton. In an orderly universe, Big Steel was his.

A.W. understood all along that giants were involved. As the Nineties ended, battering his huge desk nervously with an unlit panatela, J. Pierpont Morgan himself was contemplating The Forge of The West. He was the era's Baal, the moist-eyed omnivore of Wall Street. Railroads were already coordinated. Morgan's sanctimonious footpad, Elbert ("Judge") Gary, who had already directed the House of Morgan investment into Federal Steel, now determined that New York capital must batten on Carnegie's Pennsylvania mills.

Carnegie, sixty-five, quickly returned to Pennsylvania to establish internal battle lines. He mounted a sandstorm of a press campaign: he announced himself back in the United States to procure for his company a tube-making facility at Conneaut, to compete with Gary's, backed up by a railroad system to the Atlantic to free the Carnegie enterprises of Morgan "community of interest" pressure.

At that moment—fortuitously, it seemed to Carnegie—young Andrew Mellon had appeared. Mellon's proposal looked logical, if presented with characteristic astringency. He and his brother, Mellon remarked, had long been desirous of entering the steel-fabricating business. It happened that somebody with a background in tinplate production, William Donner, recently visited the bank to request their support in starting a rod-and-wire mill. The Mellons were willing; Andrew hesitated primarily until he could assure the venture a supply of billets, guaranteed by a five-year contract, at a fixed price reasonable enough to protect their investment. Carnegie—who'd just finished telling reporters that he expected to enter that line to contest the outfit Morgan bought from Gates—was happy to encourage the Mellons to risk their capital, and take his profit selling ingots. He'd drawn up contracts and bestowed upon the Mellons' fledgling Union Steel his heartiest benediction.

This proved an expensive mistake. Soon afterward Frick left; within that very week, the Smithfield Street banker startled Pittsburgh by calling in newspaper people to announce that he and his brother had now turned over to H. C. Frick 25 percent of the voting securities of their Union Steel Company, on whose behalf a million dollars of a projected ten million was currently on deposit. The newly founded enterprise was not merely about to construct the biggest wire-and-rod mill in the world; plans were well advanced to secure two "monster" blast furnaces as well as "batteries" of open-hearth facilities.

This left Carnegie obligated to supply his renegade manager a five-year supply of pig iron. Another pesty competitor: as much as anything this turn drove Carnegie to invoke his "ironclad" clause. Once, Frick conceded to reporters that Carnegie Brothers was close to bankruptcy to justify the Pinkertons. Now he produced figures which demonstrated that Carnegie could roll steel rails so cheap the tariff was unfair to consumers. Worse, his lawyers hinted, he'd left with documents that underscored Carnegie profiteering throughout the Spanish-American War.

Bluffs were exploding everywhere. Carnegie pondered into summer. Naturally, the Founder announced, he'd never really intended to bind his cherished Old Pard into defunctive "ironclad" arrangements. He'd recapitalize the company: Frick's rewards should total just over $31,000,000.

Frick's rehabilitation had begun. There was a misleading lull through most of 1900. The unmoved mover, Morgan, was checking into details. Then—heralded from every trading pit—birth proclamations went out to certify the formation of the Brobdingnagian United States Steel Corporation on March 31 of 1901. Carnegie had secretly sold. Somebody rustled the bedclothes; out tumbled Henry Frick, beautifully attired as always.

If Mellon got caught, he'd obviously been misled by acquaintances much dearer than exhausted Andrew Carnegie. Frick had been Morgan's idea of a negotiating partner; the regal Pierpont loathed the mercurial Scotsman. Morgan abandoned this hope once Frick left Carnegie; Frick remained in touch.

Then Pierpont blundered. The Rockefellers currently owned the iron ore deposits across the Mesabi range; no monopoly could stick without the Rockefeller properties. Rockefeller didn't mind selling, but the peremptory J.P. quickly alienated Rockefeller senior and junior.

Upset, Morgan asked Henry Frick to try to intervene. Frick arranged his audience. The thin-skinned pendragon received the syndicate's little envoy just inside the gateposts of Pocantico Hills. Rockefeller had a proposal. Let Frick suggest some reasonable purchase figure. Frick priced the Rockefeller properties five million dollars higher than Gary himself had. Gary fumed; Morgan now recognized salvation once trumpets commenced sounding, and settled immediately.

The United States Steel Corporation slouched into industrial America. As recipient of more than $61,000,000 of Big Steel's original issue, Frick deserved his position upon the Corporation's first board. The naïve might question the propriety of having one man both oversee the steel trust and direct its overheated local challenger, Union Steel. Frick's conscience remained tranquil. He ignored directors' meetings. It was Frick's conviction, divulged frequently to insiders, that interest payments alone were going to sap this billion-dollar merger. If the Corporation survived. Frick regarded its president, Charles Schwab, as qualified primarily by optimism.

Frick dumped his Corporation paper on successive rises.

Union Steel was solid, the familiar Mellon mélange of banking opportunities and industrial windfalls. Utilizing Frick's Morgan connections, the brothers pushed Donner into operation in two echoing plants the Pennsylvania Railroad abandoned in Johnstown and Harrisburg. They paid in long-term notes, having recognized at once that so long as principal was outstanding they need not anticipate the sort of ruinous freight rates that earlier threatened Carnegie. Frick helped them acquire the Republic Coke Company, cheap. A.W. traded credit on a million and a half dollars with Corrigan and McKinney Company, iron miners, to secure a reliable ten-year ore contract. Meanwhile they broke ground conspicuously for their enormous works at "Donora"—a facility they named, careful about Presbyterian balances, partly after President Donner and partly after A.W.'s frisky young wife.

By late in 1902 the brothers had concluded an exchange of stock with realistic Boss Flinn to acquire Sharon Steel; Sharon was itself diversified: shipbuilding, railroad cars, structural steel engineering.

As 1902 ended, the monster Morgan loved was all but waterlogged. Nobody needed Union's competition. The pre-negotiation dance began. Soon after the great mill at Donora opened, a delegation of U.S. Steel notables which included Judge Gary, Rockefeller wrangler H. H. Rogers, and Morgan partner George Perkins, bestowed their communal visit. The conversation worked awkwardly around the possibility of Union/Sharon Steel coming into the trust. Donner mentioned a figure. Gary balked. Persistent rumors soon abounded to the effect that Union was about to add a giant rail mill at Donora and expand its railroad and harbor network. Through all this (to the discomfort of U.S. Steel's new President Corey), Union continuously took shipment of all those contractual Carnegie ingots.

Union flourished; the trust looked sicker; between 1902 and 1904 its common slid off from over forty-six dollars a share to less than nine. Frick had already unloaded; he was diverting himself with anonymous tips to reporters like Clarence Barron which explicated the extent to which Chairman Schwab now depended on misstatements of the earning figures.

The worshipful George Harvey had provided the denouement. His tableau spotlights intimately the badly humbled Pierpont Morgan, two wobbly tears outflanking that cerulean landmark of a nose as he and Henry pace off the deck of *The Corsair*. The divinity of finances is close to undone. They face the *prospect* of passing the common's regular dividend. Frick—himself unburdened—urges sacrifices for integrity. Well—Morgan chokes it out—perhaps that is unavoidable. Only Frick promises redemption, he *must* assume control of the steel trust *at once*.

"Mr. Frick," George F. Redmond reported in his *Financial Weekly*, Wall Street's contemporary harbinger, "was deeply touched. He then realized how keenly Mr. Morgan felt upon the subject and assured him that not another word should be said. At once he threw himself energetically into the task of aiding in steering the great organization through all its trouble." But there was one widely overlooked condition. "For the purpose of inducing Mr. Frick to become active in the Steel Corporation, Mr. Morgan purchased the Union Steel Works," and at a price which Mr. Mellon is quoted as having conceded "yielded a fair profit to all concerned."

Another fair profit. Probing by a committee of the House of Representatives in 1912 demonstrated how fair that profit shone. Judge Gary shrugged off the Mellons' original high offer. But pressure succeeded pressure; the Mellons wouldn't "push"; once Morgan silently capitulated, the Steel Corporation's attorney, Mellon familiar Judge Reed, concocted a serviceable agreement. An imaginative asset reappraisal jacked up the Union/Sharon debt from nothing to $45,000,000 and elevated its capital stock projection from one to twenty million dollars. This simplified the financing when U.S. Steel took over some $45,000,000 in bonds Union abruptly owed itself. Of the approximately $75,000,000 selling price, audits by the United States Commissioner of Corporations could justify precisely $30,860,501. The rest appeared profit, half to the Mellons. They'd long since unloaded their Pennsylvania Railroad mills on Bethlehem Steel.

"Andy Mellon wound up with a hell of a block of U.S. Steel securities in his portfolio from that old deal," one associate reports. Once Frick stepped aboard the Steel Corporation righted itself. The Mellon participation rebounded.

3 | THE INVESTMENT BANKER

1

WHY HAD THAT UNION STEEL settlement churned eddies of resentment? Even A.W. noticed. Meddlesome blabberers—who circulated such piffle? People resented their astuteness.

People liked to exaggerate, though even the banker had recalculated his assets from fifteen million dollars in 1902 to twice the amount by 1906.

He hated singling out. People demanded some excitement; Frick was slipping away; he'd reestablished his family in George Vanderbilt's charming Manhattan brownstone. His interest was real estate, balanced off by blocks of railroad securities, which Frick often dubbed "the Rembrandts of investment." Morgan required Henry frequently.

Mellon still liked Pittsburgh. That iron-front facade, by now a blackened antique, was flanked by squared-off contemporary masonry. The bank now occupied the entire city block. Upstairs, remote, A. W. and R. B. Mellon did business from plain commercial offices, separated by a café door.

Nothing disturbed the routine. An employee would remember the gray little president stepping quietly onto the floor of the banking room in the midst of a panic to hand out loans of "$30,000, $40,000 and of larger amounts when this man did not know where the money was coming from to make them." The employee would "go home at night feeling as though a rat were gnawing at his stomach; Mister Mellon would go home and sleep like a baby."

He preserved a lonely child's attentiveness. Age tightened Mellon's skin; every crease and patch of shadow was now as articulated as cords along the snout of a whippet. Alert, prepared—a lozenge of daylight bobbed keenly in each pale iris, the mouth characteristically parted a hairsbreadth to test the air for exaggeration or vulnerability.

Thinking each situation through, analyzing every contingency beforehand. Ideally all would benefit. Should losses become inevitable, let risks be assigned. Mellon could countenance sacrifices, although seldom for himself.

Sometimes word leaked out—certain misadventures became notorious. It took some time, for example, before the investors around town stopped whimpering over Crucible Steel. Such results were accidental. One day in 1900, soon after the bank started working with Frick to grind down Carnegie, a delegation of minor alloy processors showed up on Smithfield Street to see what aid the Mellons might provide their projected amalgamation. A.W. was considerate. A merger like this might endanger Carnegie's markets. He prepared the paper work, and shortly after that the brothers bought out the dozen small alloy-producing firms for nineteen million and recapitalized the combination as Crucible Steel. The bank passed along its fifty-million-dollar stock issue to conservative investors.

A.W. assisted Crucible as the sustaining director. It quickly needed help. The battle-ready Carnegie immediately subjected the heavily indebted young alloy manufacturer to ruinous price-cutting. Mellon had an idea: let Crucible assure its source of supply by constructing a mill. He proposed a location: that Peter's Creek frontage which Carnegie dumped back on Frick and himself. To generate the cash for Crucible's Clairton subsidiary, the Mellons authorized Union Trust to issue $2,250,000 in bonds; the bank took over the underlying mortgage paper.

The crash of 1903 shook Crucible to pieces. Orders faltered; the half-erected mill had proved a ten-million-dollar mistake; officers of the Union Trust Company processed Clairton into receivership.

By that time Carnegie was gone, and Morgan was reconciled to meeting the Mellons' brutal price for Union. A.W. appreciated that, and fattened the sale of Donora by throwing in the shell at Clairton. Then Mellon helped negotiate a ten-year contract between the rump of Crucible and the Steel Corporation which left the alloy manufacturer sapped. Banking often required evenhandedness. A.W.'s big block of Steel Company securities deserved consideration now.

Others noted secondary aspects: ". . . a lot of Crucible stock," the Mellons' own attorney Judge Reed would testify in 1911, "which was the favorite investment with widows and orphans around Pittsburgh because of the respectability of its directors, dropped from 90 to 10. There was a lot of trouble all around."

Neither liked to complain, but both the bankers were irked at criticisms of steps they'd taken to stabilize the community. Their exploits with coal were equally typical. By 1899, with Frick so restive, it only seemed sensible to go after coal deposits. A.W. secretly commissioned the Pittsburgh broker George Whitney to buy up the mines of most of the donkey-shaft independents with an accessibility to water. Mellon capitalized Whitney's scavengings as the forty-thousand-acre Monongahela River Consolidated Coal and Coke Company—"River Coal" —and retailed its thirty-million-dollar stock offering. He recovered the ten million dollars he himself laid out by authorizing a bond issue. Mellon kept the mortgages on land.

The Chicago speculator Judge Moore came in and canvassed for similar properties within reach of rail transportation. More securities went out—$64,000,000, to found the Pittsburgh Coal Company. A.W. and Moore divided 30 percent for managing the promotion.

Inevitably coal too died in 1903. Operating cash ran low. When Pittsburgh Coal's president came around for money, Mellon bought a ten-million-dollar bond issue—20 percent discounted. There was one limitation: of the eight million dollars Pittsburgh Coal would receive, the company must devote $6,750,000 to purchase of the collapsed securities of River Coal.

This intricate boardroom mazurka left River Coal pretty largely a subsidiary of Pittsburgh Coal, which the Mellons dominated. Once things picked up, the Steel Corporation ran short of quality metallurgical bituminous. The Mellons were ready. Heavy Steel owners themselves, the bankers roped Pittsburgh Coal into a disastrous contract which obligated the company to supply the trust with cheap coking base for twenty-five years; the Steel Corporation subsequently bought up Pittsburgh Coal's important properties and retired the Mellon bonds. Exhausted stockholders shook out like perspiration.

Coal mining wasn't lucrative. Nobody really expected that. Their moves in coal were calculated to ensure that the brothers continually risked less while steadily owning more. Coal symbolized industrial manhood. It wasn't an investment. It was an investment in other investments.

2

Steam from the abattoir, stenches off life's necessaries. "It makes me proudest to realize that I never built my fortune on other men's bones," Mellon told somebody afterward. Who remembered dubious episodes? He'd forgotten them himself—he'd forsaken all that, his supple patrician's fingers passing absentmindedly across the bib of his smock to remove clotted gristle.

There were pleasanter memories. "Dear Paul," he wrote his son in 1931, "I have transferred as a gift to you seventy-five thousand (75,000) shares of Aluminum Corporation of America common stock. . . . I consider this Aluminum stock more highly as a sound and dependable investment than I do any other of my holdings."

Aluminum did stir feelings. He'd been a hopeful himself just then— about thirty-five. Still thinking things over; one otherwise uneventful day in 1889 three secretive young fellows showed up on Smithfield Street to sound Mellon out about assuming a four-thousand-dollar obligation they owed at one of the banks. Their tone was despairing. Their leader, "Captain" Alfred Ephraim Hunt, was approximately his own age, a big grave metallurgist Mellon recalled having supervised the installation of the first major open-hearth furnace in the Pittsburgh area.

The others were younger. The chemist, George Clapp, evidently kept their books. It hadn't taken long before the third man, Arthur Vining Davis, twenty-two, was monopolizing the conversation. Davis was a cheeky little dynamo with plenty of nose and a complexion like oatmeal, set off by ibex-horn moustaches he waxed to dramatic spear-points. He opened characteristically: "I'll tell you the worst. I am a college graduate and the son of a minister, but I mean to pay."

With that, Davis plucked from a pocket a biscuit-shaped object, smooth, still wrapped in tissue paper. Much concerned with effect, he slowly unwrapped the shiny pewter-colored thing and laid it reverentially into Mellon's outstretched palm. It seemed almost weightless. This material was aluminum, Davis confided—the metal of the future. It retained much strength, it obviously was light, it was an excellent conductor of electricity, and traces of its ore were present in many common earths. For nearly a century scientists had been searching for a way to separate this substance from aluminum oxide clay. Now they —the proprietors of the Pittsburgh Reduction Company—had developed a technologically feasible technique for producing it by means of the electrolytic process.

Their twenty-seven-year-old inventor and patent-holder, Charles Hall, was detained, in fact, tending his regular shift in the ramshackle iron building on Smallman Street, where day and night the row of carbon-lined vats sent up its penetrating stink of hydrofluoric acid as current from primitive steam-powered generators wavered through the baths of melted Greenland cryolite to precipitate the alumina from batches of clay.

Hall remained their zealot. His persistence was unearthly—along with his jealousy of the technique that he and his sister had come upon in the "winter woodshed" out behind the family parsonage in Oberlin, Ohio. It seemed a consummated miracle to the stripling inventor, his loaves and fishes. Upon graduation from Oberlin, Hall had begun a kind of agonized pilgrimage, from businessman to businessman, packing and unpacking his incredible aluminum globules, one day to become the "crown jewels of aluminum." Commercial people dismissed him. He'd come the closest in Lockport, New York, in which the brothers who ran the Cowles' Electric Smelting and Aluminum Company allowed him to tinker with apparatus in a makeshift laboratory. They expected Hall's patents. Hall's looks were misleading; his carefully scissored bangs and pretty, pensive features disguised his fundamental stubbornness. When Hall wouldn't surrender, the Cowleses pushed him out.

At Lockport, Hall met one Romaine C. Cole, who was himself friendly with Alfred Hunt and George Clapp of the Pittsburgh Testing Laboratory. Cole introduced Hall there. Hunt was well qualified to appreciate Hall's discovery, and in 1888 he organized the Pittsburgh Reduction Company and rounded up eight local businessmen, including several Carnegie Associates, to supply twenty thousand dollars of start-up capital to help them inaugurate production.

Only inexperience and fanaticism had gotten them by those break-in months on Smallman Street. Their primitive generator kept malfunctioning; the journeymen they employed were neglectful about "balancing" the current, and left the cryolite to harden at times to the consistency of gelatin. Captain Hunt lured Davis, the son of his one-time pastor, to work in Pittsburgh with cajoleries and temptations: "Don't think you are going to be a doctor or a lawyer. You want to come along with us out here and make some money in the aluminum business." Soon after Davis arrived he and the exultant Hall success-

Captain Hunt
ALCOA

The primary vats
ALCOA

Young Arthur
Vining Davis
ALCOA

The original ingots—the
monopoly's family jewels
ALCOA

Charles Hall
ALCOA

fully molded their first aluminum ingot. But production was discouraging, and whenever—rarely—they managed to produce their quota of fifty pounds in twenty-four hours they locked it up. Even Hall felt defeated. "Captain Hunt got Davis to take my place when we work nights," Hall wrote his sister. "He is a boy from Boston and fresh from Amherst College. He has a good deal of ability as well as grit to stand it working all night in the dirt and grit and worse."

Pittsburgh Reduction's immediate market was owners of blast furnaces, who instructed their foremen to keep feeding chunks of aluminum into the bubbling crucibles to ward off blowholes. The capital ran out; the company borrowed four thousand dollars; it soon had problems in meeting the interest on that. Their creditor now threatened to close up operations.

They'd descended on Mellon. He listened very closely; his questions were alarmingly precise. Had he been waiting? He agreed to assume their four-thousand-dollar note, and then he volunteered, meekly, "I am interested in your company. Couldn't I buy a little stock?" They watched his delicate long fingers caressing their biscuit of aluminum.

The September of 1890 Pittsburgh Reduction pushed up its capitalization to one million dollars. Ten thousand shares, 40 percent in reserve to recompense Charles Hall. The sixty shares the Mellon brothers acquired they got from Hall. They awaited much more. One day young Davis rushed into the bank flourishing orders for 7,200 pounds of aluminum. They'd need larger facilities, more power, fresh capital—A.W. looked around and arranged for one of the bank's building-lot affiliates, the Burrell Improvement Company, to present Pittsburgh Reduction with four level acres in one of its developments north of the city, in Kensington. Burrell Improvement supplied a ten-thousand-dollar bonus to the company; the Mellons contributed seven thousand dollars against moving expenses. The building cost money, close to a quarter of a million dollars. The Judge was diverting himself in distant Kansas City. His capital was handy. The Mellons traded dollars for Pittsburgh Reduction stock. Soon they were in for roughly a third.

With production approaching a thousand pounds a day, the problem became one of offsetting their output with ever-ascending sales. In 1890 the company lost $687; by 1893 the profitability was up to $139,000. As late as January 1, 1897, Captain Hunt wrote Mellon that his own analysis "showed an excess of available assets over real liabilities of $2,014.69. In the ready assets are $70,000 of bonds unsold and $142,521.69 worth of metal in store."

The banker realized early what they must do to make an industry of this. They virtually must invent their market; any hope of that depended on massive utilization of another infant discovery: controllable electricity. Production had started abroad. The Mellons' good friend Senator Cameron of Pennsylvania saw after a fifteen-cent-a-pound tariff on aluminum imports. In 1895 Pittsburgh Reduction opened operations in an enormous facility at Niagara Falls, complete with custom-designed Westinghouse equipment to switch from alternating to direct current, which kept a much smoother flow passing through those seething cryolite baths. By 1899 they needed a site adjacent to the falls at Shawinigan, Quebec.

Hall's fair-weather employers, the Lockport Cowles brothers, were producing aluminum too. Pittsburgh Reduction claimed patent infringement; the Cowleses countersued, insisting that Hall grabbed *their* secrets. The federal judge in Cleveland, William Howard Taft, found for the Mellons, but a decade of follow-up litigation led to the loss of a secondary case brought by the Cowleses, who claimed key patents on fusing and decomposition processes. Mellon bought them up.

By 1901 the North American aluminum business was Pittsburgh Reduction's. They started with ingots. But aluminum was brittle stuff, unfamiliar—customers demanded finished products. Davis pushed the company into merchandise from man-of-war superstructures to die-cast teakettles. By 1898 the army of the Czar was packing Pittsburgh-molded mess kits. When brass-plate manufacturers balked at rolling aluminum the company set up its own extensive mills. With automobile manufacturing and the advent of the airplane additional markets opened.

Before Hall's process triumphed, aluminum sold for upward of twelve dollars a pound. Pittsburgh Reduction changed that. As early as 1888 the price had dropped to two dollars a pound on larger shipments; by 1893 it went for seventy-five cents. Production was becoming enormous; and lesser competitors couldn't make a profit. They intended to dominate.

Hall's patents would expire in 1906. They must secure themselves. "But in addition to advancing money," W.L. would write, "A.W. frequently reminded me that the real way to make a business out of petroleum was to develop it from end to end; to get the raw material out of the ground, refine it, manufacture it, distribute it. He believed in that scheme of operation not alone for petroleum, but for many other types of business."

Control in every direction. By 1897 Hall perfected a method through which "we can make as much aluminum per unit of horsepower from bauxite (of which we can obtain large quantities) as from pure aluminum (oxide), then it would seem that this is the field which is now ripest for us to investigate for increasing the economy of manufacturing." The grade of bauxite they needed was laden with 40 percent or better alumina. Such lodes were choice; they weren't, fortunately, plentiful. To control the aluminum business, Pittsburgh Reduction needed merely to control the significant bauxite finds.

They started by acquiring the Georgia Bauxite and Mining Company, followed by General Bauxite and the Norton Company. As other deposits surfaced the company recompensed prospectors, who knew their ore was salable in only one place. A.W. funded metallurgical laboratories; products from aluminum foil to high-explosive ammonal emerged.

A.W. himself conducted critical negotiations. Pittsburgh Reduction worked up an arrangement with British Aluminum according to which the two formed the Aluminum Supply Company, Ltd. Neither must sell the other's home government. Pittsburgh Reduction would desist from peddling its manufactured wares in England; British Aluminum must take three million pounds of metal a year from its American partner. By 1908, through its Canadian Northern Aluminum, Ltd., subsidiary, the company had divided the Continental market with the German amalgamation Aluminum A. G.—25 percent to 75 percent, proportions reversed in North America. The producers went fifty–fifty on Asia, Africa, Australia and stipulated major islands. Monopoly was now cartel.

All this was enterprising—if completely illegal. The details were provided in a 1912 Department of Justice settlement which enjoined the aluminum trust from continuing to engage in an awesome repertoire of forbidden industrial practices—price-fixing, lethal price-cutting, international collusion in restraint of competition. The procedures slipped into focus as Governmental evidence compiled, like strings and nodules across the screen of a fluoroscope. Who would have looked for *this* fantastic concentration behind Andy Mellon's cough?

Aluminum became his pride. By 1904—three years before the company renamed itself The Aluminum Company of America—its capitalization was up to $3,800,000. The next stock dividend established the capital base at $20,000,000; during 1915–1916 the company reinvested that from profits alone. By 1917 Alcoa's stock, the Mellon block outstanding, hovered around $150,000,000.

A 1907 reorganization installed R. B. Mellon, briefly, as Alcoa's titular president. Arthur Vining Davis served then as general manager. Captain Hunt died consequent to service in the Spanish-American War; Hall went in 1914.

Vining ran the company. When infatuated French capitalists came in with five and a half million dollars to build the Southern Aluminum Company in 1912, the court-embroiled Aluminum Company ignored the transgression. War started; European capital got tight. Southern Aluminum's president, Adrien Badin, ransacked the American money market; nobody dared to help. The bedraggled Frenchman inevitably turned up in Pittsburgh. After a long, upsetting negotiation, Southern Aluminum sold out at a million dollars below its start-up costs. A rough riverside settlement was already in place. Davis tagged his North Carolina company town "Badin."

3

Other ventures opened similarly, although who could predict? Even A.W. blundered. In 1895, for instance, a cunning and resilient inventor named Edward G. Acheson came by to impress the banker with a thumb-sized chunk of iridescent material so hard that Acheson was able to set a corner of it against one of the facets of his big ring diamond and incise another scar. Only a diamond could scratch a diamond, Acheson reminded the banker. Acheson had made his.

Mellon's foxy, balding visitor was back in Pittsburgh after years at Menlo Park with Edison himself and nearly a decade as Edison's representative on the Continent, filling orders for electric light generators. He'd continued to experiment; his patents included plans for a revolutionary boring machine and an anti-induction cable.

Important commercial possibilities, Acheson sensed, were implicit in the technique he'd hit upon for producing those ultrahard flecks by subjecting a mixture of sand, coke and salt to heavy doses of power in an electric furnace. Acheson had come home and raised enough backers to found his Monongahela Electric Light Company. His directors started grumbling as Acheson drained juice from the company's little 135-horsepower steam generator into the production of chips and specks to fabricate the grinding powders and abrasive wheels he could not merchandise at forty cents a carat. Losses mounted. When Acheson visited Niagara Falls and secretly contracted for ten times the electricity, his investors stormed out.

Mellon followed Acheson's reasoning. Carborundum's markets would expand once production reached levels that allowed them radically to slash their prices. That required fresh capital, obviously. Acheson wanted the banker to underwrite a bond issue for $75,000. Mellon carried it further—he'd buy fifty thousand dollars' worth of the bonds himself, if Acheson would meet the standard underwriting fee and present the banker with a sixteenth of Carborundum's stock.

At first the arrangement followed Mellon's normal resuscitation procedure—capital out, ownership in. They dispatched Frank Tone, a trustworthy electrical engineer, to design for Carborundum the world's biggest transformer at the Niagara site. A bookkeeper they trusted, Frank Manley, kept them in touch with the flow of orders. Business did pick up, although nothing like expenses, and representatives from Carborundum seemed to alight from every smoking car to demand more investment in urgently needed improvements. Then the Mellons discovered that Acheson had retained the patents to his various processes in important foreign markets, and expected the bankers to buy those out before the company could manufacture abroad. They invested, morosely; when Acheson got strapped for cash to retool for Carborundum paper and Carborundum cloth, the bankers wouldn't accommodate until he had released enough of his stock to leave them plurality stockholders.

W.L. never forgot the August morning in 1897 it all broke open. He entered the bank to encounter his florid uncle Dick bellowing onto the telephone to Acheson: "I don't care whose fault it is. I only know that the whole concern is sadly in need of push and energy and unless an immediate improvement is shown we shall have to put in someone to protect our interests."

An extreme outburst. A.W. was equally provoked. He wrote Edward Acheson: "I am sorry to see the disposition on your part to treat the Carborundum Company as if it were an outside concern in the welfare of which you were not interested. . . . In the last six months it showed a real and actual loss in operations notwithstanding the fact that considerable progress had been made in treating carbons. Now the company is in a crucial state, having made changes in its methods, etc., and should it show no improvement, what will be the result? My brother and myself will have lost an immense sum of money, while on your part you would have received in one way or another a very considerable amount. . . . I am only mentioning these things to show that you have been getting your returns while the company has never earned anything and while it was practically bankrupt and would have been wiped out of existence beyond any doubt, had it not been for our support."

Mellon was fearful secretly that the cagey inventor had foreseen their losses and unloaded his process. The spring of 1898, alarmed by Manley's reports, the Mellons sent up Frank Haskell to look matters over. Haskell reported that Acheson seemed honest enough, after his fashion, but much too disjunct to run anything profitably. There was no sales manager, quality control was irregular, and Acheson was forever being distracted by technical minutiae. The Mellons forced Haskell in as the effective operating officer.

Profits followed. Carborundum's hones and stones and wheels and grinding blocks of silicon of carbide soon provided the microscopic tolerances the new technology required for interchangeability of parts. It became their oracle. When Carborundum sales declined, national averages generally followed.

4

Substantial misjudgments were rarities. Soon after he returned to the bank Andrew authorized a long shot. "I think I would like Andrew to lose that loan," the Judge had confided. "It would teach him a lesson." Thomas recovered his principal, and Andrew continued playing those meticulously studied hunches.

The trick was identifying managers. A runt like Davis couldn't really be stopped from *becoming* the Aluminum Company. But how to tell? It didn't take long before the banker evolved approaches. He presented certain . . . ordeals, pressed new people unexpectedly to surprise their characters. Reactions yielded "Mellon men."

W.L. stood by the bright spring day in 1900 he herded two disgruntled young engineers, Charles D. Marshall and Howard M. McClintic, into his uncle's retreat to explain their problem. They'd both just resigned, thrown up their jobs at Shiffler Bridge. The management over there had deceived them badly, turned over the place to Morgan interests. Nobody paid them bonuses. They'd work for themselves.

A.W. lit up a bitter little stogie. So. The two were aggrieved. They entertained some thoughts of looking into steel fabrication. That required . . . additional calculations. Meanwhile, A.W. proposed, it happened the bank was acquiring by foreclosure the Saylor Structural Steel Company, out east around Pottstown. He and his brother were frankly at somewhat of a loss as to how to develop this property. Was there any chance the engineers might inspect those premises and venture some recommendation? A thread of cigar smoke rose above A.W.'s chair and occupied a coffer. He propped one seamed, spare cheek against the heel of a palm. The counter of a shoe had little by little squeezed under the banker; he now half sat on it.

They looked over Saylor; the report they submitted was cogent, succinct: the company was dragging, its books were waterlogged with unprofitable contracts. The plant appeared decrepit.

Mellon met them both in Philadelphia to make his proposition. His brother and he had worked up preliminary numbers. They'd back the pair—in the Saylor facilities. Start-up expenses should run around $100,000. T. Mellon and Sons would supply half, and expected 50 percent ownership.

The engineers seemed troubled the day they reconvened in Pittsburgh. Neither man could put his hand on anything beyond five thousand dollars. Mellon's glance was sharp. Perhaps mortgage their homes? Parents—hadn't their parents savings? "Your reluctance," Mellon said with gravity, "makes it appear as if you do not have faith in yourselves or in this enterprise." Both applicants agreed hesitantly to mortgage their homes.

The banker was probing. "Neither of these steps will be necessary. My brother and I will loan you the additional money. You should be able to repay us out of the profits of the business." When papers for the McClintic-Marshall Construction Company were drawn, the Mellons reserved 60 percent.

Throughout thirty vigorous years McClintic-Marshall laid up epochal structures from the George Washington Bridge to the Panama Canal locks. McClintic supervised the engineering; Marshall provided the "business head." When installing the locks eventually lost the company two million dollars, Mellon himself appeared impressed. "Well, it's some company that can swallow a loss like that," he allegedly said. He invariably appreciated scale.

It went that way—great boldness of conception, followed up by financing. So why the hesitations—local proprietors tried anything before dragging toward Smithfield Street. People knew the soft-spoken banker's touch could dispel financial agonies. His ministrations were expert. Disillusion set in afterward.

People remembered the Schoens. They'd been industrial pioneers, a onetime letter carrier from Philadelphia and his nephew who built the company that manufactured the first truly all-steel railroad cars. The uncle, K.T., had developed the company into the foremost of its sort. Schoen's Allegheny banker, Frank Hoffstot, had talked the gruff-spoken German mechanic into putting him in as president and assuming the chairmanship of the board. Then Hoffstot selected directors who eliminated Schoen's post.

The outraged Schoens rallied to promote a corporation, the Standard Steel Car Company, with which to crush their perfidious competitor. They capitalized this enterprise at three million dollars, a step which represented more bravura than cash. They committed themselves headlong to a million-dollar foundry. Then one of their debtors went under without attending to bills, and matters became acute.

By 1902 the Schoens needed $200,000 urgently. They told the engineer Leonard Woods, on whom W.L. had depended throughout the transit skirmishing. Woods mentioned their extremity to the bank's untiring "outside man"; Willie arranged their appointment. A.W. made Standard its loan from leftover traction reserves.

With generosity went conditions. Leonard Woods would occupy "a position where he could be in constant and close touch with all the details of its finances." As reorganization proceeded, the bankers quickly identified the employee *they* intended to direct the outfit— John Hansen, a runaway butcher's son who learned the business as a blueprint boy and designed the equipment with which to manufacture its hopper-bottom and gondola cars. Once business flowed in, the Mellons themselves absorbed stock until they owned 80 percent. The Schoens were through—within four more years they'd relinquished all involvement.

Standard Car plunged onward behind its high-kicking supersalesman—Diamond Jim Brady. Brady was already legendary, the gem-encrusted palomino whose romps enlivened the tabloids. Brady's expense accounts alone would fling most enterprises into receivership. The Mellons were sympathetic: Brady called on trade in Newport and Palm Beach, whose habitués would countenance his craving to hand out Champagne by hundred-case lots and confer gilded bicycles upon demonstrative show girls. Intimates thronged his siding at fashionable Saratoga.

Vouchers regularly reached Pittsburgh for million-dollar orders. Plants dotted the East. Whenever customers fell short, Mellon bankers normally financed. The brothers remained current. "Through all those years," W.L. would write, "A.W. was frequently consulted by the Standard Steel Car executives, normally at least several times each week."

Finally nothing seemed impossible. They built a complex of steel mills to pour and roll their periodic heavy requirements. Early in the Twenties automobiles appeared en masse. A.W. had already gone along to Washington. Standard started making cars.

5

Leaving . . . Gulf. A tale in itself. Their misfit, their changeling. The whole thing started with indefatigable John Galey. Galey was a regular, a sturdy old "creekologist" who had been roaming western Pennsylvania since oil drilling erupted around the furor at Titusville. The Galeys and Mellons went back, and John was long accustomed to barging into Negley Avenue to gab with Thomas. A.W. himself always liked the prospector, although his assessment was hardened: "He is careless and always has his affairs at such loose ends that it is very seldom he is prepared to meet any payment for which he is liable. . . ." Andrew answered one inquiry. Nevertheless, periodically, he handed over cash enough to bail the wildcatter out.

The stringy old oil speculator was resolute, taciturn, with one of those beaky cigar-store-Indian countenances right out of a Western of the period; his partner, Colonel James McClurg Guffey, was mostly a promoter. Guffey dressed the role. Gussied up in his Prince Albert waistcoat and stovepipe trousers and wide-brimmed black felt hat, he looked like an escapee from one of Buffalo Bill's sideshow extravaganzas. His locks ran berserk; the sweeping white moustaches set off an infant's complexion; in protectionist backcountry Pennsylvania, Guffey trumpeted his devotion to free-silver populism. W.L. openly distrusted the showboater. The unpredictable A.W. seemed fond of Guffey too.

That frenetic, early march to the sea had convinced the Mellons the oil business inherently was much more likely to flare off capital than generate regular profits. Producing was especially hazardous, a motley of lunatics with divining rods and grabby tinhorn promoters. These gamblers were elusive—in 1894, soon after the bankers slipped in and bought enough shares to assure themselves control of the Pittsburgh Petroleum Stock Exchange, its faithless, scabby founders merely abandoned the floor, and collapsed their companies, and reorganized their marketplace somewhere else.

Then along came Spindletop. Outside Beaumont, Texas, below a hillock the natives called Round Mound, springs off the Gulf Coast swamps bubbled up some volatile, iridescent agent. Children from the neighborhood sneaked into the bog to ignite the water. In 1899 a battered Yugoslav mining engineer named Anthony F. Lucas, né Luchich, answering an ad, took over the crumbling rig of a disillusioned veteran named Patillo Higgins and subsurface rights to a reedy corner of Round Mound Higgins dubbed Gladys City. The winter after that, down 575 feet and broke, Luchich surfaced what looked to him like oil-bearing sands. Luchich contacted John Galey.

In Galey's seasoned judgment, what Luchich needed next was one of the newly developed rotary drills to tap the reservoir. Soon Galey and Guffey had arranged a credit at the Mellon bank for $300,000. This involved little risk, since for the moment Guffey's assets exceeded that.

Galey himself inspected Round Mound and selected the spot. By October of 1900 their fishtail bit was squeaking through, successively, sand, clay, hard rock, soft rock. Then, approaching 1,700 feet, preceded by whistling gas, an earthquake of oil-saturated muddy slime expelled Luchich's telescoped casing. Just short of eight hundred feet lifted majestically before toppling; a rusty black gusher then flooded the earthworks with more than forty thousand barrels daily. Somebody struck a match; out fanned a lake of fire; once that burned off a gang of laborers rolled close a cylinder of sand and upended it against the head of the well. Their monster was capped. The dunes of Spindletop looked like the Klondike of oil.

For Galey and Guffey a strike like this promised vindication for a lifetime. The two had speculated in 1895 in oil fields around Corsi-

cana, Texas. They stopped too soon and resold their interest; in 1897
Joseph Cullinan, the suave, mobile, ambivalent front man for Rocke-
feller interests, stopped over in Corsicana and developed the bonanza.
At Spindletop the Pennsylvanians would stanch their humiliation.

If they hung on. Rambunctious Guffey always recognized that control of this meant pipelines and refineries. Word of their gusher
reached Pittsburgh in January of 1901; Guffey devoted his winter to
plaguing the Mellon brothers.

They elbowed Guffey off. Oil was too risky. Nevertheless—curiosity needn't be stifled, and R.B., in New Orleans anyway soon after
the strike came in, stopped off at Beaumont to see Spindletop himself.
He recommended staying out.

Guffey kept dropping by. He seemed so positive. Reconsidering,
A.W. now decided to organize a syndicate among certain of the
cronies, a limited financial framework for Guffey's assets in Texas.
Mellon lawyer James Reed was interested, and stony William Flinn,
and other venturesome businessmen. The syndicate raised $1,500,000.
The Mellons committed $600,000; half recaptured their loan. The
syndicate was incorporated as Guffey Petroleum in Texas, and eval-
uated its 150,000 shares of treasury stock at fifteen million dollars.
Fifty thousand shares went out to members at thirty dollars per share;
Guffey retained 70,000 shares plus $634,000. The syndicate bought
Galey and Lucas out, which gutted its capital.

They'd need new money. It struck the Mellons that perhaps the
30,000 leftover shares of treasury stock might fetch some premium.
They pegged the offering at sixty-six dollars and palmed it off overnight on Carnegie's ex-wards, that gaggle of "Associates" Morgan
abruptly made gentlemen. Frick (who distrusted the flamboyant
Guffey, and recognized watered paper) declined politely to participate.

Buccaneer financing. They'd bought no pipe, leased nothing, disposed of all the developers except Guffey, and already the bankers
owned over 13 percent of a company which controlled the century's
biggest oil strike and now had available over two million dollars to
consolidate its assets.

Guffey forged on west. The spellbinder's Prince Albert bulged
grossly with treasury notes. He had his $634,000 in cash. He bore
down grandly upon that Beaumont salt marsh of city whores working
double shifts and mechanical lease hawkers. Guffey pranced the
dunes, snapping up outlying leases, studying pipeline routes, grab-
bing off 375 acres in nearby Port Arthur to secure a deepwater port

and a storage tank and refinery site. Cullinan and the Rockefeller strategists were already beginning to infiltrate the area; Guffey met with onetime trustbuster Jim Hogg, by then ex-governor of Texas.

The two were born to communicate. Hogg was a Texan with sensibilities to give an Easterner heartburn—he dubbed his daughter Ima —and one of the most persistently decorated palms west of the Pecos. Guffey quickly noticed both. "Northern men," he reflected, "were not very well respected in Texas in those days. Governor Hogg was a power there and I wanted him on my side because I was going to spend a lot of money." Guffey sacrificed the promising fifteen-acre Page lease to the Hogg-Swayne syndicate for $180,000, obviously a giveaway; the Mellons went along.

By November of 1901 the bankers in Pittsburgh had founded a corporation to construct the Port Arthur refinery, the Gulf Refining Company. Cash was again low. To tie everything together, the Guffey directors issued $5,000,000 in bonds. Holding a million back as treasury reserves, the Mellons invested $2,500,000; Boston's staid Old Colony Trust Company came in for $1,500,000. Even then, Will insists, "I cannot emphasize enough that, although they were willing to lend money against oil as security, neither Andrew nor Dick Mellon wanted to get back in the oil business."

By then they were. Themselves; worse, their intimates around Pittsburgh. Quite near the close of banking hours one sweltering August afternoon in 1902 a diffident A.W. tiptoed to the threshold of the office in which W.L. was clearing out some residual transit paperwork. He waited some seconds before he let himself cough. The troubleshooter looked up. "Will," Andrew Mellon said softly, "those Texas wells have stopped flowing." Nature itself had reneged.

When Will reached Beaumont the boomtown was exhausted. Derricks infested the horizon on lease land so subdivided the wildcatters were gyrating to keep from tapping one another's casings. Muck had become sludge; a pall of sulfurous effluvia was peeling the paint off tenements in shags. Even fast-talking lease salesmen who haunted the Crosby House lobby wandered around too groggy to pitch at visitors.

No groggier than Guffey. W.L. wasn't surprised. The Colonel had haphazardly acquired rights to over a million acres of land without taking the trouble to protect their investment at Spindletop; "doormat" operators were siphoning the reserves. Debonair Joe Cullinan had subcontracted a part of the Hogg-Swayne acreage and was con-

Spindletop
Since Spindletop—
GULF OIL CORP.

Willie in early manhood
JAMES R. MELLON II

structing a refinery. Guffey traded away Beaumont before they could repossess their capital.

Worse, the big costly refinery at Port Arthur was equipped for good Pennsylvania crude, nothing like the inert sour asphalt-ridden coagulate which Spindletop was issuing. Nobody had any idea how practically to "crack" the stuff for kerosene lubricating base. Title searches were botched. And worst of all, the befuddled headstrong Colonel had signed a twenty-year contract with Marcus Samuel's Shell Transport and Trading Company of London to supply the Englishman four and a half million barrels of Texas crude at a quarter a barrel. Guffey claimed a coup. At home in Pittsburgh, the Mellons foresaw bankruptcy proceedings.

Family throats became parched. There was some hope that peripheral wells might yet be nursed into marginal production. But rescuing Guffey Oil could require an additional twelve to fifteen million dollars.

A.W. anticipated all along that Standard would have to buy them out. Spindletop's depletion now surprised the Mellons before they could tie off southeast Texas and constitute a threat. Guffey blew the seals: future giants—Texaco, Sun Oil, Humble, Amarada—seeped up all around that Hogg-Swayne acreage.

This left them weakened. They got their comeuppance in a hotel room in New York's Holland House from H. H. Rogers and John D. Archbold, the jovial minister's son who had already "laughed his way to the top" of Rockefeller's monolith: "After the way Mr. Rockefeller has been treated by the State of Texas, he'll never put another dime in Texas." Hogg's fining of Standard's Water-Pierce affiliate left the Anaconda writhing. "We can't do anything about it," Rogers told A.W. and Will, "so you'll just have to do the best you can with it yourself." He bestowed on the aggravated Pittsburghers a limp little parody of a blessing. A.W. exited, choking; W.L. murmured hopefully that now at least their hands were untied. Their raid had folded, completely.

Everything depended upon Willie. He'd never appreciated Guffey, refused stock, distrusted Guffey's known friendships with Standard agents as remote as London, detested Guffey's constitutional slipshodness. Now he braced quietly to tolerate the promoter—still their plurality stockholder—so that his uncles could rebuild the financial side and squeeze Guffey out. Another bad mistake could gut the fortune.

They'd paid a price for picking their manager and letting him alone. They convened a directors' meeting and formally installed William L. Mellon as executive vice-president of Guffey Petroleum, to assume working control. Guffey went along, grumpily. Guffey's manager was sacked; W.L. went west. He replaced Guffey's staff with George H. Taber, a temperamental refinery expert, the hearty Gale Nutty, and meticulous Frank Leovy, a fussy ex-station agent whose responsibility was production.

In 1902 W.L. was barely thirty-four. Such concentrations of responsibility were settling his spirit. W.L. led easily, his touch so experienced few resented the reins.

Colonel Guffey was already delicate about the mouth. "From the beginning," W.L. would concede, "Colonel Guffey had never regarded the investigation or the charges with a friendly eye and there had long been a coldness between us." As Mellon's grip firmed the temperature continued falling: "Consequently, in my position . . . I was obliged at times to be quite arbitrary with him. It is very hard for me to be patient with incompetents." Chafed, the Colonel provoked dissension, countermanded W.L.'s orders, held out vociferously against reorganizations that pruned more authority. He advertised his performance: on paper the company had shown a 1901 operating loss of $28,000—excellent, the Colonel felt, at such early stages.

W.L. was able to reactivate those inert Spindletop wells with supplementary gas. They brought in producers in Saratoga, Humble, Batson, Sour Lake: each strike demanded pipelines. A.W. visited London in 1903 and familiarized Marcus Samuel of Shell Trading with the probability that holding Guffey to contract would bankrupt the company. If the company complied. Mellon gently encouraged Samuel to consider for himself what justice an English Jew might anticipate from rural Texas courts. Samuel agreed to renegotiate.

Around the Port Arthur refinery Taber was experimenting gloomily with mixtures of oils, new types of "cheesebox stills," novel industrial applications. The thick, tarry glop that poured, if briefly, out of those dunes was fuel for battleships, supported power plant combustion; the Mellons were lucky little coal was handy. The hulls of tankers they commissioned from their New York Shipbuilding affiliate floated empty off coastal piers. The refinery losses compiled.

Then, in 1905, word spread of discoveries throughout the Glenn Pool section of the Oklahoma Indian Territory. Oklahoma oil was "light," "sweet," easily reduced to kerosene and—automobiles were commoner—gasoline. But Oklahoma was more than four hundred miles north. Hard-bellied leaseholders up there weren't likely to succumb, like Spindletop's primitive Luchich, to A.W.'s percussive negotiating.

Rockefeller's Prairie Oil and Gas had already snaked pipelines; Teddy Roosevelt's vigorous Secretary of the Interior Ethan Allen Hitchcock was eager to assist the Mellons if that would convert the Indian Territory into a seller's market. Inevitably this would necessitate one very long pipeline and costly producing properties—another five million dollars within perhaps a year. Such outlays were unthinkable so long as Guffey stayed in.

Guffey's ownership was diminishing. Whenever the exultant buckaroo showed up at 512 Smithfield Street, rabid with new proposals, A.W. seemed understanding. He lent Guffey anything, but insisted on stock for collateral. By 1905 the bank held 24,000 of Guffey's original 70,000 shares against a million dollars in principal and accumulated interest. Guffey also borrowed elsewhere. The Mellons prohibited dividends, but they were remorseless about demanding that the bond coupons which they and the Old Colony held be retired on schedule. Guffey was starving out. Nevertheless, when the Mellons approached Guffey in 1905 and 1906 to urge systematic reorganization, the Colonel proved cantankerous.

Glenn Pool wouldn't wait. A producer with pipelines and refineries of its own could rupture the Standard monopoly; government officials in Texas and Washington stood prepared to help. Will dispatched Frank Leovy to Oklahoma to organized an independent "little company" and start to acquire promising tracts. In Pittsburgh, a Guffey stockholders' committee composed of A. W. Mellon, William Flinn, Emmett Queen, James D. Callery and J. H. Reed now circulated a notice which recapitulated the bookkeeping and concluded, "So it is necessary for the Company to enter the Indian Territory field if it aims to meet the competition of other companies." Most of the original Guffey stockholders agreed to form a successor, incorporated in New Jersey, provisionally called the Gulf Oil Corporation.

Leovy formed the Oklahoma Gypsy Oil Company; W.L. ran pipeline. His Pennsylvania sidekick Davison directed the construction of a 413-mile, eight-inch line which originated just outside the hog wallow called Tulsa and wound toward Texas's Sour Lake. While Will manipulated Interior Department bureaucrats for permission to cross the Indian reserves and bolt their pipeline to struts under railroad bridges, Mellon lawyers were incorporating the unaffiliated Gulf Pipe Line Company of Texas and, in Oklahoma, the H. Y. Arnold Company.

Reorganization proceeded, inexorably. As winter came on in 1906 it took a romantic like Guffey to dream of staving it off. His plurality had frittered away—by now the bankers were voting more shares than Guffey still controlled. Not that it mattered. Like its fretful promoter, the Guffey Petroleum Company was primarily a vestige— terminus to the pipeline, tank farm and refinery for all that Osage production.

The brothers took over. They capitalized the Gulf Oil Corporation at fifteen million dollars and claimed something just over a third to compensate their six-million-dollar outlay in Oklahoma. Shares came from Guffey stock. The tousled Colonel's percentage of the reorganized company suddenly looked, relatively, puny.

The Colonel mounted tantrums. How could the figures break down like *that*? The promoter was convinced he'd plowed in millions of his own. Where were they reflected? And wasn't the *original* company worth fifteen million dollars? What made them capitalize so low? To swell the Mellons' percentages?

They attempted to explain. Wholly a bookkeeping convenience. If the Colonel objected, the bankers stood ready to accommodate the Colonel. Guffey sold. The expanded Gulf Oil Corporation came into existence formally on January 30, 1907, A. W. Mellon president. The cost of buying out Guffey supporters totaled $3,413,911— largely to Guffey personally.

He lost that too. "They throwed me out," he lamented throughout Pittsburgh, and over the next twenty years he alternated between suing the Mellons and sidling into their banking chambers to solicit his handout. After he went under, the brothers provided Guffey a kind of annuity through their Reliance Insurance affiliate; he survived anybody's expectations, as if to defy their actuarial tables too. They meant Guffey well. But enough was enough.

4 | THE HUMAN PARTNER

1

OSSIBLY WILLIE learned first. Maybe that was appropriate: young Willie was thirty-two by this time, important to them all. He combined the Larimer appetite for adventure with in-grained Mellon thoroughness. He inherited the Judge's great ears. These—together with Latino-style moustaches that drooped across the corners of his full lower lip and the misleadingly sleepy poise—now imbued this roustabout with something of a style—ascendant, patent-leathered. Rockefeller nut-cutters, who earlier in the decade told W.L. to hightail it to Pittsburgh and summon an adult, wouldn't dismiss him currently.

W.L. was shrewd. Decades afterward Will recalled his worries the afternoon in 1900 A.W. had appeared at Willie's Philadelphia hospital to propose a buggy ride. Andrew Mellon in love! Will could remember registering, as they jounced along, his astonishment to find his shrinking uncle "skillful in describing the fine points of an English girl. . . ." Pleased, presumably, except as he writes the memory encumbers itself with his own anguish because the pressure he'd withstood beneath a stumbled Indian pony has ballooned his leg with a terrifying sarcoma. Willie's fright, the section of fibula the surgeons clipped away—his mood that afternoon takes awkwardly to Andy's revelation.

This may be afterthought. Yet from the beginning, other relatives report, W.L. had . . . reservations. Once he could travel, Willie and his wife hurried over to London at A.W.'s bidding to meet the McMullens—Nora's family, Andrew Mellon's prospective in-laws. Willie examined the Castle—majestic, one of that succession of Crown properties ringing London, the ancient fortification which commanded the River Lea above the long flint wall thrown up by William the Conqueror. Nora and her seven brothers, as children, sometimes amused themselves grubbing among the site's ancient mounds to unearth Roman campsites.

The McMullens were leaseholders. Hertfordshire was agricultural, an undulating countryside of rolling chalk hills with thatched little villages filling out the hollows and carefully preserved stands of beech and hardwood to edge the alluvial pastures. Grain crops were prevalent; good barley made "malting" important as early as the *Doomsday* inventory. The McMullens—also from Northern Ireland, early in the nineteenth century—started in as brewers.

W.L. might lack his uncle's developing sense of format, but this he understood. "Our first sight of Nora McMullen is unforgettable," he would note afterward. "As we stepped down from the train to the platform, there she was, high up on the box of a dog cart, entrancingly blonde and lovely. The harness on her horse was silver mounted and the horse's tail was docked. It was a smart turnout: everything correct, including the angle at which she held her whip." The family was likable. "The McMullens were good, substantial people. Hertfordshire is a beautiful piece of England, and there is little smoke in it, except that rising from the chimneys of its thatched cottages, if one excepts the smoke from its numerous breweries."

W.L. foresaw. Could she possibly survive, this tomboy of a sister, ready at any moment to throw herself into a sailboat for "ballast," bouncing across surrounding pastureland above the flanks of a horse? That bloom of complexion, those golden inviting eyes—what might Pittsburgh's crematoria subsequently make of *them*?

What about the Mellons? W.L. looked in on the holdovers around the old place at 401 Negley often enough. It was a waxworks, frankly —gloomy, a mortuary of Brussels carpets and thick draperies holding back the light. Old Sarah perhaps bustling up a corridor, beyond the unused parlor, hunting down the boys as escorts to church services. Ma. Well used, baking bread, her stubborn old face all hooded and puckered with resignation, military in her fashion underneath the thickly plaited white helmet that represented her hair.

Understated, their world of intimate formality. Meals served a purpose. The aged Judge (after carefully blowing out the semicircle of candles upon his desk within which he attempted to read at times, if

The survivors—(left to right) Sarah Jane, James,
Andrew, the Judge, Richard, Thomas Alexander Mellon
JAMES R. MELLON II

only a little) painfully threaded his path into the dining room; the
ones still living at home sat waiting. All would commence eating.
Dick, naturally animated, usually liked to converse, often with his
mother. Andrew was always watchful to seat himself at the extremity
of the table, where nobody would object because he himself ate
silently, neatly, privately absorbed.

Ritually, at holiday time, there was a common meal. Such meals
were bleak. A kiss on the cheek between an uncle and a niece would
put the others off; younger relatives still recall the utter and agonizing
silences. One maintains that all the others disapproved of compli-
ments to the cuisine as superfluous, infatuated.

Revealed emotion lost integrity. There remained some undertow.
Old Thomas and Sarah still struggled into their big upstairs double
bed. The Judge grieved particularly over the premature deterioration
of the eldest, Thomas Alexander, who erected his residence next door.
The younger boys could see him often enough, rocking on his porch,
distance in his gaze. He was characteristically perusing his newspaper,
having a little drink, puffing reflectively on a Juan Fortunado cigar
from his humidified cellar storeroom. He remained quietly genial, but

he kept away. Bit by bit, he stopped coming around the lumberyard as often as he had. He wasn't much use.

"You leave that be, it's a wolf in lamb's clothing," the Judge warned Matthew when W.L.'s eldest youngster started reconnoitering the egg-nog. He had in mind Thomas Alexander. In 1899 Tom died—carried away, doctors said, by cancer of the mouth and throat. Doctors suspected cigars—one replaced the next, a cake of ash protruded every waking moment from that unclippered shag of hair that concealed Tom's nonchalance. The father had other explanations. Imbibing betokened a slacker.

As for James Ross? Not to the Judge's tastes either, completely. He looked all right, knew enough to trim his moustache. But he was definitely odd. Once he and Tom were foolish enough to acquire an exposition buffalo, for example, and transported the hulking thing to the piece of property they owned together, the Sneeder farm, just outside of Greensburg. The buffalo would rampage, charging around the orchard, kicking over heavy fences, unless provided with cows.

That wasn't sensible investing. The buffalo wound up on spits at a local beer-garden barbecue, but the Judge's misgivings abided. J.R. was given to an occasional addled philanthropy—he had a gravestone carved in Pittsburgh to commemorate the legendary slave Stephen Bishop and shipped to Mammoth Cave to commemorate his life. He indulged that doughy wife—smug, that one, cluttering up their gabled residence across the street with artistic bric-a-brac, painting, forever filling the place with poseurs who inevitably sent Willie slinking out the back door to join his uncles.

In 1897 Mother Sarah's purported favorite, Dick, married the sociable daughter of a prominent East Liberty fellow parishioner, the importer Alexander H. King. The Kings were solid. Jennie was the daughter of a second family old Alexander raised after the death of his first wife. She wore her much-admired rust-red hair upswept, into a fashionable topknot, which added at least a hint of elegance to Jennie's broad uncomplicated yeoman face, and Jennie knew what she thought. She was quintessential Pittsburgh. When Jennie got married, a lot of the better-connected people around town turned out to wish her well. Here was the kind of celebration at which the expansive R.B. outdid himself: he moved among the guests, telling stories, leaving people bent over with laughter, at his very heartiest.

With R.B. well into a household of his own, living with the old folks had to be wearing, even for the reclusive Andrew. The Judge attributed Andrew's social listlessness to a depression that succeeded his engagement to Miss Fannie Jones of Pittsburgh's longtime ironmongering family: "This marriage . . . entirely satisfactory to both families, would have been consummated in the spring of 1882, but her health began to fail. . . ." Fannie died. "Since then he has gone but little into ladies' society," the Judge concluded, "and become more and more absorbed in business pursuits."

The Judge got matters turned around. Acquaintances insist that Andrew simply came to the conclusion one day that he, pressed by a matchmaking aunt, had bespoken himself unwisely to this decent if ordinary daughter of the industrial gentry, and diplomatically scuttled the arrangement with no more concern than unclumping his pocket handkerchiefs. That had been careless: the limpid young banker henceforward confronted personal overtures with a notorious bleached stare.

"Society" made him nervous, produced a positive anguish of self-consciousness at times. "I would rather have a panic day at the bank," one early letter iterates, "than the burden of an evening function of that nature." Almost any nature. Business aroused his imagination, inspired certainties no pair of western Pennsylvania eyes, coy above a fan, came anywhere near approaching.

He received his visions at the bank. It managed the "properties," and little by little the bank itself showed signs of becoming a phenomenon, called out of Capitalism's misty deep, answering Andrew's preternatural voice. A mere idea originally: "The business as organized by my father was a banking business in which his credit was the capital," he informed Government lawyers, patiently, in 1935. "He received deposits and loaned money and the business grew, and he did not put in any specific capital and there never was any capital stock item on the books." In good years they divided the profits; in bad years they replaced the deficit. At first the Judge had allotted young Andy 20 percent of the bank's end-of-the-year net plus seventy-five dollars a month, but after he turned everything over to his son in 1882 any kind of salary was pointless. Except for a few dollars every now and then for serving as an officer of the Ligonier Railroad, A. W. Mellon never drew a salary. Salaries were for clerks.

T. Mellon and Sons remained wholeheartedly a family shop, their reputation fitted out with tellers' cages. This kept things personal, which all of them wanted, but there were problems of scale. Tremendous industrial consolidations were already rising into view, and family banking of itself couldn't satisfy the calls. They'd have to reorganize. The summer A.W. brought Willie to England to appraise the McMullen family, James McKean, who ran the Union Trust, dropped dead and left their underwriter untended.

Another breakthrough, Union Trust—financial magma. Two hundred seventy-four dollars and seventy-five cents' worth of forgotten floor space upstairs in the Fidelity building (including the bill for fixtures) had metamorphized, behind its Delphic-temple street-floor facade at 337 Fourth Avenue, into a deal-making sanctum under-capitalized at a million and a half in 1902. Deposits neared the $20,000,000 range, and there were undistributed profits on the books approaching $15,500,000.

A.W. was much involved. When word of McKean's passing caught up with Mellon in England, he cabled Frick immediately to suggest that McKean be succeeded by Henry C. McEldowney. McEldowney was a constitutionally dumpy if remorselessly jovial bookkeeper A.W. once spotted slumped over an assistant cashier's desk at Pittsburgh's Bank of Commerce. McEldowney was thirty-two.

Frick, like Mellon, sat on the board of the Bank of Commerce. He could identify McEldowney. He cabled back immediately: "We think he's too young."

Mellon wasn't much fazed. McEldowney was his man. Mellon reminded Henry Frick of what a high opinion Frick nourished of himself when he was thirty-two, and voted his own 2,413⅔ shares. Frick held 1,503. McEldowney received his post, but Frick was disgruntled. Word got out subsequently about one board meeting at which the coking mogul muttered nastily pertaining to A.W.; R.B. lunged. Bystanders broke things up.

Andrew conceded Frick's quirks, but restructuring local banking mustn't relate to personalities. Mellon decided to wait. His sixty-one million dollars' worth of Steel Corporation negotiables left Frick better balanced. By July of 1902 the family accepted federal supervision, and converted T. Mellon and Sons into the Mellon National Bank. Its first year the Mellon National acquired the Pittsburgh National Bank of Commerce and headed the western Pennsylvania clearing-house list.

By then Mellon National had itself become subsidiary to the Union Trust. The brothers traded in their ownership of the Mellon National to Union Trust for 3,000 of the 10,000 original shares. They let

Frick buy. Everything was again reorganized; Henry Frick and Andrew Mellon claimed 2,750 shares apiece; Richard B. Mellon held 1,500. The leftover 3,000 shares were pegged at two thousand dollars each, and distributed, by invitation, among businessmen of substance.

This produced twin banks. McEldowney provided a boardroom. Pittsburgh's commercial leaders forgathered as Union Trust directors. After Duquesne Club luncheons, most nodded away good-naturedly at whatever the plodding chief executive officer proposed. Anybody looking for debentures? The bank would participate as underwriter in the Allegheny and Western refinancing. The Erie had talked to the bank about another first consolidated; there would be opportunities to pick up thousand-share lots at quite a discount.

Few neglected such opportunities. Traffic ran both ways. Where there were risks, where crises might require the Smithfield Street brothers personally to put things right, sometimes the two expected *gratis* securities enough to guarantee voting control. Then Union Trust refinanced. Then directors got involved. Everybody respected making money.

Reorganization *was* a relief. Let McEldowney dicker. Mellon National became freer for less pedestrian undertakings. A. W. Mellon appeared intact—courteous, remote, that empty gaze wandering among the flowers of the carpet, the swinging café door which communicated with R.B.'s suite beyond partitions of etched Victorian glass. Mellon's patiently nurtured stogie wanes—too quickly; the petitioner must press. "Well," Mellon would piercingly ask, "what makes you think so?" The acute glance lingers. "There are five good reasons, gentlemen, why your undertaking is bound to fail," he informed one delegation. He interrupted a chemist, aloft in the theoretical, with one stammered question. "Can-this-thing-be . . . owned?"

Owned—ownership acknowledges reality. Substance—compounds for the beaker, assets they might borrow against.

Afterward? Government attorneys would isolate, so many years later, the fussbudget who maintained the embattled "Yellow Books." These were the ledgers, lanky Henry Phillips explained, in which, since 1896, he itemized their securities. He tended the stock certificates in one of the larger Mellon National "boxes" in one of the vaults in the basement. There were three "wallets," dried from the airlessness, flaking, in which the securities of each of the brothers were kept, along with their common holdings, their "joint account." The wallets were stuffed eventually, bursting, "pouches."

Offices at the bank
ONE HUNDRED YEARS OF BANKING—
MELLON NATIONAL CORP.

Andrew Mellon—banking prodigy
JAMES R. MELLON II

Swollen, teeming, testicular—alone upstairs, cocked in his desk chair, merely remembering the accumulation might twitch at Andrew Mellon's moustache, force moisture into view beneath that sere, clenched underlip. Alone, he couldn't prevent himself from working up periodic "trial balances." How much was he . . . was Mellon really *worth*? The numbers were tantalizing; he must be conservative. In 1902 he arrived at fifteen million dollars. Thirty million by 1906. By 1920 . . . $135,000,000 . . . and that probably understated.

Projections! One stood up dizzy. Banking . . .

Such exercises were depleting. The banker was relieved each afternoon to board the dingy Pennsylvania Railroad local. Pick out a seat, by himself. Sooty bluffs, stacks passing in series, Ukrainian shanties —not much to distract the eye. East Liberty was now a noisy, settled neighborhood. Ma waited their supper.

Diversion wasn't especially important, although the banker didn't protest an evening every once in a while underneath the balustrades of Clayton. This usually involved poker. Along with Henry Frick, Jack Leishman and Philander Knox rounded out the basis for the table. There were fishing trips. He stayed in touch with grammar-school acquaintances—Pennock Hart, Charles Orr, John Lyon. Once Andrew Carnegie had endowed the institutions which carried his name—the Library, the Institute, the Institution in Washington, the Institute of Technology—he delegated much oversight to the well-regarded Mellon. The responsibility was burdensome.

Decades turned. Andrew discovered one escape. He fled each summer to holidays in Europe.

He was accompanied, usually, by Henry Frick.

Frick was almost respectable. The stripling entrepreneur with the hollow jaw and demanding eyes who slept on the Tinstmans' supply counter was gingery with industrial acclaim. Success reinforced boyhood promptings. Corey, the Judge's footpad, hadn't liked the import of all those "prints and sketches" he discovered pinned up around young Frick's clapboard hovel. Frick didn't really care. In 1880 both Frick and Andrew returned from the Continent with thousand-dollar paintings. "No picture ever painted is worth that!" Judge Mellon broke out.

Frick knew better. Andrew wasn't so sure. Throughout the Nineties, trailing Andrew, Frick dogged the galleries. He commenced to buy—art, important things, Vermeer, Hobbema, Cuyp. He introduced A.W. to Roland Knoedler and Charles Carstairs. A.W. bought too. He accumulated paintings, John Walker says bluntly, "which can only be described as mediocre, and which have all mercifully disappeared."

2

Canvases A.W. acquired in 1899 at Knoedler's suggest a call for furnishings. Troyon's *Cows in a Meadow*, Van Boskerck's *Sunset, Pulborough, Sussex*. The banker was splurging. That followed the summer, of course, when Andrew met Nora.

Again Frick was implicated. On holiday from Pittsburgh, Frick's deadly murmur gave way to courtliness. Frick climbed. Crossing over to Europe on the *Germanic* the summer of 1898, Frick ingratiated himself easily with a pleasant pair of English, Mr. and Mrs. Alexander P. McMullen, sailing home just then on the last leg of a round-the-world voyage with their youngest child and only daughter, Nora Mary. Frick introduced Mellon.

To Frick's bemusement, the one who interested Andrew was the McMullens' provincial twenty-year-old. The girl was fetching, Frick acknowledged that. She was terribly young, but something about her pursed smile and those languorous stricken eyes melted away the baby fat. A.W. suffered oceanic enchantment. "It was like a fairy story," he would admit afterward. Sea-changed, the tight-lipped banker retained glimpses of himself sitting endlessly at tea, animated, telling Nora everything. Science, politics, the resurrection of Nature through Industry. He touched on art collecting. Nora was confusingly moved. The trip itself constituted her introduction to maturity after a few months in a German finishing academy. To awaken such interest in somebody important was . . . flattering.

Dangerous. The boat docked. Andrew accepted the invitation to visit the McMullens at their leasehold castle in Hertfordshire. The surroundings were bucolic, windmills, moldering Renaissance abbeys across a sweep of rolling barley. Nora was everybody's baby. Family life was riotous, each of the seven brothers was full of teasing and enthusiasm, the children were horse-crazy.

In autumnal Pittsburgh again, the banker sent Alexander McMullen a copy of his father's autobiography and corresponded with Nora. In 1899 he reappeared and proposed. Nora sent him away. "I have been thinking long and earnestly about what you have said to me," she opened the letter which overtook him in London, "& it pains me, more than I can tell you, to say that I have come to the conclusion that I do not love you enough to marry you." Nora professed great honor and respect, "But it would be utterly unfair to you to ask you to wait at all, because even if you asked me again in time to come, there might be no change in my feelings & then you would be just as unhappy as you are now, whereas if you take my final answer now, you will get over this sad mistake you have made. For it *is* a mistake I am sure—you only know the best side of my character & I feel certain that if you ever got to know me well you would be terribly disappointed. I am simply telling you this because I sincerely think it. If I thought that we should be happy, it would be different, but it would be downright wicked of me to promise to marry you when I knew that I do not love you as you do me. You must see that it would mean nothing but unhappiness for us both. So do not waste your life in waiting for me, for at present I do not see any probability of changing my mind. But I do hope you will write sometime when you can spare time, & also when you come to England you will come to see us. Please forgive me for all the trouble I have caused you, & do not think of me as being hard-hearted. I am sure you will see things as I do if you look at them in the right light. If you have time before you go back, please write a few lines—I shall be back at Guiness on Wednesday. I cannot tell you how unhappy I have been; it seems cruel not to be able to give you what you ask. Please forgive me."

Nora's country breast inflates to answer with honesty. Her door is bolted, and there is vapor on the mirror. Nora wriggles after frankness. You're contemplating disaster. Beware. It would be "downright wicked" for me cold-bloodedly to involve a person who recognizes merely . . . "the best side of my character." Abandon hope—but write. Forget this "sad mistake"—come back. A.W. replied urgently.

Other letters follow. He persists. She weakens. Her parents are troubled too. "A strange family!" exclaims the easygoing brewer, perusing the Judge's volume, pondering the old man's courtship of Sarah. Such relentlessness—his girl seems unprotected. She attempts to listen. "I do wish I could have made the voyage a happier one to you," continues the follow-up that catches Mellon's boat. "Of course I cannot prevent your still hoping that I shall someday change, but I am afraid I cannot give you any encouragement for at present I do not see any likelihood of my altering. You see, I am rather young still & have never thought much about leaving home." The retreat abandons commas.

"I still think that if you ever got to know me better I should bore you terribly. You see you really do not know anything about me and I do not know you very well—but you must be tired of hearing me say all this as I'm sure I have said it before." Mellon reads with pleasure in Pittsburgh. A dying fall. Generosity is imminent.

They correspond. In April of 1900, finally, her inveterate "Dear Mr. Mellon" slips uncommented into "Andrew." He catches a liner. They decide on nuptials in September.

Over for the marriage, W.L. quieted misgivings. Everybody appreciated the pageantry. This was Dick's element. Plenty of party-loving loyalists from A.W.'s Duquesne Club group got into London early. Gustators from the Carnegie, in town to drink. Stags were really lively, although H. J. Heinz was adjudged "too prominent a figure in Sunday school to have a leading role." Pittsburgh strutted. Willie secretly took pride in the blowoff R.B. hosted, a gala to tempt even the starchy London art dealers "to make notes on their cuffs."

On wedding day the Pittsburgh delegation tumbled into a chartered railroad car and ventured the twenty-mile commute. After brief rites the guests were conducted from the medieval Saint Andrew's Church to Hertford Castle. Villagers lined the road to espy Nora's bridegroom. From windows flackered banners. The grounds of the Castle itself were open for feasting, a Breughelesque scramble of townspeople, catcalls against the Royal Artillery brass. Events began with speeches and toasts. Soon enough the contests—wrestling, bowls, boating, ending with a tug-of-war during which Nora's five staunchest brothers dragged five Hertfordshire lads over the line.

By then the newlyweds had detrained. W.L. lingered, disturbed. "The mother was an exceedingly nice person," Willie later observed of his preliminary meeting with the McMullens, "but she kept telling us she was afraid her daughter wasn't ready for marriage." For all Nora's freshness, Will couldn't stop wondering. The way the girl fluttered in and out of guests at the reception, seeking boys her age, bestowing such warm kisses—possibly that was traditional. This wasn't like Pittsburgh.

One wedding portrait survives. Glossy, shorn, the triumphant banker asserts his mature nose toward Nora's smoldering plumpness. No bushiness of moustaches could conceal such regard. Above An-

A.W. newly married
PAUL MELLON

drew's satin lapels a spray of lily of the valley picks points of light against the dark flocked ivy of the Castle walls, the black clerestory window. Across the lawn, where they are posed, a worn, fine Oriental.

This gratifies.

They honeymooned in Berlin. Traipsing around the Continent involved over a month. One dreary November morning, accompanied by a banged-up collection of hatboxes and steamer trunks, the two climbed off a Pennsylvania car at the familiar East Liberty commuter station. Familiar to A.W. Nora was badly startled. "We don't get off here, do we?" she reportedly asked. "You don't live here?"

There was a welcoming breakfast on Negley Avenue, a typically muted meal, bereft of small talk. Nora attempted to understand. They took up housekeeping in an undistinguished three-story residence, visible through mature plantings, step-fronted, brick, at 5052 Forbes Avenue. Space inside felt cramped. "The house," Paul Mellon later wrote, "was late Victorian and very dark—the halls were dark, the walls were dark, and outside, Pittsburgh itself was very dark." Paul remembered the paintings best. "There were one or two English landscapes, and about ten of those formal portraits, large and small. These very urbane and always self-confident personages in their classical landscapes and autumnal parklands smiled down at me with what seemed a warm and friendly glow." Outside, on schedule, tramcars of the Monongahela Street Railway clattered by the house, squealed downtown. Fly ash infested April breezes.

3

A.W. slipped back into banking hours. So much needed pondering. Until the Nineties expired, things hadn't seemed complicated. Banking involved common sense—looking applicants over cautiously, getting deposits properly placed. Underlings watched the real estate. The brothers had gotten into business themselves—the W. L. Mellon Special, the transit network, Union Steel—in about the spirit in which as boys they raised a beef occasionally behind the Negley orchard. Calculated risk—lay in enough oats, and market when hindquarters jumped.

With the Aluminum Company, and subsequently with Carborundum and Standard Steel Car and Marshall-McClintic and Koppers and Gulf, they'd locked themselves into enterprises they couldn't quite abandon. Their days of slaughterhouse financing were finished. Everything now was interconnected. Bank money—what publicists later celebrated as the self-replenishing "Revolving Fund"—flowed through the banks to whichever of the properties wanted capital. Without argument, invariably at advantageous rates. They'd started with cash from the Judge, supplemented by whatever they could borrow; once Big Steel consolidated, the city was aslosh with Carnegie millionaires, tossing about with fortunes very few quite comprehended. Mellon was completely sympathetic. He reinvested Frick's divestitures into the acquisition of banks, kept Schwab's dollars working to help them rupture the Rockefellers. Only he comprehended everything, and until the war, whatever his emotional dyspepsias, he never quit exploring the intricate financial hydraulics which multiplied not merely the Mellon empire but prewar Pittsburgh.

They tried out managers. When necessary, they slipped on financial rubber gloves and excised scattergood visionaries. Markets grew; profits collected. Wasn't "profits" inexact? "Retained surplus" looked better. Reinvestment money—they kept the payout meager. "Mister Mellon," one pup got up his nerve to regale the financier shortly before he died, "did you ever, you know, just sort of grab a little cash, fifty thousand dollars or so, and take a flyer in the market? Speculate?"

Onlookers gagged. Mellon didn't object. "Well, the truth is, I always wanted to try that," he informed the youngster. "Never had the capital. I'd get a few dollars ahead, and then the oil company would need some pipelines, or somebody wanted a reduction tank. . . ." There was always something. More plant, larger ownership. Much better to declare a stock dividend from time to time and conserve the excess. Ambitious cells divide. Fools dissipate.

Financing loosened unwelcome influences. "We found it necessary," A.W. confided to John G. A. Leishman, his crony from Carnegie, "in order to comply with legal requirements, that the new issue of preferred stock should be issued pro rata to stockholders and that was done. . . ." This was in 1899; Pittsburgh Reduction was succeeding. A covert purchasing campaign by Mellon had fattened the "joint account" to nearly 30 percent of the voting securities, but the original developers, dominated by Alfred Hunt, were stubborn about control. By inflating the capitalization with an additional $600,000 issue of voting preferred, the banker hoped secretly to subscribe enough to corner "very close to one-half of the entire capital stock; but whether I will be able to obtain a clear majority, I am unable to say as yet. The other side has been alert and may continue to dominate the business. . . . Kindly keep the information relative to competing for control confidential. I think it would not be well for parties on that side to become acquainted with just what is going on and, besides, what I am doing is in the nature of a still hunt (no pun)."

Hunt expired of malaria that year, which left daily administration passing back and forth between the puerile Charles Hall and pushy little Davis. They might not follow this reapportionment.

Both followed. After the 1907 reorganization R.B. went in as titular president, but Alfred Hunt's son Roy and the increasingly masterful Davis never neglected anything important. Succession within the Aluminum Corporation developed "internally." Spokesmen for the Mellons nosed this about later, along with a retrospective pride in how much money Charlie Hall accumulated before his early demise. Other backers were ingrates. By then A.W. acknowledged Elder Statesmanship.

4

He deserved the recognition. The kind of "still hunt (no pun)" for which the banker kept creeping into position took patience and strategy—work, especially for a planner who admitted to mental processes, however profound, of unvarying slowness. His pen scratched privately all day at Smithfield Street; he took papers home. He ate the evening meal reflectively. After that he tended to closet himself, very often with confederates. Smoke escaped the keyhole.

Nora provided human attentions. "We became much occupied socially," begins the memorandum which appears among the banker's private papers, part of his endeavor to establish what happened. "My mother, Mr. and Mrs. Frick and several others gave receptions for us and for her. Later in the winter we settled down. I had before our arrival engaged a housekeeper, but Mrs. Mellon after a few months expressed her preference to manage the household affairs herself and the housekeeper was dispensed with. She did the marketing and managed everything beautifully. She had the English instinct of economy which appealed to my admiration but I made everything easy and smooth. She kept the accounts and paid the bills carefully. In the evening when not going out she would play or sing and sometimes read the papers to me. We were devoted to each other and it seemed to me to be a state of happiness seldom reached. Of course there were at times trifling differences for the moment, but nothing to disturb our happiness. Next June 28 (1901) Ailsa was born and in August we went abroad with the baby, staying in England at Hertford Castle and returning home in September. Through the winter of 1901 everything continued lovely. We did not go out or entertain a great deal and I haven't much recollection of events during that period—however, our life was all that could be wished."

All *he* could wish, at least just then. Nora twitched. A contemporary studio photograph reveals her with delicately opened arms, trailing gossamer, her thick hair upswept, and holding a spray of roses just under a chin tilted expressively with longing. Her braided-silk accents emphasize her décolletage and encircle her lithe formed waist to trace the suggestion of a knot against the point of her loins. This was a picture Nora saved. One moment, salvaged from a time of confusion throughout which she attempted to adjust herself to soot so pervasive it blackened her underwear in its wardrobe drawer. Distracted by her giddiness, she surprised flat disapproval regularly on matronly Pittsburgh faces. Andrew was so capable; certainly he deserved better. Frivolous—she could storm back, tartly. Nora tried. R.B.'s devout Jennie, awed by such fire, turned into a confidante. But Pittsburgh's commercial inversion reposed like a headache upon her unhappy eagerness to find an existence with warmth enough and music, with pleasure and landscape. Her retained letters brim over with enthusiasm for "the full moon over the sea," her delight that today has been "more perfect than any other day; everything is golden —golden—golden." She thrived on riding, laughter, skating.

Turned upon himself, the keel of his magnificent fortune laid, the banker was preoccupied jockeying ribs into place. He responded, fitfully. . . . Almost all their summers, months at a stretch, they engaged some palatial country house, rode horseback, entertained friends, took trips. Nora required an operation the winter of 1906 and the financier took an adjoining room at Manhattan's Roosevelt Hospital, stayed on through weeks of convalescence. In 1907 Paul was born. Children woke something up, and throughout the jottings which constitute Mellon's diaries are notes like "With children at stable with rabbits," and "Play house with Ailsa and Paul. Taffy pulling," and "Talk with Ailsa about changing cretonne for her room," and "Tried to fly kite."

Both parents were devoted, but after little Paul was born the restlessness got worse. Andrew simply wasn't listening. "Will business

Nora
PAUL MELLON

A moment of domesticity
PAUL MELLON

A.W. and Nora—1901
CONSTANCE MELLON BURRELL

Ailsa as Martha Washington
PAUL MELLON

Nora, with Ailsa and baby
Paul

PAUL MELLON

always have to come before me?" Nora wrote from Sunninghill Park, England, the summer of 1908. "Why must that loathsome business take all the strength and vitality which you ought to give me? Why should you only give me your tired evenings? Why should I give you all my strength and health and youth and be content with nothing in return? For I am not content and never shall be as long as I have to be second—always second. I am feeling so desperately lonely tonight I could almost kill myself. But I would rather be lonely here than in Pittsburgh."

The dreamy little banker tended to accommodate outpourings like that. Missus Mellon sounded fatigued. He'd get her away more often. The winter passed uneventfully. Over Easter of 1909 the two were weekending in New York at the Plaza Hotel when Nora indicated at Sunday breakfast that she had already promised her intimate Grace Chadbourne that she would accompany her to Easter-morning services. Mr. Chadbourne, Nora told the banker offhandedly, "wanted to see [him] about something and intended calling at the hotel."

Chadbourne was an attorney. "He opened the conversation," Mellon subsequently recorded, "by saying he had a very unpleasant task in what he had to communicate—that he came to me as one friend to another, and hoped I would appreciate the delicate and unpleasant nature of his position." Nora demanded a divorce. She appeared utterly resolute—Chadbourne and his wife had attempted to reason with the woman. They found her "hard as a rock." Missus Mellon had declared that "she had been unhappy for the past two years, and said she couldn't stand it any longer; that she had kept from saying or doing anything about it from month to month because she could not bear to pain or hurt me, but that the suspense was killing her, etc. etc. To his question whether we had disagreements or quarrels, she said, no, there was nothing of that kind, that I had always been good to her, but she was unhappy in this country, wanting to live in England and could not bear going on as she had been doing. . . .

"It was a bolt out of a clear sky to me," Mellon observes. "I had been going happily along without the slightest misgiving or knowledge of any trouble, nor had I the least intimation of any unhappiness on her part." He confronted Nora immediately. "She came and burst into tears as she came in; asked me to forgive her, but that she could not help it. That I had always been so good to her, and that it was breaking her heart to hurt me as she was doing, but that she had been so terribly unhappy that it was killing her and that if she did not leave me she would die. I kissed her and tried to reason with her, but without any effect. I told her I did not want her to live with me if she felt that way about it. We must go home and consider what was to be done. She said she could not go back to Pittsburgh, but I answered, she must be reasonable and she consented. . . ."

Nora was terribly distraught. When the unhappy banker attempted, during the ferryboat ride to the train, to discover what possessed his wife she jumped from her seat; he prevented her leaping overboard.

Several days after that Chadbourne came out to Pittsburgh. Judge Reed sat in. They worked something out according to which Nora abandoned the Forbes Street premises on October 4, 1909, to establish the grounds of technical desertion a divorce action required. Nora received $250,000 immediately, augmented by the income from $1,150,000 in trusts. Residence periods for the children were established. People looked on sympathetically—who anticipated such misfortune?

It became a travesty. Once Andrew actually recognized how critical things were he requested a week or ten days to think through his part. The laws of Pennsylvania required a two-year separation period. Nora retained an attorney, Paul Ache of Philadelphia, who negotiated an arrangement according to which the children would allocate four and a half months a year to their father and seven and a half to Nora. Liberated, Nora indulged her transatlantic curiosities. Mellon was still ruminating. Frowning up, he summoned the indispensable W.L. Willie crossed her spoor in England. He returned with documentation.

The banker lay back. Early the following summer, according to long-standing arrangements, Mellon brought the children to join their mother on the liner *Oceanic* for embarkation to Europe. He shooed the youngsters on board; suddenly, among the milling passengers, he spotted Alfred George Curphey, a chesty bravo who had been hangign around Nora since her saucy adolescence. Curphey visited them once at Forbes Street; the ladies of Pittsburgh were soon enough privy to all his Boer War exploits. Lawyers would bicker subsequently over whether the separation agreement had prohibited Nora from Curphey's expansive company.

That morning in June of 1910 A.W. was enraged. He collared the children and hurried them back down the gangplank and into his limousine for Pittsburgh. Nora, waiting in her stateroom, grew puzzled, then frantic. Finally, gathering herself, she left the steamship and boarded the next train for Pittsburgh and swooped through the doors of 5052 Forbes Street and took over the premises.

So Nora was back, her square shoulders white within those poufs of embroidery, the quizzical expression softened and delighted the moment she embraced her babies. Abashedly the banker withdrew. The puzzled family spaniel nuzzled ankles as ever. Had everybody reconsidered? Summer, Pittsburgh's grittiest season, settled in at Forbes Street.

Unwilling as he had been to accept separation, the banker now reconciled himself. The woman was flighty, promiscuous, unfit for motherhood. There would be divorce, too late for anything except that, but as for leniency and access to the children—she wanted too much, her conduct since departing Pittsburgh precluded anything like that. Mellon had the specifics. The sequestered divorce action the Reed, Smith lawyers filed in September was based on adultery, a calendar of infidelities with Curphey which proceeded from staterooms in the *Kaiserin Augusta Victoria* to hotel accommodations in, successively, New York, Pittsburgh and London. The two had allegedly settled through the winter in private quarters along the Bois de Boulogne. They'd been brazen enough. For one holiday, the lawyers pointed out, Mrs. Mellon hadn't scrupled to hire the Vale Farm in Windsor under the name of Mr. and Mrs. Curphey.

Nora waved everything away. Alfred was terribly sweet, but whenever she traveled she moved with members of her family. Andrew was just upset.

A.W. was frantic. The humiliated banker was agonized by the notion that despite Nora's return she intended still to cuckold him. He insisted on knowing. That anguished summer he smuggled surveillance experts into the premises to install some $32,500 worth of "acousticons" throughout the domicile. These led by wire into a closet in which a secretary recorded Nora's every sigh. One of the domestics soon pointed out the little black boxes to Nora, who passed the languid summer days hinting at worthless leads to keep Andrew's flunkies hopping about.

When that grew tiresome Nora asked a girl friend to procure several hatchets and assist her in "warming the ears of the eavesdropper." Heartily, they shredded the acousticons, including the transmitter wired through a boring in the leg of Mellon's baby grand piano.

They left one little black box intact to provide Nora's attorneys.

The siege on Forbes Street was good for talebearing that winter in sullen, fascinated Pittsburgh. Relatives were particularly incensed. There were excited whispers involving liaisons with servants. No motivation went unexamined. Those youthful trips home, on which the banker's bride sometimes invited unmarried Pittsburgh girls—that was sinister too, when you considered a moment. Wasn't it just possible the Jezebel intended to pauperize the community by conveying its naive heiresses to grasping British aristocrats?

With Nora dug in, the days were intolerable. Mellon settled on detectives. Three retired municipal regulars and a professional "sticker," Barney Devlin, a barkeep and mainstay of the Allegheny County Retail Liquor Dealers' Protective League, abruptly occupied the house. Devlin was stationed inside, a heavy-treading Irishman whose responsibility it was never to let Mellon's unreliable missus stray far from view. He shadowed her earnestly, up and down the corridors, half-snoozing on one of the drawing-room divans when somebody stopped over for tea. He survived the winter, but something was amiss, and one spring day he abandoned his beat and materialized subsequently crawling up the aisle of Pittsburgh's Saint Paul's Cathedral, muttering "I am Saint George; I am Saint George of England, and I am going to kill the dragon." Priests helped him away.

Nora was bearing up, endeavoring to fluff away this nightmare wherever her children were affected. Ailsa suffered in particular. She was already ten, no longer the plump little mistress everybody dawdled over, primped up in ruffles and brocades. Beneath her schoolgirl headband Ailsa's eyes were watchful and adult; her mouth wasn't sure which expression to register. Too much was happening. For sixty more years she shuddered at details. There were those bellowings in the night, while she lay writhing, from men stamping up and down the halls; above the commotion a sharp female voice, perhaps of a servant, shrilled again and again, "I think they're kidnapping Paul, they're going to take him awaaay. . . ."

Next morning they never really had. But on her lawyer's advice, Nora herself hired detectives, a very tall policeman and Owen Moran, world champion lightweight. Meanwhile, the implacable banker had filed an application in the orphans' court demanding that a guardian be appointed as his representative in the household to prevent the children's mother from poisoning their attitudes. In December, Fräulein Bertha H. Meyer appeared. In January, bringing forward new

Young Paul and Ailsa
PAUL MELLON

evidence of his wife's earlier dalliances, Mellon asked the court to establish Fräulein and his children in a separate residence. The court
agreed; Nora's attorneys appealed immediately on grounds that the
orphans' court was no place to be issuing these orders.

His divorce was pending; Mellon looked into the possibilities of
assuring not merely its outcome, but also its *dignity*. Why create a
sensation? The newspapers around Pittsburgh were disciplining themselves—Mellon retained their mortgages. But out-of-town dailies were
starting to uncover the details; coachmen from some of Pittsburgh's
solidest families were haunting the Pennsylvania depot platform whenever fresh editions were due. The substance of the financier's allegations spread; suddenly there was mention of "serious" countercharges.
Mellon counted on privacy; Nora, worried about Mellon's influence,
had already successfully petitioned the Superior Court to require the
insertion of all charges into the public files.

That must not happen. Reed produced the tactics, a proposal to
elicit a grunt even from Boies Penrose, who delegated cloakroom
details and dispersal of monies to an organization flunky, Cyrus
Woods. After reviewing the colleagues, Woods selected an obscure

Representative named Scott, from Philadelphia, to introduce Reed's draft. Liaison was nonpartisan; the so-called Scott divorce bill got by 168–0 on April 20, 1911, and was immediately signed by Pennsylvania Governor Tener.

It seemed rather technical. Since 1815, the law in Pennsylvania had permitted either party in a divorce case to request a jury. Now, should either party wish, the proceeding must occur before a court-appointed Special Master. The amended procedure was applicable to any action pending.

Nora understood at once. The banker was maneuvering her little by little into some airless hearing room in which his Pittsburgh Special Master would impoverish her and seize her chickadees. She must fight back.

Inflating like a gorse hen, Nora rained emotional breast feathers. Each recrimination fluttered separate, bitter to the quill. Hadn't she a constituency? "Gold and politics appear to have conspired against me," she pressed a Philadelphia *North American* reporter, "and I hope only the voters of Pennsylvania and the sons of Pennsylvania who have mothers that they love will realize that the law just adopted in this state, abrogating the right of trial by jury in divorce cases, is not only directed especially against me but is also a blow at every mother in Pennsylvania."

The injustice she suffered, "all alone in this country with my two children, my two babies," at finding herself the victim of a manipulation to "adjust the laws to fit my particular case" would soon enough be visited upon any woman with a "worthless or merely bored husband" determined to "free himself from the marriage obligation."

"And what have I done to bring all the powers of the commonwealth against me? My sin is only that I have failed to realize the dream of a foolish young girl. At 20 I thought I should come here as the mistress and good angel of a wealthy and powerful husband's vast estate. I had the robust health of a girl who had spent her life out in the country, and the man of many millions and thousands upon thousands of servants suffered from a weak family constitution. He pleaded for my health for his children, for the heirs of his great fortune.

"Was it foolish of me to accept with pride the call to give new life to a family of great wealth and power? I saw myself in the role of the mistress of the manor who lightens the burden of the peasant. I imagined myself as a link between the old and the new world. . . .

"But I was only 20 then, and I married into my dream, and so we came over here, and he named a town after me, Donora. I was at last in my station as the human partner of my husband in his great financial empire. And I loved him, too; I admired him and looked up to him as a great man, a master mind.

"My first great disillusion came when I learned that his people were not of his people at all. I had dreamed of another Hertfordshire, with Hertfordshire lads and lasses; I had arrived in a strange land with strange people, strangers in a strange land. 'They are foreigns, Huns and Slavs and such as that, and you can't do anything with them,' I was told about the people whose affections I had dreamed of winning for my children."

Increasingly "sick at heart to live in the middle of so much I was told to despise," where "The whole community spirit was as cold and hard as the steel it made, and chilled the heart to the core," Nora took her baby girl and fled "the gray world of cold steel" for "the green fields of Hertfordshire." On returning to Pittsburgh she had "won friends," made "converts for the Hertfordshire ideas. . . .

"Then my boy was born, as fine a baby as any mother ever was blessed with. But my joy was saddened by the dread of the thought that this baby was to grow up to stand all alone as the master, not of a loyal set of workmen . . . but . . . an unreasoning horde of wage slaves, with an instinctive hatred for the man in the manor who knows them less than they know him.

"I took my baby boy to Hertfordshire. I wanted to nurse to life in him my own love for the green fields and the open sky. I wanted him away from the gray-smoke and dust-filled air of my husband's gold and grim estate. I wanted him to grow big and strong, prizing health more than wealth in himself and others. I wanted him to grow up as master not as slave of his fortune; to use it not as a club to dominate with, but as a magic wand to spread health, happiness and prosperity with through his land among all those already dependent on the enterprise of the fortune my boy was to inherit.

"Nights that I spent in my baby boy's bedroom, nursing these thoughts for his future, my husband, locked in his study, nursed his dollars, millions of dollars, maddening dollars, nursed larger and bigger at the cost of priceless sleep, irretrievable health and happiness.

"In that way, each attracted by the pole of his own magnet . . . we drifted apart." Sometimes there were quarrels, disagreements over whether the babies should be "trained into the Pittsburgh atmosphere, become drenched in it," or "rise above . . . the Pittsburgh clouds and let sunlight in when they came of age. He became more and more inattentive, and finally forsook me altogether for his dollars.

"It crept over me that perhaps I too, a foreigner like his Huns and Slavs, had been weighed coldly, dispassionately on the scales of demand and supply, and as a wife ranked merely as a commodity in the great plans of this master financier's lifework. The babies were there; even the male heir was there. Was the wife to be laid off like other hired help when the steel mills shut down? The manner in which I was treated at this period convinced me that my husband at least regarded my marriage as a contract that could not be broken without pretext. He sought the pretext, and when I learned that he was seeking the pretext, it drove all my dreams away, and I faced his world of reality to fight it in defense of my mother rights and my babies."

Nora welcomed the separation. "I felt as if I had saved my son from a fateful future. I had almost seen him dragged into the money whirl and drown in the bottomless dollar pit, but I had rescued him and restored him to a life in God's sunshine." Then, "my money-wise husband must have regretted the bargain. . . . He sought a divorce not on the grounds he had agreed to, but on absurd grounds of infidelity," and attempted "every means and artifice to get my babies away from me." "He is a powerful and a resourceful man with a money will to conquer, regardless of cost," Nora admitted, summing up. "Gold may crush me. Gold and politics may take my babies away from me.

"But if they do, it will be because the manhood of Pennsylvania has sunken so low that it is willing to surrender the motherhood of the state to the pillage of gold and politics. I don't believe it. That's not American, and I don't believe it is Pennsylvanian."

Here was a performance—stem-winding, reverberant with contemporary voices from William Jennings Bryan to Susan B. Anthony. It appeared May 7; that same day reporters cornered A. W. Mellon personally. Had he any rejoinder? Would he deny publicly that the law just enacted that made it easy for "rich men to get rid of their wives" was "adopted especially in your behalf . . . ?"

" 'Nonsense,' " the financier "almost whispered, and looked away from his interviewer; across the room.

" 'Do you know if the law was introduced at the request of one of your lawyers?'

" 'I don't know anything about it, but why do you come here and ask me such impudent questions; what business of yours is it?' "

By that time the banker was already quite upset: "His emaciated body shook like a window pane in a storm." This wouldn't work out. The next morning, in separate statements to the newspapers, even grandees in Pittsburgh were mouthing open disapproval. Cortlandt Whitehead, the local Episcopal bishop, "denounced the changes in the divorce laws in strong language." Petitions were going around. Mrs. Enoch Rauh herself—weighty dowager, presented in the write-ups as "Pittsburgh's most prominent social worker, member of the Juvenile Court Association, President of the Council of Jewish Women of Pittsburgh; president of Nathan Straus's Milk and Ice Association, and famous throughout the country as the leader and originator of esthetic sex hygiene as part of children's education"—waded to the fore. "With the suppression of publicity by the newspapers, the miscreants will no longer have publicity to fear," Mrs. Rauh worried aloud.

The publicity he'd encountered was nothing but "a lot of lies" whoever put it out, Mellon was still muttering. Mrs. Rauh was already scheduled to address the Homestead Women's Club; Mellon shrugged her pure, heavy gaze.

The State woke up. The Scott bill repealer slid through the legislature as quickly—if not so stealthily—as Reed's original proposal. Attorneys for Mrs. Mellon soon extracted a ruling from the court that she as an individual, should she so decide, might demand a normal jury proceeding.

Nora filed. The banker was whipped. Negotiations among the lawyers quickly produced a settlement according to which, if Nora's representatives would agree to the privacy of a Special Master arraignment, representatives of the banker would guarantee to return the grounds to desertion and accept the earlier financial dispositions. The decree was granted July 2, 1912.

Now—after Nora won? Escaped the miser's clutches, made permanent in equity her freedom to desert this heartlessness and grime, take up those seething youthful energies in gallops across English meadows, giggles among the bibelots along the Bois de Boulogne? Nora relocated. After 1912, until the decade ended, she occupied a small but charming residence behind an inobtrusive garden wall on

Howe Street, walking distance from Forbes. Her intimates were mystified. After such an outburst? It made things easier vis-à-vis the children, Nora occasionally would indicate, but there was an ambivalence about that too which veiled her rich, maturing face. Conceivably Pittsburgh was improving.

5 | BETWEEN THE ACTS

1

EVEN BUSINESS CONTACTS saw how Nora's flight afflicted the banker with listlessness verging on the morose. His moustache drooped untrimmed; the eyes looked heavier-lidded from aging and loneliness. He abandoned buying pictures. A.W. was mumbling so much the younger relatives suspected some undiagnosed speech impairment.

The Judge finally died. He'd grown more patient with religion the last several decades; old-timers recollect that diminished figure, pawing along the pews, squinting up the transept at East Liberty Presbyterian. He awaited occasional visitors among the heavy carved Victorian set pieces which dominated his sitting chambers, a perpetual coal fire glowing inside the fender below the hem of his blanket. The male nurse watched; when people were around, Thomas exerted those plowman's tough fingers to keep himself upright, fiercely throttled both armrests, his plucked scalp tilted. Wary as a gobbler, ready anytime to pounce on blather with an appropriate homily.

He went in 1908—well prepared, taking very little savor from those last stunted mealy kernels—and orderly old Sarah joined him the winter after that. Andrew saw them buried. Were things slowing down? The campaigns and strategies that fascinated him while Nora was there were losing their immediacy. Paul Mellon would claim never to remember his father bringing work from the office.

The banker was . . . consolidating, perhaps. The moves were reliable, that perfection of timing. He just wasn't eager. He really didn't appear to want any more. Pittsburghers approached him leerily. In 1917 he sold off New York Shipbuilding; there were substantiated

The final Judge
WESTERN PENNSYLVANIA
HISTORICAL ASSOCIATION

rumors that he was prospecting for buyers for Gulf. It took an extraordinary combination to hold his interest.

Then one came along. Mellon encountered a manager. Henry Bedinger Rust—stocky, nosy, demanding, imaginative, and such a driver that when he was gradually to develop palsy and started to manifest that symptomatic pill-rollers' chafing of the fingertips it seemed to people merely one more gesture to express Rust's congenital impatience. Rust positively couldn't wait. History-haunted, the impoverished offspring of an important Virginia family intermarried with the Lees, Rust as a child had seen his West Point-trained colonel of a father, Armistead, lose everything they had after Appomattox. The boy drifted north to Pittsburgh and began his professional life as a municipal laborer, chopping brush. He struggled through night school to claim a post as an assistant city engineer; he was barely twenty-one when he was put in charge of developing Schenley Park.

Rust stayed in charge after that. He shouldered his way into business—boilers, a type his brother designed. Rust's push was such that Babcock and Wilcox was forced to buy Rust out in 1908 to protect its share of the lucrative Pittsburgh market. Idleness annoyed him, he craved something sizable, he looked into situations. Then, gossiping at the Duquesne Club one day with Harry W. Croft of Harbison-Walker Refractories, Rust heard that a regular Croft customer, Heinrich Koppers, was avidly hunting capital to enlarge the American subsidiary of his international company, which designed and constructed by-product coking ovens.

The hint was galvanizing. Rust knew who Koppers was, that autocratic little tinkerer from Essen with the great bobbing scalded-looking head whose brilliantly engineered apparatus not only increased the output per ton of coking fuel but also drew off those noisome yellow gases with which Henry Frick peacefully contaminated whole counties. It reduced their compounds to base products from tar and benzol and sulfate of ammonia to recirculated coal gas.

Rust had, in fact, sounded out a competitor; once this looked substantial he met A.W. But matters never jelled.

That brush with Croft led directly to Koppers. In 1908 the United States Steel Corporation had helped the German set up a plant in Joliet, Illinois. Koppers' innovations were debated; at centers like Pittsburgh a shift in metallurgical technique made life as wobbly as a resettling fault. But economies were indisputable; Joliet was booking orders. Koppers desperately needed plant; money was painfully tight;

Heinrich Koppers
THE KOPPERS COMPANY

Henry Rust
THE KOPPERS COMPANY

remarks the harried founder exchanged with Croft, whose refractories supplied firebrick, made clear how enticingly little capital the German would take in exchange for control of his American operations.

Croft and his partner, Hamilton Stewart, had venture money—close to a half-million dollars—but Koppers demanded another million. Perhaps New York?

"Do you know anyone who will put it up?" Croft ultimately asked Rust.

Rust mentioned Andrew Mellon.

"Do you know Mr. Mellon?"

"If Mr. Mellon walked in that door I don't believe he would remember me, but I met him several years ago and he was going to help me in a business, but somebody else got started before we did," Rust said.

"Do you think he will back you in this new business?"

Rust thought he might.

Obscure personage. Waiting in that bank somewhere, quietly thinking and smoking, and Pittsburgh was smoking, and who dared approach? Rust summoned up courage. The banker seemed attentive, mildly. The year was 1914, summer was already started, and Mellon quietly volunteered to think the whole thing over while taking his vacation at Prides Crossing, Massachusetts. That August the First World War began. Koppers got trapped abroad. Mellon returned to Pittsburgh in October; not long after that he bumped into Rust. "What was that business we were going into with you? I remember that it was to take about a million or a million and a half dollars, but I have forgotten just what it was." Rust stiffened. "I remember it was all right," Mellon said, "but I have forgotten just what it was."

"By-product coke."

"Oh, yes, I remember now, I talked to Tom Lynch about it. When you are ready come to see me."

Intimidating nonchalance. Mellon had, in fact, been pondering coke deeply. Tom Lynch of Frick's old concern had mentioned the technological possibilities; Mellon's personal notebooks reflect a summer of long walks spent listening to Frick. Henry Rust mustn't suspect. Capital's mode was Queenly; She ennobled Her enterprises with restraint and indirection.

Koppers-Pittsburgh came into corporate existence on November 3, 1915. Its stockholders in America were Hamilton Stewart and H. W. Croft (42½ percent), and both the Mellon brothers (37½ percent). In Germany, fuming, Heinrich Koppers arranged through Stockholm intermediaries to barter his rights and patents for currency and 20 percent of the Pittsburgh company's stock. "This fellow Koppers has been in a hurry to get his money," A.W. told W.L.

Pittsburgh couldn't wait either. By March of 1915 the thing looked solid enough to think about relocation, and sixty-seven of Koppers' original eighty-five-man technical staff moved east. Rust accepted the presidency. Would things be easier? In Joliet the saturnine little German inventor had typically rushed in from Essen brimming over with innovations, spread out his American designers' working drawings across an office floor and crawled all over them on hands and knees, peering through the bifocals, then hauled his chunkiness to its feet and fired whoever made *that* mess.

Rust appeared unexceptional—another center-combed Episcopalian manager, his rigid little smirk weakened fatally by one of those Million Dollar Roundtable moustaches as sparse as grit on sandpaper. Then Rust began functioning. They were, employees realized, embarked on the reconnoitering phases of a protracted guerrilla campaign of sales and acquisition their starchy new boss intended to conduct from parlor cars. Koppers must become *important*. Long before the Armistice the tales were circulating. Executives whispered across bullpen desks about the greenhorn engineer gagging down a smoldering cigarette rather than explain his dissipation upon confronting his chief, scuttling down the aisle, up early to herd his groggy little sales force into a dining-car pep talk.

Rust got results. In 1915 alone Rust pulled in twelve separate contracts—more than the company had landed since 1908. A.W. underwrote a fellowship for Koppers at the Mellon Institute, and along with basic coking ovens the company soon offered complete by-product facilities, from coal-handling equipment to light-oil refineries. Then Koppers researchers discovered that the carbon monoxide and hydrogen mixture they captured by forcing steam through coking furnaces was salable as household fuel. Then—history couldn't stay away—several of the key light-oil by-products, notably toluol and benzol, fell into desperately short supply once Allied scientists realized that they alone might supply a practical chemical base for TNT and picric acid. The value of toluol, normally a waste product, hopped up to six dollars a gallon. Finally America became combatant. After that the only problem was whether Koppers could build enough of its explosives installations in time, and within two years an estimated $192,000,000 in government expenditures was directed by the company into dozens of plants it managed and, unavoidably, inherited.

Koppers was gigantic overnight. But Rust was one with visions to match his appetites. He saved and reinvested. Like so much recaptured gas the ever-richer profitability superheated the company's capitalization, reappeared as stock dividends.

Fanaticism this stubborn elicited the vestige of a smile even on Smithfield Street. Here was an alchemy—to exploit their patrimony, that diabolical back mantle on which their world quite literally rested, and produce through science and capital this completely new, redemptive universe. Explosives, certainly, but also the dyes and medicines, the illuminating gas and insecticides and preservatives. Original sin was cured!

With Koppers, as usual, prudence demanded successive winnowings. Heinrich Koppers went first. In April of 1917 the United States entered the hostilities, and Congress quickly legislated to confiscate the holdings of "enemy aliens." Koppers–Koppers' 20 percent, at least —was judged to qualify. At an October directors' meeting Heinrich was voted out.

Fortunes of war entirely; Heinrich would presumably understand. What happened after that reportedly aggrieved the German. The procedure in such cases required the Alien Property Custodian, just then Mr. A. Mitchell Palmer, to seize the foreign property to sell at auction. The bidding for Koppers' share took place on September 13, 1918. There was a solitary bid, for $302,250, and it was tendered, to nobody's surprise, by an existing syndicate composed of H. W. Croft, Hamilton Stewart, and A. W. and R. B. Mellon of Pittsburgh.

In 1918, had earnings been distributed, the helpless Koppers' fifth would have approached $250,000. Koppers took this poorly, and afterward Koppers-Essen made itself a pest to Koppers-Pittsburgh with demands for secondary payments and threats of patent-infringement suits.

Dispatching Heinrich like that bothered Henry Rust. "When Mr. Rust was last in Washington," A.W. wrote Charles D. Marshall the autumn of 1921, "about two weeks ago, he brought up the question of Mr. Koppers being allowed to again acquire an interest in the Company. I took the same view which you express, and stated that it was unfortunate that he should have discussed the question with Koppers in a way which may have held out hope to him. I see no reason for giving the proposition favorable consideration."

So far as Mellon could see the dealings were finalized. He and his brother had emerged with the greater part of Koppers' stock—their holdings put together to 55 percent. They met subsequent obligations. The official who actually conducted the auction was Joseph F. Guffey, nephew of that picturesque old plunger who dragged the Mellons into Texas. The temptations he encountered as Director of the Bureau of Sales were formidable, and he was shortly "indicted for embezzling from the alien property custodian's office" larger sums of money than he could easily replace. Guffey approached Judge Reed; Judge Reed called Mellon. In March of 1921 the pair quietly agreed to underwrite the $150,000 guarantee the Government demanded as settlement.

Business was guttering badly. Five years of assuring the salesmen that "We'll have to sweat blood on this" because "We've hardly scratched the surface" left Rust with shopworn adrenals and much of industrial America scratched virtually to bedrock. Engineering wasn't really enough. Rust hankered for ownership, and he was already starting to piece together the deals which cut him personally into several subsidiaries and involved Koppers-Pittsburgh with operations at an illuminating-apparatus plant the company had built in Fort Wayne and the advanced coking ovens in St. Paul and Kearny, New Jersey. These involved municipal contracts: coal roasting supplied gas; gas must be produced whether there were customers for coke or not.

Once business began to deteriorate the New Jersey contracts were forcing the company to compile a mountain of by-product coke that approached a landmark. Even Rust was frightened; Stewart and Croft panicked completely, and sold their holdings to Mellon at $131 a share, just about their investment. Mellon accepted them philosophically, having "never yet seen a big pile of fuel that didn't find its way into furnaces." Not long after that there was a strike of miners, and coke-short Bethlehem Steel wanted the by-product so desperately it shipped over steam shovels on flatcars and hauled everything away along with thousands of tons of Jersey meadow mud.

Again Mellon reorganized. This time he and R.B. held onto 49½ percent of the stock and allowed Henry Rust, Charles Marshall and H. H. McClintic to divide the rest. The public wasn't invited; Koppers remained "firmly held." A number of Rust's recent moves had left the conservatives around the bank cowering in the safe-deposit boxes whenever the Virginian made proposals. A.W. appreciated motility; nevertheless, since he himself was committed by then in Washington, he installed the hardheaded Charles Marshall as chairman of Koppers.

Then boom times started.

2

Before the war. Pittsburgh encounters this jumbo decade as sated as the Mellons. Downtown, between the onslaught of cheap tin lizzies and those relentless foundries flaming at the mouth, the smog gets heavy enough to tempt pedestrians to chew. Commercial posters on crumbling brick walls advertise Good Gulf and Beeman's Pepsin Gum; alongside the Pittsburgh docks the barges and tour boats nudge in beside the warehouses like unhappy animals, craving the dignity of avenues. Automobiles burn their headlamps at noon.

There is industrial peace. Frick—in carpet slippers now, browsing among his New York cloisonné—has abandoned this backdrop to his display of nerve, but his meticulous specter is omnipresent. A velvet of fly ash coats masonry facades all the way to Oakland. Dumb, languageless, the Przbylskys and Cavazonnis still migrating to the Forge of the West now cause no disruptions as they expend their brief sweated manhoods into twelve-hour days and seven-day weeks the gallant little coke baron made mandatory to the industry. A ladle of bubbling slag tips and boils a laborer. A court case develops; the mill owner escapes damage claims on grounds of contributory negligence.

In 1913, in a sparsely populated, largely agricultural America, an estimated 25,000 people die and another million are injured through industrial accidents. When workmen's compensation bills come up for debate in Washington, Pennsylvania Senators Knox and Penrose re-

Dignitaries of 1910—R.B. at left
STEFAN LORANT

Smoke rising
CARNEGIE LIBRARY

main inexorably in the forefront of the opposition. Fiscal responsibility continues uppermost. Meanwhile, in Pittsburgh, a third of the children are dead before they reach five years, and miners who collapse, coughing, near auto-asphyxiation, are almost always diagnosed to suffer from Mycobacterium tuberculosis. The sputum they expel, usually, is puttylike with coal dust, riddled with fragmented steel. This, officials think, represents a recurrent anomaly.

In 1910 Richard Beatty Mellon, whose many responsibilities now included keeping an eye on Mellon coal properties, was photographed formally with five other Pittsburgh community leaders. His hair has silvered, he is wearing a blazer, and even in black and white no viewer could mistake that "elegant, but oh, so well-fed" look W.L. loved tweaking. Dark circles underscore heavily R.B.'s melting Latin eyes, and along with all the well-advertised amiability there are, obviously . . . hesitations.

Perhaps it has something to do with an adult lifetime of furnishing the filler for that Siamese my-brother-and-I pronoun. The Pittsburgh royal *We*, a device the ever-reticent A.W. favored to soften decisions he—he alone—reached. They adhere to the formalities of a discussion; on Sundays there is almost always a ceremonial meal at one of the mansions followed by a raking-over of events. W.L. drops by. But, although there is usually an automatic pairing-off of investment between the brothers, A.W. remained the deal-maker, the comptrolling eye, never really very far from an updated balance sheet. R.B. gets legwork.

Not that Dick groused. "This is the last time you'll see me in this office," an acquaintance heard R.B. sigh one suffocating afternoon after he finally assumed the presidency of the Mellon National Bank. Skylights made the wainscoted little room unbearable. But he and A.W. never minded the heat before, and Dick could wait until the massive-columned new home for the bank was ready in 1924.

Jennie, R.B.'s outspoken wife, wasn't so habitually patient. "My husband always has to work so hard!" she complained to a friend. "A.W. just couldn't seem to *help* but make money." R.B.'s private secretary totaled the number of days her boss spent shuttling to and from the coast one year to attend directors' meetings of the Pennsylvania Railroad and American Surety and Guarantee Trust and came up with seventy-six nights on the train. Dick hadn't really needed those twenty-dollar gold pieces, but it seemed important that the Mellons remain in systematic touch with compatible power centers.

The load his brother kept sloughing onto his broad hocklike shoulders weighed more than R.B. admitted to himself. Increasingly, he and his brother both had gotten into the habit of negotiating through lawyers. In A.W.'s case, a legal opinion helped identify what he intended to do. Lawyers who worked regularly with Andrew Mellon complained at the way he would sometimes ask a question, get an answer he didn't care for, then later on rephrase the question in hopes of loopholes. A.W. was polite, but he could be a trial at times.

R.B. was easier. "R.B. was not just not smart, he was stupid," says one attorney whose senior partners enjoyed unceasing contact. "He was the least attractive of the group. He did not want to take responsibility. The name was good enough." R.B. evaded confrontation. "You never had any dealings with the Mellon family if they could help it," one associate says. "It was always with somebody else."

Cares piled up. "I've always thought everybody was happier than ourselves who had just a little bit more than they needed to live on," Jennie told one friend. Paul Mellon was to remember his gusty uncle as a man with a wonderful sense of humor who "lived in the most enormous house. He said once that if he ever built another house he was going to have a mail chute directly from the slot in the front door to the furnace."

Exasperation broke through regularly, often disguised as lavishness. When prohibition was pending R.B. once stunned the membership of Manhattan's Links Club with several boxcars of Old Overholt whiskey. His wardrobe was opulent, his days were full of incidents like summoning an employee his comptroller caught defalcating serious banks funds, hearing out the frightened man's domestic problems, and making up the loss from his own pocket until the employee could pay him back. Yet he could erupt into tantrum, swipe up an inkpot and hurl it blindly at the nearest secretary.

Even in an era when new-money Pittsburgh potentates were so confident their residences were destined to become landmarks they gave them names—LYNDHURST, SOLITUDE, RU-NA-CRAIG—rather than street addresses, the Richard Beatty Mellon fortress at 6500 Fifth Avenue was of a bulk and blatancy that astonished. "I guess Uncle Dick didn't really have it so good," an upstart second cousin would later gibe, touring the Residenz at Salzburg. As late as 1940, when property taxes induced the next generation, young Dick and Sarah, to tear the great pile down, the wrecker who got the contract turned to his brother and confessed, "This job just throws me."

What could you pry out first? Sixty rooms, eleven bathrooms. The entrance atrium opens gracefully onto the marble staircase—up which it would undoubtedly be possible to roll a flatcar sideways. Posts at the landing are cupids with inset mother-of-pearl trays. Aeolian organ consoles, two, one manual and one for player-piano rolls, lurk below the stairs to pipe their harmonies throughout the mansion. There are a workshop and a regulation-length bowling alley and gold-plated fixtures in Jennie's famous marble bathroom. The wreckers discovered a number of elderly hunting prints and a photograph of the Mellons' racehorse Glengesia—fourth in the 1930 Grand National. R.B.'s bedside volume is a college algebra. "Among the classics in the very pleasant upstairs sitting room," the Pittsburgh *Bulletin Index* reports, straightfaced, "were books like *Self Culture for Young People* in 10 vols., *Mad Marriage* by George Gibbs, *Art Out of Doors* by Mrs. Schuyler Van Rensselaer." There are two elevators, one freight.

Not, the report concludes, that there was anything "ostentatious" about the place; everything was "comfortable, even homey, in the best English manner." The judge, too infirm and blind to fuss about "shoddy-ocracy," passed on during construction. And indeed there *was* a feeling of preponderating Hanseatic intimacy about the Mellons' great brownstone mansion with the crenellated tower. People enjoyed themselves there. Johnston, the house manager, often said that everything around the place moved effortlessly on "roller bearings." It reflected R.B.'s touch, that about him exactly that made him invaluable to his ethereal brother. R.B. was earthbound. Everybody else hired butlers. For R.B.'s establishment, only a "house manager" sufficed.

Ribbed groins, architraves and recessed molded foyer ceilings which appear to require Corinthian columns virtually shoulder to shoulder to support such weight; overhanging battlements just perfect if ever the thirty-odd retainers tiptoeing around with folded sheets or stacking forks must rush to the parapet to crossbow coal miners. Ivanhoe reconquers Pittsburgh. Partly, one concedes, because the Mellons like everybody else are victims of the digestion-defying Gothic Revival pretensions of the period. Like intricately coiffed upswept hairdos for women and paunches dubbed "corporations," pseudo-castles represented the greedy innocence of a time when even the humblest moiler would probably have agreed—if asked—that barons of industry undoubtedly deserved fortresses.

Rich feudal interlude. Yet somehow, when finally the First World War blew that mood away, it lingered in Pittsburgh. Feudalism *felt* right. In their subtle manner, never much gone into, the Mellons were stealthily withdrawing from the older, more establishmentarian cliques in Pittsburgh society—propertied families like the Schoyers and the Hillmans and the Chalfants and the Olivers, the crowd that congregated mostly at the exclusive Pittsburgh Club and the Pittsburgh Golf Club—and nurtured a countervailing set of social institutions undisguisedly their own. The Duquesne Club still served as a collecting point for the steel and railroading men scrambling together their fortunes while Mellons were framing theirs. R.B.'s big house on Fifth Avenue turned quickly into another center. Finally, in 1921, the three great wings of the Clubhouse were punctuated by another of those round crenellated towers—the 6,200-acre Rolling Rock Club.

3

Rolling Rock. "I remember my grandfather asking me," Larry Mellon says, " 'Do you ever covet anything?' " The boy couldn't think. " 'I only covet one thing,' " J.R. confided. " 'When I pass a big pile o' manure.'

"That's how they were," Larry Mellon says. "They spoke like farmers, they used the terms."

Land hunger. Richard felt it powerfully. Age brought it on—the way one's hair got frailer, opened up the temples and started to snag into bristles around one's close-set eyes. He looked more daily like what he suspected he was: Andrew's beadle. Somebody's overpaid floorwalker, voluble with the help, checking to make certain clean blotters got dropped off Fridays.

He needed a tonic. Saturdays, he liked to order up the family four-horse brake and bump along the fifty miles of Greensburg turnpike, to rummage the Ligonier countryside in hopes of discovering property suitable for their personal "retreat." The terrain was ancestral. They'd pushed the railroad through; a couple of years after that the Judge picked up one 131-acre parcel not far from Burnett Springs; one of his steerers divined coal. The hunting was there—cover for the game was abundant, and winters were temperate. Young quail were multiplying and white-tailed deer could nibble early buds to fortify their stamina against roaming barnyard dogs.

R.B. was looking for a shooting preserve. J.R. had property nearby, Rachelwood, a tangle of Allegheny ridge on which he'd convinced some architect as whimsical as himself to erect his Black Forest castle. R.B. wasn't joking around. He wanted something impressive. By 1915 R.B. had acquired the Burnett Springs holding and several neighboring properties—the Saltzmann place, the Stitley and Anderson farms. People turned up weekends—the men were bivouacked at the original Pine Cabin, a plain log shelter with rockers on the porch, wry with surrounding hemlock. The women got bedrooms inside the Stitley farmhouse.

It gratified the banker that he could offer hospitality to Pittsburgh's sporting families. People like his in-laws. The Kings were sportsmen; Alexander King joined syndications to develop area thoroughbreds. Both R.B.'s brothers-in-law were shotgun adepts. Now *he* had something! But people he wanted wouldn't continually accept invitations.

He broached his idea. Why not go ahead and incorporate a club, named for a landmark through which "the water comes rolling down over the rocks," avowedly for "social enjoyments and to provide and maintain facilities for shooting, hunting, fishing, riding, golf, tennis, and other athletic sports"? He'd maintain the premises. Club members could sign whenever they passed the night or charged a dining-room meal—token obligations, for decades one dollar.

It took four years to prepare his Elysium. The scale was characteristic—monumental. Once everything was ready the banker released title to the Union Trust; the Rolling Rock Club leased back the "demises to the club some 6200 acres, the clubhouse and appurtenances, swimming pool, manager's residence, garage, trap shooting range and gun house, golf course, tennis court, water wheel and water pumping machinery, pheasant coops, bridle-paths and appurtenances."

Nor was that everything. Club members often spotted the banker astride his elegantly cropped Baywood, checking out the grouse bags of hunters emerging piecemeal from cover at dusk. He turned up everywhere. He encouraged favorite visitors to climb in alongside him on the buckboard's seat and have a gander at the surrounding twelve-thousand-acre Rolling Rock Farms. He kept after groundkeepers. A grove of pin oaks there might accent the curve of horizon. Why not some big Belgian horses, a herd of Brown Swiss cows? Poultry? A reconstituted buckwheat mill!

Something finally was satisfied. Pheasants broke from wild rose

Young Jennie King and her brother, Robert Burns King
STEFAN LORANT

Jennie King Mellon
PAUL MELLON

The R. B. Mellon four-horse brake
CONSTANCE MELLON BURRELL

R.B., R.K.
CONSTANCE MELLON BURRELL

Baby Richard K. Mellon with parents, Garden of the Gods, Colorado
CONSTANCE MELLON BURRELL

hedges and skittered over pachysandra. Passersby identified that portly old frame, too decrepit to hunt, trudging behind a plow to cultivate the tillage.

This made no economic sense. When gamekeepers and grooms became apologetic about how expensive certain refinements ran, R.B. became peremptory: "Never mind about that; I manage to pick up a little change here and there." But bills were mounting, and he was relieved one day when Andy mentioned Ligonier. Couldn't he buy half? R.B. dubbed *that* one the best business deal he ever put over.

One justification for all the fuss was young Dick's enthusiasm. He'd had his troubles. Relatives remembered the child—something of a pantywaist, cuddled up against his mother's generous hip whenever there were visitors, dangling high-button pumps and immersing those square little King jowls in flops of velvet. His blandness was unnerving —a kind of docile, glazed look—something from the mother, an over-abundance of white to the eye. Dick fled from thunderstorms into Jenny's great bed.

He assumed his role. Behind Grandmother King's estate at Highland Park he loved to direct his shaggy little Shetland pony through gaits and maneuvers, fighting back his smirk while baby sister Sarah watched enviously. He handled a shotgun early. "Some afternoons," W.L.'s oldest, Cousin Matthew, remembers, "we'd go around in an automobile, and Dick would sit in the back and shoot the street-lights out."

Education made Dick fidget. He started at several local places, including Shady Side Academy, and finished his secondary education at military school—Culver Academy in Indiana. He relished the discipline. The war was on in Europe, and R.B. installed a major to instruct over a hundred local boys in military fundamentals on Rolling Rock property. They marched alongside hedgerows, crawled around an obstacle course, took hikes for seasoning and endurance. Dick loved the drilling in particular. With this began a lifelong brute appreciation for all qualities military. Punctuality, orderliness, a fussiness about dress—these gave life perimeters. . . .

School became even drearier. In 1917 he dropped out completely and joined the Third Pennsylvania Militia. There was a student pilot program just coming into being at the Great Lakes Naval Aviation Station, and Dick was learning to fly when his instructors discovered

At ease—(back row)
young Sarah, R.B.,
young Dick
CARNEGIE LIBRARY

Baby Sarah
PAUL MELLON

(*Above left*) R.K. and sombrero

Richard B., Richard K.

the boy was underage and shipped him back. He joined the Army and completed his service a private at Camp Lee, Virginia.

Dick attempted Princeton. "By that time," Cousin Matt emphasizes, "his ideas were those of an English country squire. He had a wonderful sense of humor, and he was not serious about anything except the military. He was quite a dude, he liked to dress. People liked him. He was very conventional, everything had to be just proper." Individuals he favored considered him easygoing and openhanded, quick enough to turn his quarters into "a clubroom, where everybody sat around and mooched."

It didn't last long. "Dick was never very good academically," Matt concludes, "and he flunked out after the first term. His father sent him to Carnegie Tech, where he took some courses, and finally his father shooed him into the bank."

He became a bank messenger. "A man can't just go to his son and say, as my father used to say to me, 'You're going into this organization.'" he told a reporter afterward. Not that he complained. "No snob," observed an admiring writer, "he threw a memorable party for his fellow messengers, while the Mellon family was away. He dressed up as a butler and announced each new arrival." The intention was hospitable. Still—what did his companions think, eyeing those Aeolian keyboards?

He represented a gentleman. His hair was clippered to the nape and parted in a line—perfectly, a born Head Boy. Friends of the parents often commented on how his looks hadn't really changed since heaven-knows-when. The bangs were absent; the mouth was wholly recognizable, a delicately mocking line, its carved lips peaking underneath the nares. The young socialite's cheeks had retained their Germanic ruddiness, seemed boyish with enthusiasms. Which complemented strangely, as years went on, that fatalistic pugged quality. He kept his china blue gaze.

Dick was universally agreeable; little seemed worth extending himself for. For close to twenty more years, until he finally married, he kept his suite of rooms at 6500 Fifth Avenue. He saw R.B. virtually every day and digested by measures the curdle of heritage. When he was twelve the banker started pushing on the boy responsibilities for the coops of White Rock and Plymouth chickens he himself was maintaining behind the Fifth Avenue mansion. Dick added squab pigeons. When Dick was seventeen R.B. informed the boy that there was fifty thousand dollars in a checking account the boy might employ whatever way he liked. Dick left the money untouched.

"Father revered Pittsburgh," he told a reporter when R.B. died. "I can recall our visits together in New York. He would hire one of those old-fashion slow-moving Victorias, and we would ride down Fifth Avenue. He would point out to me the grand residences of former Pittsburghers.

" 'There,' he would say, 'that is the home of So-and-So, a Pittsburgher. Nearly all of these fine homes are owned by former Pittsburghers. And there isn't a one of them, who, if he could, would not gladly sell and return to Pittsburgh.'

"Always he held up Pittsburgh to me as one of the world's greatest cities."

That wasn't just R.B.'s idea; A.W. agreed. "In the practical side of business," Dick later said, "I had two remarkable tutors—my father and my Uncle Andrew." After Nora left, the restless A.W. had taken to walking over the hill from his home on Forbes, to enjoy his evening meal with R.B. and Jennie. He brought company executives. On Sunday, at breakfast, A.W. was fond of conversation before church. "I would be invited," Dick remembered, "to sit in and listen to their talk, which almost always was concerned with business."

To listen. His contribution wasn't solicited. On Smithfield Street, he proceeded from messenger to bond clerk, teller, assistant cashier. Vice-president in 1928. Sometimes the elders listened: R.B. was receptive to instituting aviation-camp-style inspections of the premises; at two-week intervals a trio of employees and officials reconnoitered the building. "And they miss nothing," Dick told a reporter. "Even my private desks are not inviolate. Everything is scrutinized. Ledgers are looked over and ink blots noted. And then a detailed report is made. I haven't been one of the inspection crew for some time, but my turn will be coming up soon." His list of corporation directorships occupied almost a column. Nevertheless, after 1921, when A.W. went East, R.B. wasn't interested in relinquishing the authority he'd coveted a lifetime.

Young Dick was resigned. Journalists of the period would characterize his approach as "friendly" but "subdued." Much remained held in.

He let it out on horseback. "Like most 'thoroughbreds,' " wrote the admiring J. Blan van Urk, "he is sensitive, nervous, and high-strung, although he tries to keep such qualities hidden. He also attempts to cover up a large and generous heart, but in this he is not so successful." Ligonier meant elbowroom. He'd scoured that country-side—he still liked reminding people about the afternoon their four-horse brake foundered suddenly while fording a stream and jounced his nurse and himself, between coachman and footman, over the padded sidebar and into the muck. Dick's baptism—at that point he must have been eight or nine, because nodding old Sarah was along that day; the shaking-up helped finish her.

Dormant at the bank, Dick considered Rolling Rock. Exactly what he intended out there, even he couldn't conceptualize. By 1920, on a whim, he'd come into five decent hounds he hoped were good enough to chase some foxes, invested in wire cutters, and acquired a hunter of his own. "It wasn't too bad, once most of us got good enough at riding to keep from parting company with our horses whenever we went over a panel," one remarked years afterward. They started with drag hunts. "And that was fortunate," Cousin Matt says now, "be-cause in those days, if ever they caught up with a real fox it turned into a calamity, those dogs ran away with everybody and up the mountain."

Nobody got that solemn. "There was this one occasion," a vet-eran observes, "when they'd all been out there galloping around, and they all wound up, full of booze, at a hunt dinner in Johnstown. Dick, 'Moon' Murray, Alan Scaife, Matt Mellon. This dancer came out and, you know, took off all her clothes, and carried on, and every-body was yellin' and screamin', and one of the boys sort of slipped behind the couch there, and took off all his clothes except his socks, and went up there and *danced* with the girl. . . ."

So things started informally; fox hunting changed that, and relatives have theories. "Well, there was Sewickley, down the river, and some of the people there, or some of the better, older families who live in Allegheny, who might not be so wealthy as the nouveau riche Mel-lons. . . . Aunt Jennie felt that, she thought she'd been snooted by some of those people, and she wanted everything about Rolling Rock to be bigger, and better. . . ."

Nobody'd hunted real foxes. The sport was costly. There was a pomposity—aping English gentry, duded up in phony pink coats and immaculate breeches to exhaust a pack of otherwise worthless dogs in hopes of rending a vixen. His father's trustee, A.W. was impatient with the whole idea. Nora as a bride had ridden with the short-lived Pittsburgh Hunt. Her husband still believed "A horse was not made to jump over fences. You need only look at him to see that." It made his Presbyterian stomach nip. "The unspeakable in pursuit of the uneatable," as the British gibed—wasteful, the sort of frivolity no industrial revolutionary tolerated.

Dick shrugged that off. On holiday in England with R.B. the summer of 1921, he rode to the Quorn, Belvoir, Cottesmore and Hampshire hounds and joined in several of the hallowed Irish hunts. He returned in August, on the S.S. *Olympic,* where he kept poking about the hold to check the "eight and a half couple" of crated foxhounds he'd requisitioned from top British kennels. He wanted them pampered —the boat's head chef was providing their victuals. All the dogs arrived. That autumn the Rolling Rock Hounds put in for recognition as an official pack; he himself became Master of Fox Hunting.

R. K. Mellon, M.F.H. Now *that* had tone. He contracted with farmers to open to the Rolling Rock Hunt country ten by twelve miles, Chestnut Ridge to Laurel Mountain. Grounds crews installed panels; Britishers lent their showmanship as Huntsmen and Whippers-in.

Interruptions upset Dick savagely. One disgusting afternoon, according to Rolling Rock journals, "strange gunners" came upon and killed their quarry before the baying hounds struck. The Huntsman was irate. " 'This was a case where one man spoiled the fun of fifty men and ladies because he had a gun; or a case where one good little sportsman (the fox) was shot by a dirty cur of a so-called sportsman.' " This flouted Nature itself, who expected the valuable imported hounds to eviscerate the sportsman.

It was some satisfaction, frozen November twilights, sitting around over "tea," to recollect the session ol' Stormer snapped up a fox doubling out of a cornfield. And didn't that straight-necked little bugger just curl right up and sink those canines of his right into that yowling hound's *nose*? And *he let go*!

Their jodhpurs felt stiff with splashed-up mud; everything thawed out gradually, and meanwhile the devotés speculated as to whether it was Herb May or his horse Last Chance who got "his face in the mud first and farthest." Nobody counted drinks. The Englishisms felt natural through ever number lips. Who "cut a voluntary"? Who won the "crumpler" championship?

Outside, beneath last light, teams from the grounds supervisor's office were patrolling the frosted stubble to count the rails kicked apart, shovel in the gullies behind reined-in hunters.

A day of sport
CONSTANCE MELLON BURRELL

Rolling Rock
CONSTANCE
MELLON BURRELL

Richard K. Mellon—the bachelor years
CULVER

Other members looked on. Congressman William Moorhead, whose father had served on Rolling Rock's original board of governors, remembers that Dick Mellon and "a cousin of mine, Jim Bovard, were very close friends." Bovard was a fox hunter. To Moorhead as a boy, the two were "dashing, handsome young men. Great athletes, right out of F. Scott Fitzgerald." With fox hunting there developed a special, inner group, which before too long turned Rolling Rock into the basis for a community. Along with the Flinns and Joneses and McKinneys and Callerys, Alexander Laughlin, Jr., joined up, and before too long he had begun to take an interest in W.L.'s Peggy. Madeline Walton was involved. Alan Scaife, nephew of another governor, rode enthusiastically to hounds.

The Scaifes were legitimate money. For more than 120 years the descendants of Jeffrey Scaife worried over a metalworking business which began in Pittsburgh in 1802 with oddments of japanned tin and utensils for the scullery. The Scaife product varied over five generations among steamboat pumps and conical ventilators, life-boats and water heaters and oil drums and water-purification apparatus and five-hundred-pound bombs. The Scaifes were Episcopal-Methodist, very community-minded, old-fashioned enough to run the sort of patriarchal shop in which too many employees remained on the pay-roll during marketing lulls. Much of the equipment got outdated; dividends in good years were over-liberal. This led to scraping when-ever the economy did lag, and *this* meant pressures. There were nervous breakdowns.

The Twenties were uneven. Business faltered continually, and after William Scaife passed along in 1924 there developed a policy strug-gle among family members; young Alan, his nephew, showed real practical possibilities. He'd finished his mechanical engineering course at Yale by twenty, and started right out installing water-purification plants in places like Mexico.

Alan appreciated young Dick. They shared early bachelorhood; Alan cultivated an Edwardian moustache and secured his pilot's li-cense. Dick's sister liked Alan.

This Alan saw. Sarah was normally withdrawn. Her aversions were obvious, and because of this, perhaps, she had a way of attaching herself to people who stirred her stubborn, rare trust. Others really didn't matter. "She could be very cold, very sarcastic, she had a tongue that people didn't like," Cousin Matt says. "Sarah was plain-looking." She had the sort of indeterminate large features that tend to run together into a vinegary expression anyhow; the squint was omnipresent, even beneath the fashionable rolled brims.

Alan was a balm. Wednesdays, when mostly the women hunted, drag hunts were customary: they could not responsibly waste foxes. Alan started riding Wednesdays. "Alan was a wonderful rider," remembers Matt Mellon—happy enough for any reason to jump off his stool at the bank, where W.L. found occupation for him cross-checking the clearances, and take the bus Dick chartered to Rolling Rock. Alan rode out too. "He held his horse back deliberately to be with Sarah. He was a big fellow, very attractive, who loved practical jokes. She just adored Alan."

The Club itself solidified. R.B. was fond of the Log Room in particular, its coarse old timbers brought back the family's earlier existence in ramshackle mountain farmhouses. He liked to ease himself down to visit a little with members beneath the fanning wild turkey, the stags' heads bestowing their calm, opalescent stares. People seemed so appreciative. "They sent the cards in January," recalls James Bovard. "The first of every year, everybody wondered whether he was going to get one of those cards."

Jennie lost her figure. She'd become the dowager; some found her self-important. "That's a pretty little thing," she conceded, perusing the engagement ring Larimer gave his bride. Her burnished, ageless coiffure wasn't her subtlest device. Jennie had gone bald. A friend of Matthew Mellon's, out for a weekend, blundered into the dressing area where Jennie stored wigs, one for each morning of the week, kept shapely on dummies. Groping for a light, his hand closed instead upon a distinctly human scalp. Revelers overheard him screaming, aghast, banging along the chiffoniers.

Jennie coveted her son; her grip never loosened. "His mother broke up a wonderful romance with a girl in Philadelphia," Matt says. "Dick was just a little bit afraid of girls. The girls had to push their way to him." Relatives recall subsequent courtships. None survived Jennie's veto.

Rolling Rock. Larimer sighs. "So many people came out and visited. I'm not sure they foresaw what turning it into a club entailed." It served its purposes, nevertheless. After World War II, Dick attempted it again. This time, with Pittsburgh.

4

As international war threatened, James Ross was relinquishing his East End Deposit Bank to his insatiate younger brothers. He retained titular presidency. He seemed an astringent holdover—those wasted-looking eyes, like a bemused vicar's. Obituary writers later called him the "dean of the Mellon family," but any family including Andrew didn't require a dean.

James alternated between public frigidity and a quirky warmth toward whatever stirred memories. People remembered him—a quaint old soul in button-front vests, reliable about attending national get-togethers of Theta Delta Chi. Strolling about, very quick to suggest to anybody who paused that he was a Pittsburgh brother, so anybody visiting Pittsburgh . . .

With less to do, J.R. was freer to indulge the sort of prankishness the Judge had detested. His grandchildren cherished the elaborate leg-pulls with which their "Foxy Grandpa" kept taking them in. "He was as funny as a crutch," maintains one of them, Larimer, W.L.'s last. Early in the century J.R. picked up a distressed estate of 3,500 acres, flowing up and over a rugged Allegheny ridge about sixty miles inland. Rachelwood provided him a setting for the macabre. Construction puttered along steadily, and before many years J.R. had turned the property into a Transylvanian movie backdrop. The house reared ominously, all batched-together stonework overlooked by a square hulking tower, ventilated with archers' slots, topped by imposing crenellations. Upon the boulders which supported this sprawl, facing the valley side, the vast white "cairn-like" symbols $\phi\Delta\chi$ appeared and puzzled farmers. These unearthly symbols betokened nothing more than J.R.'s college fraternity. Soon after its construction that flat crest leaked. It rotted interior ceilings, and J.R. authorized a kind of umbrellalike pagoda top. The thing looked ridiculous, but J.R.'s ego could support the strain.

Whenever the grandchildren arrived he had something ready. There was the "Roc's egg" on one visit, a white-enameled cannonball he led them to, waiting in a nest of Plymouth Rock feathers. The old man swore the great bird rose beyond the trees upon hearing footfalls. Working loose a low cellar brick, he allowed them to peer at the entrapped skeleton he'd brought out, gingerly, on the commuter train a few days earlier. "When we remodeled this," he breathed to the youngsters, "we think we walled a workman in there. Can you see anything?"

There was a flat heavy rock puddled into the garden earth into which some agency had carved: "TURN ME OVER." After the children labored and pried and tore their fingernails the great rock's bottom offered another inscription: "STUNG! TURN BACK. FOOL THE NEXT ONE."

Decorations around Grandfather's haunted castle included trophies —a stuffed crocodile, hung along a wall, a robin's nest perched between its fiery jaws. There was a huge stone Buddha along the entrance drive, a totem pole, a fourteen-inch naval shell, a graveyard for dogs just off the sunken gardens, which J.R. wasn't above suggesting to the rustics held Mellon ancestors. Along garden walks, off forest paths, the trickster positioned freshly whitewashed classical statues, bought up from bankrupts, although when visitors rode around the place in J.R.'s coach-drawn Black Forest park drag, serenaded by a groom on a postilion horn, he loved to hint that these were antiquities measureless in value. Privately, he called the place his "dollar-ninety-eight-cent Versailles."

J.R. was cheap. "He was a timid fellow," says Grandson Matthew, "and he didn't want to take a chance. He had plenty of advice from Andy and Dick about cutting himself in on some of those things, but he never did."

He bestowed and economized, by fits. "Father, being then President of the Ligonier Valley Railroad," W.L. records, "had a pass on all the lines in the country and was eager to travel about and use it." The track gave out in Jacksonville, but a correspondence with the southern poet Sidney Lanier had gotten J.R. to nosing around Palatka, another fifty miles up the St. John's River.

Palatka was drowsy. The place J.R. acquired there in 1885 abutted the board fence of a grocery store in the back, but around its other three sides there was a high, imposing Creole railing, and it was between these rails that Willie's future father-in-law, Matthew Taylor, angrily introduced his cane in 1894 to knock away one of the paper roses that J.R. wired to the bougainvillaea vines to deceive the tourists. Taylor snorted. "Whereupon my father began to laugh and emerged from his ambush to share the joke," Will wrote much later. It was in Palatka that Willie met Mary—May—Taylor, and soon enough "my mother was just as delighted with my moonstruck behavior as if she herself had taken me on a light line with a feathered

Matthew Taylor
MATTHEW MELLON

Old J.R.
JAMES R. MELLON II

J.R. (left) after birds
MATTHEW MELLON

Four generations—(left to right) May, W.L., baby Matthew, J.R., the Judge, Rachel, old Sarah Jane

lure." May's sweet, regular features burnished handsomely underneath the welcome sun; after years of scrambling for oil leases, W.L. grew listless envisioning the delicacies of the lure, and devoted himself "to finding out what was going on in the depth of this girl's eyes."

The two were married in March of 1896. They toured the Continent. By 1901 they'd produced three "chickabiddies"—Matthew in his steel-rims, Rachel, Peg—urchins, barefooted in cheap straw hats, scampering along the beaches with bags for shells, trolling with cane poles off W.L.'s old paddle-wheel steamboat, the original *Vagabondia,* fiddler crabs skipping behind for bait.

"Grandpa enjoyed the role of being a big frog in a little pond," Matthew Mellon writes. "He gave Palatka its library and they named the school after him." J.R. had philanthropic principles. He refused all requests when others might contribute, and reserved his donation for projects like the Pittsburgh planetarium.

A devoted churchgoer, J.R. once joined a soliciting committee to assist East Liberty Presbyterian in meeting a three-thousand-dollar mortgage shortfall. He tramped around town, explaining the gravity of things to the eighty to one hundred well-fixed members. Cash came hard; a surviving elder summons up J.R.'s anguish, the way he literally wrung those long bony hands in fear of foreclosure. This was especially engrossing, the elder observes, insofar as J.R.'s own bank actually held the note, and the worried parishioner might easily have "written a check and relieved himself of the anxiety right then and there. He definitely was tight across the chest."

He played on that. After portly Rachel died in 1919, the era of genteel frumpishness quietly ended. Soirées became rare. At Rachelwood J.R. built a nonsectarian chapel dedicated to her memory, modeled after the tomb of Rachel near Bethlehem. His maturing grandchildren found him still raffish and benighted, a tattered laird, tirelessly inspired with ruses. "After I got married," Larimer says, "I remember one time we were having dinner with him, Grace and I, at his place. He had an old butler named Sam. Something spilled. He called Sam. He said, 'Sam, come on in here. I don't want to waste any napkins, just bring a wet bed quilt and mop this up for me.'

"He made it a point always to buy a secondhand car, usually a Pierce-Arrow he got from some junk dealer. Once, I remember, when he was already pretty old, he telephoned my older brother Matt and told him, 'Matthew, I'm sick unto death.' He was groaning. 'You better come by here.'

"Naturally Matt was alarmed, and he walked right over. J.R. was in the room he used as a bedroom, lying there under one little green light, looking very weak against the pillow. Matt asked him what was wrong. 'Well,' he said slowly, 'I just found out that that chauffeur of mine went out and spent my money getting himself a new uniform without telling me a word about it.' "

He went in 1934, unrepentant. "J.R. was on an ocean voyage a year or two before he died," another relative says, "and somehow the boat got caught in a terrific hurricane. It practically foundered— the alarms went off, they dropped the lifeboats. . . . The incident was widely publicized. When he got back to Pittsburgh an old friend asked J.R. what passed through his mind when things were roughest.

" 'Just before I left,' J.R. said slowly, "I sent in twelve thousand dollars to pay for mausoleum space. I'd spent all that, and here it looked like I wasn't going to lie in that thing after all.' "

The eminence of Gulf boosted Willie into influence. He inherited, in time, Henry Frick's old place in A.W.'s luncheon group at the Duquesne Club. Pittsburghers joked around, guardedly, about a Mellon "triumvirate."

Willie shrugged this off. Things hadn't fundamentally changed. Anybody got too close might catch an afterwhiff of all those boardinghouse beds. Chasing leases—he loved to tell people later about the afternoon he stumbled into a remote Texas farmhouse, out of a cold prairie rain. There was a wedding in progress; he edged his big wet feet onto the grate above a hot-air register, and when he moved tore away the soles of his boots. . . .

Homespun. "Father showed me a bar and told me that women drink gin and hang about bars as men do in the U.S.A.," his sixteen-year-old, Matt, wrote in his journal halfway through a leisurely Continental tour the summer of 1914. His impudent nose wrinkles above the page. W.L. as cosmopolitan—incredible. Matt caught himself starting their first morning out while W.L. donned, successively, white shoes, a soft collar and a steamer cap.

"Will is not one of those showy fellows," J.R. had admitted to bushy-bearded Matthew Taylor, "but you have to respect him. Will is sound and true." That much, at least. "Uncle Dick was actually very jealous of my father," Matt Mellon concedes. "He resented the fact that A.W. trusted my father. Everything he did he had the feeling Uncle Dick didn't like it too much."

By World War I the Gulf was stupefyingly opulent. W.L. oversaw everything. He looked on balefully—that dark and wiry organ-grinder's moustache of his atwitch with suppressed amusement, his narrow weather-beaten satchel of a head impassive—and let his irritable chief chemist, George Taber, peck away at moonfaced Gale Nutty. Frank Leovy, precise, shrugged off the other two. Big, rumpled, plucking one jutting ear, W.L. kept order. Then W.L. decided.

He had a knack for fathering. "He was a man who did things by hunches," his eldest says, "and that was the thing that brought the company along. If a man came in and looked down at the carpet and not into his face, he was no good. He could tell a weak character just by talking to him. He never pressured us, he'd been around. . . ."

Ben Elm in Squirrel Hill was hellzapoppin' by everybody's report, a kind of new-rich bruised-knee celebration of the world, carried north to nonstop summer weeks of bass fishing around the big camp on Lake Muskoka in Ontario. Winters brought extended Florida sorties in quest of red snapper or sheepshead or bonefish, casually harpooning rays, peering into the tide by lantern light to scoop up crayfish. Blasting alligators. "It was," Matt wrote later on, "a wonderful world of unrestricted slaughter without a thought to disturb our consciences. The oil wells were gushing over in Texas and we could keep every penny they made because nasty things like 'income taxes' had not yet been thought of and capitalist was a proud name and not, as now, a dirty word."

W.L.'s chickabiddies flourished, gore bespattering little snouts. They accepted every trapping—the nurses and governesses, the unendurable family "teas," Sunday school. "No escape was possible," Matt wrote. "We were locked in closets and spanked with hairbrushes when we offended the code, yet we knew intuitively that our parents loved us and were doing it all for our good, which reminds me of an old hymn we sang down at the Presbyterian Church: 'Trust and obey, there's no other way.' "

May, W.L.'s wife, understood that trapped feeling. "She used to say that when she first came to Pittsburgh it was a great hardship to be among these Mellons," recalls W.L.'s youngest by nine years, Larimer, God's afterthought. "She meant they weren't very couth people. She found them very absorbed in business, a totally different set of values. She would have said business people, and that would have put them down several notches. But she was loyal, she'd signed

W.L. in prime
MATTHEW MELLON

Matthew Mellon as cadet,
Larimer as kid brother
MATTHEW MELLON

W. L. Larimer astride
MATTHEW MELLON

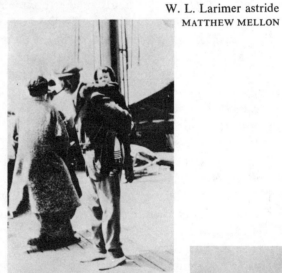

Andrew Mellon hunting
crocodiles
MATTHEW MELLON

The Grand Tour—Alec Mellon in knickers
MATTHEW MELLON

The Chickabiddies—
Rachel and little Matthew
MATTHEW MELLON

up. Father told me once, 'I've been lucky, my wife never interfered in my affairs. I couldn't have taken that.'

"Mother thought that Pittsburgh was a good place to be out of," Larimer says. "But she was first and foremost a pacifist. Anything to avoid a row. She was extremely charitable—I remember she worked for the crippled children's home, put in her afternoons at the Women's Exchange. . . . She very often said what a sacrifice it was to adapt herself to life as a Mellon, who really didn't have the kind of manners her mother and father had."

May's father, Matthew Taylor, began as a civil engineer in Glasgow and amused himself, successively, surveying railroads throughout the British Isles, keeping books, selling on the road, and as a railroad superintendent, a principal in a Wall Street brokerage house, and head of a mining concern. Engaging, competent—nonetheless W.L. would observe, "Over and over again, through hard work at one project or another, he had made sufficient money to form the basis of a fortune, but he had never been much concerned with accumulating a fortune. Assured of sufficient income for the needs of his family for the space of months or a year, he would treat himself to a period of leisure and then actively enjoy his home, his family, and his hobbies, which were legion."

Astronomy, mathematics, navigation, stenography, poetry, photography, the cultivation of birds, telegraphy, botany, parlor tricks and —unabated, cropping up in all six children—a devotion to music which supplied the obbligato to Taylor's lighthearted family life. Pittsburgh adjudged music insubstantial. "Father used to maintain, 'I couldn't whistle the tune the old cow died on,' " Matt Mellon says. "I remember one time Uncle Andy and my father got socked for twenty-five thousand dollars by the symphony or somebody, and Andy said, 'I can't see givin' money to those funny little men with beards blowing on those horns.' "

Education, too, remained suspect. Matthew would later memorialize the honorary LL.D. which W.L.'s old-time military academy at Chester—from which he had shown "the good sense to run away after a short exposure"—conferred upon its distinguished nongraduate once W.L. became chairman of the Pennsylvania Republicans. "The degree amused him," Matt says, "and he called it his 'Goat feather.' "

Underneath, W.L. could no more stifle an uneducated man's kowtow than any other Hottentot. It came and went. W.L.'s oldest boy,

Matthew, suffered through a jerky upbringing—shipped out of Pittsburgh at "the tender age of thirteen" to boarding-school loneliness at St. Paul's at Concord, New Hampshire. Then, just as he grew to appreciate the lovely Gothic detail of the place and memorized the Church-Latin responses to Handel, he lost his natural soprano. Something about his skeptical dark eyes and full, pouting lips began to disturb the Rector; W.L. became afraid his son was turning into a "worthless 'dreamer,' destroying his hopes that I would someday follow him as a successful Pittsburgh businessman." Matt found himself enrolled in a military academy. He survived by learning to play a bass clarinet in the academy band during drilling hours.

An existence in commerce seemed unchallengeable as Presbyterianism. "Thinking he was doomed to become a businessman in Pittsburgh for the rest of his life," Matt observed nearly sixty years later of himself on the 1914 Grand Tour, "the boy wrote desperately about everything he saw and did each day, and photographed a great deal of it too, with an old Kodak camera that had a black bellows on it like an accordion."

Matt felt many pulls. He served during World War I and became an ensign, went successfully through Princeton, straggled back to Pittsburgh and worked for the bank and then for Gulf, where, "mildly interested," his brother says, he looked into auditing and managed a department which sparked the development of specialized products from sealing wax to trombone oil. As Rolling Rock improved, Matt was an officer of the Hunt during the middle Twenties—bottled up, seething gusto, his loose, volatile, often sardonic manner irresistible to many women. But finally, Matt says, "I didn't want to sit around Pittsburgh and ruin my life." He took a degree at Harvard, studying philosophy with Whitehead, and soon after that he left the country to pursue a doctorate at Albert Ludwig University, at Freiburg im Breisgau, in the Black Forest.

By then Matt's sisters were grown and married—the elder, Rachel, to John F. Walton, Jr., and Margaret (Peggy), a good-natured, strong-minded girl, to Alexander Laughlin, who died of shock in 1926, having a tooth extracted.

This left only W. L. Mellon, Jr., Larimer, the baby, finishing up his adolescence. Bony, clumsy about things sometimes. Already thinking unlikely thoughts.

Possibly W.L. was more of a go-getter than J.R. expected; his youngest, Thomas Mellon II, made up for that. After St. Paul's preparatory school and several unnerving months at Harvard, Thomas returned to Pittsburgh to dabble, when cornered, in practicing the law. After officing quite briefly with Reed, Smith, Shaw and Beal, Junior, as people called him, found space for himself in the Frick annex across the street. "He really didn't want any business," a contemporary recalls, "but he got some anyway." Whenever this would happen, the paper work arrived by messenger for subcontracting to one of the Reed, Smith fledglings. One of the few occasions on which A. W. Mellon was seen to burst into public rage was upon opening an envelope from Junior—whom Henry Phillips solicited—and choking at the bill.

Thomas junior had outside interests. He was a historian manqué. He could prove sweet and diverting, and surprised a great many church congregations around Pennsylvania by conferring on them stained-glass windows of his personal device. Once World War I broke out, he equipped himself with a flat-brimmed khaki scoutmaster-cut infantry hat and an overcoat with pockets generous enough to hide his nervous little hands, and enlisted in the Y.M.C.A. Headquartered at the Willard, in Washington, D.C., he devoted the war years to escorting unoccupied sailors to lunches in hotels and replenishing the tips on unseemly pool cues.

Thomas never did marry. He lived on quietly in J.R.'s old place on Negley Avenue; his nephews remembered him as a mama's boy grown querulous, driving an elderly Stutz. Weeds overran the gardens.

Namesakes are always risky. Willie delighted during adolescence in cupping one ear against a sort of one-wire intercom that stretched between J.R.'s residence and that of Uncle Thomas, the Judge's eldest, just over Negley Avenue. Uncle Thomas was exacting. Most enjoyable by far was overhearing the squawks the device gave out when Tom laid aside his Juan Fortunado cigar a moment to elucidate his principles. Will pictured it easily—those fierce brows regnant, the bales of moustache writhing alongside Tom's tiny, bellowing mouth.

Noise had its place, evidently. Uncle Tom's children—the boys, anyhow—came along on schedule. First Thomas Alexander II (Alec), then Edward Purcell (Neddie) served out their regular apprenticeships, starting with the ticket booth in the amusement park. They inherited the East Liberty lumberyard, and over the years Alec augmented their Mellon-Stuart engineering sideline and built a company. Ned became increasingly restless, and left for Europe a few years before the outbreak of war to become an architect. Young Matt would photograph him, a sly-looking expatriate in knickerbockers, perched against his Alpenstock, on holiday in Switzerland. Matt notes, much impressed, how Cousin Ed's Parisian establishment offered "printed bill-of-fares so you could hold back for what you liked most."

Early in the Twenties the time was arriving to consecrate their properties in masonry. Ned Mellon was back, pleased enough to work on headquarters blueprints for Koppers and Gulf. And these—like the Mellon Institute, like East Liberty Presbyterian—McClintic-Marshall girded and Mellon-Stuart raised.

Malcontents weren't above whispering that every time one Mellon broke down and pledged some church-building money, another cousin was around to present the construction bid. Yet among the relatives resentments were privately sputtering. "Neddie's brother, Alec, he got the idea one time," Matt Mellon says slowly. What were the details . . . ?

"Alec's sister, Mary, married several men, including this lawyer, Samuel McClung. And he was the one, as I understand it, got that whole branch of the family riled up. They were going to sue Uncle Dick and Uncle Andy, they said they had a right to a quarter of the bank.

"Nobody was about to tolerate that, of course. Cousin Dick wasn't absolutely rabid, but he never cared for that branch of the family at all. We never could mention that branch. They had a pew at East Liberty Presbyterian, and they'd slink in and out and nobody would notice."

Only Ned escaped ostracism. "Neddie came to Father," Paul Mellon says. "He made it clear to everyone that he personally didn't want any part of the suit."

Neddie understood the world.

5

A.W.? Aging, into his ashen sixties. Recognizable, a personage you ran into around town, taking his Sunday constitutional between residential avenues while—at a following distance—his coachman

The Mellonmobile, with passenger
UNDERWOOD AND UNDERWOOD

mashed unhappily through the gears of that boxy green-burnished aluminum limousine Alcoa machinists pieced together around a Pierce-Arrow chassis.

Nobody thought he'd died; that wasn't it exactly. Nevertheless— what made Reuben Rosenthal's cigar customers stop cold, shrink back, on confronting that pinched spine? Those unsteady fingertips, selecting from the counter canister an afternoon's Marsh-Wheelings? Cars bleated; soot gusted up; onlookers caught for breath. A simulacrum, much like the morsel some abbot labeled Saint Barnabas' toe. Businessmen gasped at discovering the *number* at Mellon's trading account—Number 48, at Moore, Leonard and Lynch. Unexcelled vibrations. So many miracles!

Such celebrity could immobilize a less preoccupied man. Old Mellon stayed busy. Smoked, visited the Duquesne Club, honored banking hours. Decisions seemed endlessly required. Mellon Construction needed refinancing; their closely managed Pren Brook real estate subsidiary took title ceaselessly, subdivided, posted bids, disposed. War threatened; every company across their smoldering empire felt Governmental expenditures updraft—plant, capital, production capability gushed, sprayed unbelievably. Uncontrollably—A.W. was worried. Overproduction threatened glut.

Busy. Automatic. Drying up. Even friendly sources conceded that the banker could become "ruthless in banking and politics," mostly a legend . . . whose name is mentioned only in whispers, "Mr. M."

Mellon remained achingly disappointed. "Duncan," he demanded of the chemist who ran the Mellon Institute, "are you happy at home?" Duncan said he was. "Then you are a far richer man than I am," the banker said quietly.

Emotional roots were cropped, and regrowth was unpredictable. "My little girl is also getting along finely," A.W. had written Frank Haskell not long after Ailsa was born. "You must see her. I never took interest in babies before but now find myself comparing every one I see and shall take pleasure in having a look at yours at the first opportunity." Mellon's fascination lingered. In Ailsa in particular the banker sensed attitudes patterned after his. She too was standoffish. Nobody could budge her either once she had settled on something.

Mellon engaged a housekeeper. "Mrs. Sylvester was more of a housemother," one of the cousins recalls. "She tried to take the place of Aunt Nora. Mrs. Sylvester was very straightlaced and elderly. I can't imagine that she was a hellova lot of fun, but she kept the house running and the children out of trouble." A.W. knew his part, and among his notes are references to evenings of blindman's buff, hours with the children crawling in and out of the "jail," in the playhouse, on the grounds. They received a pony cart. Ailsa expressed the desire for horses of her own—workmen constructed a stable. There, virtually in the middle of town. "You can imagine," Paul Mellon muses. "Even in those days."

"They were very spoiled," Peggy Hitchcock stresses. Peggy—Margaret—was W.L.'s third. "We had our big place in Squirrel Hill. There was a lot to do. Little Paul and Ailsa came up sometimes. We did not look forward to it. Of course, we were hellions, and they arrived all done up in lace. Neither turned a hand."

His obligations could fluster the prosaic banker. One afternoon a relative telephoned to invite Ailsa over for a children's party. "Now, Andy," the woman urged, "you make sure that Ailsa has a nice new dress so she can look her prettiest."

There was an unaccountable pause. "But Ailsa already has a dress," the banker finally said. The laugh that roused left Mellon nonplussed.

With Paul, if anything, companionship proved more confusing. The scribbles are commonplace throughout Mellon's perfunctory journals emphasizing his determination to father the boy—fishing trips, weekends together in Atlantic City, uncomfortable hours at a time on horseback because Paul appreciated riding. Once Rolling Rock started, the banker built Paul a cabin out there. Something simply didn't take; intimacy escaped them both. "Business really was his whole life," Paul puts it simply. Even in the earliest of family photographs, his level eyes shadowed by the shallow brim of his puffed, soft Buster Brown cap, the composed little boy stands in his riding habit with one hand draping protectively over the shoulder of the forlorn-looking banker—there is traceable amusement, Paul's intuition as regards the absurdity of things.

Paul certainly wanted closeness. English summers with Nora meant satisfaction, partially with the countryside. Before World War I he started at summer camp, Marienfield, near Keene, New Hampshire. One of the counselors there was also a master at Choate, in Wallingford, Connecticut. At Marienfield there was military drill, something Paul had already experienced as part of Cousin Dick's little army at Rolling Rock. They let Paul perform as bugler. In 1918 the banker took Paul and chum Jimmy McKay to Concord, New Hampshire, to look over prestigious St. Paul's. It didn't pass muster. "We really didn't like it very much," Paul now says. "The idea of living in those cubicles . . ." He remembered that his counselor at Marienfield had been a master at Choate; in Choate's formal catalog he was excited to discover a listed cadet corps. Marching! He hurried to enroll.

By 1919, alas, the war was over and Choate's little cadet corps had already been disbanded. He remained at Choate six years. "You have good times, you have bad times," he says now. Privately, young Paul couldn't stomach Headmaster St. John's mission to the pubescents. What touched his memory was Mrs. St. John. "She used to read at night to the boys in the lower school. It was always some good but reasonably exciting book, like *Ivanhoe*. She was . . . she was sort of pre-Raphaelite, like some Rossetti painting." One imagines the long-headed little boy quietly listening in the darkness, toes stretching his blanket, basking in her voice.

At Choate, "I had a very hard time with Latin, for instance, but I ended up thinking that what I'd done in Latin was enjoyable, interesting to me." Math was hard, chemistry was almost incomprehensible. The lightly built Paul played lower-level football at Choate

Attempting to grow up—
young Paul, Nora, Ailsa
PAUL MELLON

An outing—Paul, A.W.
PAUL MELLON

A moment of conjunction—A.W.
(rarely astride), Paul (rarely afoot)
PAUL MELLON

for two or three years but never was "really good enough to be on the varsity. If you weren't good enough to be on the varsity, you really weren't anybody."

He suffered from acute literary visitations. Alone in a classroom one evening he scrawled several quartets on the vacant blackboard:

> From dreams and visions, heaven-sent,
> From simple faith and Godly trust
> Great empires, yea, each continent,
> Has risen from the dust.
>
> To those who saw this spire arise,
> This composition out of nought
> Is like a light from Christ's own eyes,
> A glimpse of Christ's own thought. . . .

The unconscious acolyte. "Years later," Paul complained, "I found the poem pasted in the school hymnal and the boys singing it. But I never received the poetry prize. Instead they gave me the most insulting thing—a leather-bound biography of Lincoln with the inscription, 'For earnest and persistent effort.' "

Ailsa finished boarding school. Her first years away she'd joined Cousin Peggy at Low-Heywood. Matt Mellon recalls pranks, and especially the afternoon the girls "telephoned every rich person in Pittsburgh to tell 'em the Mellon bank had gone bust." To her rowdier cousins, Ailsa's deliberate, self-conscious diction sounded "English"; they pronounced her "prissy." Intimidatingly clean, "always dressed in a fluffy, girlish dress, very *femme*," Larimer notes. "I remember one funny event. Where we lived in Pittsburgh, on top of Squirrel Hill, we used to put manure to cool in water to make mulch out of it. One time Matthew and Rachel decided to give a party. They cleaned up the manure pit, whitewashed it, and filled it with water."

Old Matt still remembers the sight of fastidious Ailsa, her swimming suit dripping, appearing at the main house. Even he was amazed.

Matt knew Ailsa over the years. "When I was at Princeton she came to the proms," Matt says. "One time there was this boy McFarland, and afterwards we went to Philadelphia and stayed at the Bellevue-Stratford—Ailsa, myself, this boy, and some little girl I had in tow. When it was time to go along to Pittsburgh we decided to take the Pittsburgher overnighter. There were two trains at the time—the A. W. Mellon and the R. B. Mellon. We got there late, and I remember the cars had already backed into the Broad Street station, and the conductor, who had a lantern in his hand, had started to yell at us. We all began running. Then Ailsa said, 'Matt, I'm going to walk to that train, and if that train goes out, I'll wait another day and take the train tomorrow.' "

Ailsa was then enrolled in Miss Porter's School for Girls in Farmington. She favored her father. For all the chiffon, her looks were arriving and there was a waxen fleshiness about the planes of her face, the masculinizing assertion of too much bone. Her neck jutted forward. She already displayed, Matt Mellon notes sadly, her father's heavy nose. The alterations were profound. "I remember my sister as a child as being very cheerful, outgoing," Paul Mellon says. "She was very enthusiastic about riding, she liked the country. And then she went away to school, and I've never gone into it psychologically, she became very much of a hypochondriac. She went to Farmington. She was ill a great deal of the time. She was a little bit like Father, quite animated when she got interested in people. But on the whole, she was withdrawn. On the whole, a great deal of anxiety. I would assume that it had a great deal to do with the divorce. In those days there was much more stigma attached. You know, you went to school, you saw other children with their fathers and mothers. I don't want to exaggerate. . . ."

So far as Andrew could judge these things his daughter was perfect. He appreciated her dignity, and whatever she needed he contrived to produce. He relieved their summers by taking the palatial Quay house in Sewickley Heights. There were European tours, episodes of vacation residence on Long Island and at Prides Crossing on the Massachusetts North Shore. The children kept urging, but involving himself in some pretentious "country place" was tantamount to desertion of Pittsburgh.

Perhaps they could compromise. In 1916, when Ailsa's debut was already under discussion, Mellon succumbed and investigated the suburban estate of Alexander Laughlin on Woodland Road. Laughlin accepted the bid. There was some delay while a swimming pool and bowling alley went in; Mellon took up residence on December 23, 1917.

Woodland Road helped. Space—they had escaped finally the Burgundy carpets and all that grit and the trolley's roaring. The main house alone was thirty-odd rooms of impregnable Pittsburgh Jacobean —fireplaces and mantels everywhere, accented wherever you turned

A relaxing vacation—Paul, Ailsa, Andrew
PAUL MELLON

by knights in bas-relief and Medusa heads smirking polished from black-stained oak. Inside those sweeping windows, beyond timbered brick—a private ballroom. The grounds were elegantly landscaped. Watercourses, well-established hedges to mask the tennis court, the bridle paths which overlooked the gardens.

That Christmas was exciting. "After breakfast look at presents," notes the banker's diary, "R.B., Jennie, Richard and Sarah came. While showing them house Mrs. M. comes. I show Mrs. M. through house—cruel."

Nora. Nosy, what cheek. The events in Europe made travel unsatisfactory, and Nora was around. She still roused whispers. "Nora chose a lover," a relative confides. "She remained very close to R.B.'s wife, Jennie, and regularly Nora used to write her letters that were filled with the most intimate details. Jennie used to savor them, something she herself couldn't imagine doing, it was like the movie magazines these days, the scandal magazines." When Jennie finally died, she left the letters in bundles in a little bedroom safe for which nobody knew the combination. A technician was found, and he worked open the safe and removed the letters. In time, he got in contact with certain of the family members and sold the packets back at a prearranged fee. "Which we all thought was very decent of him," the relative recalls. "He could have let us have the letters one at a time."

Andrew's life remained austere. Under Ailsa's fond prodding he attended debutante balls, joining some little clutch of elders in an anteroom, chatting and smoking, ankle across a knee, into the morning hours. She brought down schoolgirls for New York theater parties her father would arrange, good seats courtesy Diamond Jim Brady. They investigated Southampton, Long Island: Ailsa arranged her debutante presentation there.

Nevertheless. Ailsa appeared so desolate much of the time.

6 | THE TREASURER

1

FTER WARREN HARDING'S offer, A.W. dropped hints about having taken on that botheration in Washington because Ailsa needed something. As regarded himself? Mellon recalled his father. As early as 1880, when Frick made mention of considering a nomination for Congress, the Judge brusquely rang down *his* opinion: "He is getting ambitious. But he would be foolish to take it."

A stern night's deliberation convinced the coke magnate that would be brainless. In 1904 Frick again peeked, this time at an available Senate seat. Again Frick tripped away. After that the suave little industrialist confined his politicking to salons.

Frick manipulated; A.W. stood by. Between Philander Knox and his prestigious law partners the Reeds, western Pennsylvania was scrupulously looked after. Not that the Mellons were provincial. Boies Penrose, the giant in Harrisburg who poked through the Scott divorce bill, had long before occupied, unbudgeably, the U. S. Senate seat reserved for the coast. "He made frequent trips to Pittsburgh," W.L. reports, "keeping his fences in repair, and he always visited us. We saw much of him." Penrose fastened on interlopers the stolid and apprising glint of a Bavarian meatcutter.

Upon Mellons he smiled. "We've got to have $250,000 to make this fight," the boss reportedly told A. W. Mellon.

"Can't you get along with $150,000?"

"Oh, I suppose I can if I have to."

Mellon wrote the check. "I just made $100,000," he told somebody afterward. A.W. was secretly delighted. For all his bulk Penrose processed matters deftly—who else in Government would demonstrate the brass to scribble into the *Record* in 1918 those twenty-one precious lines which defined an oil company's depreciable assets as the value of its "proven fields," yet untapped, then bluster into legislation the company's right to deduct its development costs, over and over, against such hopeful guesses?

A coup like that made politics more legitimate. After Frick deserted Pittsburgh the banker agreed to shoulder the titular leadership of the Allegheny County Republican organization. He supposed he should; he took it on with the kind of resignation with which a man becomes a deacon, dreading to think how that will devastate Sunday mornings. God has been reliable, one's obligation is clear. Long after A.W. accepted Secretary of the Treasury, one of the few remarks that roused any furor was his observation that he gave to the Republican Party, because, to him, it was "like giving money to a church." Expected, club dues on grace.

The banker was temperamentally apolitical. In Pittsburgh especially, where the Magee machine was careful about patronizing leading Democrats. Mellon reserved his name for forums much elevated from common political favor-trading. He served during wartime as one of twenty dignitaries on the State Committee of Public Safety, chaired by the scholarly George Wharton Pepper. Why split token hairs? In western Pennsylvania, Democrats and Republicans both espoused the high-tariff anti-union capitalism agreeable to the Mellons: individuals who opposed *that* were properly termed "anarchists." The level of production at which resistance to the owners normally gathers—shop foremen, machinists, intermediate managers—went locally to Pennsylvania Dutch—Germans—with their inherited knack for technical innovation and regularity and their ingrained submissiveness. The unformulated Pittsburgh *entente industriale* stipulated that the bohunks and Irish slaved; the Germans kept order; the Wasp community possessed. This appeased God's will.

At times, it appeared, the Lord needed underwriting. Frick told one when. A.W. uncomplainingly stepped out in front and walked the seven-mile parade route to solicit for war bonds; the bank bought up more bonds than anybody. Frick intervened at the behest of Bernie Baruch, chairman of the Price Industries Board, and negotiated back the cost of steel plates for which the Steel Corporation was mulcting the Government. For his part, Mellon simply told Baruch to have his bureaucrats pay the Aluminum Corporation whichever price per pound the Government called fair.

Then, the spring of 1919, just as the victorious nation mounted history, Frick introduced A.W. to gross political satisfaction. Wilson, adored everywhere, seemed destined to sweep the enraptured populace into the League of Nations. A Senate cabal which tumbled western Progressives like La Follette and Borah and Johnson into unaccustomed blanket parties with reactionaries like Lodge and Knox scrabbled about the hustings to ignite "backfires" under colleagues most likely to support the President. This meant spreading dollars which guaranteed the support of small-town editors as well as handouts by the boxcar of anti-League propaganda flagrant enough to roil the Yahoos.

By May this campaign was guttering. Money was running out. Gambling, Philander Knox quietly proposed to a New York confederate that he draw Henry Frick aside at a Manhattan fund-raiser for General Leonard Wood and nerve him up against American League participation. As Frick's own creature, Knox had his doubts about approaching Frick personally.

Frick was predictably incensed. Perhaps, the New Yorker then suggested to Frick, the like-minded Mr. Mellon of Pittsburgh might tender a contribution.

"That's rather odd," the slugger from Connellsville observed. "I understood you to say that Knox was going to see Mr. Mellon; why didn't he?"

"Well, as it happens, Mr. Mellon was here tonight; for some reason or other, the Senator seemed to think it might be well for me to pull your leg first."

"Come now, do you consider that a compliment or a reflection?"

"Oh, a compliment surely." Frick was not fooled. He was a cog— a wealth of contacts, a stagnant estate that approached a hundred million dollars in real estate and securities. But A. W. Mellon—who fifteen years earlier had seemed an unprepossessing backwater banker with a weakness for long shots—now Mellon *really* mattered. Powerful, a fortune already into the hundreds of millions, each dollar of invested capital exerting leverage on how many more? Mammoth companies, cartelized industries . . .

Billions. Nobody you troubled unsolicited.

Frick chuckled. He touched up Andrew; when Knox eventually

contacted Pittsburgh he recovered a ten-thousand-dollar donation equal to Frick's. Other "irreconcilables" like Medill McCormack bucked up. Woodrow Wilson grew twitchy.

Mellon's maiden indulgence—nationally. As recently as 1916 he and his brother had pledged $2,500 to the Republican campaign; a token amount. The family preferred local contributions, where issues festered nearer the bone and money went further. But with the European war the ideological ground had started to shake. The Progressive movement, the income tax, the Federal Reserve System's involvement in banking, the "suffocating" surtax levy, unrest on the farms, Wilson's efforts to hemorrhage sovereignty. Pittsburgh demanded more done.

Penrose arranged the necessaries. Boies, who had been anchoring the intransigent Old Guard around the Senate cloakroom, now recognized that he and the reactionaries really had better bully themselves into working control. Postwar malaise was general; the ward-heeling head-knockers on whom the Interests could depend were groggily dropping off.

Penrose roused himself. He was deceptively indolent, like somebody's cherished twelve-year-old Saint Bernard who one day bestirs himself from that sunny place just beyond the curtains on the rug and bites off the face of one of the children. Unmarried, the obese Pennsylvania boss was such a habitué of whorehouses across the Commonwealth that several hung his photograph out as testimony to the goods. The towering politician's baggy pants and that close smudged look of unmasked contempt had represented the coarseness of Pennsylvania politics since well before the turn of the century. Genteelly born, devoted to clandestine practices like bird-watching, Penrose had remained since anybody could remember the paymaster for the oligarchy. Whatever the Rockefellers needed, a hint from Frick was enough. District leaders with problems, simpering little representatives waiting for their money now that a reformist bill was suffocated in committee —his people were forever hovering about the Great Fixer's narrow shoulder as he ruminated indifferently through seven pounds of beefsteak, rare, moistened as he supped by a quart of bourbon.

He lugged his standards to Washington. Penrose became so heavy finally his colleagues decreed a special divan be established for him toward the rear of the Gallery, upholstered to support his crushing 350 pounds. He ended a caricature, so obsessively Old Guard he reeled beyond cynicism. By 1919, overtaken by debauchery, Penrose

Boies Penrose (left), anchorman of public order

was clearly dying. He needed to do something, leave something. Idealistic lard stirred. Bedridden much of the time, arranging matters by telephone, he demanded terminal impact. Harding became the President. The League went down. Andrew Mellon turned up as Secretary of the Treasury.

Boss Penrose's earliest efforts concerned the Republican front-runner, General Leonard Wood. Theodore Roosevelt, still young enough, appeared the Party's candidate just after the war. Then Roosevelt died. The bearer of his tangential momentum was Roosevelt's longtime aide-de-camp, General Leonard Wood. Wood attracted the business classes initially, the watchful Harding decided, "because they want a bayonet user in the White House when that dreadful American revolution comes off." Frick's 1919 get-together had been to give his Establishmentarian friends the chance to look Wood over. He certainly looked stiff enough: Wood dressed in khaki and carried a dogheaded riding crop underneath one arm.

The anxiety about the Russian Revolution had started to subside. Security now wasn't enough. Wood was starchy. After reviewing John King, Boies Penrose's close associate and T.R.'s personal "liaison with the ratholes of politics," Wood sloughed him off and put his campaign in the hands of William Procter, the Ivory soap magnate. Procter, an amateur, had ideas of his own. Did Wood have? The Old Guard bristled.

Fearful of another maverick, Penrose auditioned candidates. Instinct drew him immediately to the flaccidly glamorous Warren Harding, to whom he announced, without ado, "You look the part. You can make a front-porch campaign like McKinley's and we'll do all the rest." But Harding faltered badly throughout the primaries. From the Senate cloakroom Penrose and Right-wing confidants like McNamara did whatever they could. Harding's parasite Harry Daugherty fed the unbending Senator Borah details of Procter's heavy spending on the Wood campaign: the Kenyon Committee was pushed hard to rush an exposé statement to tarnish Wood's brass. Concurrently, the reactionaries flagged through the campaign expresses of the Illinois reformer Frank Lowden and the tiring Progressive Hiram Johnson. Anybody, anything—block off Wood's lead!

Somehow, amazingly, Wood was able to sustain himself through Convention week. Lowden, whose wife was a Pullman heiress, was built up enough to prevent an early nomination; as late as Friday, after a deadlocked week, the general retained what appeared to be a plurality not even the muggy June days were melting. The Pennsylvania delegation was formally under the leadership of favorite-son Governor Sproul. At home, sick, grumping around unhappily under a welter of bedsheets, Penrose endeavored long-distance.

While reactionaries gathered in the suite in the Blackstone Hotel which entered political legend as the original "smoke-filled room," Penrose on the telephone pursued the fading chance that something might *yet* be arranged with the unbending general—a political deviate so extreme, political gossip ran, that he had repeatedly refused to purchase the relatively few delegates he continued to require. Not even simple bribery, most primary of professional building blocks. The evening was steamy, but Penrose wouldn't down. "You may say to General Wood," the Boss opened immediately, "if he were nominated tomorrow would he give us three Cabinet members?" Wood, across the room, snorted. "We" intend, Penrose made clear, to have a Republican President, and "we" insist on naming three members of the Cabinet. Then Penrose hung up.

In Colonel George Harvey's suite at the Blackstone better-tempered heads were butting together. Senators, from the clipped Lodge to the ingratiating Brandegee, marked up and re-marked the dog-eared list of possibilities, individuals the general public might stomach who still would "go along." Joseph Grundy, heavy industry's self-appointed chaperone, looked in from time to time to make sure nothing untoward was happening. *His* regulars had also arranged to spend the week in Chicago. Elbert Gary was around, and Thomas W. Lamont, and Atterbury of the Pennsylvania Railroad. And R. B. Mellon, a banker of Pittsburgh.

At one o'clock sharp, by "standing vote," the stalwarts resolved on Harding after all. Penrose kept calling in. It took Harry Daugherty's considerable gift for wheedling to talk Penrose out of releasing a statement for Harding before he was solidly nominated. The Convention already looked like enough of a bag job. A few hours afterward it was the Pennsylvania delegation that slid Harding over the top.

Boies Penrose was not a man to restrain himself at spoils time. Once Harding had affirmed his landslide it looked as if Boies might trisect the leadership with his wheelchair if all three conservatives he demanded didn't come from Pennsylvania. Here was a demonstration of power to Penrose's appetite completely: raw importance, chewed openly, unashamedly spattering one's vest.

To a certain extent the frail publicity-loathing Andrew Mellon was picked, protesting, from his sooted-in little life of empire building and converted all but overnight into the most influential figure of the decade to propitiate this dying ogre. Penrose bustled him forward; every time the boss turned his attention elsewhere Mellon mumbled something and disappeared.

The fault was partly Mellon's. Ptomaine poisoning and a cold had led to the heart attack that ended Henry Frick's life in early December of 1919. Once his political Doppelgänger was no longer involved, there really was little Mellon could do to avoid the repeated requests, the closed-door visits. The gathering public uproar over plutocratic gifts to candidates had already caused the invention of assorted "committees" to receive great blocks of cash from the wealthy. The three important Mellons became prime contributors. In addition, A. W. Mellon reportedly set an extra $25,000 of undisclosed funds before the party scavengers. When Will Hays, the Republican treasurer, determined that the Harding campaign had run the Party $1,600,000 into the red, the Mellon bank reportedly underwrote $1,500,000 of the deficit. To political cognoscenti, there was no mistaking this.

The regulars were undoubtedly wrong. Harry Daugherty claims he first brought up the name of the mysterious Pittsburgher, whom he espoused to the President-elect as "the richest man in this country . . . the only man the big interests, the Rockefellers and Morgans will not bluff." Daugherty's credentials for disinterested civic-mindedness didn't look like much under even the palest of lights, but undoubtedly he, like Pygmalion, adored his clay-footed masterpiece too much to destroy it himself. Once Knox and Penrose took up the idea, of course, and especially after Knox broached the possibility to A. W. Mellon in a telegram very late in 1920, it quickly became *their* major ego priority, the altarpiece in their temple of devoted patronage.

Early in January of 1921, Mellon took the train to Marion, Ohio, to confer with the President-elect. In Daugherty's sketch the unobtrusive banker got off the train in Marion, discovered nobody from the Harding entourage to pick him up and, after asking around, quietly walked the mile or so to the house on Mount Vernon Avenue. The close front hall of the place was full of reporters and visitors. After Mellon had sat there patiently for a while a newspaperman remembered who he was and told one of the ushers, who located his name on the appointment list and took him to the President-elect. Mellon had his interview. He ambled throughout the neighborhood while Harding talked to another of the callers and turned up again later on for lunch. After lunch he refused a ride to the station because he would "rather stroll along and look at the town."

As soon as Daugherty had the chance he asked Harding what Mellon had said. Mellon had claimed, Harding recalled, that ". . . he'd be criticized because he owned interests in so many different enterprises over the country." Harding asked whether there would, in fact, be any conflict between Mellon's duties and his interests.

"He tried to smile and couldn't quite make it," Harding said. " 'I wouldn't let them conflict, of course,' " Mellon had maintained. " 'But honestly I don't believe I'd make a good Secretary of the Treasury.' "

Knox was already urging Mellon to hustle signatures among Pittsburgh business leaders. Penrose, letting it be known that *he* had first urged Mellon to consider public life, clucked away every demurrer. When Judge James Reed came up with an 1889 statute that prohibited the office to anybody engaged in "the business of trade and commerce," Mellon thought he saw a way out. Knox supplied court decisions which invalidated that.

Afterward, inundated by posthumous revelations, the advisers Harding collected were dubbed the notorious "Black Cabinet." Harding hadn't wanted that. A political rhinestone like himself—somebody who simply could not resist tucking a chaw of tobacco behind a wisdom tooth during press conferences or serving the world's Great chipped beef for breakfast—he needed hyperreputables. Only modesty could possibly have prompted the selection of the glacial Charles Evans Hughes as Secretary of State, Mellon for the Treasury slot, the orotund and scrupulous Herbert Hoover as Secretary of Commerce.

Hoover in particular maddened the Republican Old Guard. Until he permitted his friends to promote his nomination to the Presidency, the prim, pudgy international mining speculator affected a superiority to politics so extreme that he refused to affiliate himself with either of the parties. His Quaker background, his high positions in the Wilson Government as European and, later on, U. S. relief and food administrator, and his overall humanitarian biases had so aroused the revulsion of the Right that such a conservative strong-arm as Mellon lawyer David Reed, during his Senate incumbency, accused Hoover of soliciting graft while he was Relief Commissioner in Belgium. "Hoover gives most of us gooseflesh," Brandegee wrote the President-elect.

Brandegee had gooseflesh; when *he* heard, Boies Penrose's hackles turned into the Rockies of post-election politics. The inexhaustible Daugherty went along to quiet him. Daugherty, dodging lunges, reminded Penrose that the Keystone State was to receive two Cabinet places—the inoffensive James Davis was already slated for the Department of Labor. The Mellon appointment, Daugherty suggested, wasn't really that firm.

"Penrose got my ultimatum—no Hoover, no Mellon. And rose to heights of profanity I have never heard equaled. He swore in every mood and tense. I had 'cussed' a little at times when unduly provoked," Harding's personal tapeworm conceded, "But I listened in awe to my master's voice."

"If Uncle Andy gets wind of this hesitation over his name," Penrose said finally, "nothing will induce him to accept the place." The thing was serious. A. W. Mellon himself was sent for—Hoover as Commerce Secretary was too ominous an appointment to be OK'd by underlings. Daugherty and Mellon talked in Philander Knox's office. Afterward, Mellon having evidently agreed to hold down the Pennsylvania representation, Daugherty telephoned Warren Harding and informed him that Senate opposition to Hoover's selection "would be discontinued." Mellon received his summons the morning following.

2

Lacking a truly compelling reason to refuse, Mellon gave his consent. Not that he was particularly pleased. Close associates were astonished. "Why, A.W. doesn't even read the newspapers anymore!" H. C. McEldowney insisted to his lawyer. The earliest official photographs betrayed a pasty-faced old moneylender, the long Scottish upper lip well protected from politicians and bureaucrats by a still-dark close-chopped businessman's bristler of a moustache. The look approaches ugly: photographers are particularly detestable.

Subsequent magazine profiles mention the new Treasury Secretary's way of referring to whatever was left of the Harding Presidency as the rest of his "sentence." In fact, the surroundings were not, tonally, at least, completely to Mellon's tastes. Washington was quickly infested by the "Ohio Gang," lackluster men with dewlaps who shared a communal cunning at scooping clean the change drawer while bussing the cashier. Their chief, Warren Harding, was finally a malleable small-town publisher who regarded his own ascension to the Presidency as one of history's more flamboyant accidents—as if, Harding maintained, he had drawn three and filled a straight. Bemused by any of the larger concerns of Government, Harding occupied his mostly unscheduled days fussing with his chip shot and tupping his appreciative mistress, Nan Britton, whom he stood bravely among the coats and hats and flopping galoshes in one of the White House cloakrooms.

Mellon's reliable Presbyterian stomach permitted him to tolerate just about anybody while he remained serviceable. Still, one correspondent remembers the new Treasury Secretary, emerging from his first Cabinet meeting, blinking into the mob of reporters before he "ran into the crowd" to make his escape. "He didn't know what it was all about. He had never seen such a gathering outside of any directors' meeting he had ever attended." He was quickly characterized as a man who invariably looked as if he were on the point of leaving the room, or "like a tired double-entry bookkeeper who is afraid of losing his job. He gives the instant impression of being worn and tired, tired, tired."

Breakings-in are tiring. But even that first year, moments came worth retelling. There was that episode in the Cabinet room, when the discussion turned to what ought to be done with a munitions plant left over after the war. Other members lobbied their opinions. Mellon was as reticent as ever: the President ultimately turned to him and wondered what he might think.

The Secretary of the Treasury hesitated to make a recommendation. The situation was unfamiliar to him. It was not exactly in his department. Nevertheless, it happened that a question of just about the same order of magnitude had developed in one of the businesses in Pittsburgh. He and his brother had also owned a war plant that ran them fifteen or sixteen million dollars. The decision had been whether to put that much into revamping it or simply wipe it off.

Everybody strained to catch the low, dry intonation.

"I told 'em to scrap it," Mr. Mellon said.

Thus ended all discussion. If liquidation had proved the sensible course for Mr. Mellon's empire, that certainly was that so far as Mr. Harding's was concerned.

Another incident that was to pinch up Mellon's trace of a smile came out of a Cabinet discussion of the Chinese Eastern Railway

Colleagues under Harding—(Harry Daugherty on right)
LIBRARY OF CONGRESS

Among the military
UNDERWOOD AND UNDERWOOD

question. "Now we've got him," Harding's bustling crony, Attorney General Daugherty, whispered in the President's ear. "Surely he wasn't in on this."

"I don't suppose, Mr. Mellon," Harding asked, "that you were interested in the Chinese Eastern Railway, were you?"

"Oh, yes. We had a million or a million and a half of the bonds."

"It's no use," the President exclaimed to Daugherty. "He's the ubiquitous financier of the universe."

If Washington remained strange, divinity had its satisfactions. As things settled down, it was gradually borne in on the rubes from Marion, Ohio, that they had somehow enticed to Washington if not the richest, most likely the second-wealthiest individual in the country. This desiccated little frail bird in his old-fashioned stiff linen collar and cuffs and subdued dark suits and boned black shiny oxfords turned virtually overnight into a kind of Moloch to the slapdash Administration. "Harding's feeling for him," declares the biographer Francis Russell, "was sacerdotal."

Mellon envisaged his President in somewhat plainer colors. A.W. "liked" Harding, W.L. insists, and took a hand himself once in a while in those knock-down poker games in the White House library which Alice Longworth subsequently characterized as transpiring in a general atmosphere of smoke and spilled whiskey, "waistcoat unbuttoned, feet on the desk, and spittoon alongside." The jovial Harding, relaxed in his *métier*, saw to the nation's affairs and passed out pardons between promising hands; he once cut cards with a divorcée and lost a barrel of White House china.

Other items from the national storehouse got equally offhand treatment. One of Harding's quirks that gave his Secretary of the Treasury pause was his habit, after he had heard one of Mellon's proposals out, of receiving the memorandum that set down the pertinent facts and skating it into the litter of everybody else's paper work with a mumbled "I'll look into this." Maybe. Sometime.

It certainly wasn't Pittsburgh style, but why be priggish? Harding's paramount oversight, allowing his Secretary of the Interior Albert Fall to barter the Naval Oil Reserves to Harry Sinclair and Edward Doheny in return for something over a half-million dollars and an assortment of cows and pigs, alarmed Senator Walch's Subcommittee much more than it had Fall's colleague in the Treasury. In November of 1923, a month after the original Teapot Dome investigation opened,

Will Hays, treasurer of the Republican Party, had telephoned Mellon from New York to advise the Secretary that he was sending him a "valuable package" from New York. The next morning, during his first free minute, Mellon ripped the package open and discovered fifty thousand dollars' worth of Harry Sinclair's 3½-percent First Loan Liberty Bonds. Mellon scurried home and clapped them in a safe.

The bonds were, obviously, hot: part of that short-lived issue with which Sinclair had originally purchased Fall. The Secret Service was on the scramble attempting to trace their numbers. As publicity swung closer Sinclair had pushed bonds worth $185,000 as a "loan" on the Republican National Committee. The GOP certainly needed the money; Hays had barely wit enough to perceive that the securities had better undergo some sort of laundering before the money showed up in the Party's books. His idea, Hays explained to Mellon, was for the Secretary and several other heavy political benefactors to accept—quietly—fifty thousand or so each in Sinclair bonds and contribute the equivalent in cash to the Party treasury.

Mellon shuddered. Refusing to have anything to do with the certificates that operatives from his own Department were just then combing the Republic to locate, he wrote a check for his part. But he said nothing.

On thinking that whole thing over, Senator Walch later demanded, hadn't the Secretary become "incensed?"

"Incensed?" That caught Mellon up. "I do not know that I am of that temperament, and I do not become incensed. If you take things in the world as they are, and according to your own conscience, I do not see that there is much use in getting incensed. At least I do not recall anything of that nature."

This world—politics. Familiar enough maggots—only a woman or a western Senator would expect anything else. It was like anticipating that the intestines of the Grand Old Party's elephant were lined with patriotic bunting. In truth, much of the Secretary's energy those early years had gone into preventing the overmanicured mitts of Harding's more aggressive flunkies from finding their way too directly into the national till. Secretary Mellon, it transpired, had ideas of his own.

As always, they were gestated slowly. Boies Penrose had assured Mellon that, once he had assumed his duties in Washington, he would not actually have to work "more than a half hour a day." It was to provide Pennsylvania's foremost citizen with an honorific between his business career and retirement. He could enjoy himself.

3

Unlike the fleshy Penrose, Mellon enjoyed work primarily. A.W. had dropped into Washington as inconspicuously as a corner spider, scarcely attended at all in the clamor of the turnover. He had resigned his sixty-three directorships; since he would serve ex officio on the Federal Reserve Board his lawyer suggested that he sell his critical Union Trust holdings. These, too, he divested—to the compliant R.B.

Before he was sure completely which among this bewilderment of corridors led where, the reluctant appointee started orienting his web. Few noticed. Harding would take office in March. Weeks earlier, Mellon sat down quietly with his predecessor's undersecretary, S. Parker Gilbert, and discovered the future Morgan partner agreeable and properly assured about political/financial niceties. Gilbert would stay.

Washington regulars were annoyed, but probably the inexperienced Treasurer couldn't help himself. He was raised parsimonious: why fire some sensible fellow who seems to know his job and replace him with a chairwarmer from Ohio? Such policy was wasteful.

As Mellon envisaged it, the economy altogether wasn't anything more complicated than a collectivity of enterprises quite similar to those around Pittsburgh. Accordingly, it was subject to about the same working principles and most of the dangers likely to beset any undertaking. Search out good men, avoid excessive borrowings, keep surplus invested, hitch acquisitiveness to innovation. After that, stand away.

Admirable theorizing, good filler for commencement addresses; to the discomfiture of stalwarts all over the capital this peaked-looking sparrow Harding lured onto the perch at Treasury took traditional cant seriously. He gave them all their first real cramp when he decided on his Commissioner of Internal Revenue. Mellon had no sooner set out his pen stand and blotter than both the Republican Senators from Illinois started to drop around to recommend a home-state man. They felt quite sincere; within a few days Mellon got a letter from Harding, stipulating that, unless the Secretary objected, he would confirm the appointment.

Mellon stalled. Meanwhile, immediately, he dispatched his personal factotum, the sinuous Colonel Drake, to Chicago.

Drake was forty-one that winter. The Colonel had barely been involved with the family three years by 1921, but the aging brothers were watching this self-denigrating New Hampshirite. Drake had appeared originally in Pittsburgh on assignment from the U. S. Army to expedite massive ordnance contracts between the mills and the Government. When, November 11, the hostilities ended, "like that," there was frantic renegotiation, a long winter of hearings before the claims boards.

J.R. noticed the lieutenant-colonel first. Frank Drake, a devout Theta Delta Chi at Dartmouth, remembered old James Ross from the national meetings and called him up. He got his Friday luncheon invitation. J.R. introduced Drake to W.L.; W.L. saw to it that the Colonel stopped over at R.B.'s house, "a regular palace," and not very long after that R.B. invited Drake to join him over a Saturday night at his cabin at Ligonier, where he was thinking about setting up some sort of a club. That evening, just before R.B. turned in, who should wander unexpected through that remote cabin's door but A. W. Mellon himself?

Drake stiffened; it probably hadn't required much Yankee perspicacity for Drake to grasp what that might mean. "A.W., he was like *God* to the Mellon group o' companies," Drake said much later. Then, invoking whatever up-country wiles might satisfy this gray hesitant hollow-cheeked banker who hadn't even begun to run out of inquiries long after R.B. shambled away to sleep, Drake admitted that he brought along, in his attaché case, a curriculum vitae that sketched the main points of his "very brief and very unimportant career."

The proper note precisely. The Monday morning after, W.L. called Drake at his desk in the Army ordnance offices and asked the Colonel whether he might just have a minute during the next several days. Drake did. When he and W.L. "visited," the president of Gulf Oil worked things around. "Let me ask you," W.L. said finally— "you're going to be mustered out of the Army before much longer?"

Yes, Drake agreed, anytime.

"Well, if there should be an opening with us, would you be interested? 'Course I don't know now that there will be a place."

Drake, feeling by this time as if he had been eaten cautiously by a shark, indicated that he would indeed be interested. It was then December, 1919. Winter came and went; spring wore on; a group of businessmen in Springfield, Massachusetts, wrote Drake and offered him the presidency of a bank. With "trepidation" Drake turned them away, twice. He arranged to stay on in Pittsburgh as a civilian adviser to the claims board. By April, stubbornly as he had hoped to "get in with the Mellon family, little fella like me from the sticks," Drake was just pulling his clothes together to return to Massachusetts when W.L. finally brought him over. Nothing had actually opened up for Drake, so he was creating a new position, Assistant to the President of the Gulf Oil Corporation. Drake accepted immediately.

For nearly forty years the subtle and energetic Colonel—wide-eyed, gifted with a native American repertoire of smooth bald reassuring gestures—plied among Mellon properties with the inobtrusive ripple of an electric skate, all swoops. Underlings feared his silences: his brush of disapproval was lethal. Drake developed the moves on instinct that made him the corporate infighter deluxe—nobody sensible ventured close. Humility alone can paralyze. "Cold, a cold man," one longtime Mellon adviser remembers. "In Pittsburgh Colonel Drake was said to speak to nobody except his secretary and W. L. Mellon."

Overdrawn. Nevertheless, besides the ambition, what looked so promising to all the Mellons was the bookkeeper's ruthlessness, the calipers for stinging out of a degenerated mush of policy profit and loss information. They moved Drake around.

He started in at Gulf, the Colonel raved, with "the greatest piece o' luck that ever happened." Legislation had just passed permitting the oil companies to charge off, retroactively, depreciation on their oil fields—the original version of the embattled depletion allowance. "The oil companies had to take every lease they had, evaluate it, and estimate reserves in order to multiply 'em by a discount factor that had to be pulled out of the air." Drake toured the producing fields and carted his ledgers to Washington. "We had so many books, big, piled clear to the ceilin'. Took us all of 1919, clear into 1920. We were just wrappin' it up when we heard that A.W. might get the Treasury. Just by the grace o' God I managed to wind it up in time. Led to a terrific refund, several million dollars, all approved by the Democrats."

The Colonel was just rediscovering Pittsburgh when A.W. called him in. "I'm going to be Secretary of the Treasury," the banker announced. "I don't want this job. They tell me I ought to take it. They tell me you know the Treasury Department. W.L. and I have talked it over. We will go down about March first, two weeks before the inauguration. I've reserved a suite of rooms at the Willard." Drake repacked.

The new Secretary's entourage those early months included his valet, Flore; the amiable Arthur Sixsmith, who looked after "personal" errands for the banker; and Drake between missions. Not in need, particularly, of homegrown reassurance, A.W. kept on a seasoned administrator named Kiley, who had been around the Department twenty years and on whom he soon relied heavily. Miss Barnes, his secretary, had also served under his predecessor. S. Parker Gilbert stayed put and brought to A.W.'s attention a discovery of his, a sprightly little Democratic attorney from the hunt country of Virginia, David Finley. Finley, who started out largely as a speech writer for the taciturn Pittsburgher, became, little by little, intimate with the family, ultimately the central hierophant of their stupefying fine-arts bequests.

Initially Drake was critical. Checking out the Illinois candidate for Internal Revenue Commissioner, Drake ignored all references. Mellon knew some people; he himself had a couple of well-placed friends around Chicago. "I found," Drake reported, "the man is just primarily a politician."

"Well," A.W. said, "we just won't do it then." Mellon paused. "I've had about thirty men in to see me. One impressed me, David H. Blair."

Drake caught the train for Winston-Salem. After soliciting the opinion of people from the president of the Wachovia Trust to conventioneers in the lobby of his Greensboro hotel, Drake attempted a balance sheet. A Republican in post-Reconstruction North Carolina, the attorney was well regarded. Blair was obviously honest; the fact that he had married into the Cannon family, the wealthiest in the area, might prevent his being "influenced for compensation."

"That's my man!" the new Secretary declared when Drake submitted his recommendation. He presented Drake's analysis to Harding at once.

"David Blair turned out to be the salt of the earth," Drake later reported. "He just worshiped A. W. Mellon."

Mellon briefed Blair immediately: "This place is just full of Democrats. If there are efficient men here I don't want them kicked out."

Political horseflies hovered. Internal Revenue—twenty thousand job slots, open, suppurating. Blair was no sooner installed before Party regulars packed Mellon's appointment book. Wasn't this a Republican Administration? Individuals received . . . promises.

Mellon listened. The beleaguered President soon asked him in. Embarrassed, Harding nudged across the desk a "round-robin" declaration, signed by 164 Congressmen, making clear that, to the undersigned, David Blair wasn't satisfactory.

Mellon pushed it back.

"Well, Mr. President, what about it?"

"Mr. Mellon, you are Secretary of the Treasury."

A.W. picked up his hat. For weeks after that individuals whose signatures appeared on Harding's petition sidled into Treasury offices to tell the immovable old man that they had signed that thing under a misapprehension.

Mere administrative procedure. Harding underwent opposing tugs. "God," he supposedly mourned, "I can't be an ingrate." In December of 1921, worked up by Daugherty, Harding found the courage to sign another document, appointing Elmer Dover Assistant Treasury Secretary. By that time Mellon was immersing himself in the responsibilities of the Department, and if he noticed Mark Hanna's onetime Columbus errand boy at all, he dismissed Elmer early as another of those embodiments of patronage, unavoidable as polyps, which spotted Harding's regime.

Except that Dover was inflamed. His post was scarcely announced before he was strutting before reporters his resolve to "Hardingize" the Treasury Department. At a Gridiron Club banquet he received an ax. A list of more than a hundred Democrats "holding key positions" in the Department was circulated among Congressmen and released to the newspapers, and Mellon was forced to scare up letters of his own influential constituents to protect the employees.

Dover was brought in as Assistant Secretary of the Treasury in charge of Customs and Internal Revenue; the I.R.S. was quickly sapped. Any pretext served for Dover to fire a competent tax man and appoint a hack. Case-load averages collapsed. Dover leaked word persistently that Blair was on the point of resigning. Blair held fast; Dover imported Gaston Means, a pernicious Münchhausen on temporary duty from Daugherty's Bureau of Investigation.

Gaston was extra special. Heavy, smiling, the cherubic con man from Concord, North Carolina, fluttered like a plump moth through court records as early as 1911, when he sued the Pullman Company for damages received when falling out of an upper berth whose defective supporting chain—one link allegedly sawed—let go and tumbled him into the aisle. His last recorded offense was larceny—he convinced the gullible Evalyn McLean, Harding's patroness, that he had contact with the kidnapper of the Lindbergh baby in 1932, and hornswoggled the credulous dowager out of $100,000.

Means, a spender, enjoyed money. Almost as much, he relished the chance to inflate just one more of those political hallucinations so fantastic he couldn't help giggling between puffs. Explaining his brief presence around the Treasury Department to a Select Committee chaired by Senator Wheeler, Gaston maintained that he had been sent over personally by President Harding to investigate Secretary Mellon for selling liquor permits.

Like many of Gaston's better inventions, this represented a kernel of truth—popped. Means had come into the Government as a private investigator in the employ of the tough-minded and not overly scrupulous detective William J. Burns. Burns, a friend of Daugherty's, took over the Bureau of Investigation within the Justice Department. The two had worked together closely as recently as the war years, when Burns had passed as a British agent and Means as an operative of the Kaiser, and Burns appreciated fully the Southerner's utility when it came to bluffing officials and jimmying file cabinets.

Means's original mission had been to poke up something damaging against I.R.S. Commissioner Blair. Blair remained depressingly clean. But the office of the Commissioner of Prohibition, a truffle the recently passed Volstead Act exempted from Civil Service restraints, lodged inside the Treasury Department multilith, and so was subject to the Commissioner of Internal Revenue. Harding had appointed as head of the prohibition unit an Ohio hill-country dry named Roy Haynes. One of the Prohibition Bureau's powers was issuance of the notorious "B" permits, which allowed the recipient to draw an allotment of alcohol from Government warehouses: these were shortly being traded so freely, Francis Russell notes, that they "became a form of negotiable security, like Liberty Bonds."

Payoffs went everywhere. To dimpled Gaston—bestowing lagniappe among Cincinnati heartburn cases and apprenticing bootleggers—bliss seemed universal. On orders, reportedly, from Harry Daugherty's crony Jess Smith, Means trailed Senator Caraway and rifled La Follette's files. Before Smith committed suicide, he emphasized to associates that he and Harry "had the Senate stacked." Intra-Governmental panic peaked when Gaston told shakedown victims that a quarter of the money he took went out to Chief Justice Taft himself.

Secretary Mellon appreciated color, but everything around the Department looked smudged with Means's funky pollens. Dover, who invited the fellow, wanted to be watched. A.W. summoned the all-purpose Drake and told him to find out what Dover was doing. "I got on his good side," Drake recollects. "He didn't do much."

Meanwhile, Commissioner Blair betrayed stress. "He was frightened to death about the prohibition thing." Drake remembers a series of meetings with Blair and the head of the Secret Service that led to the identification of people the bootleggers had planted among the Treasury Department employees to help secure vouchers with which to deplete Government liquor warehouses. As the Secret Service began to run the underworld contacts down and comb them discreetly out of the bureaucracy, gangsters on the outside realized that the Department was "spiking their guns." Pressure built. A Secret Service observer called Drake's attention to an anonymous figure who routinely fell into place behind him whenever he left the Treasury Building. Both Senators and Representatives, beholden to their home-state bootleggers, hounded the worried Blair. "It was not," recalls Drake, "a very happy situation."

Mellon waited, watchfully. Nearby, the Man in the White House toyed with his venerable putter and grieved about what people must think of a Chief Executive still ignoring the hopes of regular golfing partners. Daugherty worked this hard. Mellon was a noble figure, but the President had political responsibilities. Why should the quaint little Pittsburgher find himself involved in politics at all?

Emboldened, Harding discharged the director and twenty-eight longtime employees of the Bureau of Engraving and Printing. There was a powerful backlash around Capitol Hill against the action, which was attributed to Mellon. The Secretary said nothing. An appropriations bill passed late in the Wilson Administration had authorized the Treasury Department to expend $18,600,000 for veterans' hospitals. A.W. had brought in several reputable Pittsburgh hospital administrators and had largely completed the construction when, according to the Sweet bill, the hospital-building program was passed over to the Veterans' Bureau and into the exceptionally willing hands of Colonel Charles R. Forbes.

To the uncertain Harding, young Colonel Forbes—boyish, an enthusiastic womanizer, invitingly redolent with after-shave—epitomized qualities to which the befuddled President aspired. The two became acquainted when the then-Senator visited the naval facilities at Pearl Harbor and Forbes gave Harding a ride in a submarine. After that they stayed in touch. With the American Expeditionary Forces in France, Forbes acquired his much-mentioned Congressional Medal of Honor for efficient communications work. He had taken up residence in Spokane, Washington, when Harding solicited him for help during the Republican primaries. From then on the colonel's big glad hand remained outstretched.

Within the new Administration, "Charlie" was visible, during the early months, mostly around the poker table on H Street. Harding appointed him director of the Bureau of War Risk Insurance, despite Forbes's insistence that he actually hadn't any background whatever in the insurance business. But Forbes knew contracting, and once Harding centralized the Veterans' Bureau and appointed the colonel director, Forbes went devotedly to work. His background in logistics expedited a wholesale sell-off of "war surplus" properties to individuals who understood where dues needed paying. Construction was Forbes's *métier*, and he soon convinced the impressionable President to allot him the $17,000,000 appropriation.

It would be February of 1923 before a misdirected visitor, happening into the Red Room of the White House, came upon the berserk President choking the life out of his card-playing intimate and Veterans' Commissioner. "You yellow rat! You double-crossing bastard!" the enraged Chief Executive was croaking at the smoothie to whom he entrusted the management of so many millions of dollars and monkey wrenches and rolls of gauze. All disappeared, all quasi-legally hijacked out of warehouse cities like the one at Perryville, Maryland, to selected single bidders who understood without an excess of prompting what kind of a good time Colonel Forbes required, how much of an unsecured "loan" was in order, where valuable real estate was available at artificially low prices without collateral, what percentage of the markup had better be tacked onto the top of any construction contract to cover the colonel's consulting fee.

Earlier, when Secretary Mellon forced a confrontation, all this was something the experienced Pittsburgher sensed before anything was provable. Attempting to complete the veterans' hospitals authorized by the earlier allocation, Mellon discovered that his bureaucrats were frustrated drawing from the Veterans' Bureau supplies and equipment enough to stock the institutions. New complications, patently imposed, stipulating such addenda as an iron fence and a greenhouse, pushed Mellon's suspicions to the point at which his "confidence in Mr. Forbes dwindled." Mellon insisted on a three-way evening presentation in front of Harding. Harding decided for Mellon.

The fever broke. The previous spring, after having disregarded the obsessive feather-pulling to which Elmer Dover kept subjecting David Blair and his apolitical accountants, Mellon issued a letter to all Internal Revenue employees in which he observed, dryly enough, that his "attention had been called to the reports which have been appearing in the press predicting a general reorganization of the Bureau of Internal Revenue and the removal of certain officers and heads of divisions." Not true at all, Mellon asserted. Then he stepped over to the White House and asked for Elmer Dover's resignation. Between singeings, Harding complied. At the next scheduled Gridiron dinner one of the speakers asked Dover to rise and observed that, when the reporters had given Dover his ax, nobody expected him to use it on himself.

Politics, like any Mellon venture, meant insinuating himself deeply enough into something unfamiliar to educate his timing. Shortly, just as the sink of scandals was starting to drive piling rats into view all across the Administration, Mellon reappointed the careerists around the Department of Engraving and Printing the President had fired. This too reflected nothing more profound than taking "things in this world as they are, and according to your own conscience. . . ." As moral ballast, A.W. arranged indirectly to discount two notes, for over a half-million dollars, with which two young Ohio newspapermen bought Warren Harding's little newspaper in Marion, the *Star*. The purchase price was subsequently appraised as much too high, an "indirect bribe." Matters of this world, as A. W. Mellon saw commerce, involved many balanced transactions.

4

Little by little intimates made out signs that A.W.'s resistance was softening. A couple of months of coffee-shop breakfasts with Colonel Drake in the basement of the Willard was enough. Mellon engaged a fifteen-room apartment on Massachusetts Avenue. Ailsa moved in.

"Mighty nice apartment you've got here," the elderly J.R., stopping over on his way to Florida, remarked after surveying the good English paintings and selected porcelains with which the place was stocked. "How much are you paying for it?"

"Twenty thousand dollars."

"And how much do you make from the Government?"

"Twelve thousand dollars a year."

"Hmm," J.R. reportedly sighed. "Good thing Father's dead. He'd never have let you hire the place."

James Ross had something. Miserly "Mister M" had started to relax. He let his moustache grow. Shortly—overnight—it appeared to thicken and whiten, assume a swan's-belly downiness, become that benign pediment that overhung the Republic. "Uncle Andy" was arriving.

He was discovered. "Of no other man in public life have we been asked so many personal questions . . ." the editor of *Collier's* will maintain as the decade closes. His profilist can barely get through even a short paragraph without jerking into the prose *some* kind of a salute. Mellon's ruddiness, the mile he habitually walked to the Treasury offices, his desk once there (that "monolith to work"), even the *entire* glass of water—"not a measure"—he drinks at seven. And the heroic breakfast. ". . . two or three fruits and he will indulge them all." Followed by orange juice "in large portion" and the favorite hominy grits and hot cereal and eggs and little pork sausages and French toast . . . A digestive Siegfried, at *seventy-five!*

A plainer man was never eulogized. Much owed to Mellon's performance—he'd done his duty to his class. Partly—the terrain was different. After fifty years of dodging inquiries Mellon had now admitted to himself, as he told W.L., that there was "a fairness in the desire of people to know about him since he had become their employee." Besides, were he too aloof, the wary banker guessed what he might anticipate from all those pup dingoes the newspapers sent around. He would distribute tidbits.

Reporters found Mellon abashed as advertised, but gentle and forthcoming. He was quite scrupulous about not misleading press, which spared reporters problems, and whenever a city editor sent him advance copy he endorsed what he said. Mellon never minded controversy—he said right out that prohibition was unwise and fundamentally unworkable. That $300,000,000 veterans' bonus for which the American Legion pumped was revenue wasted. Reporters believed Mellon; he rarely ducked. Fortunately for the Secretary, press people weren't well enough informed to divine which questions to ask.

Real trouble usually came from schismatic Republicans. While Penrose and Knox survived as Congressional point oxen, Mellon was looked after. Both were already failing when the Treasury Secretary arrived; within a year or two David Reed and George W. Pepper had taken their seats, although not their places. Politics soon broke out.

Except for clubhouse spoilsmen and frustrated bootleggers whose plight wrenched Harding, not many around Washington grumbled during Mellon's inaugural months. The Secretary himself was focused on what then seemed an incapacitating federal obligation— $27,000,000,000, coming due in relatively short order, War Savings Certificates tumbling over Victory Loans, with many of the instruments sagging, well below par, in the postwar slackness. Nearly half a billion dollars in Treasury notes was due eleven days after the Secretary took over, and an aggregated $2,500,000 during 1921—twice the predicted revenue. Such problems Mellon understood. By thoughtful refinancing and a judicious coaxing down of the Federal Reserve rediscount rate, Mellon was quickly able to stretch out the federal obligations and cut the percentage the Government had to pay on its borrowings from 5½ to 4¼. Most people liked that.

But then! Moderates swallowed hard—God knows enough black-eyed liberals exploded from every hedgerow. Then the tongue-tied Secretary appeared at southern bankers' conventions and before Congressional elders to *propagandize* in behalf of what the shocked press soon dubbed the Mellon Plan. Not at all, the Secretary kept emphasizing. Both his immediate predecessors, Carter Glass and David Houston, had the impeccable Wilson's blessing in recommending equivalent rate relief. "The problem before us now is not so much one of tax reduction as tax reform," Mellon maintained. But something felt clammy, and a 1924 *New Republic* supplied lemon juice: "Tax reform—a multitude of strange notions has advanced under this banner. Secretary Mellon is the first financier in history to apply it exclusively to the detaxing of the rich."

Lines for a generation. The front went backward and forward, but well before he gave his Cabinet post up, Mellon pried and pressured through Congress just about everything the editorialist meant by "detaxing the rich." The excess profits tax and an assortment of entertainment and luxury "nuisance" measures went in 1922. Coolidge's election produced a Congress euphoric about the gathering boom, and by early 1926 it had already cut the fixed "income" tax of the period to 5 percent, revoked the gift tax and income publicity clause the previous Congress pushed through and which Mellon interpreted as a personal affront, lowered federal inheritance taxes and authorized up to an 80-percent credit on state taxes, and dispensed with a number of exactions the business classes especially hated like the capital stock tax. Most gratifying to Mellon, the graduated "surtax," the progressive skimming of the higher incomes that once had reached 65 percent, a loss of income Mellon compared with money "taken by a highwayman at the point of a pistol," now sank to 20 percent.

Hadn't everybody expected that? Wholesale payment reimbursements, favors to the rich? Why was Mellon grumbling?

Politicians never understood. Devoutly as the aging Treasurer detested the utilization of Government as "a field for socialistic experiment . . . a club to punish success," he was just as suspicious of all the inducements and deductions and depreciation allowances which already—1921—were infesting legislation. Sapped the entire system, sponged up necessary capital. Obnoxious—the war was no more than settled, and all that blood money the Government kept printing was already reabsorbed. Gone. Leached into—municipal bonds largely, a billion dollars each year thrown away on civic opera houses and playgrounds nobody cared about. Except crooked contractors, or millionaires too gutless to venture beyond tax-exempts. Revenue levels showed it: taxable incomes of more than $300,000 a year had fallen off by two-thirds between 1916 and 1922. Mellon requested an amendment.

It failed of adoption. In that case, Mellon reasoned, wouldn't it be provident to cut back deductions on interest payments and non-business losses to "the amount the sum of these items exceeds tax-exempt income?" He proposed a sharp limitation of capital losses —12½ percent of the total, the obverse of the prevailing capital gains rate—as applicable against other gains or income. Why not "tax community property income of the spouse having control of the income?" The Secretary repeatedly urged a steeper rate of taxation on "unearned" income than on "earned" income—salaries. But familiar abuses already sat like arthritis at all the joints of the code, and Mellon got nowhere with this notion either.

Taxes, the cost of services, Mellon insisted were subject like any other commodity to pricing mechanisms. Too high, and the customers go broke or escape through loopholes. Too low, and a meager collection arrives. Mellon raised the floor of the "surtax" to ten thousand dollars a year, still a comfortable income in the 1920s; like later Republican pipe dreamers he endeavored to slough some sort of sales tax onto the working poor. Congress disposed of that.

A dry business. Technical. Yet there were times, with people who understood, when A.W.'s blue and watery eyes glittered in their hollows, perspiration bedewed his chin. "There is no escape from the fact that 'death taxes' are capital levies," he told one reporter. "When carried to their highest limit the inevitable result is the destruction of capital. When merely excessive, the effect differs from destruction only in elements of time and degree."

The destruction of capital! A leukemia, eating out the industrialism's marrow; "properties" are prosperous limbs.

Because capital is final. Even credit, bewitching credit, comprises capital's spiritual emanation, its testimony of faith. Anything that consumes cells—taxation, confiscation, inflation, errant and conspicuous consumption, mismanagement, misguided charity, repudiation of debt, undue demands by labor, asinine veterans' bonuses: diversionary, wasteful, dangerous to capital's life-giving accumulation and recirculation. Insanity, a violation of God's own order, at least since Nature shifted primary valuation from land to money. Mellon subscribes to Marxism without the State.

5

Warren Harding initially faltered while making a speech in Seattle the summer of 1923. After a halfhearted rally or two Harding died within the week, the evening of the second of August. News of the President's apoplectic seizure first reached his successor while Vice President Coolidge was preoccupied in Vermont, in shirt sleeves, doctoring an iffy maple.

The Republic, after some perfunctory mourning, forgot the gabby roué who liked to push down a hearty plateful of overpeppered chipped beef in cream sauce for breakfast, and accommodated the stoop-shouldered Mountain Yankee who sent the White House chef to the produce market to secure for him a peck each of wheat (whole) and rye (whole), some of which the Chief Executive expected boiled together every morning at eight (sharp). Not glue, not watery. Bland.

Harding, for all his crossbar eyebrows, had about himself the guilty, perennially worried air of a small pudgy boy whose mother is forever pulling his fat little hands into plain sight on top of the counterpane. Rich political sensations, what incredible oily possibilities down there—Warren simply couldn't help himself. Coolidge, on the other hand, evidently felt few compunctions. His grain was beyond dispute, and certainly he had the discipline to conserve himself for ambitions that mattered. Harding was—almost—corrupt. Coolidge was dangerous.

Coolidge's fundamental attitudes, in the opinion of his shrewd biographer, William Allen White, were traceable to a philosophy White calls his Garmanianism: stay clean and make yourself useful, and luck will come biting like bluegills between raindrops. His ruling *political* axiom, in White's phrase, was to allow "no advertised crooks to stand too close to him." Throughout Coolidge's long twenty-year climb through the political chairs he had always taken his gratuities in favors, not money, but that in no way invalidated the fact that, "generally speaking, property, once it had gathered itself under a charter and was guarded by a silk hat, was sacrosanct to him."

Mellon, always a quick study, realized long before the autumn was over that Coolidge was acceptable. Constitutionally silent men, a consultation between the two wasn't vivid. White on white. Coolidge maxims are collectors' items, but one that got a lot of play was the discovery that "The business of America is business." Anybody who believed that would obviously be inclined to defer to Mellon, business's archon, the choice of economic directions. Coolidge did.

Pop historians joked that "three Presidents served under Andrew Mellon." Contemporaries, Mellon in particular, disparaged an idea like that. A case was there. "Indeed," says the judicious White, "so completely did Andrew Mellon dominate the White House in the days when the Coolidge administration was at its zenith that it would be fair to call the administration the reign of Coolidge and Mellon."

If A.W. fidgeted at petty larcenists, perhaps his own intentions were disturbingly grand. Mellon saw no reason the country couldn't be run like a transcontinental Pittsburgh. With a commercial oligarchy looking after the blundering Government, he anticipated the creation of an enormous industrial/financial webwork invulnerable to invidious foreigners—the Fordney-McCumber tariff of 1922 established at least the bottom tier, the footing, for a protectionist policy that eventually adumbrated world trade. Inside, the Administration kept the farmer debt-ridden by permitting the wholesale importation of food. Labor rarely sneezed. When the Railroad Trainmen's Union went out and the grandstanding Harry Daugherty euchred a federal judge into issuing an injunction that violated the workers' simple rights, Mellon sat in silent approval while Daugherty squealed away in a Cabinet meeting against the "Red borers" who riddled the industry at the behest of Zinoviev. Even Hughes was sickened.

Yet Mellon remained popular. Moviegoers, catching sight of this worried-looking little Edwardian setting forth one overpolished toe outside a limousine in a grainy newsreel, sent up a tumult no other public figure came anywhere near evoking. He was the moment's totem. A percipient official in Hoover's Department of Commerce remarked the "amazing transformation in the soul of business" into "a thing of morals," and if such a thing came anywhere near occurring, Mellon was most definitely its prophet. Something *was* going on, one of those cyclic preconscious authority-surrenderings our Teutonic impulses require. Mellon, who understood this, took.

He created a *mood*. There was a period, early in the decade's afternoon, when just about everybody who wasn't busting clods was either getting rich or believed he was, and if in fact *that* didn't feel patriotic, you'll have to extrapolate values in another society. Mellon's welling insight—that banking and technology, combined to the alchemy his instincts might conjure, must release a stupefying abundance that would justify anything—leaked like a scandal and fertilized every weed.

That bald-headed ticker-tape machine with its world-girdling, ever-extending tongue was obviously the recognizable sign and aftermath of all of this. But first, as Mellon supremely recognized, something was necessary to dislodge impacted capital, tempt money beyond savings accounts and out from under mattresses and beguile out of active portfolios those detestable municipal bonds. Get people investing, developing, borrowing, dreaming. Cutting back taxes helped, but beyond this the important thing was to make credit so free and so generally available—to the investment classes—that anybody who hoped to hold his position in society would have to get out there and build something, push into something.

Get that money *working*. It was an era when a New York advertising man, in perfect seriousness, could write a best seller which presented Jesus as History's Most Successful Hustler. Republican toastmasters, having made the Treasury Secretary wince by presenting him as "the Greatest Secretary of the Treasury since Alexander

Hamilton," soon got to reminding the worthies that the unpretentious speaker who had just passed an hour among them ignoring his food was the administrative genius who brought our greatest prosperity while reducing the national debt from $24,000,000 to $16,000,000. One figure nobody mentioned was the increase in private debt during the same period from $106 billion to $162 billion. The 40 percent increase in productivity and the practical revolution the automobile produced generated profits that showed up largely in a rapidly consolidating heavy industry, its plant expanding fast, and in the increase in profitability of financial institutions, by an impressive 150 percent. Wages rose a little over one percent a year. The value of shares sold on the New York Stock Exchange tripled between 1925 and 1929.

Much the din obscured. This was the epoch of Fatty Arbuckle and giggling flappers in black silk stockings who kept their liquor flagons nestled just under their garter rosettes. "Petting" made inroads. Swamp acreage in Florida sold amazingly by mail. An elevator operator celebrating with his cutie his ten-thousand-dollar profit from a tip he overheard resists diversion *in flagrante* even from Eugene Debs. Few interrupted.

One expanding ancillary function that kept disturbing Mellon's cornucopian credit machine was its overseas annex. The First World War had left the United States virtually a universal creditor, planted permanently at the big end of that rickety telescope of debt that proceeded from war reparations at its Weimar Republic extremity through the endless series of war loans among the onetime "Allies" that fed into money the lesser nations owed the British and French which they in turn owed us. The Germans, peeping through all that, got so economically demoralized that their whole society fell into hyperinflated berserkness; when this happened the whole pastiche of Western European debt, which depended at many points on the German payments as collateral, threatened to come apart and leave the ultimate creditor, the United States, with a big portfolio of uncollectable obligations. The two great American financial interventions into European finance, the Dawes Plan and the Young Plan, with their stretch-out payment provisions and their moratoriums, were, under all the rhetoric, efforts to forestall collapse.

With this overhanging the transoceanic atmosphere, Mellon, with the extreme venturesomeness which characterized him as a banker,

manipulated trade and foreign investment by ratcheting downward
the Federal Reserve rediscount rate. Once it leveled off at a little over
3 percent, capital-starved Europeans simply couldn't help coming
here to borrow to rebuild the Continent. We got it back by selling
Europeans grain and industrial products; *their* industrial products,
"finished manufactures," or "competitive articles," as A.W. called
them in one extended defense of American trade policy, our duties
kept out. Europe ran a deficit. We let Europe borrow to keep on
buying.

The form these lendings took was long-term bonds between U. S.
banking institutions and individual foreign governments and corporations. Some were remarketed to private investors; others, banks
hung onto to secure their portfolios. These investments were quality;
they were as good as their domestic governments.

Here lay the danger. Mellon grasped right away the interinvolve-
ment between private debt structures and leftover war paper. One
of his earliest requests of Harding was for authority to settle the war-
debt questions himself. Senator La Follette heard about that in time
personally to make sure the issue got settled by an intragovernmental
debt commission. But Mellon soon proceeded anyhow with deal-
making with his opposite numbers in the Western European governments on his own authority. W.L., who looked into Washington,
remembers the way his uncle thrashed privately when mountebanks
like Lord Balfour and Winston Churchill suggested that it would be
sporting of the United States, since it had merely "lent" the Allies
money to purchase American supplies and armaments for use against
a common foe, to cancel outworn paper and take the pressure off
everybody.

Mellon was publicly aghast. Repudiate *obligations*? His alarm at
notions like that activates even his press releases, seething as they
shortly are with genteel vituperatives like *debility* and *thriftless* and
ne'er-do-well. When the operatic Frenchman Joseph Caillaux
shrugged, hinting default, Mellon hadn't minded mentioning that
the American money market could quite easily be closed to a country
which ignored her commitments.

Risking mental burnout, Coolidge trod the pith: "They hired the
money, didn't they?" Walter Lippmann was quick to join the chorus
of Columbia and Princeton educators caroling under Treasury Department windows by 1927 to hit at the absurdity of those sixty-two-

year debt retirement schedules which Mellon had little by little concluded with assorted debtor governments. The academic economists were particularly alarmed at the disquieting wobble the whole Western economic system was evidencing as European gold and promissory notes mounted in incredible piles upon the United States side of the machinery. At the extreme opposite, Germany, pounded by those recurrent reparations demands, was looser and looser financially and politically.

Mellon obviously was torn. "Europe is our largest customer," he wrote apropos the whole issue in 1931. "Unless the finances of Europe can be restored, her currency placed on a sound basis, and her people able to earn and spend, this country will not be able to dispose of its surplus products of food, materials, and goods." And Europe must sell, except . . . not here. But Europe must buy from us, since we couldn't survive without her markets. So—more credit, appended finally from the ten billion dollars the Europeans had owed us ever since the war. The threat of which, for all the schedule delays and the rescaled interest charges the understanding American Treasury Secretary tinkered into the promissory notes, still depressed the European capital marketplace and helped to prevent a durable European recovery. We extended more loans. Lend, certainly. Repudiate, never— no son of Judge Thomas Mellon condoned evasions that blackguardly.

Mellon wouldn't budge; Germany—and, because of Germany, the onetime Allies—simply could not pay. They could only borrow.

6

Like Marley's ghost, reminders of Teddy Roosevelt had a way of turning up in Republican caucuses or stampeding conservative lawn parties throughout that whole drunken decade. He'd given them offspring—his anomalous scattering of Progressives, insurgent political mules with absolutely no feelings of Party solidarity at all, kicking out in every direction. Grandiose, most of them. Sterile. At the 1924 Republican Convention in Cleveland, days after the sheer ovation he got had caused Andrew Mellon's emotions to seize and those patrician hands to shred the speech he was unable to give, the Party chairman, William Butler, asked their reigning plutocrat what, in fact, he thought of Idaho's maverick Republican Senator Borah.

"The Secretary," Nicholas Murray Butler reported, "looking dreamily off in the distance, took his characteristic little cigar from his mouth and said placidly: 'I never think of him unless somebody mentions his name.' "

Progressives thought about Mellon. In February of 1924 Michigan's sturdy Senator James Couzens, who had been spatting with the Treasury Secretary over the desirability of municipal-bond interest deductions, stood up and proposed a thoroughgoing investigation of the new Internal Revenue Department policy of going back and reassessing, according to "liberalized" procedures, the taxes both owed and paid by major corporations and wealthy individuals. Largely unpublished tax interpretations and retroactive amortizing methods were resulting in enormous refunds to needy Americans from John D. Rockefeller ($457,000) to the Treasury Secretary himself ($404,000). Once the Senate authorized the investigation, Couzens proposed to import, at his own expense, the pugnacious prosecutor Francis J. Heney, of San Francisco, a good friend of that primordial conservationist and sworn Mellon hater, Gifford Pinchot.

Pinchot, to the annoyance of the Mellon group, had gotten himself elected governor of Pennsylvania. A devout dry, it was Pinchot's conviction that Mellon was deliberately ignoring his prohibitionist duties, owing to the family's longtime involvement with the Overholt distilleries. He had no trouble crediting rumors that Gulf was importing booze from Europe in oil drums and distributing it at gas stations. The Mellons were corrupt; the broad-brimmed black hat of the energetic Pinchot and the resources of the State of Pennsylvania were placed squarely at the disposal of Couzens and his investigators.

Here was a threat; Mellon rushed, "trembling with rage," to confer with Calvin, and that evening Senator Reed discovered him "hardly coherent." The Secretary obviously struggled with his dignity in the formal protest he wrote the President, but even this letter ripples with Mellon's deep-seated fear and outrage. ". . . From the line of investigation selected by Senator Couzens and by the atmosphere which he has seen fit to inject into the inquiry, it is now obvious that his sole purpose is to vent some personal grievance against me. All companies in which I have been interested have been sought out. . . . In effect, a private individual is authorized to investigate generally an executive department of the government. . . . If the interposition of private resources be permitted to interfere with the executive administration of government, the machinery of government will cease to function. . . . When, through unnecessary interference, the proper exercise of this duty (efficiency) is rendered impossible, I must advise you that neither I nor any other man of character can longer take responsibility for the Treasury. Government by investigation is not government. . . ."

Enclosing Mellon's implicit threat to quit, Coolidge sent the Senate a letter of his own, protesting its effort at "unwarranted intrusion." Nevertheless, Couzens' Select Committee persevered. "This is worse than Teapot Dome," Heney is quoted on perusing the committee's evidence. But although the Select Committee did elect to conduct its inquiry, it backed off Heney, and the nearly seven thousand pages of testimony which resulted were solicited largely from Treasury Department employees like amortization chief S. T. de la Mater and chief solicitor Nelson Hartson and his dexterous successor Alexander Gregg, who thus seized A.W.'s personal attention. Gregg, like a few other individuals the Secretary regarded during his Washington years, was silently marked for service in realms choicer and more rarefied than Government. Gregg became a Mellon man.

Massively documented, hotly disputed, the catchall of evidence the Select Committee investigators produced suggested that, however wittingly, Mellon had converted much of the Internal Revenue Department into a welfare apparatus for businessmen. Its principles were flexible; each mining depletion rebate or plant amortization allowance was determined, as legislation permitted, according to the "merits" of the case. Almost a half-billion dollars was returned to enterprises and individuals who discovered their opportunity. Among the principles that informed the Secretary's "wide discretionary power," according to Hartson's testimony, was "the point of view of getting all the money that can be secured . . . of keeping the company a solvent and going concern."

While acknowledging that, except in one case, "the questions involved in the allowance of nearly $600,000,000 of deductions for amortization appear to have never been called to the attention of or to have received any consideration by the commissioner, the deputy commissioner, the solicitor, or any other higher official of the Bureau of Internal Revenue until these questions were brought to their attention by this investigation," the report makes clear that Mellon people stood waiting when kickback time came. In 1919 Gulf Oil's ratio of depletion to net income ran to a staggering 448.66 (Drake's achievement while the Mellon appointment was pending), and over the ensuing four years the Aluminum Company, Gulf, and Standard Steel

Car together compiled refunds, tax credits and abatements that totaled just under seven and a half million dollars. The notation "This is a Mellon company" turned up on dossiers. The august Secretary might tiptoe by the accounting department doors, but Union Trust lawyers like W. A. Siefert enjoyed "uncanny" luck in tax readjustment cases. Senate liberals fussed enough about the $91,472 in taxes the Union Trust avoided by declaring its wholly owned affiliates as independent banks to compel the Treasury Department to recall its beneficence. Couzens' probe had little immediate consequence.

Except to Couzens. The afternoon of March 7, 1925, the Treasury Department informed Couzens that a retroactive Department study revealed him to owe the Government an additional $10,861,131.50 on the 1919 sale of Ford Motor Company stock which constituted Couzens' forty-million-dollar fortune. A lawsuit was pending.

Mellon could actually *bite*! He hadn't wanted this. Hadn't he been patient enough? Kept quiet, taken record political gas while orthodontists from Couzens' miserable subcommittee "probed" his Internal Revenue files. Chiseled calcified financial bones, sawed across innumerable nerves. Out came the old Shumway leases so important to Gulf's Gypsy Oil subsidiary, salvage value estimates from Koppers, postwar tonnage breakdowns from the Aluminum Company.

The thing wouldn't end. Politics recognizes few accidents; nobody in Washington could miss the connection between the Senate's extension of Couzens' authorization to investigate after March 4, 1925, and the abruptness with which, three afternoons later, Internal Revenue Commissioner Blair himself and one of the Department agents pulled Couzens personally from the floor of the Senate to present his arrears bill.

Even deferential Carter Glass stated that his successor pounced "simply because he and the Senator from Michigan hate each other. I don't believe the Secretary has a foot to stand on in a court of equity or law, or that he can recover one dollar." Mellon wasn't after money. Fumbling with a microphone shortly after Couzens got started, Mellon told a Pittsburgh audience, "I haven't had experience as a broadcaster. I think I have rather been accused of being a receiver." And truthfully, that hurt.

Mellon let a year elapse. Even the tight-lipped Coolidge had the generosity to push his hard Yankee mouth in the direction of the

Treasury building when visitors mentioned prosperity. Credit—Uncle Andy. ". . . a wistful, appealing figure," *Collier's* maintained, "kindly and a little pathetic; wishing to be loved; enjoying like a youth the fame that has come to him late in life; courageous; free from that political ambition which gives a certain meanness to almost every other figure in Washington."

Autumnal nobility—A.W. undoubtedly appreciated that. Saw value —enough to lie back, wait out a year of investigations, crouch shuddering with anger and dignity. Nothing else made sense. What, claw out? Affect remoteness while gift wrapping Capitol Hill in Couzens' fiduciary entrails?

Mellon had to anyway. Colonel Drake was around the offices the afternoon it ripened. Drake attributes to Garrard Winston, the newly appointed undersecretary, their breathtaking lummox counterstroke. Back Couzens off? Simple. Pull his Internal Revenue file, and work up stupefying back taxes. Couzens would undoubtedly countersue in the newly instituted tax appeal court, and someday he might exonerate himself. Meanwhile he could wriggle.

His friends could watch. Mellon signed the thing, scratching off his signature as if that paper among the late-afternoon sheaf of directives were an administrative detail. Eased into his topcoat, mused as he ambled the customary mile home to his Massachusetts Avenue apartment. He got about halfway, Drake says, when little by little the *nakedness* of what they were about literally stopped Mellon. Where might this lead? "Mister M" had dematerialized in the effulgence out of which doddered "Uncle Andy," Boniface of the Exchequer, whose best-known foible was forgetting his billfold on the chiffonier. The billionaire was reported in debt to bemused Negro cabdrivers all around D.C.

Mellon pondered. Decided, flicked away a crater of cigar, bustled immediately, topcoat flapping, toward the deserted offices, stop the thing, prevent this . . . too late! Winston prevailed. Perhaps everything was ruined!

Nothing changed. "His controversy with Senator Couzens on the subject of tax reduction," conceded the *Saturday Evening Post*, "was unfortunate." The Government's devouring lawsuit? Most probably, "a mistake," since "the Government eventually lost its case in the courts." Everyone makes mistakes. Why, Senator Couzens' own wife, following a delightful dinner-party chat with the courtly Treasury

Secretary, was quoted in print as bemoaning the way "Jim" was forever getting into quarrels with "people I like." Inconvenient. Nothing to take seriously.

7

Did anybody care? By 1925 that Coolidge bull market, though really a calf yet, had started to snap at flies and butt up averages with promise and energy enough to keep experienced pool manipulators like M. J. Meehan and William Crapo Durant swearing quietly to themselves as they watched, jaws dropped, the stubs of forgotten cigars annealed to those ever-mobile lower lips. This thing had *punch*! Pretty soon a crowd was gathering.

By now everything began and ended with moneylending. Historians tended to blame the outset of the boom on those two fateful visits of the European financial magi, Montagu Norman of the Bank of England, Schacht of the Reichsbank, and Charles Rist of France. In 1925 Winston Churchill, Chancellor of the Exchequer, insisted on repegging the British pound at prewar standards, too high, payable in gold. English exports fell; gold vanished to reappear in America. In 1925, then again in 1927, the Europeans were able to persuade the chairman of the Federal Reserve System, Daniel ("Dick") Crissinger, Harding's boyhood chum, to crank the federal rediscount rate way down, to scarcely more than 3 percent, so Europeans could keep borrowing. Crissinger in real life had served as corporation counsel to an Ohio steam-shovel company, and he was possibly as qualified as anybody from Marion, Ohio, to manage the international monetary structure. Unavoidably, he listened with care to advice from his legendary Treasury Secretary, who, through his Debt Commission work, was already an intimate of Norman's. The rate went down.

Europe kept borrowing. And not only Europe: with cash so available nobody in America saw any sense in dissipating his own. On the cuff, most of the major corporations undertook plant expansions. Once these had grossly increased their "underlying bases," the majority "went public." So much new capital rushed in, company treasurers went after the market in other people's stocks. *They* quickly started climbing. Goods sold; employment jumped; by the middle Twenties a largely agricultural society had half its wages flowing through enormous corporations. Mellon gave credit; now Mellon got credit. Let him profit too.

Examiners around the Department weren't afflicting their status reports by keeping Pittsburgh satisfied. But rebating tax money, like A.W.'s other policies, came down to redirecting abandoned capital into living investments. The demand became voracious, murdering. Automobiles. Oil production. Utilities.

Pure growth, what appetites—black holes of capital-absorbing antimatter. They could swallow everything; when financing hesitated the gagging was unbearable, the industrial earth shook. A.W. tittered: unruly creatures, but his. Could we deny them?

We couldn't responsibly afford them either, and little by little, from the mid-Twenties on, knowingly, Mellon oversaw a metabolic alteration in the country's finances. We turned from reinvestors of our painfully assembled capital hoard to embezzlers from the treasuries of enterprises to come, borrowers off the future. Traditional virtues reversed. "The desire to accumulate," John Maynard Keynes observed the decade afterward, "is a social *fact*, to be taken as such." And in a consumerist society, one to be deplored. Uninvested savings retard production. Mellon agreed.

Uninhibited, Mellon did not restrict his closet Keynesianism to peeling taxes away whenever the economy slowed. By advocating a meager rediscount rate and an unattractive level of federal bond yields he squeezed reluctant capital out into things, ready, available at banking multiples to fuel the expansion.

Anything looked worth trying. Every time the great Bull balked in any way, reassessing another lunge, a horde of bond-house impresarios and trust-department picadors hurried close to affix fresh inspirations. A plethora of margin accounts, a string of "investment companies" comprised largely of huge issues the mother bank was barely finished writing, a syndicate to insure a colossal broker's loan no bank would even touch on some banana-republic mining speculation. Everybody wanted a ride; nobody feared whiplash. The fees were enormous. Interest differentials split 5 or 10 points sometimes as money got borrowed and reloaned; investors scuffled for a place in line. Quick—the scuttlebutt was, good stocks would soon be unobtainable. Double your capital now.

New Capital—in essence, a chattel loan against tomorrow. Old Capital didn't have any place anymore, insensitive cysts of fussed-over savings. No growth to those. Certainly no leverage. Ride the Bull up.

Mellon had to approve: things were too advanced, New Capital and New Capital alone would keep their world from consuming itself. A.W. understood this administratively. He understood it privately as well. Gulf was refinancing massively, and Koppers was taking shape as one of the utilities pyramids. Mellon hadn't any choice.

Mousing history, Professor Galbraith cornered something and observed how "By the summer of 1929 the market not only dominated the news. It also dominated the culture." And this was noteworthy, since "Then, as now, to the great majority of workers, farmers, white-collar workers, indeed to the great majority of all Americans, the stock market was a remote and vaguely ominous thing."

Hurricane Andrew, moving powerfully offshore. Keep out there— even common people grasped, via the industrial unconscious, how in the end the electric, and linkage for the threshing machine, and Pa's fi' dollar a day they gave him over to the Ford assembly place, got back to "prosperity." Some'n ta do with "stocks."

People adored their novelties. Restlessness unified. John J. Raskob of General Motors and Du Pont moved in as chairman of the Democratic National Committee. John L. Lewis of the United Mine Workers stumped hard for Hoover in 1928 "so that the unprecedented industrial and business prosperity which he inaugurated may be properly developed and stabilized."

Hoover! If ever that tousled labor pighead scraped tipple ash enough out of those shaggy Welsh ears, he'd know like everybody else how often the Commerce Secretary was working his disapproving cud whenever anybody whispered speculation. Lewis was probably affronted. The Mellons had barely finished starving the Mine Workers out in much of western Pennsylvania.

Mellon liked to dismiss his own influence out of hand. "I can remember when Shaw was Treasury Secretary," he told one acquaintance. "He was also supposed to be the greatest Secretary of the Treasury since Alexander Hamilton. We're all entitled to that. I saw him afterwards on a ferryboat. He looked like a retired drummer. Nobody remembered who he was." Mellon was working late. "Public office is just like that electric light," he concluded. "It looks fine while it is on. But afterwards—"

A dab of emollient—power dried one out so. Sometime during that period he reminisced for one of Paul's young friends, conjured up the nights he passed in Brown's Hotel in London, carriage horses outside rumbling through his restless sleep, and ". . . I thought as a melancholy boy will, that they will still be clopping on the pavement long after I, and perhaps my money, are gone."

Perhaps my money. But perhaps not—stirring, the Treasury Secretary went back to clearing his desk. Harlan Stone, Daugherty's replacement—hadn't he said something recently about bringing the Government's investigation of the Aluminum Trust "down to date"? Refuse, buried Federal Trade Commission garbage, bandy-legged Progressives like Walch and George Norris were already bellying up to venture a sniff. Evidently Stone didn't understand. Stone needed something substantial to occupy that solid legal mind. Before the year was out Stone transcended the mundane upon a Supreme Court bench. The new Attorney General, Sargent, understood political limitations better. He relegated the entire intricate matter to his more cosmopolitan assistant, Colonel William ("Wild Bill") Donovan, who worked the thing through quietly, and to everybody's satisfaction, by means of conferences in which Coolidge and Mellon himself participated at times and which were reported on the Senate floor by Pennsylvania's David A. Reed. Violations of that 1912 consent decree? A misreading. ". . . no proceedings in contempt," Donovan had determined, "can be successfully maintained."

This meant unusual exposure. Mellon was more comfortable in administrative shadows. Throughout his tenure, the Secretary served as ex-officio chairman of the Farm Loan Board. Recognizing early how inflation threatened profits unless agricultural commodities stayed down, Mellon endorsed approaches which augmented the unmanageable rural debt as farmers floundered to keep up technologically. When, momentarily, Progressives ruptured business lines and passed the McNary-Haugen bill to peg domestic commodity prices and lend farmers cheap long-term operating funds, Mellon helped provoke Cautious Cal's rasp of dismay. He vetoed the mischievous thing. Nobody dast immobilize capital!

One day the worried Judge Cooper, head of the Farm Loan Board, enticed the complacent Coolidge out of the cellar of the White House, where the Vermonter liked to pass afternoons sorting good from bad among the apple larders his constituents kept stocking. Coolidge heard Cooper patiently. "Well, Governor," the Chief Executive concluded when everything was said, "I don't know enough about the subject to advise you one way or another, but if I were in your position, I think I would yield my views to that of the Treasurer and make the Treasurer assume the responsibility." The Treasurer wouldn't mind. Recently, he'd recommended in passing that the Federal Bureau of Investigation might work much better within the Department of the Treasury.

7 | AS IF I DIED

1

As 1921 ENDED, propped up under comforters in Washington's Wardman Park Hotel, the emaciated Boies Penrose nodded off for good while giddy revelers below hooted in the season.

Who could replace Penrose? Those puffy giant fingertips, thrusting inside his rumpled suit-coat lining to retrieve more bank notes, patting soiled pockets grumpily to isolate the wad while reps and heelers glanced daintily away—Harrisburg mourned its loss. They'd underestimated his devotion. Each year since 1897, it developed, the boss had expended $150,000 in funds of his own to keep his Pennsylvania machine operating.

His contribution in Washington was no less invaluable. He dominated the Congressional Old Guard; he reigned as chairman of the Senate Finance Committee; his special-order davenport between the cloakroom doors supplied the ideal command post from which to nudge toward floor debate or wink into oblivion the measures his protégé, Andrew Mellon, might require or disparage. Whatever escaped the caucus, Boies's colleague Philander Knox rushed up to envelop in respectability.

So everything looked ready-made, so far as Mellon could tell. Then, before 1921 ended, Knox too passed away: both Senators were gone, Pennsylvania erupted with squabbles, and A.W. was frustrated for years with efforts to effectuate the Mellon Plan.

The lapse was peskiest in Pennsylvania. Pennsylvania had been orderly. Since 1862, when Simon Cameron assumed control in Harrisburg after Abraham Lincoln had put him out of the War Cabinet for profiteering on munitions orders, the "Pennsylvania system" obtained, uninterrupted, throughout the bustling Commonwealth. There was a "Boss"; he—first Simon and Donald Cameron, then Matthew Quay, finally, most grandly, Penrose—looked after "the interests" and distributed their alms. Regional concerns were balanced by allotting a U. S. Senator apiece to Philadelphia and the industrial west. Good liaison made sense between owners and representatives. The "organization" leadership remained "protectionist" and Republican.

A.W., musing, hadn't doubted all along that legislatures served emblematic purposes, like molehills cast up after vigorous commercial activity. Their role was easy to misinterpret, however, and contacts were important. Selecting public servants was far too rife with consequences to leave to people on the streets. Whenever Penrose appeared, A.W. prepared somberly to contribute his share. Strictly cash and carry; A.W. expected word whenever something sizable portended.

Without Penrose, coordination faltered. Contemplating interim appointments, Governor William C. Sproul had looked into Mellon's Senate preferences, then ignored them completely and proposed the names of George Wharton Pepper and William Crow.

Pepper looked all right—a constitutionalist and canon law buff from Philadelphia. But Crow was ill, relatively unknown, certainly not the figure to represent the trans-Allegheny counties. Pittsburghers consulted: Judge Reed's son David decided to challenge Crow in the Republican primary. The boss of Philadelphia, Representative William Vare, also resented Sproul's high-handedness. In April of 1922 there began in Philadelphia a series of closed-door conferences to negotiate a "harmony ticket."

A.W. sent Willie. From then on W.L. was saddled with the burden of representing the Mellon interests at periodic secret conclaves. This he accepted good-naturedly. "I don't think W.L. ever liked politics," Thomas Mellon Evans says. "That's just the Governor of Pennsylvania," W.L. once explained to onlookers at the Muskoka Lakes camp after finally hanging up. "Fisher. He has to make a speech and wants to know what to say."

Politics teemed with individuals no businessman could penetrate. Arrangements slithered. Factions were forever maneuvering, promises wriggled with ambiguity. Landing bonefish offered clues—most of the fry were susceptible to gaffing close to the bank account, but many of the leaders necessitated maddening guile.

W.L. was direct. At the April meeting W.L. barged in backed up by Pittsburgh's Ninth Ward chairman, State Senator Max Leslie. They struck a bargain and replaced Crow with David Reed; in return for that W.L. would back Vare's choices for governor, lieutenant governor and Pennsylvania Party chairman.

All this seemed equitable; then Joseph Grundy heard. Grundy was Penrose's legatee, his wily, withered paymaster, a hand in Washington for marking up tariff schedules since the previous century. *Vare* pick the *governor*? The hard-bitten worsted maker recoiled; he insinuated the extensive Manufacturers' Association of Pennsylvania funds at his disposal in an effort to elect the renegade Gifford Pinchot. Pinchot looked dangerously rattlebrained—blindly conservationist, a fanatic dry, a detested Progressive. "Can you imagine me supporting Gifford Pinchot for anything?" Grundy cackled that spring. After a long lifetime of assiduously "fat-trying" donations out of Pennsylvania industrialists to underwrite their interests? But Pinchot was transitory, whereas if Vare got in . . .

Vare frightened Grundy. He was jellyfish meat, a wan encroaching presence from Philadelphia's scummy Neck who managed, supported by his brothers, to develop his landfill and reclamation business into a political organization. Ultimately they squeezed Penrose. Originally Boies was contemptuous; he scoffed at payoffs until the Vare brothers brought down a melee of blackjacking which left Penrose's home precincts throbbing. Boies demanded police protection; a patrolman got riddled. Penrose came to terms.

Vare craved larger dignities. He won a seat in Congress; it didn't take long before that wasn't sanctification enough. "He wants to go to the U. S. Senate," Penrose railed, unbelieving. "Not while I live. Not while I live. By God, they won't carry me off in their ash cart."

Grundy's intervention stopped Vare in 1922. The next several years the infighting was largely between stiff-necked Governor Pinchot, who accused the Treasury Secretary of ignoring prohibition (unreconstructed distiller that he was) and the preoccupied A.W., who retaliated by keeping Pinchot off the Pennsylvania delegation which helped nominate Coolidge. Unhappy, smoldering, Vare felt left out. His remaining brother died; resentful ambition plagued him; he realized he wasn't getting comelier: "a little pudgy, rheumy-eyed, thin-haired, squeaky-voiced Pennsylvania boss," to one journalist's observation.

From what Philadelphia heard, the Mellons couldn't even keep track of Pittsburgh. Republican totals were faltering; the Progressives worked up a quarter of their nationwide vote in Allegheny County alone. Who counted *those* ballots? Vare ran Philadelphia classically, a regime of Christmas turkeys and muscle from Scranton to vote the tombstone constituency.

Once Pittsburgh's rulers admitted to themselves that Vare seriously intended to take his seat from Pepper in 1926, there began a lethargic stir. Vare was moving powerfully. A.W. and W.L. met to map their strategy, "away back before the first of the year a considerable time," as W.L. later testified. An autumn of hotel room meetings slowly convinced the Pittsburghers that Vare wouldn't budge. He intended to win. He intended to select the governor. Vare's choice was Edward F. Beidleman, the sitting lieutenant governor.

Now Grundy intervened beforehand. Beidleman was wholly obnoxious, he informed the Mellons. Beidleman's thinking was addlepated, he'd become a nuisance around Harrisburg with hints about replacing the traditional levy on anthracite—the Mellons owned bituminous—with something menacingly broader. "No, Mr. Beidleman had, in our judgment, always been antagonistic to that settled policy of the party," Grundy stated in hearings, "and we believed that if he had been nominated—and of course that would have been the equivalent to an election—that he would have been for the imposition of a tax on the capital stock of corporations in Pennsylvania."

Capital stock! Western Pennsylvania broke tremors; familiar cues missed setups across the Duquesne Club gloom. The Treasurer himself summoned George Wharton Pepper to inform him that the Mellon-Grundy coalition had settled now upon a candidate for governor, John Fisher, a well-used pleader for New York Central interests. Fisher and George Pepper would share the ticket. The polished Pepper demurred.

Mellon glanced over, pale-eyed. "Of course," A.W. suggested, quietly, "I can get along very well with Mr. Vare." Pepper came around.

Not that reducing Pepper would get them far. Leslie announced for Beidleman. A.W. undertook one, uncharacteristic effort. In March of 1926 he convened a two-day bargaining session in his apartment on Massachusetts Avenue. Vare was beyond trade-offs. When the diffident Treasurer held open a box of cigarillos, the aroused little guttersnipe reportedly "scooped a half dozen into his paw, tied a rubber band around them and grunted, 'A fair smoke, Mr. Secretary.'" Then Vare scuttled away in hopes of converting Coolidge.

They'd fight Vare openly. On March 24 both Mellons broke tradition and supported in public a Pepper-Fisher ticket. His role, Will shrugged, involved "just helping along generally." He had donated $25,000 himself, as had both uncles, and what with the generosity of several "business associates" and an additional $158,000 the Mellon banks loaned, much of the $306,000 the Pepper-Fisher campaign laid out in western Pennsylvania looked easy to trace.

Mellon's chin was out; in Pittsburgh the Secretary attempted his sole avowedly political address. Speechmaking wasn't Mellon's forte. At the 1924 Convention the Treasurer had accepted the podium to propose a motion. He mumbled with stage fright; after a decent interval the clerk stepped forward and repeated the Treasurer's proposal.

These nightmares were chronic. Endorsing Hoover over a nationwide radio hookup in 1928, the very conception of all those invisible people out there was enough to freeze his epiglottis—millions heard an extended, thin, sibilant choking sound they must have confused with static. Once, well into a presentation ceremony at the unveiling of a statue of Alexander Hamilton, the Secretary lost his place and stood there thumbing desperately among the unfamiliar pages, perspiration beading. Nothing audible came out. There was an honor guard; its commanding officer concluded that the address was finished and enunciated shoulder arms. Suddenly Mellon peered up. "Looks as though they didn't like my speech," Mellon observed, quite distinctly.

Mellon's performance in Pittsburgh that afternoon followed precedent. A mob of thousands packed in to observe this frail, legendary incarnation. Mellon strained for partisanship, urging that his listeners send back to Washington a Senator "who staunchly supported the policies of the Republican Administration . . . ." Fisher was effectively ignored, and after the introductory paragraphs the Treasurer moved on to rarefied, governmental matters. People pressed to hear. He turned the final page over, paused, riffled back for certainty. "Well," A.W. decided aloud, "I guess that's all there is." His hometown audience bellowed.

Speaking up for worthies like Pepper was easy enough, the skeptical Grundy insisted. Fisher's nomination was important. "I have always felt that the issues involved in the campaign were the fundamental things," Grundy piped up later, horrifying a Senate Committee, "and that the candidates, or whatever might go with the candidates, were what you might call an accessory after the fact."

Criminal nomenclature in public life? The Committee chairman bridled; Grundy brushed him off. Where interests were involved nobody fussed over personalities. They'd started honorably—the hope had been that a flagrant media bombardment might push Vare out. But Vare kept coming, and soon even W.L. concluded there wasn't any profit in overstuffing mailboxes. Philadelphia professionals moved around—political cadre was defecting.

Big Bill showed up mouthing one puissant slogan: "Beer." He campaigned wringing wet; troublemakers reminded the millworkers how Mayor Kline's municipal detectives stood by for protection whenever a bootlegger's van unloaded. The graft that involved!

This left one recourse, and Mellon accepted it: buy stiffs. Rates were already up, especially in the gubernatorial battle, where Fisher was losing support to Pinchot among the drys while Beidleman was hinting of relatively lax alcohol-law enforcement. By primary morning a dependable Fisher "poll watcher" might expect ten dollars. Pepper devotees got $4.14 apiece; Grundy, who hated Pepper's starch, knew where to economize.

The polls had scarcely started closing before heavies formed lines which meandered out the door of Pittsburgh Republican headquarters, back-switching around the block in so many parallel files that it would literally require days to unbind and surrender those bales of ten-dollar bills. Grundy later reminisced archly about all the trouble it involved to produce the final $90,000. Devotedly, weeks before, W.L.'s new-found intimate, Mayor Charles Kline, pushed out municipal employees to assist the canvassers; cops working the bars below Liberty Avenue were registering some unlikely patriots. Once polling places closed, Kline assigned his detectives to help "complete the returns from their districts."

Then—uniquely—there was a dramatic delay. Wholesale recounts were demanded. Sacks of sequestered ballots kept disappearing and resurfacing; finally—but not until vote counts throughout the Commonwealth were tallied and confirmed—Pittsburgh reported in too.

Vare carried, easily. But Fisher won also, although by stingier margins—ten thousand votes out of a million and a half. Why overspend? "Interpretations abounded," remarks the historian Lawrence Murray, who cites Senator Reed's view that prohibition was decisive. Pinchot had plainer ideas. "Partly bought," he scrawled across Vare's mandate, "and partly stolen."

A.W. watched phlegmatically. When editorialists complained, he authorized an official release in which he "expressed a pained surprise that anyone should object to the expenditure of a million and a half dollars in an attempt to nominate Senator Pepper . . . ." Sometimes democracy meant sacrifices—he reminded Senate investigators that it had cost $42,000 per statewide mailing. The fuss was unfortunate, but everybody was satisfied. He would accept Vare; the Philadelphian was agreeable to W. L. Mellon as state Republican Chairman.

Big Bill appeared quiescent. "Let me ask you this question," Senator King asked later, once Senatorial inquiry began. "Was the contest between you and Mr. Pepper and Mr. Pinchot for the senatorship, or was the paramount contest between the Mellon interests, if I may say that without any offensiveness—and I do not want to be offensive—and the Vare interests, for political supremacy in the State?"

Vare staggered for syntax: "It did not hardly get in that shape." Vare tried again. "A great many people—with apologies to you distinguished gentlemen—think the governor is the important part of the ticket, by reason of the amount of patronage, for instance." Even that sounded lame; Vare lumbered after heart's blood: "While I have no right to speak for Mr. Mellon, my personal opinion is that he is a very, very busy man."

The prospect of infesting the Club on the Hill with Big Bill Vare roiled bipartisan senatorial stomachs. The inquiry soon started. Its justification was expenditures—$1,804,070 on Fisher-Pepper alone, with $785,934 on the Vare ticket and $187,029 by Pinchot. By 1926 few Presidential campaigns boiled off amounts like those. Hauled before the Senators, W.L. appeared stunned at Senator La Follette's imputation that there was something dubious about spending those epic donations to "successfully elect the ticket": "It depends on what your contributions are and what your collections are and what the conditions are. I do not see how I could answer that."

A.W.'s coeval David Reed—fearful that the "ash-cart statesman" might oppose *his* renomination—condemned the Special Committee's findings as "thoroughly unreliable." Vare was unseated anyhow; Governor Fisher appointed Grundy to finish the senatorial term. He'd understand the responsibilities.

A.W. was less blasé than he would normally let on about that "Mellon-Grundy machine" talk. He shrank from exposure. W.L. intervened desultorily. He undertook the chairmanship, W.L. allowed, only "because of urgent requests from a large number of leaders in various

The "Vagabondia" at anchor
MATTHEW MELLON

parts of the state." He'd consider any devotion, except when fishing was good. Lackadaisically, W.L. lent his name to metropolitan reformist measures.

The emboldened Mayor Kline now decided to take over Pittsburgh: perhaps the Mellons wouldn't care; and in fact, in 1929, while Kline pulped Leslie, W.L. sent along a telegram from Canada that ordained, "As such a large number of candidates are my friends, I have determined to take no part in the primary campaign unless some unexpected changes should occur."

In 1930 the same cast reappeared. But spirits were uneven, and even the betrayals had rather a road-company quality. Big Bill floated reports that he was again after Grundy's seat. But Vare was ailing. The expiring spoiler decided to support the U.S. Senate candidacy of Labor Secretary Davis, himself technically a Pittsburgher; Davis's victory, everybody knew, would jeopardize Reed's franchise. The Mellons courted Vare by persuading Grundy's selection for governor to renounce his own bid in favor of Big Bill's favorite, Francis S. Brown. On political tiptoes now, the Mellons openly endorsed the Grundy-Brown ticket.

This riled old Grundy. It was his habit to *present* faits accomplis. Joe silently moved over; again, mischievously, he pledged his tithe to Pinchot, whom he again administered to business-oriented Pennsylvania like a Quaker emetic.

As for the Mellons? At least a mention, perhaps, ought here be made of the fact that on December 3, 1928, there arrived in New York harbor, for W. L. Mellon, from the great Krupp shipyards at Kiel, the plaything of a lifetime, the great sleek double-hulled, teak-planked yacht that became the ultimate *Vagabondia* (224-feet long, 856 tons, a crew of thirty-two). The winter of 1930, observes the troubled Murray, "delicate negotiations" were "hamstrung much of the time by W.L.'s inexplicable absence on a late winter Florida vacation." The empire would keep.

In fact, it wouldn't. Grundy lost; Brown lost. By 1931 the resurrected Pinchot had progressives like himself running even Allegheny County. The hegemony was over.

2

After the 1926 upheaval a profusion of smells, some misleading, came off the decomposing Pennsylvania Republican Party. Many floated toward Washington. Even conservatives sensed problems. Some, newspapers lapping their knees, squirmed in their reading-room club chairs at realizing how frequently probes originating far afield came around to sideswipe the inarticulate Treasurer. Others couldn't help pondering the run-up in valuations the Wall Street professionals accorded certain "closely held" Pittsburgh enterprises. Were there . . . undisclosed relationships?

By March of 1929, with assorted Senators outraged at Herbert Hoover's insouciance about smuggling the Treasurer back into his Cabinet, Mellon sent his spokesman David Reed a letter which met the question few yet dared ask. He did possess, Mellon submitted, a "substantial amount of stock." But as regarded any trespass of the ancient regulation which specified that no Secretary of the Treasury "shall directly or indirectly be concerned or interested in carrying on the business of trade or commerce . . . or be concerned in the purchase or disposal of any public securities of any State, or of the United States"—nothing there was relevant. He'd assisted various enterprises, yet "As far as these companies are concerned my active connection with them was severed in 1921 as completely as if I had died at the time. I have not concerned myself with their affairs and I have not endeavored to control or dictate their operations in any way."

This unequivocal statement rose, rectilinear as a sandbar, and provided considerable shelter against the incessantly nibbling Congressional tides. Then the prosperity broke. Angrier winds came up; with people going hungry the threat to Mellon was beginning to originate, not with the stately old Progressive carpers around the Senate who disapproved all along, but from among depression Congressmen, their empty bellies whining.

They needed explanations. Their leader in this, a pink-cheeked newcomer from Texarkana, Wright Patman, ached, for all his mannerliness, with wanting to establish how everything for plain people had gotten so down-in-the-mouth. The lanky western Democrat had appeared in 1928; before he even ran for reelection he identified one culprit. In 1924 the Congress pushed through a bill which provided "adjusted compensation," a bonus, to World War veterans. Mellon didn't like bonuses. Bemoaning sizable oncoming deficits, he worked enough legislators around to block off payment for twenty years. Then, relieved considerably, Mellon manipulated a respectworthy surplus.

Wright Patman was incensed: "Filthy rich, didn't lack fo' anything on earth, and there he was, attemptin' to keep needy veterans who fought and bled fo' their country from gettin' what was already theirs." In 1930 Patman introduced a measure to require the Treasury to pay off those certificates. When even an American Legion convention in Boston refused to endorse Patman's proposal he couldn't hold back. "The invisible hand of Mellonism was present," he erupted to reporters, "misleading, and false statements were circulated that the Legion should not take action on my proposals because it was strictly a partisan matter and I was attempting to throw mud on the administration. This was false, but Mr. Mellon's cohorts were successful in applying the gag rule to the extent that free discussion and a fair vote on the merits of the proposal were denied."

Another session started; months passed; times worsened; one day in January of 1932 Texarkana's dust-bowl Ichabod slid into the aisle his long country shanks and moved a "question of constitutional privilege." He took this opportunity, Patman explained, to urge the assembled House, upon his own authority, to proceed with impeaching Andrew William Mellon for "high crimes and misdemeanors." Important details needed airing, Patman maintained, and he was prepared to make his case before whatever forum the members designated. Scarcely a week afterward, on January 13, Patman began to justify his charges before the full House Judiciary Committee.

Patman's documentation was scant, colleagues realized, but he was sputtery with indignation. Everywhere little mean pecks. Offspray bespattered morning newspapers.

Initial scraps looked paltry. Coast Guard irregularities. Control of the Office of the Supervising Architect had positioned the Treasurer to steer important Government business toward selected Pittsburgh suppliers. Shares in an East St. Louis bank turned up in the Aluminum Company treasury. Rye from the Overholt inventory was occasionally dispensed, according to the provisions of the law, by Union Trust, trustee, and receipts credited automatically to the account of A. W. Mellon. One swollen rumor, which alleged a two-hundred-million-dollar Koppers contract to oversee the erection of villages of coking ovens in the Soviet Union by convict laborers, broke down on investigation to a $383,000 sale of engineering plans and the transitory reassignment of seventeen unemployed technicians. Stymied, charge after charge, by Treasury expert Alexander Gregg and A.W.'s personal estate man, Donald Shepard, Patman's case appeared forlorn.

His mild gaze sickened at moments with unfulfilled recrimination, Patman ransacked collateral staff work. There were Senator McKellar's appendices, the rough material Senator Watson surfaced. Senator Walch had unexplored beginnings somewhere in his 1929 eligibility inquiry. That Aluminum reorganization, the so-called Haskell proceedings.

Patman hauled it out. Depositions in the Haskell case had a sort of intermittent, even a conjectural quality, like bits of Rorschach material. Various interpretations were possible. Haskell's proof, examined critically, ran like disastrously exposed jurisprudential Super-Eight across which indecipherable huge shapes were seen by Haskell forever converging and departing. Haskell hadn't really understood—attorneys for the Mellons tended to treat Haskell like some sunstroked hobbyist, who overdid things attempting to photograph Loch Ness. His pictures were . . . uneven. Was his emulsion rotten?

George Haskell lacked practicality. Shortly after the war, with very little capital and no more plant than the modest quarters provided by his Baush Machine Tool Company in Springfield, Massachusetts, Haskell evidently had decided to challenge the Aluminum monopoly.

Originally Haskell bought rights to an aluminum-based alloy called Duralumin, with which he attempted to entice a specialty clientele for items like airplane propellers. Salesmen for the Aluminum Company quickly identified his customers and undercut his costs.

Haskell ignored this warning. His timing in any case indicated purity of soul—the trust's chief impresario was managing the economy, Fordney-McCumber tariff hikes coddled aluminum, antitrust was dormant, the I.R.B. was well along in rebating fifteen million dollars to the receptive monopoly. All this sounded muffled, so far as Haskell could discern, against the drumming of adrenaline when Ford's head engineer made mention of multi-ton contracts for aluminum engine blocks—if only some outsider could defend large customers against Aluminum's cutthroat pricing policies.

Purchasing agents everywhere nodded. Hot *damn*! This thing could integrate. Haskell priced the makings. Then, rummaging Quebec for waterpower, he stumbled into George G. Allen, head of the Quebec Development Company. Quebec Development, which overseas the Île Maligne vastness of the Saguenay River wilderness, looked after the results of decades of Canadian land grabs by faltering James B. Duke.

Once, long before, the baronial North Carolinian had been the Hotspur of the tobacco monopoly. Triumphs dim; overshadowed, old Duke was sensitive. He insisted on reminding visitors, offhand, that the fountains which dotted his rolling estate lawns gushed filtered water exclusively. Not that he scanted enterprise—his Southern Power Company, alone, was "turning five million spindles" by 1922.

Haskell guessed. Duke's kingdom in Canada was humiliating, empty weight. An affiliate was harvesting trees, but what Duke demanded was immoderate, visionary, one culminating financial wallow. The International Aluminum Company, which Haskell would run and Duke would bankroll, got slapped into paper-work existence so quickly that operatives for the principals kept running into one another, cramming reduction techniques in Europe or verifying Guiana bauxite strikes.

Old men get carried away. Then, usually, they reconsider. Lulled by Allen's reassurances, Haskell caught on last. Information taken in testimony pinpoints the autumn of 1924 as bringing Arthur V. Davis's exploratory overtures to Duke. Aluminum was complicated business. Technicians were almost unobtainable. Marketable bauxite was rare —in fact, the concession in Dutch Guiana one Duke-Haskell agent

uncovered had just been optioned by the pervasive monopoly. Surely
. . . some rearrangements were possible?

Duke hadn't considered selling. Quite possibly, however, there was
some basis for entertaining the notion of an exchange of Duke's Saguenay property for holdings in the Aluminum Corporation. Meaningful holdings.

"I'm not going to worry my head about what you do," Duke informed Aluminum's lawyers, "but I want ten percent." Ten per*cent*!
Of the trust? Fifty years have passed, but Aluminum attorney Leon
Higby still develops a dryness along the larynx just recollecting his
astonishment. This required, whatever anybody preferred, that "A.W.
had a hand in this deal along with Davis." A block that size—they
might as well go public after parting with that. Bubbling to the surface
from stark corporate depths, both mating parties ignored one minor,
hysterical onlooker. George Haskell, "honestly convinced that Alcoa
had beat him out of the deal of his life," came forward to embroil
everybody involved in litigation even brusque little Davis pronounced
"a great embarrassment." Proceedings continued for years; they focused the attention of Haskell's dogged, contemplative lawyer, Homer
Cummings, upon assorted Mellon activities.

Legal millstones commenced grinding; on July 2, 1928, A. W. Mellon personally stopped by a hotel room to answer a subpoena and
contribute his deposition. He proceeded with aforethought, lapsing
into autumnal forgetfulness at times, then stirring himself periodically
into a dreamy flow of unwanted statistics. Duke, certainly. Davis had
already verified having opened negotiations with Duke formally on
November 6, but it was sometime after that that Mellon became
aware, dimly, "that Duke had this large water power and wanted to
negotiate with the Aluminum Company." In Pittsburgh to relax a day
or two, the Secretary naturally visited the office his brother still maintained for him around the Mellon National. "There is a daily meeting
there, and Davis comes to that daily meeting, and that is usually the
time I see him." Davis requested a favor. "Well, I recall that he said
that Mr. Duke would like to come to Washington and talk this business over in Washington."

Duke arrived for dinner on January 16. G. G. Allen appeared, and
Davis. Insofar as Mellon remembered, "The conversation was principally, almost wholly, on the part of Mr. Duke and me."

Mellon recognized, of course, that "there was always the possibility

The leadership of Alcoa—(Arthur Davis,
sixth from left, top row)

ALCOA

of his [Duke's] going into the [aluminum] business," but neither
tycoon was so unfeeling as to broach a subject like that. Bauxite
sources remained available, the Secretary observed passingly, "in Italy
and in Austria and Yugoslavia, and then in South America, and also
to some extent in this country, although there is very little in this
country of the grade of metallic content that would make it profitable." But why fret this, since "So far as the aluminum business is
concerned, for a great many years I have depended entirely on Mr.
Davis . . ."? Almost entirely; in this situation, "Well, I suppose he
recognized whatever was done would be—that I would be a factor in
it, whatever it was."

Mellon had urged Davis to get after that Île Maligne power. But
Duke demanded merger. A.W. would recapitulate that supper on
Massachusetts Avenue as largely an inspirational by Duke: the steps
he followed in acquiring the perimeter of Lake St. John, his franchise
to raise the water level seventeen feet, the anticipated million horsepower, the way the paper industry, like the electric business, tapped
nature's "perpetual motion" for benefits—and profits—ad infinitum.

The rearrangement took proportions. A.W. left R.B. the drudgery of "making the reappraisement of the Aluminum property and making an exchange with Duke."

By April 15 rough documents were drawn; the restructured corporation allocated "Duke and his associates" a ninth of the shares distributed, with provision later on to allow the North Carolinian in for up to an additional 4 percent. In July (railroad cars jiggling tandem throughout the pull to Quebec) officers of both companies as well as Mr. Duke and Mr. A. W. Mellon and his brother perused these breathtaking united properties. Davis had already drafted orders to dredge a regulation tidewater harbor at Chute à Caron. Rolling south, legal papers to recapitalize the entity, with $150,000,000 of common and $150,000,000 preferred, appeared upon a table in one of the smokers. Everybody present recalled signing. Even A. W. Mellon; unaccountably, afterward, his signature had disappeared.

Passingly, counsel for the plaintiff wondered whether the accommodating Treasurer remembered anything about "one George D. Haskell, of Springfield, Mass., or of any other place."

Mellon suspected he did. "Well, I have read—not during all this time, I have not heard of him"—clarity here was important—"but I have read of the suit in the papers."

3

Mellon's Aluminum involvement, enshrined in printed testimony, loosened up serious interest all around the Hill. It attracted the first wary drifting of reporters toward Patman's hectic antechambers. Was the Treasurer . . . implicated? Innumerable wowsers chafed. The old fellow *looked* immaculate, but for a public official who announced himself as uninterested in commerce "as if I had died," his specter wafted vivaciously.

Historical moments collide. Patman was barely under way before a concurrent Senate inquiry, chaired by Hiram Johnson before the Senate Finance Committee, broke open a series of diplomatic and banking coincidences which involved the Treasurer. In his self-justifying hurry Patman couldn't be put off waiting for galleys of Johnson's hearing; he tore the information he spotted directly out of the Baltimore *Sun*'s communiqués. "Senator Johnson," ran a January 7 story, "also elicited the information from Governor Jones, chief of the Finance Division of the Commerce Department, that a $20,000,-000 credit had been extended to Colombia by the National City Bank simultaneously with the granting of a clear title to the Mellon-owned Gulf Oil Company for the famous Barco concession. This tract, held to be one of the most valuable oil reserves in the world, had been withheld from the Mellon firm just prior to the granting of the credit, but was restored to the company immediately afterward, Mr. Jones admitted."

Johnson, a burly California Progressive, was bumping around a succession of pretentious commercial flunkies, hoping for unintended divulgences. Something buried was trembling. He'd surfaced one lead. Early in 1931, at a State Department banquet, A. W. Mellon had encountered President Olaya Herrera of Colombia. There had been exchanges.

"I explained to him [Mellon] how we were going through a grave situation . . ." Olaya was directly quoted during an interview in *El Tiempo* of Bogota. "Mr. Mellon told me then: After you settle those questions pending in matters of oil; after you settle in a just and equitable manner the difficulties confronting you in this respect; and as soon as you adopt a policy to give stability to the industrial activities of those enterprises, there will be open for Colombia without any doubt wide roads for its economic progress and its financial restoration."

The Treasurer himself, struggling, was able to recall the sketchiest of conversations with the esteemed Olaya. Nothing about the Gulf Company. Or State Department officials. No New York bankers, certainly. Mellon's subordinate Alexander Gregg produced a cable from Doctor Olaya in which the Colombian president specified that he had never discussed either the Barco concession or credits to his government with Mellon; the "mention" by the Treasury Secretary "regarding the possibilities that the petroleum riches of Colombia offer for its restoration were incidental. . . ."

Washington chopped everything overfine, so far as Pittsburgh could judge. Gulf people in particular couldn't see how arrangements they'd worked so hard on could somehow prove improper. Ordinary commercial manipulations, provocative in this case because Olaya shot off his big slack Latino mouth, then backtracked under floodlights.

Such maneuvers as reactivating the Barco concession for Gulf were dictated by *policy*. National-interest considerations, not merely what oil people demanded. After 1918, ventures Ferdinand Lundberg, "it was also evident that Wilson's 'Copper Administration,' dominated by the National City Bank, was to be succeeded, no matter what figurehead adorned the White House, by an 'Oil Administration.' "

Even Hoover recognized that. "As our United States oil reserves were estimated by the Geological Survey at only twelve years and new discoveries seemed to be diminishing, the subject came up in Cabinet. President Harding asked me what could be done. Mr. Hughes supported a suggestion of mine that the practical thing was to urge our oil companies to acquire oil territory in South America and elsewhere before the European companies preempted all of it. As a result, a conference of all the leading oil producers was called, and such action taken that most of the available oil lands in South America were acquired by Americans."

Not that the majors awaited prompting. By 1913 lease buyers for The Gulf had followed in Edward Doheny's stunning Potrero del Llano discoveries around Tampico and optioned adjacent countryside across those promising Mexican marshes. While armies of mercenary brigands on tick-ridden pintos with legs like dogs' blasted away on behalf of Standard Oil or the British Mexican Eagle, contract technicians from Pittsburgh labored unnoticed, blending into historical shadows, with nothing to volunteer unconnected with ramming down casings. As talk of expropriation became general after 1924, those Mexican Gulf straw bosses had tied into epochal gushers like Toteco Number 4; half of Gulf's production suddenly originated in Mexico.

Too suddenly, perhaps. By 1927 a welter of confiscatory export taxes and abruptly rescinded drilling permits compelled a begrudging Coolidge to sacrifice his private angel, Dwight Morrow of J. P. Morgan and Company, to charm the requisite concessions from Mexico's sticky President Calles. Gulf moved warily on.

Venezuela appeared inviting. Geologists for the company selected the "Marine Zone" just inside the beaches of lush Lake Maracaibo. Subequatorial politics were staple. The calcified Venezuelan dictator, Gomez, held down inflammatory speechmaking by suspending his nation's more obstreperous malcontents all along La Rotunda's mitered stone interiors with meat hooks peeking through their jaws.

Committed to the area, planners around The Gulf glanced over from time to time to see what Harry Doherty had made of that mountainous million-and-a-half-acre bulge he'd optioned in 1917, General Vigilio de Barco's fief along Colombia's Venezuelan border. Doherty kept 75 percent; the Morgan bank came in for most of the rest. Wall Street dubbed the speculation the Carib Corporation. The terrain appeared promising, but exploitation was delayed in Bogota by a hysterical Upper House and successive presidents, traditional gringo-revilers, who insisted that production flow west over a projected 350-mile pipeline through Motilón Indian country. The stone-age Motilón were inaccessible to anthropologists, but they were represented by artifacts—stubby little poisoned arrows, winged from behind trunks, bursting beyond marsh leaves, with punch enough to perforate whole gangs of terrified coastal laborers. Costly rigs suffered vandalism, and there were incessant and mysterious fires.

Doherty curtailed preliminary planning. The concession was available; in January of 1926 Gulf exercised a prearranged option on Doherty's share of the rights for a million and a quarter dollars. Colombian officials, alerted, unilaterally canceled the concession.

The acquisition was distressed; nobody blamed the underlings. "Do you mean, Mr. Gregg, that Mr. Mellon was never consulted by the Gulf Oil Corporation officials with regard to the Barco concession, worth about two billion dollars?" Patman's sympathizer, Congressman Oliver of New York, demanded of the astute Government attorney.

Gregg recovered tellingly. "No sir, I did not say that at all. That is what I was very careful not to say."

Mellon wouldn't be rushed. Fresh strikes in Texas and Oklahoma filled in the production on line from Mexico and Venezuela; accumulated capital was earmarked for five huge refineries. Standard too had properties in recalcitrant Colombia, so both companies retained Arthur Loomis and Allen W. Dulles, recently of the State Department, to take their grievance directly to President Coolidge. The President was compassionate; soon afterward Secretary of State Kellogg, in formal diplomatic protest, urged that the American companies be allowed to pursue their claims before the Colombian courts. This immediately loosed squalls of anti-*norteamericano* publicity.

Mellon kept his counsel; that same week the Department of Commerce issued Special Circular of September 29, 1928. Investments in Colombian bonds, the Circular advised, were, in all probability, unsafe.

Gunboat diplomacy works overnight. Economic strangulation requires patience. Recessions, taking hold, snuff marginal economies first. By early 1930 the coffee aristocrats and banana cultivators who dominated Colombia were secretly wondering whether they hadn't overindulged their emotions as they selected Dr. Enrique Olaya

Herrera for president. A disastrous deficit opened; unless the government could arrange support from foreign-capital centers, national bankruptcy portended. For nearly a year Olaya toe-danced discreetly among Victor Schoepperle of the National City Company, State Department officials, a Princeton financial expert, and George Rublee, the lawyer at Dwight Morrow's elbow while he was straightening out the Mexicans.

Olaya's was a courtship dandle, a lift of invitation, macho's traditional alternate opening. Washington prepared its machine. Tensions must be eased; afterward, propriety depended on secrecy and amnesia. The congress in Bogota had never quit fulminating. Subsequently, a City Bank employee conceded, all innocence, to Hiram Johnson's investigators that his organization routinely "took no interest in foreign loans," and only went along with the twenty-million-dollar credit to Colombia because "State Department officials had mentioned various things President Enrique Olaya was doing for American interests, including a favorable settlement of the Barco concession."

Secretary Mellon's nudge? The Treasurer's misunderstood observation, under clouds of crystal, that what was inflamed might yet be assuaged? Disinterested advice, received appreciatively. Hadn't everybody benefited?

That was what mattered. "He didn't think of his fortune as a big pile of money just sitting there," Paul Mellon said afterward. "He thought of it as working for all the people the companies employed, the economy." If, circumstances permitting, A.W. could help—who respected outdated legalisms?

Pondering Patman's charges, his head cocked sideways, A.W. often shrugged at how most reformers got everything hindside to. Those piratical oil-company machinations! One longed to explain what actually was happening.

One obviously never could. The so-called American majors were reminiscent of a neighborhood society of overendowed little boys, convened whenever need arose by a hollow-cheeked State Department zealot. Unhappy, sitting along the outstretched lower branches of a buttonwood tree, ankles banging, forever whining with demands, but then not pleased at all to discover the favors Their Government expected *them* to perform. Few appreciated the challenges. Gulf, the podgy fellow, already bulky but insular, still tended to moisten his britches every time some rite of manhood looked unavoidable.

The zone for risks and initiation once World War I got settled was patently the susceptible Middle East. Unlucky Turkey had taken its chances with the Central Powers. One theater of British Expeditionary Force maneuver had been the Arabian subcontinent; that big dangling Ottoman remnant, Byzantium's final sandy hope. Tribal war and subterfuge left Britain overweening among the sheikdoms and sultanates.

Dependable Middle Eastern oil had become a Foreign Office fixation as early as 1908, when crude spurted up quite near the Mosque of Solomon in western Iran, and prompted geological surveys which predicted the oceans of petroleum trapped under the limestone along the Persian Gulf littoral. Prodded by Winston Churchill, the government of Great Britain bought in for 51 percent of the Anglo-Persian Oil Company; this arrangement survived reorganizations into the Anglo-Iranian Oil Company in 1935 and, finally, B.P. (British Petroleum) in 1954. It, along with half-English Shell, kept discreet employees prowling throughout the decade before Versailles. Brushing Arab expectations aside, the French and British convened diplomats to carve the petroleum-laden area into Gallic (blue) and English (red) protectorates.

Officialdom in Washington turned over. The document of dismemberment, the 1920 San Remo agreement, couldn't be suppressed indefinitely. When details escaped, the American Ambassador in London delivered a "strong note," which accused the Foreign Office of scheming to hog the democratic world's principal reserves. The U. S. Geological Survey bemoaned the American position as "precarious." Affronted Londoners might protest that 82 percent of production just then came from the United States or Mexico. *Americans* hadn't fought Turkey.

Nobody's heart appeared softened. American interests demanded protection. Andrew Mellon was Secretary of the Treasury. The troublesome Winston Churchill was out; refinancing the British war debt in America on salutory terms was critical to the incoming Conservatives. The economic survival of Europe overall, and the United Kingdom especially, was coming to depend, and pressingly, on access to American money markets. Montagu Norman visited America.

Jibbed, bludgeoned, pestered endlessly by couriers and drowning in communiqués, the Foreign Office reconsidered. Let the Americans participate. After 1922 as much as 20 percent of the Turkish Petroleum Company, Anglo-Persian's principal affiliate, opened to American investors.

And then? "The State Department had gradually pushed the door into Iraq open," Anthony Sampson writes, "but the oil companies went through it with some reluctance." One was particularly hesitant. "As the Gulf representative, Charles Hamilton, described it, 'representatives of the industry were called to Washington and told to go out and get it.'"

"It" looked forbiddingly exotic. The Turkish Petroleum Company, a syndicate which started up initially to explore for crude along the banks of the Tigris, lay in the dominating squat shadow of one quirky visionary, "Mr. Five Percent," Calouste Sarkis Gulbenkian. Since 1914, through wars and politics, the nimble Armenian deal-maker bounced all over Europe and the Middle East, playing hunches, joining irreconcilables, brokering industrial modernity. Those delicate Balkan eyes beneath brows like starling wings bulged with enough curiosity to tickle answers from a sarcophagus.

From Constantinople to Aden, that decade, reality was pretty much what Gulbenkian decided it was. This bothered the Armenian's new partners. Of the seven American companies which participated in the Iraq concession, five, including Gulf, quickly sold their shares. The business was unmanageable enough—east Texas ruptured prices; once profitability looked stronger the Bolsheviks flooded markets. During lulls the majors diligently ripped one another to pieces.

One day in 1928, under cover of grouse shooting, the leaders of most of the world's important petroleum producers appeared at Achnacarry Castle in Scotland to divide the oil business. The "As Is" agreements established, ad perpetuity, pricing and production quotas. W. L. Mellon attended.

Months later, in Ostend, the successor to Turkish Petroleum, Iraq Petroleum, convened the historic conference at which the sprightly Gulbenkian picked up his legendary red pencil and defined for the interests—Gulf was a noninvested signatory—the perimeter of the prewar Turkish Empire, whose resources Iraq Petroleum reserved. Gulbenkian's demarcation excluded Persia and an arrowhead-shaped jog inland which verged on the northwest beaches of the Persian Gulf.

This jog was Kuwait. In 1923 a plump and beguiling New Zealander knockabout, Major Frank Holmes, bought himself an option for mineral rights throughout the Persian Gulf island group of Bahrain. The territory of Bahrain was completely a British protectorate, identified more closely with India than the Arabian subcontinent and presided over by His Highness Shaikh Sir Ahmed al Jabir al Subah, K.C.S.I., K.C.I.E., ruler of the Kingdom of Kuwait. Holmes picked up traces of petroleum among the islands, and bustled to the United States to cash right in. The Americans were hesitant. Standard Oil of New Jersey turned down the major's firm asking price of fifty thousand dollars. Finally, in 1927, Holmes approached Gulf Oil. Gulf dispatched Ralph Rhodes, the company's chief geologist and ultimately its president, to investigate Holmes's findings and submit his recommendation. Rhodes saw some promise, and W.L. authorized the commitment.

They owned it; suddenly Bahrain roused shivers. Geologists for Anglo-Persian clucked over the absence of significant "Oligocene–Miocene" formations. Consultants from Iraq Petroleum, where Gulf retained affiliations, rolled out Gulbenkian's map to show the bottom of one red French curve which clearly included Bahrain as part of the earlier Turkish suzerainty. Sheepishly, Gulf repossessed its original fifty thousand dollars by remarketing Holmes's option for Bahrain to an American outsider, Standard Oil of California. The British interests balked, but State Department heavyweights quickly extorted a compromise.

Gulf retained first refusal on deposits underneath the Kuwaiti mainland. W.L. sent Holmes back. British technical men insisted the fly-ridden little jetty for dhows was barren of petroleum. They ridiculed the tar sands the Bedouins still plastered all over their beasts to remedy camel mange. Still, Holmes noticed, a young bemonocled Anglo-Persian representative, Archibald Chisholm, was around a lot, attempting to ingratiate himself with the wary Shaikh. Then oil was struck in Bahrain in June of 1932.

That broke things open. Sir John Cadman of Anglo-Persian and Gulf's Frank Drake came together to negotiate a joint bid to the Shaikh for mainland concessionary rights. A mysterious third party, Traders, moved in to jump the bidding until the persevering Holmes got to the Shaikh, who preferred American participation, and convinced him Traders was Chisholm's device. In fact, it wasn't—though certainly it might have been.

By now the British Foreign Office had hopes of enforcing a British nationality clause. Gulf officials alerted State; Secretary of State Henry Stimson immediately telegraphed his newly appointed Ambassador to the Court of Saint James's, Andrew Mellon, to urge the British to respect the "Open Door" policy toward Middle East oil. This produced more pained English policy reappraisal—the pound was softening. Mellon did not falter. The authoritative Sampson reports that negotiations to protect Gulf's foothold were pursued by A.W.'s Minister, Ray Atherton, "but Mellon's interest was evident in the background, and at one point he personally sent a stiff note to the Foreign Office for which he was reproved by the State Department."

Politics lifted; businessmen sat down. The resulting agreement divided the Kuwaiti pool between Anglo-Persian and Gulf. The great British holding would set the schedule of exploitation to ensure that production didn't upset returns worldwide. Gulf, whenever necessary, might draw on crude from Anglo-Persian's Iranian wells. The U. S. majors now gave the Open Door its decisive bang shut.

Unmentioned on distribution lists for coded diplomatic cables or seal-embossed attaché reports, Wright Patman continued tugging loose the information he needed from court transcripts and newspaper speculation and overlooked security registration forms. Whatever bore on Mellon, whatever ripped free details.

He spied something additional. The bond thing, the rearrangement they dubbed the Union Gulf Corporation—ol' Mellon in office, and back in Pittsburgh they're movin' his securities around. The Congressman hectored witness after witness to elucidate that bang-tailed monstrosity.

There were business explanations. By 1930 The Gulf had outgrown mere measurement by profit and loss. It was an institution. Automobiles proliferated; the arithmetic of oil dictated unstinting production. Frank Leovy earmarked millions for tinkering with gravimeters, working up geological biopsies of slushpit residues, coring sequences which graded the richness, the promise, of layers of shale and veins of metamorphic float. A scraping of sludge was frequently enough. The scrawl behind a seismograph needle along a curl of graph paper read like a suicide's testament to geophysicists among the hundreds of technicians who worked the Harmarville laboratories outside Pittsburgh. Ship out the instruments, new risk was justified.

Buy! Leases cost; breakthroughs left accountants shaken. Gulf-pride alone, their massively advertised motor oil which utilized the Alchor process, emerged from a multimillion-dollar struggle to re-arrange a hydrocarbon molecule in caldrons of chlorine and bauxite at temperatures so fierce the firebrick got blasted each time to a bubbled husk. Undergoing spinal tap worldwide, Nature whimpered secrets begrudgingly. Her demands became exorbitant. Mushrooming tank farms, pumping stations by hundreds, a navy of carriers from river barges to tanker fleets, balloon-wheeled marsh buggies wobbling deep into bayous. . . .

Most staggering—those refineries. Rounding off a decade in which the company's own bookkeepers admitted to an asset rise from $200,000,000 to half a billion, the managers at Gulf bought up the Paragon Refining Company for seventy million dollars. The acquisi-tion added three new refineries, including a prime facility at Toledo, Ohio. This ran off cash reserves, but planners were adamant: Stan-dard Oil of New Jersey had already overtaken Gulf with respect to the crude it lifted. A big Middle Western refinery would soak up Gulf's Texas and Oklahoma surpluses and provide a marshaling point from which to go after Standard throughout the industrial heartland.

This meant a pipeline across the South to Toledo. Pipelines were invariably expensive; preliminary estimates ran up around sixty mil-lion dollars. They'd have to borrow. Currently, months after the '29 blistering, this was no marketplace to peddle negotiables. Attorneys for the company sat down with Union Trust underwriters. By June of 1930 the paper work was drafted which authorized an issue of sixty million dollars' worth of Union Gulf Corporation collateral trust sinking fund 5-percent bonds. To reassure regular customers and keep the interest low, the bonds were backed to 130 percent of face value with personal securities put up by all three Mellons. The formula required A.W. and R.B. each to maintain enough certificates to cover 46 percent of seventy-eight million dollars. W.L. pledged 8 percent. Gulf reimbursed the backers a fraction of a point.

This guarantee was window dressing. Gulf's net for 1929 ap-proached thirty million dollars, and not even A.W.'s own attorneys saw fit to quarrel with the indignant Patman's charges that by the start of 1932 the oil company's assets still ran around $761,000,000. Conservatively—even that late—holdings by the brothers ran into several hundreds of millions. Union Gulf would certainly never default its interest payments. Only a nit-picking yokel could find anything questionable.

4

Yet Patman wasn't misled. Union Gulf itself materialized because the joint account was plump with a congeries of recent trading acquisitions, impervious packets of securities the brothers picked up by disposing of well-used secondary companies. Leading the Union Gulf "trust indenture" was a 200,000-share block of shares in Pullman, Inc., half the financial remains of Standard Steel Car.

"On January 23, 1923," Colonel Drake remembers precisely, "I happened to be home from Washington for the weekend, and R.B. sends for me. 'We got a new job for you. We're going to send you over to Standard Steel Car. They're in bad shape. This damned Standard automobile has cost us a lot of money, lost millions. We want you to go over as of tomorrow morning. We three have talked it over.'

"John Hansen, the president, tipped his elbow once in a while. He had a fine technical organization, and he was much beloved. I was as welcome as a skunk in a lawn party. They elected me a vice-president, and assigned me to a little office in the Oliver Building.

"I went right back and talked to R.B. I said, Mister Mellon, I can't do what you want with the title of vice-president. He gave me authority. I went back and had a little talk with Hansen. I told him, they're going to make a little change around here in the titles. Would you like to be president or chairman? I don't want any credit, I don't know anything about engineering, so I'll handle the financial and administrative side, you stay with sales and the engineering."

Hansen wanted chairman. Drake rebuilt the company. He moved the Pittsburgh Equitable Meter Company into the abandoned automobile plant and imported a lively engineer, Willard Rockwell, to take that over. "Somebody in the bank poisoned R.B.'s mind about Rockwell," Drake says, and subsequently the Mellons sold off the business. Drake kept his stock and wound up heavy in Rockwell International.

"Making railroad cars," Drake determined, "was not a very happy business. Always peaks and valleys. You'd lose a lot, and then you'd gain a lot. It got to be 1929, and by that time the Mellons were looking around for assets they could put into that Union Gulf thing. It seemed to me a merger with Pullman made sense all around. I told R.B. I'd like to get to work arranging a merger. The Mellons would wind up with a lot of marketable securities they could use as collateral, and Pullman would have forty-one percent of the railroad-car business."

By then the Morgan Bank had control of Pullman. Drake and David Crawford of the Pullman Company pieced out the rearrangement. Once that was agreed, J. P. Morgan, Jr., and George Whitney and Drake shook hands in London. Just before the three climbed aboard the liner *Olympic* to return to America, the stock market crumbled. Morgan and Whitney invited Drake to cocktails once the boat was asea. "B' God, I didn't bring the deal up," Drake stresses. "I was afraid they wouldn't go through with it."

Whitney asked to present himself to A. W. Mellon "to tell him how pleased we are to hook up with the Mellons." Drake scheduled the meeting. There were introductory pleasantries, and then Whitney added " 'one other thing. We'd like to have Drake head up the Pullman Company as chairman.'

"I never saw A. W. Mellon actually fuss before," Drake says, "but it took him a little while before he admitted that that could be arranged." But briefly, since " 'We have other things in mind for him.' "

Drake, rehearsing openmouthed, concedes, "I was flabbergasted." He summons up that year of regular board meetings; the membership included Whitney and Morgan and George Baker and Alfred Vanderbilt and Alfred Sloan of General Motors.

"Can you imagine," Drake marvels, "a little squirt like me presidin' over fellows like that?"

On March 30, 1930, Pullman took possession of the manufacturing assets of Standard Steel Car; the Mellons acquired Pullman stock, 400,000 shares altogether, and a little over eight million dollars in cash. Each brother got 40 percent, and W.L. got just over 6 percent of a settlement worth $38,700,000.

The divestment of Marshall-McClintic proceeded simultaneously. Family members would cherish Charles Marshall's fine statement that "All we ever had to do was to state and explain our problem to Andrew Mellon. Invariably, he replied with a double-barreled question: 'How much do you want? And when?' " Increasingly, as engineers launched projects as vast as the seventy-story RCA building in Manhattan and the sprawling Tata mills in Jamshedpur, India, both Marshall and McClintic fell out of the habit of consulting as fully as both their bankers wanted.

John Buchanan, the company's attorney, never forgot an exchange between Marshall and A. W. Mellon inside the Massachusetts Avenue apartment. Marshall, rushed, himself authorized new preferred. Complications unleashed a stockholders' suit, which the construction company lost. Marshall expected the brothers to absorb the damage judgment, but the affronted Treasurer remained "persistent and argumentative," although he agreed in the end that he and his brother would pay off their 60 percent of the $180,000 settlement.

By then Andrew Mellon was accumulating the dowry of the National Gallery. While Charles Marshall pleaded, Buchanan had "ants in my pants because I wanted to see those paintings so badly. He never showed us around. I thought that was not up to A.W.'s stature."

By 1931 the McClintic-Marshall operation had repaid its founders eight million dollars in dividends. Capital requirements were prodigious. Union Trust generally provided, if not too eagerly. After a touchy negotiation, the mills and most of the secondary assets went along to Bethlehem Steel; the partners took seventy million dollars. Better to hold capital. Unpredictable times were rising.

8 | A PERMANENT GIFT

1

IN UNEXPECTED WAYS, the years in Washington slowly regenerated emotions A.W. imagined were over. The heart aged whimsically. Once, scorched, the best one hoped was that civility would survive.

A surprising amount did. Shyly, he resumed his correspondences with Nora's jovial brothers. Paul remembered boisterous uncles like indefatigable Percy, who took him up in an airplane he'd engineered for himself. It survived its takeoff, although it arrived at very little altitude before it settled its nose abruptly into a neighboring meadow, tail erect. After that Paul grasped the indulgence with which his father treated the assorted ex-brothers-in-law, to whom he regularly extended advice and cash, until, in the end, it actually seemed simpler to set up most of them with adequate little trust funds. About the brothers (as about Nora) he and his affectionate ex-mother-in-law remained in effective agreement.

Nora had been foundering. The passage of years had taken them little by little from telephone conversations kept strictly to arrangements for the children, through appointments for tea, until, just about the time A.W. reached Washington, they started to exchange regular birthday greetings and telegrams and chatted long-distance whenever either was tempted. Without ado, the banker ultimately sent his free-spending ex-wife securities enough to boost her income an extra thirty thousand dollars a year. As the children matured he presented Nora with country homes. There were successive residences near Hudson, New York, as well as Litchfield, Connecticut. Ultimately,

A.W. bought Nora the four-hundred-acre Rokeby estate of Admiral Cary Grayson, near Upperville, Virginia.

Then, without warning, in November of 1922, Nora sent her ex-husband word of her imminent marriage to Harvey Arthur Lee, a New York art dealer. Mellon found himself bereft; he immediately wrote Nora and asked her to consider, then, the possibility of re-marrying him. Her reply was galvanizing. "If only you could have given me the faintest hope during all those years," she began, "I would have waited till I died, but the hope I had had gradually died and it was then that I felt I could no longer bear this dreadful loneli-ness. This is not a reproach, dear Andy. I have not the shadow of one in my heart for you. It is just a dreadful tragedy, at least for me. . . . Dear, dear Andy, even though I feel I have a mortal in-ward, bleeding wound, still I am so grateful not to have died without telling you how much I have loved and missed you all these years. As long as I live, it will always be the same. I shall try very hard to be brave and regain some peace when I am once more among my flowers. Think kindly of me sometimes and, if you can, write me."

Mellon replied:

Dear Norchen,

I have read your letter and it has grieved me deeply, while at the same time bringing solace and abiding comfort.

I have been sadly wrong but must tell you how it was that I did not speak sooner. In the years of contention there was on your part a seeming animosity and bitterness which I did not believe could dis-appear.

When suggestions were made of conciliation I believed you un-feeling and did not think you could really care for me. However wrongly, I attributed to you motives of expediency and convenience.

I did not believe that any love existed for me, and so when I heard of your engagement to Mr. Lee it only gave me a heavy heart. When I learned that the day was close at hand I had a twinge of pain and felt that I must see you. It was then the revelation and understanding came to me. It proved too late—your letter was so *final*.

The old love was in my heart even while I was so obtuse and blind, and it makes me heartsick to think of you in all this time suffering so sadly alone. The past can not be brought back and we must now look to the future. You have had more than your share of unhappiness and are entitled to brighter days.

I want to be helpful to you now and always. You must look forward and not allow anything of the past to distress you. Interest in the farm and garden will do much and your married life can become a happy and contented one.

For myself, aside from all else, the truth of our understanding remains, and it is an abiding comfort in my heart. I shall be interested in your life and pray for your happiness.

I hope you are now feeling well and strong again.

God bless you, dearest Norchen,

Your ever loving
ANDY

In 1926 Ailsa married. "She had a lovely glamorous time in Washington," her cousin Peggy remembers. "She never was really a *gay* person, but she was very wise, a lot of the men told me. She had a lot of common sense, she thought things out and didn't agree with everybody." Her energies went into managing their floor of 1785 Massachusetts Avenue. She planned the increasingly frequent dinner parties and accompanied her father to social events and ceremonials. "She was a beautiful young woman," the man she married says, "full of spirit, with a model's figure, and seemingly in perfect health. She rode horseback almost every day, went to innumerable parties, and had a large circle of friends and acquaintances in Washington and New York."

Ailsa's fiancé was David Kirkpatrick Estes Bruce. David Bruce at twenty-eight could probably have brought out anybody. His was a cultivated coltishness, chipper and well brushed, overflowingly eligible for recognition. The Bruces were people one took into account. David first met Ailsa at a dance while visiting his father, William Cabell Bruce, an established Baltimore lawyer and enough of a writer to have won the Pulitzer Prize in 1918 for his biography of Franklin. In 1923 the father began a term as U. S. Senator from Maryland (Democratic), and David, just out of law school himself after Princeton and two years of artillery duty during World War I, was regularly around Washington.

He had the impulse to experiment. In 1924–25 Bruce got himself elected to the Maryland House of Delegates. Meanwhile, "I fell in love with Ailsa. In the latter part of 1925 I began to call on her frequently, especially after I had moved to Washington to prepare for my entry into the Foreign Service. There was an interval between the time I passed the examinations and actual assignment to a State

Ailsa enjoying Washington
PAUL MELLON

Department position. During it, I returned to my law office in Baltimore, but saw Ailsa as often as I could."

Their wedding ceremony was, inevitably, a mid-decade event. Ailsa
looked almost happy, exiting on the sleeve of her zestful bridegroom's
cutaway, her squint and lankiness and the precise turbaning of her
veil giving her the thrust, momentarily, of a contented goose smelling
water. The rites had occurred at the Washington Episcopal Cathedral;
President and Mrs. Coolidge were among the attending. If there was
discussion of staging the ceremony in Pittsburgh, or Presbyterian, no
mention comes down. Such decisions were Ailsa's. What concerned
the Treasurer, who worried about fortune hunters, was the selection
itself, and Mellon identified immediately upon the cultured, tactful
young patrician the imprimatur of practicality. "In Pittsburgh and
elsewhere," Bruce characterized the banker, "he was famous for his
judgment about men and affairs. His often dreamy look cloaked a
will of steel."

Right after the wedding the pair went directly to Italy, where
Bruce took up his duties in Rome as a Vice Consul. They leased a
sumptuous residence. And there, within weeks, she succumbed to the

Pushing off for Bermuda—Paul,
Ailsa, Sir Robert Horne, A.W.
LIBRARY OF CONGRESS

Mrs. David K. E. Bruce
(with bridegroom)
LIBRARY OF CONGRESS

The Bruces receive
LIBRARY OF CONGRESS

mysterious ailment which was to blight her life and reduce her to struggling semi-invalidism. Bruce describes it nicely: "Her indecision, that some people remarked upon in her later life, was, I am convinced, a product of ill health, which commenced within a couple of weeks of our arrival at Rome in July, 1926. She began to run a high fever daily and nightly. At first Italian physicians diagnosed it as 'sand-fly fever,' at that time a frequent malady during Roman summers.

"As her condition persisted, yielding to no applied treatments, she lost weight, could take no exercise, and was advised to go to the Doctor Kocher clinique in Berne, Switzerland, for further diagnosis. This famous doctor at first thought she might be tubercular, but after many examinations that speculation was dropped. By then it was evident that she was dangerously ill, and no diagnosis either then or in her later life ever revealed the true cause of the almost incessant temperature that made her health subnormal. Finally, her state was such that Dr. Kocher informed me that she might die within two or three weeks, and felt I should so advise her father. I did so; he immediately came to Berne from Washington and remained there until it was clear that although she was still seriously ill, she was no longer in immediate danger.

"For a year there was no marked improvement, so we arranged to go back to Washington to live at least temporarily."

Ailsa returned to service, however unsteadily, as her father's chatelaine. David Bruce stood by. Helpful, if making no pretense of hiding his belief that before much longer he'd better start redeeming chits. David felt his breeding—that good, lank, hunt-country mane of hair, his height, those wide-set light eyes of such unembarrassed gravity they appeared at moments to dispense with blinking. Everybody accepted David's credentials. He demonstrated a connoisseur's quickness, a gut for speculations, a gift for badinage and unbudgeable good humor when that was necessary. He displayed, in fact, the moves of a natural courtier.

New York seemed appropriate for trying them out. Bruce "maintained," as the saying went, "business interests" in the city. His service in one government interrupted, he assumed his position in another. Still officing in the house in Jackson Place in Washington where Donald Shepard and, later, David Finley and the young Paul Mellon maintained their desks, Bruce's business importance radiated until he ultimately served on twenty-five boards of corporations, from Westinghouse Electric to the racetrack in Rockingham, New Hampshire. He "was associated" with various banking houses, including W. A. Harriman Company; he served on the board of the Union Pacific Railroad. Averell Harriman was grooming Bruce personally.

He'd acquired a brother-in-law. As regards Paul Mellon, Bruce writes, "I have known him since his college days. My personal feeling about him and affection for him is that I would have had for a younger brother." A brother whose priorities, Bruce realized, differed sharply from his: "It appeared evident in his early youth that he would not engross himself in strictly business occupations except out of a sense of duty. His inclinations were more toward humanistic concerns."

Paul was at Yale. Classmates identified Paul's gait—his way of edging, with the barest of smiles, toward undiscussed enchantments. The family made out Paul's inherited wiriness, along with the instinct to spare the emotions. Paul too wouldn't argue with destiny. George Wyckoff still laughs about the afternoon the schoolboy—not much at athletics around Choate, and mortified about that—decided to look over hockey, and trudged to the rink. A puck lifted immediately and banged him in the eye. Paul never went back.

Bystanders subsequently pegged Paul as one to keep to himself except for durable, culled friendships. He exhibited that sharp Mellon widow's peak, the drooped strong nose which obscured (halfway) a sidelong lens-avoiding narrowing of his look. He was, by reputation, shy. His mood was cautious; an ambivalence played fitfully across his tiny Mellon mouth, uneven as a scar, like an excised beak.

Paul was, like Andrew, of such preoccupying tastes it took some effort to confront responsibilities. To regard himself seriously. At Yale he became a candidate for the *News*, an ordeal which cost him plenty of sleep and kept him scurrying among shopkeepers to solicit advertising. He survived the healing and—with typical doggedness— eventually became vice-chairman. An essay on Donn Byrne won Paul the McLaughlin Prize during his freshman year; he crowned his undergraduate work by becoming an editor of the literary magazine, an important honor.

Popular distinctions seemed artificial. When Skull and Bones tapped Paul as preeminent among the fifteen "glamour people" in his class he turned that down and proceeded with several friends into Scroll and Key. No gentleman did that. He acquired a reputation, like Kipling's famous Cat, as one who walked by himself, and all places were alike to him.

All but a few. "It was a bad system," Paul Mellon said afterward, "and the fraternity system was a bad system. I had two roommates. One, Lennie Mudge, at least was accepted by one of the clubs. The other, Jack Douglas, was left out of it entirely." Paul wasn't really egalitarian; he was just doubtful of any arrangement which favored the football captain over people he thought had something to say.

"At Yale," Wyckoff says, "there were six or eight of us. The rest are gone now—Chauncey Hubbard, Carmody, Nick Brady, Moorhead. Paul was a pretty good student. He could have been better. I remember one time I found out late in the afternoon I had to have in a paper in the history of art. I didn't know about that stuff. I borrowed a paper of Paul's and changed it around a bit. I got an A. He'd gotten an A-minus, and he was really annoyed." Wyckoff also remembered Mellon's problems when he got caught with liquor in his room. "They told him to go home and tell his parents. That was a doozer, what with A.W. in charge of prohibition. Paul informed his mother.

"Everybody who really knew Paul liked him," Wyckoff concludes. "He had a great sense of humor. He just enjoyed life." This constituted Paul's secret—for all the modesty, those gestures of habitual self-effacement, his personality was nourished by freshets of pleasure. In his quiet way—elfin even at moments—this somehow got over. Paul's company was disarming; he made your bones feel lighter.

2

Paul's father was rightfully proud. Occasional visitors in Washington were pushed to appreciate odd scraps of editorial matter from the *Yale News*. One thing and another, the Twenties had provided much emotional vindication. Life gave; he gave.

Philanthropy required exceptional craftiness. The old man's beneficences, Lucius Beebe reports, were widespread and considerable. They ran from pianos for music students to support for deaf-and-dumb asylums. These he shrouded scrupulously, recoiling in "patrician hatred for anything savoring of personal popularity or seeming to cater to good will." Beebe mentions private Christmas celebrations devoted to burning the obligations of bad-luck creditors.

Burned them—like rags from lepers. Calvinism stirred. Certain generosities were unnatural, sops to the undeserving. Those Capital has rejected, no earthly measures redeem. Unconsidered exactions meant "destruction," as A.W. told Hoover while struggling to dissuade the engineer from recommending an inheritance tax. "It wiped out capital."

Wasn't there something productive? The summer of 1909, with Nora suddenly gone, the banker had been endeavoring to learn rudimentary French during his unused hours. One evening his effervescent tutor brought around a letter from a father in France, who thought he'd discovered something. Mellon sent the note around to a chemist at Gulf; within a few days the man reported that the supposed discovery was of no commercial value, and buttressed his opinion with a recently published volume called *The Chemistry of Commerce*, written with surprising charm by an Ontario-born professor of chemistry at the University of Kansas, Robert Kennedy Duncan.

"I read the book with interest," Mellon said much later, "but the part which particularly interested me was the last chapter in which Dr. Duncan described his plan for industrial fellowships, by means of which industry could utilize the services of qualified scientists. . . ." Mellon sent for Duncan.

Duncan appeared. Bones mostly, his crest of unearthly white hair tousling untended into wings. Would anybody really listen? The professor was wearying—too many approaches already to "manufacturers of the last generation" in hopes that one of these, "endowed with great natural ability but of small education," might overcome his disdain for the "theoretical fellow" and help rescue "American manufacture" from its "chaos of confusion and waste." None had; nobody understood. It worked both ways. "You are not going to let the jungle in here?" a mathematical physicist at Clark came back at Duncan's proposal that industry underwrite postgraduate research.

Mellon at least listened. Asked a few questions, grasped easily Duncan's thesis that "mechanical contrivances are but a small part of the operations of modern industry. Since every manufacturer deals with the modifications of substance and substance is the business of chemistry, every manufacturer is just exactly to that extent chemical." Understood idea and bearer—those burning hazel eyes, that fierce rejected vision.

Much fitted. "I was very much interested in these ideas of Dr. Duncan's," the banker said later, "for as a result of all my reading and observation it seemed to me that improvement in the standard of living of the human race could come about in the future only by reason of new discoveries and inventions, just as, in the past, the steam engine and other inventions had been responsible for many improvements in the standards of living enjoyed by the average man today. It was these things and not governmental or political action, that increased production, lowered costs, raised wages, elevated the standard of living and so had brought about a greater participation of the human race in these benefits."

Duncan returned to Kansas. Once, life meant breaking in on Mme. Curie in her Paris laboratory to hear personally "all about radium." *"Mon Américain,"* she'd labeled him fondly. Mellon shared her affection.

Samuel Black McCormick, chancellor of the renamed University of Pittsburgh—that same defunctive institution both Mellon and his father attended—had been tugging away at the uninterested banker for years, preaching at him, appealing to his sense of duty, even offering to pray for him. The buildings were decrepit. There were such deficits. Mellon bought him off with token amounts.

Duncan offered something practical. He had already established, in Kansas, a program within the department of industrial chemistry, a fellowship program that made available, to an industrial "donor," the services of qualified research people.

In Kansas the insurgent Duncan had felt himself crowded into a few basement rooms, underfunded by a stingy legislature, limited to such mundane problems as those which beset the bakers of salt-rising bread and inquiries into the diastatic content of dried alfalfa. Pittsburgh promised something fundamental. He accepted Mellon's offer. At first, the banker set him up in a rather disappointing two-story hutch of a building on the university grounds and provided, that initial three years, $52,000. Always attracted by building, R.B. matched that. By 1913 the laboratories were overcrowded. Responding to a call from Duncan, A.W. arrived in time to watch one scientist being hoisted by block and tackle into an attic workshop inaccessible by stairs.

"It looks to me, Dr. Duncan, as though you needed a new building," the banker observed. Duncan couldn't but agree. The brothers allocated $325,000 plus maintenance expenses to construct the Mellon Institute, dedicated to the memory of their father.

Muckrakers challenged their motives. "The Institute solved admirably the research problems of the Mellon corporations," suggests Harvey O'Connor. "Manufacturers wait their turn for access to its facilities." Success draws a crowd, and didn't the public include family companies? When a malignancy killed Duncan in 1914 his successor was Raymond F. Bacon, whom Duncan recruited personally to push his researches into the "cracking" of gasoline. The automobile was proliferating, and work at the Institute supplied Gulf key answers.

"We ultimately developed hundreds of patents for the Gulf," admits Bacon's successor cheerfully. Dr. Edward Weidlein, who'd helped Bob Duncan in Kansas, took on the Institute's presidency in 1921 and still bounces in and out of the laboratories, ebullient once, dismayed lately. "Time came they got so big I told them they'd have to move out. Mr. Leovy used to kick at the amount of money he had to pay in here. Later, when the Gulf set up their own research, Leovy called and said, why, it's costin' us four times as much!"

The brothers seldom interfered; the times they did they predicted their needs. Weidlein remembers a day late in the Twenties when R.B. summoned him along with Arthur Vining Davis. "I'm going to insist that the Institute develop a process for chrome-plating aluminum. It's going to be valuable in automobiles. I want Aluminum to endow a fellowship and find a scientist to work up the technology." One concocted a finish.

Nevertheless, Weidlein insisted, most things just followed. After World War I broke out, Weidlein developed the equipment that permitted the recovery of toluene from carburated water gas for TNT; such equipment became obsolete until a Mellon Institute Fellow discovered how to modify it for purifying gas. This technology fed research R.B. kept pushing into smoke abatement. Each step benefited Koppers.

Weidlein cites a trip to Washington to meet with Henry Morgenthau to assure the Institute tax-free status. The most amazing thing the Treasury people saw, Morgenthau remarked, was all that research for competitors. Work at the Institute had long since demonstrated the viability of petrochemicals. "Gulf saw no future for the discoveries, I've got the letter," Weidlein says. "Well, if they don't have the intelligence to see that, go ahead and develop it for Union Carbide," Andrew Mellon told Weidlein. A giant escaped.

Whatever technology offered, both brothers took eagerly. It is to brutalize their intentions to dub the Institute their service organization. Both bankers loved serendipities. "We stumbled upon something that was the basis of a cure for epilepsy," A.W. told Clarence Barron, "and we turned that over to somebody else." Fellowships arrived for dental caries. They got into *pure* research in 1922, and four years afterward established their Department of Research in Pure Chemistry.

Months before he died, a failing A.W. himself dedicated the monumental structure which houses the Institute today. It adjoins the university, soot-permeated now, its gloomy hushed architectural pomposity a throwback to standards of another epoch entirely, its solidity and decor, its expectations of men from Nature. The brothers pledged $8,400,000, half each, and exacted it from depression-contracted holdings their bookkeepers resented invading. R.B. initiated construction. "My hog pen looks a lot better than this," R.B. was heard to remark as the four-story bunkerlike bottom half sank between the avenues. He wanted the paneling in the library to show a carving of every known variety of fruit and vegetable. To assure himself that the sixty-two $10,000 monolithic limestone columns would look just right marching along the exterior, R.B. constructed full-scale plaster casts—each sixty tons—in Ligonier and moved them around until they satisfied his eye. When limestone replicas arrived, railroad beds were lowered and bridges raised.

Nonetheless there were limits. "I stopped by yesterday to look over what you've been up to," R.B. was heard to greet the architect, Benno Jansen, in the Duquesne Club. "I loved those chows' heads." Benno's bas-reliefs represented lions. They disappeared.

A.W. had visions of his own. The Institute's famous accomplishments—the gas mask, artificial rubber, the cellulose sausage casing which replaced Chinese hog intestine, research underlying Dow Corning—he saw as way stations. "If somebody had to sell it today, this place probably wouldn't fetch ten cents on the dollar," the banker told Weidlein at the 1937 dedication. "But it will be worth many millions to humanity." He appreciated his investment. He put it as fully as he was ever able by approving a plaque which commemorated the short-lived Duncan's aspiration: "Every new significant fact is a permanent gift to the human race in its struggle for that unknown goal toward which it is proceeding."

Other claims Mellon sidestepped. Delegations of the elders filed into the bank incessantly, aboveboard in their conviction that it was time A.W. did something for East Liberty Presbyterian. Wait until the holidays, the banker muttered finally. That Christmas there arrived, to deck the altar, the handsomest poinsettias obtainable.

A.W. did join R.B. in donating a parcel of choice Negley land to the congregation when a Presbyterian cathedral was under study. Once R.B. announced his four-million-dollar gift to the building fund his brother deplored that. He refused any contribution after trustees of R.B.'s depression-shrunken estate reneged on payments. Malcontents quickly dubbed the vast Gothic cruciform the "Mellon fire escape." Relatives insist that Jennie, who had been impressed by the tomb of Napoleon in Paris, demanded a place magnificent enough for genuine cellar crypts—she craved burial "dry."

In 1921 a gallant innocent, John Bowman, turned up to head the ramshackle University of Pittsburgh. Its trustees were frank. One, Henry McEldowney, hadn't made a meeting in over five years. ". . . the place is run in such a slipshod way that I'm ashamed to be seen inside it," the uneducated bank president responded when Bowman closed in. Unless the deficit was met, the property was due for foreclosure. McEldowney expressed the businessman's view: "You seem to think that Pittsburgh could not go on quite as well if there were no university here. You're wrong."

Bowman started probing elsewhere. "He rose from behind a small desk," the chancellor wrote subsequently of A. W. Mellon, "a man slender and straight; eyes blue and direct; hair and short moustache grey; and although his face and hands with long slender fingers suggested sensitiveness and inherent fineness, he stood there with a dominant over-all rocklike quality." Bowman mentioned the university. "In a soft voice but with amazing finality he said that he was busy, that he was not interested, that he did not care to talk about the subject." They discussed something else. "Austere, alone, serious —I had not seen so much of these qualities in any man before. He had said, in effect, 'no,' but it seemed somehow to be a revisable 'no.' "

Bowman opened his campaign. Both A.W. and R.B. were on the university board. At Bowman's first meeting, with all the trustees sitting down to quibble over means for raising the $300,000 deficit, the chancellor demanded fifteen million dollars to give the institution a boost. While stipulating this amount Bowman felt somebody tug sharply at his coattails. R.B. was seated immediately to his left. "Sit down. You can't talk to us about fifteen million dollars. You're simply crazy." Next day the banker had thought it over. "Talk about a plan— a plan, not money. Get a plan."

The chancellor initiated skirmishes. Once events gained momentum, the brothers would undoubtedly have preferred to stop with fund raising. Bowman's proposal soon appeared. "Why not record in stone what Pittsburgh, an Inland Empire, really is?"

"A tower—why not build a tower?" Its scale and movement, Bowman later said, had come to him during a phonograph rendition of *Die Walküre*, "climax rising on climax, when you felt that each was the top of human achievement." Fifty-two Gothic stories, 680 feet high, an epiphany in carved, arched stone. Mellon, unwilling during the early stages to discuss such idiocy, purchased from the Frick estate for $3,500,000 the fourteen and a half acres of the Civic Center Bowman felt were suitable.

By then A.W. had relocated in Washington. Bowman took his drawings to the capital and confronted the Treasurer.

"What is the cost of the proposed building?" Mellon demanded.

"Eleven million dollars."

"What is the debt of the University of Pittsburgh at present?"

"Two million dollars."

"This plan is so absurd that I ask you not to mention it to me again."

Bowman showed up repeatedly, well stocked with allusions to Lorenzo the Magnificent. "You want to put up a high building," Mellon attempted, later on. "Colleges have never been built that way. You want me to be a pioneer or a frontiersman in college building. I do not want to be a frontiersman in anything. In business I always let the other men have that part."

Was Mellon hinting something? Once the engineering studies were available Bowman called a trustees' meeting. Important people were alarmed. Officials at the Carnegie Institute were petulant at the prospect that Bowman's skyscraper would literally overshadow them. The University's own chairman got board agreement that nothing rise higher than a hundred feet.

Within a day Bowman popped into R.B.'s office. He'd come on an unusual errand; he expected no reply. Simply: "I'm going ahead at once with the construction of the high building."

R.B. caught up with him halfway out the door. "Wait a minute. Do you mean what you say?"

"Yes."

Mr. Mellon, Bowman records, "laughed heartily. '*You* might get away with it,' he said."

A.W. returned home. Responding, as ever, to the Mellon initiative, the business community rallied. But Bowman's pretentious "Cathedral of Learning" idea grated still on Andrew. Bowman *must* reconsider.

The chancellor now demonstrated an acumen which approached the Treasurer's. "Tell me, if the plan is to be changed, may I announce that the change is yours?" If not, Bowman promised, he would "leave with good will and without fuss."

Mellon immediately backed off. To control was necessary; to exert control openly was out of the question. The Cathedral went up, if slower and closer to the earth than the chancellor once dreamed. Mellon remained dubious. Nevertheless, the corporations did contribute, and when a half-million dollars was needed to buy the stones to pave the Common Room, A.W. quietly inscribed for Bowman one last conciliatory check.

As the Twenties progressed the Treasurer gave six-figure amounts to a variety of western Pennsylvania institutions. Paul's experience with Choate was heartening; A.W. earmarked several hundred thousand dollars and provided a library. When his son joined Chi Psi at Yale the financier contributed a fraternity house. He and R.B. set up a fund, in the end, to placate a besiegement of shiftless local relatives. This could become embarrassing. Once, in a shop in Bermuda watching Paul being fitted for a polo coat, the father was unable to resist— under his ancient breath—the temptation to stammer his proposal that if any of Paul's friends standing around just watching might enjoy a coat like his . . .

3

Wasn't there something more? Occasionally Bowman sensed dropoffs. "What did you see on the prairie?" he asked the Treasurer, returned from the Middle West.

"Corn, so many fields of corn, so many stalks of corn—they fill me with wonder. My mind cannot take hold of them." Mellon paused. "And not a single stalk was an accident. Outside the mystery of growing, each was the result of order—plowing, planting, cultivation, sunshine. How strange that order is in growing things and in rocks, in rivers, in waves on the sea, in the movement of stars."

An underlying unity. Religious intuitions—to a less activist mentality. Mellon will comprehend literally—to grasp, to close his hand upon. Must materialism itch? The old man's spirit scratched. Perhaps beauty offered salves. Once, offhandedly, the penetrating Bowman asked what led the financier into art collecting. "Every man," divulged the banker slowly, "wants to connect his life with something he thinks eternal. If you turn that over in your mind you will find the answer to your question."

The indulgence of collecting. Exotic reminders; intimations from moral Borneo.

It began so early. "I learned much about that from Frick," he confessed to Bowman, "while we were in Europe together. How he could buy a picture! Sometimes he would dicker with a dealer until he got the price way down. Then he might decide not to buy even at the low price. Well, at such times I would occasionally slip back after we left the dealer and buy the picture and not tell."

Frick's leavings. Like serving the public, collecting in a major way was something to defer until his cocksure mentor died. Mellon's purchases were fitful. Early in his marriage, along with an assortment of modish Barbizon decorations, he acquired for seventy thousand dollars Corot's excellent *Le Lac de Garde*, and secondary works by Reynolds and Raeburn. Then, in successive years, he bought *Herdsmen Tending Cattle* by Albert Cuyp, *Mrs. John Taylor* by Gainsborough, and George Romney's lovely *Miss Willoughby*.

Mellon's marriage came apart; for ten bitter years he bought no paintings. In 1917 he and his children took over the house on Woodland Road, which presented, along with better moods, a lot more wall space. Mellon reappeared in galleries. The conservatives at Knoedler's respected his desire that nothing Mellon saw be tasteless or troubling. They stocked him up with lots of elegant long Gainsboroughs, good Raeburns, an unimpeachable little Turner (*Mortlake Terrace*), and Hals's powerful *Old Lady*. Vermeer's touching *Girl in a Red Hat* stood upon the piano. Mellon was acquiring courage; one notebook entry indicates a 1919 meeting, through Frick, with the still-untitled Joseph Duveen—he of the bowler hat, that great burst potato of a mouth surmounted by its authoritative frizz, dealer in objets d'art both minor and beyond all price, already intent on making Mellon his pupil as he had made Berenson his hireling.

Congenitally, Mellon could always wait. Except for El Greco's *Saint Ildefonso,* the walls of 1785 Massachusetts Avenue filled slowly with luminous perspectives, with parks and ruffles and sycamores and overdressed little aristocrats like the Treasurer's favorite *Lady Caroline Howard* by Joshua Reynolds—exquisite child, beneath a black silk cape in a garden to pluck a rose. Then came several Turners, a

Hoppner, *Lady Derby* by Romney. A few American portraits. Mellon bought quite cautiously. Price frightened him. The Gainsboroughs and Lawrences he coveted most went to other collectors because he felt the amounts asked outrageous.

He bought what pleased him. "I have no gallery with paintings or tapestries," he wrote the Duchess of Rutland in mid-1926. "I have only those paintings and a few tapestries which I have acquired from time to time when I had suitable places in my residence. I have not had occasion to consider acquisition of such for public purposes." Mellon's eye was broadening nonetheless. The redoubtable David Finley recalls works by Rembrandt and Hobbema among the apartment's early glories. By 1925 the Treasurer could bring himself to commit nearly half a million dollars to the acquisition of a single painting, the younger Holbein's historic *Edward VI as a Child*.

Mellon felt Finley's influence. His petite "special assistant" brought into Mellon's life the pecky discriminations, the pitch and chirp, emitted by a Southerner native to expensive amusements. Little David was cosmopolitan. Son of a Congressman, descendant of good South Carolina cotton people, he crackled with the diffidence and politesse one expected from somebody with a brother named States Rights Gist Finley and another famous wherever magnolia blossomed as co-owner of the foxhound Sir Galahad. Finley teethed on protocol; his reflexes were irritable. As Mellon acquired canvases, Finley admits, "I could be useful. I had gone abroad every year. I actually preferred art to the law, but my father insisted I go to law school." After World War II, Finley set himself up in Washington in a little practice which specialized in income taxes. "It was all a terrible bore," he told a reporter afterward. "I hated to make out my own income tax report, and I certainly wasn't interested in anybody else's."

Sorting Andrew Mellon's callers and writing his speeches and organizing the seating arrangements at official entertainments was far closer to the fastidious South Carolinian's notion of an amusing life. He understood A.W.'s style. "Everybody always seemed to want to do what Mr. Mellon wanted," Finley said years later. "He had a way of making you feel badly if you failed him. Whenever a group of people would get into an argument, and he was called in to settle it, he would listen for a moment and then say, 'I think it ought to be this way, don't you?' And they would all quiet down and say, 'Yes, Mr. Mellon'—because he was usually right!"

It helped, Mellon found, once he started contemplating a purchase, if he might retain the painting until his decision hardened. Dealers encouraged the indulgence. When Carman Messmore of Knoedler's picked up the Duke of Buccleuch's great anguished and philosophical self-portrait by Rembrandt, cheap, and offered it to Mellon for more than twice the cost, the markup alone was enough to make the financier tighten and accuse the dealer of "a big nerve." Some weeks went by. Worried, Messmore carried the canvas to Washington, entered Mellon's apartment and hung the portrait conspicuously in the Treasurer's dining room. The two ate lunch; there was no mention of the portrait. More time passed. "I will buy the portrait," Mellon told the dealer, "but not at the price demanded. You will have to make a considerable reduction." Ultimately, Mellon proposed that Messmore take back a Pieter de Hooch of which the banker was tired and shave 10 percent off the asking price of the Rembrandt. The fatigued Messmore capitulated.

While contemplating something new, A.W. fell into the habit of taking Finley home for lunch to solicit his opinion. Finley's preferences were classical. He was especially fond of great Italian Renaissance masters. These canvases were costly; moreover, they catered to impulses it made Mellon queasy to confront. Nudes put him off. Crucifixions he found painful; the idea of having religious pictures of any sort in his drawing room, where people were smoking and drinking cocktails, offended his notion of fitness.

That left very little. When A.W. did ultimately acquire a major madonna and bambino it was by Memling, strained through those pious Flemish breads. His Perugino *Crucifixion* was leeched of suffering, more perspective than foreground, beyond tragedy. For some months his drawing room exhibited the portrait of Guiliano de' Medici attributed to Raphael. "It seemed to me a strong work," he wrote Helen Frick, "but not particularly attractive for a private living room." He resented its subject's "evil face." Mellon turned it back.

One day in 1927, with regrets, Finley told the Treasurer that he was thinking over a job offer from a New York law firm. Mellon sat him down. "I won't try to stop you, David," the Treasurer began, "but I want to tell you a secret. For a long time I have felt that there should be a great national art gallery here in Washington. It is a disgrace that we don't have one—I am really mortified by it. If necessary, I am going to build it, and I would like you to be here and run it when it is built."

This was both offer and confession. Finley's sophistication was indispensable. To collect "for public purposes" meant gratifying tastes worldlier than his own, and snippy little David was just the intermediary. Finley rigged the snares. In 1931, for example, a friend put David into touch with Mrs. Walter Schoellkopf, whose husband was Counselor of the American Embassy in Madrid. Spain was boiling politically. An irreplaceable Goya, the full-length beribboned *Marquesa de Pontejos y Miraflores,* was up for purchase through a Pontejos descendant, about to flee Spain ahead of the Republican take-over. Two days of telephone negotiations ensued. Mellon set a limit; Finley and Mrs. Schoellkopf bargained. By then the Republicans had seized the painting. The new leadership consulted with the muralist José María Sert as to the advisability of letting the picture out of the country; Sert recommended the Goya as the regime's best imaginable ambassador.

Originally, both the Pontejos family and the Treasurer had hoped to arrange the sale without any dealer commission. "When the purchase was made, however," notes John Walker slyly, "Andrew Mellon found that he still had to depend on Knoedler's for the Spanish export permit. This required months of negotiations and certain payments over and beyond export taxes—delicate deals, for which the word 'bribe' might seem too brutally descriptive. Such 'reimbursements' only an experienced intermediary could possibly arrange. In the end the commission Mellon paid, somewhat peevishly, was what he would have been charged had he not intervened."

Evidently dealers were unavoidable. Not temperamentally a customer, Mellon resented them keenly. They always knew. Let a collection decompose, and dealers squirmed out like flukes from livers.

Profits originated with rogues, after all—was loveliness any different? Hadn't Mellon's greatest triumph—to skim the sweetest curds of Russia's unrivaled Hermitage collection—started out among dealers?

Each step was maddening. The five-year plan had just been initiated; insurgent Russia needed tractors, and credits for machine parts were out of the question in the unfriendly West without frozen foreign exchange. The Soviets were ragged. Calouste Gulbenkian, who appeared in Moscow to direct the worldwide Soviet dumping of oil, brought to the attention of the leadership its dowry in canvases.

The clue that these were obtainable originated, evidently, with the chameleon Zatzenstein, a nerveless rascal of a Berlin appraiser the Soviets then imported to price their holdings. This occurred in 1928.

A few months later, in Paris, the elated Gulbenkian, slipping up for once, could not resist exposing to Zatzenstein a bust and some superlative silver the wily young connoisseur recognized instantly. The Russians were retailing the Hermitage collection! Zatzenstein scrambled into London and negotiated a partnership with Knoedler's agent there, meanwhile dispatching a footpad of his own, Hans Mansfield, to poke around Leningrad's Department of the Treasury.

The commissars were skittish. Again and again, Zatzenstein insists, the Soviets had emphasized that they intended to dispose of nothing. Despoil that storehouse of masterpieces where Catherine the Great, replenishing those heroic loins, had strolled with Encyclopaedists and relieved her heart? There would be recriminations; superiors would review prices; news would inevitably leak.

Russia still needed money. Perhaps something very minor? An unnamed Soviet Treasury official secretly authorized the sale of a single canvas, as an experiment, to see whether confidentiality was possible. Mansfield contacted Zatzenstein; Zatzenstein passed along word to Charles Henschel of Knoedler's in Berlin, who received the discreetest of nods from their client in Washington. Within months *Lord Philip Wharton* by Van Dyck, badly in need of cleaning, appeared in Knoedler's New York vaults.

It arrived in March of 1929. Everybody was jittery. The Treasurer himself, who trusted no dealer very far, had negotiated a letter contract from Henschel which authorized the firm to purchase certain paintings from the Hermitage collection. On whatever he retained he agreed to pay a 25 percent commission. "In the event you do not wish to keep any of them," the letter concluded, "it is understood that we will sell them for your account, and pay 25 percent of the profit on the price we receive for them." Additional paintings, which Henschel wanted to import, Mellon would underwrite. On these, should they be resold elsewhere, he reserved a 50 percent profit.

The commissars feared profiteering; that, and selling too low. Remorse was phasing in. Hermitage curators were aghast at each new depredation; the flat-headed bureaucratic revolutionaries fidgeted. Nor was this paranoid. A Hals and two Rembrandts arrived in New York in April. Then nothing was forthcoming. Violating the agreed procedure, Mansfield telephoned his ministry acquaintance. The call was pointless, responded the official who answered finally, since the original contact had already been liquidated. Superiors questioned the prices.

Everybody implicated was fevered: greeds alternated with chills of regret. The American stock market collapsed; Henschel began fretting aloud that he might find himself stocked up with overpriced Soviet masterpieces; he struggled to bargain. Rival dealers haunted Soviet ministries. In May of 1930, Charles Henschel personally set forth for Russia. Halfway across the Atlantic he got a radiotelephone call from Mansfield in Berlin, who told him that the Soviets' Nicolas Ilyan had arrived in Berlin and announced himself prepared to turn over the panel A.W. wanted most, the matchlessly spiritual *Annunciation* of Jan van Eyck, on receipt of half a million dollars. Henschel and his uneasy associates pushed through to Leningrad and perused the museum. There was serious negotiating; Finley intercepted cable after cable. During the following months the paintings that would become the soul of the National Gallery landed in New York. For something over six and a half million dollars, Mellon acquired twenty-one indisputable masterpieces, ranging from Raphael's superb *Alba Madonna* and *Saint George and the Dragon* to Botticelli's *Adoration of the Magi* and Titian's semi-nude *Venus with a Mirror*. He had surmounted Pittsburgh.

Then Mellon stopped. Throughout 1931, both Henschel and Messmore prodded urgently in hopes that still another shipment of masterpieces, headed up by a unique Giorgione and two fine Leonardo da Vincis, might complete Mellon's raid. The fading Treasurer stalled, shifted, bargained. He denied all press reports that he was accumulating anything. Mellon would not buy. Zatzenstein was particularly distraught. He knew, as certainly as Knoedler's people, that what the Russians around Antiquariat were still prepared briefly to offer was genuinely priceless, an irrecoverable opportunity. What he did not know—what nobody knew—was what was steadily happening to the Treasurer's own holdings as the collapse swallowed assets.

9 | THE CRASH

1

IN LATE JULY of 1927 Calvin Coolidge, vacationing in the Black Hills of South Dakota, took up a handy blue pencil and presented his secretary Everett Sanders a slip of paper on which was scribbled the period's most sibylline press release: "I do not choose to run for President in nineteen twenty-eight." At that moment Herbert Hoover was winding up a stint of western flood-relief duty which refreshed his dusty reputation like warm sweet rain. Coolidge had barely resettled in Washington before he understood that he had not merely cut short his Presidency; he had anointed his successor. "That man has offered me unsolicited advice for six years," Coolidge soon whimpered privately, "all of it bad!"

It was dangerously late. That mightily overstimulated Mellon bull market, egged into a frenzy by Wall Street and sanctified by the Treasury Secretary's regular public asides about how "orderly" and without "evidence of over-speculation" the rampage was proceeding, kicked free of Reserve Board sanctions and began its charge into a commercial empyrean for which the past was barely admitted to furnish even historical antecedents. Few demurred; among these unimaginative complainers the persistent and obdurate Commerce Secretary—still exercising the franchise he wrung from Harding to involve himself wherever he liked—disapproved of the spectacle of the day and waddled around the Government like an unhappy barnyard pug to eat out of everybody else's dish.

Once, as S. Parker Gilbert groused, Hoover probably had justice in regarding himself as "Secretary of Commerce and Under-Secretary of all other departments." This patent was expired. In the early years the Cabinet "liberal" had euchred Harding into allotting the Government rights of review of all major foreign lendings (temporarily; Mellon intervened later on) and in fact managed to kick shins heartily enough around the departments to embarrass the industrial leadership into giving up the eighty-four-hour work week. But once Mellon helped Coolidge establish his grip on policy a lot of Hoover's meddlesomeness evaporated. He became more tractable. His theoretical disapprobation of "over-reckless competition" evidently made it easier for Hoover to leave the trusts alone; he lent his serviceable dense outrage to Mellon and Coolidge against the McNary-Haugen proposals.

Hoover still provoked gooseflesh. Backing up that torrent of "unsolicited advice" it made the beady-eyed Vermonter so uncomfortable to hear was an engineer's recognition that this runaway financial machine had thrown its governors. Hoover himself was troubled by the extent to which his own Department of Commerce had managed to promote exports for which the disgusting Europeans simply returned borrowed dollars. The pygmies his predecessors attracted might revere whatever the tongue-tied Mellon struggled into words; Hoover had another opinion. "He was," Hoover later wrote of Mellon, "in every instinct a country banker." The hard-bitten international mining promoter certainly appreciated Mellon, granted him what credit was coming on "the balance sheet of national welfare." But judgment was judgment.

Much needed redressing. "Unsocial and uneconomic," Judge Gary exploded, splenetic over Hoover's proposal that working people get Sundays off. Hoover plumped insistently for development of the tremendous western river basins; although Coolidge "could not bear the high outlay of public money," the Commerce Secretary quietly undertook engineering studies. He proposed to "cure" the business curve with variable public employment.

Hoover was forever proposing; the fact that Coolidge appeared to devote himself to something just above and beyond the Commerce Secretary's shoulder didn't slow Hoover down. Annoyingly, others accepted Hoover's views. As early as 1918, admitted to that peripatetic seminar which collected naturally around the much-publicized Humanitarian, young Franklin Delano Roosevelt pronounced the administrator "a wonder, and I wish we could make him President of the United States." Hoover was regularly able to excite enthusiasm among individuals as unalike as young Robert A. Taft, Louis Brandeis, John L. Lewis, and, late, the embittered Joseph P. Kennedy.

He remained as political as flu. Progressives who might have seemed his natural political allies he dismissed as misguided reformers who "no doubt hoped for the growth of Socialism inch by inch." He dubbed one Cabinet colleague "in truth, a fascist, but did not know it . . ." for espousing agricultural price-fixing. Yet something there was irrefutable about the man, a technique for planting a foot of argument squarely in the path of whatever he disapproved. Hoover disliked the speculation; pretty soon he'd gotten his old friend Roy Young of the Federal Reserve Board to push for a sharply higher discount rate. Experience abroad convinced Hoover of the futility of milking Germany to replenish the rest of Europe; he converted Ogden Mills. When, against expectation, Coolidge presented the country with his pixilated scribble of abdication, Mills shouldered immediately into the forefront of that odd but widespread constituency which surfaced to promote Herbert Hoover for President.

Odd by American standards: informed, influential men. Weeks after Coolidge's announcement Hoover had invited into being a clubhouse network which threatened the Old Guard's dominance of the GOP for the first time since 1920. Mellon himself was shocked.

After Coolidge reneged, Mellon quietly involved himself. Tried to involve himself; the trouble was, advisers around the lame-duck President kept conjecturing that Coolidge's reluctance was largely perverted coyness, that no matter what he said the Vermonter secretly expected the Party to heave him upon its collective shoulders and bear him triumphantly, prim with disclaimers, into another four years.

This wore on Hoover. By May of 1928 Hoover's "Boy and Girl Scouts" reported as sure four hundred out of a total of one thousand convention delegates. Herbert paid a call on Calvin. He was already close, Hoover admitted, but even now he was prepared to reinstruct these delegates according to Coolidge's whim and continue to haul his oar, "entirely content" under the Navigator of the Great Prosperity. Coolidge read that contemptuously. "If you have four hundred delegates, you better keep them." Hoover backtracked, swallowing vinegar.

He might be stymied; he recognized by now that he would undoubtedly require backup support within the great eastern industrial blocs. The Pennsylvania delegation, seventy-nine votes, looked like the makeweight. Unhappily, "The Pennsylvania delegation had a meeting late in May and decided to vote as a unit and not to come to any conclusions until they reached the convention. Secretary Mellon dominated the delegation, and I was of course sitting with him in the Cabinet twice a week. I was aware that he was constantly pressing the President to run again and assuring his friends that the Coolidge acceptance was a certainty. Also, Mr. Mellon participated in constant meetings with Charles D. Hilles of New York, who controlled a large part of the New York delegation, and with Henry Roraback, the Connecticut boss, and with others in the opposition groups. These men formed a circle of opposition which collaborated with the Senate in opposing me."

"He [Hoover] is too much inclined to have his own solution of problems," Mellon informed his diary, "frequently unsound." But reservations went deeper. "You know," Mellon observed, subsequently, "in all my business enterprises I have never once put an engineer in charge. The trouble with engineers is that they deal with specific facts and with problems that always have specific solutions. . . . In business, however, the human element is very important and incalculable. You never know what men are going to do. For this reason engineers are not much use in handling human problems."

Engineers relied on instruments. Management was an art—one apprehended the mystic, the immeasurable. Any shrewd businessman's hunch arced beyond a galaxy of "scientific formulas and mathematics." These oriented one later, mostly with moppings-up.

Efforts by the Soviets to engineer an entire society drew Mellon's saddest scorn: "Before the Revolution, Russia was one of the wealthiest countries of the world. Then the Soviet thought they would grab this wealth, and they destroyed the structure of credit, and found only the dregs of gold. The wealth had evaporated. It was as if you had burned down the house to get the nails."

Stop Hoover. Definitely; when might his replacement appear? Mellon never liked Lowden; Hughes was getting old. W.L. propagated rumors that A.W. himself might contemplate the nomination. Mellon ducked any commitment among Pittsburghers through several autumn months and reportedly commissioned a campaign biography. But not very long after *The New York Times* dismissed his nomination as "absurd to the point of impossibility" he stated publicly, "I am not a candidate and won't be one." Even W.L. couldn't protect A.W.'s clout after that.

Dawes, maybe? By June the Treasurer was still eating lunch with the inexhaustible Dwight Morrow in hopes the two could evolve a strategy which would lead to Coolidge's reconsideration. On June 10, the day the delegate train from Pennsylvania pulled into Kansas City for the Republican Convention, Mellon was still awaiting that communication from the White House. It never came through. The evening before the Convention opened, A.W. quietly clutched, and telephoned the importunate Hoover, and confided his decision to commend to the Pennsylvania delegation on the following morning a vote for Hoover on the inaugural ballot. Hoover must say nothing.

Hours later, tasting something sanguine foaming the pre-Convention political waters, that corpulent Philadelphia scavenger, patient William Vare, called in the newsmen to announce that, whatever Mellon decided, his coastal delegation was solidly behind Herbert. With that, William Allen White observed, "Mellon, the richest man in the world, was left suspended on a limb, his political feet dangling in the air."

W.L. remembered him tenderly, a corpse at his own political wake, propped up in fresh pajamas in bed in a suite at the Muehlebach Hotel, puffing stogies and presiding over a court that included David Reed and Senators Smoot and Borah and William Butler, Coolidge's seasoned manager. Charles Curtis, the Senators' choice, looked in to urge his own candidacy. By 1928 David Finley had established himself as A.W.'s companion, and he remembers the chuckle it gave him to overhear Curtis's indignant downturn of Mellon's suggestion that he consider the Vice-Presidency.

Curtis left; Mellon turned to Finley. "He'll take it just the same," A.W. decided. And Curtis did.

2

So detachment survived, however violently Mellon's fingers sometimes trembled with overwork. He'd enjoyed his season; after Hoover's inauguration he'd relinquish Treasury affairs.

But afterward, Mellon wouldn't. Equally stubborn, Hoover wouldn't relieve Mellon. They were a historic mismatch, Jack and Missus Sprat, working each other over in genteel tones underneath the familiar wattles. The way the winds died made voices carry. The horizon looked tidal.

It pounded the stock markets initially. For at least three years Hoover had been with difficulty compressing his lopsided lips, sucking in compact jowls, whenever the boom in securities prices came up in Cabinet. Coolidge continued to declare that the prosperity was "absolutely sound" and stocks were "cheap at current prices." Mellon admittedly knew better, but it was only at the prodding of the newly inaugurated President that Mellon publicly confided, in a kind of editorial whisper, that the "prudent" investor might contemplate switching part of his holdings from common stocks to industrial bonds. Nobody was really listening. Shortly before the break he joined the minority on the Federal Reserve Board in favor of raising the discount rate; by that time the Bull was out of control.

The slump in market prices began on October 29, 1929. Dignitaries like amiable Chairman Charles E. Mitchell of the National City Bank of New York—busy, selling to his wife and repurchasing securities also pledged to J. P. Morgan and Company to double up tax losses—were climbing all over each other to reassure the nation's bucket-shop customers. Mellon felt complicated emotions.

Like Hoover, Mellon despised "certain varieties of New York Banking, which he deemed were too often devoted to tearing men down and picking their bones. When the boom broke he said, 'they deserved it.' " Pool manipulators and raiding sorties had very little to do with reputable accumulation. Furthermore, since the important Mellon holdings were closely held, scarcely traded on exchanges, the 40 percent the highflyers relinquished just after the break seemed mere investment sanity. Business was holding up.

Capital, Nature's descendant, was fang and claw. "Mr. Mellon," Hoover wrote much later, "had only one formula: 'liquidate labor, liquidate stocks, liquidate the farmers, liquidate real estate.' He insisted that, when the people get an inflation brainstorm, the only way to get it out of their blood is to let it collapse. He held that even a panic was not altogether a bad thing. He said: 'It will purge the rottenness out of the system. High costs of living and high living will come down. People will work harder, live a more moral life. Values will be adjusted, and enterprising people will pick up the wrecks from less competent people.' He often used the expression, 'There is a mighty lot of real estate lying around the United States which does not know who owns it,' referring to excessive mortgages."

Mellon blinked what Hoover dreaded. Hoover had been involved in Paris in May of 1919 in much of the haggling that produced the Treaty of Versailles. He himself pleaded earnestly with the faltering Wilson not to involve American prestige in a reparations stratagem

Presidential material—Coolidge (left), Hoover (right)
PAUL MELLON

which left greedy allies feeding for capital upon a decomposing Germany. Reparations sapped Central Europe continuously, provoked feverish inflations incurable with poultices like those administered by Dawes and Young or A.W.'s own stretch-out schedules or suppression of the Federal Reserve discount rate.

Compounding this, as the decade ended, higher European returns tempted American capital abroad. Some bounced right back, redirected by manipulators into the rampaging American stock market. Ersatz capital, puffed with speculative salts, made all the economies logy. At Mellon's insistence, no specifics were permitted.

Crisis quickened Hoover; as 1930 opened he rallied, shook off the torpor which already had business leaders in despair. There were Presidential jawbonings to keep wage levels up, an intervention to forestall the threat that imported Russian wheat might collapse farm prices. Even this, Mellon felt, constituted interference with a proper adjustment of values. He disapproved specifically of Hoover's intention to convene a conference of industrialists. Alarmist; when Hoover insisted, the elderly Treasurer shrugged. "By that time he was getting used to having his advice ignored," W.L. says.

The stock exchange started rallying a little. "Steels remind me nowadays of Robinson Crusoe's prick," Charlie Schwab mused privately. "They have a tendency to firm up sometimes even when there really isn't any market available." It proved a gallows erection. European washouts were impending. Contemporaries, gathered around the Bull, were fussing a great deal more about every little snort and eye-roll that might betoken a recovering "business indicator." The yearned-over "averages" were looking better before 1929 was out; the Great Thing's rump, at least, propped up its bones and switched its tail most promisingly.

By that time even the most adoring were starting to hedge a little as regarded Mellon's sainthood. Several carped at unreliable budget projections. Another leaked reports about the jeers and "razzing" he received from a still-Republican House of Representatives when he again appeared to oppose the veterans' bonus bill. "Mr. Mellon may be a poor politician, an indiscreet adviser and a small, wistful, disillusioned 'old man' right now, but money talks in Pennsylvania politics—and nobody has yet suggested that the Secretary of the Treasury is insolvent, financially."

The public was turning. Between March of 1930 and March of 1931 unemployment deepened from four million to eight million. This made Hoover sorrowful, and he undertook fresh efforts to reassure the laboring community, catch farm prices before they fell permanently below production costs, and quietly encourage fuller state and municipal employment. Even these "remedial measures," Hoover noted, meant bucking the " 'leave it alone liquidationists' headed by Secretary of the Treasury Mellon, who felt that government must keep its hands off and let the slump liquidate itself."

Hoover still, like Mellon, vouchsafed that Old Testament economic dust bowl where tender grapes were followed by droughts and sandstorms. Nature needed replenishing too. Hoover and his advisers were downcast, in their ways, at how the poor economic climate persisted. As he had earlier, Mellon recommended strongly that personal income taxes be trimmed even further, so "bottled up" buying power could be released and money start finding its way into "good, sound securities"; and that measure was probably the easiest to accomplish. It didn't particularly help. The leadership followed up with what the unappreciative Galbraith termed the "no-business meetings of the great business executives."

These convocations, like the Presidential Commissions of a later period, involved the much-publicized calling-together of individuals the newspaper reader might respect. To emphasize the high level and historical seriousness of these occasions, the meetings were often held in Andrew Mellon's palatial apartment on Massachusetts Avenue. Underneath Mellon's accumulating masterpieces, the hardest heads around Wall Street and an occasional labor statesman were forever determining that recovery was irrepressible.

This made hopeful copy. Practical men; whatever advice anybody offered between glancings-up at Mellon's Hals, many of the nation's business leaders were now concerned privately with stocking getaway yachts or, like the ever-resourceful Albert Wiggin, chairman of the board of the Chase Manhattan Bank, coordinating bear raids against the holdings of their own banks' stockholders. The skeptical Lundberg notes that Hoover's "two principal advisers" were Dwight Morrow and Thomas Lamont, both key Morgan partners at precisely the time "the Morgan banks, alone of the nation's banking institutions, were almost one hundred percent liquid, i.e., had almost all their resources in cash or government securities."

Lundberg concludes from this that the Morgan managers remained, at their most innocent, cheerful bystanders around the securities slaughterhouse. They waited with money; they anticipated choice cuts. That certainly was likely enough after a collapse which saw General Motors end up at eight dollars a share the summer of 1932, down convincingly from 73 three action-packed years earlier. General Motors did well; U. S. Steel was off from 262 to 22.

Actually, Morgan undoubtedly got out early because it was troubled by the same tremors of impending disaster which made Herbert dyspeptic. Europe, those forever-whimpering Europeans. Those extensive European borrowings, privately solicited, discreetly granted, had already been flowing so long through the important American banking houses nobody really knew how much they represented. That train of private and governmental loans, reparations, interest payments coming due—whenever he really thought about it the orderly Quaker felt his Presidency teetering. In May of 1931 it went. A dispatch reached Washington that Vienna's largest private bank, the Kreditanstalt, was openly in trouble and depositors were rioting.

Historiography often extends choices. In Hoover's version, the longheaded badly worried mining engineer, well versed after decades of flooded shafts and rubble-choked corridors about the underground interconnectedness of things, got news from Vienna and recognized instantly that frigid economic waters were lapping his garters. He called Mellon in. The Austrian banks were already in convulsion; capital was fleeing Germany; there were approaching runs on banks in Hungary. A temporary shoring-up effort attempted by the New York Federal Reserve Bank and the Bank of England was undermined by the uncooperative French. American exports were low, partly because of retaliatory tariffs the Europeans instituted in response to Smoot-Hawley levels. American borrowings, the capital with which the Germans had been making their reparations payments and rebuilding their industry, were effectively used up. Transatlantic bankruptcy threatened. The upcoming billion-dollar payment on the European war debt would unquestionably throw the entire system into catastrophic default. Hoover recommended a moratorium. What did Mellon advise?

"Mr. Mellon objected that it was Europe's mess, and that we should not involve the United States."

Even Hoover blinked. "As Mr. Mellon was leaving for Europe next day on a vacation, I suggested that he look into the situation abroad. I was also relieved to be able to deal directly with Mr. Mills, who would be acting Secretary of the Treasury and had a younger and more vigorous mind than Mr. Mellon."

"When I returned to Washington on June 18," Hoover wrote subsequently, "Mr. Mellon, now in Europe, had reversed his views and was telephoning frantically that action must be taken at once or American financial safety would be seriously involved."

As W.L. recollected, A.W. was secretly first in the U. S. Government to be genuinely alarmed. "Hoover and A.W. had discussed this terrible situation . . . before A.W. had sailed from America and their views this time had been pretty much in harmony." Germany obviously wouldn't pay the $400,000,000 reparations installment coming due July 1. Paul was finishing Cambridge. After "hours and hours sweating in a telephone booth in the lobby of his little Cambridge hotel," and extended consultations with most of the really important moustaches, A.W. incorporated his recommendations in a five-page telegram to Hoover. France hoped to play the spoiler. Nevertheless, "Acting on the theory that we could not afford to let these nations destroy their power to trade, however willing they were to do so themselves, A.W. recommended a moratorium."

Even that wasn't enough. As Central European banks closed, lenders in the West had started to demand gold for deposited Eastern currencies. Reserves were depleted overnight; smaller countries jumped off the gold standard like fleas off a drowning dog. Hoover, shaken, demanded of the Comptroller of the Currency accurate figures as to the extent of unsecured short-term borrowings from American banks about to sink inside these quagmire economies; something about the relatively low estimates submitted by the Federal Reserve officials just hadn't felt plausible. "Twenty-four hours later I received the appalling news that the total American bank holdings probably exceeded $1,700,000,000," much of it by banks for which large losses would critically "affect their capital or surplus and create great public fears. Here was one consequence of the Reserve Board maintaining artificially low interest rates and expanded credit in the United States from mid-1927 to mid-1929 at the urging of European bankers. Some of our bankers had been yielding to sheer greed for the 6 or 7 per cent interest offered by banks in the European panic area."

Events approached the vortex; we were the dog; Mellon's policies would drown us all. By this time apprehension was widespread enough around the Western capitals to necessitate the convening of a conference, the international equivalent of one of Galbraith's no-business business meetings. It met in London, at the British Foreign Office. The honeymooning David Finleys came over from Paris; Secretary of State Stimson joined Mellon. The conference produced Hoover's "standstill" agreement. "As a result of it," W.L. notes, "Germany was given about a year in which to cure her ulcerous financial condition; and the relief manifest as the conference was concluding its work found expression in editorials in the newspapers of London and Paris devoted to Mellon, the diplomat."

Hoover tells another story. Behind all the official posturings that July in London, everybody involved had arrived agreed as to the operative difficulty (Germany needed money) as well as the amount ($500,000,000). The important question was, Whose? Mellon, Henry Stimson in tow, urged that the money be raised through a "joint loan" participated in by several governments. "I replied," Hoover wrote, "that this was a banker-made crisis, and that the bankers must shoulder the burden of solution. . . ." Mellon dug his heels in; the exhausted Hoover promptly subjected the longtime Treasury Czar to a transatlantic ass-kicking. By telephone he informed Messrs. Stimson and Mellon "emphatically that we would not participate in such a loan and that I was publishing the gist of the standstill proposal to the world that very minute. They protested against the publication as undiplomatic. I issued it nevertheless."

The negotiation specified that earmarked funds, originating in private banks, be provided the Germans through the Bank for International Settlements at Berne. Stimson's Wall Street legal clients didn't like the proposals any more than he and Mellon. "A group of our New York banks informed me," Hoover would conclude, "that they could not agree to the standstill plan and that the only solution was for our government to participate in a large international loan to Germany and other countries. My nerves were perhaps overstrained when I replied that, if they did not accept within twenty-four hours, I would expose their banking conduct to the American people. They agreed. . . .

"On July 23rd I made a statement expressing satisfaction with the acceptance of my plan by the Conference."

Satisfaction was rare; briefly, the pudgy Humanitarian hand broke triumphantly above the "bath of ink" Stimson called Hoover's mood. Then it went down, permanently. Just as the apprehensive President suspected, the undeclared European debt was greater than even he had discovered, as high as ten billion dollars, as great as the total of intergovernmental indebtedness which for so long had originated with the German reparations and proceeded by pass-through arrangements to the ultimate creditors—the French and ourselves. The settlement in June of 1932 at Lausanne, which amounted to the abrogation of most of the German obligation, inevitably forced on the United States—however waspishly Hoover spun his negotiators away from even a peep at the Medusa of linkage—*de facto* cancellation of the payment schedules Andrew Mellon had struggled to perfect. Public debt evaporated; what hopes for private creditors in the United States, their trust departments hopelessly abscessed with Budapest debentures and Transylvanian revenue anticipation notes?

By that time Mellon was out. Banks were everywhere defaulting. Early in 1932 the Congress gave Hoover authority to bring into being the Reconstruction Finance Corporation in hopes that the Government could do something about the collapsing credit structure. The President offered Mellon a directorship, but "Mr. Mellon, advancing in years and having served as Secretary of the Treasury longer than any other man, thought he would like to have some less strenuous appointment." Hoover didn't argue. "The shift to Mills as Secretary was of great help, for he warmly supported my views on handling the depression."

Flat-footed. A memoirist's decency requires Herbert to bestow some valedictory pat of appreciation upon his silky little financial vixen, but he cannot resist twisting one of Mellon's ears even in bidding good-bye. Even this was charitable. Why inflame the thing?

That January of 1932 there had been . . . other aspects to consider. The flow of news that season was dilatory—nobody wanted reelection tidbits, finance was between cataclysms, and loiterers from the press were giving column after column of front-page exposure to everything Wright Patman's investigators all over the Hill could conceivably poke up regarding Mellon's business involvements. Seriously taken now, letting the evidence collect, Patman absorbed himself with all the painstaking inertia of a crossroads storekeeper picking currant weevils out of a deposit of lard. Each newly documented malfeasance provoked its equivocal half-smile. The Duke merger. Union Gulf. The Barco concession. Patman buttered it all into his Judiciary Committee reports.

Hoover summoned David Reed. A natural Hoover sympathizer, Reed had a second-generation retainer's sensitivity to Mellon's brittle ego. Charles Dawes had quit the embassy in London without warning at the beginning of January. Ambassador to the Court of Saint James's—the ideal Mellon capstone, the post from which he still might involve himself in those international negotiations which appeared at times to flare the old man's interest. An appropriate transfer, Hoover urged it strongly—and as expeditiously as possible. Electioneering would start soon. The House of Representatives was evidently going to return the probe to Patman and the Judiciary Committee for exhaustive and extended investigation.

David Reed went through his presentation; the Treasurer was neither convinced nor fooled. He thought he'd wait. They played the investigation out. "I still can remember the way they arranged that hearing room," Patman maintains today. "There was this huge table, semicircular, and I was on one side and Mr. Mellon and his thirteen lawyers were on t'other side of the thing. Fo' two full weeks I presented my case. After that I yielded to Mellon, but he refused to go on the witness stand. We recessed until one-thirty. Ev'body thought old Mellon would be on the stand at one-thirty, there was lots of interest. By one-thirty that afternoon the newsboys were runnin' around an' yellin', Mellon resigns, Mellon resigns, appointed to the Court of Saint James's—

"Hoover supposedly received his resignation, but you can't find hide nor hair of those papers. When he was back at the Treasury to take the oath of office a friend o' mine, a newspaperman from Corpus Christi, kep' on askin' him was he happy about the new appointment. Mellon finally turned on him. 'Young man, you don't seem to understand what is going on here, it's not a marriage ceremony, it's a divorce proceeding.'

"Once Mellon was out there was no point in any more investigation. It was felt nothing could be done, it was a moot case." Patman folds his immaculate old hands. "I don't believe there has been a day since then I haven't been under surveillance by the Mellonites."

3

Well before that even Pittsburgh's reporters noticed how the financier had "aged perceptibly" since Hoover took office, the way the "slender, artistic fingers with which he brushes his face while seeking the words that come so haltingly to his tongue have fluttered with fragile feebleness. The closing of his eyes as he gropes for ideas has been more frequent and of longer duration." In fact, blurts the Baltimore *Sun*'s Washington man, "Mr. Mellon had not been in the Cabinet for three years or more, tho he did not know it." Undersecretary Ogden L. Mills was doing the real work. Well characterized as "cocky, somewhat hard-boiled when he is not glassily suave," the New York yachtsman didn't balk at referring to his chief as "the old man." Affectionately, reporters insisted. Mellon hadn't commented.

He reserved himself. The reporter who discovered that Mellon's "enthusiasm has been tempered by recent reverses and the President's studied neglect of the financier's advice" concluded that his "golden throne is beginning to irk him, we are informed, and he is contemplating the comforts of private life."

"Comforts" weren't the inducement, but something *was* happening. Once he had simply alighted in Washington and taken up Treasury offices whose reception rooms he shunned for months. Now, as methodically as ever, Mellon prepared his departure. Wafting, falling away. The first true indication came when individuals who caught his eye, such as Donald D. Shepard of the Internal Revenue Department and Nelson Hartson, left Government service and reappeared as private Mellon attorneys. Government investigators subsequently traced the much-traveled route that allowed attachés to come and go from administrative offices at the Treasury, via a labyrinth of private elevators shut away behind discreet grilles that barred the general public, and emerge in Pittsburgh to shuttle smoothly up the secret elevator tucked into a pillar among the massive Ionic columns that overlook the Union Trust's banking lobby.

After 1927, it developed, office space was provided on the third floor of the Mellon National Bank for D. D. Shepard. The abrasive specialist in cooperative reorganization also practiced out of a suite he maintained in Washington. In time, the indefatigable David Finley shared the Washington offices, along with Andrew Mellon himself. From 1927 on, quite clearly, Mr. Mellon of Pittsburgh intended to remain Mr. Mellon of Washington too, as inconspicuously as possible.

There were other stirrings. That same year, David Finley would recall, he got the job offer in New York that tempted him. "He told me don't do that," Finley said, much later. "I wasn't interested in money, I had some of my own. I saw he needed me, my strong young legs. . . ."

Finley glances up suspiciously, nervous as a little old stewing rabbit who senses a hand overhanging his cage. Impressively wizened, his fine protuberant connoisseur's eyes are ravaged with pink all the way around the rims: he is obviously worried that sentiment is about to jeopardize his crustiness. He entombs many memories. Over fifty years already since A.W. spotted something about this strong-minded bantam attorney from Virginia whom Parker Gilbert brought into the Government as part of the War Loan Staff. A resignation caused Finley to replace the fellow who handled the public statements and taxation policy. Before long Mellon created the post of Special Assistant to the Treasurer and moved Finley in. Finley handled nearly everything—appointments, speech writing, that expensively nourished accretion of canvases and public ambitions which was to become the National Gallery.

There was a resonance. "He took me abroad often," Finley says. "He was lonely." There was the never-forgotten tour of France in 1928. "He always treated all us young ones just the same. He expected us to tell him things." Curiosities—sensitivities—were awakening the financier; Finley was present. "Mr. Mellon had a dry but delightful sense of humor," Finley later wrote, "and a very infectious laugh. He disliked garrulity or serious talk that made no sense. He had a disconcerting way of saying 'Why?' when someone had been making statements or proposing something to which not too much thought had been given. 'It sounds well,' he would say, 'but it won't work.' "

Finley dismisses clichés testily. Mellon had been "described by people who did not know him as a shy, silent man. . . ." Even this is unfair; he was "a reticent man but not shy, and he was a very forceful character."

Finley became the servitor, guardian of the chalice, very likely the first person since Frick infected measurably by Andrew Mellon's laugh. Benefaction started casting cells.

Invisibly, then. What renewed energies A.W. could summon now that the economy looked bad he lavished on Pittsburgh. "By the time I got involved with 'em," recalls Frank Denton, who went to work for R.B. in 1929, "A.W. was coming home frequently, and whenever he did he sat down and went over business in a big way." Denton was another find, an out-of-the-way Kansas banker's son with a breezy personality and a head full of stainless steel accountant's dies that threaded anybody's books. Denton was established around the Government as an administrative prodigy—he'd been the youngest National Bank Examiner in the Department's history at twenty-four. At thirty, after stints that permitted him to poke his famously cold nose into the world's financial complexities from the reorganized National City Bank of New York to the China Sea, he'd ascended to Assistant Chief National Bank Examiner. Then R.B., who was already absent-mindedly elbowing his way into ownership of a lot of the little local western Pennsylvania banks, suggested to his brother he certainly could use one real good man. A.W. asked around.

"I guess my name came up after A.W. indicated what he had in mind to the Comptroller of the Currency," Frank later surmised. "He said right out, '*Denton's your guy.*' " Soon enough after that Denton took the B & O to Pittsburgh on A.W.'s recommendation— "It's got a better roadbed and it gives you a better ride, so take it, even though we are interested in the Pennsylvania." By prearrangement, Denton stopped off for breakfast at the Duquesne Club. Then he reported to the bank, where R.B.'s Dick, just Denton's own age, came off the "platform" to welcome the youthful bank examiner and show him around.

Denton came aboard originally to piece together the Mellbank Corporation, the bank holding company through which the Mellons hoped to impose everything from centralized purchasing to standard auditing procedures on their gathering accumulation of country banks —Wilmerding, East Pittsburgh, Butler, Donora, New Kensington, Charleroi, Latrobe, Ligonier, Washington, more than twenty nearby localities before very long. The bank's own history ascribes the formation of Mellbank to "R. B. Mellon's profound concern for the economic stability and growth of the Pittsburgh area." Ears nearer the ground overheard that throughout the Twenties it was the banking side that interested bustling diffident young Dick (R.K.), very nearly as much as breeding up a premier strain of American foxhounds or drinking or hanging over the split-rail paddock fence to stopwatch his trotters.

Even neighborhood banks, as R.B. realized, had use for a reliable interest-paying city depository for their unneeded funds; by picking up as little as 5 percent of their stock the Mellons not only obligated cash they could reloan but held down competitors. After 1927, when the McFadden Act legitimized branch banking for banks with national charters, it was not only necessary for the Mellons to branch out themselves; they became very wary about letting another national bank attempt to colonize the trans-Allegheny region. Mellbank forced the march. This thing was business; there was no hesitation about squashing hillbilly stockholders or blanketing them into mergers with dummy Mellon corporations. Pittsburgh murmured. Had this been pursued by a less public-spirited gent than R. B. Mellon, citizens might have bellyached.

Testifying, Andrew Mellon would emphasize that Mellbank was mostly R.B.'s baby. There was one incident, A.W. recalled clearly, when R.B. was picking up those distressed country banks at quite a clip. He came to Andrew for cash. Andrew, momentarily "in funds," lent R.B. a million and a quarter. It was 1931; there certainly were bargains around, but capital was uneasy. The brothers were cautious. A.W. was especially guarded about whether he'd been the official pushing legal branch banking. Ground was getting scorched. It wasn't anybody's business that half of Mellbank's original issue of stock disappeared into an ephemeral legal entity entitled the Smithfield Securities Corporation—A.W.'s pass-through holding company. With meddlers like Patman around, publicity could be nasty; twice, at least, bargainers from Bethlehem Steel very nearly gave up their efforts to establish a price for McClintic-Marshall; the brothers were simply too vague about one half-million-dollar item on the books—a loan to Mellbank.

Bit by bit, Mellbank turned into the Mellon boys' culminating cattle drive. Whatever the failing Henry Phillips could dredge from the depleted pouches of the "joint accounts" got worked in there. Assets sealed into Coalesced, the holding company A.W. had devised to get his biggest blocks of securities around inheritance taxes, came out of retirement for the moment.

They almost trampled themselves. Indulging surmise, Andrew Mellon would observe from a few years' vantage point that "The fact that he [R.B.] had kept all of those stocks, and the obligation for them, may possibly have kept him from investing in some other direction, and that other investment might have been unprofitable; and consequently the fact that he had all of those stocks and had that indebtedness, may have been a fine thing for him personally, in his personal affairs."

This certainly plays flat; A.W. was smarting from open-market losses in outsider securities like Western Public Service with which his brother had loaded up the joint account. Mellbank was premature. Those suburban banks whose stock looked like such a bargain at 1931 prices were shortly treading water. Soon after his move to Washington, A.W. had installed a private wire to his brother's desk at the Mellon National. It was seldom idle, but once the market collapsed traffic on the line picked up.

4

They misapprehended—grossly. Even A.W., the Administration's liquidationist, quoted around town for his belief that time was long past to return the money in the country to appropriate hands. He had anticipated, W.L. reports, something every bit as cataclysmic as the break in '73. Throughout 1931, discerning bottom, all three of the Mellons moved in with whatever assets shook loose, went after the holdouts around Pittsburgh as important companies became vulnerable. Unsmiling as a bloodhound, W.L. assumed his overdue place on the Westinghouse executive committee. Thomas Mellon Evans, hanging around The Gulf as W.L.'s office boy, remembers one buy order intercepted from the *Vagabondia*. Just as he rounded Tierra del Fuego, it hit W.L. that this was the turn at which to go after Pittsburgh Plate Glass. "The stock was cheap as hell," Evans says, "but as it happened W.L. didn't have any more money in his account. The clerk just carried the voucher over to R.B., and he put his name on it, and after that they put the checks through. On the account of the bank."

Tiptoeing; neck-deep in transcontinental ooze. Unexpected costs erupted. In order to assure "resources" to keep depositors from shying, the branch banks needed municipal accounts. But municipalities wanted guarantees, surety bonds, and by that time, as Denton says, "banks were going under all over the place and the insurance companies were running like a rabbit from insuring banks." The American Surety Company wanted "personal indemnification" from A.W. and R.B., the equivalent of cosigning their own note. That they wouldn't do, and before long Denton was also managing the Mellbank Indemnity Corporation. This tied up another five million dollars and left the cashbox emptier than ever.

In March of 1932, accompanied by the Finleys, Andrew Mellon had boarded the *Leviathan* to assume the Ambassadorship to the Court of Saint James's. Even W.L. conceded that "the work was less heavy than he had anticipated." This long year approximated, in fact, political exile; Congress and the distracted Hoover appeared to conspire to keep the wily ex-Treasurer as far as possible from problems of the debt. The best of it was helping Ailsa repanel the library in the Prince's Gate residence, luxuriating in badinage with the Queen about his choicer pictures.

Mellon testified subsequently that "I was in London for over a year during the worst part of the depression. I never had information about those companies over there." Weariness became his style. He nevertheless kept track.

"They did their business the way they always did," Denton admits. "R.B. remained the inquisitive fella, the one with the human touch, a contact salesman by inclination. A.W. still picked and chose among the ideas. Whenever he was in town A.W. would sit at the desk and R.B. got the visitor's chair. A.W. decided anything big. Even when he was Ambassador, when banks all over the country were really in trouble I remember how R.B. got me into his office one time and put me on the phone to London to tell his brother how bad it was. Union Trust, the Mellon and the Farmers Deposit were in pretty good shape, but I told him, if we wanted to save the country banks it was going to take seven or eight million dollars. A.W. said, go ahead."

Sour news—that rash of tormented country banks now prickled like white spots across their shrunken Mellon tongue. It was becoming disagreeable to swallow. They might have anticipated. Shortly before Mellon sailed, in middle September, he'd appeared in Pittsburgh just as a run on its deposits was threatening the Bank of Pittsburgh. Nothing quite that size had gone under anywhere. The Comptroller of the Currency, John Pole, was around town as inconspicuously as possible with a couple of Government examiners to help clearinghouse representatives pick over the Bank of Pittsburgh's collateral.

At the time, R.B. headed up the fifty or so banks which constituted the clearinghouse. The ordeal of directing the examiners went, uncontested, to Frank Denton, who sneaked his subordinates into the deserted old bank's executive chambers soon after closing hours for a week to attempt an appraisal of its ramshackle portfolio. By sometime early Sunday they'd repriced the bond list and taken a hesitant look at its assorted equities. "It was perfectly obvious," Denton says, "that the bank's assets amounted to millions less than its liabilities."

R.B. put word out. Suave old H. C. McEldowney, still looking after the Union Trust, appeared at the Forbes Avenue mansion, along with his tightly buttoned brother A. W. McEldowney, serving at the time as senior vice-president of Mellon National. The audit was leaking, and there was pressure from most of the other big Pittsburgh banks to issue a clearinghouse guarantee to support the Bank of Pittsburgh. The Mellons anticipated this. They also realized, because Andrew divulged it, that the following morning officials of the Bank of England would bust the dike by abandoning the gold standard. It required no economists to predict worldwide dumping of securities. With that, any but the stoutest bank would also slide under.

"We knew that most of the other banks pushing us to help assume big losses were liable to come up insolvent themselves," Denton maintains. "As you looked at the list of the Pittsburgh clearinghouse banks, only the three big Mellon banks were sure to survive. So there we were.

"There wasn't any question that world finance was going into debacle on Monday. The error was in the way it was done. A. W. McEldowney was the spokesman for the clearinghouse. He was a cold-blooded guy anyway, the sort who wouldn't loan anybody a dime because he was afraid he wouldn't get it back. No diplomat. He didn't really confer with the other clearinghouse members; he called the press in and he said, *Well, we've looked it over, it's just too big a loss, the bank has to be closed.*

"It appeared so cut-and-dried. He just didn't give the other clearinghouse members a chance." Denton molests his cigar. "This caused a lot of people around town to start talking badly of the Mellons," Denton says thoughtfully.

Capital also suffered lows. The inundation of unwisely managed banks was like the periodic flooding that swamped commercial Pittsburgh. Somebody with enough nerve suggested to A. W. Mellon that he retain a publicist like Ivy Lee to fabricate for him the smile Lee attached to Rockefeller. "No, that won't work," Mellon responded immediately. "In the long run you just have to do what is right, you can't hire somebody and get it fixed."

Properties risked alluvial burial; others came into view. Late in the Twenties, inveigled by the opportunity to acquire nearly eighty thousand shares at an insider price of just about half the open-market level, R.B. bought deeply into the Pittsburgh Coal Company. A.W. held 30 percent.

"I do not think," A.W. would reply to a Government investigator, "anyone could have a great sentimental interest in a coal company." Mellon management perpetuated the "patches" that disfigured this leper among industries. Common people carried stories about the troublemaker with black lung his comrades discovered pulped, the scurvy Appalachian children. Hauled into one of Senator Wheeler's committee rooms to account for excesses of the company's brutal coal-and-iron police, R.B. batted answers like a tranquilized grizzly. "You could not run without them," Senator Eaton enticed Mellon to admit, alluding to machine guns.

That caught some headlines. Then, touching near something important, Wheeler provoked a flurry. "Nobody has accused me of drawing dividends in the coal business," R.B. suddenly lashed out. Here was the crux of the matter: whoever suffered, he and his brother certainly had not profited.

They kept the faith as industrial trustees. During even the best of years Pittsburgh Coal lost capital. Generations of contracts with U. S. Steel made certain of that, although the brothers saw nothing amiss about borrowing from deficit-ridden treasuries. True motivations touched deeper. When New Deal attorneys probed the sale of 123,000

shares of the Union Trust at four dollars a share in 1931, they ragged
A.W. for turning down the offer of one hundred dollars a share from
Frank E. Taplin in 1929.

Mellon seemed surprised they asked. "I had enough knowledge of
Mr. Taplin's operations in the coal business, and of Mr. Taplin generally, to feel that his proposition, if accomplished, would not be
beneficial to the Pittsburgh Coal, or to its stockholders; and besides,
it would be hostile to the interests of this community, to the business
interests of Pittsburgh, or the future of Pittsburgh."

Business interests—the heart, the pump. Workers' lives are nail
pairings. Gifford Pinchot got reelected; he appeared suddenly, without
appointment, wrought up as Jeremiah before the startled old Secretary.
Destitution everywhere was nauseating. Pittsburgh even—one place
where a man with a back on him and sense to tip his cap could always
find something. Families survived in culverts, when cars went by
children squirmed out from underneath upturned dinghies or the
muddy end of mildewed tarpaulins, all dull-eyed, remembering food.
Citizens secreted themselves in the weeds around dumps until the
refuse was unloaded and the trucks rolled out and they might freely
claw open the steaming piles with boughs and sticks.

Hoovervilles. Unemployment in Pennsylvania approached a third,
worst around the soft-coal areas. Pinchot flaunted a state report testifying that among Pittsburgh Coal Company families charitable relief
was negligible, the women wandered barefoot, starving children were
normally too lethargic to whimper. "This is a hell if there is a hell
anywhere," Pinchot quoted one miner. "No work, starving, afraid of
being shot, it is a shame for a man to tell such bad truth."

Would Mellon pledge a million-dollar loan to the State? Mellon
wouldn't promise. Pinchot exited, markedly flushed, too angry to respond to Mellon's claims that "many of the unemployed are so because
of their own improvidence," or "united drives" would "meet the need."

Pinchot wouldn't understand; charity sopped up capital. That
winter the Mellons contributed $750,000 and sponsored efforts which
furthered the "Pittsburgh Plan." Money hawked from local manufacturers and whoever still drew wages went into a multimillion-dollar
account with which the unemployed were put to work at Allegheny
County public improvements. Such arrangements, Mellon pointed out,
helped "maintain the self-respect which is so essential if people who
are willing and able to work are to be spared the bitter experience

of receiving money for which no compensating labor has been given in return."

The dole—this was the insanity. The disruption would pass, Mellon assured the English-speaking Union in May of 1932. "Today, like other nations, America is bewildered in the face of forces which have overwhelmed the world. We have found that the machine civilization which has been evolved in recent years cannot be made to function with ever-increasing speed, and that new inventions and over-production have necessitated a period of slowing down until the world adjusts itself to the conditions that have arisen since the war."

The long view. Not even the Mellons could overlook the wretchedness of the moment. Pittsburgh was bombed out. Its smogged old neighborhoods waited, empty. What light got through lay dull as suet along deserted tracks in the train yards, picked at the forks with which lumpy returnees in Father Cox's "Hunger Caravan" to Washington went after their soup-kitchen dumplings. The city was scraping. The political apparatus seized.

Nothing was finally dependable. W.L.'s stooge Mayor Charles H. Kline, by now a meaty little seraph with quite a curl across his shiny browline, got convicted on forty-nine counts of misdemeanor in office. What seemed to everybody a perfectly sensible graft-redistribution arrangement rubbed a depression jury poorly. The Mellons' own State Senator James Coyne hung around until an appeals judge reversed Kline's conviction, but at the human level the damage was already done. A "defeated and broken man," Kline returned to City Hall briefly but turned his powers over to the City Council president.

Then came the deluge. That year, 1933, disgruntled Pittsburghers approved a constitutional amendment which empowered the state legislature to draft a new metropolitan charter: this lifted the level of control from the family dooryard to statehouse politics, where even the overendowed Grundy was ranting his last. Mayor Magee's nice manner of keeping the city's serious Democrats docile with table scraps was suddenly outmoded. The autumn of 1933, in one of the few real errors of judgment to mark his career, the aspiring Democratic boss David Lawrence set up in Pittsburgh as mayor his onetime campaign manager William McNair.

McNair in office evinced the reflexes of a porcupine. The mayor was much lambasted for having sold out secretly to the Mellon interests. He lacked this consistency. Once Democratic Governor Earle took office in 1934 Lawrence initiated a "Ripper bill" in the state legislature designed to tear McNair from office. McNair barricaded himself in, bed and all. "I put him in, and I'll take him out," the headstrong Lawrence growled.

Eventually Lawrence did. With the irrepressible "Davey," the Mellons encountered a personality equal if opposite to both their own. He represented the coming leader. As what the surviving forecasters now called the "terminal trough" plowed deeper and deeper into the dilapidated national "plant," workers crawled the ruins like dizzy shocked ants. Idle men joined unions. Invigorated mightily by the ascendant New Deal, C.I.O. agents went out and organized the needy, from college instructors to insufficiently expended wet nurses.

Reexamination was universal. In the middle Twenties, in one of those outbursts that justified his habitual closemouthedness, A.W. had expressed enthusiasm for the emergent Mussolini, "A strong hand," come in to reestablish in Italy "Government by party and not by bargaining." "Many of his measures," Mellon now observed, "are unique indeed, but they are effective."

5

Solidity, effectiveness . . . The frolic had subsided. Coming to, rolling over, one glimpsed immemorial visages, foreheads blotting the glass. Who had not transgressed? Even the cautious ex-Treasurer, in honesty, would have to recognize about the period just ended certain mistakes they'd made. Overexuberances. Like encouraging Henry Rust.

For years, with Rust, each time he got his backers quieted down, something would inevitably break which gave the rest of them a scare as regards the direction he intended to take the Koppers company next. It could be anything—rumors of a proxy fight, an unexpected tombstone insert in one of the financial dailies. Henry blurted things himself. Occasionally, invited out to Rust's refurbished homestead at Leesburg for luncheon, A.W. would listen while the high-strung little manager—exalted, gossiping about the staff, that temple vein athrob and his forgotten butter knife vibrating along the rim of a plate— absolutely could not suppress some business tidbit so replete with risk and questionable in judgment it soured Mellon's digestive processes throughout his winding ride home.

The problem remained—Henry achieved such results. It seemed like anarchy. "Rust seldom bought anything for Koppers without a preliminary battle with his board," concedes an early *Fortune* appraisal, "especially with his cautious Chairman." Charles Marshall was A.W.'s selection for chairman; he and McClintic and the Mellons controlled the preponderance of the voting stock, although Rust soon found a way of participating personally. Still, whatever Rust really wanted, throughout the Twenties, he might expect to receive.

Because the Mellons went along. Knowingly, if from a sympathetic financial distance. Rust demanded autonomy? Fine—inexhaustible, all wound up, he skittered around industrial America. Grinding away out there, their hollow tin mongoose. Henry found things; Mellon banks located financing. Located, which wasn't the same as *providing* financing, a distinction people missed throughout the delirious mid-Twenties.

Take the Milwaukee area, where H.R. had accumulated enough equity in The American Light and Traction Company to get him browsing among the deeds and liens which bound this Middle Western generator to its enormous maternal holding company, United Light and Power. Henry spotted a weakness—Frank Hulswit, United's high-rolling president. Rust bought Hulswit's debts, backed up by Clevelander Cyrus Eaton. The 1926 shake-out left Rust teetering contentedly from the apex of United's half-billion-dollar pyramid.

Rust's progress was unpredictable, he ignored all breakage. Rust swapped his Milwaukee ovens for title to American's Brooklyn Union Gas installations; his enamel-drop eyes now fastened upon a dowdy Boston-based fuel hauler, The Massachusetts Gas Companies. The collective's bituminous properties could double Koppers' output to eight million tons a year. Henry darted in, committing Koppers for twenty million dollars before his partners woke up. Too committed to renege, Koppers produced its $125,000,000 parcel of bonds, prior preference, and preferred securities, renamed the giant subsidiary Eastern Gas and Fuel Associates, and purveyed this mountain of engraving months before the crash.

Too fast, too clever; when had a mutant's cunning built anything that lasted? His empire, like Rust, quavered pitifully with conglomeritis. Important units ignored Pittsburgh. In New Haven and Philadelphia the overselling of Koppers gas had all but destroyed the market for Koppers coke. Freewheeling among his subsidiaries, Rust himself invested heavily in American Tar and battled The Gulf for asphalt contracts. A move into creosote produced timber losses. When Marshall-McClintic developed a waterless gasholder which outsold Koppers' model, Koppers gobbled it up.

A.W. lost patience. "Take that back to Mr. Rust and tell him I never in my life bought anything I had to buy on a time limit," the Treasurer dismissed one messenger, pushing across his desk some figures on gas-company securities. By 1930, expecting downturns, A.W. had instructed R.B. to dispose of whatever they'd accumulated underwriting various Insull operations, including whatever came down via United Light. They'd better be watchful. "After the break Rust approached the old man two or three times with new acquisition ideas," one Koppers man remembers. "A.W. wasn't interested." In 1932 Mellon imported Parker Gilbert, long since a Morgan partner, to locate somebody competent.

"After looking everywhere," A.W. admitted, "we found we had the best man around already working for the company." J. T. Tierney had been Rust's vice-president in charge of operations. "Rust always was more of an acquisition and sales type," one insider says. "A real Wasp gentleman. Obviously the Mellons decided they needed a guy who could consolidate the thing, and so they went with Tierney, who came up through the coke ovens and was a rough tough Catholic who liked to drink and, to tell the truth, was not above roistering a little."

Who managed matters better? One mid-depression afternoon Arthur Davis of the Aluminum Company looked up to discover a pair of familiar pince-nez aflutter upon a very long nose. Roosevelt's Attorney General, patient Homer Cummings, watching—the homespun Connecticut attorney who'd represented George Haskell. Cummings never liked "consolidations"—an aberration acquired early from unrealistic Louie Brandeis.

Davis didn't need Cummings. The pachyderm was deep into financial lily pads. Production was way off. A.W.'s favorite palliative, cutting back the workers to two or three days after successive wage reductions, merely loosened fresh violence around New Kensington's mills.

Nothing muddled them loose. The profitability slid from $10,-868,000 in 1930 to a $6,763,000 1932 deficit. There was still capital, enough to cover the preferred. But how much longer? In hopes of controlling events the Aluminum Corporation joined the worldwide cartel in 1930, buckled on firm shackles of quotas and formulas. The

Europeans were cleverer: by 1934 even bankrupted Germany exceeded the Corporation in ingot tonnage. By then the U. S. Department of Justice was preparing broad antitrust proceedings.

6

The depression settled in. On Pittsburgh street corners too, entrepreneurs in spattered cravats were interrupting holiday shoppers with offers of diseased-looking apples. Whoever couldn't look, bought. Movies seemed relatively cheap; in Kansas in newsreels the cattlemen were lining up their livestock alongside gullies shallow enough for bulldozing. The soup in soup kitchens looked lifeless as water. In industrial New Kensington, unemployed from the aluminum mills marched noisily upon borough hall to insist on gestures of relief.

Around Prince's Gate, between strolls with royalty, the Ambassador received information but managed his "ice-water smile." Little endangered his equilibrium. In May of 1931 he sent his son 75,000 shares of Aluminum Company stock. "It is not paying any dividends at present," A.W. pointed out, "as the Company is expanding and using its surplus earnings for that purpose; but this course is better for the stockholders than would be the present receipt of cash dividends."

Let the wind blow. When Gifford Pinchot responded to the newly inaugurated Roosevelt's lead and decreed a Pennsylvania-wide banking holiday in March of 1933, the Mellons were unshaken. Other banks might close. The Mellon National and the Union Trust opened promptly that Saturday morning. Beaming, stalking the banking lobby of the Mellon National to squeeze as many hands, oversee full payment to as many of the bank's customers as cared to withdraw, the spruce and florid R. B. Mellon presented an embodiment of confidence as irrefutable as the "open cage, in plain view . . . used to stack money in bundles so that everyone could see that there was plenty of it."

Across Smithfield Street, H. C. McEldowney presided. A later-day photograph displays the lieutenant himself, benign, white tie. The portly vizier's squint tightens now with fatigue. He remains, after everything, what nourishes everything else.

It was that ill-advised Union Gulf fiasco. When Henry wasn't present, insiders blamed him personally. He demanded personal collateral.

"That was really something," admits Colonel Drake, ninety-five. A hand as veiny as a mummified contour map taps its emphatic forefinger, drums the interviewer's wrist. "It very nearly ruined the Mellons." Uncertain breath draws close, drops. "It got so, here was the bottom, that was the graveyard. I remember old Henry Phillips, who had access to the safe-deposit boxes, saying, 'If this thing goes any further we are going to be broke.' "

What popped the bung was that $78,000,000 in demand collateral; just covering the bonds required assets that once approximated nearly $300,000,000. Between faltering corporations, Union Gulf reabsorbed wholesale whatever the inner Mellon group legitimately called theirs, the rewards for everything.

They turned it over. The Little Bull market, like its parental Great Bull market, was ground into headcheese. Originally, the bankers and W.L. had made available five sizable blocks of securities. Large, although odds and ends so far as the bankers' wealth counted. In three years Pullman had dropped from a per-share high of 99 to a bottom of 10. Alcoa, the most valuable segment, fell from 539 to 22. The U. S. Steel and Pittsburgh Plate Glass securities also underwent the shift of a decimal. The call for Pittsburgh Coal Company (preferred) was especially weak. Buyers were so novel shares stopped getting financial-page mention.

The surrender of equities too deserves a moment in history; while A.W. served abroad the family scented Appomattox. Gangling Phillips remembered keenly those months of delving among the portfolios. Moving over ledger entries, "taking down" fresh certificates to the Union Trust to protect those oblivious Pittsburgh businessmen. Cornered by Government investigators, old Henry let slip who else had provided. Securities appeared en masse from every holding company. R.B.'s wife Jennie, foursquare, sent collateral in batches from King family repositories. As safe-deposit boxes emptied, R.B. walked in on H. C. McEldowney and emerged with three hundred shares of McEldowney's own Union Trust certificates.

He'd better help out. This was McEldowney's doing. Let them fall short for even one trading session; the stir of air behind some yokel bank examiner could explode their water. After that, what prospects? Everything would dump spontaneously, befoul Wall Street's spats. The banks as well—their stock was committed. And who would buy? Millions of unwanted shares? In London A.W. woke up and asked an emissary, "Who ever got me into this awful scrape?"

Such reports made H. C. McEldowney morningsick.

He was reminded often. " 'Damn you, Henry,' " an insider caught R.B. erupting at McEldowney just as the market was scraping its 1932 June lows, " 'I'm going to get the last municipal bond out of the box, and that's *it*.' If the market decline had gone any further, that issue would have defaulted." Possibly. The Mellons stood fast.

Their attitude was privileged. "We've moved to these new office buildings," W.L. reportedly wrote his uncle in London, "and that looks pretty bad in these times, but I'm pleased to tell you, although we show a paper loss, there is no cash loss." Whatever that might indicate, the deficit Gulf reported in 1931 was $23,658,000—not precisely heartening news. Oversupply around the Southwest induced red-neck legislatures to "prorate" the amount of oil each producer could pump; the expanded refinery complex and all those pipelines Gulf borrowed to underwrite now ran at crippling undercapacity.

The Mellons were justified. Under the detested Roosevelt the ordeal was passing. After the 1932 lows the securities market, bleating audibly, started pulling itself together. Family stocks and bonds went back to original owners. Gulf inched into solvency. In November of 1934, a year before its managers dared show an operating profit, the Gulf Oil Corporation paid off the Union Gulf loan. Sighs arose like prayers.

They barely slid through; A.W. continued anticipating. He'd prepared them carefully; he tipped one intention the afternoon George Whitney had jarred the Treasurer by declaring the Morgans would like to retain Frank Drake as chairman of Pullman.

The Colonel managed Pullman. He knew the Mellons quite intimately by then, and he awaited developments. "In March of 1931 I went home to Pittsburgh, and my good wife told me, W. L. Mellon would like to see you. W.L. had a way o' waggin' his head. 'I'm gettin' tired of workin' so hard,' he said. 'I want to spend six months in the winter on my yacht. We're goin' to make some changes. I'm going to be chairman, you're going to be president of Gulf.'

"Can you imagine a worse time? Even the Gulf company was losing money, they were cutting off their dividends. That was the baptism that I got. I was lucky. The only way I could go was up." W.L. had also promoted Frank Leovy, to vice-chairman, still responsible for crude.

Drake took on refining and marketing. Gulf had been shaped by Leovy's fixation on drilling, and virtually every other activity of the

Jennie, R.B., leaving Pittsburgh funeral
PITTSBURGH *Press*

A.W., conventioneer (Henry McEldowney on right)
CARNEGIE LIBRARY

company was cluttered with overcapacity. "Naturally," a writer for *Fortune* asserts, "there was wholesale firing, pensioning, overhauling." The Colonel decentralized.

The Barco concession had yielded more publicity than oil; in 1936 Gulf traded its interest to Texas and Socony for $12,500,000.

There were vicious moments. "Leovy was a strong little man, and Frank Drake was determined to alter things he had to do with," summarizes another Mellon operative. "He wriggled this way, and that way, in his usual style. He got Gulf into Finland, and Sweden, and Denmark. He's always been a great maneuverer." In 1935 Gulf netted $10,500,000—its first true profit since the inception of the slump.

Mellbank settled in too. Federal legislation in 1933 and 1935 prohibited commercial banking houses from underwriting securities. Few retained much appetite. That too would change, the Mellons expected; in 1933 they formed the Mellon Securities Company. As vice-president of the Mellon National, young Richard—R.K.—was ineligible, so Denton became president. Before the Thirties ended, offices for the Mellon Securities Company occupied two of Mellbank's three floors. "We did a hell of a big business," the unvarnished Denton proclaims. "Made a hell of a lot of money for the family. We got to be one of the three or four biggest in the country." The zest was back.

10 | THE TAX INVESTIGATION

1

VIA FLUKES OF HISTORY Mellon escaped the worst. He'd left a bourgeoisie in paroxysms, its symbol the matron grumpily shoveling potatoes from a municipal pile into her surviving beaded handbag. The ex-Ambassador returned in March of 1933 to an intimidating militancy. Demolition squads were forming to make an end to the discredited Old Order.

A story was going around. According to one version, Andrew Mellon and ex-President Hoover were strolling. "Could you let me have a nickel, I'd like to make a telephone call to a friend," the recent Greatest Secretary of the Treasury Since Alexander Hamilton ostensibly asked his superior.

"Here, take a dime, call all your friends."

Very few weeks elapsed before signs of Mellon's new status became sharply personal. A.W. was scarcely unpacked before "unofficial sources" leaked word that his tax return for 1931 was up for auditing. Shortly, May 5, Congressman Lewis McFadden, a longtime Mellon assailant, read into the *Record* a letter from David Olson, the man who instituted informer proceedings against the Treasurer for failing to tax foreign shippers.

Olson accused the financier of racking up large market losses on paper sales of securities he arranged to convey to the Union Trust Company, an organization "under the control of Mr. Mellon and his associates." There, after the stipulated thirty-one days elapsed, the stock passed quietly to other Mellon entities, notably the "Coalesced Company, which is owned 100 percent by Mr. Mellon and his family." These transactions were not "bona fide sales," Olson charged.

They resulted, in fact, in the "fraudulent withdrawal of income taxes from the government."

Mellon spokesmen squawked.

Poppycock. Nevertheless—something pernicious was gathering. Soon after McFadden spoke the new Attorney General, Homer Cummings, waved in the reporters and emphasized the thoroughness with which he expected to poke into Mellon's "specific tax evasion of $6,700,000." Newspapers coursed with innuendoes. On June 16 the affronted banker wrote the Attorney General personally, demanding such an inquiry and extending his fullest personal cooperation.

Nothing happened. Only newspaper stories and radio attacks, "a campaign of character-wrecking and abuse," as Mellon wrote the off-hand Cummings, "based, apparently, on information furnished by someone in either the Treasury or the Department of Justice." A muckraking biography of Mellon by Harvey O'Connor came out and sold very briskly. Quite late in October three F.B.I. accountants showed up on Smithfield Street and kept the employees on edge for weeks. They announced nothing irregular. Bombardments in Congress continued. On January 6, 1934, there were press reports that the Justice Department was going after Mellon for twelve million dollars in delinquent taxes. Mellon again wrote Cummings; Cummings summoned the press to reflect, not obliquely, on new Justice Department procedures when "The Treasury's investigation discloses a situation. . . ." A year of this, yet so far not even the "thirty-day letter" which normally heralds a Treasury Department audit.

Was anybody in doubt? The Roosevelt Administration was mounting a campaign of nerves. The elderly banker's neat little peaked ears lay back very flat by this time; those well-seamed hackles were stiff with apprehensions. Taxes furnished their excuse. They simply wanted . . . everything, the affair wouldn't end until that crowd around Roosevelt had conducted its autopsy, spread Mellon's intimate arrangements across the pages of tabloids so good-for-nothings could gawk. They required their Judas goat. Henry Morgenthau, Jr., A.W.'s successor as Treasury Secretary, subsequently made that plain: "I consider that Mr. Mellon is not on trial but democracy and the privileged rich and I want to see who will win."

Mellon awaited events nervously. Cummings peppered out interviews—hints, references to action pending against the "100 percent Aluminum monopoly," the concession that any tax prosecution of Mellon just then would probably be "borderline." Nevertheless, on

May 7, 1934, the Department of Justice instituted proceedings before a Pittsburgh grand jury in hopes of establishing that Mellon's 1931 income tax return might provide the basis for an indictment for defrauding the government. The federal attorney lost. The Allegheny County grand jury quickly dismissed the complaint as "not a true bill."

"I am, of course, gratified," Mellon murmured just afterward. "The fact that the grand jury reached a sound conclusion, notwithstanding the unusual methods pursued in my case, is proof of the good sense and fairness of the American people." He'd reiterated this throughout. In Washington, Homer Cummings scourged "these highly improper assertions," which Mr. Mellon made "so as to be current while the grand jury had his case under consideration."

The exposure had taken them all beyond forgetting about Mellon. A special task force was already in being within the Justice Department to collaborate with Treasury in preparing "acquittal-proof cases against suspected tax evaders." Its attorneys were embarked on proceedings against luminaries from Jimmy Walker to Thomas Lamont. Mellon *must* be cornered. They backed themselves up. Long before the grand jury convened, the Department of the Treasury sent Mellon his belated "deficiency letter," which specified a 1931 underpayment of $1,319,080.90. Ten points were alleged. One, which carried with it the imputation of deliberate fraud, involved an additional 50-percent penalty.

Tainted bait. A taste implied culpability. "I will spend the rest of my life in jail rather than do that," Mellon then declared. His decision followed quickly. He'd shrunk back pitifully, mailed one unanswered explanation after another to the high-handed Attorney General. Tremulous, aged, even that restorative appetite had dwindled to a yen for bread in milk. But this was insufferable. Mellon summoned his attorneys. He instructed the lawyers to institute an action before the U. S. Board of Tax Appeals for recovery of $139,045, the amount a reexamination of his personal records indicated he *over*paid his income taxes in 1931.

Let the public see. The Government promptly countersued.

Mellon's case, Docket Number 76499, came up before successive three-judge panels of the Appeals Board throughout the winter and spring of 1935 in Pittsburgh. Witnesses appeared in Washington into May and June; the last few testified in reconvened sessions in February, 1936. The documentation was massive. The trial yielded over

9,900 typewritten pages, and briefs from Mellon's lawyers alone comprised five separate volumes.

Even minutiae were strategic. The Government's mapping expedition dallied over each nightshirt transaction, picked apart the holding companies over which Mellon's specialists labored. Let the ragged consider.

Earlier, just after the grand jury acquittal, a righteous Walter Lippmann condemned the Government's tactics as contemptible and idiotic, a "low and inept political maneuver." Yet as the columns reprinted testimony and magazines summarized detail, opinion shifted of itself. The experts on Ways and Means incorporated what they read into the Revenue Act of 1935. As Robert H. Jackson, the Government's prosecutor, commented once things quieted: "The great service to the administration . . . was to demonstrate that the tax transactions of Mellon had been handled so close to the edge of the law at least that the administration was justified in pursuing him. After the trial, nothing more was ever heard of the claim that Mr. Mellon was persecuted, a cry which until that time had done the administration some harm."

The case made Jackson uneasy. "They brought him into the Government for that, to prosecute political enemies, and when he finished they gave him what they promised him for it," one Mellon lawyer growls. Jackson wanted no inducements. Even as a Supreme Court Associate Justice the attorney from Jamestown, New York, never relinquished his pugnacity—those hemispheric temples lifted easily, the mouth was resolved. His reputation for scrappiness got Bob Jackson started—personable in the anteroom, but dogged before quixotic country juries. He began his education with a crusty old Democrat of a father who never could resist a bid to exchange some horses. "But how do you dare trade that way, Pop, when you don't know what you are getting?" Bob asked him once while they were riding the buggy home.

"It's sometimes enough to know what you are getting rid of."

By 1932 Jackson and his friends were eager to rid the public of influences like Mellon. He came to Washington as general counsel to the Bureau of Internal Revenue. He'd pleaded limited background; Morgenthau turned it around. "We want somebody who hasn't had tax experience," Roosevelt's Treasury Secretary maintained. "We think there ought to be a fresh viewpoint in the Treasury." Fresh, and persevering.

Jackson's were frankly nostalgic. Thomas Mellon might nod. "I think the end of all this enormous concentration is government ownership," Jackson himself would write. "I don't believe in it. I don't think it is a good system. I like people who aren't too rich but who are looking out for themselves."

Mellon was avidly trying. Patriarchal, eyebrows grizzled, something of the old, half-humorous gleam crept into his look as he put together defenses. This might cost money. Brushing off the implications, he imported the most flamboyant defense lawyer of the period, Frank Hogan, and paid a seven-figure fee to repel his attackers.

Hogan's sympathies were professional. "My definition of the ideal client," declared the mouthy little Brooklyn attorney shortly after he cleared Edward L. Doheny of charges of kickbacks to Interior Secretary Albert Fall, "is a gentleman of unlimited resources who is really scared." Hogan bulwarked his practice by partnership with Nelson Hartson, A.W.'s old Treasury solicitor. When Hogan came in he ingratiatingly elbowed Mellon's more subdued retainers out of the planning sessions. A.W. ignored dissension. The case on paper was never the issue. Only two things mattered. Would his holdings survive? Mellon's ghost and residuum, guardian of his children.

What about his reputation? He'd never trusted fame very far, yet life in Washington, his place in history, Ailsa's nagging vision—he wanted something major. His brush with ruination the summer of 1932 had left him financially short of breath. But things were mending. He had more time, he'd make the bequest. Only—on his terms, not something they'd think they'd bullied him into.

Jackson and his Revenue Bureau attorneys had torn the stuffing out of five prime components of the 1931 return. These the Government labeled: "(1) the McClintic-Marshall Issues; (2) the Bank Stock Issue; (3) Stock Loss Issues; (4) the Contributions Issue; and (5) the Fraud Issue." As points under dispute they seemed rather legalistic. Laid out in charts and documents, overlaid across the record, they presented a fortune newly overhauled for passage. Suddenly readers caught glimpses.

Sympathizers accused the Government of providing "ammunition for the radicals." Word was gotten out that Jackson himself had argued, on tactical grounds, against the fraud charges. It was Mellon's employees. Hadn't he himself neglected to witness his tax return? Who drafted that intricate phased liquidation of McClintic-Marshall over which the Tax Appeal judges were poring those hundreds of hours? The arguments became technical; even cheeky little Hogan gave up the courtroom to Reed, Smith drones.

The lawyer who understood it all was young Paul Rodewald. "I know A.W. was fully aware of what we had in mind when McClintic-Marshall passed over to Bethlehem Steel," Rodewald says flatly. "I remember spending twenty minutes or so with him, going over the status of the transactions when we were getting the deal together." The version the family prefers would center the problem on establishing the 1913 tax base so as to compute the 1931 capital gains. "The proper amount of tax to be paid by a citizen necessarily may be subject to dispute," conceded A.W. himself.

The issue was fundamental. Roughly, the liquidiation of the McClintic-Marshall Corporation involved disposing of assets Bethlehem Steel hadn't acquired to Mellon-dominated Union Construction Company and Pitt Securities Company. Then, Union Construction Company was collapsed and its primary assets credited into the treasury of The Koppers Company, which in return distributed 83½ percent of *its* shares of beneficial interest among the four original McClintic-Marshall stockholders. A.W. and R.B. got 30 percent each.

All this, including A.W.'s big bundle of Bethlehem certificates, left him with something like $35,000,000 in funds and securities. The entire display was essentially a "reorganization," the Mellon lawyers intoned, and accordingly no taxes were due the Government.

Jackson prepared the wringer. The previous Internal Revenue Commissioner had "erred in favor of the petitioner," admitted the Government's brief. That would be rectified.

The regulars in Pittsburgh were prepared to forget the McClintic-Marshall proceeds if that might close the ledgers once and for all. What dried the lips of Mellon's longtime financial man, Howard M. Johnson, was Jackson's intimate questioning. Auditors were searching everything, the admissions so raw at moments the rustle of a bailiff pushing out the door in the back could convulse an afternoon.

Hadn't they been provident? "During the time I was in the White House," Herbert Hoover would record, "we had occasion to recommend an increase in taxes. I suggested to Mr. Mellon that the upper brackets of the income and estate taxes be increased and mentioned a very substantial increase. 'That is not enough,' Mr. Mellon replied." Enough for the others. His own estate, the Treasurer had decided, had best be earmarked for higher public purposes. As the Thirties opened, Thomas Mellon Evans remembers, there was a call from Andy in Washington. "They're going to put that inheritance tax thing through," the Treasurer tipped Will. "You better get out and give some stuff away." Jackson produced a list of twelve tax-avoidance angles David Blair worked up for him in 1923.

By 1931 the Treasurer had well-developed plans. With his usual prescience, Mellon had, in 1927, drawn aside A. W. Gregg and instructed him to send to the Secretary's offices the Government attorney he gauged best fitted to reorganize an estate. Gregg forwarded Donald Shepard—daring, gruff sometimes, quite willing to invent a procedure when one was lacking.

Central to A.W.'s planning became the Coalesced Company, a family holding corporation in which the financier anticipated that the greatest part of his securities would arrive, as lawyers say poetically, "at rest." Coalesced was organized first in December of 1929 and reorganized barely two years afterward. Its common was divided between Paul and Ailsa. Mellon retained the preferred, which disgorged as dividends whatever *it* collected on securities it held. Virtually all came down as gifts from Mellon's own holdings.

Some discovered beneficial detours. In several situations, their uneven routes had not only allowed securities to escape all inheritance taxes, but also provided deductions to offset Mellon's income.

Such transactions, Jackson's brief often hinted, took place in an unearthly Middle Region, set out to accomplish effective transmigration of capital without basically disturbing ownership. These moves Jackson stigmatized as "phantom" or "shadow" sales.

A simple specimen involved the 54,000 shares of Western Public Service common R.B. had added to the joint account just at the crest of the boom. Its value utterly collapsed. In early 1931 R.B. had established a loss by selling the stock off directly to a Union Trust subsidiary. Soon after the mandatory thirty-day waiting period expired, the Coalesced Company stepped in and repurchased A.W.'s half. The banker put in a $402,000 capital loss.

A.W.'s 123,622-share plurality of Pittsburgh Coal Company common draw similar challenges. Barely two years earlier, Jackson emphasized in court, the chairman of the Pittsburgh and West Virginia Railroad had approached the Treasurer and offered him ten million dollars for 100,000 shares. Mellon hadn't been receptive. Yet late in 1931 the financier had accepted $500,000 from the Union Trust

Company for his entire 123,622-share block. Howard Johnson himself hand-carried it over. Then, "On April 25, 1932," notes Jackson's brief, Johnson reappeared at Union Trust with a check from the Coalesced Company for $517,278.21. "This alleged 'price,' " writes Jackson, "was exactly the 'cost' of the stock, plus expenses for transfer stamps, Pennsylvania five-mills tax, *plus 6% interest* for the number of days it was held by the Trust Company." The italics are Jackson's. So much for claims by petitioner that coincidence alone dictated his loss sale late in 1931, that afterward his children, studiously reviewing the Coalesced portfolio, took up an identical position scarcely four months later.

Meanwhile, before the pending gift tax legislation passed into the law, the Treasurer had divided his 34,000 shares of Pittsburgh Coal preferred between Paul and Ailsa, and they had remanded it to Coalesced.

Auditors were combing numbly through something over $400,000 in losses which Mellon had claimed on scattered stocks which wound up in Ailsa's personal holding corporation, the Ascalot Company.

Ascalot itself, from time to time, sold some of these same securities back to A. W. Mellon for further tax losses, which led to entries "so hopelessly confusing," Jackson wrote, "as to defy understanding." Why had he dubbed it *that*, somebody queried the banker.

"So people like you will ask a lot of questions."

Mostly, throughout his five-day courtroom extravaganza in April of 1935, the Government's prize witness came across as autumnal yet winsome, bemused in the flow of all these memories. The banker's usual reticence, those wary, stammered responses, gave way to spurts of recollection. His crafty mouthpiece, Hogan, strained regularly to cut him off before he rambled dangerously. Mellon wanted to help.

Often he appeared lost. When Jackson pushed Mellon to admit that the 1931 capital losses had cut nearly a half-million dollars from his tax obligation for the year, the old man repeated the figures aloud. "I do not know," he finally admitted.

"You see the difficulty," Hogan quickly put in, "in having three of us up here who do not know anything about this return. The—"

"I have—" Mellon began.

"I think you had better call in an expert," Hogan said.

"I never did take any interest in going into a complicated set of figures like that," Mellon observed.

"I do not either, Mr. Mellon," said Robert Jackson.

It seemed the moment to elucidate a principle. "Somebody else—" Mellon began. "I never believed in doing anything that somebody else could do better than I could, and there always was someone who could do these things better than I could."

One detects regrets. Not very long afterward, sounding out the financier about the Pittsburgh Coal Company's prospects, Jackson wondered whether a loan effected cost reductions.

"No doubt," Mellon remarked. "That could be better testified to by someone in the company who knew something."

"We have not had such a witness, Mr. Mellon," Jackson explained. "You are the best-informed man we have had up to date."

"Oh, you are at a loss."

So Mellon answered patiently, and session succeeded session. His visage appeared ghastly at times, all bone and hollows. His haberdashery never changed—very lovely and completely dark except for the pinpoints on his invariable tie. He remained much interested. The explanations he offered for all these complex dealings relied wholly on fundamentals. He frequently needed money. He desired to simplify his affairs. He had been glad to dispose of certain of his securities through Union Trust because his holdings were large, and any real effort to throw them back on the open market during 1931 or 1932 would probably have broken away what little support such issues retained. Yes, he conceded rhetorically, sooner or later somebody might possibly have picked them up, at grossly depressed prices, in about the spirit that speculators grab "unclaimed baggage."

Couldn't this be plausible? He sat so still, that neatly clippered old head propped up by fingers like fine, knobbed chalk or—as when he reviewed some banking proposal—cradled lightly with chin capping palm. The eyes looked curious as an infant's; from time to time, when matters got technical, the ancient cobbled eyelids closed. Still the informed bystander, attempting gently to explain away Jackson's reminders that every single share of stock Union Trust took in at less than Mellon's basis was "repurchased" by Coalesced, while nothing the bank acquired over basis ever got passed through. These things happened sometimes, Mellon would quietly suggest. Weary priest. Such mysteries seemed otiose.

Mellon had his effect. After eleven weeks Jackson submitted the Government's preliminary brief. Even Jackson's heading blazed: "PERFECT PARALLELISM EXISTS BETWEEN THE PITTS-

Target of the Government—A.W. with David Finley and David Bruce

Preparing defenses (Donald Shepard, left)

BURGH COAL COMPANY COMMON STOCK TRANSACTION OF DECEMBER 30, 1931, AND THE SIMILAR FRAUDULENT TRANSACTIONS OF DECEMBER 29, 1932, in the following respects: . . ." Charges flew both ways. Mellon had "sold short"; Hogan claimed an annotation by Cummings which singled out this case as one the importance of which transcended "its merit." Jackson's brief aroused everybody. Hogan rose in indignation, a peppercorn pulverized. "This," he reportedly shouted, "is vicious, scandalous, scurrilous, impertinent, and malicious." That was probably expected, but immediately afterward Ernest H. Van Fossan, chairman of the Board of Tax Appeals, labeled Jackson's document "false, ill-tempered, and not useful." He threw out Jackson's brief.

Not *useful*! "It is Mr. Mellon's creed that $200,000,000 can do no wrong," Jackson told the reporters. "Our offense consists in doubting it." Jackson telegraphed his resignation to Morgenthau, who wired back his "emphatic desire" that Jackson proceed "with no abatement" to insist that Mellon's transactions "be judged by the standards of common business honesty." Meanwhile Hogan jeered publicly at Jackson's "swan song," when "the board . . . would not allow his slanders to foul its records."

Jackson was particularly incensed that elements of his case which clearly proved *generations* of chicanery were being dismissed so errantly. That bank stock issue! If statistics could march!

This effort to mislead the public went back to 1921, when Andrew Mellon discovered he'd better be relieved of bank stock holdings before he entered the Treasury. He'd sold the securities—to R. B. Mellon. This detail he'd kept to himself throughout his tenure in office. After the Frick estate came onto the block A.W. acquired Frick's surviving bank stock. This left A.W. with 3,300 shares of Union Trust voting securities and R.B. with 1,000.

According to the "written instrument" which bound the brothers, R.B. was liable to pay $10,520,495.00 for these securities "six months after demand." Meanwhile, he agreed to reimburse A.W.'s account at the rate of 5⅓ percent "interest." As Union Trust increased its payout, A.W. started receiving more "interest"—the very amount, and to the penny, he would otherwise have gotten had he remained the owner of record. Clauses in the "instrument" provided that, in case of A.W.'s death or "legal disability," his "representatives" would recover those Union Trust securities.

Throughout the Twenties R.B. was aggressively buying into and reorganizing the banks around Pittsburgh. While A.W. was precluded by statute from participating directly, he did supply much of the cash. These "temporary loans" carried forward by means of a series of meticulous accounts. Mellbank pulled this together.

By 1930 the time had come to "simplify" the banking interests. "It first came to my attention from Mr. Johnson," the financier told Jackson, "who said that my brother had come to—had said to him that he would like to be relieved of those bank stocks, that is, to sell the bank stocks, and in that conversation my brother had suggested that Paul should acquire them, and when Mr. Johnson spoke to me about it that was agreeable to me. It was in line with what I was—"

"Willing to approve?" Hogan broke in prudently.

"And I approved it, yes."

Paul assumed the "interest" payments. The open-market value of the 3,300 Union Trust shares and an assortment of other bank holdings had just about doubled. Nevertheless, they went to Paul for what R.B. had paid. Jackson could only marvel: "The contentions of the taxpayer are worthy of Alice in Wonderland." Then, in March of 1932, weeks before the imposition of the federal gift tax, Paul turned over two thousand shares of the original Union Trust issue to a new Shepard creation, the Smithfield Securities Corporation. Smithfield also picked up half interest in the Mellbank Corporation in return for forgiveness of much of R.B.'s indebtedness to his brother the Treasurer.

Barely two weeks later the Smithfield Securities Corporation, at Paul Mellon's recorded suggestion, turned over *its* entire capital stock to the Coalesced Company.

Such generosities boggled Jackson. The power that represented! Dominion over western Pennsylvania. Yet throughout this awesome, secret passage, as Jackson's brief indicates, and until those last several weeks, "Paul Mellon, like R. B. Mellon, did not receive possession of any of the stocks, and did not receive even the record title to the most important of them."

2

Somehow that wasn't startling. "Paul Mellon found it expedient to be absent at all times during the trial," Jackson observed, perhaps balefully. "Paul Mellon is a beneficiary of many of the transactions and could have thrown upon them the light of a young, alert mind.

Whether he was unwilling to initiate his business career by attempting to make testimony which would fit with that which we have heard, or whether it was feared that he might on cross-examination fail to sustain his father's case, we do not know."

Probably Andrew didn't either. "And on those occasions," Jackson prompted the banker, "you discussed the various business transactions, and the relations of the Mellon family to the different industries, I take it?"

"I do not think we ever discussed questions such as you have indicated. That is not usual between father and son. What I mean by that is that we were congenial, and I do not like the word, but say comrades. I mean we discussed matters which were of interest."

"Well, that included, of course, the business interest to which you had given a large part of your life?"

"Very little of it."

"Very little?"

"Yes."

Very little. In 1931 Paul returned to Pittsburgh. A.W. was impatient. "My father had a theory that too much education was debilitating," Paul says, "and he always used Childs Frick as an example. Childs went to Princeton. His father always emphasized to him he could become whatever he liked. So he became a taxidermist. I got quite tired of that story, which was supposed to be a lesson to me.

"I wanted to go to graduate school. I was interested in books, possibly in publishing or teaching. I'd talked to the professors I knew at Yale, teachers like Chauncey Tinker, about possibly attending Harvard and getting a Ph.D. I got to thinking about it, I thought, Mother being English, and I persuaded Father that Oxford or Cambridge was a good idea. One of my uncles in England had a cousin in Clare College, Cambridge."

Paul began at Cambridge in 1929. "My father really wasn't very keen on my going to England to college. Then, after I had spent a year there, I really couldn't see much point to it unless I got a degree. You know, you don't really get to know anybody in England for a year. I convinced him. He was pretty reasonable, so I stayed. I have to admit I didn't do very much work over there. I made the mistake of thinking I ought to know more about history. English economic history had a very good man, a very good lecturer, but the other people there were really pretty ghastly. I gave up the lectures and merely did the reading. My tutor really wasn't much of a help.

"I got a third-class honors, just scraping through." His essay question saved him.

Paul was squirming loose. "He got to drinking at one point," Cousin Matt says. Matt had left Pittsburgh years before and wound up teaching philosophy at Albert Ludwig University, in Freiburg im Breisgau. "Paul ruined his stomach temporarily, so he came over to the Black Forest and got himself treated at a sort of clinic they had there. They got him up at six in the morning and played a hose of ice-cold water all across his belly. I took him around a little, showed him the town of Staufen, where the Faust myth started. I could see everything in Germany was repellent to him. There was something really wrong with Paul when he was young."

English anonymity. One more callow undergraduate in a dressing gown, hurrying through the drizzle of the quadrangle to schedule a bath. People took him up. They liked the wryness, Paul's low-key delivery blighted by a faint lisp at moments very like A.W.'s. Nobody wanted anything particularly, and one might try things. He'd rowed at Choate; he made the college shell, and returned to America with oars. A crowd of Pennsylvanians coming over had got Paul interested in fox hunting. "I had never hunted before," he says, "and barely could jump. I didn't know a thing about fox hunting except what I had read in books. But I went to Leicestershire, hired a horse and tried it." After that he kept a hunter in a Cambridge livery stable. Paul accumulated sporting books. He bought a picture—George Stubbs's lively portrait of the racehorse Pumpkin.

Nevertheless—Pittsburgh appeared inescapable. A.W. had made him promise to begin his banking apprenticeship between academic sessions. Freshly disembarked in Manhattan in July of 1930, Paul divulged to interviewers that, honestly, "Commerce and banking hold no interest for me. . . . There are other members of our family who are far more fitted than I am to look after the family interests." He genuinely preferred publishing. This made the newspapers. Once Paul reached Pittsburgh, A.W. was tapping his fingers. "I really don't know what I'm going to do," Paul admitted soon afterward. "I'm going to have to talk with Father tonight."

Paul understudied Frank Denton that summer. "He really worked," one of "young Mellon's associates" tipped off a reporter, excited at how the scion "quickly grasped the fundamentals." Co-workers detected airiness—when Paul lost money shooting craps, none of the runners would accept his check; he settled with discounted Irish

Serious effort—Paul Mellon in banking
U.P.I.

Visions
CULVER

Sweepstakes tickets. Officials maintained he loved the work. Paul himself wasn't commenting.

In December of 1931 the Treasurer again came in from Washington to conduct his reluctant heir personally to banking quarters. His career in publishing had become, Paul divulged, "old stuff." Reporters arrived to see. "I didn't do much, really," Paul wanted to emphasize after the initial session. "Just looked around, mostly." Photographers led him upstairs. A shot at work? "Oh, no, no, no. Why, everyone on earth would know it was a dreadful fake. They know it isn't my desk. They know I haven't any desk. I'm not a banker, and everybody knows it." The accompanying cut portrays the prince of industry scrolling up one corner of some statistical document, his tight little banker's four-in-hand a threat to respiration, venturing an official peek. His brows are taut with controlled repugnance.

"I went through all the departments in the bank," Paul remembers. "I enjoyed a lot of it. Two or three of my Yale friends came along to Pittsburgh, and *socially* it was nice.

"Father made a misjudgment. One day while I was doing something he and Uncle Dick called me up to their offices and told me there was an opening on the board of the Pittsburgh Coal Company. I thought it looked kind of silly, a minor employee of the bank sitting on the board. Then I went on the bank board, and on the board of Gulf. I never really knew what was going on."

Paul's Coal Company directorship came up several times during Jackson's ranging cross-examination. The Judge had coal works among his holdings, A.W. reminisced, and they had invariably "given him a lot of trouble." Andrew took them over. Now, with Paul coming along, the president of the Pittsburgh Coal Company approached A.W. and indicated that "there was a vacancy on the board and whether it would be satisfactory to me if my son—if they should elect my son a director and I said that would be all right, and I told my son that he was going to be elected a director and I was in full accord with the idea because I did not know of any business that was harder than the coal business, and I thought if he could get interested in it and learn the coal business he would learn a great deal about carrying on industrial businesses."

Hadn't that seemed sensible? Not very long afterward Howard Johnson escorted Paul and George Wyckoff to West Virginia to examine real mines. "We crawled through coal-mine shafts on hands and knees," Wyckoff recalls. "It was a pretty frightening thing."

George was a friend from Yale. He'd been around Pittsburgh anyhow, working at Union Trust, and then the summer of 1933 he got a letter from Paul, who said his father was interested in having a younger person come into the office. Wyckoff took the job of assistant secretary of Coalesced. George was a Canarsie Dutchman with a powerful, equine face—nostrils flaring, bottom teeth on show—and clanging ebulliences that made his jaw bridle, eyes rolling, as if he startled himself. He spoke his mind, and he was devoted to Paul. Both he and Paul were aware that A.W. brought him in in hopes of keeping Paul deskbound.

Paul lived at home on Woodland Road. He applied himself—up early, struggling to understand discounting and come to terms with sliding interest levels, sitting in on meetings of the branches in Donora and Charleroi. At one point he and Wyckoff and fellow Yale man Nick Brady went over to Manhattan and took a three-month course in accounting at Bankers Trust. Paul suffered. "He's the first one to admit that figures confuse him," Wyckoff says. "That I didn't like at all," Paul Mellon says.

They dabbled with investments. Paul's childhood friend, Jim

McKay, somehow convinced the others that a downtown Pittsburgh hamburger stand could be a money-maker. "We hired a Greek fellow to run the place, Al Seraphic," Wyckoff says, "and he hired his girl friend as the cashier. She had her hand in the till. A White Tower opened across the street. Business wasn't what we hoped for. We hit upon the idea of sitting my wife and Leonard Mudge's wife in the window. As a draw, we wanted a quality trade. People still wouldn't come. It was the hamburgers. You simply couldn't eat the darned things.

"The time came when somebody had to go tell Seraphic to fire his girl friend. Mellon and Mudge happened to be out of town, so I was elected. I walked over there and started to talk with Seraphic, and then I noticed that he was raising one hand slowly, and that there was a pistol on one of the shelves.

"It really seemed easier to just go out of business. We went broke. It took me five years to pay Paul back. We'd called the place the In and Out Restaurant. Most appropriate."

Paul tried something else. "He came to me," George recalls, "and he said, 'I've got an invention. There are an awful lot of injuries in the bathtub. What would you think about a rubber tub?'

"I thought he was kidding. He got rather provoked. But he is like his father, he wouldn't have an argument with you, he just went his own way. He actually set the thing up, The Rubatub Corporation. It even had its own little plant.

"I believe it lasted about as long as the In and Out Restaurant."

After hours was best. Several of the older cousins found Paul personally disheveled, obviously afraid of people. It required real friends to release in Paul a kind of infectious gleefulness, his way of reddening heartily and shuffling with appreciation when something was apt. "When Paul was young," John Walker insists, "he went to a great many dances and parties. He always liked girls very much. These were not always the richest or the most socially acceptable girls—which isn't to say that they were ladies of easy virtue. At least I never found their virtues very easy." Paul relished a drink; sometimes, like Andrew, he indulged in poker. A.W. played expertly. Paul, Walker reports, did not. "The stakes we played for were low, but even so Paul started at an early age sharing his wealth."

Diversion simply wasn't enough. "I would have been happy if I really liked it," Paul muses. "Father had very definite opinions about this. He didn't mind if I disagreed, but I respected his opinion, I was perfectly willing to try out what he thought I should do. But I kept feeling that there wasn't enough time for reading, or really any of the things I'd been interested in in college."

On arriving in Pittsburgh George Wyckoff and Chauncey Hubbard both stayed several months with A.W. and Paul. "I got to know Mr. Mellon," Wyckoff observes, "if you can say that. I remember one incident. A.W. always had a huge breakfast. The three of us were talking about horses. He was always an intent listener. He looked up and he said, Paul, why do you have this interest in racing?

"Paul gave a plausible answer. The old man thought a minute, and took another mouthful, and said, Paul, any fool knows one horse càn run faster than another."

Their minds met awkwardly. Early in 1935 Paul married a divorcée named Mary Conover Brown, whom the discreet Walker characterizes as "a somewhat exotic though beautiful creature" who found herself unable to dispel the "slight feeling of estrangement" Pittsburgh aroused in her. Paul understood. The couple spent increasing stretches at Oak Spring, the farm in Upperville, Virginia, A.W. bought Nora. By then the tax investigation was under way. "One day that winter," George Wyckoff reports, "a fellow turned up at the bank from the Federal Government. Paul had already gotten word that there might be a subpoena served. He crawled out his office window that day, and along a ledge. Then he left Pittsburgh, and in a certain sense he's never come back."

"A.W. never really gave Paul a chance," says Dick's widow, Connie. "Whenever something would happen he'd call in Dick. And Dick would say, let's talk to Paul. And A.W. would say, no, he's not interested.

"Dick was A.W.'s pet."

Things landed on Dick. R.B. was ailing. Pittsburgh after the mills started closing was grisly, overseen day by day. Jennie set aside tables just off the service entrance, and indigents started trooping through the Fifth Avenue mansion for tasty hot victuals. Then, late in November of 1933, R.B. couldn't shake a chill he got inspecting a construction project in Nadine. It went into pneumonia. He died December 1.

Reporters confronted "Young Dick." He received them humbly. His bland doll's face was taking on flesh. Gray marked his temples. "We" hope, he repeated, "that we can do half as well as they have done." A week hadn't passed; Dick gazed out unselfconsciously from behind his father's expandable desk.

Dick had more problems than Pittsburghers realized. R.B. left just over eleven million dollars outright and shares in the Aloxite Corporation worth about seventy-five and a half million dollars, divided equally among Jennie, Sarah and Dick. Then the Commissioner of Internal Revenue stepped in. When Aloxite was founded, R.B. acknowledged heart problems. Therefore, all gifts of stock were made "in contemplation of death," and all of Aloxite's assets were liable to estate tax assessment. Between state and federal exactions the death tax totaled $37,567,602.59. Interest added another three million dollars or so. Everybody staggered. Who had the cash? "They had to arrive at values," Frank Denton explains, releasing his machine-gun laugh. "There was the problem of blockage—you'd bust the market high, wide and handsome if you just sold." Frank ran Mellon Securities, already their key financial-operations man once Henry McEldowney went in 1935. The authorities demanded settlement. "The lawyer for the R. B. Mellon estate, W. M. Robinson, had developed the idea that a big block of Gulf had better be sold before the end of the year. Mellon Securities looked into it. We got a Reed, Smith opinion that this was not 'hot stock,' that is, that by acquiring it we'd control the company. It cost us fifteen or twenty million dollars. We got some Scottish trusts interested, but the British Treasury wouldn't let anybody export sterling. Things finally worked out with A.W. taking a whole bunch of the Gulf stock, and all of his interest in Mellon Securities winding up on the R.B. side."

The shake-out made everybody fractious. "R.B. had left the East Liberty Presbyterian a million-dollar endowment," John Buchanan says. "But he had given away so much money late in life, and in failing health, that after taxes the estate was insolvent. We didn't get the million. We sent our chairman of elders over to see whether A.W. wouldn't make his brother's promise good. He got very mad, it was the turning point in our association with the Mellons, he said if R.B.'s family would support him in some impossible grant, as to the National Gallery, he'd help them out. Later on R. K. Mellon and Sarah Scaife each gave five hundred thousand dollars to replace the original commitment."

With R.B. gone, worries devolved on Dick. He had the experience. Up from the platform, conversant with the language. Paul couldn't be bothered, although Paul and Ailsa, once A.W. died in 1937, came

Dick Mellon at ease

into assets at least four or five times greater than those of Dick and Sarah Scaife. Dick liked business detail; he'd enjoy a life on trains to board meetings.

Dick wouldn't let on. His sleek straight hair looked glossy as pewter; every day those round blunted features and the increasing floridness brought back R.B. more. He became R.K. That color, at times, owed something to an additional drink or two to offset his overcrowded business day—a habit that troubled his father the final few years. But Dick buckled down. His morning started early; his habits were regular. Newspapers profiled him regularly now, always the Princeton alumnus. He craved real importance: resistance hurt his feelings. When, after 1929, he offered to open the Rolling Rock acreage to several of the neighboring hunts, they preferred to fold. In 1937 adjoining farmers whose land they'd paneled for fox hunting attempted to close it off; the help on Rolling Rock farms went out on strike and picketed the access roads. R.K. was upset, and denounced the "impossible and ridiculous demands which they are not going to get," and threatened to close down permanently. The strikers gave in.

He fought off nightmares of incompetence. Months after A.W. died, relates the doting Van Urk, Dick "dreamed he was surrounded by hundreds of people, all mounted on beautifully groomed horses. The highly polished tack and the sea of red coats dazzled him. He heard a tremendous crash of music which sounded like the cry of hounds. Then somebody blew 'gone away'—and kept on blowing it. Hounds were running, but none of the people or their horses seemed to move from the spot where they stood. What was worse, everyone was staring at him with cold beady eyes. He began to blush and perspire. He was embarrassed—perhaps, he thought, because he was standing in the middle of a dance floor in his pajamas."

One young, alert mind whose light Jackson missed was that of David K. E. Bruce. This was a loss—Bruce grasped the details. He attended court proceedings virtually every day. Photographers caught his stately profile regularly when snapping A.W. Solicitous, gently attending his father-in-law.

Bruce made a fine reputation later for delicacy in negotiation. He came fully prepared after marriage to Ailsa. "Perhaps they began badly," one intimate suggests. "She got so ill in Rome when they were first married, some weird kind of allergy to insects of some sort, sand flies perhaps, that came out of the plaster in the walls. She was obviously running a fever a great deal of the time. It was a difficult period—Mussolini was just starting in, their wedding presents got stolen. If you've heard other people describe her she wasn't exactly Little Miss Fixit. She wasn't going to concern herself with her husband's running of his office.

"Besides that, you know, here you had David . . . always a brilliant student, the highest averages everywhere. And Ailsa? That school in Farmington. She wasn't sufficiently prepared to be the wife of somebody like that. And still, you know—they were very sympathetic, and very close."

One luxury wealth provides is pliable relationships. Both Bruces had accompanied A.W. throughout his tenure in London, but much of the time, their friends agree, "they lived more or less apart." David favored Staunton Hall. Ailsa leased Ann Morgan's old apartment on Sutton Place in Manhattan, and usually spent weekends at the manicured estate her father gave her at Syosset, Long Island. She dressed herself beautifully, but makeup couldn't cover the flushed, drawn look, the premature pallors. After 1926, Bruce maintains, Ailsa was a "semi-invalid." Courage, along with that unabashedly haughty sense of who she was, kept Ailsa functioning.

That, and her affection for David. He called her, ominously, "The Princess," and remained the "central fact of her life." The friend who insists on that also says "she saw his limitations. She anticipated his career in diplomacy, although she didn't think he would have been a great Secretary of State."

The ice-water quality, A.W.'s firstborn. Refinement lowers the temperature.

Bruce's grasp was warmer. He turned up, cheerful as usual, when Sarah Mellon married Alan Scaife in 1927. He worked with Shepard, setting up the Ascalot Company to receive the fourteen million dollars which A.W. turned over to beat the gift tax. He was an early director of Mellon Securities. Stocks came and went. At one point A.W. strongly urged his son-in-law to take a block of his own Koppers preferred—the dividend was solid—and sell Southern Pacific.

David didn't mind gambling, now that he had some information. Board meetings were instructive. There was a play in Ward Baking stock—chemists at the Mellon Institute had produced a very economical "yeast food," and with his father-in-law's backing David made good money. "His judgment was sound," an acquaintance confides, "but in 1932 his brokers were after him for collateral, and he didn't have it. 'I went to Rolling Rock for ten days,' he told me, 'and played some golf until the storm blew over. They never got me.' "

To Andrew Mellon's delight Ailsa produced a daughter in 1933. Audrey's trust was waiting. "You got a present for her?" somebody asked A.W., eager to look.

"Why, should I?"

The failing banker's fixation had now become philanthropy. Here Bruce was perfect. "David had law training," Lauder Greenway says, "and he had a wonderful personality, which Mr. Shepard did not have. So A.W. depended on him, David could do all sorts of things for A.W. He was interested in history, he had a wonderful eye for furniture, English silver, pictures. So knowledgeable, and he always has been marvelous with his brother-in-law, Paul." Bruce left the executive committee on Ascalot, to reappear in Washington. He wrote a history of the Presidency and won a seat in the Virginia legislature. "When we were getting the National Gallery organized," John Walker says, "Paul was on the building committee. The person who made the practical decisions was Shepard. The one who made the *ultimate* decisions, of course, was David Bruce."

11 | SOMETHING ETERNAL

1

L ATER THERE WAS TALK that recriminations from the tax suit produced the National Gallery. This depresses the Mellons. The slosh of assets through familial holding companies seemed unreal to newspaper readers. Remote maneuver—Atlantic whales sieving plankton. Of far more color just then was what the Government lawyers labeled the "contributions issue."

They meant the art collection. The "issue" was dragged in anyhow, Jackson and his team insisted, a "red herring" Mellon's brain trust had tossed out late to mislead public attention, an attempt to "smother the whole thing under an art gallery. . . ." As late as May 16, 1935, there had been no documentary mention whatsoever of the alleged "five valuable paintings" whose donation to "The A. W. Mellon Educational and Charitable Trust" constituted all but the last half-million of the over $3,800,000 which Mellon had requested be deducted from his income in 1931. And this, even, only after receiving word that the Government wanted additional taxes.

And why so reluctant? It was entirely paper work, "A trust with as little substance as a summer cloud," according to the Government's brief, which left the paintings "donated" in 1931 still locked away in the vaults of the Corcoran Galleries, less accessible than Leningrad. Subsequent gifts still glowed in their accustomed places on Woodland Road or Massachusetts Avenue or around the walls of Ailsa's apartment in Manhattan. Mellon grasped the keys. And after he died, was there any hope that the designated trustees—Paul Mellon, Donald Shepard, David K. Bruce—would change the policies according to which "No enjoyment or benefit whatever has inured to the people of the United States as the results of the alleged gifts . . . ?"

Mellon wouldn't bother lying. The vociferous Frank Hogan kept referring to the banker's secret intention to grace the country with a "Temple of Art." But when the trust was recorded, the registry was Pittsburgh. Worse, when confronted with statements he had issued as recently as November of 1934, in which the financier went out of his way to proclaim that "The report that I have arranged to build an art gallery at Washington is entirely unfounded," Mellon conceded that, indeed, he had been "waylaid by a reporter, and I think what I told him was substantially true." No commitments, no architects, no plans so far.

Why misrepresent? Mellon was content answering. Yet even these bare courtroom responses hint at the disruptions, the churnings and collapses in valuations, the disparities between what was intended and what, suddenly, was evidently left.

He himself hired Shepard, A.W. admitted readily, to oversee the reorganization. This was 1927: "At the time I was seeking someone, some additional assistance or support in my affairs; and one of the items was the matter of an art gallery which I had in mind to build, and to give my art works to, the collection which I had; to give them to that institution." Clues reinforce this. There is a diary entry in 1928 in which the Treasurer makes note of a telephone call from Ailsa at Sutton Place, eager to find out whether her father has announced the gift. In Herbert Hoover's memoirs, the fair-minded Quaker records Presidential conversations pertaining to such Gallery; Mellon wanted to reserve a site.

Then came the bust. Assets shrank; income diminished; Union Gulf opened under them. Shepard's precedents were ready, but "It transpired then that I did not go on with it, as at the time I intended to, because there were other matters that prevented . . ." On December 30, 1930, The A. W. Mellon Educational and Charitable Trust surfaced. The next four years the trustees took in a smattering of cash and oddments among the securities like shares in the Monongahela Street Railway Company. Young Paul made contributions. The trust engaged, desultorily, in trivia like freighting Father Cox's shattered lumpen-Army back to a Pittsburgh soup kitchen, the underwriting of scholarships between Yale and Clare College, Cambridge.

In truth, just then, the "E and C" was obviously providing the financial holding tank for Mellon's art collection. In 1931 it received the disputed $3,241,250 worth of Hermitage old masters. In 1932

Mellon gave the trust just over six million dollars' worth of art; in 1934 he added paintings appraised at just under nine million dollars. Nobody took these later deductions against income, but nobody could question that here, too, the banker was unloading assets in anticipation of estate taxes. The salient doubt remained: was this, too, technical? Another "shadow sale"?

Evidence speaks against that. "For many years," proceeded the banker's late 1934 statement denying having already "arranged" to build a gallery, "I have bought paintings from time to time with the idea that eventually they would be made available to the public." This prompted the trust. "The trustees have absolute discretion to dispose of all these paintings for the benefit of the public by way of either public gift, exhibition or sale. In case of sale the proceeds will be used for such public educational or charitable purposes as they, the trustees, may determine. The trustees are not likely, under existing conditions, to come to any decision for some time as to what will be the eventual disposition of these pictures, and no further details or lists of the pictures will be given out."

Crisp. That had been November 13, 1934. Yet six weeks later, at a December 31 meeting, the trustees resolved formally to "further increase the Trust's charitable activities during the year 1935 and to make plans for the erection of an art gallery to house the Trust's art collection."

Now wasn't that suspicious, such overnight turnabouts? Robert Jackson wasn't placated. His thick forefinger outstretched toward stacks of evidence, he conveyed the urgencies of top federal officials. The situation was awkward, even for a tough curly-headed young provincial with a shallow grinding naturally prosecutorial jaw. Between his heel-dragging Tax Commissioner, Elmer Irey, who thought that Mellon was innocent, and all the courtroom card tricks he had to confront against Hogan every session, Jackson kept making telephone calls to get himself relieved.

It really didn't help to cross-examine irresponsibles like picture promoter Joseph Duveen. The contraction of values had precipitated a flight from masterpieces too. As owners lost confidence, Duveen—unflagging in his protestations that the truly priceless was cheap whatever he charged—now exercised a corner on major old masters. His indebtedness was colossal; like farsighted Mellon he very rarely worried. Pedestrian shake-outs were inevitable. He enjoyed life meanwhile, amusing more calculating men with, as his biographer Behrman notes, "big, colorful splashes of untested generalizations and unpremeditated gusto."

All this proved spectacular in court. The recently elevated Lord Millbank loved testifying. Innocently, the Mellon legal staff had decided to bring on Joe Duveen to help establish Mellon's intention to found a public gallery prior to 1931. Nineteen thirty-one? Why, Duveen could assure the auditors that he could remember personally statements the ex-Treasurer ventured, making this quite clear, as early as 1923. They'd talked the whole thing over; Duveen offered consistent guidance, showing up every fortnight or so until Mellon went off to England to guard the banker from possible judgment errors. He'd introduced the prospective architect, Pope, "who is doing work for me in England," and consulted with the Treasurer, who'd presented him with a kind of rough sketch to which the more experienced Duveen contributed the refinements. He'd selected the site, naturally—"by the obelisk near the pond." He meant the Washington Monument, so far as anybody could tell. The courtroom broke up.

Duveen seized the chance to improve Jackson's tone. "Real art works, my dear fellow, don't rise and fall in value like pig iron or sheet copper or tin mines." Attempts to pin down the worth of a Raphael led Duveen to reminisce that the price, $836,000, had seemed to him "rather a low price; I was quite disappointed that I did not get more. But Mr. Mellon rather persuaded me that it was a very high price, so after lunch one day I gave way." This aroused no sympathy—Duveen in the box, his riven face impudent with bluffer's composure, a rat's bold eyes, lacking only the panatella he normally fondled reverently, as if he'd discovered it intact while perusing a richer man's cuspidor. Seducing Joe was routine. As for that Raphael? He'd offer three quarters of a million for the canvas right here and now, with everybody looking on. It was, after all, "one of the most famous Raphaels in the world, or in the universe."

"The witness was not," sighs Jackson's brief, "one of those conservative witnesses who give qualified answers." He seemed too preposterous to discredit. Evidently nobody cared that in 1911 Duveen had paid penalties in excess of a million dollars for smuggling goods into the United States and issuing fraudulent invoices. When Government lawyers mentioned that Duveen's company had lost a million dollars in 1931 and two million in 1932 he himself appeared surprised. Mildly—figures didn't interest him.

Duveen's testimony wowed onlookers; Mellon's lawyers were apprehensive. "What could we do, impeach our own witness?" Paul Rodewald asks. Nattering away up there, the Gatsby of Artifacts kept nudging into doubt the time-line the attorneys were struggling to confirm. Duveen couldn't help himself. Embellishment was his instinct; truth was ghastly pallid. He supplied the brightwork.

One claim was accurate. His association with Andrew Mellon dated. For many years, long after Frick succumbed, Mellon gazed back, "inscrutable," Behrman insists, not impressed at all while Duveen drummed away, vehemently, upon the "importance" of something Mellon fundamentally didn't like. Knoedler's was your agent—glad enough with uncomplicated transactions to accept 10 percent. Duveen was your equal. One bought from Duveen, not through him. Effrontery was his medium, the way a haberdasher's was serge.

Duveen pushed; Mellon wouldn't be rushed; early negotiations boggled. When the affronted Treasurer stalled about paying the high price Duveen required for Lawrence's *Pinkie* after Duveen ran up the cost by refusing to bid with Knoedler's, the dealer blandly withdrew the offer and telephoned H. E. Huntington.

This left Mellon wistful. But Mellon required disciplining before he would be conditioned to acquire, and without those questions, the works of art their processor labeled "Duveens." By finally turning back that Raphael Medici portrait the Treasurer displayed immaturity. Its replacements—a Gainsborough, a Vermeer and the quiescent Memling—they didn't add up.

One impediment was Finley. "I liked Lord Duveen," Finley now says. "He was always extremely polite to me. I didn't socialize with anybody who wasn't polite to me. . . ." Duveen remained, observed Finley, "rather an arrogant person. I remember one occasion, Mr. Mellon asked me to go up there and see what pictures he ought to send down from the Dreyfus collection. He brought down the tall Saint Paul picture. Duveen said, this is a Giotto. I said, no, this is a Follower of Giotto.

"Duveen said, no, I say this is a Giotto, and that makes it a Giotto.

"I told Mr. Mellon. He smiled. He bought the picture. He bought it as a Follower of Giotto."

It was already late. Life itself was guttering. Suddenly, the triumphant Duveen worked loose a Giorgione, *The Adoration of the Shepherds*, owned by Viscount Allendale. The economy was improving, and Mellon was visibly eager to compensate for the chance he lost the day the Soviets quit selling. A Giorgione was rare, priceless almost. Duveen committed half a million dollars to procure the canvas, and offered it immediately to Mellon for $750,000. Mellon prepared to buy, subject only to authentication by Duveen's longtime adviser Berenson.

"Never mind about that," Duveen reportedly rapped out. "*I* say it's a Giorgione. *Everybody* says it's a Giorgione. And there isn't a doubt in the world that B.B. will say it's a Giorgione!" But Berenson didn't. With mischievous integrity the circumspect little scholar sent along a letter to Royal Cortissoz at the *Herald Tribune* in which he recalled the moment during which, "Finally, some ten or twelve years ago, the light dawned on me, and I began to see that it must be Titian's, perhaps his earliest work, but only half out of the egg, the other half still in the Giorgione formula—the landscape, namely."

Mellon sent it back. "I don't want another Titian," Behrman quotes him, "sourly." "Find me a Giorgione."

So that went bad. Duveen broke with Berenson. Yet now, belatedly, something critical caught between the reticent banker and this effervescent English Jew whose guts now made him custodian of so many masterpieces. They were ultimately similar—commercial men, traffickers in creative mysteries. Outsiders, sharing an outsider's melancholy. "*Why* is this picture marvelous, B.B.?" the dealer was wont to ask as he and Berenson poked about some gallery. Such forbidding dark varnishes—no millionaires liked that.

Mellon was uncertain too. John Walker wrote later of evenings around Woodland Road, where "one had a general sense of gloom, the darkness broken by patches of light where reflectors on paintings illuminated the muted colors of English and Dutch portraits and landscapes. I remember on one occasion seeing emerge from the shadows a frail, fastidiously dressed man with high cheekbones, silver hair, and a carefully trimmed moustache. He was inarticulate on the subject of art. Even the names of the artists whose works he owned occasionally escaped him. But from the way he looked at his paintings, from the sheer intensity of his scrutiny, I knew that he had a deep feeling for what he collected, a relationship to his pictures which I have rarely found in the many collectors I have known."

This intensity of scrutiny, this *wanting* to penetrate, Mellon understood about Duveen. They were perforce collaborators. Once, pressured to repay an overdue loan of three million dollars to the Guaranty Trust, Duveen arranged a sixty-day note to cover the amount through

Lord Duveen with patron
U.P.I.

skeptical Henry McEldowney. His London credit reinstated, the dealer again borrowed the three million at Guaranty and paid in Pittsburgh. Mellon fed him hole cards.

The tax trial, oddly, would leave the ancient ex-Treasurer more purged than vindictive, his affairs much simpler. "Well, I gave 'em everything except my laundry slips," he told one friend. Whenever, rarely, lawyers on either side were able to interrupt the sprightly fantasies which had Lord Millbank guiding Mellon's every move, the dealer needed only glance for reassurance down among the visitors. Mellon was usually present, prepared at all times to meet Duveen's impudent if beseeching stare with a nod and—sometimes—a very perceptible wink. Let Duveen rave on. Mellon would make good.

Events gained momentum. The testimony obligated Mellon to leave his collection to a public museum. His Hermitage acquisitions, stored in the Corcoran Galleries, would be the nucleus. Meanwhile, he had gone ahead with working drawings of the building itself and retained John Russell Pope to oversee the architecture. The preeminent designer of neo-Classical structures, Pope had directed construction of the lovely Archives building while A.W. was Treasurer, as well as annexes to the Tate and the National Gallery in London.

A very long lifetime of footsore browsings down malls of canvases had left the banker with notions of his own about museums. They must be stately; they must be comfortable. While acceding to Pope's initial model of a double-H-shaped building patterned after the post-Colonial Hadfield courthouse with a domed rotunda, Mellon eased Pope away from an overimposing envelopment of columns and flanking pediments and intermittent niches for statuary. Genuine elegance required severity. There were few galleries; he envisioned, for intimacy, a hundred rooms, their decor varied subtly from oak for the Rembrandts to plaster and travertine for the Early Italian pictures. "I don't care what it costs, so long as it doesn't look expensive," Mellon once informed Finley. Mellon chose, for facing, great blocks of pinkish Tennessee marble. They looked quite blotchy going up and so were necessarily—and at unexpected expense—picked over and matched to align the reddest along the base and bleach in tone as tier by tier they approached the cornices. The structure cost fifteen million dollars.

The projected hundred rooms, a labyrinth whose width exceeded the Capitol itself, would inevitably leave Mellon's personal collection dotted sparsely around one of the suites. To entice other collectors—and because he shrank from monumental self-advertisement—Mellon insisted on keeping his own name off the architraves. True generosity was disinterested.

The banker had some idea of what was necessary for complete historical range. He'd roamed enough collections; at Henry Frick's urging he'd sat with Vasari's *Lives of the Artists*. He had earlier acquired, for himself, a gentle Lippi portrait, a Luini, even a small Titian Madonna. He must fill in. Mellon expected that; so did Joseph Duveen. He'd protected his monopoly, bankruptcy sniffing his heels.

By 1936 Duveen was dying. Mellon still appeared sphinxlike; Joe Duveen remained coarse. But sympathy had developed, and when, the summer of 1936, the financier stopped off at Duveen Brothers in London, both realized the dealer was irrefutable. "I am going to retire from business," he opened quite simply, "and you are getting ready to give your collection for a National Gallery. This is a combination of circumstances that can never happen again."

What Mellon was after was evident from a sale which followed. The Nazis were sloughing off "non-Aryan" museum holdings, and Duveen procured the important little altarpiece painting *Nativity with the Prophets Isaiah and Ezekiel* by Duccio di Buoninsegna. The financier was preparing to take Duveen up on his London proposal that they peruse the treasures Duveen held "hidden in storage during the Depression" in New York, with an eye to helping Mellon "round out" his collection. Then Mellon caught cold. He dispatched David Finley, with instructions to route through Washington "everything you think is good enough for the National Gallery."

The cue of Duveen's professional lifetime! He bustled to Washington and wangled a lease on the apartment immediately beneath Mellon's own. Overseen by a caretaker, looked after by guards, he arrayed among furnishings to taste the thirty paintings and twenty-one Renaissance sculptures, mostly from the Dreyfus collection, David Finley liked best.

In Duveen's recollection, needless to say, such underlings as Finley dematerialized. "You and I are getting on," he reports approaching Mellon. "We don't want to run around. I have some beautiful things for you, things you ought to have. I have gathered them specially for you. You don't want to keep running to New York to see them; I haven't the energy to keep running to Washington. I shall arrange matters so that you can see these things at your convenience and at your leisure."

The apartment's own contents make clear whose judgments were conclusive. After "much agonizing," Finley relates, he settled on specimens which he believed "not only fine examples of the work of great artists, but were needed to fill the gaps in the Mellon Collection, so that it would give some idea of the achievements of Western painting from the thirteenth to the nineteenth century." Some were Mellon's favorites, the Van Dycks and Lawrences he loved. To Duveen's relief, Finley's choices now included many unsalable acquisitions—holy, exquisite, drab—the intimidating Bernard Berenson once pushed on Duveen Brothers to wind up neglected in the vaults, their radiating gilts and smoky umbers repugnant to Duveen's regular following of railroad speculators and shoguns of the press.

How long they'd languished is evident from John Walker's exchange with Duveen about one of Finley's selections, Masaccio's *Madonna of Humility*. At one point, the happy dealer blurted, he became so incensed at his inability to palm this canvas off that he instructed an employee to rend it. Dissuaded by an assistant, Duveen "decided to destroy it partially by having it repainted to make it prettier."

Like the Renaissance statues from the Dreyfus collection—which Duveen kept pushing to populate the halls which led to the Gallery's garden courts—the *Madonna* by Masaccio escaped Mellon's natural purview. Duveen worked him over, of course, but the decisive influence remained the ever-present Finley. His appreciations were Berenson's; as regards Early Italian both Joseph Duveen and A. W. Mellon functioned substantially as middlemen. The list of purchases speaks largely for itself. Among the acquisitions were an exemplary thirteenth century Byzantine canvas, an attributed Cimabue, and choice paintings from Antonello da Messina, Lippo Memmi, Pisanello, Allegretto Nuzi—masters only to connoisseurs, denizens of that parish, as Berenson observed, where he alone baptized.

The lot Finley summoned hung downstairs at 1785 Massachusetts for several months. Mellon came to meditate for several hours daily. Duncan Phillips stopped by, and Paul and David Bruce, and Mellon's ubiquitous lawyer Donald Shepard. When everyone was satisfied the financier told Finley to ask Duveen to lunch. "Of course," Duveen had instructed Mellon, "these things don't really belong to us. They belong to the people."

Or would—hopefully. Just one more thing. Their solitary auditor, Finley relished the bargaining. "Lord Duveen asked astronomical prices. Mr. Mellon countered with lower ones. At one point Mr.

Mellon said: 'Well, Lord Duveen, I think you will have to take all these things back to New York,' and Lord Duveen replied: 'Mr. Mellon, I would give you these things for the National Gallery rather than take them away.' "

Of the thirty paintings, Mellon bought twenty-four. He bought eighteen sculptures. Behrman sets the bill at twenty-one million dollars. For once, the settlement left A. W. Mellon in need of cash. He paid in securities. After this nobody doubted his seriousness of intent.

On December 22, 1936, the increasingly unsteady financier offered in a letter to F.D.R. to build a National Gallery and donate his own collection to provide the "nucleus." Mellon rounded things out by purchasing the entire Thomas Clarke collection of American portraits. He owned 369 pictures, of which only 115 were subsequently judged worthy of the Gallery.

For some months Finley had been negotiating quietly with an association previously allocated the site Mellon wanted, between Fourth and Seventh streets just off the Constitution Avenue Triangle. There had been Citizens' Association opposition to the projected blockage of traffic, and A.W. had talked that through with the President's uncle, Frederick Delano, chairman of the National Capital Park and Planning Commission.

Getting back to Mellon the day after Christmas, Franklin Roosevelt was nevertheless able to insist that "When my uncle handed me your letter of December 22 I was not only completely taken aback by surprise but was delighted by your very wonderful offer to the people of the United States." Perhaps Roosevelt felt playful. Mercurial President. Upon returning from London in 1933, Mellon had accepted the new Chief Executive's offer to stop by the White House and chat a little about the country's finances. Overall, the retiring Ambassador had tended to condone Roosevelt's emergency proposals, even those more controversial, like the disputed bank holiday. Their tête-à-tête was cordial. Roosevelt was particularly solicitous of what Mellon thought about the workability of the Federal Bank Reinsurance Bill, which just then awaited the Presidential signature. "My father was against it," Paul remembers. Roosevelt couldn't agree more.

"What a charming man Mr. Roosevelt is!" Mellon exclaimed to friends. Next morning, on the radio, Mellon listened to the signing ceremony, during which the President was vibrant while praising the act as the most progressive piece of legislation to clear the Congress.

The litigation which followed made plain Roosevelt's resolve to keep his likes and dislikes from sullying his politics. The populace wanted retribution. Above a filling-station urinal in 1934 Paul Mellon spotted evidence:

> Hoover blew the whistle.
> Mellon rang the bell.
> Wall Street gave the signal
> And the country went to hell.

It made no sense to ignore the Old Order's primary bell-ringer. The tax investigation began. Then Mellon saved himself. Resurrected under courtroom lights, he seemed a spectral little thing, a visitor from much better moments. His answers were endearingly vague, he prattled with gentle archness around five days' inquiries. He made an unserviceable villain, and before the trial was over there was a silent, national applause.

Washington heard it, resoundingly. This tempered politics too; when Franklin D. Roosevelt received that Christmas letter he accompanied his surprise and delight with a suggestion that Mellon or his delegate "come to see me some afternoon this week." Finley wasted no time. By five that afternoon the banker and Finley were installed for tea in the White House library across from their President and watchful Homer Cummings. There was a companionable fire. Roosevelt was again "charming," but throughout the preliminaries the fretful old banker kept tugging at a corner of envelope tucked in his suit-coat pocket.

It contained the provisos. Like every Mellon formula, its terms were generous. Mellon offered his Government everything except control. The essentials quickly reappeared in Donald Shepard's sharp, well-practiced legislative draft, introduced in the Congress as House Joint Resolution 217. To start with, the Constitution Avenue site was appropriated legally. The adjoining area, on the Third Street side, was reserved for future additions. Mellon pledged an endowment, originally five million dollars, the income of which was earmarked to pay the five top gallery officials and fund purchases later. In addition, "the faith of the United States" was committed by statute to guarantee that the Government would provide money for upkeep of the premises and administrative and operational expenses. Formally, the National Gallery of Art was to remain subsidiary to the Smithsonian Institution.

It would be overseen by a board of trustees. Four served ex officio—the U. S. Chief Justice of the Supreme Court, the Secretary of State, the Secretary of the Treasury, the Secretary of the Smithsonian Institution. Five general trustees "shall be chosen," in Finley's transposition, "on first taking office, by the Regents of the Smithsonian Institution." And they would serve "subject to the approval of the donor, Mr. Mellon." These selected general trustees would, accordingly, hold effective control; as their ten-year terms ran out they would be extended or succeeded by other general trustees, "chosen by a majority of the general trustees." This meant, in effect, that three general trustees from the self-perpetuating Mellon group could effectively control policy decisions by the eleven-member board as regarded a National Gallery built on a monumental site donated by the federal government and maintained by taxpayers. Salaries, and presumably loyalties, among the top administrators would flow from that endowment provided by The A. W. Mellon Educational and Charitable Trust.

So the financier fidgeted as his inconsistent President pored paragraph by paragraph over the conditions set out in Donald Shepard's letter. One imagines the heavy head lifting, that rich monarchic smile. Roosevelt handed the pages to Attorney General Cummings. "I think this is all right, and I see no reason why it should not be put through as Mr. Mellon has outlined it," the President finally said. Cummings read the letter. The tea began arriving, accompanied by Jimmy Roosevelt's wife and children and Missy LeHand.

They passed an hour in conversation; Mellon and Finley left. "What a wonderfully attractive man the President is!" A.W. couldn't help conceding. Then, wryly, "I came through it much better than I expected to."

Who ultimately prevailed? The National Gallery opened in 1941. Roosevelt took to teasing Robert Jackson about "his art gallery," and joked about sending Jackson to dedicate the place.

By that time too the original general trustees had long been selected. Besides the banker himself they included David K. E. Bruce, S. Parker Gilbert, Duncan Phillips, and Donald Shepard. Predominantly Mellon people—then, and today.

A.W. fell subject ultimately to what his countrymen might imagine. His evolving standards accommodated. Certainly he wasn't impervious. "I remember very well one stormy winter Sunday at the Rolling Rock Club," Frank Denton says. "The fireplace was goin', a bunch of us were sittin' around in one of the bedrooms, killin' time, not really even drinkin', the door wide open. . . .

"Then, from down the hall, lookin' in, hesitantly, as always—A.W. appeared. We younger men got to our feet. He said he didn't mean to interrupt. And then he said, to me, 'I understand you've had a little trouble with the law recently, Frank.' I'd gotten a speeding ticket."

They left one wizened, such evaporations of grace. Doubts, after a custodial lifetime. His works would justify.

Personalities mustn't enter in. "I'm not going to be deterred by the way I've been treated," the banker told Finley while awaiting the verdict. "Some day the people involved will be dead, I'll be dead, the National Gallery will still be there."

It was the reverie of somebody who'd absorbed a warning. "The spring of 1937 Father fainted a couple of times," Paul Mellon says. "Once, just walking around, he fell and cut his chin. He would insist on walking from the bank to the Duquesne Club. In May he gave the dedication speech for the new Mellon Institute. While we were starting, going from the house to the car, he had one of those lapses people get with arteriosclerosis—a lot of words were coming out, but nothing made sense. When we were partway there he tapped on the glass and signaled to the chauffeur to go right, and I had to tap to tell him left. We rushed a doctor to the Institute. I didn't know what to expect as Father mounted to the podium and started to speak. He read it perfectly, and for the week after that he was absolutely fine, I've never seen him better."

Summer found him reverting. He attempted to muster. He cheered up noticeably each time the Bruces brought four-year-old Audrey around, but that became wearing, and now he had no appetite, gave up his constitutionals, abandoned overnight those rank little rattail stogies he'd puffed since adolescence. A specialist from Baltimore thought he could substantiate a tumor. A.W. would concede he didn't "feel quite right," but he was irritable about advice.

Ailsa was finally able to convince him to escape the worst of the Washington mugginess and join her household in Syosset. A.W. resisted that; blueprints for the Gallery were getting their last markings-up, and Pope had daily questions. En route to Union Station he passed the excavation. Special comforts were ordered. "I have never before hired a private car for my own use," he observed, stepping aboard. Pottering about in Southampton, he continued to refuse medical attention, and his resourceful son-in-law explained away the physician who took up residence as merely a houseguest. Probably Mellon wasn't fooled. A bronchitis hung on, but the increasingly shaky old man wouldn't stay in bed, and late in August it went progressively into pneumonia. Uremic poisoning set in. "The end was perfectly peaceful," David Bruce commented afterward. "He was very weak."

Important funerals mean curtain calls. The forty-four honorary pallbearers trooped up the aisle of East Liberty Presbyterian, sticky in their morning clothes, flaunting top hats. A lifetime of captains—John Bowman, Arthur Davis, Colonel Drake, Frank Denton, Childs Frick, David Finley, ex-Governor Fisher, Benno Jansen, Howard Johnson, Frank Leovy, Ogden Mills and S. Parker Gilbert, Edward Weidlein, Frank Tone, David Reed. . . . R.K. got stranded, hunting bear in Alaska, but most of the immediate family had hurried to Southampton to accompany the body on a Pittsburgher.

Nora joined her children in Pittsburgh. Her marriage to H. Arthur Lee hadn't worked out either, and after another divorce in 1928 Nora reassumed the name of Mellon. Other mourners sneaking looks could tell how heavy she'd gotten, but obviously her delicate English complexion survived. Those soft cat's eyes. Anybody who offered condolences might enjoy again her genteel musical phrasings, so close to teasing with people she liked. Her existence was reportedly quiet these days, rural, mostly flowers and dogs.

It had been A.W.'s wish that his funeral be open to the public. Throngs pushed in, sweltering workers in shirt sleeves and women in bright, damp frocks elbowed toward the closed bronze casket. Up under the nave over four hundred floral pieces, including shipments from President and Mrs. Roosevelt, stood banked with colors filtering down through stained-glass windows which pictured the life of Moses. The choir did "Lead, Kindly Light." One woman ducked under a guard's arm in hopes of seizing an orchid which decorated the edge of the bier; just then the casket passed under the last fluted arches and into the glare of midday. Large numbers of patrolmen on horseback were necessary to control the mobs outside as family members squeezed by into limousines. It wasn't the sort of gathering A.W. under other circumstances relished.

The banker was interred soon after at Allegheny Cemetery, inside the ivy-covered vault which contained his brother's remains. Crowds also assembled there, and there was a police problem with souvenir hunters tearing apart the flowers. A relic for pressing. The air was close, and rites were mercifully brief.

Even testimonials startled memories. "He was a genius in finance

Nora at Andrew's funeral
I.N.S.

and a giver beyond any one person's knowledge," said A. C. Robinson, chairman of Peoples-Pittsburgh Trust Company, witness to the banker's secretiveness. Mrs. Enoch Rauh, whose snorts helped unnerve the banker more than a quarter-century earlier, conferred newspaper benedictions upon a "rare philanthropist, an ideal public servant, a tender and devoted parent, a sincere loyal friend, and a commanding industrialist."

Mellon died; numbers rose, a wraith of decomposing inventory lists. In December, following on three years and eight membership changes of its fifteen-judge panel and 10,350 pages of testimony, the Board of Tax Appeals handed down its conclusions. There was "no doubt" that "the record before us does not sustain the charge of fraud." The foundation was bona fide. The swapping of stocks to establish capital losses was perfectly all right, since "Anyone may so arrange his affairs that his taxes shall be as low as possible." The exception was the Western Public Service reshuffle; both H. C. McEldowney and R. B. Mellon, who worked the deal, passed away before testifying. The sale of McClintic-Marshall to Bethlehem went beyond mere "reorganization," and taxes on it were overdue. With interest, the estate of Andrew W. Mellon owed $668,000.

The divided verdict prompted sputterings about appeal, but, behind paneled doors, sighs of relief were general. Public interest was waning. Businesses were again hiring, and even the nippiest New Dealer quickly lost his sizzle upon confronting those cartons of stenographic onionskins. It became a noncase. Robert Jackson was up for Solicitor General.

The fortune crossed over. Mellon's estate once filed added up to just over $34,000,000 in odds and ends. The important properties were lightly represented, along with a sprinkling of traction-company investments descended from the Judge. An interest in McMullen & Sons, Ltd., brewing; advances to the six McMullen trusts for his many brothers-in-law; local school-district bonds and half a Pittsburgh Stock Exchange seat and nearly seventy thousand dollars in personal effects his will denoted specifically for Paul and Ailsa; and one mysterious two-million-dollar personal loan, given out in 1920, not yet fully repaid. Mellon's Coalesced preferred. A note for $73,000 he'd lent the Institute. His executors cut up the authorized $180,000 among servants, and approved an eight-million-dollar advance against Pennsylvania death duties. The rest went into The A. W. Mellon Educational and Charitable Trust.

This residuary estate worked out at $23,000,000. A.W. passed away August 27, 1937; a revised securities schedule quickly assessed the holdover foundation assets at $52,000,000, of which $20,000,000 had already been slated to build and endow the National Gallery. Once that was finished, the E and C retained over fifty million dollars.

The infatuated around Pittsburgh would rejoice in believing that the departed financier simply split his estate—half for philanthropic purposes, the rest for Ailsa and Paul. And that was credible, if briefly and misleadingly. The assessment on which retainers based this estimate came out of the Jackson investigation, during which a figure just over two hundred million dollars got much bandied about. Probably that veered close, for a historical instant.

How quickly that passed once the market rebounded is evident from even the most offhand graphing of important Mellon blocks. Take Ascalot, Ailsa's personal holding company. Government appraisers had pegged its securities at something like $14,000,000— down well over half from the $34,000,000 portfolio A.W. had presented each child for Christmas of 1931. When things looked hopeless Ailsa's 75,000 shares of Aluminum common, for example, got down to little more than $1,500,000. Then came the recovery. By September of 1938 Alcoa was selling around $160 a share, and Ascalot's block was worth around $12,000,000. And Alcoa was one of thirty entries.

Waning, preoccupied, the ghostly old financier was never too tremulous to putter among the assets as much as necessary to ensure his "position" would survive himself. He had finagled expertly. Jackson never quite understood why Mellon would borrow a tide-me-over million or so from a Gulf affiliate or plunder the tottery Pittsburgh Coal Company treasury while dividends kept accumulating in the Coalesced account. Why all the back-room refinancing? Was it so important that art collection costs and pledges toward the new Institute building be redeemed for cash?

Mellon wouldn't risk securities. Not those he trusted, not the Aluminum Company or Koppers or Carborundum or The Gulf. Certainly never the Bank. Through the depression's trough he rearranged and connived, nudged mismanaged competitors under and bore up through days of testifying, fetchingly, if that protected ownership. Capital represented his life. It must survive uncompromised. And ultimately, with token exceptions, those batches of certificates over which twitchy Phillips had humped his lanky devoted spine for all the decades, seen into and out of the tattered leather portfolios through boom and cataclysm—they handed on down. Not that Mellon doubted—they were irrevocably *invested*. He would be justified. Capitalism deserved to survive.

In Pittsburgh sources "close to the family" were convinced the children would emerge with $500,000,000. Means, sufficient to their purposes, their election properly manifest. Enough themselves to bestow.

BOOK

II

Thoughts in a Mellon Patch

If Grandpa Thomas with his plough
Could only see us Mellons now
(Especially those who misbehave!)
He'd turn abruptly in his grave.

A Puritan who had the gift
Of soberness and work and thrift,
He's scarce believe we'd be such fools
To sun ourselves at swimming pools

And ride around in fancy cars
Smoke cigarettes and big cigars,
Drink alcohol like mothers' milk,
And dress ourselves in brightest silk.

And he might think our clothes out-
rageous,
Our mini-skirts, like mumps, conta-
gious,
Our rock and roll too loud to bear,
Too wild our boys with maxi-hair.

But other days bring other ways,
And while each child and grandchild
pays
The Piper (each great-grandchild too),
Such revolutions are not new.

Each generation has its rules,
And Mellons never have been fools.
Some have thrived, a few have failed,
But hardly *any* have been jailed.

Though some of us are fond of horses,
And some have scandals and divorces,
And some like fishing, some like art,
Our paths are never far apart.

We mind our business, love our
friends,
Grow old, collect our dividends,
Nor do we shrink from healthy toil,
(Though sometimes it is eased with
oil!)

Each generation has to face
Its triumphs or its faults with grace.
Each, as it labors or relaxes,
Itself is faced with Death and Taxes.

So though he was a stern old Judge,
I'm sure he wouldn't now begrudge
Our foibles and extravaganzas,
(Or even these poor foolish stanzas!)

Perhaps he'd smile from up above
With ancient grand-paternal love
To see us dance and dine and wine,
All Mellons on his fruitful vine.

—Paul Mellon
Ligonier, 1970

*A living belief in anything produces corresponding ac-
tion: the loose band slips on the pulley . . .*

—Thomas Mellon, 1885

THE THIRTY-NINTH FLOOR

1

"IT WAS A DAY like this," recalls R.K.'s widow, Connie, "but worse, and I said, 'Dick, I just cannot ever come back and live in Pittsburgh again.' He always said afterward that I was the one that started him thinking."

The war had ended. This was their first night back; they'd taken a flat high in the William Penn Hotel, one that looked out over the murky Golden Triangle. At night the smog closed in and blotted the lighted windows of the surrounding office buildings into fluctuating specks. The entire dilapidated downtown smelled like a tunnel.

Connie had been game. The two were married in April of 1936. If rich people do differ particularly from anybody else, the difference is easiest to spot during mating procedures. They pair so conscientiously, reconciled in the end to this discharge of responsibility too.

Perhaps this sounds heartless. But wariness starts early when money is involved. Bad judgment afflicts status. Dick had finally chosen, and even his close friends will confess that his selection had involved a lot more venturesomeness than people anticipated.

Somehow Connie surprised people. Her credentials stood up—she'd prepared, releases stated, at "fashionable Miss Bennett's school in Millbrook, New York," a place well suited to finish the daughter of Mr. and Mrs. Seward Prosser of New York and Englewood, New Jersey. Connie's father was influential—as chairman of the board of the Governing Committee of Bankers Trust, his was a name the leftists rarely omitted when selecting the dozen prime manipulators who stealthily ruled America. Connie's marriage, her second, provided the newspaper readers of Pittsburgh with quite an array of pictures on which to base their impressions of this slim, delicately muscular little woman, sprightly as a nuthatch, whose "darkly beauteous" fine looks had attracted the affable if reticent young Master of Fox Hunting and president of the Mellon National.

Constance did photograph nicely. In person, even then, a tendency toward leatheriness and suggestions of a carved, stubborn force about the features of her heart-shaped face sometimes put provincials off. They expected less . . . immediacy. Connie's approach was freestyle; when things got ridiculous she had a way of shrugging her shoulders, and lofting a comedic roll of the eyes, and expressing her opinion no matter who looked miffed.

Her accomplishments were undeniable—she was a devoted sportswoman, solid on a horse, a seasoned and reliable shot. She was obviously intelligent, openhearted, gracious. Still—for Dick to up and marry this independent-minded divorcée so soon after Jennie herself had waded into his romance with "Weesie" Reed, whom everybody in Pittsburgh knew and liked, except that she was Catholic. . . . People were taken aback.

Perhaps Connie was too. "She said she was completely through with marriage," one relative says. "It left a bitter taste in her mouth. She could see that Dick was kinda gun-shy and she's supposed to have told him, 'You don't have to worry about me, I'm not going to marry anyone!' That made her even more attractive." The pair met largely by accident at a Madison Square Garden horse show. Then Dick and James Bovard took some time off and visited Nassau, where a mutual friend, a daughter of R.B.'s longtime companion Thruston Wright, reintroduced the couple. "He courted her there," Bovard remembers, "and then he saw a good bit of her in New York."

The girl had already been through one harrowing, benighted liaison. In 1929 Constance Prosser married Vance McCaulley, the adopted son of a wealthy Denver businessman. McCaulley's stability was precarious. After Yale, McCaulley had gotten into the brokerage business in Manhattan, selling bonds for Lee, Higginson. Peddling securities can produce uneasy moments for even the most flexible of moralists, and McCaulley, Connie says, was "warped about honesty. It must have been something in the family. If a telephone operator misled him he thought the entire phone company was crooked." McCaulley's mind wandered; his habits became vagrant. Early in the

Thirties the McCaulleys separated, and in September of 1935 Mc-Caulley killed himself in his New York apartment.

Connie was badly upset. "My father and mother felt sorry for me and wanted to take me to Honolulu for Christmas," she remembers. Her mood was vulnerable. Then R.K. appeared, and unpredictably their courtship took on a momentum of its own. One weekend in Ligonier Dick proposed, quite abruptly; the two were married as soon as practicable after that.

Overhanging even their courtship was the awareness that natural children were out of the question. Connie had undergone operations during her years with McCaulley, and word had gotten around. Some-body close to Dick felt duty-bound to mention the situation shortly before the nuptials. Dick knew; finding out others did shocked him, and he reacted angrily.

An exhibition of temper like that from Dick just then wasn't really characteristic. Even R.B.'s death hadn't freed him much from the inhibitions of scionage. "Dick seemed no better than a boy to the likes of A. V. Davis," one companion remembers, and although no-body opposed his ascension to the presidency of the Mellon National, the importance of the bank itself had fallen off steadily. "Seventeen years ago, this wasn't a bank at all—it was an investment trust," one officer would exclaim in 1963. His observation was even more apt about the years immediately before the war.

R.K. was careful. Blandness required little energy. His impulses were generous, but he protected sensitive feelings. "Also," sums up the dedicated Van Urk, "in spite of a genuine love of people, he 'stands off' familiarity. Very few can get close to him despite his being 'sweet to everyone,' as one person expressed it."

The handful who knew him better recognized ambivalences. For all his mouthings about duties in western Pennsylvania, he shied at leadership. At Wharton in 1953 to receive an award, R.K. would "recall the circumstances that made me a Pittsburgher rather than a Philadelphian." The family had established on South Broad Street a small investment banking business. "I thought to myself that this was my opportunity to move away from Pittsburgh and go to work in the city which I admired so much. . . .

"However, just about the time that I was endeavoring to convince my parents that I would like to undertake this move, my father came to me one day, or rather he sent for me, and said, 'Look here, young man, we can't buck the trend of those good friends of ours in the Philadelphia banks.'

"Consequently, we retreated over the Alleghenies back into Pittsburgh."

Pittsburgh mustn't be abandoned. Periodically, a kind of vehemence would threaten. Uneven performance, sloppiness by some underling —rage pounded. More often, just then, unguarded energies broke loose when Dick was relaxing, particularly when he drank. Playfulness, crashing through the barrier. "I remember one time," Frank Denton says, "a bunch of us met in that marble hallway at the foot of the staircase of the house on Forbes. I was there with a girl I was courtin'. We had on dinner coats, and one of the fellows started pullin' bow neckties. One thing led to another. A little bit o' roughhousing started. I was standin' there protectin' my necktie when I was attacked from the rear. Dick tackled me. He cracked his ankle, and that was the way he missed a whole fall's huntin'."

Sports provided reliable outlets for backed-up adrenaline. One of Dick's great satisfactions during the early years of the marriage was the extent to which Connie took to even the most rugged situations. There were repeated trips to the Yukon to kill or capture animals, often after new specimens for the Pittsburgh Zoo or the Carnegie Museum. The summer of 1940, operating from a yacht and searching for bear along the beaches of the Alaskan off islands, the banker shot one large male just as it was advancing on the party's unsuspecting guide. Their last day out, in hopes of flanking several cubs catching salmon in the riffles beside a sandbar, R.K. and the guide, Bruce Johnstone, had separated in hopes of hemming in the babies and taking them alive. Scrambling through the underbrush beneath close-set hemlocks, Dick heard the explosion of a rifle. He struggled to the top of a mound. ". . . A ghastly sight," the naturalist who accompanied them would write soon afterward, "met his eyes. . . .

"Bruce was down on his back in a shallow mudhole, with his rifle under him and a bear on top, snapping at his face. With only his bare hands clutching the animal's lower jaw and the hair of her right cheek in a death grip, Bruce was holding her head away from his face and yelling to Dick: 'Shoot, shoot quick! I can't hold her much longer!' With prompt decision, Dick put the muzzle of his Springfield close to the bear's shoulder, but noticed Bruce's leg sticking out underneath the bear in direct alignment with the rifle barrel. With a quick change, he lowered the butt of the gun and poked the muzzle up under the bear's throat, firing upward into the brain and killing her instantly.

"Bruce's face and hair were covered with blood. . . ."

Fierce satisfactions! So much was involved—Dick's appetite for danger, his pleasure in nature, acting in a world where everything was comprehensible. "Mr. Mellon can get along anywhere," one Alaskan guide recalled, "and under the most rugged conditions. He is one of the few men who don't need much, and he can do with as little as anybody." In wilderness one escaped, or fled, the middle-aged side-parted silver figurehead whose cheeks were slipping season by season into the anchorage of jowls, across whose noncommittal lips a rigid chiding expression sometimes caught between pleasantries. Wasn't there something better?

There was, it developed, the Second World War. "Three things actually mattered to Dick," George Wyckoff said later. "The Army, Rolling Rock, and the bank. And in that order." After war broke out, R.K. quickly volunteered and received a major's commission. He began his service as an assistant to General Phillipson, helping organize the Army Emergency Relief Fund, the precursor of the U.S.O. "Dick was amazed to find himself in the world of entertainment," Joe Hughes recollects, "but of course he took the assignment on and worked to get that whole thing off the ground." About a year and a half into the war Pennsylvania's governor Edward Martin, a military man himself, under heavy criticism because of the state's Selective Service procedures, put in a request for Lieutenant Colonel Mellon to run the office in Harrisburg. Mellon imported Joseph Hughes, a dapper Pittsburgh lawyer he knew by reputation, from John McCloy's Japanese loyalty program. The two solved drafting problems, and Hughes became a confidant to Mellon for the rest of his career.

These years of service were perhaps the happiest in R.K.'s life. He had the chance every day to display his salient abilities—picking men, smoothing over difficulties—without the strain of all but unlimited responsibilities. He loved the crispness, the ritual, the pomp and ceremonial. He made full colonel—gratifying too, not bad at all for somebody who busted out of Princeton. Nobody finagled that.

There was even talk of making the Army a career. Connie balked. "Ye gods, what she put up with," one relative observes. "She was one woman who could fill any role." After the war ended, R.K. stayed on at the behest of Governor Duff to administer Pennsylvania's civil

Constance and R. K. Mellon
PITTSBURGH *Post-Gazette*

Military appreciations
PITTSBURGH *Post-Gazette*

defense. This helped him secure promotion, finally, to lieutenant general in the Pennsylvania Guard in 1961 and then the U. S. Army Reserve (Retired).

Immediately after the war he bucked for advancement. Each summer he oversaw a National Guard encampment at Indiantown Gap, sported ribbons, reviewed troops. "I disliked it so," his widow admits unhesitatingly. "After a session or two I said, 'Well, *I'm* not doing it.'"

Her days were full enough. In 1939 she and her husband had taken Richard Prosser—Dickie, the first of the four babies they adopted from The Cradle, an agency near Chicago. Cassandra King was adopted in 1940; her sister, Constance Barber, in 1941; and little Seward Prosser—Pross—in 1942.

People sensed right away that fatherhood wasn't something Dick warmed to naturally. "You have to bear in mind that he was a supreme egotist," one associate emphasizes. "The children were essential to him to round out his place in history." In Germanic old Pittsburgh, with all that reverence for blood and authority, adoption chiseled against nature. "A lot of people were sore at Dick for splitting up the fortune by bringing in those children," one family member says. "Connie pushed him into that, you know, she wanted a family so she went out and bought one." It made him uneasy. "One day Dick told me about one of them, that it actually came from much better stock than we do. You know, he said, its father was a bishop."

"Relations were not close," Connie concedes, thinking back. "Dick wasn't an affectionate, loving father. He adored the boys, although I think they were scared of him. He just wasn't easy with them. If anything went wrong he was frightfully upset about it. When he'd come home at night the conversation was the office. And you and I know little people aren't very interested in that."

Dick's obsession remained Pittsburgh. Its wharves and neighborhoods seemed utterly mined out. Subcurrents tore the wastes of two million riverside inhabitants, while over the scum scows dribbled into wakes, and barges flushed unmarketed petroleum. At night, on schedule, convoys of rusty gondola cars pulled up not far from the makeshift Pittsburgh airfield and laved glowing slag across the terrain of years. It cooled in layers, through weeks, and passengers flying in could judge the age of the deposits by tonalities. Fresh ridges were scarlet.

The haze of soot was itself a blessing. The inversion sometimes lifted, and from the office buildings the leadership could see, crawling alongside the Point, the tenements and whorehouses of the dilapidated black Hill. The area had attracted a half-million rats. Approximately 40 percent of the city's downtown property stood completely untenanted. "Odors of the middle ages," to one reporter's nose, slucked through the pilings. Nylons melted from calves. The "smoky city" compounded its reputation, and corporation executives wavered between retaining their unhappy wives and accepting promotions to Pittsburgh. Townspeople understood either way.

Pittsburgh received a visit from Frank Lloyd Wright. "It would be cheaper," pronounced the famous architect, "to abandon it."

Dick Mellon understood that. "We've either got to do something about that place or give it back to the Indians," he had already told Edward Weidlein in 1943; the bouncy little director of the Mellon Institute and Wallace Richards were attending an informal breakfast meeting of the Pittsburgh Regional Planning Association, convened

Depression

with wartime informality in a hotel room in the District of Columbia. In 1941 R.K. had accepted the presidency of this private reform committee. The freewheeling Wallace Richards was involved as planner Frederick Bigger's assistant. To neck-trimmed Pittsburgher businessmen, Richards, with his soigné pallor and theatrical silver crest, exemplified the yawping of collectivism. An outspoken New Dealer, Richards emphasized this himself—a finger of cigarette ash slumped from a corner of his mouth, he loved to expound upon his years as Green Belt administrator, his tricks of publicity agenting. Openly sizing Pittsburgh up, he rammed home proposals for multimillion-dollar skyways, for vast slum-clearance projects.

R.K.'s contemporaries were shocked. It wasn't *Richard*'s money. Mellon couldn't be serious! The taxes this suggested? The dislocation, the shift of property values? Still—even then, who intended to balk this third-generation banker, step up and confront the lank Teutonic hair laid back in perfect pewter strands, the baleful, imperious eyes? Argue until annoyance blouses Mellon's mulish upper lip?

What attracted the high-pitched Richards to Mellon was the need to plan. Why underplay the problems? "My forebears created it," he observed one day, nodding above the squalor; that defined the atmosphere. "Let's say selfish interests are involved," he informed another interviewer. "We have a lot of property here. We can't very well move out banks." Things must be reversed: Mellon companies required professionals—brought in, kept happy. It was too late to cater to every passing whimperer. When smoke abatement turned into an issue, dividing lines became overt. "Some of the boys down the line —the older men—haven't got wise yet that the boys at the top really mean business on this," one local hand remarked. Midway through the war R.K. lined up the activists around town and constituted the Allegheny Conference on Community Development.

Until peace settled in, the Conference seemed mostly a graveyard for initiatives. With Dick Mellon's reappearance the Conference buckled down. Wallace Richards became secretary of the executive committee. A public-affairs strategist, Park Martin, took on the buffeting as permanent director. Martin understood executive mentalities. He insisted that corporation chiefs and institution heads alone, not deputies, show up at meetings and speak for record. A full-time technical staff would define the problem areas, project expenditures, draft legislation. Martin demanded operating budgets—$355,000 to get them through the inaugural three years. Nothing must be authorized without funding first.

Mellon refused to participate—directly. He would dispatch delegates—originally Weidlein and Jim Bovard and Alan Scaife and Joseph Hughes and Ted Hazlett and Adolph Schmidt and, emerging now as *primus*, genial Arthur Van Buskirk.

"Van" established himself naturally as Mellon's alter ego. For thirty uneven years the attorney's round clippered scalp and rimless spectacles set off that youth-leader eagerness, bridgework locked characteristically open, as if in fairness to inhale any argument. R.K. saw himself as "lowest common denominator." He was cripplingly undereducated—speeches he wrote ran on, went nowhere, each sentence became paragraphs. Assistants chopped out phrases like short-order cooks whacking shark meat into scallops. Arthur spared Dick embarrassments.

An accommodating, cultivated man, his endeavors in Washington helped to efface for Van Buskirk (as undoubtedly for Mellon) shibboleths concerning public funds. Republican regulars condemned Van for contributing to Mellon's delinquency, for enticing this bell cow of the business community into connivance with David Lawrence.

Criticism remained sotto voce—Dick supplied the money which kept the local party operating.

R.K. had notions all along. "I'm a Republican and a Presbyterian," he informed one interviewer, "and I don't think I'll ever change." Then, quietly: "I'm not a fanatic about either. Each man has his own individual right to do as he pleases, but businessmen have no influence over voting. It they did it would be the downfall of the nation."

What Republicans hated most, of course, were R.K.'s dealings with Lawrence. In 1945, unpredictably, Pennsylvania's reigning Democratic leader stepped down and ran for mayor of Pittsburgh. David Lawrence was fifty-six, a big grave Scotch-Irishman with an enormous head he tended to throw back augustly before launching his extraordinary speaking voice. He'd been the overwhelming influence in the Democratic Party in Pennsylvania since 1932, when Al Smith's increasing conservatism pushed Lawrence into Franklin Roosevelt's column. Lawrence wasn't above appointments—he'd been Pennsylvania's secretary of state midway through the Thirties—but like most kingmakers he preferred to contrive. He left-handedly booked insurance. His proper education ended when Lawrence was fourteen. Lawrence's "private life" deteriorated—his wife drank heavily, and two of his sons died soon after an automobile crash. Very little remained important. Davey avoided easy confidences, bore down, despised graft, and granted an interview to a reporter from a fashionable magazine while staring at himself in one of the lavatory mirrors in the City Hall men's room, suspenders dangling alongside his solid hips, sleeveless in his undershirt and splashing up water to soften his inexpressive face so he could shave it before some ground-breaking ceremony. His memory was sharp, he commanded invective, and normally his air of dignity and control were such, his executive secretary emphasizes, that "he quickly and naturally dominated any room he was in."

There was no hope of countering such a man, and R. K. Mellon was astute enough never to have tried. Innumerable accounts would maintain that the Pittsburgh "Renaissance" was accomplished through two unlikely friends, Mellon and David Lawrence, and that has meaning, if *friends* be italicized. "I really doubt myself that Lawrence and Dick Mellon were ever alone together more than a few times," Jack Robin, who should know, maintains. They met to ratify.

Traditional barriers washed away. Shortly before Lawrence's elec-

David Lawrence (left), Arthur Van Buskirk

tion in 1945 the planners at the Allegheny Conference identified projects. A new arterial traffic system to divert the cars that clotted the business district. Estimates for the proposed Penn-Lincoln Expressway started out at fifty-seven million. Since this would bypass the no-man's-land between rivers, the planners envisaged ripping out the sprawl around Fort Duquesne to install a triangular green park. They projected *its* cost at another four million dollars.

Stumbling blocks were political. For over a decade the state's successive Republican governors had denied Democratic Pittsburgh. The summer of 1945 Arthur Van Buskirk came back from Washington and took his place as Mellon's official factotum upon the Allegheny Conference. He became in addition finance chairman of the Republican County Committee. It was in overlapping capacities that he descended on Harrisburg and acquainted the governor, Edward Martin, with the high probability that unless the Commonwealth released to Allegheny County its proportion of funds, the party out West might forget about housekeeping money.

Martin signed executive orders, pleading with Van Buskirk that any announcement be timed to benefit the Republican mayoralty candidate. Lawrence called in reporters. He acknowledged considerable delight at finding the state even belatedly cognizant of Pittsburgh's need, and assured the Allegheny Conference businessmen that he himself, once elected, would assist wherever possible.

By that time Park Martin and Richards and Arthur Van Buskirk were booking a series of "quiet little luncheons" in the Mellons' private dining rooms. Local Republicans were dished. "I heard a lot of rumors throughout that time that the Mellons were getting out of politics," Leon Higby says. "Obviously that was nonsense. They simply had too much money to just get out of politics. They didn't dare." What R. K. Mellon expected was to *transcend* politics. The old tired crowd of workaday Republican courthouse idlers would predictably obstruct progress. Let Davey get in.

"I remember the day Lawrence was sworn in as mayor," says Lawrence's Democratic successor as mayor, Joseph Barr. "I came back to the council chamber, and the telephone rang, and it was Dick Mellon calling. He wanted to give this piece of ground on Fifth Avenue and Beechwood to the city." From 1946 on, Mellon's devotion was plain. "Whenever Dick left town after I became mayor," Barr says, "he would call me and tell me where he would be in case we needed him."

They needed him most, obviously, during the early years. By 1947 the Allegheny Conference technicians had worked up legislation to empower the "Pittsburgh Package." The motor for everything was obviously a muscular "Pittsburgh Urban Redevelopment Authority," capable of seizing property by eminent domain to negotiate its rehabilitation. Once plans for the redevelopment agency were under way, Van Buskirk stopped in at City Hall and proposed a shocker: Lawrence should be chairman.

"I'd be laughed out of town if I appointed myself," the boss shot back. The lawyer was prepared: "If we condemned people's properties, it was better for the mayor with his popular following to be responsible, rather than someone with the Mellon or U. S. Steel nameplate." Van Buskirk lined up the Chamber of Commerce and pushed through an Allegheny Conference resolution that urged the reluctant mayor to assume the chairmanship, and himself became vice-chairman. The log was spinning. Lawrence reciprocated by appointing a majority of Republicans.

Richards headed the Parking Authority. A kind of shadow government gradually came into existence now, staffed, without important exception, by people satisfactory to the Mellons. Jeanne Lowe sums up the Conference itself: "The directors of this and other Renaissance agencies were paid to make local public service competitive and sufficiently attractive to high-caliber public servants. They moved with a flexibility uncharacteristic of government, and developed, forwarded and coordinated the new programs; these were the men who, as former Conference director Martin put it, 'move the kings and queens around.' "

Let pawns beware. Shortly after taking office Lawrence attempted to enforce the dead-letter smoke-abatement ordinance the City Council passed in 1941. "Little Joes"—slumlords, realtors, petty union leaders, homeowner groups—particularly resented the provisions requiring that they go first in converting from bituminous. Gritty air meant jobs; soot itself, according to private studies, subtly benefited the lungs. Lawrence himself wasn't amused. When coal interests boycotted, Mellon interposed as a plurality stockholder in Consolidation Coal; Lawrence nudged the Mine Workers. This became Mellon's part —that low, definite voice on the long-distance telephone which hinted of recourses nobody preferred to consider. The bank held paper on just about everybody.

How indispensable Mellon was became clear the week Lawrence and a delegation from the Conference got together in Harrisburg to lobby through countywide antismoke regulations. At a preliminary dinner meeting important Republicans balked. Lawrence laid it out: "Now, speaking to you fellows as a politician, I'll be perfectly happy if you don't go along with this. . . . We are going to pass these bills anyway and I have the word of the governor that he's going to sign them." In Harrisburg others jackknifed. A Pennsylvania Railroad representative had assured Park Martin the carrier would accept the empowering amendment; then at a crucial hearing Rufus Flynn, the railroad's assistant general manager, enraged the remaining delegation by declaring himself opposed.

"Wallace Richards was greatly upset," Lawrence later wrote, and "dashed to the telephone and reported to Mellon in Pittsburgh what had taken place at the hearing. I understand that after this Mr. Mellon called the President of the Pennsylvania Railroad, who happened to be in Florida, and told him in no uncertain terms that the Pennsylvania Railroad must change its position. Benjamin Fairless too was on the phone talking to the heads of the railroad—so it was related to me—and told them how distressed he was by their position. He let them know that there were other railroads besides the Pennsylvania that would be only too happy to ship the products of the Mellon enterprises."

The Pennsylvania buckled. Pittsburgh railroads dieselized. Still, once the emphasis started shifting from stopping hallowed abuses to rebuilding the city, simple coercion wasn't enough. Suave Arthur Van Buskirk might cajole the governor into signing through components of the "Pittsburgh Package" that permitted the nation's first parking authority and rescinded the long-standing prohibition on insurance-company investment in center-city real estate. That wasn't the same as enticing a sponsor; this effort, which R. K. Mellon had pledged to work on himself, left Dick as edgy as any frustrated petitioner.

The planners now visualized a brand-new, handsomely gardened residential buffer between Point State Park and Pittsburgh's compressed downtown. Joe Barr well remembers the struggle to reclaim these twenty-three acres of rooming houses and railroad overpasses. "It was a festival of grease and dirt," Barr says. "Van Buskirk was really great, but that thing was always on again, and off again. . . ."
The expense of acquisition went down when a providential fire wiped off about eight million dollars of valuation in 1946. Van Buskirk quickly shepherded a delegation of Pittsburghers to Manhattan. Managers at the Equitable Life Assurance Society listened, but soon their real estate men insisted that the Allegheny Conference's projected "Gateway Center" made sense only as commercial property. Wasn't it about time to replace Pittsburgh's dowdy home office buildings? Landlords wriggled; the Mellons themselves—confirming plans just then to erect a midtown headquarters for Alcoa and double up with U. S. Steel to build a modern forty-one-story skyscraper off William Penn Place—regarded Equitable's proposal forlornly. But backers weren't appearing, and in the end the Pittsburghers took twelve million dollars for the land and a million more—Van Buskirk's inspiration—for exercising eminent domain, and guaranteed the Equitable twenty-year leases and 60-percent occupancy on a million square feet of projected office space.

Later everybody nursed afterthoughts. Van Buskirk went onto the Equitable board. There had been plans, when excitement was up, to hedge the skyline with eleven cruciform office structures. But even the three initial buildings held stubbornly at 70-percent occupancy.

The crotch of industry—renaissance Pittsburgh (industrial
Monongahela on right)

An executive of Equitable was frank: "There was not anything like
the demand for space to fill the rest of the buildings. It's not a big
city. The thing about Pittsburgh is that its appetite exceeds its digestion. We were stuck with it."

2

Perhaps Manhattanites were surprised. "The best thing about this
town is the fact that it's big enough to mean something but small
enough to manage," one communitarian said later, not without a
wink. Pittsburghers understood the reference. It was another form
of "the accepted and respected community leadership," a phrase
Jeanne Lowe ran into so often she included a translation—"This was
a euphemism for Mellon." Awe congeals. The responsibility closed
in so tight at times those postwar years that van Urk stumbled onto
R.K. one afternoon, avoiding telephone calls, hiding in the waiting
room of the Pennsylvania train depot. It couldn't be helped. "You
and I know," his widow admits, "that anyone who gets to the top
must be egotistical, in the sense of power. Not for his personal estate

but for the bank, the companies the Mellons were interested in."

The companies, too, needed comprehensive shaking out. The cousins were dispersing. Paul wanted to pursue his interests based at his Virginia farm. Ailsa wouldn't be budged very often from her Manhattan apartment. Of W.L.'s children only Rachel and her husband, John Walton, Jr., lingered now in Pittsburgh.

Of all the relatives, the one Dick really couldn't dismiss was Paul. Paul's estate was tremendous, and after 1946 he spoke for Ailsa. Even before Pearl Harbor he and his sister each retained securities valued at upward of $200,000,000—many times the inheritance of Dick and Sarah. Paul's share of the pivotal bank alone was virtually double R.K.'s—14.64 percent as against 7.95 percent. It disquieted R.K. to think about that.

"R.K. was irked that Paul should have so much," George Wyckoff saw. "R.K. was buying up bank stock all the time." He sought a way to contain such preponderance. Dick consulted his advisers, and early in 1946 Pittsburgh's impressionable business community was told about a new kind of nonprofit institution—T. Mellon and Sons. Besides sentimentalizing their grandfather, T. Mellon and Sons was intended to look into social and economic needs, promote discussion and coordinate results. Dick assumed the presidency, and at his elbow vice-presidents were Alan Scaife, Adolph Schmidt, Van Buskirk and Wyckoff. Assurances went around town that such an operation, while unfamiliar in America, was popular "in England to serve old industrial families."

Paul wasn't fooled, particularly. "I'm not so sure Paul wouldn't have said no to the whole thing if it hadn't been for my goading," recalls Wyckoff. "We met once a month. R.K. was head. To me, it represented a sense of insecurity." The meetings went on until Dick had died, but insofar as R.K. intended it as a means to subordinate his cousin, it wasn't much use. It never was necessary. The overworked Pittsburgh banker was heard to mutter a wish that Paul might return and give him a hand. Insiders knew better. "In fact, R.K. was always concerned with the possibility of Paul's coming out here and getting into the situation," Wyckoff says. "I knew he never would."

Paul normally seemed airy, but reliable. "There'd be disputes, differences of opinion in the office," Connie says. "When it came to the critical point, Dick would say, 'Well, I will speak to Paul.' Paul always went along with Dick's decisions." Paul kept himself current

T. Mellon and Sons—(back row, from left: Luther Holbrook, Arthur Van Buskirk, E. B. Clarke, Nathan Pearson, Donald Shepard, Joseph Hughes, Adolph Schmidt) (front row from left: George Wyckoff, Paul Mellon, R. K. Mellon, Alan Scaife, John Walton)

PAUL MELLON

chatting regularly with Wyckoff, who over the years went onto the boards of Gulf, Alcoa, Carborundum, and the bank.

For all George's bubble, a job which posted him between the Mellon heirs produced memorably flat moments. "On most practical matters," Wyckoff says, "Paul Mellon wouldn't really *have* a point of view." Sometimes he had. "Who the hell are you working for, Dick

Mellon or me?" George remembers his employer bursting out, piqued once too often at hearing whatever was going around the offices on the thirty-ninth floor of the stark new Mellon–U. S. Steel building.

Wyckoff watched each turn. "When T. Mellon was formed, R.K. wanted to put everybody on the same payroll," George says. "I said no to Paul, 'I don't want to be in a position where I'm beholden to R.K. Where he can fire me.'" The support Wyckoff represented— indispensable, yet exempt from R.K.'s chain of command—threw Dick Mellon off. He reduced the risks where that was possible: "Paul would be told by R.K. that, subject to his veto, things would be so," Wyckoff's successor, Nate Pearson, remembers.

Even this remote shadow made Wyckoff's presence unsettling. "R.K. being very difficult to work with," Wyckoff says, "if I had a problem I'd talk to Arthur Van Buskirk. Then he'd go in there and get an answer. You couldn't just go and ask R.K. anything, he simply wouldn't make a snap judgment, he was always afraid that somebody was trying to pull a fast one, although I think he realized in later years that that was not true. If he stopped in your office, that was dandy. If you went into his office and asked about a problem he might answer, but he was just as apt to get us talking about Rolling Rock or some complete *non sequitur*." Approaches were roundabout. "If R.K. was asked to give one hundred thousand dollars he'd work through me to get Paul to go along for fifty thousand dollars."

In office politics too Van Buskirk moved untiringly. "Frequently insiders didn't like him," another adviser adds. "He would do exactly what R. K. Mellon wanted. I've heard Van do a lot of enthusiastic agreeing with Dick when I was well aware he couldn't have agreed less." Van Buskirk was invaluable at departmentalizing Mellon's affairs; he contributed his share of advisatory infighting. Joe Hughes had returned to Pittsburgh on terms of great confidentiality with Mellon, and although he continued the practice of law on his own, he emerged before long as an important idea man for Dick and a governor of T. Mellon and Sons. Colleagues found him bumptious. "He acted as if he were R.K. himself," one says. "Van Buskirk and I went to him twenty years ago and told him he was making mistakes. He told us he was no messenger boy, he had a good background and the rest of it. After that he and Van Buskirk were always at logger-heads. Neither of them knew what the other was doing."

Hughes helped confer structure on T. Mellon and Sons, and was particularly effective at implementing Dick's philanthropic urges.

Sources near the top were fond of dismissing T. Mellon as largely a get-together beneath the founder's portrait, "a very simple arrangement that works, a kind of family sewing circle." But R.K. clearly had grave commercial intentions. "Since T. Mellon and Sons is a business organization," he wrote another member after a decade of operation, "I do not feel that a woman should be either a Governor or an officer. A daughter could and should become a Principal, but it should be limited to that."

Yet deliberations there failed to incubate the sort of bold common departures such wealth and advice promised. It became a sounding board, a place its president, Richard Mellon, could explain his reasons for turning down a merger offer or budgeting for petrochemicals. It provided some protection from ripsawing charitable requests. R.K. got tired of overseeing a parking lot full of automobile tops and rounded up a million each from Sarah and Paul and Ailsa and underwrote Mellon Square Park, a block-square pour of aggregate designed with a protractor. T. Mellon approved grants by the local A. W. Mellon Educational and Charitable Trust like the multimillion-dollar bequests that created the University of Pittsburgh Graduate School of Public Health, where Jonas Salk developed the antipolio vaccine.

But aspirations to maintain the spirit of the "joint account" through another broad generation were misbegotten. "When Paul and R.K. got together they were as thick as thieves," one go-between says. "On the surface." The family had divided. There were funky departures— Joe Hughes still remembers a flyer into the film business in Rochester, New York, Kryptar, and an enterprise called Island Packers, a South Seas fishing venture in common with the Rockefellers after Jean Paul Getty came back with word that there were tuna out there. "The tuna were around, but so were the sharks," Hughes reflects, typically matter-of-fact.

As matters developed, T. Mellon and Sons helped most by providing a meeting ground on which to ratify disentangling. "R.K. would never touch a business deal we went into," George Wyckoff says, referring to the investments he made for Paul and Ailsa. When Wyckoff went on the board of Carborundum, R.K. got off. He sold his Carborundum stock. The Rockefellers bought heavily into Pittsburgh Coal; when the reorganized Pittsburgh-Consolidation in turn took a big position in Chrysler, "R.K., who owned a lot of General Motors stock and sat on its board, thought that was a terrible thing. He sold his coal stock and didn't go into Hannah Mining, which became a very good thing." Meanwhile R.K. bought into Pittsburgh Plate Glass, and later set Frank Denton onto its board.

Dick's fussiness carried over into workaday business ethics. He shied at conflict-of-interest situations. Insofar as feasible he kept the family away from politics beyond the formal-registration honorific-to-the-party good-guy Republicanism people identified with Eisenhower. "He thought the job of a fellow who ran a Mellon company was to run the company, not sit on outside boards," one insider emphasizes. This preserved the insularity of the empire, especially since R.K. normally kept his boards of directors small, compliant, and weighted with operating officers and staff from other Mellon companies. Genuine disputes were settled at executive committee meetings or presentations before R.K. personally. He watched the banking detail closely. "R.K. didn't normally permit any of the other officers of the bank to sit on any of the company boards," an associate says. "He felt that when a company has a large loan with a bank its officers are likely to feel somewhat beholden to a banker who sits on its board."

Mellon bankers naturally regretted these extremes of abstinence. In Denton's case especially such restraint was noticed. Frank's status was unique. A.W. had selected the blunt-spoken Kansas banking prodigy and moved him into things before the bad years started. The young banker's nerve and discretion and thoroughness and his *frisson* of humorous Middle-Western materialism tailed into the family's own wry, agricultural character. Frank had been around six months before he strolled in and informed R.B. that he could use a little more pocket money. "What's the matter, don't you think we're paying you enough?" R.B. said.

Denton had his doubts. R.B. investigated the complaint and found that nobody had informed the treasurer of Denton's employment, and he had never been paid.

Denton and R.K. became intimate personal friends. They drank together, shot quail together, slid into their matching scarlet coats every season and rode after foxes. Denton married; bachelorhood started to weigh on Dick soon after, and he married too. "Wouldn't you like to borrow a little something and make a few investments of your own?" the aging R.B. had suggested to Denton once everybody was familiar. "You know, you can't make any real money unless you're willing to borrow money." But Denton thought not. He'd already seen leverage drive able men under. His reputation for prudence solidified.

Once war was declared both bankers got in. Dick emerged a colonel, but Denton was mustered out a brigadier general, "which certainly didn't hurt me any" with the military-minded R.K. The bookkeeper at Mellon Securities kept paying Denton a portion of his regular salary well into the war. Frank stopped it; Dick had it restored, with back pay. Embarrassed, Frank went to Harrisburg and informed R.K. that he didn't want any obligations to return to Pittsburgh after the war ended.

"Uncle Andy sent you," Mellon told the Kansan, "Father adopted you, that makes you a Mellon. I've got obligations, you've got 'em too, and you can't quit any more than I did."

Frank stayed. Through long, bantering, well-lubricated wartime bull sessions in hotel rooms in Washington and Harrisburg, R.K. and Denton and occasionally Alan Scaife traded projections about reorganizing. They had things largely thought through before the fighting ended. Important changes began in 1946. That year the surety affiliate the family had started up to guarantee Mellbank's member-bank assets, Mellon Indemnity, went over to the General Reinsurance Corporation of New York for an important block of General Reinsurance equity. This turned out brilliantly—R.K.'s insistence over the years that General Reinsurance make money selling insurance, not merely through investments, rode up the value of their 20 percent from scarcely ten million dollars to something over $300,000,000 at the market's top.

Their next divestiture, Mellon Securities, represented a major shift. Underwriting was the dowsing rod of the family fortune while A.W. lived; to give that up implied a new generation's shortfalls. But facts were facts. "Dick Mellon was not a builder, in the sense of acquiring anything new," Denton will state flatly. "He worked at improving the assets they inherited."

By 1945 they decided to combine the banks. To replace himself at Mellon Securities, Frank arranged an interview with the managers of New York-based First Boston Corporation. They needed a very good man in Pittsburgh, Denton informed his auditors, and the fellow he had his eye on was George Woods of First Boston.

"But they said no," Denton recalls. "I said, 'Well, keep him if you can. We'll pay through the nose.'

"They said, 'Let's merge. You're primarily industrial, we're utility.'

"We made a deal with the S.E.C. that Dick Mellon and Sarah Scaife could own up to twenty percent. We drew down the capital, and the Mellons still own twenty percent." Another very large percentage is held by Rockefeller interests, which provide the underwriter the best information anywhere.

The reconstituted bank, known as the Mellon National Bank and Trust Company, took up corporate existence in September of 1946 and expected to compete for customers with even the Chase and the Bank of America. Its resources neared $1,200,000,000. As vice-chairman and chief operating officer, Frank Denton exercised control. R.K.'s fox-hunting sidekick, Lawrence ("Moon") Murray, went in as president.

Time featured Denton's picture in its financial section, his thinning hair parted over the center and a half-smoked cigar suspended, in a gesture of commanding delicacy, before his wide, strong mouth, just open, about to utter something. Globules of intensified light gleamed across his irises. He understood his position. R.K. became chairman. "Dick said he'd be chairman as long as I'd run it," Denton says. "W.L. helped persuade him to take the chairmanship. Connie wanted him out. He took it on, but he didn't even have an office in the bank."

W.L., in town between fishing trips, still exerted the charisma of holdover patriarch, a keen, husky opinion from the age of miracles. His approval remained important, and he immediately became a "strong" member of T. Mellon and Sons. Age fortified his courtliness. When W.L. recommended something, R.K. was hard pressed not to agree politely.

So Dick became chairman, and Frank, by his own description, became the "operating guy." There was an executives' meeting at the bank every morning, at which the problems of the bank and of the companies and indeed of the entire trans-Allegheny community were thoroughly hashed around. Stipulations of the merger had required the recombined Mellon Bank to divest itself of control of the Farmers Deposit and its subordinate, the Reliance Life Insurance Company. Frank Denton was careful to pick over the talent before disposing of these affiliates, and John Mayer, who succeeded Denton in 1963, came in with Denton for grooming. The bank's printed history records growth from the time of the merger, a quadrupling of assets by 1970, a quiet, pioneering role in the use of computers to expedite the paper work, the development of Master Charge, emphasis on retailing the bank's services through the almost one hundred branch banks

Denton in the bank
ONE HUNDRED YEARS
OF BANKING—MELLON
NATIONAL CORP.

in adjoining counties, and an increasing participation with European banks in financial research and—through BOLSA, The Bank of London and South America—an effort to cut Pittsburgh in on the enormous prevailing profits from lending money in Europe and the Third World.

Denton's eye, like Mellon's, roved far beyond limits properly associated with administration. He did not serve on many outside boards but, insofar as Mellon companies couldn't really borrow elsewhere, Frank enjoyed his opportunities to review their balance sheets. Denton rarely backed away.

The times were trying for Koppers in particular. One of R.K.'s first decisions was not to contest the S.E.C. ruling and divest Eastern Gas. Henry Rust was gone, but even under J. T. Tierney the company's over 150 semi-autonomous subsidiaries still functioned with panache, making and losing fortunes, in Rust's earth-conquering tradition. As war profits dissipated, the results favored losing. "All through its history the Koppers Company had been too big for its britches," Denton says. "Even now, Koppers keeps one of the biggest suites in the Duquesne Club and pays its management what companies five times its size do, and flies them around in the fanciest private airplanes. . . ."

The contradictions were especially painful after Tierney became president and survival meant credit directly from the Mellons. Denton recalls one go-around with Tierney, "a big, fat man, a wild Irishman, goddamn this, and goddamn that." Tierney demanded a bond issue. Denton required sufficient coverage. "Three times he ordered me out of his office. I ignored it twice, and after that I said, 'All right, the hell with you, I won't buy your bonds.' "

Even trade-oriented *Fortune* tagged Koppers "the dog of the Mellon industrial family." By 1946 Tierney himself was retired. Surviving management reportedly "agreed that the company needed a new chief executive who could not be influenced by any Koppers tradition." R.K. proceeded cautiously. What happened with Koppers would color his prospects. Through many hectic months Frank Denton had worked with General Brehon Somervell, the four-star commandant of the Army's central procurement section. Somervell was a scorcher about lines of responsibility. The General had decided, according to *Fortune*, to "get a porch and a rocker and after a month, if he felt like it, he might rock." Somervell's month wasn't over before his onetime subaltern turned up, purportedly on vacation at Hobe Sound, and left with Somervell the 147-page prospectus Koppers' caretaker management developed to outline its intentions. Somervell became the president in April of 1946. Despite an occasional grumble about the "innate conservatism of the average businessman, who tends to underset his goals so as to reduce the pressure on himself," he took over smoothly, as Denton always anticipated. Somervell had run the New York W.P.A. in 1936, and understood rehabilitation.

"R.K. made major policy decisions," one top man says. "Everything got decided before the board meetings. There was never, in all my time, a single dissenting vote. Mellon got the company into the chemical and the petrochemical business in a big way. Except in major policy decisions the Mellon group tended to exercise more of a veto power than a directing power. It was up to management to formulate the means. In cases involving major capital appropriations they would want to see profit projections, estimates of risk. If they weren't satisfied with the figures, they would exercise their veto. The matter wouldn't get to the board. I've also heard more than once that R. K. Mellon never attended a stockholders' meeting unless he was dissatisfied with the management. It was a signal the management was due to be changed.

"R.K. was a reasonable man. He would listen, he was patient. Other people around here would sometimes use their power for vendetta reasons. R.K. never did."

Mellon had no need after 1946 to attend a stockholders' meeting at Koppers. By 1951 the company was back. Sales climbed from 113 to 285 million; book value per share was up from $26 to $50.

Aluminum had other problems. In October of 1941, extemporizing from foolscap notes, an elderly federal judge, Francis Caffey, documented in a piping voice his view that Davis's sprawling combine was not a monopoly within the Sherman Act, and that, in fact, "the evidence is convincing the other way." Homer Cummings wasn't Attortorney General anymore, but squads of Government attorneys were tempted to rise in the courtroom and claw the air. Just then four members of the Supreme Court—Murphy, Reed, Jackson and Stone —had worked at various times preparing the Government's action against the trust, and would be disqualified in the event the case reached appeal.

Davis personally felt vindicated. Caffey's statement that Arthur Vining Davis had "contributed more to [Alcoa's] advancement than any man alive" was one of the few in his endless summation nobody felt like disputing. Davis was still alive, a neckless little cocker whose fifty million dollars or so in aluminum stock became the nucleus of a fortune.

Then things started changing. The war gave malcontents one last, unexpected opening. The call for aluminum to sustain the air war had forced Alcoa itself to close to treble its capacity. That wasn't nearly enough; under extensive Government contracts the company had built and operated reducing and fabricating plants worth another $500,000,000. To these the Government held title. Soon after the fighting stopped, availing themselves of a "somewhat tenuous technicality in the Alcoa leases," agents of the Government's Defense Plant Corporation came forward and claimed its facilities. Over half the industry's capacity went on the block as war-surplus property.

Logical bidders were frightened. Alcoa controlled, beyond dispute, most of the country's high-grade bauxite reserves and the entire available range of patents on every proven process that made it possible to extract alumina from the low-grade ore the new Government plants had been constructed to process. On January 6, 1946, the tenacious young administrator of the Surplus Property office of the Government, W. Stuart Symington, publicly accused the Aluminum Company of attempting to obstruct proper disposal of the plants and "to distract the members of Congress and the public from the fact that Alcoa was seeking to obtain the more desirable government plants and thus to increase and solidify its own monopolistic position." The time had arrived, Symington stated "frankly to Congress," to insist that the company undergo a change of attitude. Otherwise, the courts must certainly step in and break the company's "monopolistic power" and reorganize the industry.

What worried Alcoa's managers about that was the probability that it would whip up the reform-minded Congress a year after a new, and binding, circuit-court ruling came down which held that Alcoa did indeed exercise a monopoly of ingot production in the United States. Days after Symington's pronouncement, crusty old Davis himself, backed up by Alcoa's shrewd vice-president in charge of operations, Irving ("Chief") Wilson, and lawyer Leon Higby, turned up in Washington to try to bargain with Attorney General Tom Clark and representatives from the Reconstruction Finance Corporation as well as Symington. The administrators stood fast. The Government might interfere even if the Aluminum Company attempted to expand its own facilities with its own funds.

The mightily irritated Davis had hopes of bringing the Government to reason by projecting a series of analogies to smalltown boardinghouses. Didn't the best survive? Higby termed Symington "pugnacious." The Alcoa men regrouped. They returned January 9 to offer a limited licensing arrangement to buyers of certain of the plants of previously stipulated capacities. There was a lot of intrabureaucratic telephoning. Symington, getting into the spirit, urged upon the businessmen one grand, sweeping gesture: Simply release those patents! Do the inevitable yourselves. The Pittsburghers ducked out to caucus for an hour, and then they returned and surrendered to Symington. Joy was reportedly "unconfined," and The Aluminum Company of America emerged from the meeting as merely another big well-managed operation in an enormous industry in which it abruptly had competitors.

R.K. never surfaced, but here as usual the movement of events reflected his impulses just then to simplify things as much as possible and accommodate changing times. Nevertheless—as long as Davis remained chairman, Mellon constituted a voice, little more, another opinion worth considering. "Dick's influence was limited as long as Davis was running the company and even when, after him, Chief Wilson took charge," one Mellon adviser remarks. As during the Aluminum Company's erratic early decades, when even A.W. couldn't capture a majority of the stock after months of conducting his "still hunt (no pun)," the great company's managers would make its decisions for themselves.

Perversely, the evaporation of monopoly probably left the Aluminum Company more susceptible to banking pressures than ever before. "After the antitrust action, there was a feeling that Roy Hunt, whose father, Captain Hunt, had been a founder, really wasn't very strong," explains Leon Higby now. Arthur Davis had retired. "Wilson was put in over Roy Hunt's active objection," Higby says. "Then, in 1951, I went to Alcoa full time from Reed, Smith. The antitrust decree had given us until 1956 to divest ourselves of certain big properties. I talked at the time to Hughes and Van Buskirk. The Mellons wanted to make sure that the company wasn't handicapped any more than it had to be, and they felt that the law firm found it easier to say no than yes. Not that anybody wanted me to disregard the antitrust decrees.

"I became the chairman of the finance committee. It's important to realize that aluminum is a game played by elephants. You have to invest a hundred million dollars at a clip. With the Mellons involved you didn't have to worry about money. If we needed a lot of money, more than the Mellons could handle, they would use First Boston or put together a consortium of New York banks. If the question had come up and we could have borrowed at a quarter of a percent cheaper somewhere else, I wouldn't have wanted to do it and jeopardize our fine relationship with the family.

"R.K. just tried to see that competent men were in control. He didn't try to help them make their decisions. R.K. would be consulted not because he represented the biggest stockholder, but because he and the bank could give us so much help. They understood the aluminum business quite well, and knew the economics of the industry. You have to remember that during the Fifties there were a lot of corporate raids and proxy fights. When you sat there with the Mellons owning thirty-two percent of the stock, you didn't have anything to worry about as long as what you did satisfied them. Once Kaiser and Reynolds got into production there would be times of overproduction, of glut. Profitability went off sharply. When I was active at Alcoa we had a steadily rising debt, we loaned ourselves up to the maximum rate, I'm sorry to say.

"Working with the bank was a blamed easy way to work. We never had any question as to whether we got good attention."

Developments around The Gulf were similar, but different. As Aluminum shrank, relatively, the Gulf Oil Corporation spread across the world's financial landscape. By 1951 it was the country's eighth-largest enterprise. The emergence of democracy in outposts like Venezuela tended to crimp possibilities there, but the accession to control in Iran in February of 1951 of volatile little Dr. Mossadegh, ranting in his pajamas and goading the angry members of the Iranian parliament, the Majlis, to expropriate the Anglo-Iranian concession, set off a train of events enormously profitable to Gulf.

The British Government reacted by permitting Anglo-Iranian's management, led by the dynamic Sir William Fraser, to organize a boycott of Iranian oil, in which the Aramco companies gladly joined. To meet its requirements Anglo-Iranian turned immediately to its enormous reserves in Kuwait, where the discovery in 1938 of the legendary oil fields at Burghan assured a close-to-limitless supply of crude so light and pure it scarcely needed cracking, waiting in vast pools under just enough seismic pressure to convey it spontaneously, without benefit of pumping stations, to tankers in port.

But Gulf owned half of the Kuwaiti concession. Then serious production started—from six million barrels in 1946, liftings in Kuwait jumped abruptly in 1952 to 273 million barrels, more than Iran had ever provided in a year, and by the end of 1953 Kuwait had surpassed Arabia. Since Gulf had plenty of domestic oil to meet its North American needs, it sold a great part of its half to Shell for half of Shell's eventual profits, and subcontracted the rest to Socony and Atlantic. Between 1950 and 1953 Gulf's sales nearly doubled, to close to two billion dollars annually.

Meanwhile, influences governmental and quasi-governmental were focusing upon Iran. While Truman remained President, and lawyers in Thurman Arnold's antitrust division were poking through oil company documents preparatory to mounting an attack on the maturing cartel, even Acheson's flavored protestations that some manner of intervention by the West was indicated for national-security reasons didn't prompt a reprisal. The break came quickly after Eisenhower had entrenched his Administration. One blistering August day in 1953 the rumpled, rather academic young chief of the C.I.A.'s Middle Eastern desk, Teddy Roosevelt's grandson Kermit, drove over the wild, neglected passes on the road between Baghdad and Tehran with an estimated $700,000 and a headful of strategies. Months before, Mossadegh had taken over the army and sent the terrified young Shah scrambling for his life. Soon after Roosevelt's arrival supporters of the Shah, well directed by professionals, battled the Mossadegh loyalists in street fights throughout Tehran and returned the Peacock Throne to its stripling of a sovereign.

It happened that Churchill personally, looking after the Government in England while Eden recuperated from an illness, had sanctioned the American operation which Eden abhorred. Roosevelt stopped off briefly in London to visit the implacable old hero. "In so splendidly conceived and executed a mission," Churchill proclaimed, snifter aloft, "it would, indeed, have been an honor to have served under your command."

Roosevelt would shortly receive the "ultrasecret National Security Medal" from Eisenhower. Beyond that, "I always stayed away from the payments side," he told one friend. The benefits of this caper— beyond setting the intelligence community an example the repetition of which would lead to decades of national disasters, and completing the humiliation of the Shah—accrued to American oilmen. Extended negotiations, lasting into 1954, produced the device of a consortium, composed of Anglo-Iranian (40 percent), Shell (14 percent), and five American oil companies, including Gulf, each of which might buy up to 8 percent of the production of the National Iranian Oil Com-

pany. This saved Iran's face, but everybody involved was aware by
then that Western interests could determine Iran's liftings—and profits—by juggling worldwide sources.

The career of Kermit Roosevelt would touch at so many points
where industry and Government confirm their placental relationship
that perhaps it deserves an extra moment's examination. After Groton
and Harvard, Roosevelt taught some history, then brought his proposal
for the foundation of a "propaganda and intelligence agency" to
Colonel William ("Wild Bill") Donovan, the same high-spirited and
well-connected New Yorker who helped allay Congressional suspicions
about Andrew Mellon's extragovernmental tinkering. Well before the
war, probably during his stint of Red Cross administration, David
Bruce was understudying Donovan and preparing himself, as second-
in-command at the Office of Strategic Services, to run this elite unit's
European branch from London. As war years passed, an assortment
of Mellons turned up under Bruce's command.

After 1945 the O.S.S. evolved into the C.I.A., the covert operations
and intelligence-gathering agency which was to prove so fascinating
to televiewers throughout the Watergate hearings. "Kim" Roosevelt
stayed on. His services in Iran were only the most glamorous of his
contributions. In 1958, with four children to put through school and
some well-researched ideas about how that might be expedited, Roosevelt found employment "outside." He became a vice-president of Gulf
Oil in charge of governmental relations—the critical lobbying job in
which Claude Wild later showed such bustle. In 1964 Roosevelt set
up his own consulting firm, Kermit Roosevelt Associates, Inc. He spe-
cializes in Middle Eastern contacts.

But what about Pittsburgh? Appraisal here gets complicated, a
mixture of knowing and not-knowing that seems as mottled at times
as one would expect of politics repeatedly tinctured with oil money.
For R. K. Mellon, avowedly provincial and moralistic, the machinations of Gulf Oil's secondary managers in unfamiliar surroundings are
exotica to avoid. The family had involved itself too deeply, for much
too long, in Gulf's intimate affairs for Dick to risk getting spattered.
He preferred a broad brush anyhow. "I hire Company Presidents,"
he reportedly snapped when asked what he did for a living, giving in
to hubris for once, and that was meant to suggest not only how powerful he remained, but how remote. He sat, as expected, upon the oil
company's board of directors, yet Mellon would accept no seat on

Colonel Drake
GULF OIL

the critical executive committee itself, where, at exhausting morning sessions, the real business of the company was thrashed into condition for presentation in the afternoon.

Still—finally, R.K. knew. The bank, after all, processed the important numbers. "I had a hell of an argument with W.L. and Drake and Leovy about the bookkeeping of Gulf," Frank Denton recalls. "I accused the bookkeeper of showing a better report than was justified, and I made a believer out of the comptroller." And that in innocent, transitional times. In June of 1948 W.L. turned over the chairmanship at Gulf to Colonel Drake, and Drake in turn put into the presidency a Harvard Business School graduate and production expert from Standard Oil of Ohio, Sidney Swensrud, 47.

Very likely the scholarly and punctilious Swensrud was simply too impersonal, too much of a technician, for the rowdy, bourbon-sippin', shoot-the-moon oil fraternity. The companies were separate, but they were also, as waves of Congressional investigations would document, parties to well-established arrangements as to markets and production, and before long managers in the industry had started to complain that Swensrud hadn't gotten word. "Under Swensrud things ultimately reached the point where the Gulf organization was falling apart," one bystander comments. "Swensrud was a brilliant guy who said hello without any trouble, but in a way he was too sharp. Employees here were unhappy, and people from the other oil companies kept criticizing him. They'd talk, and later on he'd say he'd 'indicated' something, but he hadn't really 'agreed' to anything. Word got out."

Meanwhile, Swensrud's rough-and-tumble assistant, Bill Whiteford, had started to stew quite openly about the basis on which decisions were being made around the company. "The basic thing they disagreed about," George Wyckoff says, "was this: Swensrud ran the oil business strictly on what was good tax-wise. If you had depletion enough you went out and drilled. He kept turning down what Whiteford thought were good deals, and after a while Whiteford sent in his resignation. I myself thought Whiteford was basically right, and I felt that word should get to R.K., and I went in to see him. Within fifteen minutes R.K. had Colonel Drake in, and Dick was telling the Colonel what he wanted done."

Denton watched the aftermath. "One day I'm sittin' in the bank," he reports, "and Dick comes in and closes the doors. 'What do you know about Swensrud?' he says.

" 'He's sure made enemies to the left and right,' I told him. 'The Oklahoma company, and the California company . . . He's quite a trader.'

"Dick really didn't like what he heard, I didn't think. You know he had an awful quick temper. Swensrud still had a lot of Gulf stock options. Nevertheless, Swensrud was asked to resign, and when he went back on the board of Standard of Ohio, the options were canceled."

The changeover went before T. Mellon and Sons, and Whiteford assumed the presidency of Gulf in 1953, the same year Kermit Roosevelt nudged history in Iran. In Gulf's chronicles, the *putsch* by Whiteford registered at least as much of a bounce on the Richter scale. "Whiteford was a bear cat, a roughneck who began as a roustabout in the oil business and fought his way up," one survivor notes. His family gave up what money it had to ransom Whiteford's father from Mexican kidnappers beyond the Rio Grande. Family members got everything together and passed it over the border; their father was repatriated, flung across the line, his gullet slit expertly.

"Whiteford really was amusing in his way," Wyckoff says, "but he was a wild man. He was tough, he was brought up that way, he didn't give a hoot what the law was. He made his pilot take him into Washington one time when they couldn't get any clearance and the guy lost his license. At a Gulf executive committee meeting one morning Whiteford cut loose on T. Mellon and Sons, and I told him what I thought and he got so mad he had to leave the room. Whiteford always had a squawk about something."

Whiteford's irritation with T. Mellon was merely an extension, obviously, of the discomfort he couldn't help feeling with R.K.'s supervision. He couldn't go that far; Dick Mellon had put him into his slot and probably wouldn't scruple to jerk him out again. But Whiteford felt pushed. "I remember a compensation committee meeting at which

Denton turned up and asked some very difficult questions," says another member. "Denton digs into things. Whiteford left the room."

He retaliated when able. "One day I was having lunch with Bill Whiteford," says Thomas Mellon Evans, "and I said, Bill, I read this article in *Forbes* about The Gulf, and it said that whenever anybody referred to the board of directors at Gulf, that meant R. K. Mellon. Who told them that?

" 'I did,' Whiteford said. 'I was sore, I had been assured that I would be told in advance whenever any family members were going to sell some stock, and right after that I read in the paper that R. K. Mellon had filed to sell a load of it.' "

So feelings ran high. Over on the Mellon side, pleasure with Whiteford's results was offset, from time to time, by the disquieting awareness that things were *hectic* around the oil company. Profits continued spiraling up, at twice the pace of the Gross National Product. Nevertheless—"Dick spoke of G.W.W. [George Wyckoff] going on Gulf Board," Paul Mellon would note in a confidential memo the summer of 1958, "saying he felt he would be most useful, although he was somewhat concerned with Whiteford's over-activity. . . . I said I was all for the move . . . and that Whiteford should not expect him to keep up with the social side of Gulf!"

This meant, mostly, drinking. But Whiteford was, indeed, both determined and active, and within a year had created the "off-the-books political fund," as well as a shadow staff to supervise its distribution, which he was intent upon keeping from "the Mellons" and other "Boy Scouts" around the company too squeamish to deal with economic realities. The Mellons' private Watergate had now become inevitable.

3

Throughout this postwar scuffling around, one principal intrudes rarely—Sarah Scaife, Dick's sister. R.K. and Alan Scaife kept common books in a number of holdings, and supervision of Sarah's affairs, on paper, might properly be expected to devolve upon her husband. This didn't quite happen. For all Alan's dash, his engineering background, his airplanes, his personableness and years of sailing over split-rail fences alongside R.K., Dick Mellon had very little intention of bringing any other family member into primary decision-making. Connie cites his thinking: "Alan was a most likable person," she says, "but not much business ability. He didn't listen things out, and he did not have the best judgment. But Dick could handle Alan, and whenever things got a little out of line Dick would straighten him out."

His authority for this too R.K. could authenticate. "When R.B. died he told Dick, you look after your sister," one intimate reports. "Dick didn't want Alan involved in the family businesses when it was up to him to decide. He gave lip service to playing ball with Alan, but it was an effort."

With middle age arriving, Alan Scaife had matured, on first approximation, into the very frontispiece of deliberate Pittsburgh breeding. His hair grayed theatrically to bracket his open temples, set off his public expression of amused, even cherubic, mildness. He retained a tall man's way of inclining his head an extra degree or two so ingratiating to women. He appeared at ease in any situation. Upon returning from Washington and London after several years of service in the romantic O.S.S., Alan wore the Bronze Star as well as the Legion of Honor and the Croix de Guerre. Strangers admired his modesty.

It was entirely mannerism. By Pittsburgh's lead criterion, commercial know-how, Alan wasn't measuring up. Perhaps he overmatched himself. As early as 1924 Alan had been struggling to bring some leadership to the faltering Scaife Company, where outmoded production methods and fights among the heirs edged Pittsburgh's oldest manufacturer steadily closer to bankruptcy. Alan became the president in 1930. "Father was so proud of that family company," his son, Dick, says. "The only trouble with the company was that it didn't keep up with the times. The pressure vessel went out with the Pullman car. Only World War Two and the Korean war kept the place going. He tried everything, purchasing another company, he kept borrowing, anything to keep it in operation. He wouldn't let go. After he died I sold it." Dick Scaife summons up his exceedingly mobile smile. "For a dollar."

Meanwhile, months before he died, R.B. had designated Alan chairman of the Siberia of the Mellon holdings: Pittsburgh Coal. That too was hopeless. In 1940 R.K. brought Alan into The Gulf and let him poke around the Texas end of the company before installing him in Pittsburgh as a director and member of the executive committee. That pulled him closer, but Dick was careful to protect himself from Alan's growing impetuousness. "Theoretically, Alan was the Mellon representative on the executive committee throughout those postwar years," one colleague says. "But Alan was wild, and R.K. was always so afraid that he would do something not in keeping with R.K.'s objectives that R.K. would let Scaife go only so far. W.L. and Drake both gave Alan the runaround, on orders from Dick, and Dick was forever dealing behind the scenes with Whiteford, telling him to pay no attention to Scaife. Alan couldn't get anywhere, R.K. was always there to block his path. R.K. was no team player."

Dick Scaife was old enough to understand all this: "In truth, R.K. would pick up a phone, what he wanted was done. That used to annoy my father—he was suckin' hind tit. R.K. would tell him after the fact. 'Alan, we've done this, it's OK, isn't it?' " Several decades as monkey in the middle did little to improve Alan as an executive. "Alan had this precipitation," another functionary notes. "When something went wrong he'd go get a man fired. That was his immediate reaction— bing!" Ultimately, being extremely civic-minded, Alan Scaife undoubtedly accomplished the most as chairman of the University of Pittsburgh board of trustees. But even serving there, he let his enthusiasm get the better of him sometimes, and commitments he evidently made were later to plague the Mellons.

Alan's ups and downs tended to make Sarah quite unhappy. Prosperity after the war and R.K.'s successful upgrading of the Mellon companies had made Sarah Scaife an extremely wealthy woman. By the middle Fifties her fortune, like Dick's, was pegged by *Fortune* into the baronial four-to-seven-hundred-million-dollar category. This generated ambivalences too. "To Dick, Sarah always came first," says R.K.'s widow. "Dick would always see that Sarah got more than he did. Sarah and I always got along, but she didn't always get along with her brother. She was a determined young lady. Sarah could be very vindictive when she wished to be. . . ."

One escape the Scaifes often enjoyed was travel, sometimes to the most remote, even uncomfortable, stretches of the world. "When Father overdid it Sarah would take him away on travels," Dick Scaife says. "He would be away, come back, work harder and harder, overwork, and then she would take him away again." Alan's own father, Verner, had undergone a bad nervous breakdown from working too hard. After that a trip around the world had helped.

Back home, in residence in Ligonier, the Scaifes lived most of the time in what one relative remembered as "stuffy Penguin Court. I remember walking out after dinner up there. The place was built on a flat field, very high, at the end of a million-dollar road, and I remember the view and the penguins carved out of stone in those Gothic arches. They swung some terrific parties." Sarah, who loved the birds,

Sarah Scaife (left), young Dick and Cordelia
PITTSBURGH *Post-Gazette*

Dining at Penguin Court
CARNEGIE INSTITUTE MUSEUM

From left: Alan Scaife, Mrs. Denton,
Sarah Scaife, Frank Denton
PITTSBURGH *Post-Gazette*

even attempted to raise and breed emperor penguins in little concrete igloos on the premises, in hopes that they might strut around the court-yards and keep people amused. Sarah obviously kept trying—through an inspired eccentricity, exercising her famously mordant wit. Caught in Central Europe by the outbreak of war in 1939, she nonplussed one reporter after her escape by remarking that "the only fashion note I saw was the gas mask." When Jim Bovard politely questioned the propriety of her adding to her collection a big alfresco Renoir full of rosy nudes, Sarah understood at once: "I know why you're opposing it. Because you never went on a picnic like that."

There remained that undertow, frequently expressed by gestures. She did her visiting in a big square imported London taxi. George Henderson, the husband of R.K.'s daughter Cassandra, noticed once how peaked she looked when she stopped over. "It's all right," she said. "It's just that every time we turned a corner today Moose fell off the front seat." Henderson conjectured that "Moose" was her chauf-feur for much of the visit, and was relieved to discover that he was Pamplemousse, Sarah's poodle.

In practical matters Sarah was astute, with just the restraint with underlings the family missed in Alan. Outsiders found her knowledge-able, sympathetic, alert. Her Sarah Mellon Scaife Foundation dis-pensed, between its founding in 1941 and 1974, a little under sixty-three and a half million dollars—a figure, coincidentally, not far from the estimated assets of the foundation by the later date. Emphasis was on health care and education—a lot going to Children's Hospital and the local zoo, with Pitt the heavy recipient—and, with the posthumous opening of the Sarah Scaife Gallery, cultural affairs.

Even that brought little. "She loved and hated the people of Pitts-burgh," Dick Scaife says. "I guess you might say she was insecure in her own town." Dick cherished her; Cordelia, her disgruntled, inward daughter, becomes embittered just thinking back about a childhood spent mostly with nurses and governesses, during which the droll charms even of Penguin Court wore out too quickly. "Certainly it was palatial," Cordy says, "an achievement in pure Cotswold architecture, like the structures around Stratford-on-Avon. It was the kind of home which should have generated a lot of happy memories and echoes. Nobody was happy there."

"I would guess that Mother was overprotected," Cordelia says. "She was the most unself-reliant person I ever met. She did not know how to cook, she couldn't drive, she didn't play cards. She was dependent on my father for everything. She was aghast when he went off to war. 'You would leave me?'

"Actually she was shy, she was very bright, and she had great humor, if unfailingly at someone else's expense. It was razor-honed, and it could be devastatingly amusing."

Life in the office carried over into everything. "It was just assumed that R.K. was always the lead goose," Cordy says. "My father got along with R.K. As long as my father didn't seek the spotlight all was OK. He became a drudge. Sometimes he'd come in, and sit down and take it out on the piano, and even the dog would just cringe."

The long-standing Mellon convention of an enormous, silent, family-wide Christmas dinner continued throughout Cordelia's youth. It spooked her especially. "Mother would be plastered, sarcastic, grousing," she says. "The second we all got through the plum pudding everybody shot out the door—"

Other, younger Mellons reinforce these memories. Even Sarah's formal portrait, suspended above the landing of the Pittsburgh gallery, presents a sad, pinched face above its guiltless and unadorned shoulders, unprotected in any way by the double pearl choker, a final aquiline handsomeness redeeming a lifetime of unclear devotions. People recapitulate little kindnesses. "I remember one time that I baked some macaroons for her as a surprise," one relative says. "She ate one, and a peculiar expression came across her face. She was happy to get it, and she was trying to protect me from eating one myself. They had a foul taste.

"Later, when I was living in New York, she would come to town, and before long, of course, she'd be roaring drunk. It was very painful. I'd see the aftermath."

Due bills were accumulating.

13 | A WORLD OF ART

1

PITTSBURGH RUMBLED. The meadows around Upperville, Virginia, suffered very little alteration beyond the autumnal turning of the soil, the topping off of an additional horse barn whenever one was needed. The clanging of hammers pattered down like rain among the honeysuckle blossoms. Paul Mellon was there largely, Pittsburghers would hear. Hunting foxes. Adding broodmares. Even old-time familiars rarely got a look.

It had been different while Mary was alive. Mary accepted even Pittsburgh. She'd met Paul accidentally—the two piled into a sleigh together just after the winter's first snow in 1933 to compete in the traditional race to the Central Park Casino. Their whiffletree snapped; Paul was horseman enough to hold the course until they won, and amidst the laughter something between them caught. Mary was a few years older, a Vassar graduate, a big bouncy extroverted girl of twenty-eight just getting a divorce from magazine writer Karl Brown. She'd stuck in Manhattan, unwilling to return to Kansas City, where her father, the internist Dr. Charles Conover, held perhaps too public a position. Her mother chaired the Alliance Française.

For the uncertain Paul she became a centrifuge. Paul's life wouldn't settle. His father was alive; Paul lived at home on Woodland Road, showed up for banking hours but ducked away to Virginia or Manhattan or England whenever he could arrange an excuse. Mary personified life's excitement—her big full-blooded generous face with its wide bumpy cheekbones and those magnificent lips, exuberant lips turned open to experience as if to compensate Paul for generations of primness. So much was promised! "Mary was the sort of person," says

John Barrett, who knew her while Mary was still supporting herself by working for a photographer, "who, when she came into a room, it was sunshine. It was also a little bit more. It was turbulence, she was so enthusiastic, sometimes to the detriment of the things she was enthusiastic about. By that time she had become distinctly intellectual, she already had well-formed ideas. She adored her friends, but she was quixotic. She was always able to take up a new idea, reject another. . . .

"At that point Paul Mellon was still quite . . . unusual. Shy, hard to know, but blessed and amusing as a companion." The two were married on February 2, 1935, before a Presbyterian minister in the palatial apartment Ailsa leased at 3 Sutton Place from Ann Morgan, the sister of J. P. Morgan the younger. A.W. and Nora attended, the place was heaped with lilac and peach blossoms. David Bruce stood up for his brother-in-law. The newlyweds embarked immediately on the *Rex* to travel through Europe and some of the Middle East, plagued by regular pagings on the recently developed ship-to-shore wireless by newsmen who frankly wanted to know how relations were proceeding. Even Paul became snappish.

It had been A.W.'s impression the couple would be honeymooning for perhaps a month. That winter was arduous—in April, supported by David Bruce, Andrew Mellon defended a lifetime of activity before the tax-court tribunal. Paul was still abroad. Quite late in June, finally, the couple turned up. Mary helped manage A.W.'s vest-pocket estate. "She was just marvelous with Paul," says Mrs. Joseph Horne, Colonel Drake's daughter, who herself had recently married Paul's classmate Chauncey Hubbard. "She made an *effort* to love all his friends." The crowd from Yale stayed together, their friendships rekindled often at uproarious—and very alcoholic—get-togethers. The wives would joke at times about resenting this closeness.

Mary was everybody's favorite, a dynamic woman with lots of humor. Her intellectualism impressed everybody. "She really wasn't particularly smart in her dress, she wasn't that chic," an acquaintance remembers. It was her erudition. "Paul's friends thought Mary was a living encyclopedia," George Wyckoff says. "She knew a lot about a lot of things, if none too much about any one thing."

Days after his return, Paul had wearily consented to fifteen minutes with reporters in his office at the Mellon National. A.W. was visible "poring over a stack of papers at his desk in the adjoining office," and even the local feature writers admitted that Paul was almost as colorless and uncommunicative as A.W. had always been, if somewhat less abrupt. As for his plans? "I'll be here in the office. There are many things I must catch up on."

Perhaps that was misleading. Game as Mary was, Pittsburgh clearly wouldn't do. They were marking time. A.W. was genuinely frail by now, a cadaverous old figure who shuffled into rooms to find unfamiliar young people bursting with senseless laughter. What little he volunteered was acute, if more abstracted now than ever. "That's not so strange," he inserted one night, quashing the enthusiasm with which Paul and Mary were describing the 3,200-year-old artifacts they'd viewed near Tutankhamen's pyramid, the carved amethyst bottles edged exquisitely with gold. "That's only forty times my age."

The newlyweds lay low around Pittsburgh through much of 1936. They'd acquired two cocker spaniel puppies, and Mary was expecting. Baby Catherine was born very late that year in Pittsburgh's St. Margaret's Hospital. Paul Mellon lingered, watching. A father in attendance was . . . unexpected around delivery rooms, nothing local doctors encouraged, yet this too accorded with Mary's "mad intuitions" just then, fed by her earthiness, an immediacy that all but crackled from Mary's curly chestnut hair, the unstinting blue eyes, her rich forgiving laugh.

A.W. passed on the August following. Once that was over it didn't seem important to go to the bank anymore. "I found that I was gradually trying to get out of Pittsburgh more than anything else," Paul confesses now, reddening. Soon he and Mary had transferred their headquarters to Upperville, Virginia. There was some justification for this—Paul had started Rokeby Farms, and breeding race-horses represented, in its fashion, a kind of business. They built a sizable Georgian mansion, the Brick House. Paul mounted the Clare College oars which won their class in the Henley Regatta, joined various racing associations, submitted his name to important clubs—the Jockey, the Knickerbocker and Links and River and Racquet and Tennis, the Grolier, the Duquesne and Bucks. By then the National Gallery was rising; Paul agreed to complete his father's term as president. The young couple maintained a small apartment in New York, and another above the offices Paul shared in Washington with Finley and Shepard.

They both felt bottled up, confused and a little bit anxious about what came next. "Before they were married Mary often said to me, 'What am I doing, am I going to be able to live up to this?' " Jack

A memorable sleigh ride—Paul Mellon,
Mary Conover, Lucius Beebe
U.P.I.

Mary Mellon riding
PAUL MELLON

Mary confronts the wind
PAUL MELLON

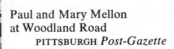

Paul Mellon with toff
PAUL MELLON

Paul and Mary Mellon
at Woodland Road
PITTSBURGH *Post-Gazette*

Barrett recalls. "She was very reluctant to make a step from freedom to what would obviously be the performance of a part. This was the young girl." They returned to England so Paul could complete a master's in history at Cambridge. In July of 1939 the secretary of the governing board of the National Gallery announced, with regrets, that several months earlier Paul Mellon had resigned as president "because his personal interests and business affairs were occupying so much time he felt it unwise to retain his position with the gallery. . . ." The same year he resigned his directorships of Gulf and the Mellon National.

That summer the family moved on to Zürich. Mary suffered from asthma, brought on most intensively by overexposure to horses. Horses rimmed Paul's identity, both as a rider and hunter and now as a breeder of steeplechasers and collector of sporting books. He rushed back season after season to Gloucestershire and Wiltshire to race and fox-hunt with friends from the Duke of Halifax to his beloved Nick Brady; at one lively dinner somebody spotted him, pink in his hunting coat, executing cartwheels along the long linen table before a leap for the chandelier, which he reportedly brought down. Horses aroused his temperament; Mary wouldn't be excluded.

They'd encountered Carl Jung during a previous stay abroad. Perhaps Jung could help. Jung himself was established as almost the only figure of his generation wily enough to disagree with Freud and survive the counterblasts. Jung's notion of archetypes, his investigation of dreams—these fed Mary's fascination with contemporary painting, her acute modernist need to intellectualize the primeval. A Dutch woman, Mrs. Froebe, was sponsoring a kind of seminar series in Ascona, on one of the bluffs overlooking Lake Maggiore. Another participant remembers the group sitting around a stone table overlooking the sweep of lake, the place "so beautiful it was almost magical." Mary herself was glowing, the type of big healthy girl who "probably played field hockey at Vassar" and now was "not overcome by her position. Paul Mellon seemed introverted, obviously in a new world, the world of psychoanalysis." There was a detective to guard little Catherine, and Paul was supposedly subsidizing the Tagung.

The Mellons went back to Zürich with Jung, and Mary gave over that autumn and winter to intense analysis. "I was never as much convinced of the therapeutic elements of Jung's work as Mary was," Paul says. "She had a feeling it had a psychological basis." It appeared to help; in April the Nazis invaded Norway, and Paul booked passage for all of them back to the United States. The September after that they rented a small house in Annapolis and Paul himself enrolled in the Great Books course at St. John's College.

All this made onlooking Mellons skeptical. "Mary had Paul wrapped around her little finger," old Matt says. "He followed her around like an agreeable little dog." Paul Mellon over thirty still had his waxen, susceptible look—long neck, drooped nose, an afterthought Mellon mouth that often hadn't decided whether it should turn up or down where it intercepted baby fat. Paul's gaze remained quizzical, mild, forgiving much in advance. He wanted to try things out, so long as setbacks didn't mark him as another infatuated rich man's son. He was vulnerable currently, with columnists and compilers of almanacs now singling him out as America's richest heir.

Mary seemed so sure of herself. Jung impressed her deeply; on returning to America she bustled about buying up manuscripts and treatises about the occult, forgotten works on alchemy. Paul himself liked collecting—besides his colorplate books he'd expanded his tastes, begun to accumulate Caxtons, unearthed a Pall Mall dealer who got him a copy of Strutt's rare *Sports and Pastimes of the People of England*. Along with Stubbs's *Pumpkin* he'd acquired additional sporting pictures, several—two Ben Marshalls and two Sartoriuses— gifts from A.W. These, like whatever drew Paul, came out of immediacy, reflected loyalty to experiences.

Mary jumped right in. Soon after their return she had another idea. "Her interest, and Paul's, was how to dispose of all their excess income just then," John Barrett remembers. One way they found evolved into the Bollingen Foundation. "The inspiration was entirely Mary," Barrett says. "She thought that if she—this *is* Medicean patronage— could have a stable of young, perceptive new thinkers and writers, and assure each one of five years of untroubled work . . . So that was how they set it up. Paul presented a specific fund that produced enough income to allow five or six writers to be able to depend on fifteen thousand dollars a year each for five years. Malcolm Cowley was one, and Denis de Rougemont, and St. John Perse came in on it."

It served many purposes. "I've always understood Paul founded the Bollingen to help Mary get rid of some of those excess energies of hers," one onlooker surmises. Paul himself was prospecting. "I've always thought that I had all this money, and that part of my vocation ought to be to learn how to spend some of it for educational and charitable purposes," he says. Days before Pearl Harbor the formation of the Old Dominion Foundation was announced. Paul became the chairman. "I had the feeling even then that all the foundations, even the big ones, were attuned to scientific things, medicine especially, and that the liberal arts colleges were not getting enough attention," he observes. "It was, for a great many years, an amateur operation. The tendency was to do things where you knew the people. That's why the Old Dominion did so much for Yale." Along with Paul, its original board consisted of Mary, Adolph Schmidt, Donald Shepard, and Wyckoff; Shepard administered.

Over twenty-five years the Old Dominion dispersed in excess of seventy-seven million dollars. Just under forty-eight and a half million went directly into education. St. John's was well remembered—seven million dollars' worth—and Yale received twenty million dollars to develop its directed study and "Scholars of the House" programs. The Old Dominion underwrote Yale's Morse and Ezra Stiles colleges. Clare College in Cambridge benefited greatly as well as Choate in Wallingford. The foundation also distributed between four and eight million dollars each to undertakings in the arts, mental health, conservation and an assortment of projects in the Commonwealth of Virginia. Gifts from the Old Dominion and Ailsa's foundation, the Avalon, made possible the creation of the first true ocean beach park, the Cape Hatteras National Seashore in North Carolina. Paul personally enjoyed sailing.

These steps would prefigure a lifetime of duty for Paul and Ailsa: the distribution of Andrew's fortune. Paul had no doubt that what he had he held by public sufferance. A story his father relished amuses him. Frank Haskell ran Carborundum. "Mrs. Haskell," Paul says, "was apparently a very demanding and jittery sort of woman. They had a chauffeur and a very big car in Buffalo. Mrs. Haskell was always telling him to do this, do that, and finally one day he got so fed up he simply stepped out of the car, when it was all locked up in very heavy traffic, and walked away from it, and never came back." Paul chuckles. Presumption is comically vulnerable.

Yet philanthropy gets touchy. Paul repeatedly observed that generosity was much more likely to damage than benefit its recipients. Underneath, like Andrew, he hated to tamper with natural economic mechanisms. Calvinism dies out reluctantly.

Largely for his own sake he intended to try. "Before and after the war I saw all kinds of things which needed to be done," he said, years later. "Besides, obviously there were a lot of advantages tax-wise in setting up foundations. They helped you do your charitable things much less haphazardly." There wasn't any choice.

Quite late in 1941 the Old Dominion announcements went out; Paul Mellon opened his during mail call at Fort Riley, Kansas. In July he'd become a private in the cavalry. "Although married and with a young child," he subsequently wrote, "I had for many months had a compulsive desire to join the Army, and more specifically, the cavalry."

Their lives were shifting. In 1940 Paul bestowed the house on Woodland Road upon the Pennsylvania College for Women. Just the previous March he'd presided over the official presentation of the National Art Gallery, awkwardly reading an address which opened, with point: "This building, which we are dedicating tonight, is the realization of a plan formed by my father many years ago, soon after he came to Washington as Secretary of the Treasury." A jubilant Franklin Roosevelt barely mentioned the donor.

Patriotism begins with individuals—at least that served when explaining such decisions. Paul enlisted in the District of Columbia to avoid undue publicity. "I have been thinking about it for a long time," he informed a reporter, who tracked him down to ask why anybody his age had willingly gone in. His wife, Paul hastened to add, also believed that this "was the thing to do."

But why the Army? "I don't know," Paul now says. "Maybe I was still disappointed about missing the cadet corps at Choate. Besides, in those days a lot of people thought the cavalry was romantic—horses could be used in the wild parts of the world." He finished basic training, tolerated the nickname "Cantaloupe," and instructed in horsemanship. He went through Officer Candidate School. By 1943 he was stultifying himself repeating his two-hour dissertation on the preservation and grooming of saddle leather. The mounts were plugs. Furthermore, "it had become obvious to me that the cavalry was not going to make any more wild charges." Donald Shepard in Washington pulled strings to get him onto the staff of a general headquartered in England. Following a three-week boat ride in a seven-and-a-half-knot convoy, Paul reached wartime London to discover his orders were lost and that the general had "either been killed or moved to another theater of operations. The people in command then found out I owned a farm, and sent me as a farm expert to the colonel in charge of all the victory gardens around Cheltenham. That almost drove me crazy, it was worse than the bank."

Paul shared a flat in Belgravia with "a great friend of mine," his Middleburg neighbor Stacy Lloyd. Lloyd had a staff assignment with the London headquarters of American intelligence, the Office of Strategic Services. David Bruce ran that. "*Naturally* I didn't want to go through David," Paul says; Lloyd arranged an interview at a subordinate level, and Paul put in his last two years with O.S.S.

Mellon likes to maintain he was in serious peril only once during all these years. Riding in a train compartment with a couple of enlisted men, bent on impressing them, he jerked his service revolver from its holster so clumsily the safety snapped off and the heavy pistol ejected cartridges all across his lap. Paul Mellon's war. In fact, his dossier mentions parachute training with British troops followed by a year directing the drop of key intelligence agents all around Western Europe. He became a major, and commanded a unit which attempted to infiltrate "block propaganda" behind disintegrating German lines. Pneumonia laid him low, but Paul took home the European Theater of Operations Ribbon with Four Bronze Stars.

Throughout the war years Mary managed the farm, read, worked on the publishing schedule for Pantheon Press, which was to print the relatively arcane manuscripts selected by the advisers to the Bollingen Foundation. The foundation's exotic name was derived from the site of Jung's retreat, with its medieval study tower. Mary taught little Catherine to read and write. Time often felt suspended, as if the mother and child stood watching the play of heat lightning from remote, secluded fields. Catherine remembers her mother—stormy and involving even to a youngster—pulling her from bed at midnight to spy an unfamiliar bird, to observe an eclipse. "We used to discuss our dreams a lot," Catherine says. "She'd write mine down. Whenever my father got out on furlough he would come back to the farm. I could never recognize him. I felt left out, I would be standing at the door and they would be kissing and hugging. . . ."

In July of 1942 Catherine's baby brother, Timothy, was born in Pittsburgh. His name was intended to recall the Judge. Once she was up and around, Mary prepared a surprise. "She was a very determined character," John Barrett says. To overcome her sensitivity to horses she went about her farm chores from a pony cart. The asthma attacks recurred. "You know," she confided to Barrett, "the doctor said if I have one of these things in a very bad way it might carry me off."

Barrett remembered his answer: "I said, 'Oh, go to hell, I don't believe in doctors.' "

When Paul was mustered out in August of 1945 she was riding well. She joined the fox hunters. One Friday afternoon, October 11, 1946, the pack formed up for a regular session of the Piedmont Hunt. "They'd all gone out," Barrett says, "and then something happened. She had a seizure, she had to be gotten off the horse. Somebody drove her back. It all went very quickly." While doctors labored, Paul telephoned close friends. "They say she can't get through the night," he told George Wyckoff. Before Barrett and Nora arrived her heart gave out. "We couldn't save Mima," he told Jack Barrett. "We spent four hours with the nurses."

"There she was lying," Jack Barrett says. "I went upstairs to see her. Paul said, 'I want you to know we will continue to carry on Mary's ideas if you'll stick with me.' "

They held the funeral inside the Brick House. Friends came, and afterward they placed her, within the pine coffin she herself requested, upon the bed of the pony cart and walked behind her up the dirt road to leave her in the traditional Randolph burying ground just above the house. "It was a scene from a novel," one mourner says, shrugging. Little Catherine was nine.

"She was a very enthusiastic person," Bunny Mellon says. Her attention wanders off. What else to say? "Very enthusiastic about a great many things. And Mary was older, of course. She'd been to school. Most of my knowledge came from having grown up in a house where girls didn't go to college. We got along surprisingly well—she with her formal education, I with my informal education. . . ."

Bunny is Paul's wife. Rearranging her stately legs, sipping mid-morning coffee, she searches her interviewer with exactly the uncertainty, the eagerness and raptness, expected of a too-tall sixteen-year-old, in town from boarding school, jittery at a subscription dance. Finishing out her sixties, her face is painfully hollow. She sets the china cup onto its saucer. Her mouth is desolate, forlorn wire.

"You know, Dr. Jung was originally a friend of Mary's, and then of Paul's. Paul became interested in him as a scholar. Basically, Paul is a scholar. That's the thing that I liked in Paul Mellon was the scholar. I'm not scholarly myself, but I do like to talk to people with ideas."

Her voice is light, well modulated, yet there are decisive little nudges of inflection to carry the important ideas, reminders of nagging force, just as her strong, supple gardener's hands belie the quavering head. "You know for Paul—the Thirties—that was a very sad time. He was in a doldrum period. Then came the war, and the war just sort of moved him around. Then Mary died, and we were married—

"My marriage to Paul? I really only wanted one life, I was very happy with my first husband. It crumbled during the war. You know, there are a lot more casualties in war than death."

Bunny had been married to Stacy Lloyd. Stacy owned the newspaper in nearby Middleburg, Virginia, but he was much more than that implied, "just about the most charming person you could know," Jack Barrett recalls. "Definitely first-line Philadelphia, which usually means, perhaps a little bit stuffy. . . ." Mary like them both. "Mary always told me, 'They're the nicest people we know in this area.'"

Separation loosens people up. The crazy, chance-taking, somewhere-across-an-ocean-and-tomorrow-we-die mood that prevailed among people on Colonel Bruce's eclectic staff was conducive to sorties, often involving adventurous women. Around the Belgravia flat Stacy shared with Paul there weren't any parietal rules. What seemed simple refreshment in London was unstomachable in Middleburg. Bunny tried to convey this, but Stacy "wasn't going to listen, to change. I couldn't remain in this state."

Mary died. Bunny, nearby, looked in as often as she could to relieve Paul's management problems. His children were still very young, eleven and six, the ages of Bunny's pair. Bunny's father, the yachtsman and Listerine tycoon Gerard Lambert, had been an exacting organizer with quite a demanding eye; this eldest daughter, Rachel —"Bunny" virtually from birth—was barely a stringy little kid scrambling among the rowboats at Hobe Sound or peeping at the workmen laying out the gardens in Princeton before he recognized in her gifts corresponding to his.

Paul acknowledged these too, and required them pressingly. "Paul and I married because I felt I could help him," Bunny states now, flatly. "We became partners to help one another, and we remained that." A divorce was prepared, and Paul and Bunny were married in May of 1948. "I've always surmised that it was essentially a rearrangement between two friends, between Paul and Stacy," says one civilized intimate. "A sort of shift. There were temporary difficulties, but when it was arrived at, everything was in perfect dignity. It was a heartbreak for the bewildered man who was being left, but that's perfectly natural. Incompatibility, which can be the grounds, can mean almost anything." There is a pause. "Those years with Mary certainly fade."

2

The dislocations of war finished another Mellon marriage. One day in London, Evangeline Bell—cultivated beauty, daughter of an American diplomat and something of a friend at Harvard—drew Arthur Schlesinger, Jr., aside and sounded him out. The two were attached to O.S.S. "She said she'd fallen in love with someone of whom she thought I'd disapprove," Schlesinger says. "It was Colonel Bruce." Schlesinger couldn't really respond—he himself regarded the tall, pale-eyed Southerner as an effective leader who, "despite his air of Border-State inconsequentiality, was much more intelligent than he let on, with a gift for moving people in the direction he wanted them to go, and rather a skeptic about established institutions. He liked bright people, and he didn't care whether they came from the New York ghetto or the southern aristocracy."

David requested a divorce. This had been pending. Yet now, it hurt. "She deserved it, she was very spoiled," her cousin Peggy Hitchcock admits; Ailsa recognized this too. "I saw the aftermath—'I wish I'd done this, I wish I'd done that,' " says another friend.

Paul was typically charitable. "As far as I could see they were reasonably happy. On the other hand, he was a very active and outgoing person. I would imagine it was depressing for him. They did spend considerable periods down at Staunton Hall. Ailsa didn't really like the country. They were on different wavelengths.

"My father always thought very highly of David," Paul says. A.W. proved it, in his way, by creating irrevocable trusts—ten million dollars' worth, by one account—from which the dividends went directly to David. David redirected the income to Ailsa's foundation. Personal relationships held up. Bruce did resign the presidency of the National Gallery, and in due course David's place among the Gallery's directors would go to G. Lauder Greenway.

Currently Lauder is aging. He moves most carefully at this point, an apparition in unpressed tweeds, smoothed hair, hazy corneas. Tall, like David, amusing still, his solicitous, genteel conversation splashes up quite snidely at unexpected moments, a reminder that bitchiness was expected once of confident old money. Behind Lauder's sprawling stone Gothic Revival Greenwich cottage a jungle of boxwood prickles through the screens, exuding tangy pollens, and across the toe of his slipper Lauder's elderly bulldog, shedding for the last time, lies limp as blutwurst.

Lauder's relationship to Ailsa? Companion? Confidant? Who dares to inquire? It should be enough that after the formalization of the divorce Lauder devotedly filled in, helped wherever he could, escorted Ailsa almost daily to the little restaurant she liked, the Passy, waited at the milliner's, gentled Ailsa even during her "off" days to dress herself and attend certain long-scheduled gallery appointments, put in her appearance at important dinner parties. Around her Syosset estate he was always somewhere—idling in his flannels beside the tranquil pool, mixing newcomers a drink. Lauder made life bearable.

Even that was something. Ailsa was getting sicker. Among people she trusted her recurrent languors, her practice of ignoring engagements, her frank self-centeredness—hypochondria, everybody conceded. Ailsa simply indulges herself. Few actually understood. "She had a condition which manifested itself in feelings of weakness," her doctor says. "Lupus erythematosus disseminatus. A fatal disease, a progressive malady. She felt *sick*. She was weak, asthenic, thin, lacked appetite, found it difficult to summon up strength to fulfill obligations, had many infections of a respiratory nature—sinus problems, et cetera." Her doctor, Arthur Antenucci, clears his powerful throat. The diagnosis is firm. "She was very dedicated, she showed an almost slavelike devotion to the obligations she thought she bore."

Depression, sustained, can lead to crippling irresolution. Ailsa's did. Tradesmen suffered. Perfectionistic about clothes, she subsidized a dressmaker whose work she liked, Sophie Shonnard, through various establishments, including, finally, her own. The requests she made—while always in imperturbable, low-keyed, cultivated diction—seemed calculated to madden. "I knew Ailsa's dressmaker," one friend reports. "She would come in after wearing a dress a year and say, 'Could you possibly lengthen the sleeves a quarter of a centimeter?' She had no idea what this would mean. What can you charge?"

Ailsa hated feeling pushed. She had been helping a group of Russian émigrés, headed by Tolstoy's daughter. Their representative kept insisting she visit their encampment and let them show her around.

Finally Ailsa lashed out: "You can be thankful for the money, but I don't really care about the immigrants at all." The invitations stopped. Ailsa had her standards. "She was extremely fastidious, she all but asked you whom you had just come from visiting," one friend tosses off. She kept herself socially for people who counted, a small circle which included over many years dignitaries from the Louis Bromfields to the Duke and Duchess of Windsor. Ailsa remained very close to intimates from childhood—Peggy Hitchcock, Mrs. Craigie Mackay Schwartz. After ten years—over the course of which Dr. Arthur Antenucci had progressed from assisting Ailsa medically to looking in several afternoons a week to help sort out the flow of foundation requests—Ailsa suddenly glanced up. "Lauder and I have been talking," she opened with hesitation. "We've been wondering whether you would mind if I were, from now on, to call you *Arthur*?"

Hauteur; partly it was apprehension, what somebody referred to as an "incapability of expressing herself emotionally." The jolts of childhood, never quite smoothed away. She traveled very little. She bought and decorated several houses in Greenwich, where Nora and Lauder both lived, but she was never actually able to force herself to pass a night in either. She also kept residences around Palm Beach. With Ailsa growing older the phobias proliferated. A cousin stopped up to find her edgy about traveling the Manhattan streets, quite certain the pavements were undermined and that their car might easily fall through. On one of Ailsa's rare appearances in Pittsburgh she discovered herself, along with the omnipresent Lauder, shooed by the freewheeling Connie Mellon into special accommodations atop the bank building. The proprieties concerned Lauder, but Ailsa had other anxieties. "Why is it," she demanded, absently, "that everything in Pittsburgh these days drops off forty stories?"

Despite this—despite everything—Ailsa retained a knack she shared with A.W. and Paul. She could enlist loyalty, provoke intense, even incapacitating affection which really had nothing to do with wealth or position. She was, like Paul, doggedly true to individuals. There were relieving moments. "I never saw anybody improve with a martini the way Ailsa did," Peggy Hitchcock said. The little she drank brought out considerable penetration; at times—with friends— a touch of insidious, tweaking humor.

There exists an inexpertly retouched glossy among Paul Mellon's little bin of pictures which portrays the "A.W. side" of the family

A present from Harry—from left, George Wyckoff, Cathy Mellon, Adolph Schmidt, Audrey Bruce, Mrs. Schmidt, Truman, Paul Mellon, Ailsa Mellon Bruce

during one uncommon moment of public recognition. The photo was snapped during 1947 or 1948, judging from the ages of Catherine and Audrey. The shot was obviously taken in the Truman White House. The President is sitting at his desk, evidently signing a paper in acceptance of a National Gallery gift from the A. W. Mellon Educational and Charitable Trust, and arrayed behind him are Wyckoff and a beaming Paul, the Adolph Schmidts, the two little girls. High, onlooking, in a flowered silk print, Ailsa oversees the others. Her expression is benign, but there is something about it inescapably remote and patronizing. To Ailsa this President is another ordinary politician, exposing his unbecoming neck, getting through five minutes, receiving one more handout.

Which represented, after all, a portion of Ailsa's own life. Perhaps, those middle years, she more than Paul felt responsible for fulfilling A.W.'s commitment. Paul was still searching. "Her father always said, from a business standpoint, she should have been the boy," records Adolph Schmidt. "There was more guile to Ailsa than most people suspected," one regular would note; Walker remarks her competitiveness.

Her instincts were parsimonious. She too loved paintings. With Greenway, who himself held posts with the Metropolitan and the New York University Museum systems, she frequently passed afternoons perusing worthwhile pictures coming onto the market. "Her tastes were not very advanced, she never surprised me, but she had a very good eye, says John Walker, another regular companion.

Her income was stupendous. Whenever she couldn't avoid getting her name in the paper it was commonly accompanied by the sobriquet "World's Wealthiest Woman." Yet making a commitment—actually purchasing something—was often nearly impossible. She stalled, she bargained, she soft-soaped dealers into permitting her to borrow major paintings for what could run into years. They stacked up, often unframed, against the scrollwork of incidental chairs, filled out the bottoms of coat closets. "It used to concern me that the dog might appear some afternoon and pee all over a masterpiece," a friend admits. Usually they went back.

"She *was* indecisive," her brother says. "She always was worried about overdoing things." She sought out reassurances. Paul tells of happening upon a very large Monet canvas, a garden scene he liked at once. He inquired after price; the dealer told him the picture was on reserve, pending Ailsa's decision. "If she doesn't want it, please let me know," Paul said. "But don't tell her I'm interested." He knew that if his sister discovered that he was prepared to make the purchase she would, and she ultimately did.

Ailsa's account in Pittsburgh—relatively static, securities her father left—compounded. Wyckoff looked after that. "She really did worry about the goldarnedest things," George says. "She'd come in and tell me, as concerned as hell: 'I spent a lot of money today.' And maybe she'd have one hundred times that much in her bank account just then."

Ailsa felt much better about giving it away. Throughout the 1960s, while Walker directed the National Gallery, paintings of international reputation abruptly became available. Walker would inform Ailsa—and Wyckoff. "We were in cahoots," George acknowledges. His part was to convince Ailsa her estate could absorb the grant.

Undoubtedly her most stunning gift remains that eerie little likeness, *Ginevra de' Benci* by Leonardo, with which the prince of Liechtenstein had long been tantalizing collectors. In time, after suffering, the terribly smitten Walker was able to negotiate its purchase at a price "fantastically high," if reportedly about half the ten million dollars the prince once asked. Ailsa sent the money.

Another acknowledged masterpiece, Fragonard's peaceful and touching portrait of a young girl reading, *La Liseuse,* went into the collection "from Mrs. Mellon Bruce in Memory of Her Father Andrew Mellon." Ailsa loved this picture. Over many years she had regretted that her father had presented a painting she adored as a young woman and hung in her bedroom, Reynolds' *Lady Caroline Howard,* directly to the National Gallery despite her wish to retain it. She regularly asked Walker whether there was any chance of working out a re-purchase or trade. Yet when she acquired *La Liseuse* in 1961, and it was easy enough for Ailsa to earmark the gift but enjoy the picture, she turned it over at once. She repeated the explanation A.W. had offered her: it "was too important to be privately owned."

Close to the end she occasionally baited Walker. "You know, John, you mustn't think you are going to get everything I have for the National Gallery," she informed him. "My grandchildren are going to have some of the collection." She meant the Impressionist paintings with which she decorated her apartments. Afterward, she'd willed the Gallery everything. "Ailsa's generosity," Walker wrote, "cannot be ex-aggerated. She gave many millions of dollars for purchases. The majority of the greatest acquisitions the Gallery has made with its own funds came from the immense resources she provided. For some of the paintings and sculpture she felt excited enthusiasm, for others personal indifference; but as long as I assured her that the works of art were needed, she urged me to go ahead."

Her efforts with philanthropy were equally wholehearted. In 1940 she brought into being the Avalon Foundation. Around New York especially Avalon became a factor. In 1968, shortly before the foundation was dissolved into the enlarged Andrew W. Mellon Foundation, it appropriated, from income on its roughly $150,000,000 in assets, $5,919,000 in grants to 102 organizations and institutions. Medicine remained its focus, but grants went out to beneficiaries which ranged from centers for the training of the unskilled of Spanish Harlem to the Metropolitan Opera Association, Inc.

"Ailsa took an extraordinarily personal interest in what happened to her money," Dr. Antenucci says. "She had a way of asking, when you had other obligations, 'Arthur, would you have a minute to go over these papers with me?' Her desk was stacked with requests to

Avalon." Throughout much of this, Antenucci was chief of medicine at Roosevelt Hospital, and followed research nationally. "She would peel off these papers and look at me and say, 'Arthur, do you know anything about this?' " She supported pioneering research; the earliest efforts to treat mucoviscidosis began to succeed only after Ailsa started contributing.

"I think her greatest personal interest was actually science," Dr. Antenucci says. "She read its literature voluminously. She was always underlining parts of books. She would ask me such things as 'Arthur, is this statement about the value of potassium in neuromuscular illness accurate?' You could always appeal to her reason. Another time she asked me if I knew anything about an avant-garde method of training nurses. The request had come from Fairleigh Dickinson. I knew the person who signed the application, Peter Samartino. I advised her to give twenty-five or fifty thousand dollars a year for five years. In fact, Ailsa processed a lot of that stuff herself."

3

The picture with Truman offers one of the very rare representations of Audrey Bruce, fourteen or so, already getting quite tall, especially in the straw Easter bowler garlanded by millinery flowers with which her mother had offset her prim, dark dress. Little Audrey is making even less of an effort than Ailsa herself. Her face is darkly suspicious. A quite pronounced swollenness shadows in just below her mouth, the consequence, undoubtedly, of years of orthodontia.

Audrey's experience wasn't conducive to joviality. Much time passed alone. "Ailsa was the most dignified person," her cousin Peggy says. "A real lady." But Peggy is honest. "I wouldn't call her a good mother." In hopes of enlivening her daughter Ailsa stirred herself at times to take her to beautiful places, Peggy recalls, "where she was the only child."

"She was a most intelligent sweet girl," Lauder Greenway remembers, "but left too much with governesses and trained nurses. She loved to be outdoors. One summer I took my nephews and Audrey and Ailsa and everybody went west to visit a ranch. Mrs. Bruce tried hard, although she wasn't exactly Mrs. Buffalo Bill, you know. . . .

"As a little tiny child Audrey went to Miss Chapin's School. She became terribly pulled into herself, I don't know why. The country began to turn, people started to refer to her as the 'Little Princess.' She'd been a beautiful child, but then her lower jaw stopped growing. To straighten it out they'd have to pull her teeth out and start all over again. They felt it wasn't worthwhile."

Her situation tortured her. She proceeded to Foxcroft, with its socially immaculate clientele and two military-style inspections a day. Audrey loved to ride. She spent her summers around Ailsa's sixty-acre estate in Syosset. Her cousin, Cathy Mellon, remembers her there as quietly mischievous: "Her mother had some kind of governess around her all the time. We'd have to come down at a certain hour, eat this enormous breakfast, ride, swim, come back, have a rest. . . . I'd see my aunt a little before dinner. We used to spend hours trying to get around this governess, play tricks on her. . . ." Oppressed, embarrassed, Audrey scurried into the back of the family limousine whenever it appeared and dropped onto her hands and knees immediately, pretending she had lost some pennies. This was an excuse so people on the street, who otherwise might recognize her, wouldn't see her overprotected like this.

"She had a childlike dimension even as an adult," one friend points out. "If, walking in the woods, she came upon a wounded caterpillar, it would concern her deeply, for days. Most of the time she was as unprepossessing as any woman could possibly be." At college classmates remembered her, if at all, trailing about the Yard in a soiled raincoat, her dark hair tangled. By then her chin was remarkably undershot.

About halfway through Radcliffe, Audrey fell in love. "Talk about pathetic boys!" exclaims the faithful Lauder. "I think it had been difficult for her to find somebody she liked whom nobody else liked or was inclined to try and take away from her. Stephen came from a shattered family; he was thoroughly insecure. Once Audrey started seeing Stephen the family looked to find out who this young man might be, he might be Jack the *Rip*pah so far as anybody knew. She brought him round. He was unfortunate, he wanted to please, but he didn't have the ability to please. His father was a mess, we never saw him, although his mother, Mrs. Eddie Warburg, was a great friend of all of us.

"Part of the problem was, Stephen kept *saying* these things. Which weren't true, but weren't exactly untrue either. For example, he told us he was living in Cambridge, which we thought meant he was attending Harvard. But Stephen was not at Harvard."

Audrey was well aware of what her family thought of Stephen Currier. "She didn't tell anyone she was married for a while," Greenway recalls. "Then she told her father, and he told Ailsa, and Ailsa and I went up to Boston."

The first Currier baby arrived the day Audrey graduated with honors. "It's a diploma," Lauder was there to assure her once she came to. The Mellons didn't appreciate Steve Currier any more as a son-in-law than they had as a suitor. "He was a snotty sort of a guy," Dr. Antenucci says, "who disagreed before he knew, for the sake of disagreeing. Audrey never answered back very much. There was some question about whether that marriage would last. None of the Mellons liked the marriage at all, and especially the fact that he finally got to the point where he wielded great influence over her wealth." Audrey was, after all, the legatee of half of Andrew Mellon's fortune; she was very young when the initial installment, around fifty million dollars, came down as principal. Family sources still joke about the day she and her husband visited the Mellon bank to all but present a withdrawal slip. The two expected cash, and right away. "Audrey had been kept in abysmal ignorance of how much money she had," remembers one of the lawyers. "It hit her like a steamroller." Part of her inheritance was the ancestral Bruce estate in Virginia, Staunton Hall. Sometime after the marriage David Bruce, by then the dean of the diplomatic corps of the United States, quietly contacted his son-in-law to begin the formality of buying it back. Currier had other ideas. He finally gave up the house and a little of the surrounding acreage, but most of the property he intended to dispose of to other, higher bidders. "If they could have gotten away with it," one familiar says, "both Paul and David would have strung Currier up."

Ailsa fared little better. "He thought he knew absolutely everything," Peggy Hitchcock says. "Ailsa might venture an opinion, and Stephen would cut her off: 'Now, Mrs. Bruce, just keep quiet a minute.'" To universal horror, the marriage flourished. "The fact was," Peggy Hitchcock goes on, "Stephen gave her great confidence. She was very happy, she bloomed like a flower. She went onto the board of Brearley. They had three children and the parents read to them, they all said prayers together. They had a *wonderful* family life." The Curriers settled into a clamorous apartment on Central Park West, says Dr. Antenucci, "which Ailsa hated, and we began to hear stories connected with a monstrous nursemaid they had, who twirled the babies around by the feet. Ailsa thought they lived like a bunch of barbarians."

Then there was one secondary objection. Peggy voices it, hesitantly: "My family disapproved of the things they were working on. Something having to do with the colored. We felt they were on the wrong side." Vague as this is, it suggests, at least, the presence of the other Stephen Currier, the bustling self-conscious opinionated can-do self-educated hanger-on and would-be social meliorist who, during the decade he had, probably induced more change and left a larger personal imprint on contemporary America than all the remaining Mellons.

Currier wasn't particularly clubbable. While still very young Stephen lost most of his hair, leaving a glistening pate, across which he piously combed whatever was left, up over one side. He tended to pudginess and he wore glasses. His features were fine, chiseled, yet much of the time he carried himself with the rigidity of an accountant who hopes that uprightness and solemnity of manner will preclude an audit. "In a sense Stephen seemed to be his own grandfather," says Mrs. Eddy, who directed his pivotal Taconic Foundation. "Always trying so hard. There *was* an uneasy self-importance." Harold Fleming, who ran the Taconic's Washington subsidiary, the Potomac Institute, finds that characteristic easy to explain: "He'd had a difficult upbringing, always in that sort of no-man's-land on the edge of the rich New York world."

To make matters worse, he had an artist's temperament. Stephen's own father was, in fact, a painter, reputedly gifted, charming, reputedly a drinker. His parents had broken up early in his life. At best, Currier's relations with the transplanted-Hanseatic Warburg family were in and out, although his stepfather had settled the income from several hundred thousand dollars on Stephen. He'd gotten into Harvard but quit. Stephen drifted among contacts, put up for fairly extended periods with liberal acquaintances like the Marshall Fields, collected prints and drawings in a small way. Audrey came across him while he was working for a Boston art dealer.

He later told intimates that he had very little notion that Audrey had means of her own until after they were married, let alone that

Audrey Currier with Michael
TACONIC FOUNDATION

Stephen Currier
TACONIC FOUNDATION

she was coming into one of the world's great fortunes. Intuitive, not analytical, Currier never had bothered to understand very much about corporate America.

About these things, according to the Mellons, he learned uncomfortably fast. Soon after the marriage, on a friend's recommendation, he turned up in the law offices of Lloyd Garrison and asked that unreconstructed New Dealer to explain to him the welter of trusts and provisos from which his wife would benefit. The conversation wandered. Garrison discovered that Currier's interests had taken a turn toward the problems of race. As onetime president of the Urban League, this descendant of the publisher of *The Liberator* was widely acquainted among the contemporary Negro leadership. He introduced Stephen around. Meanwhile, he helped Currier organize the Taconic Foundation, through which Stephen intended to funnel the bulk of his wife's enormous income to "enable"—a word he liked—masses of otherwise helpless people to piece together lives.

Currier was a newcomer, but he was determined. In real life, a dollar into politics has more genuine influence than thousands to charities. What professionals would characterize as "the spectacularly

brave and controversial Taconic Foundation" formed quickly to
events. "Sometime in 1957 or 1958, when I was executive director
of the Southern Regional Council, I got a telegram out of the blue
telling me that a Mr. and Mrs. Currier wanted to make us a small
gift," Harold Fleming says. "Twenty-five hundred dollars, I think it
was." Support from the Curriers increased with Dr. King's requirements. Before long, by agreement, Currier and Fleming limited the
Currier gifts to $25,000 a year; more would have been "distorting,"
and created "undue dependence."

With blacks taking over, Fleming moved to Washington to run the
Potomac Institute. Stephen projected its function as that of a "small,
low-profile, self-effacing institution" through the offices of which experienced civil-rights workers could share their thinking with bureaucrats. It specialized in means, the translation of enlightened legislation
into something out there. Potomac strategists were active in promoting
the voter registration project—alerting plain southern blacks to their
first chance at meaningful political choice. They designed the Contract Compliance Program, which John Kennedy implemented by
executive decree, to force all suppliers to the Government to offer
minorities equal employment opportunities. Then pressure was exerted
to compel the Government to follow the same procedures "in-house."

The whole thing fused, of course, during Johnson's early Presidency. The Civil Rights Act authorized the creation of a Community
Relations Service. Ex-Governor Collins of Florida went in as titular
head, but Johnson wanted somebody with experience on the organizing level to be his deputy. He asked Harold Fleming. Fleming wasn't
very enthusiastic. "But then one afternoon Stephen went to a White
House reception," as Fleming tells it, "and Johnson, who knew even
the most insignificant details in this town, threw that long arm around
Stephen and said, 'Mr. Currier, we need yo' man.' "

Currier called Fleming up, somewhat apologetic. " 'What can you
do when the President gives you that bear hug?' he asked me. I went
over for six months."

The person Fleming knew was sincere, impatient, unwilling to
"suffer fools gladly," a natural leader, and searching, "like Diogenes,
for an honest man, or at least for somebody who wouldn't hustle you.
He wasn't anybody's patsy." Back in New York he led the fight that
kept Breezy Point from developers. Taconic lawyers evolved strategies
to resist local "exclusionary land use" provisions; Taconic grants went
out to minority banks and struggling rural co-ops. Whatever Audrey's

relatives thought, Stephen's impulses weren't radical. "Stephen poured a helluva lot of oil on troubled waters," Fleming says, "to the extent of having been accused by some black leaders of having bought off the march on Washington."

On Park Avenue uptown, all that was distant and distasteful. "Stephen had a kind of charisma which bothered people who were used to going by the numbers," says Mrs. Eddy. Associates claim he listened to advice and had an excellent rapport with almost all the important civil-rights leaders, but "if he didn't like you it was no closely held secret." One friend observes that Currier hated situations of personal stress and handled them poorly. Either he avoided the issue entirely or confronted it clumsily. "His face would flush and he would become impetuous, uncontrolled, blurt things out. There was a kind of blurt-out syndrome. He was very touchy about the fact that anybody who would marry Audrey would be seen as a kind of potential money-digger."

Audrey supported Stephen completely. She attended foundation meetings—timid, pleasant, radiating belief in Stephen—and rarely said anything unless the grant under review concerned children or education. By the middle Sixties she was receiving the after-tax income on $250,000,000 in trust, which came to about five million dollars a year. Three plus went directly to Taconic.

The Mellons remained dubious. "They used to give these Christmas parties at the foundation offices every year," Lauder Greenway says. "Ninety-nine percent colored people. I went. Mrs. Bruce wouldn't go because she hated crowds." Another member of Ailsa's circle remembers seeing the Curriers during intermission at the opera, "looking like a couple of ragamuffins. When they spotted me they ducked behind a pillar." Early in her marriage Audrey started doing volunteer work at Lenox Hill Hospital. She was still wearing the ratty old raincoat people remembered from college. Audrey kept coming back, and after a while a group of staff members got together enough to buy her another raincoat. They were reportedly touched that somebody who obviously did not have resources of her own would volunteer her time.

When Currier started spending, that was even worse. One Thanksgiving, the Curriers mounted dinner at the Virginia estate Stephen had been developing near The Plains, Kinloch. People across the family still talk about that. Starting with a set of outbuildings and the relic of the house in which Robert E. Lee passed much of his boyhood, Currier and his architect had developed a 1,600-acre estate which unfolded very gradually to the visitor's eye among the hedges and buildings, along watercourses, through rose gardens which erupted into fountains and dropped into walled terraces for dining. "Do you remember that place in Versailles, Jack?" Paul Mellon asked Barrett as their car swung into the entrance and started the climb toward the remodeled mansion. Each room featured antiques from a different period. Beneath hand-painted Chinese wallpaper a table "as big as two entire rooms" was heaped with fruit. "Currier was going to do things in the big manner," Barrett observed. "Of course *he* knew how to do everything. The Mellons were the way they always are when they get together—you'd think they didn't know one another."

Stephen's intentions with Kinloch seem remotely—if unconsciously —feudal in their patterns. He intended to create the Currier family seat. The mansion itself "curled," as inconspicuously as possible for a stand of masonry which contains twenty-three bathrooms, down from its knoll to blend with the surrounding Blue Ridge Mountain foothills. Stephen took up fox hunting. There were 110 regular employees on the estate, black mostly, who received higher wages than other working people around Fauquier County—an irritation to neighborhood employers. Audrey kept a list of all their children's birthdays, and scrupulously sent cards. Plans were allegedly in the works to import a thousand Puerto Ricans, "as if there weren't enough around without that," says one Mellon manager. Stephen was starting up a cattle operation. They had a sprawling farm in Vermont. "The trouble with his projects," one onlooker, a Rockefeller, noted, "is that they don't have sound economic bases. They'll all fall down if they aren't kept going with outside money."

With years—and grandchildren—Ailsa Bruce and Stephen Currier attempted gestures from time to time to get themselves onto an agreeable personal footing. In Pittsburgh and Wilmington, the long-established trusts maintained their imperishable existences. Periodically, when consultation was unavoidable, George Wyckoff made appointments to rendezvous with Stephen; sometimes Currier was there. Over holidays, in winter, Ailsa received the Currier family in balmy Palm Beach. Grandchildren captured her imagination, and increasingly she cherished her sweet, introverted, sensitive daughter as deeply as she had come to appreciate generous old Nora. Life offered certain balances. The Curriers started decorating a Fifth Avenue apartment.

One Wednesday in January of 1967, ambling along a sunny harbor pier on St. Thomas, in the Virgin Islands, Lauder Greenway was startled to come upon Michael Currier, five, youngest of Audrey's babies. Stephen's mother, Mrs. Warburg, hurried up to Lauder. A chartered Currier boat, with its crew, now lay at anchor in the Charlotte Amalie bay, and Stephen and Audrey had been expected the evening before. "Don't let Ailsa know," Mrs. Warburg said. "The children are missing."

That told the story, although the week that followed would involve a great part of the eastern Caribbean—the section just south of the Sargasso Sea that forms the lower edge of the Bermuda Triangle— in one of the most massive sea hunts in naval history. Solid facts were few. On Tuesday, January 17, Stephen Currier had hired a little five-passenger Piper Apache, piloted by one of the San Juan charter service's regulars, John Watson, to run them over seventy miles of ocean to St. Thomas. This was most unusual—the Curriers had agreed never to fly together. They made an exception flying out. They'd missed the last regular shuttle flight. The children were sure to be disappointed; Stephen impulsively engaged Watson. The night became unexpectedly turbulent, and whatever went wrong, the Apache never landed.

While an alarmed Lauder stood talking with Mrs. Warburg, search operations were beginning. For over a week a coordinated effort by the military involving twenty-two aircraft, the guided-missile cruiser Boston, four submarines, and low-flying commercial DC-7's combed more than 128,000 square miles of ocean. Nothing convincing turned up, although a Coast Guard pilot reported swooping down upon some floating debris and remnants of an oil slick. One exhausting night, awakened by an attorney for Stephen, Dr. Antenucci rushed out to Kennedy Airport to catch a jet for San Juan. A body was discovered. He arrived at midday; he recalls, very sadly, pacing institutional grass outside the public mortuary, waiting for the hours of the siesta to pass so he could look. A pathologist finally returned. "The trouble is," Antenucci explained wearily, "that you may have in your unrefrigerated morgue a girl I'm here to identify."

It was the remains of somebody else. David K. E. Bruce, by then the U. S. Ambassador in London, reached New York Thursday. Things looked "pretty hopeless," he told a reporter who met his plane, and he hurried to Ailsa's apartment.

The vigil had started. Paul was already there, and Lauder, and others looked in from time to time. "I rushed over," Peggy Hitchcock says. "Poor Mrs. Bruce. She had a little brown suit on. She never said a word. Tears just kept coming down. I don't know how many days. I don't believe she moved or slept or took that little brown suit off.

"But finally, of course, they had to accept it. . . .

"Paul was terribly upset. 'She should have telephoned me, I'd have sent my plane.'" The details still rankle. "I've gathered that Stephen had some kind of a grudge against Trans Caribe," he now says, evenly. "That's why they hired that private pilot. My people checked, and they discovered that he failed his instrument test four times."

It took some months before anybody could guess what might yet emerge from the Curriers' lives. By long-standing arrangement, a mild-mannered Yale law professor and intimate adviser of Stephen's, John Simon, took over and raised the three Currier children. Even with a skeleton staff, Kinloch became a considerable drag on the Currier estate. The Taconic Foundation survived on its share of the distribution from Audrey's holdings. Its activities, of course, were radically curtailed.

Perhaps there was one other secondary effect. Shortly before he died, with racial uneasiness spreading, Stephen poured angry energies into creating some kind of forum where backlash and segregation in the North could properly be thrashed out city by city. "We started a great big fast entity called Urban America," Mrs. Eddy says, "which really was not a success. But out of it came the Urban Coalition." Andrew Heiskell of *Time* took over the direction after Stephen was lost and worked up allies among farsighted local leaders—including, interestingly, R. K. Mellon. Like-minded people collaborated; such challenges to the Nixon Administration as Common Cause found sympathy and support.

Typically Currier seemed pressed. He lived by hunches.

4

Between Mary's death and Audrey's death over twenty years—an American generation—slipped by for Paul. Little appeared to change. He avoided offhand interviews, and references to the scion identified him with better-recognized forebears. His daughter, wrote Gerard Lambert in 1956, had divorced Stacy Lloyd, of whom he manifestly approved, and then "in turn married Paul Mellon, only son of Andrew H. [sic] Mellon."

Even cuts in newspapers were commonly a decade out of date. Paul's narrow questioning stare was edged, by now, with patrician asperity. He'd started breeding thoroughbreds for racing on the flat, and joined his wife in collecting the work of recognized French Impressionists.

Pittsburgh conceded the pattern. Yearlings, and Bonnards. The "new woman," as relatives called Bunny, had Cousin Paul solidly in tow. At least with Mary there'd been an attempt. "We just weren't welcome anymore," one old-timer says glumly. "Whenever I see Bunny she just gushes. I think it's insincere." Even people Paul cherished appeared confused at times. "Whenever I sat next to Bunny at dinner we would have such a good time I wouldn't feel she could get on without seeing me a lot," one notable says. "But then I wouldn't see her for years."

This absolved Paul personally. Whenever he turned up, old friends were reassured—he was unassuming as always, as solicitous of feelings, as effervescent with puns and quips and pixilated ironies once his recurrent shyness passed. His gestures were affectionate. More often than not he dialed his own telephone calls. He himself went shopping before Christmas, decided on bits of jewelry and sent them along to the wives of his associates. When a classmate at Yale went wrong out West, Paul arranged for something to help him get started again after a stretch in prison. After he found out that another classmate's daughter was infatuated with horses he sent her an animal worth riding from Rokeby Farms. Small gifts were accompanied frequently by a strophe or two of tenderly humorous doggerel. "The best reason I know," he wrote on a reproduction of a portrait of himself he sent Dr. Antenucci, "for not eating an apple a day."

He preferred the simple, the immediate, and continued to go about his day unaccompanied, without ado. One night in 1969 a reporter intercepted Paul, just approaching the gateposts of his Manhattan residence after a return by subway. He undid the latch. "If it is very late," he jibed his visitor, "I find myself putting the collar of my coat up and kicking open the front gate like they do in the movies. I think it's sort of sissy to ring the doorbell and wait for the guard."

Not hard to imagine: Paul's head thrown back a little, suddenly ruddy as a toddler's, snuffling down his amusement at the very idea. Hilarity moistens those pale Mellon eyes—abruptly, through all the fun, there is a tremor. The joke is over. The gate swings in.

Arrogance—express arrogance—is to be shunned as assiduously as another, less self-assured man would stem any display of weakness. "One senses . . . with Paul . . . that it would be easy to overstep," a friend of many years' standing feels compelled to add. Certain reserves are impenetrable, ever, for anybody.

Bunny understands this. "He sees the idiotic side of everything," she explains, completely frank that morning. "There is a sense so often of jumping out of his own skin and watching everything. He never is pushy. He's very very nervous if things aren't done well. . . ."

This side of Paul even the employees of decades, kept at their distances, virtually never see. Pressures insistently build up. "Paul's very paradoxical," his wife continues. "A writer, a scholar, very sensitive and gentle, kind to his friends, to me, certainly.

"Then, on the other side, he's got the robber baron. It's going to be done like that and you just duck, boom! And you say, but have some consideration. But there is no consideration. His mother pointed it out to me, she put her hand on me and said, 'My dear, I understand. His father was like that.' "

Hurt constricts Bunny's mouth. Little else to say—this passage of feeling seems framed for the moment by meager ropy arms. A matron by Giacometti, in from the country, largely tweeds and chilblains. Then suddenly Bunny turns. Something in the profile—its regularity, its elongated page-boy innocence—brings back the affronted young girl, stubborn in her pride, holding out for something. "Bunny never makes a fuss," her father wrote, "nor does she even raise her voice. She just quietly insists until she has her way. She thinks everything out in advance and then opens her campaign."

The maneuverings seemed endless. To start with, there were innumerable problems associated with raising two children who weren't her own. "I took the children when Cathy was eleven and Tim was five," Bunny remembers. They were the ages of her own two, young Stacy and Eliza. "Cathy as a little child was very close to her parents, but Tim, who was born during the war, didn't have as much to do with them. As a little boy he was very gregarious. In time he became brilliantly mathematically minded, but very shy. He has confidence, but no curiosity to branch out. He is soppy kindhearted and the robber baron mixed in. My greatest regret was that their mother didn't bring them up. You're so much more strict with your own, you can't be strict with your stepchildren. A lot of things I would have liked to have seen done, Paul couldn't cope with. He'd say yes to anything. He'd leave it to me."

Cathy saw both sides. "Timmy was sent along to school very early," she says. "Bunny made things just difficult enough so that my father would give in. Her preferences were clear. There have been plenty of times when I thought she was more right than he." Tim himself is unwilling to get into personal history. Bunny? "I hope you don't want to open *that* can of worms," he says simply. His nervous sneer is offset by amused eyes, very much like Mary's. Tim will admit to fishing trips, layovers on the Cape with Paul. "He did apply discipline at the appropriate times," Tim says. "A reproach often. Usually pretty well thought out, which got to the point of the situation." Yet Bunny recalls occasions, as Tim's political and social mind-set, so different from Paul's, started emerging during adolescence, when he would literally "pray to Mary for guidance. I know that Mary wouldn't have put up with it. If Tim had an idea, and the idea was naturally radical, Paul pounced on it—'Oh, you'll learn better, you'd better change.' Paul's forgotten. He forgets everything he does."

Bunny's complaint, at bottom, isn't really very different from that of generations of ladies who married the Mellons, full of expectations, to discover how life is sacrificed to servicing the fortune. For Paul the urgency has largely been distributive. His responsibilities are widespread, and even before his remarriage the pattern was in, traces of the nomadic calendar by which he orders his years. This seems so unavoidable it puzzles Paul to hear it mentioned. "What does Da *do* all the time?" Bunny recalls little Eliza's asking. His plane was forever landing or taking off, or he himself drove away on Monday for the week. "I think he's a private detective."

When Paul next appeared Eliza asked him directly. He had been warned—he reversed his lapel and exposed his badge.

Much of the strain on Bunny bears on the way she relates to this. She is Paul's chamberlain. "She has the most original mind of anyone I know and has exquisite taste," her father wrote, and demands of taste, like any compulsion, must enslave their owners. The Mellons maintain five homes—this means that Bunny maintains them, which involves the endless supervision of five separate staffs, the oversight of menus, the direction of what appears to be a chronic round of structural repairs and additions, the tending of intricate gardens she designed herself and to which she—stooping, reaching, the floppy hat

Balenciaga designed for her shading her open temples, one gloved hand positioning a sprout for the pruning shears—still devotes hours daily. The residences are beautiful. "*Isn't* it a lovely home?" the trim little fellow in understated livery asks, stepping into the elevator of the Mellons' gleaming five-story pied-à-terre on East Seventieth in Manhattan. "So relaxed and tasteful. I used to work in England for Our Sovereign Lady, and I never saw anything like this."

While Paul is there—available for foundation meetings, or conferring with Bill Wissman, his accountant, or up to have a look at a handful of oils his contact at Wildenstein or one of the other dealers who understand his tastes has ready—Bunny is often elsewhere. Out anticipating his schedule, standing over the workmen at the Osterville house, on Cape Cod, or down at Antigua during the off season, expertly butchering some proportion into encroaching frondage. One sweltering night, watering, she reached too far over one of the terraces of the bluff and toppled and shattered a leg.

The place in Washington, which Bunny's father owned, requires much less gardening—it looks out directly upon the grounds of the British Embassy. The District makes other claims. Soon after becoming President, Jack Kennedy asked Mrs. Mellon to help him rebuild the White House landscaping system. She developed a cool, traditional, eighteenth-century-American pattern of plantings, rejuvenated the Rose Garden, and scented the air with rare piquant herbs whose winding Latin names only she always remembers. Bunny landscaped Kennedy's grave. Jackie became her intimate, and gave her a scrapbook of White House flowers. Bunny advised Mrs. Johnson. She continued to see after centerpieces for state occasions, but rumors of Bunny's distaste for Nixon were abroad in Washington, and throughout the Nixon Presidency relations were arm's-length. "Now I work around the White House surreptitiously," she said then. "The bulbs have to be ordered, the soil has to be changed and the trees have be planted for the next President. Gardens aren't political."

To Paul's irritation, Bunny evidently was. "But how can you say you don't trust the man, Bun, just because you don't happen to like his face?" one visitor to Oak Spring remembers Paul's bursting out over lunch. Politics made him squeamish. He remained nominally Republican and could be relied on for a presentable contribution every four years. Why take it personally? Bunny was like that. "One day at a fund-raising dinner I met Mr. Nixon," she recalls. "Sat two seats away from him. I thought he was just awful, I watched him all through dinner. I called up a few friends, Joe Alsop . . . I even prayed and asked God. I became a Democrat, it was as simple as that. Lo and behold, I became a great friend of Jackie Kennedy.

"Paul was very mad. . . ." So there were piques, traditional mid-marriage frustrations in each to find the other *still* hadn't understood. Herself a lifelong Francophile, Bunny worked on Paul to buy her a house in Paris. Paul wouldn't; Bunny fretted; finally she obtained capital from one of the Lambert trusts and purchased a residence on the Avenue Foch. That was by no means the end of that. "Bunny has this place over in Paris," Matt Mellon fills in, "with a whole lot of fairies running around in it. She keeps these fairies building things." Paul's reaction wasn't surprising. "And here's a photograph of Bunny with one of her decorators," he says, too quickly, tossing the picture aside to search out more historical shots. Bunny acknowledges his feeling: "When I make friends with people he doesn't like, Paul tries to protect me." Paul has refused flatly to permit Bunny's Parisian contingent onto the Virginia property. Occasionally gestures appear exaggerated. One family source insists that recently Bunny rented the Hall of Mirrors at Versailles to stage an intimate little dinner. Recently, involved with a group that underwrites a hospital for terminal cancer victims, Bunny devoted an afternoon to passing among the dying to hand each patient a remembrance from Givenchy. Everything to its style.

Who presumes to judge? A commentator once wrote that throughout his adult life J. P. Morgan reserved the tenderest of devotion for Old Masters and old mistresses. Paul Mellon is sentimental, and nobody would expect less fidelity from him.

Because attachments do rub. What persists is gratitude. "Paul and I have our best times with the very simple things we do together," Bunny says. Sunday nights in Virginia she herself often cooks. "She usually makes everything right down," one friend insists. "If they're having spaghetti she'll mix the dough and roll it out and cut it into strands. Then she goes out into the garden and picks the tomatoes to make into sauce."

Bunny's fundamentalism. "We redid the farm together," she begins. "One day I bought a Renoir of an artichoke. I began getting interested in the French Impressionists in a horticultural way. In those days things weren't that ghastly expensive. I bought mostly with my eye." Before long, Paul admitted, she "drew my interest toward a . . .

vision and technique, that was like a new wind blowing through musty galleries. . . . The artist applied his pigments in fragmented dabs so that the eye of the beholder mixed the colors." In 1958 Paul authorized what then was a very brave $616,000 bid and acquired Cézanne's revolutionary *Boy in a Red Waistcoat*. Charles Ryskamp remembers occasions on which Paul turns up with a picture under his arm. "After dinner at Oak Spring they unwrap it, and look at it, and by the end of the evening it is often obvious, without anybody saying anything, that it must go back. I've seen them turn down things which were just too high. Sometimes when Paul does buy something he wants it up right away. He keeps a hammer in a drawer. He finds a nail. He never measures—he just bangs it in."

By 1966 the several hundred canvases owned by Mr. and Mrs. Paul Mellon represented the most valuable Impressionist collection in private hands, well along toward one hundred million dollars. They added relatively little except for six major canvases which went along directly to the National Gallery. Prices were high. "Too rich for my blood!" Paul shrugged and decided. By then the bargains were obviously somewhere else. That year the Mellons joined Ailsa and loaned the French collection to the National Gallery to celebrate its twenty-fifth anniversary. Paul had become its president in 1963. Taking on the Gallery soon involved the Mellons, Bunny most, in entertaining massive delegations from diplomatic and cultural communities. This could prove taxing for two people jealous of their privacies, neither of whom often made the usual society parties. More than Paul's purse was committed: "Each dinner or reception for the National Gallery really does go beyond a White House state dinner," Charles Ryskamp says. "If there is a preview of the treasures of Tutankhamen they give a tremendous dinner for Egyptian state officials. Special tablecloths are created, they bring in New York people to design the space, flowers arrive in quantity from the Virginia greenhouses. Special floors go down so the party for the Egyptians won't look too much like the party for the French two months before."

Six friends, eight possibly, generally fill an evening. The Mellons have received on a larger scale. In June of 1961 they staged a get-together to celebrate the return of Eliza from study in Paris. The grounds at Upperville flackered pennants atop a sea of medieval tournament tents. An enormous pavilion seated more than seven hundred guests in white dinner jackets among a density of saplings set into the vast wooden ramp, their foliage threaded cunningly among wandering wire cages to reproduce the Bois at Versailles. Parisian sidewalk shops featured a Gallic astrologer and a specialist in omelets. Standing in the Brick House, Eliza and her mother received well-wishers along an interminable line before a jungle scene by Henri Rousseau. Partygoers danced until sunup while bands of Emil Coleman and Count Basie alternated, and there was an elaborate fireworks display reflected in the man-made lake. A society reporter divulged that this bacchanal cost over a million dollars and that Jackie Kennedy had arrived escorted by William Walton. That weekend the President's back ached. Soon after the party a mob of workmen sheared off the layer of asphalt with which a contractor had paved the old farm's meandering gravel lanes, and after a while the dust resettled.

Here was an experience, if nothing to repeat. Paul's farm is closest to him, the property in which his soul abides. He relishes any excuse merely to poke around, amble out a little behind his mincing little Norwich terrier Robinson to overlook the swale in which their low, asymmetrical manor house of whitewashed fieldstone nestles around its courtyard, breathe fresh pasture air. Through aisles of apple trees the 3,500 acres of meadows ripple up into foothills; the darkening of visitors will cause a cardinal to lift beyond a rail and set the glossy mares cantering, prancing up and down, heads tossing with mischief, circling away and back. Cattle crop the margins. "Those are Black Angus," Paul Mellon says. "The farm manager wanted them to help with keeping the fields trimmed, and I permitted it, as long as he kept them out of sight of the house. Too ominous, too depressing."

Serenity arises from detail. Throughout the farmhouse decor Bunny's individuality is everywhere. Softening conversation, touching laughter, the air is seasoned by tart country fragrances of thyme and santolina, of myrtle and rosemary, which Bunny has coaxed in greenhouses from threads of herbs along slivers of bamboo until they have thickened into hardy little potted shrubs Afro-clipped like bay trees. Doorways frame out successively; every prospect is harmonious. A tray of growing Corsican mint occupies a corner table above a window seat where somebody has recently been perusing a three-volume life of Eugène Boudin. A neigh sounds; outside, gloaming is already settling and barn swallows dive beyond the twilit panes. Paul Mellon eases down to start the fireplace kindling. There is a telephone; he taps the housekeeping button. "James, what are we having today, what's the meat course?" His auditor is waiting, part of that cadre of male retainers, brimming over with yessirs, rarely encountered, felt everywhere, replenishing the ginger jar, skipping around the table throughout every scheduled meal. Trained to the minuet; not blacks, certainly; barely Negroes. Colored, house servants.

Paul solicits a drink order and sidles around a corner into a sort of alcohol pantry, from which he returns dangling two bottles of Burgundy. They'll need to breathe. The telephone buzzes—somebody outside is calling, and people in the office must feel the call is important enough for him to take. The exchange is long drawn out. He returns to shrug. "Honestly, the things you do to stay out of trouble," he says, still wheezing a little with suppressed glee. "That was ——, the ex-wife of ——, an excellent horsewoman in her youth, and she is selling shares in her stallion. He's not a particularly good stallion to start with, and I need participation in another stud arrangement like I need . . . as much as I need subzero weather. But I've turned down so many of her business deals I felt I had to take a share this time. You can often sell your shares later and get *some* of your money back—"

That really isn't business as A.W. understood the word, but requirements are different. Minor sacrifices are justifiable to keep the bloodlines evolving. Horse images are everywhere—underneath the large Van Gogh above the mantelpiece, naked on its stretcher, stands one of Degas's pert little wax thoroughbreds, much of the neck crumbled from its wire. There also are two china hens, an anodized loving cup, and propped-up schedule cards for the Piedmont Fox Hounds, the Orange County Hunt, Buckland Farm. Paul still rides, hard; hoofbeats key his verses:

> I've had my share of falls and knocks
> Pursuing the elusive fox.
> I've heard the stirring cry of hounds
> From Melton to the Sussex Downs.
> Each spring I ride a hundred miles
> My tail bright red, my face all smiles.

Occasionally the smile stiffens. The competition that chafes is a three-day ordeal, the Virginia Trail Riders Association 100-mile Ride, a test of pacing and horsemanship and attentiveness to the mount. Paul Mellon has won three times, most recently in 1977. Once, having placed second, his chagrin was such that afterward he remarked publicly that he had been, quite plainly, "robbed. . . . My horse had it

Under the Tree—(from left)
Bunny, Paul, Liza
TONI FRISSELL—
LIBRARY OF CONGRESS

(*Above*)
Oak Spring
TONI FRISSELL—LIBRARY OF CONGRESS

Bunny cutting
MAGNUM—HENRI
CARTIER-BRESSON

Paul Mellon with colt
TONI FRISSELL—
LIBRARY OF CONGRESS

absolutely won, but they gave him second. Later I found that one of the judges was a close friend of the winners of three divisions in the event."

Horses whip him up. ". . . I know no more solid proof of successful breeding and racing than large black figures on the bottom line," he proclaimed, all business, to members of the Thoroughbred Club of America during an award address. That certainly sounded commercial. But unfortunately those large black figures lie down like shadows behind only the most extraordinary of racers, and these, at Rokeby, haven't matured so often. Since Elliot Burch stepped in as trainer in 1962 the silks of Rokeby, yellow and deep gray, have bracketed the girths of remarkable animals—first Quadrangle, and then Fort Marcy and Key to the Mint, Summer Guest, Arts and Letters, Run the Gauntlet. Meanwhile expenses climb continually, far over a million a year nowadays for everything from exercise boys to Saratoga paddock rentals, and farm managers are watchful about when they sell promising foals or make their best stallions available so as to isolate the two profitable years out of every seven they need to remain a business.

Major rewards are elsewhere. When Fort Marcy beat Damascus to become the 1967 Grass Horse of the Year, Paul's farm secretaries, Miss Tross and Miss Rye, telegraphed him in Britain: ROKEBY COLORS FLYING HIGH SAY THE SAME FOR TROSS AND RYE. Paul cabled back immediately: THE ATTITUDE OF RYE AND TROSS IS FAR OUTDISTANCED BY THE BOSS WHATEVER STATE OF JOY THEY DWELL IN IS MORE THAN MATCHED BY MR. MELLON.

Fort Marcy provided thrills. Then, early in the Seventies, an alert little mahogany bay Paul shipped to England to protect its uncommonly long pasterns from poundings upon the harder American tracks started dominating the European middle distances. Even as a colt, Mill Reef, whom Paul personally named after a stretch of Antigua coastline, displayed extraordinarily light "action" and explosive acceleration. Buffs everywhere around Britain soon recognized that elegant musculature and the Kentucky forelock which jounced beyond those sensitive peaked ears. Intelligent, susceptible, Mill Reef entered fourteen races in England and France and won all but two. This was an interval for Paul of dreamlike gratification. "I remember going over with him to watch Mill Reef win at Longchamps," Carter Brown says. "Afterwards we flew back in his plane, *Gulfstream II*. It really was very like a trip on a magic carpet. The plane finally landed on the airstrip at Oak Spring, and because one of their horses had won, the

The happiest day—Mill Reef, Paul Mellon
PAUL MELLON

flag of Rokeby stable was flying, and there was a fine gray automobile purring beside the landing strip. . . ."

Mill Reef was already in condition to meet the only other sprinter in Europe of comparable promise, Brigadier Gerard, when something trapped a hoof during a training gallop at Kingsclere in August of 1972 and splintered the three little bones around that extended fetlock. It required prodigious veterinary skill to save the animal. Paul put him up for syndication in Europe—an expensive courtesy. He periodically solaces himself running off his three-reeler about Mill Reef's triumphs, *Something to Brighten the Morning*, while Albert Finney's voice thickens professionally with observations like "Nothing ever moves faster than the little horse. If he were running on water he would hardly make a ripple." When Paul Mellon and Elliot Burch have punished themselves enough, they leave the Oak Spring lights untouched until their eyes stop smarting.

In 1970 an array of British horse fanciers which included the Queen of England recruited Paul to address the hallowed Gimcrack Club. Mill Reef had lapped the Gimcrack Stakes competition that year by ten full lengths. The dinner officially memorialized the two-hundredth anniversary of the group, and Paul, "Reaching into the dufflebag of memory," soon tantalized the company with vignettes from English sporting chronicles: "John Mytton coming home from the races in his coach, highly intoxicated, with all the five- and ten-pound notes of his winnings floating out of the windows like leaves falling from an autumn tree." He eased in memories of his own: "those long, soft, eminently green gallops stretching to the horizon in the slanting afternoon sun, and the late October sunlight on the warm yellow stone of the old, high stands at Newmarket—the bright colors of the silks flashing by, the sheen of the horses' coats." Mellon capped the evening by producing a sonnet, of which each line's initial letter formed an acrostic tribute to the old club's gallant little eighteenth-century namesake:

Grey was I, well-proportioned, but so small
In stature that I scarce could shade a child.
Many a master had I, from the mild
Callow young lad who rubbed me in my stall
Right on through Count Lauraguais, who asked all
And more of me, for which he was reviled.
Courage restrained me from becoming wild:
Kindness and English grass soothed my deep gall.

Swift as a bird I flew down many a course.
Princes, Lords, Commoners all sang my praise.
In victory or defeat I played my part.
Remember me, all men who love the Horse,
If hearts and spirits flag in after days,
Though small, I gave my all. I gave my heart.

Emotion recollected with intensity. "Of all the rich men living today," his wife says, "Paul is the least conscious of money as an implement of power in the wrong sense. You can't find a man with his wealth with the humility he has. . . . The day Paul won the Derby in England he didn't even have a place to sit. After his horse won he turned ashen white with surprise and delight, and then he was taken to the Queen's box." It wasn't the introduction—the British royal family had known the Mellons for several generations, and when Her Majesty and Philip visited the United States in 1967, their only private stopover had been to Upperville. Paul's satisfaction was traditional.

To breed the Derby winner—what else was left? By then Paul's other campaign, British pictures, also promised major breakthroughs. "How much poorer," he stopped himself midway through his Gimcrack Club speech to regale his audience, "in inner vision would we who inhabit the worlds of racing, hunting, fishing, and shooting be without the amusement and action of Alken, the facility of Ferneley, the homeyness of Herring, the mastery of Marshall, the mellowness of Morland, the prolixity of Pollard, the ribaldry and rascality of Rowlandson, the style and simplicity of Seymour, the sublimity of Stubbs." Stubbs—ahhhh! Stubbs, "the most superb of all . . ."

In Mr. Mellon's opinion. How many aristocratic pates, nodding after a long afternoon in boxes at Epsom, twitched as their befuddled owners attempted to identify this train of forgotten genre painters? Alken? Pollard? *Stubbs*? Just imagine the bother of thinking up so many alliterations. And frankly—about what? The poor chap's favorite, George Stubbs, hadn't even been represented at London's National Gallery until just the other month. . . .

"He *was* buying rather against the fashion originally," Sir Geoffrey Agnew acknowledges, placing aside his trifocals a moment to pinch reflectively along the jut of his nose in hopes of recapitulating those earlier prejudices. "Intimate pictures, the highways and byways of what were considered unimportant and minor painters. It was quickly obvious that he was attempting to make an extensive collection. A very touching collection, based on his youth here. He is a tremendous Anglophile."

Agnew pauses briefly. Let that sink in. Agnew remains a personage, still the commanding figure around the London art marketplace, the principal of Thomas Agnew and Sons, Ltd. He has the bearing of somebody who, over a well-ordered lifetime, has shot more grouse than he intended to eat.

Agnew involved himself early, 1959, the same year Mellon visited London in his capacity as chairman of the "Sport and the Horse" committee of the Virginia Museum of Art in Richmond and encountered, fatefully, Basil Taylor. Basil was famously eccentric, an emaciated wan uncontrollably twitchy cultural historian, very wry, who struggled to support himself broadcasting about cultural matters on the BBC, and finally was successful in garnering a secure post lecturing at the Royal College of Art. John Baskett would remark Taylor's "terrier-like quality. He could look at a drawing with you, and afterwards you'd think you'd learned quite a lot." Taylor supported an *idée fixe*. He was fiercely indignant at what he regarded as the brutal neglect by the British art establishment of England's quieter talents. "At the start," Mellon observed, with precipitous understatement, "I was interested primarily in sporting paintings, especially the work of Stubbs. The happy circumstance that Basil Taylor shared my conviction that Stubbs deserved to be ranked with the first five or six British painters made it easier for him and me to work together."

They developed, Paul wrote, "a kind of partnership arrangement that has always seemed to me completely delightful and unique." Taylor would nose around, investigate sources, check provenance, bid, option, represent Mellon "in an unofficial, unpublicized and, I am quick to say, uncompensated capacity." Then Paul would select. "Our correspondence was voluminous and often very funny," Mellon wrote. "Photographs and transparencies, to say nothing of real drawings and paintings, shuttled across the Atlantic by the boatload and trainload —and the overseas telephone knew no rest."

"Oh, yes," concedes Sir Geoffrey, "fairly early on somebody called Basil Taylor comes into the picture. A most charming man, considerable knowledge of eighteenth- and nineteenth-century English art. High-strung. Taylor got Mellon interested in English watercolors, he realized the great charm and importance of them. I'd draw Taylor's attention to things and he would alert Mr. Mellon. What was so inspiriting about Mellon as a collector was that he bought absolutely out of his own taste, out of love." Those happy earlier years, with many helping out but everybody keeping quiet, prices held. Often representatives from England crossed over and bought in the United States to conceal the push from dealers in America. At Harrods, the big London department store, a magnificent Stubbs canvas of a zebra turned up and Mellon quietly acquired it for twenty thousand pounds and hung it in his New York foyer. Word of the sale startled dealers in London, who actually hadn't cared to bid on decorative work under those circumstances. They felt the price was ridiculous. It later would multiply ten times.

Soon three hundred paintings a year were arriving in America, along with fresh consignments of Major Abbey's six-thousand-volume collection of colorplate books "illustrative of the Scenery of England, Life in England, and Travel in England and the Continent," and the Duke of Gloucester's unrivaled Thomas Girtin watercolors and topographical drawings. The duke had intended the hoard to go to the British nation, but mealymouthed bureaucrats wouldn't promise a curator. He took Mellon's offer, reserving for his countrymen whatever the export licensing authorities stopped. The authorities proved generous, possibly because the duke hadn't let them in on his patriotic proviso. Paul's man John Baskett was handling the matter on the English side, and so, he recalls, "of course we couldn't let them know in advance." The lot got through.

The stakes kept increasing; Paul was utterly committed. "I'd ring him up, very often on Sunday evening," Baskett says, "and I'd open with 'I hate to trouble you over such a small point,' and he'd say, 'No,

it's not a small point. I want to know at all times what's going on.' "
Bunny felt this feverishness. "She was terribly good about those English pictures *pouring* across the Atlantic," Agnew says. "She doesn't really like it, you realize."

It took some time before people woke up. In 1963 the Virginia Museum exhibited the take so far. "I remember it well," John Baskett says. "The English papers all asked, Why should a man this rich collect *these*?" Mellon's wholesale scavenging continued, pulling to the surface and storing in the Brick House what ultimately became eighteen hundred or so paintings, five thousand prints, seven thousand drawings and watercolors, a library of rare titles which came to include the Gunnis collection and William Blake's own hand-tipped copy of *Jerusalem*. Sixteen thousand volumes. Mellon avoided towering formal portraits, the Reynoldses and Gainsboroughs, "so much admired by museums," as he remarked, and kept after the "intimate, informal, revealing paintings that are pleasing to the eye—what are called conversation pieces." He was rounding out—by 1967 the collection included twenty-five Constables and thirty-five Turners.

Paul's approach was gradualist, accretive; the days were over in which the buccaneering A.W., upon discovering that a collection he wanted was blocked off as collateral, bought up the note-holding bank.

Major canvases involved dealers. And dealers? Decades had gone by, but Paul hadn't shaken youthful memories of Duveen, steadfastly descending the great curve of a formal staircase below which Paul and his father stood, supplicants. That lurid overweening countenance gradually fastened itself, renewing its coercive force upon the deteriorating A.W. Paul finally turned away. He simply couldn't look.

He must not let this dependency recur. "Paul Mellon is famous for never negotiating," says Eugene Thaw, from whom Paul intermittently bought over many years. "He never teases you, never strings you along or gives you a hard time. His position in the art world is such, his fairness is such, that we always try to give him the first opportunity. He buys very important things as well as the less important. If you try to explain to Mr. Mellon that a thing is historically important, that's almost the kiss of death. He buys what he likes, what he thinks is beautiful. He likes a thing to stand on its own feet.

"At the beginning, because his manner is so polite and diffident, I didn't realize that *every* word registered. He has tremendous familiarity with the market. More and more, he shies away because prices have gotten out of hand. I've sold him difficult pictures, chancy things. He will see immediately the pure painterly quality of a Constable, elements only a connoisseur could understand. He has tremendous courage. Every once in a while he sees a picture that stands above the ordinary, he sees that he has to step out for that picture. He doesn't consider himself an expert, but I think that he has long since developed an expert's eye. He has an inner confidence."

This means, with Paul, that "first opportunity" is almost always last opportunity. "They'll ask a price which he'll accept," one collaborator says, "or else it's their bad luck." Many don't really understand. "When I was in London recently one of the dealers got word to me that he had a picture he thought I'd like," Paul says. "A small Cézanne. It was a nice picture, not too special. I indicated that I wasn't buying things like that just then, and somewhat later in the conversation, casually, I asked the price.

"He said, 'Five million dollars.'

" 'Five million dollars!'

"And then he said, 'Well, for you, Mr. Mellon, I think I could let it go for four million dollars.' " Mellon twirls his fork. "Do you suppose I could have gotten it for two million dollars?"

Paul Mellon's long novitiate in Basil Taylor's crusade inevitably pushed his appreciations beyond domestic and sporting pictures. "The development of taste in all collectors is haphazard," John Baskett says. As Mellon's acquisitions compounded he needed a curator, an expert in Virginia to oversee the cataloging. Taylor sensed Baskett's promise. Scarcely into his thirties, son of a onetime partner in the prominent London print house Colnaghi's, John had put in his mandatory apprenticeship in the great continental galleries and now was studying at the British Museum when Mellon imported him. Between 1961 and 1963 Baskett managed the Brick House and tended the traffic. It kept picking up. Rowlandson amused Paul: four hundred Rowlandson drawings had begun to arrive for storage and categorization.

Baskett became Paul's friend. There was a resonance—John's asides are understated, as becomes an Englishman and an aesthete, although his brilliant hazel eyes do tend to goggle if kept under pressure too long by imbecile surroundings. An off-putting Italianate wave crimps John's dark hair. He suppresses any prejudices against alcohol, a liberality he shares with his longtime employer, who is occasionally spotted tucking a witch-hazel bottle previously decanted with gin into his jacket lining before visiting churchlier get-togethers.

Late in the Sixties, Baskett returned to London, having married a

Two cream Ponies, a Phaeton
and a Stable Lad
YALE CENTER FOR BRITISH ART,
PAUL MELLON COLLECTION

Sir Geoffrey Agnew
GEOFFREY AGNEW

John Baskett
JOHN BASKETT

South African girl who came to Virginia to join the Brick House staff; and with his brother-in-law Richard Day, John subsequently formed an art consulting firm. Baskett was everywhere suspected of being Paul Mellon's ears, his eyes, his taste (on occasion), and—frequently —his nod at major public auctions.

Agnew readjusts the trifocals. "That is a very close personal friendship," Sir Geoffrey will state. "The sort of relationship those two have I should have thought was rare. John Baskett has given Paul very good advice. Very high standards of integrity, very impartial." Then—Agnew's commentary preserves its self-righting quality, like a transatlantic liner—"On occasion he's recommended a picture of mine because he thought it was so good, so important."

There have been several of those. Paul and Sir Geoffrey both acknowledge a nodding acquaintance at Cambridge, although their professional association, as patron and tradesman, did begin in 1959. Paul had come across a magazine cut of a work by a nineteenth-century English primitive which depicted rustic life. He liked its character, and through a friend he contacted Agnew. "I looked at the picture," Sir Goffrey says, "and frankly it wasn't very considerable. An itinerant artist." He alerted Paul; when Mellon was next in London he looked into Thomas Agnew and Sons, Ltd., and asked whether there might be something else. There was. "I showed him a beautiful Canaletto of Walton Bridge," Sir Geoffrey recalls, "and I told him the price, and he said he'd like to buy it."

He discovered Paul modest, serious, reasonable. "I've never pressed him," Agnew says. "I don't believe in the Duveen technique of selling, the dominating role." Others, closely involved, will cite at least one incidence of Agnew's having urged most earnestly that he had better function as Mellon's sole agent. Paul didn't think that.

As things worked out, Agnew labored as middleman in acquiring a large proportion of those more formal oils that anchor the collection. "I bought him the best of the Constables," Agnew says. "*Hadleigh Castle*. I found it in the home of one of the descendants of the Vanderbilts, on Massachusetts Avenue in Washington. After Mellon bought it he needed only to transport it to his house on Whitehaven Street, two hundred yards away.

"Taylor and I came upon that Stubbs of the two cream-colored ponies pulling a phaeton in a private house. Paul saw a transparency of it, and he liked it very much. I said, the only thing to do is to *shock* it off the man's walls. I wrote the owner offering a high price. He wrote right back. 'Of *course* I couldn't keep the picture if it's worth that much.' That is the sign of a very intelligent collector—he's willing to go beyond the conventional."

For Paul, obviously, the picture was irresistible. That knobby little stable lad, all ruffles, very concerned and tugging on those balky ponies against an enormous black breaker of sycamore, while deep light glistens across the indistinct fens, and a dog yips. A moment in nature, inklings of a civilization, like bathers in Paul's lovely Boudins or one of Degas's dancing urchins cocking up a slipper. The mood is eternal—between urgency and nostalgia.

Other purchases could provoke less complete satisfaction. To arrange the acquisition of Turner's ponderous midcareer masterpiece, *The Dort,* from the Horton-Fawkes family, Sir Geoffrey was forced to accede to a very high demand. "He doesn't want to pay a silly or excessive price," Agnew says of Mellon. "He's obviously been affected by how cheaply he bought during the early years. Sometimes, when I have made finds, often at public auction, I've said to him, 'I must warn you that I bought it at less than its value, and I'm selling it to you at a very large markup.' He appreciates being told. When we finally did get *The Dort,* I remember, he queried me. Funnily enough, I was only making five or ten percent."

It wasn't, basically, Paul's kind of picture. He was rounding out, buying for institutional purposes. A week before Christmas of 1966, President Brewster of Yale announced a gift by Mellon to the university of his British collection, along with a gallery and library to keep it in. There was a ceremonial. Paul didn't attend. "I'm sure personal modesty prevented Mr. Mellon from being here," Kingman Brewster announced. "He's so modest he won't talk about his modesty." Mellon held back comment.

5

Scarcely a month afterward the Curriers both died. Ailsa admitted it, finally. She removed her little brown suit, and attempted to divert herself. Much of the energy she had went into the appointments of a palatial apartment at 960 Fifth Avenue. She turned her current, smaller flat into a kind of warehouse and showroom in which to bide her time—while suppliers paced—and select the curtain materials and boiserie, the appliqués and carpetings with which to furnish, she confided to Walker, a home more beautiful even than the celebrated apartment of Charles and Jayne Wrightsman. She had, after all, an item or two with which to decorate its many rooms—some from her father, and whatever held up best from the ninety or so little Impressionist pictures she'd bought en bloc from the Parisian couturier Edward Molyneux.

John Walker stopped by and was completely appalled. Ailsa had "surrounded herself with crates, boxes, samples of textiles, pictures on tables and on the floor, objets de vertu half unpacked, a medley of works of art. . . . I can see her now seated in one of the two chairs still available in her living room as she served tea, doing it as she did everything, with an air of distinction, always, even in her late sixties, looking very beautiful, with her father's high cheekbones, slender figure, and long tapering fingers."

Ailsa also could see that it was time now to institutionalize, to discard. In 1969 her foundation, the Avalon, merged with Paul's Old Dominion to constitute the Andrew W. Mellon Foundation. It retained a full-time director, Nathan Pusey—fresh from rioting Harvard—to assist the family in enlarging the benefactions beyond the concerns of the donors to assure the wider impact of a mature public trust. By then the invested assets approached $700,000,000. "At Avalon Ailsa had made *scores* of little gifts," Pusey explains. "Directors of hospitals would come in and say, 'See here, Ailsa cared more about our hospital than anything else in the world.' Everything, girls' clubs. We had to work out of this, we made a terminal gift to each of them, enough for two or three years, to give them time to turn around. . . ."

While Pusey, a classicist, was president, emphasis favored higher education. His successor, John Sawyer, has a historian's background. Sawyer tends to search for starving research areas, and attempts to select the "best instrument" for pushing into these. Conservation is now uppermost; the Andrew Mellon Foundation has funded such projects as M.I.T.'s effort to monitor the earth's albedo, its reflectivity, so as to anticipate ozone injury. The foundation underwrote a Brookings Institution study of the Japanese miracle. Paul attends the board meetings, Sawyer reports, but intervenes "with a very light hand. When we ask him we get a response. Nate Pusey said he couldn't get a reading out of Paul when he wanted one."

Pusey certainly wasn't unique in finding Paul indecipherable. "Well,

Jack, what do you hear of my poor little rich boy?" wondered the elderly Nora. John Barrett, her neighbor in Connecticut, shared whatever he knew. "She had a gentility you miss in the youth," Barrett observes, "and not the slightest interest in wealth or display." Everybody agrees on that. "She was a very romantic person. Money never impressed her," says one who knew Nora well throughout her final decades. "I had to be very, very careful. She had a funny class insecurity. If anything came along which was an upper-class English thing, it caused in her some of the difficulty which was born into Ailsa. If I said Lord Humpty-so lived in such and such a house, she'd say, 'I don't know those people, I don't want any part of that. . . .'" Nora would not renounce a commercial Englishwoman's skepticism about the frivolous aristocrats.

She relented toward Americans, with blanket exceptions. "I wouldn't say she had the greatest head in the world, but she had a wonderful heart," Lauder Greenway says. "She had a nice house in back of Stamford. She became a cult, everybody took her up. The Cushing sisters, Mrs. Vincent Astor. I'm not saying she was Cleopatra—she was tall, she wore glasses. . . . To the very end she hated Pittsburgh, she always said so many of the Pittsbourgeoisie couldn't wait to supply bad bits of news."

In later years both Paul and Ailsa made sure to supplement Nora's allowances, and George Wyckoff endeavored to follow her financial affairs. She saw a handful of people; toward these, as ever, she was unfailingly generous. "She went too far," Wyckoff says, "she became quite prodigal. She was always spending more than she had. There was a standing order at Maison Glass for delicacies—hams, caviar, that sort of thing—and bills would run around three thousand dollars a month. Everything for her friends. Finally I had to go to the guy and tell him to stop."

It may have taken a lifetime to compensate. "Whenever we went anywhere by train," she told her daughter-in-law, "and it was time to get the luggage down, Andy would give all the porters a dime, and I would follow behind and give them each another twenty-five cents." Memories of the desert. One mustn't be grasping. Often of an afternoon, when Ailsa dragged in for tea after many fruitless hours of trying things on, of looking things over, her comfortable old mother couldn't help but twit. Shouldn't wealth give pleasure? Why exist for renunciation? She teased her abstemious children, subtly. Whenever Paul came by, "Muttie," as Paul and Ailsa had taken to calling her, would insist on one more cocktail than Paul really liked to see to draw his attention, brooking his glassy disapproval, sipping blithely. "She would laugh so at some of the things Paul did," one regular insists. Nora was approaching ninety.

Sometimes Ailsa became upset with Paul for not seeing Nora. David Bruce dropped in—couldn't Paul find time? Ailsa seemed nerved up. She fussed over details of an unlikely trip to Europe. Her echoing Fifth Avenue apartment was virtually complete; there had been small trial dinner parties there. Her intimates agreed—the place was splendid.

There was periodic talk of marriage between herself and Lauder. "It came back and went away, came back and went away, right up to the end of her life," Greenway remembers. They'd picked a date, one version ran, but then the morning of the event Ailsa could not find one of her shoes, and everything was canceled. "Ailsa really was lucky we didn't marry," Greenway reflects. "She did not know how ill she was." Matt Mellon, in Manhattan, came by one day early in the summer of 1969; Ailsa saw him off; just as the elevator doors were about to close she gave Matt a kiss; he looked up sharply and saw that tears were running down her cheeks.

Very soon after that Ailsa entered Roosevelt Hospital for what the family believed was nothing more than a recurrent hemorrhoidal complaint. "She'd put it off, and put it off," Peggy Hitchcock says. "She had this operation, and then they called me up and told me she had to go through another operation. Paul came up." Dr. Antenucci provided a room for Lauder, and everybody waited. After that was bad. "She was just riddled with cancer," Peggy Hitchcock says. Her long, sympathetic face, very like her father's, manages to remain composed. "I never saw such a death."

The funeral was held in Ailsa's newly decorated apartment. Ailsa's furnishings were shipped to the Carnegie Institute Museum in Pittsburgh. Smaller bequests were paid—to servants, to Lauder, to David Bruce. Her residual fortune, most of a half-billion dollars, went to the Andrew W. Mellon Foundation. Gifts and earlier trusts had provided for Audrey's three children, each of whom could expect the income from securities evaluated at approximately one hundred million dollars. Years before Ailsa's death Paul removed his father's remains, as quietly as possible, from the Pittsburgh crypt, and had them reburied in the little plot at Oak Spring where Mary now lay. Ailsa rests there too.

| # THE CHICKABIDDIES

1

I T WOULD HAVE PLEASED Ailsa, Johnny Walker maintains, that Pittsburgh would house at least the furnishings of her desultory later life: "She was always troubled that her father had taken his own collection away from the city which had been the source of his fortune." Even during the Twenties, with another generation maturing, older Mellons began worrying that upcoming family members might forsake this tabernacle, settle elsewhere, become schismatics. "My father was fiercely loyal about Pittsburgh, and bitter about the people who had made their money here, the Phippses and Carnegies, then skimmed it and ran," Cordelia May says. "We all know it's not the garden spot of the nation. I received a lecture—this city has given you your livelihood, you will stay and put it back." She recalls one bleak tour the spring of 1936—by then a long-legged eight-year-old, considered self-possessed enough to accompany the stricken Alan—around the Scaife Company plant in Oakmont, where rows of very expensive boilermaking machinery had already been buried a week in thick Allegheny mud. The floodwaters were receding that March from a record crest. The Mellons were not amused by the prevailing speculation that anything that inundated Pittsburgh was likely to test out seven parts gin to one part vermouth. Ownership rarely seemed humorous.

By then, of course, A.W.'s two children were going or gone. R.B.'s were entrenched. W.L. had four, but insofar as his was largely the offshoot fortune—it ran, according to well-placed sources, to something like fifty million dollars before he died in 1950—the responsibilities of his line were regarded as supportive. Nevertheless, W.L.

made money, and he, at least, was obviously not pleased when both the boys and Margaret, the younger of the girls, wound up living unfamiliar kinds of lives in places the family didn't care anything about.

Not that Willie meddled. In 1942 his wife passed along, and after that his older girl, Rachel Walton, and her family stayed with him in the big house on Squirrel Hill. "He still was vital," Jimmy Walton remembers, "always working. Lots of vacations, but people coming in and out even on those, and letters and telegrams." He was physically slumping; his elongated face had become more hangdog than ever now that the tissues were swollen with age, and with those heavy broomlike moustaches and ears like leather flaps his younger grandchildren saw him in exploded dimensions: "When I was a child," Jay Mellon says, "and I said my prayers, I believe I half-consciously said them to W.L."

His acumen was unimpaired. His daughter Peggy laughs about the way her father always defended Thomas Mellon Evans. "Tommy was very shy and very thin," Peggy says, "and his head looked too big for his body. We liked to make fun of Tommy, he didn't look too bright. Father would say, 'He's got ability, he'll go beyond all of you.'" Evans remembers this himself: "When I decided to leave the Gulf company, W.L. said he'd always have a desk for me. I appreciated that. Unfortunately, the only one that appealed to me was his, and it was already occupied.

Late in the Thirties, W.L. found out that the Union Trust had gotten back 80 percent of its investment in a defaulted City of Chicago tax anticipation note after he himself had sued the City—and lost—to recover a million of his own. He instituted an action against the board of directors of the Union Trust itself—on which he served—for not tipping him. A referee was appointed, W.L. came into a sizable award, and prospects for the Union Trust's chairman, at the time Clarance Stanley, didn't improve after that. When the banks were reorganized in 1946, W.L. nudged R.K. into the titular chairmanship with Denton as chief operating officer. Clarance Stanley was finished.

"W.L. was astute," Joseph Hughes points up, "not only running Gulf. The family had long before gotten itself into the street railway business, and by 1946 and 1947 it was a mess around here, already headed into reorganization. The whole thing came up at T. Mellon and Sons—W.L. put it out there on the table, what do we do about those traction companies? They asked me to make a study, and I recommended that the family get out. W.L. agreed. The operations themselves had long before been turned over to the carriers, but the family still owned the basic rights-of-way, which made them vulnerable to suits by creditors. But then I discovered that W.L. had been wise enough even during those early negotiations to arrange for guarantees on the leases from the still-solvent holding companies—Duquesne Light, the Philadelphia Company, et cetera—which made it possible for us to maintain at the S.E.C. hearings and before the bankruptcy courts that we, as leaseholders, could liquidate our interests."

By 1948, just short of eighty, Will knew he'd better tuck everything in. He resigned The Gulf, left Drake as chairman and the punctilious Swensrud managing day to day. With W.L.'s retirement the far-flung company would lose its unifying intuition. Without bothering to apologize, W.L. had selected a number of blacks as Gulf station operators, and promoted a Jew to control of one of the refineries. "A group came in," Matt says, "and told him, 'You ought to get him out and put a Presbyterian in there.'" But all they got was W.L.'s fulsome chuckle, and the gentle suggestion that they go find a better-qualified Presbyterian.

He lasted long enough to complete a privately printed narrative, *Judge Mellon's Sons*, in collaboration with Boyden Sparkes. In this the elderly cousin searched Mellon family history since the dotage of the Judge. There was one major philanthropic stroke—W.L. came up with twelve million dollars to found the Graduate School of Industrial Administration at Carnegie Tech. And there was one last precaution. "Addison Vestal has been a significant part of this family's affairs for quite a while," Jay Mellon emphasizes. "He was a little man my grandfather picked up somewhere. My grandfather had a very keen appreciation for business qualities in somebody." Denton had spotted Vestal among the New York employees of Mellon Securities, and brought him west to supervise the tax accounts. Vestal maintained an office on the thirty-ninth floor. "He sort of adopted our family," Larry Mellon says. "If any of us winds up in trouble, financial or otherwise, he's in there pitching."

The last few years of his life W.L. mostly enjoyed himself. Sat around over cards, read mystery stories into the night. The *Vagabondia* was gone, but Jay remembers well enough the winter of 1947, throughout much of which his grandfather had chartered a

W.L. and May

houseboat, *Windswept*. "We lived on the boat like one big clan," Jay says, "Grandfather by himself, although we all ate at one huge table. By then he was very hard of hearing. Everybody had to yell. He spent the whole day out on the water in a canoe with a colored servant he'd had for many years, Dave, and fished for bonefish. I remember that he and Dave had the same kind of wide straw hats, and after a while my grandfather was burnt almost black, so that, what with the glare off the water out along the horizon, you really couldn't tell the two of them apart.

"I myself was seven when W.L. died. Dave was the first person mentioned in his will."

On paper, at least, the fellow who represented the interests of W.L.'s heirs was Rachel's husband, John Walton, Jr. He became a governor of T. Mellon and a director of Gulf, serving on the finance committee, and impressed the others, in Hughes's phrase, as definitely a "kindly soul, if never a factor in the family business." Richard saw to that. "Jack Walton was actually a helluva nice guy," another of the T. Mellon governors remarks, "but he was always opposed to Gulf expanding its debt, he swore at Whiteford regularly as the indebtedness got to one hundred million dollars, then five hundred million dollars, after that a billion. Fifteen or twenty years ago he had a breakdown and went to Silver Hill for shock treatments. I believe he went back two or three times."

Swore? Protested, made out his case with unintended shrillness possibly. One watches Walton aging through three wearing decades of official board photographs. Bleached, dignified-bald, by early middle life Jack's chin looks steady above his spike of a bow tie, but there is flatness behind his wire-rims. He finally has established for himself just what he can and cannot accomplish with all these power gobblers. Life is largely duties. Sometimes duties become onerous.

Willie's eldest, Matthew, had been the first to abandon Pittsburgh outright, although he liked to return occasionally, to the chagrin at times of more conventional relatives. He arrived in May of 1936, for example, after crossing the Atlantic on the Zeppelin *Hindenburg,* and informed a delegation of press at Lakehurst City-County Airport that his voyage through the clouds was "splendid but a trifle monotonous." He was the first known Pittsburgher to make the trip by dirigible. The newsmen had heard, young Dr. Mellon ventured, of one violent air storm which shattered the crockery, but "outside of that, the journey was the usual airplane ride. Much of the view was shut off by small windows." Dr. Mellon was wearing a tan tweed topcoat, the resulting article noted, "upon the lapel of which was pinned a small American flag, and a Germanic insignia, red with a small swastika."

Matthew's espoused political sympathies were certainly no revelation. Barely a year earlier he'd responded to an invitation by the *Pittsburgh Press* with an extended essay in defense of the Third Reich, over the course of which he did not hesitate to proclaim that "Personally, I rejoice when I hear that Germany is again rearming . . . using her inalienable rights to defend herself against the whims of her dangerous and heavily armed neighbors. . . ." He characterized President Roosevelt as a "big, simpleminded boyish optimist slowly giving America the hemlock of inflation." Pushed by his "skeptical and amazing keen" students to name an American contribution to Western culture, Matt wrote, he "threw out my chest" and cited the skinless wiener. For Germany, just then, "A strong man who shows the way is at this time preferable to the eternal chewing of the

Congressional cud. . . . Being a property owner in Germany I regard Adolf Hitler as having saved my home from the Communist rabble that would have spread all over Europe had he not come into power in 1933." He too resented "the influx of foreign financial parasites, the reparations, the inflation, limitations of armaments. . . ." Matthew's party-line observations were accompanied by a portrait of himself, white tie, his shirtfront boiled, those sensual lips crimped at the corners and Matt's somber pupils leaden and defiant.

Yet even the sincerity of Matthew's Naziism is open to challenge. "Doctrine turns him off," his kid brother, Larimer, insists. "The minute a thing is accepted by everybody, and becomes the established social custom, Matt stops going along. It's part of his talent for making fun of people, but it's not funny. A sort of basic disrespect." Mother May, Larry remembers, was particularly distressed during her last, semi-invalided years by what she regarded as Matthew's "cynicism." Why should the Nazis escape? It happened that Larimer was visiting Matt in Freiburg im Breisgau, the beguiling little Black Forest community in which his brother had settled by the early Thirties, completed his doctorate, started lecturing on philosophy and American literature, married a teacher's daughter, the serious, freckled Gertrud. One day in 1933, while Matthew was having a haircut, the Nazis took control. A few minutes afterward Matt led his brother into the local bank to cash a traveler's check. "Even the postman suddenly began to click his heels and say Heil Hitler," Larry recalls. "Matt felt all that was sort of a boy scout thing. He had his tongue in his cheek, as with most everything he did."

"I was taken in," Matt himself will confess, "by a lot of the propaganda. When I was very young my mother had gotten us a German governess, and she had read to us all about Frederick the Great and Goethe and so forth. Naturally all this Heiling Hitler every five minutes was a hell of a bore. But even Martin Heidegger, who was around—he ate it hook, line and sinker. There was a rhythm about it that the Germans enjoyed, it renewed the pride of the German people. I was an editor of a German magazine, put out by the Karl Schuetz Gesellschaft, I had a German wife, and I really didn't know much what I was talking about. My wife was born a Catholic, of course, and she and her family hated Hitler."

It seems a long time ago—forty years. At eighty one does not scruple to admit certain blunders. A retiree currently, in lush Coral Gables for half the year while maintaining a *Landhaus* near Kitzbühel

Matthew Mellon with overcoat

summers, Matt manifests even now a kind of good-natured cold-blooded beside-the-parade mood, a state of waxen preservation which suggests the Oriental. If anything absorbs him, it is the Mellons' own history. He himself has published privately several other elaborately done volumes of family memoirs. Like most smoldering iconoclasts he staves off sentimentality. In certain respects the years in Germany represented perhaps his last genuine attempts to turn his refined intelligence, his independent means, to something of account. Things seemed fairly promising—he received a post, taught, translated *Immensée* and Daudet's *The Last Class*, was elevated by the administration of Albert Ludwig University to the dignity of *Ehrensenator*, a kind of honorary trustee. It seemed a status worth defending.

This became a chore. There came a time when even as apolitical a man as Matt would notice that the authorities were "throwing the Jews on the faculty out right and left. Some of the ablest teachers. Once several of us formed a little delegation and paid a visit to the head of higher education in Baden. He sat there, in his armband, and we told him that he was getting rid of the best people we had. And he told us, 'If you don't like it, you get out too.' "

Certain of Matt's statements in support of the government had caught the eye of the ubiquitous Dr. Goebbels, who invited him to be a guest of the State at the *Parteitag* in Nüremberg in 1936. "It was a tremendous experience in certain ways," Matt says. "When Hitler arrived it was like the second coming of Christ. I just didn't like the class of people he had around himself, like Julius Streicher, with his blacksnake whip. With all those colors, and lights, it was like a stage setting for the *Meistersinger*. The enthusiasm! There were people invited from Sweden and from the Eastern European countries. At my table there sat the woman who was the head of the German *Bundesmädel*. While we were eating, I remember, she was telling this Polish count, 'You know, I have two million women under me.' The affair was beginning to drag a little by then, and I remember that the count just looked at her a second, and then he piped up, 'Well, I wish I had one under me right now.' Oh, boy," Matt says, roused by the memory, "she definitely was mad as hell."

In 1938 W.L. got word to Matthew that things were obviously worsening, and he had better get home. He returned with Gertrud and the newborn Karl in time for Christmas. Their second son, James ("Jay"), was born in 1942. Even during the years in Germany, Matt liked to return for summers of yachting off the coast of Maine. He resettled his expanding family in Philadelphia and bought a seasonal residence in reliable Palm Beach, already a sanctified purgatory for supernumerary great rich. He indulged his curiosities.

The direction these took is evident from *The Watermellons*, a kind of compounded log of the voyages of all the boats and ships he and his father and his son Karl had owned since the Palatka days. Characteristic of Matt's sallies were the expeditions he underwrote during the winter of 1947, and again in 1948, to the Republic of Honduras, "to collect birds." Two Carnegie Museum scientists were invited to accompany him on this ornithological quest. The team bagged hundreds of specimens, but food and drink and some of the sultrier of the Caribbean's social amusements receive far more coverage: "After a wonderful supper at Mr. Perrin's hotel we went over to Kirkconnel's house and were shown into a large unfurnished room with many chairs and a bar at one end of it plentifully supplied with bottles of rum and whiskey. Here all the elite girls of the town were lined up and we danced with them to recordings until 2:00 A.M." Matt's report is unfaltering—"Kingston is full of women on the make of every race, color, and variety of disease"—and on one remote island

On vacation—James Mellon,
Matthew, W.L., Karl
JAMES R. MELLON II

The open sea—Matthew
Mellon on right
MATTHEW MELLON

A layover in Kitzbühel—Karl Mellon
(left), then wife, James R. (Jay) Mellon II
JAMES R. MELLON II

he and his companions found themselves importuned by "a whole boatload of girls," who led them into a dance hall behind a grocery store. "There wasn't much choice inside," Matt notes, "so I asked a young woman who was breast feeding her baby to dance. She laid the baby flat on the table while she danced and then returned to nurse it." Matt manages a heroine, the imp-faced twenty-five-year-old wife of a mainland mahogany-plantation owner, Melba Jones, who lives on outlying Bonacca and laments the way "the town is filled with young women whose husbands have run away to the States or to sea and left them stranded here." The yachtsman is compassionate, and soon the two are regular dancing partners. Melba appears several times in the accompanying photomontage, invariably beneath a pith helmet, a shoulder nestled comfortably against her rakishly grizzled-looking admirer, his black eyebrows diabolical, not overdressed for once.

Wherever facilities will permit, the traveler is scrupulous about radiotelephoning his Trude in Palm Beach, he marks her birthday with a cable, and once he leaves the other scientists to return to Florida briefly "because of my duties in Palm Beach as President of the Society of the Four Arts. I had many meetings to call and attend as well as many dinners with a few charity balls thrown in." But facts were facts, their marriage had broken down irreparably. Gertrud received her uncontested divorce in Reno in 1951, a large—sealed—settlement, and custody arrangements as regarded the boys. Two years after that Matthew married again. He'd bought a house in Greenwich, Connecticut; his neighbor, Mrs. Rensselaer W. Bartram, Jr.—Jane—soon wanted a divorce herself and subsequently married Matt. The pair moved into the ninety-foot yacht, another *Vagabondia*, which Matt both commissioned and captained, and for eleven years, except for a farm in Jamaica the two visited occasionally, they lived on water.

Gertrud took an apartment in Manhattan and tried to form the boys. It was already evident there would be problems with the elder, Karl. Despite his grandfather's gift of an orchestrion, Choate expelled Karl early, and after that, ingenious as he was, recurrent depression and bouts of periodic derangement soon reduced his life to episodes of freedom between sieges of psychiatric care.

The family tried everything. Karl's cousin Billy Hitchcock ran into him while he was taking a course of psychotherapy in Vienna. The two were ensconced in Sacher's, embarked on their third gin and tonic,

when a messenger appeared with a telegram from Matt: "PSYCHIA-
TRIST FRAUD," it said. "CALL ME COLLECT." "He does the god-
damnedest things sometimes," his father exclaims. "And he has absolutely no idea of the value of money." *The Watermellons* refers—
dryly—to Karl's seagoing ventures. There was the gigantic barkentine
Karl and his militia of volunteers—college students, weekend guests—
planked up and bolted together, its lines closely resembling a massive
whaling dory, under a decaying apple tree behind Karl's house in
Greenwich. The thirteen-sail vessel, Matt adds, survived its inaugural
"grand run over to Maine, where she caught fire and burned, much
to the distress of her owner and his friends, who were anticipating a
cruise around the world."

One tanker provided "a wonderful addition to his collection of
antiques." In 1973 Karl and "his wife and her six children" sold out
in Maine and purchased a 138-ton converted ore carrier, which they
"brought down from Maine" to the Bahamas "without a crew," Matt
writes, admitting that "how they did it I don't know." Rangy once,
Karl had become portly, and grown a clipped gray-shot beard.

Karl divorced several times, always an expensive habit. "For quite
a number of years it seemed that every time I returned from Africa I
had another sister-in-law," says his brother, Jay. Jay's tone is fatalistic,
in this and everything—his is a romantic, even a Byronic condescen-
sion to anyone gullible enough to think human experience sustains
hope. Such resignation accords well with Jay's native reclusiveness,
his shock of startling pewter hair, those burning auburn eyes, glitter-
ing in dark pits oily as a Hindu's against his boyishly flushed face.
He exudes existential fatigue.

"I'm sure you've realized that within this family there is a tremendous emotional stultification," Jay says, watchful of being abrupt.
"We don't marry well because we're only able, finally, to look within
ourselves. This repression of emotions within the Presbyterian ruling
group is contagious, not hereditary. It comes from Pittsburgh. One
mustn't show feelings, it isn't even polite to observe that the food
is good." He issues a sharp relieving cackle, paradoxes make him
giddy. "In human ways we lack the ability to live well. We are all
islands, even to each other, even within the family. Perhaps the saddest thing is that everybody wants what we've got, but we want what
everybody else apparently has, and obviously there is no way to make
the exchange."

He shoots his blazer cuffs, too well-bred openly to consult his watch. "I'm not complaining about my lot in life," Jay says. "If there were some button I could push to become the man in the street I wouldn't push it." Even spoiled priests persevere. Some awareness of calling abides, if not to what.

No wonder Karl wavers. "My brother and I have always been the greatest imaginable friends," Jay says. "I was nine and he was fourteen when my parents were divorced. I remember the summers in Maine in particular. Beautiful boats, digging for clams, picnics. I believe that if one has a happy childhood it has a quieting effect on one's whole life. Father adored me, but he didn't get on so well with Karl. He was the first child, and I think he got caught between Mother and Father."

Jay's own career complements his weary diction, certain end-of-the-empire locutions he tends to favor. He appreciated St. Paul's, but Yale, where he studied philosophy "largely to satisfy Father," seemed "drab, dull," and even then, during summers, he started to amuse himself "east of Suez." In 1964 he skipped his graduation and "flew right off to Africa for a hunt." He passed the next five years establishing a reputation as an accomplished white hunter, "slept on the front seat of my Land-Rover, shot my own food. It really was hard to keep a girl friend under those conditions," Jay says. "One's mind goes to pot in that part of the world, it's too much of a backwash, the people know nothing except farming, shooting, and flying a plane." In 1969 he relocated in Delhi, a base from which to go after specimens in India, Kashmir, Nepal, Java, Thailand, Cambodia, Afghanistan, Pakistan, Iran, Outer Mongolia. But "in the end, living in the void became a completely nauseating thing and I came back."

Jay even considered Pittsburgh. "I set up in hotels and talked to my cousins," Jay says, "and decided I couldn't survive there. There was a certain intolerance for people who are not doing office work. If you're not a businessman you're sort of a weak wart." He repaired to Manhattan, purchased a Fifth Avenue apartment, and labored with his vast, definitive volume, *African Hunter*, a compilation of photographs and essays by himself and his friends, members of perhaps the last generation to pursue the sport. Sometimes commissions tempt him—he accepted the challenge of taking a very rare upland goat for the Shah of Iran recently, an undertaking which involved a large percent of the Imperial Army as beaters—although that is ending. Jay sees a few friends—Peter Beard has been an intimate since the Nairobi days, and Jay is particularly fond of Princess Radziwill and her sister—although he hides out much of the time in his enormous apartment, its vaulting rooms fitted with trophy cases which remain as empty as the rooms themselves. A magnificent stuffed peacock fans before the entrance. His collection is stored in a Mount Vernon warehouse. "I've never seen it," Jay says, and represses a shudder. "I'll probably put it in the Carnegie in Pittsburgh. I really can't imagine living with all those *heads* around myself."

2

"Don't worry about this," Larry Mellon says, blinking out from under his impromptu turban of soiled hospital toweling, which he delays a moment or so to wind around his freckled Scottish pate and lap across the nub of vertebra below his scrawny neck. "I had an episode of skin cancer last year, so I'm being a little careful." He hits the starter, white dust clouds up all around the Jeep, it bounces into gear. He has those reedy, self-abashed, patiently suffering inflections helpful in the tropics, like an underactive thyroid, to conserve one's stamina. Blessed are the meek. The morning becomes hot, and down in the village the woman who bakes the bread for the Hôpital Albert Schweitzer may start to wonder just when the *Docteur* will appear to receive her loaves.

Of W.L.'s four—of all the Mellons, perhaps—this is the unlikeliest, the real genetic sport. William Larimer, Jr., the saint, Dr. Mellon of Haiti. Such characterization galls Larimer, earthy as he remains, for all the hereditary dryness. "Whatever you wind up writin' about me," he suddenly says, and gives the wheel a jerk to sideswipe a gully, "don't make me sound as *insipid* as the others have. We're not sacrificing anything. We'll run the place as long as we can. We intend to die here, because we really can't see anything better to do."

The comparison nobody stresses is unavoidably with Pittsburgh. For Larimer especially the estrangement was early, deep-seated. This puzzles him too; he attempts to follow for himself the primary derangement of personality, thoughtfully reviews his toes, still in their battered, dust-caked sandals. Those unearthly flat ears and something of the gleam of a visionary schizerino make Larimer resemble alarmingly a reclaimed Henry Miller. He too was raised in W.L.'s mansion, Ben Elm, marched around by governesses, referred to as "Baby Larimer" for an uncomfortably long time by both his sisters and sardonic Matthew. Larimer was an "accident"—everybody laughed about that. He appeared to understand, better than the older children, the qualms his gentle, ailing pillow of a mother couldn't keep from feeling about the enveloping commerciality. Things became so impersonal. Larry pushed that further. "Take wealth," he begins. "It really can't work for you. Either you get a cockeyed notion of your own importance, or you get an inferiority complex. I guess that's what I got. It obscured the better aspects of the members of my family. Once I got the idea that dollars were foolish, the people that were chasing them seemed foolish. The fact that the servants kowtow to you makes you think that you're a little different from other people. That difference is embarrassing. What actually would give a child the cockeyed notion that the servants were real people, but the people who came to call on Sunday were stuffed shirts, that people who pulled up to the East Liberty Presbyterian Church on Sunday in Rolls-Royces didn't have their feet on the ground?"

All this was subversive, confusing and hard to translate into anything. Larimer got through Choate, began to display an ingrained Taylor aptitude for music and languages, even consented, under W.L.'s prod, to enroll at Princeton. Crosscurrents surfaced. "I didn't relate very well to Princeton," Larimer admits. "Most of the boys I knew there wanted to be bond salesmen. Our family was important, and all you had to do was go to parties and push 'em up." Besides, "I was in touch with a girl at the time, and weekends I was there." The girl, Grace Rowley, "seemed very inappropriate to my family," Larimer knew. Grace's father, Elmer Rowley, fabricated artificial limbs. "To me it was an attraction, I used to help the old man make rubber feet down in the cellar," Larry says. "I could have seen myself doing that a lot sooner than working for Gulf. The mother was a particularly strong character, and I remember that Grace's grandmother lived right under the steel mills, in the smokiest part of town. Wealth, social position—to me it was just one more snare.

"I guess I was cowardly, I took her down to Wellsburg, Ohio, one time and we got married." Larimer himself was nineteen, and Grace was several years younger, fetching, and squirmy with prospects. Larimer rented a bungalow, and they agreed not to tell either set of parents. Before long another Pittsburgher ran into their names upon the register in Wellsburg, and arranged to blackmail Larimer in a small way. Then, after almost a year, the older Mellons relented and permitted the pair to announce their engagement. A major society wedding went into the last few days, "lavish entertainments" had

Young Larimer with Grace
PITTSBURGH *Post-Gazette*

started, the maid of honor arrived from Newark, and even A.W. scheduled a "hurried trip." Shortly before the event the minister who ran the marriage mill in Wellsburg tipped off the papers. W.L.'s personal secretary would devote the remaining hours to urgent telephone calls disinviting the guests.

Their marriage was equally discombobulated. One child, William Larimer Mellon III, was born in 1932. "It seemed to me that what Grace really wanted was things for her home," Larimer noticed. "She engaged an interior decorator to do over a small house Father had bought for us in Sewickley. He designed a table with a very thick top which had to be especially cast at Pittsburgh Plate Glass and cost a good many thousand dollars. Highly stylized kinds of pictures kept arriving, big bills. I got less and less enthusiastic—the very thing I was trying to escape was just what Grace was trying to cling to."

After giving up Princeton, Larimer tried the bank and then hoped to please his father by starting in as a messenger for The Gulf. "I rather liked that, I got to carry a lunch," Larry says. But after six months W.L. promoted Larimer to the sales department. He stayed at that for two or three years, and life emptied completely. One day he told his father he thought he'd better head West. "Father was disappointed—Matthew had flaked out too—and he said I ought to have my head examined. He also said, before I went, to go see Dr. Foot, who was the head of the geophysical department of Gulf. Dr. Foot pulled down a big map he had of Pecos County, Texas, and he told me, 'If I were a young man, this is the area I would start out.' I knew that he was trying to tell me that there was so much oil in that section that if I bought three acres there I'd soon be rich enough to buy up the state of Arizona, if I still wanted it."

He attached his horse trailer to his car, loaded his mare, Goldy, and started for Pecos. "All I could see was baking clay, and derricks, and a few skinny old longhorns just standin' there, lookin' at the sludge comin' up. So I kept going." He alighted in Rimrock, where he was quick to commit to a big enough spread to remain land-poor indefinitely. To secure enough income he agreed to fatten a thousand head of cattle from over the border in Mexico, where range was skimpy, and dehorn the lot of them for fifty cents a month per steer. "They delivered 'em to me, and we started in during April and May of 1937. Big, age-y cattle," he recalls, "with horns this long. We dehorned the entire thousand head. Blood all over the place. It rained that summer, and pretty soon the animals were covered with blow-flies, and after that we spent most of our time chasin' 'em around so we could doctor them."

He lived very plainly, first in a chuck wagon, then in what his disgusted sister Peggy termed a "one-peg shack." W.L., sympathetic, agreed to put in money enough for a thousand head for half the profits and, to the old man's surprise, beef prices firmed up over the next several years and it became an investment. By that time Grace had filed a divorce action on grounds of desertion. Larimer noticed in passing. Riding into a sandstorm alongside his hired man, Bill Jones, he remembers Jones asking, "How did we ever get into this goddamn business?"

"I don't know, but look at the fun we're havin'," Larimer remembers forcing out.

Satisfyingly gritty; nevertheless, when war broke, young Mellon was eager to get into that. While unimpressed Navy technicians were losing his blood sample, the solicitous Peggy happened to attend a dinner party with David Bruce and Wild Bill Donovan. She mentioned that Larimer had picked up Portuguese at Choate. The Office of Strategic Services was on the lookout for somebody to post in Lisbon to log Axis shipping. From there Larimer moved on to Spain as a "commercial attaché" and worked as a liaison with French underground representatives, smuggling downed Allied fliers back over the Pyrenees, then joined Allen Dulles's staff in Geneva to provide the inducements to the German generals listed in Edda Mussolini's captured diary as inclined to surrender.

In 1942 his mother had died, a loss which troubled Larimer in a number of ways. "If she did sin it was because she didn't stand up," he would reflect afterward. "Avoid a row. She thought that espionage in particular was a very low degree. 'Son,' she'd say, 'I know you would never stoop to becoming a spy.' She said the best thing was to become a medical missionary."

This was on Larimer's mind after he returned to Arizona, bought up the 110,000-acre Fort Rock Ranch, put in a sizable house which overlooked a swimming pool. He felt himself slipping toward something he distrusted, yet he was attempting to be fair. Shortly before the war, in his backhanded style, he'd started keeping company with a spunky ex-Smith girl who arrived in Arizona with three young children to maintain herself as a riding instructress at a neighboring dude ranch while obtaining her divorce. She'd seemed to understand so much, Gwendolyn Grant Rawson, a loose-jointed tawny woman with pale witchy irises and a decisive sashay, a cheerful offhandedness that ran to the snippy every once in a while. It amused the self-effacing Larimer to watch her examine an intruder balefully, then unload what's what. She also craved immediacy. "If you want to do something for me while I'm away," Larimer told her as he was processing into service, "learn to be a good cowgirl." This represented a promise; after he was back he made it good.

"Surely you don't want me with three children," Gwen said.

"I wouldn't take you without them," Larimer said. The pair went East to celebrate their marriage, an event which provided Gwen her first real hint the Mellons were affluent. Larimer built the ranch house. Young Billy, his son with Grace, came out to spend the summers and learned to appreciate Gwen's affectionate tartness. The ranch itself prospered. "I had become a domesticated cowboy, a dude, and that spoiled the whole thing," he remarked later on. Gwen sensed his restiveness. Months after their marriage his duffel bag, packed, still leaned in place against their bedstead. "You had better get rid of that," she finally told him. "It makes me nervous."

Larimer began learning Arabic. Never really a churchgoer, he

Older Larimer with Gwen
A.P.-WIDE WORLD

found a Bible in Arabic and pieced a translation. The passage from Luke in which Jesus exhorts a rich man to sell whatever he has and give the proceeds to the poor stuck in his head. In 1947 he read an article in *Life* about Albert Schweitzer, and from then on Schweitzer's image, his work, dragged at Larimer's thoughts. Matt, a director of the International Bach Society, had repeatedly contributed organs to the Aula in Freiburg, and met the world-famous humanist during meetings of the society. His letters mentioned this. Larimer brooded. His ranch manager at the time was a Frenchman; on a vacation trip to France he agreed to look over Schweitzer's hospital at Lambaréné. "He hated it, the mosquitoes especially," Larimer remembers. But in his halting, stubborn way, Mellon pursued the idea. He wrote Schweitzer, whom he suspected of "getting more out of life than I was," and asked what the chances were of attempting such a thing himself, inquiring finally whether mankind were "really worth saving."

"Many men have sent me the question you ask, but I have always avoided advising them because the choice is difficult and there are hardships," Schweitzer replied. "It is the plight of the do-gooders of this world that others should throw rocks in their path. But you seem courageous. I urge you to pursue your new goal."

Not long after that a Pittsburgh friend, a salesman, came out and the pair went camping and talking for a day or two. " 'Gee, you got it bad,' " Mellon remembers him saying. " 'You're obviously going to do something like that.' That startled me, it put a bee in my bonnet."

Once they got back he looked for Gwen, busy on a ladder at that moment, straightening up some curtains. "Darling, I think I'll go to become a doctor and then practice in some underdeveloped part of the world," he blurted.

"Is that what's been on your mind lately?" Gwen said. "I wondered what it was. All right, how do we start?" She is a powerful assimilator. "You're right, Larry," Gwen reportedly continued, "we don't want to sit around here and look at those damn cows for the rest of our lives."

Of ordeals that followed, the worst was eking out Larimer's neglected education. He had the equivalent of one undergraduate year at Princeton, and suffered interminably once he was back in school at Tulane, even fortified by Schweitzer's advice to "Be satisfied by simply sneaking through honorably . . . just what is needed to wangle the degree." The sciences in particular resisted every approach. "Nights before examinations," he later said, "I'd memorize whole pages, but the next day I'd see the questions and be convinced I had studied the wrong material. Then later I'd check my books and find that the answers were there; I had simply forgotten them." His hair whitened; he developed an ulcer; he seemed far older than he was. "I remember one time I was sitting in a medical movie," he says, "and next to me was the youngest guy in the class. There was a character on the screen, and I said, 'Hey, that guy looked like Wendell Willkie, didn't he?'

"And the fellow beside me said, 'I don't know, Grandpa, he died before I was born.' Another fellow made a very comforting remark to me. He said, 'You know, it's harder to stay the last in your class than the first.' I thought that was a very kind thing to say."

Mellon finished up somewhere in the lower half of his class. He spent the summer of 1951 at Lambaréné. Gwen took a degree as a laboratory technician. Both joined the Disciples of Christ. They began to prospect for the right place for Mellon to install a hospital of his own. One sojourn, which involved an attempt to cross the Andean highlands from Peru in a decrepit taxicab to inspect the headwaters of the Amazon, came to very little when Mellon realized that the indigenous Indians were not merely sparse, but also discouragingly healthy.

There were no setbacks like that in Haiti. They first looked into the Republic so Larimer could research his thesis on jungle ulcers. The summer of 1952 he and Gwen put ashore in Haiti with a Dodge power wagon and began to scour the wasted central plantations to isolate an area destitute enough to justify a hospital. Almost anywhere would qualify. "We made some friends in the American community," Larimer remembers, "who got us into a party the then President of the Republic of Haiti, Paul Magloire, was giving for Somoza of Nicaragua. I stood in the receiving line and when I got to Magloire I said, "Hello, I'm very happy to meet you, sir, my name's Mellon, I'm a medical student, I'd like to build a hospital in your country.'

"And he said, 'Good evening, you're holding up the line, come see me in the morning at eight.' I went, obviously, and he made his position clear: 'I'll tell you, this is the way it works here in Haiti. If Mrs. Magloire is for it, you'll get the green light. If not, you don't. If she is for it, write a brief proposal, and I'll run it through the Congress and turn it into law.' "

Mrs. Magloire nodded. The government of Haiti offered Mellon land enough and a scattering of low stone headquarters buildings left behind when the Standard Fruit Company abandoned operations in Deschapelles, halfway through the blight of the Artibonite Valley. There wouldn't be taxes, personnel might come and go, and whatever installation Mellon erected would tie into electricity "if it ever came down the road. The new hospital itself cost about two million dollars," Mellon says, "with another two hundred thousand for special equipment. I gave what I had in my pocket, which got the buildings up, and donated the income from the trust my father gave me to keep it going. We knew that wouldn't be enough, and so we established the Grant Foundation, which is a clearinghouse operation, with no endowment, to collect and hold donations to what we had decided to call the Albert Schweitzer Hospital."

By 1955, while Larimer finished residency, Gwen and her teenagers came out to supervise the last details, largely in native stone and concrete, of a fifty-five-bed complex of rooms and wards, the outpatient clinic and X-ray cubicles and stores and kitchens and a medical library and air-conditioned operating rooms, the vast diesel generating plant. She also made sure there was a house for them, a sprawling one-story mahogany residence far enough in back to encourage privacy. The district they expected to service was an eight-hundred-square-mile patch of rolling desolation in the geographic midst of the Republic, perhaps ninety thousand abandoned souls. They'd looked for volunteers, but "volunteers didn't generally last very long," Larry discovered, "they don't have enough of what Father used to call *traction* under 'em." The key operating staff, nurses mostly, soon came from religious orders—the Mennonites, the Dutch Protestant Dienst Obergrenzen, and Catholic sisters the Bishop of Haiti, Monsignor Robert, believed might be helpful. American medical schools made residents available. Dr. Mellon commenced practicing.

Before too many months Thomas Evans flew in. W.L. gauged correctly—he'd manipulated his success, built an industrial empire. He'd become a conglomerator, true to his overheard preference for seeking out a "family company run by a third-generation Yale man who spends his afternoons drinking martinis at the club," and packing it in.

Beaming elf, monstrous burly, he planted his feet and surveyed the swarm of lethargic-looking natives camped across the gray-flagged hospital turf, asleep on stone benches before the outpatient entrance of the Hôpital Albert Schweitzer. Many crossed by raft the night before. The rabble looked greasy and ashen despite the high-color rags, overperspired, hunkering in silent clusters to eye the locked clinic doors. "Larry," Evans decided aloud, "you're never going to get yourself out of this one."

Mellon relishes the anecdote. It acknowledges his achievement— they'd finally shaken Pittsburgh. Just thinking about that can rouse an appreciative little whinny—relief. Making ordinary rounds, the *Docteur* takes pains to route himself through a courtyard between two of the wings of the hospital, and interrupts his hunchy progress to nod at a small memorial tablet. It says, after Schweitzer, "Help life wherever you find it." Mellon pauses. "I believe that," he says. "We see a lot of gonorrhea around here, and I never give anybody an injection of penicillin without reflecting for a second about all those bacteria that are going to die." That might sound sappy, but obvi-

ously Mellon feels this too had better be included. Above the unattended corner desk which serves as Larimer's office there is a snap-
shot of his mentor, also in lumpy wash pants, his pith helmet dingy
and the Alsatian moustaches adroop, shuffling up the path at Lambaréné toward the leper colony.

A door stands ajar to what is obviously the pediatric clinic. Benches
line the wall, occupied by nursing mothers. At a very large low stain-
less-steel-covered table wait thirteen children under two, naked except
for name tapes stuck one to a forehead, bellies puffed, withered legs
like chicken wings drawn into their crotches. What tufts of hair the in-
fants have left have turned an electrifying rust color as starvation re-
jiggers their body chemistry. Several struggle to crawl. The air is laden
with feces and alcohol. When babies prove impossible to feed, families
around the island who live in the leaning little huts the passerby keeps
noticing behind the great flowing breadfruit trees adjacent to the
marshy places, the awesomely eroded gravel banks, simply put them
out. Prop up the extraneous ones along the margin of the road, perhaps in the shady places underneath one of the huge frilled candelabra
cacti on which the laundry is drying. Sometimes strangers remove
them, although not very often. A handful, relatively, get to the in-
firmary at Deschapelles. "We've come to think of malnutrition as a
disease entity," Dr. Mellon remarks. "We give out a good bit of food
in the pharmacy." One infant begins whimpering. Others bob, in response. "I think of that sometimes as a look at the future Haitian
Senate," Mellon confides, buoyed at the sight. "As they progress, they
get to horsin' around, pokin' food in each other's mouths, acting like
children."

A tap is dripping in a cleanup lavatory, and Larimer walks over to
tighten the valve. Budget problems keep plaguing. By the early Seventies the running expenses were up to $800,000 a year, largely because
the hospital was taking in people from much of the island. Pittsburgh's support was mixed—R.K. and Sarah were good for $100,000
a year the first five years, but the concerned Adolph Schmidt, who
ran the A. W. Mellon Educational and Charitable Trust, refused funds
unless something went into an effort to stem Haiti's compounding
birthrate. "The island is a basket case in terms of population growth,"
Schmidt says. But Larimer is aware that the Church would throw him
out if he should hand out birth control devices. Besides that, a man
who admits to a twinge of conscience each time a gonococcus expires

would make a very persnickety abortionist. "We see a great many more women who want us to help them start having babies than women at all interested in stopping the process," Mellon says.

They've worked all along to make the place as self-sufficient as possible. "We raise our own beef," Larimer says. "I'm real proud of this. The government gave us a hundred acres, we added another hundred. We use the local tomatoes and onions and melons and carrots, and we make our own ice cream. We eat a lot of goat meat. We even have a special refrigerating room for garbage—otherwise it spoils before the hogs can eat it."

Mellon's pride in the technical side of the hospital is intense. "We make our own I.V. solutions," he says. "We run a morgue." This boasts a homemade ceramic-tile autopsy table. They preserve the cadavers in refrigerated storage vaults. Mellon slides a drawer which contains six children, all trussed as neatly as so many Butterball turkeys. "We have a resident from Yale in ophthalmology," Mellon says. "Changes every three months. Somebody here does a cornea transplant every once in a while. The other day we had a plastic man come in to do a bunch of lips."

"We know we're going to get nationalized after a while," Mellon says, later on. Much of his energy these days goes into "Haitianizing" his hospital. The tendency has been for native professionals to abandon this sink of the poor, flee the political whimsicalities. The ruling Creole oligarchy has treated Mellon well, especially when Dr. Duvalier was President for Life. Other hospital employees despair. One cites, for example, the belated legislative requirement that anybody who marries must pay the government for examination for syphilis. "They asked us to run these tests," the technician remembers, "and finally we noticed that nobody came around to pick up paperwork. Turned out there wasn't any law which said you couldn't get married if the result was positive. It was another maneuver to impose more fees."

Yet year by year the hospital has generated a skilled, devoted staff of Haitian professionals. Gérard Frédérique, René St. Léger, Muller Garnier. By 1975 Garnier was the medical director. He is a round-faced, slope-shouldered man, who shambles all over the hospital, picking up on everything, keeping up the morale. "Eet's awnbee*leev*-able 'ow much good 'ee 'as dawn," Garnier proclaims of Mellon. Garnier is one of the world's ranking experts on tetanus, the developer of techniques which pushed up survival rates. Tetanus abounds in

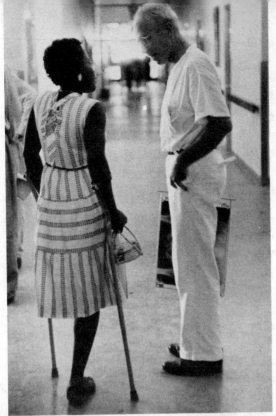

Dr. Mellon of Haiti
MARILYN SILVERSTONE—
MAGNUM

Gwendolyn Mellon of Haiti
MARILYN SILVERSTONE—
MAGNUM

Haiti, where a newborn's grandmother is likely to cut its cord, then rub the potion of ashes, dried dung and powdered beetles the voodoo bocors prescribe into the lesion of the umbilical.

Early in the Sixties an Australian journalist, Peter Michelmore, moved into the compound to study Larimer's methods before attempting a book. "Larry wanted to help these people day to day, hand to hand, mouth to mouth," Gwen told him. Michelmore concluded his subject "felt a sense of privilege that he had somehow found his way to a place where he could be so exultingly human. Never was a task too menial, a duty too unsavory. He emptied bedpans, dressed the dead, and wiped vomit from the floor. . . .

"There was the sad afternoon when a little girl came to Deschapelles with a cancer that had gnawed at her mouth and nose. She stood there in distress, looking up at Mellon, her face half pretty and half raw flesh. The doctor picked up the little girl in his arms and carried her to his house. He sat her on a divan on the front porch, and then went to the music stand to play the flute for her. After an hour Mellon carried the peasant girl back to the hospital and put her in a clean bed. He smoothed her hair back from her forehead and bent close to whisper, '*Au revoir, chérie.*'

"In the morning she was dead."

Mellon's approach is pragmatic. He tried, quite early, to educate nearby villagers to the importance of water, and himself builds primitive conduit systems to conduct what spring water exists into the hamlets for drinking. He helped set up a factory to manufacture roof tiles, which became the largest on the island. A school was started, but it became expensive and "didn't pan out too well," he says, and that was dropped. Most heartening of all was the establishment by a group of hospital employees, with money they'd collected, of a tuberculosis sanitarium at Escalle. "Quite frankly," Mellon says, "if I had TB I'd as soon be there as anywhere."

Why rule anything out? In 1963 young Billy, by then a nervously exhausted Boston University premedical student, was found in a parked car on a side road in Yarmouth Port, dead of a mixture of barbiturates and alcohol. Soon after starting up, Larimer himself began suffering acute heart palpitations. His heart stops once in a while. One cardiologist, putting in his stint among Deschapelles' regular rotation, arrived at Mellon's bedside to find him perilous, close enough to death to need a catheter straight into the aorta. This happens occasionally; what struck the visitor was Gwen's uncanny composure, the way she rarely glanced up while taking her neat, unhurried stitches; while beyond the half-open door the cardiologist was sweating.

"We're still not sure what's going to happen," Larry Mellon says. "I talked to the Mennonites about taking over the place. They said, 'You know, Dr. Mellon, we're good at some things, some things we're not so good at. What really scares us is your budget. We're not in that class. We're simple missionaries.' "

The shadowy late afternoon, when some of the stickiness goes out of the tropical air, has brought an equilibrium to the waning day. Mellon breathes this in. Sitting in his living room, with both the louvered mahogany doors standing open to the light while hills become purple and cows are grazing and lowing among the palm trees, Larimer savors this remoteness to anguish and devotion. "Those cows," he begins, "we started with the local cattle and crossed them with some Brahman bulls we imported, then bred their offspring into some Charolais. We got a big, loose-hided, short-horned animal, not over-marbled, with a fifty percent beef yield. We butcher maybe two a week, and sell them to the employees at cost." Well-doing, even without the profit motive.

This is the time of evening he likes to play his flute a little or read some Arabic, or sometimes a verse or so in classical Hebrew. Somewhere beyond the hills, sporadically, there is a stolid little passage coming off the tom-toms, an early, miniature thunder. The people are gathering to begin the voodoo. This too Mellon acknowledges. "Every once in a while we get a patient with a severe psychiatric or neurotic problem," he explains. "I very often refer 'em to the voodoo priests. They have some pretty good insights. When they run into something they can't handle, we get 'em. Of course, the fee schedule is different. We ask four gourdes, which isn't much. The priests sometimes charge thirty or forty dollars. One fellow who works in the hospital is a priest, and he asked me once, 'Do you ever wonder why the patients at the clinic haven't got any money? They stop at my place first.' "

This makes Larimer grin: everywhere much the same. Just beyond the entrance, deep in the foliage of the enormous strangler fig, a raven has settled and breaks without warning into a fierce, gargling caw. "That's only his nature," Larry Mellon says. "He just gets mad, and cusses out everybody."

3

One bystander who understood young Larimer's malaise was fun-loving Tommy Hitchcock. "I suspect it pleased him that I wanted to leave," Larry says. "He advised me not to stop until I got to Hawaii."

Hitchcock entered this picture in 1928. W.L. would write of the evening he and May were sitting in a little oval side room in Squirrel Hill, listening to Margaret—Peggy—"giggling and Tommy protesting. So both my wife and I were looking at the doorway as Tommy came through, seeming to have been propelled by unseen hands. Then he stammered as he asked our permission to marry Margaret."

W.L. was skeptical. Peggy's first, Alex Laughlin, had died a couple of years earlier while having some wisdom teeth extracted. He left Peg a son, little Alec, and somewhere between six and eight million dollars. What Hitchcock would offer was hard to predict. "I think people felt that he was a society twerp," Matt says. "We used to laugh and joke a lot about New York society, those people with names like Mrs. Stuyvesant Fish. My father didn't like the match at first, he heard that Hitchcock had been running around with chorus girls."

Tommy made a wonderful appearance—husky, burstingly san-guine, no airs, yet suave in a quietly amused Long Island way— although there were doubts around town as to the sincerity of Hitch-cock's acquisitiveness. "A.W. himself sounded me out one time about whether we could use Hitchcock at Mellon Securities," Denton notes. "I told him, 'Tommy is a meeter of people, not somebody to button up the trade.' A.W. said, 'Just forget I brought it up.'"

Possibly Frank was dubious about the likelihood of Hitchcock's absorbing himself in work because he'd done so little. Moneymaking hadn't seemed important. The Hitchcocks were gentry, a clan whose way of living "depicted the English country life as did the style of few families in America," to Billy Hitchcock's observation. One of Tommy's twins, Billy remembers the culminating decade or so of the ancestral manner, the rolling family farms in Aiken, South Carolina. There was a sweeping commodious main structure, full of "good fur-nishings," if deliberately not great, to which as many as twenty visitors a season might come, each likely to bring a servant or two, and expect to stay on right through the winter if things went amusingly.

Until perhaps 1939 French was usually spoken at the table. A great aunt, Tante Maria, lived as a spinster with the family and always took luncheon with Billy's paternal grandparents. Dinner she preferred alone. "My grandfather was first a gentleman, and then a very shrewd breeder of horses," Billy says. He was a learned man, who attended Oxford and built up the Hitchcock steeplechasers until they were the best anywhere. The Hitchcock racing colors were among the first given out, solid green. Fox hunts went out three times a week, and Grandmother organized the polo.

In summer the family repaired to the estate at Old Westbury, Long Island, where walks and gardens threaded among the great boled willow trees which drooped above the pond. Before the sprawling residence there was a mile-long steeplechasing course over trodden grass. Many friendships came down. Tommy's grandfather had been the financial editor of the New York *Sun* and his wife, a Eustis, a relation of David Finley's wife, had descended from William Corcoran, the eminent Georgetown financier who, even before the Civil War, had turned to philanthropy and art collecting. "The Mellons, by comparison, were upstarts," Billy says. "The Hitchcocks were aristocratic almost to the point of being degenerate."

When Tom married Peggy his reputation depended largely upon his accomplishments as an adventurer, a *bon vivant*, an athlete. Hitchcock learned to fly and joined the Lafayette Escadrille as a seventeen-year-old, won dogfights, bailed out and took a bullet in the hip and landed behind the German lines, got caught, escaped from a prison train and hobbled a hundred miles to sneak into Switzerland. He returned quickly after the armistice and finished at Harvard. Even then his talent as a polo player was making his legend, and the year he graduated, 1922, the U. S. Polo Association granted him a ten-goal handicap, its highest rating, which he would keep until 1940. He was the beau ideal of a generation ascending, its pampered, energetic pet. Among his closest friends were Jock Whitney and David Bruce. Gerard Lambert would write about the night in Paris he scraped his way into the exclusive artists' Quatre Arts Ball and found himself, along with Tom Hitchcock, attempting to "vault" over the shoulders of another pair of Americans. Tommy was "a bit tight"; on one effort his skull jerked forward and shattered Lambert's nose.

"Throughout the Twenties he had a couple of business investments, several associates," Billy says, "but he didn't seriously get involved in making money until the crash. He'd made money easily." After 1929 the Hitchcock fortune, like most descended estates, dwindled to a relic. Hitchcock went to work for Bankers Trust as a trainee, and then a polo-playing friend, Bobby Lehman, offered him a shot at in-

Tommy and Peggy Hitchcock
U.P.I.

vestment banking with Lehman Brothers. Although "three generations removed from business," in W.L.'s phrase, Tommy was "reverting to it." He had a hand in the financing of American Airlines and American Export Lines, became a partner in 1937, and presumably settled down. In 1939 fighting again broke out. After that, W.L. saw, "Tommy Hitchcock had no time for anything but the war." A violent antitoxin reaction prevented Hitchcock from enlisting in the Flying Tigers; he settled, briefly, for an air attaché slot in the U. S. Embassy. This produced his chance to join the Ninth Air Support Command under Carl Spaatz. Hitchcock became the chief of tactical research, and he was testing an aircraft while awaiting the opportunity to train his own group of P-51 Mustang pilots when his plane went down in April of 1944, and Tommy Hitchcock perished.

"What I remember best," Billy Hitchcock says, "about my father is like the times he'd come home on furlough when my twin brother, Tommy, and I were maybe three or four, and we really loved to climb up and ride on his shoulders and he would walk around and we would attempt to be as naughty as possible, pummel each other, make faces and grab things out of the medicine cabinet. . . ." Such memories are fragmentary. Billy also remembers a film his father brought back to show the children, shot through a camera linked to a fifty-millimeter machine gun in one of the Mustangs as it maneuvered in combat with a Focke-Wulf, which it ultimately downed. Billy's sisters, Louise and little Peggy, were old enough to retain a more complete impression of their widely adored father, but the twin boys came along in 1939, and throughout their first several years their father was usually away.

What fatherlessness brought on would become a theme to which other Mellons recurred. "Those boys were raised without any leadership," Matt says. Peggy was visiting him in Palm Beach when David Bruce telephoned, and left it to Matt to tell his sister that Hitchcock was gone. For stouthearted, attractive Peggy, life's romance had ended. Five children needed rearing, and she had remained too much of a Mellon to overreach emotionally. "I was always bothered by Mummy's loneliness," Billy begins. "I felt she was sort of walling herself off. We had a place of our own at Sands Point, and she decided she didn't want the memory of that. She sold it and bought my grandfather's estate in Old Westbury, Long Island. We lived in Manhattan in the winter, and spent the summers there."

Peggy's Laughlin capital, added to the several hundred thousand a year each of the chickabiddies now received from W.L.'s trusts, had left the Hitchcocks with a lot more income than others on that side of the family. "They lived like kings," one cousin said. "There was no authority in the household. It was perfectly obvious that Billy's mother adored him, and she spoiled them all, but Billy in particular." This favorite—William Mellon Hitchcock, "Billy" always, even to chance acquaintances—is happy to confess that too, since frankness is indicated. "The problem was, although Mother had withdrawn from things, my twin brother, Tommy, and I had an abundance of energy. We were pretty fucking unmanageable, if you'll pardon my language. She sent us off to boarding school in Aiken, a place they ran like an English public school. There was riding two days a week, and blazers. I went to St. Paul's when I was fourteen. During my junior year I had a horse go down on me while we were playing polo. I got a concussion and lost a year, and to make it up I went to a tutoring school in New York. That was a mistake. I'd outgrown the restrictions of childhood, and I was yearning to experience life."

At about this point, Hitchcock was upsettingly victimized by an elusive extortionist, who threatened Billy's life. This led local police to tap the Old Westbury telephones. The whole affair jackknifed when Hitchcock was himself arrested and charged with participating in—at minimum—a hoax. A court proceeding exonerated him; the publicity was confusing, and so with all that hanging in the air he felt he'd better move out.

He turned up presently as a tool dresser on an assortment of oil rigs around Pecos County, Texas. After a year and a half of that, an Austrian he met arranged a job for him at a refinery near Vienna, where he might resume his abandoned education at the University. He drifted to London and became a trainee at the English branch of Lazard Frères. On holiday in Venice during the fall of 1961 Hitchcock encountered his father's mentor, Bobby Lehman, and Lehman himself proposed that Billy return to Manhattan and join his brokerage organization.

Hitchcock accepted, reluctantly in a way since "I had started to fancy myself as an Englishman, with English tastes for life." Not expecting too much, rather out of touch, Billy Hitchcock at twenty-three came home to Wall Street. Few noticed. Hitchcock enrolled in Lehman's executive training program.

Even then, of course, Billy's watermark was exuberance. He was a tallish youngster with something of a musing, languid tonality, a tendency to plumpness—part of that informality his time in England helped perfect. Adored early, without qualification, he indulged the impulse to open himself up. "There is a sheep-dog friendliness about Billy," a relative quips, "so marked that when a Mellon meets him he instinctively wants to draw himself back."

This too is presentation—Hitchcock seems so unguarded sitting there, feet on the nearest coffee table, obscured by a wall of hunched-up thigh behind which his intimate nasal baritone frames explanations, blasphemes, drifts into sociological reverie, seizes words to clothe these gouts of furry universal compassion he wheels into even the most casual of exchanges above W.L.'s protruding lower lip. Billy Hitchcock offers . . . himself. This has not altered. "He is a man of great energy, dynamism, charm," Jay Mellon begins. "There is a certain excessiveness, a lack of moderation and judgment. That's the only thing that has kept him from becoming a very superior person."

This too reflects viewpoint. Soon after Billy's return to the United States a mutual friend, Charlie Rumsey, introduced him to a model, recently widowed, tall, twenty-eight, a Venezuelan national. Aurora Troconis Moore, though subdued in style, flickered intently as Billy with emotional incandescence. "I liked heem immediately," she recalls. "It happened very queek that night." Aurora is swarthily beautiful, with perfectly frilled bee-sting lips and warm Latino eyes which glow with the pleasure she takes from each fresh idea, every sincere contact. Her hair is tresses, raven. The two got married, and Hitchcock helped out with Aurora's two growing children, and soon they had a baby of their own, Melinda.

Risible as Hitchcock is, perhaps Wall Street wasn't the ideal place for him once all the dense, itch-provoking pollens of the Sixties had started to blanket the culture. Comments James Walton sourly, mindful of the aftermath, "A relative said to me once that he was the only one in the family now with a real financial genius." Looking around at Lehman's, Hitchcock thought he saw true opportunities to disburden himself: "I had one goal," Hitchcock says. "I wanted to be financially independent of the family money, never have to take one effing dime. All the years I was growing up I had had women of various degrees of intelligence surrounding me, giving me orders on things they knew nothing about. Two sisters, one mother, two governesses, five maids . . . I had the *income* on money in the middle seven figures, but I had hardly any capital of my own. I wanted some, badly."

It seemed, for years, that destiny couldn't wait to gratify Billy's hankerings. Once he was trained, Hitchcock received a desk at the institutional sales department at Lehman's, where he was quick to form a close working association with Louis Pemberton, the respected asset sales manager. Hitchcock's income depended on the level of the institutional brokerage business he provided the house. "Lehman's participated in the rise of the Sixties," he says, "and my fortunes went along with theirs." By the middle of the decade Billy's commission level was running around a quarter of a million dollars a year.

Posted where he was, Hitchcock saw that other—quicker—routes to financial success were opening all around. Late in 1964 he spent a weekend in the Bahamas with his half-brother, Alec Laughlin, and through the conservative Laughlin he met an attorney and banker, Sam Feranis Clapp, chairman of the local Fiduciary Trust Company. Clapp quickly convinced Hitchcock of the wisdom of setting up some Bahamian trusts for his children and those of his Troconis in-laws in Caracas. One advantage of dealing through such an offshore trust was that the U. S. Treasury Department's inhibitory "Regulation T," which limited the percentage of borrowed money an investor might involve, seemingly did not apply. His Fiduciary Trust, Clapp indicated, was prepared to loan a client with Hitchcock's exemplary background a very high percentage of the price of whatever he selected.

Another of Fiduciary's customers was bustling Bernie Cornfeld, whom Clapp further assisted as offshore tax consultant. Cornfeld's gifts were organizational, but at certain stages of the boom it was necessary even for the gnomic proprietor of the billion-dollar Investors Overseas Services to churn his accounts a little, to revamp or upgrade the fund lists his salesmen were hustling. Like anybody else, Cornfeld needed a broker. It became, increasingly, Hitchcock.

It seemed, just then, that Billy was irresistible—he idled among capitals, an alert, humid presence; manipulators and banking officials and promoters and businessmen of every moral stripe jostled scupper to scupper, overflowing three-piece suits, heated up with eagerness to spread raw opportunity before this personable Mellon connection. "I happened to be working around Europe, finding customers for Lehman's," Billy reflects, "and I ran into the ex-vice-president of Crédit Suisse, Fred Paravicini. He'd started a bank of his own." Paravicini was looking for good, current American ideas, and early in 1965 "Lou Pemberton and I opened up an omnibus account for Paravicini's bank in New York, and he was buying and selling a lot of securities through Lehman Brothers on our persuasion."

By 1965 the most unfettered bull rally since 1929 was gaining authority, and Hitchcock and Pemberton were ideally situated to get in early. Paravicini's goals seemed modest. "The guy was only too pleased to make five points in Xerox," Billy saw. With lots of underwriting around, the boys at Lehman's were confident that they could show the banker something better than that. "In July of 'sixty-five," Billy remembers, "Kuhn Loeb was doing a secondary of Polaroid. Everything was right. I had Lou on the extension, and we told Paravicini, 'You've just got to get on this, you're going to get a short-term trade as well as a capital gain.' They took upward of ten thousand shares." The issue reacted upward, powerfully, and not long after that, when Pemberton was spending a weekend at the Hitchcocks', Paravicini telephoned from Berne and told them that he had decided to put a percentage of the profits they made for him in a special trading account. They might, everybody understood, repatriate what they wanted.

By December, "buying, selling, going short, you name it," this numbered incentive account, 1315, contained more than fifty thousand dollars. Pemberton needed some money to buy a cooperative apartment, and moved his half into a regular account at Paravicini's and declared his gains. Hitchcock let his ride and leveraged his results with 100-percent margin loans from Paravicini. By New Year's of 1969 the account contained over a million dollars.

"Like his sister Peggy," another cousin concludes, "Billy inherited his susceptibilities from the father's side of the family. Most of us have a far sounder set of values. It's our Middle Western heritage— our standards are inimical to the publicity-mad glamour scramble that goes on in Manhattan, that floozy rootless café-society thing. . . .

"Of course Billy always adored the idea of making money. He can go through it in an awful hurry, you know. There was a time when he lived in a double-decker penthouse, and had a Jamaican butler, and he would sit in the back of his car and buy and sell securities over the telephone. He bought his own personal helicopter. By then, of course, he spent his time with a whole lot of smart-ass corner-cutting beady-eyed types. People in that business, fly-by-night, gimmee-gimmee, full of big talk about what they were going to do. Billy just likes anybody who is not a bore.

"Even Millbrook. I think Billy saw the financial possibilities of the thing, rebellion, which he loved. The facade they presented to the public was: 'This is a liberating thing, the new generation is making its war cry, moving on to a higher level of understanding.' Then, before that sunk in, Billy and Timothy Leary rented a movie theater in New York to show slides of what you're supposed to see under LSD. Commercial, they patented an LSD T-shirt. . . ."

This last is problematical. Millbrook provided Billy's anodyne. He bought the place, together with his brother, Tommy, shortly after getting back in 1962. Their mother would decide to donate the Long Island property to the cerebral palsy foundation, and Billy himself soon happened upon what had once been Walter Teagle's 2,600-acre shooting preserve in upstate Dutchess County. "During the old days," Hitchcock says, and snorts, "the place maintained two hundred employees. Until we got it. *Then* it went to pot."

Hitchcock's admission is gallant, but everywhere around the vast, fallow property fixtures crumble after decades of lawyers' remote economies, of skimping at groundskeeping. Brambles accost the fences, cocked and fractured shingles chatter before the wind. A pickup truck with "Brown" unevenly lettered along a door cruises the empty acreage, comes by on schedule to check the turreted Victorian farmhouse. Boarded up now, its clapboards turning gray as year by year it sheds its morsels of paint. The first-floor porch system is extended by bales of chicken wire which have been stretched in billows between electrical staples, connecting railings and garrisons; inside, a neurotic hound (alternately mournful and vicious) prowls before webby sashes. Halfway up the wall of the outcropping tower there is a six-pointed star, its center the nestling-comma yin/yang symbol long associated with witchcraft. It overlooks barren grounds, vestige of the epiphanies.

This is the shrine where acid was sanctified. Leary became its prophet; Hitchcock provided august backdrops. A winsome attenuated figure, Aurora now moves thoughtfully, sadly perhaps, along shadowy upstairs corridors where "LSD" stands thinly whitewashed-over in splashed-up letters higher than a man. The public rooms downstairs are altered as well. The fireplaces stand sealed, and elegantly padded walls—wine fleurs-de-lis, raked by untended cats, then slashed and tattered during the breakthrough psychedelic sessions—have had their batting poked back to accommodate rudimentary stitching. There is a stale, varnished smell. Her noble forehead awash in the refraction of high Tiffany inserts, Aurora extends her fine-boned wrist to direct one's attention outside, into the stonework garden. There Timothy Leary remarried. Each door tempts memories. Within the bowling alley, Tim and the trustworthy once lived on acid for two straight weeks.

The meaning this had! Drawbacks followed by degrees. "My twin brother, Tommy, was at Harvard toward the end of the Fifties," Hitchcock says, "and there he and my sister Peg became friends of Leary. I was considered to be the 'square' of the family because of the prewar mentality I had picked up in Europe. Peggy used to ridicule me because I was so defenseless. The summer of 1962 I met Dick Alpert at my mother's. I found Dick funny—he understood how to laugh at himself, and he had a background similar to mine. He was Jewish, his father was head of the Hartford and New Haven Railroad. He opened me up. He got me to read Thomas Mann, Salinger . . . he was already having his problems with Harvard, and he had established this community in Mexico, Zihuatanejo. Tommy and Peggy went down there, and Peggy told me I should try a psychedelic. I said, 'Why?' She said, 'That's a good question, try it, you've got nothing to lose.' "

The drug people favored at the time was mescaline. At Harvard

Medical School, Leary himself had conducted lysergic-acid experiments on undergraduate volunteers. The summer of 1963, when Hitchcock made arrangements to lease the big house to Tim and his friends for five hundred a month, Leary, although quietly leaving Harvard, still maintained professional credentials, still traveled and lectured and wrote up the results of his research for the American Psychological Association. "Tim too was like a teacher to me in many ways," Billy said. "I had been interested in things like religion even during my years at St. Paul's. You've got to remember I was working my ass off already at Lehman Brothers by then, and starting to make a lot of money, and still I sensed that this was my trap, I had no goals beyond that. The Viet Nam war had started to escalate, and I was getting alienated, I used to hear those goddamn fools get up and tell me all about the great things the effing war was going to do for the economy. Maybe I was more sensitive on the point, I remembered when my old man was killed in a war.

"Then Tim came along, and he told me what to read, and pointed out the discrepancies in the thinking that was going around. He's a real leprechaun, a real shit-stirrer. We were a group of people who were feeling that there was a whole new dimension to the space we lived in, why I was on this planet. Meanwhile, down on Wall Street, I was not receiving the satisfaction I demanded. Acid made me examine myself. I started to see Billy Hitchcock as a kind of composite —more than the person who was a Wall Street banker because his father was, or somebody who had to support a family."

Under Leary's charismatic tutelage every session was directed: the flesh screened visions. Before the ritual ingestion one of the "meditation centers" was readied, art books set out and personal mementos and flowers and passages of appropriate poetry and selections of classical music entered onto the tape equipment for when the lapses started opening. Particular foods were authorized, but during the sacrament the participants would warn each other that these as well— fruits, salads—must be assimilated sparingly. Members watched each other—there was a danger that one of the participants would wander off completely, and possibly be lost. An ashram started up. The first several years, Hitchcock maintains, he used acid infrequently; each experience ripped deeper, tore more deceptions away. Aloft, sublimely critical, he watched the aura of anger or confusion surrounding each of the others even as they attempted to misrepresent their emotions to themselves.

"Under LSD everything seemed so clear to Beelee," Aurora emphasizes. "Then after a while he didn't think it was that real, what he was doing on Wall Street. I tried it too, the first time I was shaking when they gave it to me. You see things which you have never seen before, you get into the actual notes, the colors which form the pattern. An' Teemothy Leary was part of this, of course—thees incredible man, he has a min' like somebody you have never met before, an' he took everybody on treeps, convince' everybody that with thees LSD he's going to change the whole worl'. But I had a premonition that everything would be an incredible change from this. Which it was. At the beginning Beelee and I were very close with this experience, but later he wanted to take it all the time. But I deedn't dare, because it was changing me in a way that was confusing me. It gave me so much information I did not know how to put this information to use. It's just too much, overpowering. Under LSD I started to see Beelee as very intense, very nervous, very sensitive. Acid will do that, it rob' any previous attachment. People are little by little on a different train ride, they see their partners like they never saw him before."

Leary had, Hitchcock discovered, an "egotistical" side. "Tim just couldn't resist the action," Hitchcock says. By 1965 Millbrook had become the publicized eastern campground for a cultural phenomenon; the apostate doctor, filling out what Hitchcock calls his role as "wistful guru," now became the impresario. He mounted "seminars," for which the charges ran to several hundred a week, and a procession of crazies and dignitaries, from Alan Watts to the Aluminum Dream and Peter Fonda and The Grateful Dead and Edward Hornig, trooped in for exposure, joined the collective upheaval. Leary presided, his graying hair dramatically tousled, still crackling with ideas, grainy and spare, a certified Orpheus figure, delighted to be photographed naked except for a pair of chaps upon a fine white horse, grinning triumphantly into sunlight.

On weekends, Aurora remembers, she and the others would arrive in very large groups. The Hitchcocks kept quarters in what was called "the bungalow," an ornate Tuscan villa some distance from the Big House, built by a previous owner, Dietrich, whose son, cursed by a gardener, drowned himself in Champagne in the bathtub that serviced the suite Billy and Aurora used. The Big House offered entertainment. "There was always happenings," Aurora says. "Light shows, costume parties, fireworks on the Fourth of July, Huntington Hartford and his crowd showing up black tie. There were always a lot of crash-

Millbrook once
WILLIAM M. HITCHCOCK

Aurora
AURORA HITCHCOCK

Billy Hitchcock in another season
JAMES R. MELLON II

ers. You become very confuse'. If you go for a walk in the woods, there would be horses all painted up in Day-glo paint, you would think, 'Am I under LSD? But I didn't take it today.' "

He remained a believer, but as a backer, and certainly as a landlord, Hitchcock began suppressing reservations. His mother was uneasy, and forces were obviously gathering. In December of 1965 Billy Hitchcock and Aurora had arranged to meet Leary and his new wife and several of his children to spend the New Year's holiday together at Isle de Mujeres. While processing through customs, Leary's sixteen-year-old daughter was discovered to be carrying, in a pillbox in her brassiere, a smidgen of marijuana. "Leary was still a relatively straight ex-college professor," Hitchcock says, "and he was indicted on charges of attempting to smuggle marijuana out of the country without paying any duty on it. This fired me up, I thought it one of the great travesties of American justice, and I set up the Leary defense fund. I paid Leary's legal bills. Then all of a sudden *I* was inundated with bloodsuckers, people who were furious with me for doing that because they wanted to make an issue out of the thing. I told them, I'm not paying for a lot of PR people and ads in *The New York Times*. We eventually took it to the Supreme Court, and got the case thrown out on grounds of double jeopardy.

"Then Tim let Millbrook really start to run downhill. We had hammered out a pretty good understanding with the local police. But Tim just opened up the doors, and although we told Tim we didn't want the place turned into a hippie crash pad, pretty soon there were groups camping on the property. I remember the day Ken Kesey rolled up in that bus with the Merry Pranksters. A pall settled over town, there was a rumor that eighty Hell's Angels were aboard. I told Leary, 'Look, the Hell's Angels are *out*.' He agreed. Kesey actually showed up one Saturday night—people playing flutes, sacks hanging out of everywhere, the thing painted *thousands* of colors. They were practically catatonic, a group of ten or so started to wander around the bungalow, clutching their flutes and cymbals tight for protection."

In 1966 the standoff ended. Local Assistant District Attorney G. Gordon Liddy, running for the Republican nomination for Congress, needed a flagship issue. Raids started, with and without warrants. "I had these assholes like Liddy, who stood on the platform with a thirty-eight strapped to his waist, running on a plank which was largely Throw Hitchcock Out of Millbrook," Billy says. "They were busting people because there were no treads on their tires. One Saturday they arrested thirteen people up there, and two were merely tradesmen, one milkman, I think. Making deliveries." Jay Mellon was up the day of the enormous police sweep toward the end of 1968, and remembers the dogs, troopers mounted on horses bearing down on hippies in their robes as they burst from their wigwams throughout the chilly woods while cops in helicopters honked down through bullhorns: *"You must get out, you must get out!"* Billy had already left; he returned from California to stand charges along with the crowd of material witnesses who had been waiting in jail for months. Finally charges were dismissed because the local authorities could not find Leary. It was, Jay reflects, the end of an era.

Returning east just then, Hitchcock couldn't help perceiving how quickly enthusiasms date. As early as 1965, when Leary got busted, "Aurora and I began to grow apart. This was very painful to me, especially since we had the children in common. But I had to admit to myself a tremendous discontentment, a restiveness. I met this girl, Priscilla Ashworth, who was toying with a Ph.D. at Berkeley." Hitchcock began to spend longer periods at Millbrook, where he and

Priscilla shared the gardener's cottage, and although in Manhattan Hitchcock lived with Aurora "under the same roof, we had become estranged."

"I had stopped taking LSD," Aurora says. "Because I could see that with it you sort of lose your balance. By then Beelee din' care whether the children were present or not. But I have to make sure that they do their homework, go to school, brush their teeth. Everything change' so fast. When we first got married people at Lehman Brothers, older men, would come to Beelee for advice. Then, when he start using acid, I could see that his work was not important anymore. Hiding all that money in Switzerland, et cetera, was a way of rebelling against his family background, these moral codes, the family structure. You get onto an ego trip; as Leary said, 'I'm a guru.' So Beelee got into these crazy deals. They seemed rational."

If not rational, profitable, at least at first. Alerted early, Hitchcock exploited his unlimited borrowing privileges at the Fiduciary Trust to take a very large position in some lively issues, notably the Mary Carter Paint Company, fanning out just then to install casinos throughout the Caribbean. Others, including Chase Manhattan managers, were speculating here too, and Hitchcock's 100,000 shares shot up to a value of three and a half million before the bottom fell away. "I was really lucky to get out of that alive," Hitchcock says, and laughs.

In 1969 Investors Overseas Services acquired Fiduciary Trust; Samuel Clapp left, and Hitchcock quickly transferred his Bahamian trusts to Berne. The year before, Fred Paravicini had opened a second bank in which he offered Hitchcock a 6 percent interest, and Billy was able to convince his mother of the wisdom of making the investment. Hitchcock left Lehman Brothers early in 1967, soon after Sam Clapp had suggested that, with I.O.S. salesmen being excluded by the Securities and Exchange Commission, this was the time for Billy to found a firm of his own to supply what now had become a multibillion-dollar overseas financial clearinghouse operation. "The guarantee was enormous," Hitchcock says, "but I wouldn't do it." Instead, he negotiated a partnership in Delafield and Delafield, the officers of which were delighted to process the $700,000 annual override Cornfield's purchases brought in. Billy took one-half. "The best thing that could have happened as far as Delafield was concerned would have been for me to drop dead," Hitchcock says, "so they wouldn't have to pay the commission."

Billy rarely stopped by. In 1968 he'd been suspended briefly by the S.E.C. for dealing, wittingly or otherwise, in falsified brokerage records. He moved to Sausalito with Priscilla. "I had," Hitchcock says, "lost every drop of interest I ever had in I.O.S." What financial attention survived went into the money he was illegally managing—a total of sixty-seven million dollars, the modern record, finally sloshed through Berne according to the U.S. Attorney—in connivance with Paravicini. When a friend close to Kleiner-Bell told Hitchcock that Armour was on the block and that General Host was interested, he and Paravicini undertook a large-scale speculation in Armour, then in General Host, which left them stranded when General Host was unable to grab enough of the Armour common to raid its cash position and repay its creditors. Armour was suspended briefly; its securities buckled; Hitchcock— meaning Paravicini—took a ferocious beating. Billy flew to Berne, where it took him "a week to figure out what was actually in" account 1315. By then, it developed, almost nothing was. The million was gone.

Paravicini was deteriorating overall. By 1969 the series of breaks which started the bull market down sent chancier issues tottering. Paravicini was overloaded. In November of 1969, with the market falling, Paravicini and his associate, Irving Freiburghaus, met Hitchcock and an assistant in New York at the Olde Chop House. Billy had left Delafield. The four were talking, Hitchcock remembers, when suddenly Paravicini said, " 'Billy, would you mind signing these documents?' I looked through them," Hitchcock says, "and they were opening-of-account forms, hypothecation agreements. And there was one particular thing. They all were dated July, 1965. I knew I was admitting to owing thousands of dollars of income taxes if I signed that, so I changed the date on the thing to a period in 1968 when the account was on a break-even basis."

Youthful, dauntless, Hitchcock was well embarked on yet another —overlapping—life. What Billy was after out West still elevates legal eyebrows; his cousin Jimmy Walton expresses the Pittsburgh, or magisterial, consensus: "As far as I'm concerned, there's absolutely no place for him in our family. I don't think it's fair to anybody. He just thinks it's a big joke. How the hell you can buy your way out of jail for some of the things he did is more than I can understand. He's charming. He acts like a big baby. You will think that he's naïve.

But he's not. I mean, he's simply not a productive person. What's he given to the world besides a bathtub full of acid . . . ?"

This last appears directed to Hitchcock's emergence the autumn of 1967, in dope-baked California, as lysergic acid's éminence grise, its amiable deft internationally connected middleman. This phase of Billy's career is handsomely documented, virtually week by week, through testimony that developed during the exhaustive trial of Nicholas Sand and Robert Timothy Scully that started on November 5, 1973, and throughout which Hitchcock's testimony, as an un-indicted co-conspirator, pepped up the exchanges and determined the outcome. Billy's contribution was uninhibited—he had negotiated immunity, and there was reason to believe that his performance here might ameliorate the sentences on other federal charges he faced—their resolutions thoughtfully deferred by eastern officials until Billy had spilled his insides to their entire satisfaction in San Francisco.

Hitchcock's role in California, like others he undertook, evidently sought him out. One day in April of 1967 he received a visit in his palatial Manhattan apartment from Augustus Owsley Stanley III, "Owsley," a wimp whose reputation preceded him as the kingpin of lysergic acid manufacture in the United States. Owsley's product was celebrated—"righteous," in the popular phrase—and before LSD be-came illegal in California in October of 1966, the tufty little eccentric produced millions of tablets and capsules, headlined by "Owsley blues," his five-hundred-microgram leaders, each impressed with Batman's image.

Owsley had amassed capital, some $225,000, stashed away just then in a New York safe-deposit box. Hitchcock was the investment banker; what did he advise? Hitchcock arranged for Owsley to open an offshore account at Fiduciary Trust under the pseudonym of "Robin Goodfellow," and sent Clapp's assistant there, William Sayad, and his own devoted flunky, Charlie Rumsey, to bag the cash for deposit in Nassau.

That day in April, Owsley had introduced Hitchcock to a young associate, Tim Scully, a Bay Area science prodigy flushed with the humane possibilities of the expansion of consciousness. Scully's ideal-ism was touching. After he and Priscilla moved out to Sausalito late in the summer of 1967, Billy invited Scully over. Scully could synthesize psychedelics. Would Hitchcock be willing, Scully won-dered, to lend him money for apparatus? Hitchcock had recently explored a similar proposal from Nicholas Sand, who once visited

Millbrook and now was attempting to produce the low-grade hallucinogenic "STP" in a covert laboratory while living on a ranch near Cloverdale. Everybody's bottleneck was supply; acid's two known bases, ergotamine tartrate and lysergic acid monohydrate, were all but unobtainable. Hitchcock mentioned Charles Druce, a reputable English source. That same happy autumn Timothy Leary showed up at Hitchcock's Sausalito house to present John Griggs, cofounder of The Brotherhood of Eternal Love, a quasi-religious order centered on a ranch outside Palm Springs. "The place was beautiful, full of drop-out Laguna beach-type kids," Hitchcock says now. "They were the biggest distributors of acid. Well structured, very well-organized. They ran a shipment through inside the cage of a live Bengal tiger headed for the Los Angeles Zoo."

Once things got organized, motivation itself went awry. Sand knew what *he* wanted. He authorized Hitchcock to open an account over which he would retain discretionary investment powers at Paravicini's, the "Alan Bell" account, and, midway through 1968, he took Billy along to London to provide him entrée to Druce. Sand's Hell's Angels customers were bracing him frighteningly. Sand established a Liechtenstein corporation as a blind for cash transactions; it became the owner of record when Sand's attorney, Peter Buchanan, picked up the farmhouse in Windsor, California, in which they intended to manufacture their hallucinogens. Hitchcock tucked the mailings from England into his Sausalito safe-deposit boxes.

In December of 1968, along with Tim Scully and another associate, Hitchcock carted the drums and crates, the vacuum evaporators and chromatographic columns and tightly wrapped bundles of semiprecious primary compounds into the Windsor farmhouse. Billy had recently run an additional $98,800 from Sand for the "Bell" account to Pittsburgh and handed it to Freddie Paravicini personally, steps, reportedly, from R. K. Mellon's sanctorum. In January of 1969 Scully commenced his manufacturing run. Billy pitched right in with tabbing the results. Their shelves filled quickly with high brown bottles of "orange-colored pills slightly smaller than . . . an aspirin." They'd created "Orange Sunshine," the highly respected hallucinatory which, distributed by Leary's Brotherhood, soon found its reception wherever madness was relished.

Then something went wrong. The serviceable Rumsey, reentering the United States with $100,000 in cash from an assortment of Paravicini accounts, ran afoul of customs. Most of the money originated with Sand and Owsley, but Rumsey had panicked, and told the authorities that everything was Hitchcock's. Federal examiners cornered Billy: why had not taxes ever been paid? "This is where I make my big mistake," Hitchcock knows. He accepted questionable advice. " 'Get Paravicini to say you borrowed the one hundred thousand dollars to help you with the troubles with your wife,' " one attorney supposedly advised. "It was a lie, but you might as well go for the banana. Paravicini agreed to sign a letter I dictated. It was the first real felony."

This sickened. He'd perjured himself, grossly. There had been something of the patron-of-the-breakthrough to all this initially. Even then, he confesses, he let his "greedy whims" delude him into pocketing the I.O.S. override. Then Los Angeles officials grabbed Nick Sand during a customs check, loaded down with chemicals. Hitchcock attempted to withdraw.

He returned to Manhattan and put up temporarily in the Volney Hotel. There was a passing attempt to reconcile with Aurora; by then her divorce action was under way, affidavits were compiling. She allegedly accused him of not only spending their money on drugs, and leaving them around, and infidelity with Priscilla, but also—and this was heaviest—taking cash from operatives like Owsley for banking in Switzerland. To back her charges, Hitchcock discovered, she had removed certain Paravicini documents from Billy's Manhattan safe-deposit box and included them too. "I went to Aurora," he says now, "and I said, 'Aurora, you're jeopardizing your children's future, you're going to make them front-page news.' I knew that she'd been masterminded by some fucking avaricious attorney."

Aurora acknowledges this now. "When he was with Priscilla, of course, a woman's pride gets hurt. I decided, what's the point? There was a document there, eet was not my faul', eet was the faul' of the lawyer, he assure me that the document was not to be shown, he use eet only to scare heem." In this it succeeded.

Aurora's affidavits were filed at the end of January in 1970. By then the stock market itself was in full retreat, as the saying goes, and many of the high-risk issues Hitchcock once picked brilliantly were dramatically defunct. Billy rushed to Berne, where Paravicini kept records not only of Hitchcock's own trading, but also of the bank itself. It made breathless reading, "I discovered that he had held onto all kinds of things I thought he had long since gotten rid of," Billy says. "The General Host warrants were down to two, and the bonds were around forty. . . . The bank overall was in the hole for about a million dollars. And guess what, he's looking to me for the million dollars." Hitchcock's look becomes soulful. "I have to tell you something," Billy says. "I never ever liked the guy."

Paravicini had prepared documents; they stated that whatever losses the account now represented were Hitchcock's personal obligations. "I had to sign those," Billy says, "or my ass was going to be thrown to the wolves. I'm really shook. I've put family money into this. At this point my attorney tells me the handwriting on the wall is becoming black letters."

Enter Addison Vestal. "I went to Pittsburgh and talked to Vestal," Hitchcock says. The years of looking out for the W.L. line had inured the tax accountant, little ruffled his expression or disturbed one strand of center-parted hair. Now Vestal remained soft-spoken. "He told me, 'Billy, you've got to declare this whole account,' " Hitchcock relates. "I said, 'I can't do that, he's hedging Swiss money, he's long on silver.' I knew there were a lot of unpaid long- and short-term gains."

A two-year negotiation opened between Hitchcock's representatives, Vestal and Pittsburgh attorney George Lockhart, and a string of Government lawyers. The hope was settlement through amended tax returns. To stave Paravicini off, Hitchcock paid him $120,000. But Paravicini clutched, and sued for a million dollars through Arnold and Porter, to whom he allegedly sent copies of transactions in numbered account 1315 as well as documents behind the "Robin Goodfellow" and "Alan Bell" accounts.

If Hitchcock could conclude a quiet civil settlement by June 30, 1972, the statute of limitations would apply. Then another seam ripped. An ordinary tax investigation of the affairs of Nicholas Sand led routinely to Buchanan. To official amazement, Buchanan now stepped forward and volunteered to assist the investigation provided he himself be assured of immunity, and further immunity provided for Scully and Hitchcock.

On both the coasts, Government attorneys started tearing into related Hitchcock records in hopes that charges on the tax and securities-infraction end might justify a major criminal action; the threat of this could compel his cooperation in prosecuting the drug operation. Let Hitchcock be keelhauled!

The news that Buchanan was talking to the U. S. Attorney's office alerted Hitchcock at once. Scully was especially vulnerable, since, as the prosecutor conceded, "it was not for greed or profit that he had entered that life." "He was an easy victim," Hitchcock well recognized. "He had an almost adolescent belief that it was us versus them, the Government, the straight people out there who wear plastic suits, and drive three-tone cars. He felt the world was one big bear trap." Throughout, Scully had fought shy of anything more than alternating shifts at the apparatus with the mercenary Sand. Who would believe that?

The summer of 1972 a grand jury convened in San Francisco to review the evidence that Scully, as Judge Conti concluded, "was the drug and psychedelic movement in the State of California." Billy attempted to protect them both. With money Hitchcock gave him, Tim roamed around abroad. Charles Rumsey did testify, perjuring himself, he would later concede, "at Hitchcock's request."

The indictments came down; federal authorities in Pennsylvania had beaten the deadline by filing indictments of their own against Billy for criminal tax evasion and nonconformance with Regulation T. "In February of 1973, I heard there was a bench warrant out for me," Billy says, "and I immediately hoofed it back to Pittsburgh under another name and gave myself up the next day. Who should be hanging around the courthouse but a reporter for the *Wall Street Journal*. He said, 'Mr. Hitchcock, I've seen a copy of your ex-wife's affidavits concerning your separation.' I thought that had been sealed in family court. I knew that in it she said she had seen me taking two hundred and fifty thousand dollars from Owsley Stanley." Undoubtedly the Government was privy to records from Paravicini too.

They could prove perjury; he'd have to deal. He hired a criminal attorney with background in the U. S. Attorney's office, John Doyle, and bargaining started. "We flew to California and met with the Government's lawyers, Browning, Milano, and Youngquist. They wanted the drug convictions badly, and so we showed them a little at a time. Like an experienced hooker—a little tits, a little ass. . . . And they said, 'Hmmm, we'll go along.' " Hitchcock's unpaid tax liabilities were settled for $547,000; he now accepted fraud penalties in excess of $300,000 and agreed to guilty pleas on tax-evasion and margin charges; the perjury rap disappeared and there was reason to hope concerning Hitchcock's eventual sentencing.

Hitchcock saw some change of dealing for Scully too. Tim had been dodging a subpoena; Billy ferreted him out. There had been talk of a negotiated guilty plea; Scully, as Hitchcock views things, still lacked great realism. "Tim is a kind of quiet, charismatic guy," Billy says, "and he wanted to get his own lawyer. He picks a young guy, thirty-two, who believes in Tim to the point of devotion." Then Scully pleaded innocent, his defense based largely on the technicality that when the pharmaceuticals he had been manufacturing left Windsor they were a legal compound known as ALD-52, although Scully didn't deny that within a very short period they could deteriorate chemically into LSD. The presiding judge, Conti, repeatedly remarked Scully's "smirking" and discerned an undertow of considerable "intellectual arrogance." According to the Government's brief, Scully, "under the shepherding of his own counsel . . . had thoroughly told his version of the entire conspiracy; blaming Hitchcock for everything and describing how Hitchcock, cringing with fear for his family's good name and his own patrimony, had lied repeatedly on the stand and had also asked Scully to lie to protect him from the truth of his own dark involvement as the only mastermind of the whole vast operation ever reaching the light of day."

Scully lost the case and received consecutive sentences totaling twenty years. Hitchcock paid his legal fees, saddened by the outcome. Nicholas Sand got fifteen. That bothered Billy less; Sand was beyond reform. In August of 1972, the month the grand jury conducted its hearings, Hitchcock ran into Sand in the Phoenix airport. "I hadn't seen him since 1969," Hitchcock claims. "He said, 'Listen, Bube, why don't you come out and see this new acid lab we've got in Missouri.' I told him, 'Nick, my ass is so close to the fire. . . . You're doing Tim and me a tremendous disservice, especially since you and I agreed in 1969 we wouldn't make drugs anymore in this country.' "

The Sand and Scully verdicts came down on January 30, 1974; on March 28 Judge Morris Lasker of the Southern District of New York passed sentence on Billy's tax-evasion and Regulation T infractions. Lasker's attitude was compassionate, and with a round of boosters in the courtroom like assistant U. S. Attorney Youngquist, in from San Francisco, one heard a redemptive, even a Dostoyevskian, hum to it. Assorted witnesses gave testimony pointing up Billy's unfortunate associations, his "long and troubled period"; Judge Lasker couldn't "help but observe in my own mind the irony of the fact that being very rich can sometimes be the kind of peril that being very poor can be in the sense that it leads to aberrant or socially unconstructive behavior." The fines were twenty thousand dollars, and Billy was sentenced to five years suspended with probation and consultation at intervals with a psychotherapist.

"I went into psychotherapy immediately," Billy says. "I want to tell you, that's one of the rules of the game." He settled in Tucson for a time and formed a corporation devoted to providing industry to residents of the Apache and Navaho lands. The ashram he encouraged at Millbrook started up out West. He emerged rather strapped—to pay his taxes he reportedly sold part of his holding at Millbrook to his mother. People still expected salvation whenever he came around. Midway through the 1973 trial, Paravicini dispatched an agent to haunt the courtroom antechambers; just as he entered a corridor one depleting afternoon, Billy felt the drag of an arm against his own, slumped shoulder. "Mr. Hitchcock, about that million dollars you owe us—"

Hitchcock still could laugh. "I want to give you points," he remembers protesting. "For pure chutzpah, you've just run away with the Academy Award."

With time, things improved. "Working with the Indians around Tucson I really started to like myself again," Billy says. "I began to write." Motivations of his own, little by little, started to become clearer: "You've got to remember that after 1963 the country was going through the loss of a parent, a father, a person who was a leader, who made people feel proud to be a member of a society. Then came the insane fucking war. Change came too quickly, it took people on a liberation trip they couldn't digest. You have to understand what you want to change, you really can't lay out perceptions in consecutive form."

One begins with attitude. "In Pittsburgh, protectivism is the ultimate theme of one's life. At all costs, protect. Now, I've probably chosen the other extreme, at times. Both are ridiculous. If a person is to evolve as a human being I think he has to be able to experience himself, commit for himself, make his own mistakes. Hopefully not too severe."

Aurora too has mellowed. She lives in Millbrook now, not far from the Hitchcock estate, with a gentle, somewhat Chesterfieldian French painter named Aymon de Roussy de Salles, who showed up initially during Nick Sand's early visit, and remained. Among Hitchcock's pre-

Billy Hitchcock and Jane
WILLIAM M. HITCHCOCK

sentencing statements was a strong and touching endorsement from
Aurora. "Deep down you know Beelee has a beeg heart," she says.
"Even now, after he is remarried, he's very much attentive to all the
children, the older children too. Whenever I have a problem with them
I call him, and we discuss what thing there is to be done about it."
Tenderness leaves Aurora velvety. "Beelee's very worst enemy is hav-
ing money," she concludes, and sighs. "This make' people confuse'.
They think other people love them because of that."

15 | THE WHOLE CIRCLE

1

ONE DAY IN 1958—the culmination by then of weeks of schedule rearrangement, of pacing before receptionists, of hotel-desk call-back messages—a journalist in Pittsburgh to research an article wrapped up the interview that mattered the most. ". . . word came like a command," Herbert Kubly would write, "from court: 'The General will see you.' "

The General was Richard King Mellon, "head of Pittsburgh's patriarchal clan and guardian of its $8,500,000,000 holdings. . . ." Kubly's emotions are unmistakable as, "In a stainless-steel elevator I was floated to the top of the Mellon–U. S. Steel Building and discharged into the walnut-paneled offices of T. Mellon and Sons, the corporate name of grandfather's bank now used to front the vast network of Mellon philanthropies. It was a hushed place of softness— soft rugs, soft lights, soft-toned family portraits on the walls. Even the telephone whispered. I waited apprehensively, trying to piece together my hearsay impressions: the General was modest and self-effacing; he was an imperious Napoleon accustomed to commanding; he was—said one of his friends—a frugal man who commuted daily fifty-five miles from his farm to save the cost of an apartment in town; he was taciturn and hated interviews. . . .

"A nervous attaché came to warn me that the General was somewhat tense, and then ushered me in."

Like Dorothy confronting Oz, Kubly found "the General" more human than otherwise, "a warm man, anxious to communicate." Kubly spent his interview peering out the enormous windows beside his ruddy, spouting host, who directed his attention to the turmoil of reconstruction. Masonry unevenly rising, a wrecking ball crumpling a facade, tunnel openings like wormholes beside which laborers bobbed in and out like nits. Kubly, involved, now contemplated the "city spread out so far below it looked like a museum model . . . all looked like toys."

"We're not halfway through," the General was saying. "By George, look! We get things done." Mellon wouldn't be sidetracked. Kubly asked his subject whether there were any great men in Pittsburgh. "Great men?" responded the General at once. "We've got one. Jonas Salk. He's so modest he won't even let us name a building for him."

Kubly left soon afterward—conducted to the elevators, undoubtedly, by the same attaché who alerted the reporter originally to R. K. Mellon's emotional condition. Through softly lighted corridors, by banks of whispering telephones, beyond the sanitarium-like hush.

Heavy the head. By 1958, as Dick approached sixty, one might have anticipated some cautionary lightening of the load, some inclination toward divestiture. That certainly wasn't happening. For fifteen years the man had stubbornly dominated Pittsburgh, piled obligation on obligation, draped encomiums with encomiums. By 1948 R.K. was already on *Forbes*'s list of Fifty Foremost Business Leaders. To his Distinguished Service Medal from the Army he added a matching award from the Commonwealth of Pennsylvania. In 1953 he thanked the Wharton Alumni Association for its Gold Medal of Merit. In 1958 the United States Chamber of Commerce had designated Mellon "a Great Living American," along with Jonas Salk and Wernher von Braun and J. Edgar Hoover and Calla E. Varner, the principal emeritus of Central High School in St. Joseph, Missouri. Mellon attended the dinner, although Salk, "tied to his laboratory work here, was unable to attend."

Honorary doctorates compiled; he served as trustee at one time or another of Pitt, the Carnegie Museum, the Carnegie Institute of Technology, the American Museum of Natural History, and lent his services to the National Mobilization of Resources for the United Negro Colleges. There was the Mellon Institute, of course, and all the Mellon directorships, and the Pennsylvania Company and the Pennsylvania Railroad and Pittsburgh Plate Glass and Westinghouse Air Brake and Pan American World Airways and the General Motors Corporation. There was his own foundation; he stayed on long after the war and presided over the Pittsburgh Regional Planning Association. . . .

What next? Why more? Could there be . . . overlays? Thirty years gone by, and R.K.'s secretary was overheard to deplore—very much the way R.*B.*'s old secretary did—the fact that her boss spent well over a hundred days a year on planes and trains getting to and from all those trustee and directors' meetings. While Paul Mellon—like Andrew Mellon—did whatever he pleased.

Why invoke these parallels? "He was a terrifically hard worker," Connie muses, "up at five-thirty, not back until seven or eight." She herself is aging—skinny, noticeably humped, a little weathered lady in slacks perched on the edge of her chair, her hair in two chopped graying country wings. "A hard worker and he *loved* it," says Dick Mellon's widow. "Weather made no difference to him." Her eyes gleam reminiscently, bird's eyes, and between quick drags on a succession of filtertips her pert, frank phrases arrive with an enthusiastic rush. The library at Huntland Downs is decorator Provincial—on a corner desk the shade of a lamp glows on a flintlock base. Everything here is outsize—windows, doors and jambs, panels and ceilings—as if to protect the coziness while asserting a responsible grandeur. The trim and detail seem largely of bronze, marble, fruitwoods polished to a subdued glassiness; although Connie has remarried, there is the assumption here of strict, memorial restraint. Above the unlit fire hangs another of the ubiquitous horse paintings, this within a manger, and upon the foreground straw a crumpled saddle blanket is embroidered *R.K.M.*

What can one say? "He was always a great Pittsburgher, a very generous person, Dick Mellon," his widow observes. "He didn't tell people, deep down he did a great many things to help people. Personal loans for people who couldn't afford to take things out of a bank. He made the foundation, and when that was established he said, 'No, I want three-quarters of this, or perhaps all, given to western Pennsylvania. . . .' "

Admirable. Yet more is involved, there is an urgency which resembles the mythological one's compulsion to bestow himself alive, to distribute his substance among the faithful below. "Just before he died," Cousin Matt remembers, "I was up in his office. He was showing me. 'See the Three Rivers Stadium? See, Matt? We're putting this in, and that in. . . .' " He soon discovered philanthropy. "Unlike A.W.," Joseph Hughes says, "R.B. hadn't taken charity very seriously.

He gave year-end gifts. Soon after I joined T. Mellon and Sons, I suggested to R.K. that it was time he got started on a charitable program. I told him that that way he would have the pleasure of seeing some of the things he wanted accomplished in his lifetime.

"He said, 'All right, let's do it.' We started modestly, but then he said, 'Let's do enough if we're going to do it. Let's transfer a hundred thousand shares of Gulf.' I was shocked. The Richard K. Mellon Foundation came into being in November of 1947. He didn't want to be a trustee; he said, 'You people run it.' In the beginning Mrs. Mellon, Van Buskirk and I were the trustees. As the administrative trustee I ran it. Every year Dick added to the assets, *way* beyond what would have given him a tax benefit. He said he wanted to make it *felt*. We qualified R.K. under the Unlimited Charitable Contribution Provision of the tax law—if you gave all of your income away for ten years, after that you didn't have to pay any income taxes if you continued to give your whole income away. It was the road to take for a man in a hurry. There was no tax gimmick, you had to be of a mind to help others. He could always have given seven million dollars away each year and stuck three million in his pocket.

"He was buying time." Dispersals of the R. K. Mellon Foundation ran heaviest to fund new institutions to train people to cope with the country's deteriorating cities. It funded studies by the Brookings Institution and endowed Catholic colleges. The foundation provided ten million dollars in one burst to create the School of Urban Planning at Carnegie Tech. Another program provided money enough to medical school deans to supplement the salaries of doctors in teaching positions. What became a massive effort by the foundation created the Mellon Fellows for Urban Affairs, to set up pilot projects in three metropolitan universities to develop technicians to work in cities. Heavy contributions kept flowing to the University of Pittsburgh and the West Penn Hospital.

Benefactors suffer morbid backlashes, they detect ingratitude everywhere. Godheads are notoriously impatient, the quickest of all to conclude that nobody truly understands. Disappointment blights the nerves. Whatever the explanation, such touchiness shows most around those who see the commanding figure day by day, off guard, most intimately.

"It's true," Connie says, and sighs. "I don't think he was well, really, the last ten years of his life. He worked so. Rightly or wrongly, he burnt himself out. You expected a stroke any day.

"When Dick made up his mind, nobody was going to change it. When I disagreed with him, it was an issue. I would say, 'Well, why did you ask my opinion?' I don't think Dick ever held a grudge. He would apologize if he felt he was wrong."

Their marriage by then? "*Rocky* is the best I could say about it," one relative admits, taking the usual view. "They found a way of reconciling their differences, they weren't going to get a divorce." R.K. would refer, sometimes, to A.W.'s humiliation. Others intervened, forcing choices. They stayed together.

The years turned over, strenuous with the overwork and bouts of heroic leisure acceptable to Dick. Periodically, en entourage, the couple would reconnoiter the Yukon or British Columbia and take likely specimens of black bear and grizzly bear, of Dall sheep and phantom sheep and bighorn sheep, of moose and elk. R.K. kept horses in England and Ireland. He emphasized his "timber-toppers," jumpers. There was some competition between himself and Paul to see whose 'chasers did better—not much was said about this, but both followed carefully.

So there were trips abroad, and summers in a house Connie selected at Woods Hole, where Cape Cod shoulders into the Atlantic. The Cape meant little to R. K. Mellon—in Massachusetts he became merely another businessman summering. He didn't like sailing.

Moving around seldom helped. "In many ways Dick remained a very nice guy," somebody close summarizes. "He did have problems with his wife. Both of 'em had to win each thing. They fought like hell. We'd go to lunch, and he'd pull this apart, and that apart. He was a prima donna. He had this big plantation, Pineland, a twenty-thousand-acre rectangle along the Flint River in Georgia, and it became the finest place around from the standpoint of quail shooting.

"They took people down there. They were both great shots, although maybe Connie was the better shot. They always kept track of the quail, who killed the most. In all the times I was down there I never knew them to shoot together in the field. They switched off guests."

The holdings around Ligonier remained pampered home territory. "Give Rolling Rock hell!" was scrawled onto R.K.'s calendar at six-month intervals. He rode its clipped pastures devotedly, stood with his grounds keepers and argued until they convinced him that there was no other solution except to cut off trees. The solid pillared homestead at Huntland Downs was gradually assuming an institutional, a testamentary atmosphere. Halls off the entrance were painted with hunting scenes, and along the walls of the basement gun room a dioramic taxidermist had set each specimen of wildlife that Dick or Connie had taken in the North against an appropriate backdrop. Two unique household pets frisked in and out—Lobo, half dog, half wolf; and Tahltan, a spotted little animal with beaded onyx eyes and a brush to impress the onlooker with its Indian-fox parentage.

With Dick so busy, activities at the Club slowed down, gave up a lot of new-rich exuberance. R.B. had bought back A.W.'s investment in Rolling Rock before he died—the best deal *he* ever made, A.W. would claim. Some drag hunting continued, its stalwarts still flapping their scarlet coattails before the rumps of their hunters while hounds in packs circled the paneled countryside, their flagging cry reawakened each time the newly laid spoor grew pungent again, its drying rag replenished with a splash of fox urine. On special occasions real foxes were imported, and R.K. rode out, astride again as Master. Such romps became uncommon. Those years were over when a horse could collapse of a heart attack and roll on Mellon, as his big dappled gray gelding Windsor had in 1935, and R.K. would squeeze himself out from under the carcass, brush off a slightly bruised shoulder, and take the incident offhandedly as part of another muddy afternoon.

The important sporting event after the war became Race Week, when the Club sponsored the Rolling Rock International Gold Cup Race. This began in 1935, in memory of R.B. The steeplechasing events themselves took place in early October on Wednesday and Saturday, but Race Week occasioned a society revel. Ligonier draped its shops with bunting, Pittsburgh department stores redid their windows with tableaux of the chase, and local hotels mounted hunt balls for transients. Members of the Ligonier coterie staggered dinner parties for prestigious out-of-towners. The Pennsylvania Railroad put on special cars to haul the thousands of middle-class Pittsburghers who otherwise rarely caught a glimpse of the town's elite to jam the Rolling Rock grandstand. Mellon subsidized this happily; his jumpers were making a record in competition. Trophies in his basement included the King of Spain stakes and the Grasslands International, this last with hallowed Glengesia. Glengesia had also placed a very respectworthy fourth in the premier English race, the Grand National

Steeplechase, and his Alike and Pink Tipped were internationally
respected. Yet here too Dick's accomplishments were undergoing a
faint, shadowing chill. By 1948 Paul Mellon had become the leading
American steeplechase owner, his schedule commitments to the important tracks too demanding to ship his jumpers to Ligonier.

Perhaps there were other reasons. Paul appreciated a party but,
after a week of toasting the racing results, pickin's around the Club's
rustic taproom didn't promise that much. The story was printed of
one "well-known gentleman rider and trainer" from Virginia stranded
at Rolling Rock after Race Week who doggedly kept himself "merry
and festive." He did, ultimately, show evidences of "wear and tear."
The concerned Alan Scaife arranged for the man's overdue transportation home—in a van which belonged to the "local sporting
mortician," Roy Sibel.

The rider and trainer awakened during the trip. "Who are you?"
he demanded of the mortician. "And where am I?"

"I'm the undertaker," his companion said, "and I have my eye
on you."

By then Sibel's eye was undoubtedly fastened on numerous local
pooh-bahs. Saturday nights became notorious. "It was quite a sight,
you'd drive over to Rolling Rock for dinner, and by ten o'clock half
the captains of American industry were staggering around in there,"
remarks one younger Mellon, part of the New York flank. Nobody
quarreled with that. "My difficulty with Rolling Rock," Leon Higby
says, "is that I don't drink. Everything at Rolling Rock begins with
a cocktail party. If you live there, it's every day." Connie and Dick
Mellon rarely looked in weeknights, but weekends were different,
a time to ease the weight, and drinking helped Dick recover the playfulness friends remembered. As he and Connie circulated, people
enjoyed the byplay, the hints of relaxed marital teasing.

R.K. did try to lighten things up during business hours. Power
made it awkward, that fixed flat gaze and features so hard to interpret could turn what started as a shy man's leg-pull into circumstances
which became . . . belittling, embarrassing to people. The U. S.
Attorney General, for example, had given the family ten years to
liquidate its dominant interest in either The Aluminum Company of
America or Alcan, the company's Canadian affiliate. Early in the
Fifties the option started pressing, and Dick Mellon ventured at a
meeting of T. Mellon and Sons that he himself tended to favor the

disposal of the American firm. Others understood the joke, but the devoted Van Buskirk, says one T. Mellon governor, "fell for that, and believed it until the very last minute."

R.K. wasn't above contriving with servants and underlings. Late in the Thirties, according to one source, Dick signed a remodeling contract on a cabin in Ligonier with Adolph Dupres, a tough local builder whose mother had worked as R.B.'s cook. Dupres did an outstanding job, and at a startlingly low figure. Others in the Mellon circle soon convinced themselves that much of the lumber had come from projects Dupres was completing for them, and one, Alan Scaife, became so stirred up about the whole thing that he allegedly involved the I.R.S. Dupres quickly moved on, but every December after that R.K., who continued to admire many aspects of the family, reportedly sent his chauffeur, Ed Burns, to Dupres's new home to present a Christmas turkey.

A convivial fellow, Burns understood his master well enough to play along spontaneously. "R.K. often sat up front," George Wyckoff remembers, "and as we were moving along he'd suddenly glance over. 'Say, Ed,' he might comment, 'we're going to have a bank meeting this morning. Should we increase the dividend?' " Ed grunted some answer, and whatever it was appeared to convince Dick. Wyckoff knew the routine, but the effect it had on others in the car—some curious for years about how the Mellons actually operated—was well worth watching.

Driving in with Dick had pluses and minuses. "We'd leave at six-fifteen and get here before the elevator operators," Wyckoff says. "Still, my damn train took over two hours, so every once in a while I'd call him up and ask him whether he wanted company. He'd say, 'OK, be over here by six-thirty.' I got there five minutes early, and he was already waiting on the drive, looking at his watch. This became progressive. He'd still say six-thirty, but each time he'd get there earlier, and I'd get there earlier. In the end I was getting there at ten after six, and he finally said, 'God, let's call this thing off, it's getting out of hand.' "

"He got up early, and he was in bed most nights by eight-thirty," one intimate says. "Connie, she had no life, no life whatsoever. She makes no bones about it. She used to laugh at everything, and do as she pleased. . . ." The same good friend can remember stopping by Huntland Downs for a Christmas drink. "He was so uneasy. A servant would show you through and there they'd be—the men all gotten up in uniforms. R.K. in his general's outfit, of course, with all the ribbons. Young Dickie was going to Valley Forge Military Academy, and was wearing whatever they issued him there. Pross in a Boy Scout getup. We'd stand around talking, and after a while R.K. would sort of draw me aside, and he'd say: 'I didn't actually want to wear this, but you know how boys are about dressing up. Dickie wanted it.' Then later I'd hear Dickie mutter, 'Goddamn this silly uniform.' "

The children would remember these regimental Christmases. "Dad, of course, was a military man," says Prosser, the youngest—R.K.'s replacement, insofar as anybody could be. "He always exerted a lot of self-discipline, and he expected a lot of discipline in anything you did." Prosser's mannerisms are pedantic; he rattles on compellingly, his expressive hands flopping around in front of him to wheedle up conviction. His head is smallish, quite jerky and simian. His nose snubs. Some gray is invading the blue-black of his perfectly parted hair, so tight and formed-looking that it might be a toupee, although clearly it isn't.

"I'd say we weren't an unhappy family," Prosser judges. "Everything was strict but fair. You have to have rules. If you have a lawless or ruleless society it's no good. Rules *are necessary*. And then it makes life better. If you don't like the rules, don't play the game. If you walked in at eight-fifteen, and dinner was at seven-thirty, you didn't get dinner. One day I complimented him on a new shirt. I got chewed out. It was not a shirt, it was a blouse. He hated gossip, small talk. He was always willing to listen, if you had a problem, but so often his mind was on other things . . . Mom was easier to talk to, she would drop everything. . . .

"I'd say Dad taught much more by example. He loved to be outside. He wanted you to teach yourself, to learn by observing. He could identify every tree in the forest, every animal track—" Prosser's hazel eyes labor to illuminate his point. His hearing is noticeably impaired, the result in part of decades of shotgun competition; he strains to respond.

All R.K.'s children hark back to well-entrenched eulogies. Persevering did them good. "I used to tell them, 'There are four of you, you're all from different parents, you've got to get on with one another,' " their mother recalls. The children seemingly understood. Cousins emphasize the isolation of such a childhood, the growing awareness of having no part in the adult life of your family, while distrusting outsiders, who always want something.

"Our having been adopted made no difference to any of us," insists young Connie, younger of the girls. "Our parents were our parents, and that was that. We were quite unalike in lots of ways, and yet close. Maybe even closer than other children. My kids fight all the time. I only fought with my sister over who got in the bathtub first. We were nicely told, 'You're here, you belong to us, come tell us anything.' So we did. I've never regretted it. I consider myself very lucky."

Exalted survivors, waifs after mysterious storms. "Life was very simple," Connie the younger says. "It was not something you would think of as something connected with the Mellon name. When my parents were home they were there, for anything and everything. We had our pets. Dogs were always running around, and nature was of enormous interest. There was no big deal about meals. If you worked in the garden you got fifty cents for a morning's work. We seldom spent a night with a friend, although sometimes a friend might come for supper. I suppose that later on Rolling Rock was a large part of my life. When I got sick of it, I would just run home, uphill and downhill. . . .

"Normal—you went to the doctor, you had dancing classes which you hated, then whisk, off to boarding school. I knew my father was dedicating himself to the process of rejuvenating Pittsburgh, making a crummy filthy city into a neat, clean, workable, attractive city. But even now if you plop me into the middle of Pittsburgh I wouldn't know where I was. It meant a long car ride, and, at the end of it, the dentist."

Through each child's testimony the parents loom—instructional figures, attempting to listen carefully, to commend or disapprove, before one or another leaves and the household can again relax into the less demanding routines of servants and housekeepers. R.K. seems immeasurable.

One encounters this awe even secondhand. In 1960, anxiously, a buddy of Dickie's named George Melville Henderson looked in at Huntland Downs and, bumping into R.K., blurted out the hope that the two of them might have a word whenever the father's schedule

From right, front: Prosser, young
Constance Mellon Burrell, their mother

Huntland Downs
MRS. CONSTANCE BURRELL

permitted. The son of a minor postal employee, Henderson had been taking out Cassandra, the Mellons' elder daughter. R.K. ushered Henderson through.

The thing was, Henderson told R.K., he and Sandy had talked a lot, and with the parents' permission they actually would like very much to marry each other. Sometime.

Mellon contemplated George Henderson unnervingly. Then, offhand, he recalled the occasion on which Alan Scaife had asked for Sarah's hand. R.B. was reading the newspaper at that moment, R.K. observed, and he had put the paper down slowly, and gently said no, and gone to bed.

Having aroused Henderson's interest, R.K. then made it clear that he personally had no objection. The two were married in September. Cassandra is an earthy, generous-hearted, domestic-minded girl with an allergy to horses, which is a break for Henderson, who prefers bridge anyhow. The marriage has lasted—uniquely for that generation. Henderson saw all along that he had better build a career for himself, and became a very successful underwriter and stockbroker. "You wouldn't catch me in that nuthouse on the thirty-ninth floor," one relative quotes Henderson.

He and R.K. got along. George remembers coming home one afternoon soon after their first child arrived. It had been extravagantly
carsick, and threw up all over George's lapels. While Cassandra was
mopping up the car, her husband went ahead into their house to get
things ready. R.K. was sitting there, waiting. He looked Henderson
over. "I hope you don't come home every night in this condition,
George," he finally ventured, evenly.

R,K. clearly tried. He once told Henderson that he was his favorite
son-in-law—a plaudit George cherished until it occurred to him that
just then he was R.K.'s only son-in-law. In time, George says, "he
asked me to call him Dick. It would start that way, right here, in the
voice box, but, by the time I got it out, somehow it had invariably
turned itself into *General Mellon*."

2

One problem with command, that near the top, was the recurrent
nightmare that somebody with an extra star or deeper, fringier epau-
lettes might descend on Pittsburgh, and bust up everything. This
would be Paul. Paul's shadow was fugitive during the initial decade;
before the Fifties ended, it started to sharpen and enlarge. Affiliates
sensed a reason.

Bunny spits it out. "Stoddard Stevens! He's Paul's father figure.
Whatever estrangement and loneliness I have in this family is because
of him. They're all afraid of Stevens." Bunny's facial hollows deepen,
and the intensity of her emotion on this point stirs tremors into her
feather-cut ash-blond hair. "Stoddard keeps Paul busy. He writes him
a sort of menu of events. If it weren't for Stoddard Stevens, Paul
Mellon would be a happy man today."

Complaints about Stoddard Stevens aren't limited to Bunny—various people grouse, although most aren't devoted particularly to
Bunny's welfare. Many dismissed Stoddard's involvement as a natural
calamity, unanticipated as the Old Man of the Sea's plummet through
those palmetto boughs to weave his shins around Sinbad the Sailor.

Suddenly—there Stevens was. Paul struck upon Stoddard while
maneuvering among factions once David Finley retired in 1956 as
director of the National Gallery. Finley's successor, insiders assumed,
would be the Gallery's ebullient and well-connected chief curator,
John Walker. Walker's promotion looked assured—a boyhood friend
of Paul's, a lodger at I Tatti and quite a favorite of Berenson, who

would pronounce Walker the most charming person alive, a promising enough youngster to justify a job recommendation from Kenneth Clark to David Bruce. Then Walker's fortune snagged. Shortly before Finley left, the mercurial Chester Dale became the president of the Gallery.

Dale preferred somebody else. He demanded Huntington Cairns, the orotund Platonist Donald Shepard had recruited from the Department of the Treasury and installed in 1942 as secretary and chief counsel. Chester's lifetime of manipulations, first in the bond market and later as an art collector, left him with lots of corner moves. He "rattled his will," as Huntington admits, hinting to other directors via a "circulating minute" that unless Cairns prevailed, the Gallery might forget Dale's matchless fifty-million-dollar French collection. David Finley wanted Walker. The circulating memo never made it around, and steamy little David reportedly carried his case to the Gallery's designated chairman pro tem, Chief Justice Earl Warren. There were personal allegations.

In hopes of mollifying Chester, Paul, who had rejoined the National Gallery's board in 1945, jumped onto a train and visited Southampton. Chester liked Paul—he patronized Paul's earliest efforts to collect the Impressionists, and passingly, Walker reports, had come "to look on Paul as a son." Dale met Paul's train, expecting him where the parlor cars mashed to a halt. Paul hailed him from well down the platform; characteristically, he'd ridden the coach. There were several meetings, and over the course of these Chester Dale's attorney, one Stoddard M. Stevens of Sullivan and Cromwell, drew Paul's sidelong attentions.

Stoddard Stevens, even then, was no young man. Veins etched the puckers of his face; his stare of experience was clamped in powerfully between two enormous jugged ears, either one of which, properly fricasseed, might comprise a meal. It happened that Stevens, through clients, carried over some familiarity with business in Pittsburgh, and even could remember, "when I was a young whippersnapper, not even a partner in the firm," the pleasure of taking a meal in that legendary little private dining room in the Duquesne Club with David Reed and A.W. and R.B. and W.L. and Bill Moorhead, after which they ritually "sat around and matched for the lunch. I was glad not to be included in that because my pocketbook wouldn't have stood it at the time." Stevens enjoys these reminiscences, planted in his chair behind a big solid desk in one of the larger offices Sullivan and Cromwell maintains

Stoddard Stevens
STODDARD STEVENS

at 48 Wall. The air is musty, everything dignified browns, the sort of redoubt that's honeycombed with communicating staircases. The spines of editions behind glass look regularly oiled. Steel engravings, dull corridors. Foster Dulles litigated here.

"When I met Paul Mellon," Stoddard Stevens says, "he seemed to me a very pleasant young man. He was perhaps forty-seven or forty-eight. He'd been away a lot. Paul is, I think, a very unusual fella. A very sensitive man, at that time very shy, shyer than he is today."

Mellon picked Stoddard consciously. "He came along just at a time when I realized I needed that kind of help," Paul says. Stevens had a reputation for knowledgeability about the shaping of estates to accommodate "third sector"—institutional—philanthropy; what impressed Paul initially was Stevens' adroitness at manipulating rambunctious Chester. John Walker did receive the directorship of the Gallery; Chester Dale cooled down, and left his treasures after all, and Paul was close enough to gauge the diplomacy *that* exacted. Personally, Stoddard was refreshing. "He didn't beat around the bush," Paul saw. "If he thought I was doing something wrong he'd say so. Generally people aren't forthright. Your employees, your personal friends—they want to do what you want. I've never had that trouble with Stoddard."

As for the rest? "Sometimes Stoddard's crankiness is overdone," Mellon will allow, "but that's the way he is. Stoddard Stevens is a sort of watchdog person. Being such, isn't it better to be a fierce watchdog than a mild watchdog?" John Sawyer, head of the Andrew Mellon Foundation, rounds this off neatly: "Stevens—there's a sort of interesting curmudgeon there. He's a vigorous, forceful guy, retired from our board last June. I recognize a sort of gnarled quality there. He's a fortress for Paul, Paul has used him as a sort of massive barrier against intrusion."

For that, at least. "Stoddard Stevens is really Paul's creature," says another, very close to events. "When Paul doesn't want to do something he gets Stoddard to refuse to countenance it. He's thought things out. For example, Paul is not really shy at all, he has simply found it to be in his best interests to appear to be, not to respond, to look quite blankly and forbiddingly at people so as not to have to respond to their demands. It's part of his repertory. Have you ever seen Paul when he doesn't like somebody or somebody bores him? He just sits there, saying nothing, and his eyes get larger and larger, and glassier and glassier. . . ."

Let Stevens blister dreams. In January of 1957 Paul presented Stoddard a fifteen-page memorandum, fully schematized and subparagraphed, which represented Paul's own thinking then about a number of his responsibilities. Mellon was almost fifty; he understood the folly now of promiscuous good intentions. Planning alone trapped results. Page 2, for example, gets after Mellon's devotion to one stubborn concern: "The principal consideration here is that I believe strongly some well-supported or endowed foundation or institution should be conceived to rectify the overemphasis on the physical sciences in Education. In other words, to strengthen the Humanities through education, research, publication, scholarships, grants for original work, grants to schools and colleges, etc. It seems a generally accepted truth among humanists that of all humanistic learning, the Greek and Roman Classics of Literature, Philosophy, and Science have been most neglected, and that of these, a return to and study of Hellenic thought and Philosophy is at the present time most essential."

Such reflections had earlier driven Mellon into St. John's College to "fill the gaps," and underlay the attempt in 1947 by a "Paul Mellon charitable corporation" to endow for four and a half million dollars a "new liberal arts college and graduate school" near Stockbridge, Massachusetts. But external donations lagged, projections rose, administrators jockeyed, and plans were "laid aside for a year at least," a Mellon spokesman confessed, lamely, "to wait and see whether building costs will drop."

They wouldn't. Paul subsidized St. John's; he still felt there was a need for something to revitalize the classics. Mellon delegated Huntington Cairns to poke around Europe and attempt some opinion sampling among the acknowledged great. Cairns sounded out Eliot, and Toynbee, and returned fired up about All Souls at Oxford, in effect a sanitized faculty corpus unencumbered with undergraduates. All Souls had already inspired Abraham Flexner to found the Institute for Advanced Study at Princeton, so Flexner advised Mellon's project. Paul's neighbor on Whitehaven Street, Mrs. Truxton Beale, was convinced to leave the Old Dominion twelve acres; the foundation added five milllion dollars of endowment.

One listing on Paul's 1957 "Others to Consult: ?" chart was Nathan Pusey. Nate was a Greek scholar. Informed of Paul's plan, the president of Harvard came down quite emphatically against the original proposal—the effect would be to strip senior classicists out of American academia, where they were rare enough anyhow. "Paul said, 'OK, you do it,'" Pusey recollects. Harvard assumed the administrative obligation, and in effect the Center for Hellenic Studies took shape as a Junior Fellows program, where, in Pusey's words, "harried young fellows trying to get out their first books could escape their squalling kids" and concentrate for a year in cottages behind the low, Doric administration building. Stoddard approved such tidiness of means and ends.

The Bollingen demanded revamping. "Bollingen Series now publishing Collected Works of Jung, etc.," Paul's memorandum notes. "The books began under aegis of Old Dominion Foundation, but new Foundation formed because Counsel (D. D. Shepard) believed risky to Old Dominion through possibility of obscenity (books) or subversion (books or grantees)—i.e., might become 'controversial.'"

Notoriety has already singed their exposed reputations. Despairing of the Pulitzer Committee, Allen Tate approached Cairns in hopes the Bollingen might provide money for a poetry prize administered by the Library of Congress. Paul agreed; Huntington reserved the Cosmos Club for a presentation dinner. "I hope the award ceremony will attract some attention," Cairns remembers telling Tate. Tate suspected it might. The recipient was Ezra Pound: liberals unleashed a media storm, there were key articles which labeled the entire enterprise a fascist "plot" to promote Pound's reputation by Mellon and Jung. Paul would not renege. "As far as that went," Cairns says, "Paul knew very little, and Jung knew less. Pound's always been nuts, since he was Yeats's secretary."

Paul started the Bollingen with three million dollars, but as its program developed it came to require a supplementary million a year.

"Paul put in Gulf stock, that sort of thing," comments Barrett, no financier. He himself looked after their recherché publication programs in anthropology, philosophy, aesthetics, ethnology. They projected the Series as one hundred numbered publications, many in several volumes. Fellowship money was dispensed to thirty scholars a year, quite frequently to academics over forty-five who needed the help to finish the book that assured their tenure. Paul himself, Jack emphasizes, usually "read the material. He remained immensely close to the growing interests of the Bollingen. . . . He felt it was a very personal project, dedicated to one idea, which shouldn't be changed into other hands." Titles ranged from *Mythological Papyri* to *Jewish Symbols of the Greco-Roman Period*, in twelve volumes. Except for the flabbergasting vogue of the Wilhelm translation of *I Ching*, such publication involved losses. Paul tried to stay two or two and a half million dollars ahead of the bills.

Under Stevens' fearful prodding, they eased this off. In 1961 Pantheon Books quit publishing the series. They'd respected their promises; now, during March of 1967, Paul inconspicuously presented Yale with Mary's books and manuscripts on alchemy and the occult. ". . . in 1969," according to the Bollingen's 1975 catalog, "the Series was given to Princeton University Press to carry on. The Foundation is inactive."

That was the year Congress dynamited the foundations. Its reforms owed everything to Congressman Wright Patman, chairman now of the Banking and Currency Committee of the House of Representatives, still red-eyed about "Mellonites." He dubbed the Bollingen "an organization that seems to specialize in spending thousands of dollars abroad for the development of trivia into nonsense," and cited a study of European "chthonic traditions" of the Middle Ages as well as "Acquisition of data on important proto-historic entrepôts. . . . Congress certainly cannot complain if the entire Mellon banking family assembles in one of their Pittsburgh mansions each evening for a roundtable discussion of the origin and significance of the decorative types of medieval tombstones in Bosnia and Herzegovina," Patman announced. So long as the American citizenry wasn't obligated to "give the Mellons tax-free dollars to finance their exotic interests."

It was undoubtedly years since R. K. Mellon remained awake after nine to ponder Serbo-Croatian mortuary styles, or exclaim the unappeasable cravings of medieval man to munch on soils. Patman's objections still carried. Regulations emerged from committee which required the expenditure of half of each new capital commitment during the year of its donation, and constricted foundation activities.

All this seemed hardest for Mellon to explain abroad. "One of the first things I was asked to work out for Paul," John Baskett says, "was some way to get his authority here, Basil Taylor, to accept some money. Basil wouldn't. So Paul finally convinced him to take a salary to run a little foundation in London to publish British watercolors."

"The Paul Mellon Foundation for British Art and British Studies was funded largely by the Old Dominion," Paul muses, "and to a certain extent the Old Dominion kept track of it. We'd find money from time to time as they needed it. They'd submit budgets. It wasn't too closely watched." Taylor now might occupy himself subsidizing publication of neglected fine-arts manuscripts, underwriting special exhibitions. One day John Walker approached Paul and proposed that he, Walker, attempt a series of subsidized monographs about the major British painters. "That's a marvelous idea," Mellon responded, "but not for you. For Basil Taylor." With that, Baskett maintains, both Basil Taylor and the Paul Mellon Foundation quickly "came to grief. Basil soon was very excited about developing a Dictionary of English Art, in many expensive volumes, and after a bit the cost projections got up to perhaps a million pounds. Paul certainly hadn't expected it to mushroom like that."

Stoddard bridled. "Taylor was very indignant about what he regarded as Stoddard Stevens' obstructionism," Baskett says. "But then, Basil sooner or later had a falling out with everybody." Mellon foresaw the rest. "He'd send me something," Paul says, "and either he'd forget to include the price, or possibly the dimensions, so I finally wrote him. I said, 'Basil, with all your work on the foundation, maybe you shouldn't be working on the collection so much.' He wrote me back a four-page closely written letter, and it was sort of insulting. I called him, and he calmed down, and everything was all right for another six months or so. Then later he got upset again, and he wrote me that he was resigning from the foundation. He wanted a civil service job. It was impossible for the Old Dominion to set up a pension fund, but it was understood that he was going to be taken care of."

Nevertheless, Taylor quit. Baskett and Dudley Snelgrove pitched in with collecting chores. Colleagues remember Basil dawdling—bleak, indecisive, lips jerking with tensions—about the bookstores of Leeds. Taylor's "depressive complaint" sharpened. In 1974 Taylor killed himself.

The foundation survived. Tightened funding requirements after 1969 provided Stevens his rationale to excise this carbuncle. By that time plans were already approved for the New Haven shell for Paul's magnificent British collection. Perhaps Yale would assimilate the London foundation too. "Yale's administrators were terrified of owning this foreign presence," recalls Christopher White, director of studies of the renamed Paul Mellon Centre in Bloomsbury. Paul affixed a five-million-dollar endowment, and pushed it over. English trustees fumed—one labeled the move an interference with Britain's academic freedom, and there was unsuccessful opposition when Paul, who had earlier won the Franklin medal at the Royal Society, came up in 1974 for the Order of the British Empire, honorary knighthood.

Generosity usually proved treacherous. "My father used to say, never do a good deed, it will always come back and haunt you," Mellon told a black-tie mob the night the museum at Yale finally opened in April of 1977. His sniffle reverberated. "Paul takes more stuff from people like Kingman Brewster at Yale," George Wyckoff says. "He knows deep down, and he gets burned up, but he doesn't show it." What worked on Paul, throughout years of construction, was how the administrators at the university cheerfully, even impudently, took whatever he tendered, pleaded unceasingly for more, then ignored his intentions. Roughing in, George maintains, "they never showed *Paul* the layout of those first-floor shops or the plans for the library. He discovered all that much later, when he got there. . . ."

Yale wanted a teaching instrumentality, supplemented by a financial larder into which its faculty could dip for traveling fellowships and grants-in-aid. Mellon wanted a gallery. His English collection was gaining value fast, up from his forty-million-dollar outlay to approach the hundred-million-dollar level. The original gift, twelve million dollars, wouldn't provide important services. "From the start I kept asking questions," says Charles Ryskamp; as director of the Morgan Library, Ryskamp dealt with housekeeping trivia day after day: "What is the gardening and maintenance bill going to run, what about the light bill?"

The building, Louis Kahn's last, wound up much smaller and of far less academic utility than Yale's administrators expected. Paul's donation rose reluctantly, then stopped at eighteen million dollars. At one point disagreement would reach an intensity which forced the philanthropist to stage-whisper about the District of Columbia as an alternative site. The summer of 1976, alarmed at administration presumptions that he or his estate would automatically pay budget shortfalls, Mellon wrote Brewster to propose "fervently" that the name of the institution, which started out The Paul Mellon Center for British Art and British Studies, be altered, with significance, to the Yale Center for British Art.

There was something else. Paul deleted all references to this from his ultimate draft, but he was now incensed by what his activist young museum director, Ted Pillsbury, forced to the surface as regarded Yale's treatment of the endowment assets: "Without seeming carping, I hope, I would like to point out that, when my original pledges of money and works of art were made, no special effort was made to explain to me or to my advisors that such large deductions would be made from endowment income for investment services and general University administrative costs."

Pillsbury—his cherubic temples ablaze—gets into the numbers. "The attitude around here was always that Mr. Mellon was there, he'll bail us out. When the money was originally requested in 1967, it was simply sent up. The university then put it into a pooled mutual fund, after siphoning off an investment charge, a service charge (six point nine percent), and, once the building was in, a maintenance charge. And after that, the money does poorly, the yield gets pretty low. I've been digging up all kinds of questionable practices, ways Yale has discovered of finagling. They try to make us pay for services which we simply have not requested. We got a voucher not long ago for a ten-thousand-dollar withdrawal for grounds maintenance. To mow the lawns. If we had lawns. We got that reduced to five hundred dollars."

Yale is remanding funds. There still isn't enough; the Center opened primarily on Paul Mellon's promise to replace the deficit its first five years. "What would you do," Stoddard Stevens challenged Pillsbury while he and Ryskamp were interviewing the passionate

At Yale—Paul Mellon,
Ex-Prime Minister
Heath, Jules Prown

administrator the winter of 1976, "if, once you were installed in the job, you discovered that Mr. Mellon wouldn't give the Center one penny more?"

"You really want to know? I'd resign."

"Well, I think that's a good answer," Stoddard Stevens admitted.

Not that Mellon surrendered all available leverage. For purposes of income taxes, the English collection goes over to New Haven a batch each year. This sets Yalies pondering. Where would they be if, after all the hoopla, *The Dort* and *Hadleigh Castle* and several of the Stubbses wound up on walls in the East Building of the National Gallery? Where Paul is president, to which he devotes three-quarters of his time? Would Yale provide Paul a repository into which to empty his attic? "I used to think Jock Whitney was shy and Paul Mellon was modest," Kingman Brewster is quoted, "but now I'm coming to think I had it turned around."

As chief executive officer of the National Gallery, remarks Director Carter Brown, "Paul Mellon has an office here. He takes this role very seriously." The completed East Building, apart from doubling exhibition space, will provide for an unrivaled 300,000-volume library for art scholars. Berenson's lifelong vision, a re-created Alexandria. I. M. Pei's airy, modern trapezoid is sheathed in pink Tennessee marble just like the neo-Classical mother structure. Like A.W. earlier, his son stays close to financial dispensations. "Paul Mellon has been very sophisticated about the way in which these grants have been made," Brown says. "He usually is pretty canny about acting too quickly or getting us into anything too complicated or tricky which

Thomas Beddall
THOMAS BEDDALL

The National Gallery (top),
The East Building (foreground)
NATIONAL GALLERY

may come around and hit us later on. He has a great feeling about the quality and dignity of this place."

Wasn't this Paul's birthright? Here *he* exercised judgment. "Stoddard was a member of the building committee," Mellon reminisces, "and he said we ought to leave the Study Center until last. Leave it unfinished, and see later on whether the money was still there for it. It was a good idea, on paper. The trouble was, our people said, if you don't do it as you're going along it will cost three or four times as much later. It got so that the amount we were saving, $800,000 as against something more than $90,000,000—that was ridiculous. We talked to Stoddard. He agreed by then. . . ."

It had become characteristic of Paul—without changing his intention—to bide his time until facts converted Stoddard. Paul abhors personal confrontations; anecdotes he embroiders gleefully often concern resulting mishaps. One Paul especially likes memorializes his sojourn in a hospital after a trivial operation. He'd reserved a room; a very militant nurse barged in each morning to direct his gargling. There was a blue and obnoxious fluid inside the sizable bottle that dominated his night table. Mellon refused to object. One afternoon the nurse dropped by and discovered the bottle was all but empty. She demanded to know which mouthwash he'd brought. Paul brought no mouthwash; the stuff, it developed, was Windex an orderly left.

These things kept happening, though much less frequently whenever Bunny was along. Is anybody really interested in how he acquired his British nickname, Watermellon? One morning in 1969 he'd joined the Duke of Beaufort's hounds late. His mare was skittish; she shied at jumping, and before he was able to overtake the pack Paul found himself planing down her neck and into a couple of feet of very frigid ditchwater. His hat floated off. Paul abandoned the muck and remounted, miserably. "It was embarrassing," he admits, "and it was desperately cold. I wanted to go home but I thought they'd say I was afraid of their ditches. And actually I *was* afraid because the mare disliked jumping them. But finally it got so cold I didn't care what they thought, and I left."

Owlish behind dainty bifocals, Mellon very nearly giggles. A WASP Woody Allen. He considers another martini. The roles one plays! Paul belies this personally—there is a sinewy jauntiness much of the time, and powerful horseman's hands. Once, on a bet, he scaled the front of his bookshelves and squeezed himself into the uppermost tier, seven feet up, squared off, staring out, his formidable nose overhanging like a gargoyle's beak.

Humor mimics the anxieties. Paul shows, like Andrew, symptoms of universal stage fright, awareness of too much power. This takes its expression in his exaggerated unwillingness sometimes to push on people. "Paul doesn't just call and say, 'I want this done by one o'clock,'" Bill Wissman observes. Wissman coordinates the financial side. "You never get those calls. He'll say, 'Bill, would you have time to do this for me?' He's so darn thoughtful. You wouldn't think he would notice things, but he does. Everything."

The key with Paul is establishing the intervals. "He doesn't like people opening doors for him," Wissman says, "or helping him on with his coat, or keeping after him about things. The way I look at my relationship with him, he knows where I am, but if he's away we don't call him and say, 'Is there anything we can do for you?'

"Don't misunderstand that. We keep him informed. He takes part in the planning also, he's busier than any three of us. He's very well-organized, he has a slot for everything. Just keep in mind that R. K. Mellon went to the office every day, but Paul Mellon goes many places."

Many places. There are, Wissman notes, a pretty steady two hundred employees rotating through the payroll, and these may range from exercise boys at Belmont to Pearson around Pittsburgh. There are balanced staffs—the Oak Spring office, a suite presided over by Tom Beddall in the Kiplinger Building in Washington, the Paul Mellon Collection supervisors on Whitehaven Street. These coordinate with Baskett and Day, with the National Gallery professionals and experts at Yale, with racetrack managers and stallion syndicators.

While copilot Art is settling Paul's fifteen-passenger Gulfstream II into an approach pattern over the Antigua airstrip, and the beloved Walt is wedging back into place the seat cushions after once again demonstrating to Mrs. Mellon—whose only brother died in the wreckage of a private aircraft—that nothing is smoldering, Paul is just capping his ancient Parker pen—every component of which except the part he pinches to write he has replaced over the years—after composing another of the extended, gracious, quietly probing little notes he favors. Paul is constitutionally tolerant. This, too, has limits. "There's quite a strong autocratic streak," one associate suggests. "He knows what he wants when he wants it. I've seen him with people who didn't do what he wanted. It's quite frightening. He can be very cross. He's a man of strong feeling. He will be very loyal, and stick by people, but once it's broken, and he loses confidence, you've had it."

That would be understandable. "Attention to these interests is a full-time and at times exhausting job," Stoddard Stevens maintains. What Stoddard admires most is balance of temperament: "He is highly educated, he is sympathetic, thoughtful, generous, loyal to his friends, intelligent and has a good sense of humor with an underlying sense of shyness. I have never met another person who had *all* these qualities to the extent that he has."

3

Once Stoddard got oriented, it only made sense to investigate the personal side of Mellon's affairs. Estate planning seemed overdue, and Mellon was agreeable: "Before I knew Stoddard, George Lockhart in Pittsburgh, a very fine lawyer, did Ailsa's and my legal work. Then I began switching over to Sullivan and Cromwell, and after a while I persuaded Ailsa to let Stoddard take a crack at her will. He talked to her, and I talked to her. We got that settled a year or so before she died, which was a very fortunate thing."

Not everybody was pleased. Outsiders made Dick wary. Wyckoff was being supplanted. Bunny was notably miffed. Stoddard received the blame for Paul's having denied her a house in Paris, largely on the ground that owning the residence might make him subject to unpredictable French taxes. "If I say to Paul, I'd like this and this, Stoddard Stevens will see that it is not done," Bunny Mellon rages. "Always wants to pry into everything, into my life. I have my own lawyers."

It wasn't just herself. "You realize that both of the Mellon children have independent income," Bunny says. The holdings of both—via hundred-million-dollar trust instruments—come down in part from A.W.'s bequests, and partly from Paul's. "Paul has no strings. He's been very generous to my children, of course, and set up a trust for each of them, but I limited it. I learned from my father that there is a limited amount of money that can bring joy. You have to reach out a little.

"It's hard with children who are on the same economic level. They simply don't *have* to listen."

Mostly this means Timothy. His stepmother remembers Timmy as an extremely gregarious *little* child. But removal to boarding schools can have a smothering effect, and once he finished at Milton and got a political science degree at Yale, Tim's manner was smoldering, if with an attentiveness which does not conceal distaste. "Tim really is *so* much like his grandfather A.W.," George Wyckoff marvels; the parallels here go beyond the sallow complexion, the delicately carved features, the uncompromising jaw. There is an absoluteness, a curtness with small talk, an apprehension of events so locked into ethical focus any disagreement seems futile.

"I applied to law school in New Haven," Tim says, impatient with personal detail, "and spent three days there. Didn't like it. Then I walked down the street and enrolled in the department of city planning. The reason I didn't stay in city planning as an occupation is that it turned out to be more politically oriented than I expected, less to do with architecture." Computers interested him; he got a job and worked for three years at the Yale computer center, and then, in 1969, went in for himself. Nobody among the Mellons had quite tried that for precisely a century. Tim sold his services. He developed an array of systems programs for small computers, time-sharing arrangements, to fit the needs of little educational institutions. Rumors passed among relatives that he was operating from a pickup truck and already was earning in excess of the fifteen thousand dollars or so a year he and his wife require.

Timothy himself can't see why this should surprise people. "I can't find fault with anybody who wants to be comfortable," he concedes. "I live comfortably. Enough heat, enough food. As far as I can see,

Catherine, John Warner
JAMES R. MELLON II

Tim Mellon
TIMOTHY MELLON

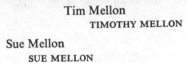

Sue Mellon
SUE MELLON

the more people you've got around you the more you have to worry about them. You spend more time worrying about them than doing the things yourself. We've got a housekeeper who comes in three times a week and does most of the laundry."

"He has fallen heavily under the influence of his wife, who does not have much time for us as a family," says one cousin, a bachelor. "She doesn't really grasp that you can no more get out of this club than you can get into it." The two got married in 1963 after meeting at a party Bunny threw in 1957 for Tim and Stacy junior. Sue is a sweet person, a Bryn Mawr graduate, earnest; the hope that marriage might "bring Tim out" guttered soon enough. Sue clearly wasn't overwhelmed by seignorial life-styles. She ignored the pictures, and this hurt Bunny. Onlookers pronounced the girl rather a knobby little thing, with all that blue-black hair and something of a musty, Slavic look, accentuated by alarming sincerity.

Paul's man in Pittsburgh now, Nate Pearson, also advises Timmy's foundation. He dismisses random talk. "Tim lives the way he does because he's just built that way," Pearson says. For some years now the pair have occupied a two-bedroom house upon a point of land along the Connecticut coast in Guilford. They sail a boat Tim helped to design. They share a Mazda. She does the cooking, which is allegedly superb, and weaves and designs jewelry and works hard on projects involving Tim's foundation, the Sachem. This too rouses comment. "Are you aware that the head of Tim's foundation is now a *colored* man?" one Mellon retainer asks. "It's strange!"

The Sachem Fund's executive director, Ernie Osborne, conjectures that Susan and Tim live plainly because "they're very concerned with the whole energy issue as a social problem. They're worried that they might use up more than their share. They ask, as individuals and citizens, don't we have to make some sacrifices?"

The Sachem Fund directs its million or so a year of Tim's trust income into a kind of social ecology—efforts to redress the balances where vested-interest power has become abusive. "The Sachem Fund tries to do its work in any area that is screwed up," Tim comments. "A major grant to me is one that has a lot of effect."

One early Sachem allocation was $7,800 to the American Civil Liberties Union in 1970 to bring a preemptive civil suit against the Mitchell Department of Justice, which had recently rammed through a badly cowed Congress the District of Columbia Court Reform and Criminal Procedure Act. This authorized a court to jail suspects for sixty days without trial to assure the "safety of the community"—the "preventive detention" procedure. "A thing like that is so blatantly ridiculous it jumps at you out of the newspaper," Tim remarks. Osborne immediately made inquiry, and found that although "the Washington ACLU chapter had people running around and yelling and screaming, no foundation people wanted to touch 'em. We read about it, and we went after them. The whole thing was incredible to us—it wasn't an awful lot of money they were looking for." The suit went in, the Supreme Court nullified the procedure, and after that most of the hysteria-induced "law and order" provisos with which Congress had been doctoring the Bill of Rights since 1968 dripped off the laws like fever perspiration.

Sachem money subsequently funded a feminist law firm to initiate class action over the credit issue, underwrote an inquiry into squalid Navaho housing conditions. Grant holders explored probationary alternatives, counseled adolescents, provided experimental facilities for the brain-damaged. As Osborne gained experience Sachem offered vital clearinghouse services for combined foundation studies like the attempt to forecast social side effects of the enormous public-works water project known as the Tennessee Tom Bigbee, where predictions of barge traffic and provident organization of cooperatives might yet improve the existences of some of the country's poorest people. With sympathetic philanthropic entrepreneurs like John Simon of the Taconic Foundation, Sachem helps guarantee "high risk" minority enterprises.

Who makes these decisions? "We vote," Osborne says. Sometimes the others disagree, but "Sue and Tim are a very close couple. A *very* close couple. They both are interested in ecology and energy, and in that sense they feed off each other. At times Sue may be more strident on some particular issue. But Tim's hardly ever strident about anything." The money flows through. "I may have technical title to an estate," Tim says, "but I don't really feel it's mine, personally. It's more of a responsibility than an asset. I can't just go sell some of the Gulf stock. I'd have to file with the S.E.C. And if you can't sell your own stock— It's more like money in a savings account. Dorsey, the chairman at Gulf, called me one day, and I had a long harangue with him about Angola." Tim had instructed Pearson to vote his securities against the management. "Dorsey told me, 'There are a lot of Communists running around over there.' I said, 'The way to do it is not to play the typical colonial company and support the corrupt government.' I don't even buy gas from Gulf anymore. They've got such crummy-looking gas stations."

Tim's politics, at times, seemed worse than arbitrary to other family members. He'd given money publicly to the campaign to rebuild the Bach Mai hospital in North Viet Nam when hostilities were fiercest. This was an embarrassment to his brother-in-law, John Warner, subsequently Secretary of the Navy. Warner isn't a man to harbor any grudges. "Tim has a good mind, independent, good habits," Warner says. He is a tousled, rawboned-looking fellow, a lawyer years earlier at A.W.'s old defender, Hogan and Hartson, fifty, with just the sonorous all-things-considered official's delivery to complement his pipe. "I suppose that I have to say I wish he had participated a little more in family affairs," Warner frowns to admit. There is a cassette recorder whining on the table—his years of service in the Nixon Administration have made John sensitive about quotes. John's divorce from Cathy has recently been finalized, and before anything else he intends to convey his admiration for everybody in the Mellon family. He admires Paul devoutly: "I have been with him many times fox hunting, and I have seen him performing with great style, and stamina, and perfect etiquette. I think that everything he does—eating or drinking, his personal habits, his dress—is done in a modest manner. I have never seen him overindulge in any way." Might that sound stiff? Warner's voice drifts lower. "Of course he thoroughly enjoys a laugh," Warner divulges. "A laugh of the sort men enjoy out of the presence of the ladies."

Warner married Paul's daughter in 1957. "In certain ways," Jack Barrett says, "Cathy really is very like her mother. An independent thinker. Now she is separated from Warner, whom she actually married very young"—Barrett's observation is often of such a subtlety that it can pass without disturbance through virtually any subject, like quality piano wire— "if perhaps thoughtlessly. An enchanting though somewhat difficult person. Three adorable children."

The children are teen-agers, and Cathy is openly worried about what breaking up housekeeping will mean for them. She is an unassertive woman, and as matters go the breakup is without savagery. After their formal separation Cathy herself moved into the little frame Georgetown house next to the big brick place she occupied with John. The children are in and out. The big, rich, defiant Brockhurst portrait of Mary overlooks the cluttered rear library. Cathy agrees with John that disagreements about the war in Viet Nam damaged their relationship badly. "I'd have these arguments with John. I'd say, 'But I'm right.' And then it would turn into something else."

One senses that Cathy—until her recent remarriage to Ashley Carrithers, at least—struggled to reorient herself. "I hate to spend my income," she says. "It's easy to do, though, it's hard to get out of the habit if you've grown up that way." Her gifts are large but anonymous, recently through her Island Foundation, very often to medical groups or Indians. Part of the uneasiness with Warner came from his thumping political ambition. "I'm not very social," she confesses. "Although John and I used to have"—she opens her thin palms upward, a craziness/hopelessness gesture—"*dinner* parties. Then John and I got into the horse business, and that became one more thing we argued about. It seemed a little too much like what people would expect. I'd say, 'If you're going to run for the Senate, don't expect me to give those teas.' And he'd say, 'All you have to do is sit there while I'm on television and look pretty.' "

Just thinking about that evokes a historical sigh. "I have lots of friends who are divorced, and now are starting to do things we wouldn't have done ten years ago. Like changing my name. That's another argument I have with my father. I'd like to go back to Conover. I like the name. My father felt it would be too much trouble, too difficult to explain to people."

Warner was reportedly overbearing during their matrimonial years, but after the divorce he found it within himself to abstain from judgments. Gratitude blends with understanding. "When the time came, during the later stages of our situation, when we had to face up to the fact that the marriage had to be terminated," Warner says, "she looked at it as comparable to the loss of her own mother. She did not want to thrust on her own children a parallel loss.

"And at every stage Paul Mellon remained the *perfect* father-in-law. He gave me an absolutely free hand with respect to taking care of the children, using the financial resources made available by himself. And he was *very* generous to me. Through his generosity I am now able, and will be able, throughout my life, to pursue a career of public service."

Warner shared these thoughts in October of 1975, not long after assuming the chairmanship of the Bicentennial Commission. He was quite enthusiastic about organizing that. His romance with Elizabeth Taylor had yet to begin.

"Cathy?" Stoddard Stevens reacts, "I don't feel I know Cathy at all. Personally I find Tim an attractive sort of a fella, very intelligent, at least he's well-read. Paul sees him rarely. He asks me sometimes, 'What's Tim been up to lately?' Tim was a very good student, although he has never had any interest in Paul's affairs in any way, shape or description. Married Sue Tracy, a girl from out our way." Planning for the children was completed a long time ago. At Sullivan and Cromwell, other concerns press harder.

4

What bunched Stoddard's hackles was all those posturings around Pittsburgh. To avoid all that! Whenever Stoddard pressed, Paul affected a true rentier's disinclination to get in close, a kind of humorous shrug, not unallayed with earlier humiliations.

Nevertheless Stoddard made headway. Paul's 1957 memorandum touched on the personnel—"Nathan Pearson is assistant to George W. Wyckoff, in my personal office; also a Director of Carborundum.

They and *one* bookkeeper attend to all of my personal business in Pittsburgh. . . ." But was this economy? Stoddard made Paul reconsider. "Now, I had respect for Wyckoff's ability, his business acumen," Paul says, "but when it came to a change of management, how would he be protecting my interests?" Stoddard pushes this further. "I doubt whether in this day and age these fellows need representation on boards. The days of conspiracies are over. Ever since the little fellow hopped up on J. P. Morgan's lap things have been open, open, open. Let's suppose he was a big owner, and he had a representative on the board, and the representative said things weren't so good. What can he do? After all, his representative is only one man, he can't do anything like throw the management out. He can't sell, because now he's got inside information. I think Nate Pearson is an excellent director, for example, but as for forwarding Paul's concerns, he would be mighty ineffective. He can only attempt to cause the corporation to flourish."

Back in the office George wasn't that busy. There were some municipal bond issues to watch, an occasional industrial borrowing. Whenever Paul went overboard on paintings, or operations around Rokeby boosted expenses for a while, Wyckoff checked the advisability of taking out a short-term loan, or possibly selling stock. He retained outside people to invest Ailsa's surpluses. Wyckoff showed Paul's flag, and that was important, but keeping him around to monitor R.K. and make the directors' meetings scarcely justified the salary. Stevens served on boards himself. Most directors were window dressing. After the Andrew W. Mellon Foundation was under way Stoddard proposed to Paul and Pusey that the three of them get together before the actual meetings and work things out and tell the others how everything would be. When Pusey said no, Stoddard was mystified and provoked.

He'd visited Pittsburgh enough to see how things worked there. The evening the Scaife Gallery opened, Paul gave a graceful little speech which began, "I am a Pittsburgher." He was as much a Pittsburgher as John Kennedy was a Berliner—symbolically, hit-and-run. Jack Barrett would remember visits to New York by Adolph Schmidt, full of swarthy intensity, who ran the vestigial Mellon Educational and Charitable foundation in Pittsburgh and also went onto the Old Dominion's board. They always needed money for western Pennsylvania colleges, Barrett recalls, and "Schmitty was always bringing that up. We'd say, 'But isn't the E and C helping them? Why put it on the O.D.?' That's the way it used to go."

Paul gave out West, that wasn't the point. His concerns were cosmopolitan—retaining Stevens was simply the first of a series of moves to institutionalize the shift. In 1968 Paul bought the building at 713 Park and moved his accountant, Bill Wissman, to Manhattan. Stoddard restructured the wills. "George Wyckoff was very close to Paul at one time," Stevens observes, then picks another subject. Stevens is eighty-four. All relationships are transitory.

What Stoddard had hoped for wasn't so much an unpublicized détente with Pittsburgh as something more direct, perhaps a more aggressive pattern of connections. He'd spoken up promptly as re- garded that T. Mellon boondoggle: "T. Mellon and Sons was really a fiction," Stoddard explains, "in that it had no assets except its office furniture, its lease on the thirty-ninth floor. When I first saw it, it seemed to me that it was not wise. The public had an idea it was the Mellon group sitting down and conspiring to control this and that and the other thing. When, as a matter of fact, it was not there. They were all paddling their own canoes. The boys down the line, the help- ers and employees who also became the 'Governors'—they had an interest in keeping it alive because it gave them some dignity."

The approach Stevens preferred is abundantly clear: "I think some- where along the line Paul just wasn't interested enough to go out and make the fight to take over from Dick." Stevens all but sighs. "I was meeting a man who had never been in business, was bored by business, had a very keen mind, it seemed to me at the time it would be better if instead of just signing on the dotted line, he knew what he was doing, who was running what." But Stoddard is realistic. "The only thing he's ever done is go on the bank board. Because I suggested it to Frank. I said, 'He's a big stockholder, he ought to be on the board.' That hasn't turned out as I hoped. After all, bank meetings are a bore."

The centennial history of the Mellon bank includes a diplomatic paragraph or so, which touches, hopefully, upon the accomplish- ments of A.W.'s son. There is a picture. An effulgent studio pho- tograph represents the scion in a nicely tailored pinstripe suit of a much earlier period, his ear cocked out and one of his eyes noticeably astigmatic. A gentle if pixilated demi-smile humanizes Paul's features. For unintentional contrast, the compilers of the volume have included across the page a cut of two of the bank's regular executives, "shown in a recent loan policy discussion," typical saturnine early risers. Along with his charitable work, the squib notes finally, Mr. Mellon is "a very active and influential Director of the Mellon Bank."

What interested Paul more out there were problems of philanthropy. The sympathetic Adolph Schmidt helped focus the income from the E and C—already in the process of liquidating its forty-million-dollar endowment subsequent to the earlier public-health grant—into humanistic enterprises like a community theater and liberal arts professorships at the University of Pittsburgh. Paul's 1957 memorandum proposed the transfer of ten million dollars from the foundation's assets to "Strengthen Mellon Institute of Industrial Research and provide endowment for basic research, chemistry and physics."

Even before Stoddard intervened, some kind of fundamental decision-making obviously couldn't be deferred. "The Mellon Institute was just plain antiquated," George Wyckoff says. He was a trustee there too. "In this day and age for the Mellon family to be subsidizing research for Union Carbide and the Koppers Company—that didn't make sense." Paul himself wasn't watching. "They made me a trustee in 1930," Mellon recollects, "when old Dr. Weidlein was actively involved. He was lively, and I used to enjoy those meetings. I sort of forgot about it after I left Pittsburgh. Wyckoff used to tell me a little bit about it from time to time. After Dr. Weidlein retired they decided to have an appraisal made. They set up a committee—Dr. Conant, Lee DuBridge, James Killian, Bill Baker of the Bell Telephone labs." At this point even the Koppers Company had withdrawn its hundred full-time researchers, and competitors like Arthur D. Little were complaining to government agencies about the Institute's tax-free status. Almost every important corporation had laboratories of its own now, many of them developed under Institute supervision. "The scientific advisory board produced a report," Paul continues, "which said we ought to get into basic research. They decided we needed twenty million or so, and Dick and his sister each put up five, and the E and C produced the other half. I got a little interested and began to go to meetings."

The Institute bought land twenty-three miles east of town and commissioned the Bushy Run radiation laboratories. "Dick had a great friend," Paul says, "Matthew Ridgway." After the Korean war General Ridgway was available, and "Dick and Alan Scaife decided he was the man to run the place. Then they got a good research man,

Paul Flory," who divided the authority as executive director of research.

"Then, to my horror, there got to be a big schism between Ridgway and Flory." Resentment became so intense that the pure-science people and the applied-science people wouldn't sit together at lunch. "Flory got the impression that the family was going to put up a lot more money," Paul says, "and do away with practical research. He felt that research for the benefit of the companies was beneath anybody's dignity. It got terribly political between him and Ridgway. Nobody was paying any attention to us, so one day we had a meeting." Paul had become the chairman of the trustees in 1960. "It became very obvious this thing wasn't going to work. I got along with Flory, I used to hold his hand. So I got Ridgway to retire a year early."

The horrified Dr. Weidlein remembers a lot more drama. "That's where the Mellons went wrong," he emphasizes. "They raised that endowment, and used the money to import a lot of old, worn-out scholars, who got in here and loafed. The whole thing blew up. Real friction developed, and one day Paul came to the board meeting, and afterward he took Ridgway aside, and he told him, 'General, you're fired.' I had to rush back from Europe, and it took six months to get the place on any kind of a footing. Finally they put Flory in charge. Then R.K. got into it, and he fired Flory. It caused a terrible split."

"At about that time," Paul goes on, "I got Stoddard involved." Stevens became an Institute trustee; George Wyckoff, caught in the middle, went off the board. Stevens terms his own opinion of R. K. Mellon as "a little hard to describe. I think that's a professional matter I would rather not go into. I saw a great deal of him at that time. . . ."

A few minutes later Stevens drops a hint. "I knew Dick as a boy around Rolling Rock," Stoddard reminisces. "I was a counselor to West Penn Electric, the railroads, Babcock and Wilcox. I saw him occasionally at board meetings. He was very often shooting birds when I was around. Not really too bright a fellow. Had half a semester at Princeton. There was an adviser, a lawyer, Van Buskirk, kind of an alter ego for Dick. He made the snowballs for R.K. to throw. Dick Mellon was quite an emotional man. He'd got to the point where he thought he was a lot more important than he was."

Stevens' appraisal wasn't lost on the increasingly edgy General. His emotionality was heightened as it became clear that Paul now intended not merely to relieve himself of Ridgway; he intended to dump the Institute itself. This looked past enduring. Their temple to invention, the technological dream factory Dick and his father had watched going up, driven out to Oakland each time a monolithic limestone column came in by rail, all shrouded, to stand there together while the enormous booms babied the gigantic shaft of wavering stone into an upright position between base and lintel. What could Dick do, at that point? "Once Paul got involved," George Wyckoff says, "R.K. couldn't bring himself to attend the board meetings. He left the Institute to Alan Scaife."

Nor was Paul indirect. "Paul came to town in 1966 to attend a party for me to celebrate my eightieth birthday," Dr. Weidlein notes. "People were amazed at the way he handled himself. He got off a good one at my expense. There was some mention of work I'd done in ductless gland research, and about the extracts from camphor, then Paul spoke up and he said, 'The best thing this man ever did was to extract greenbacks from the Mellons.'" Such gibes were affectionate, but they were rarely idle. After assuming the chairmanship Paul wheedled the sour R.K. into building up the trustee list with dignitaries like DuBridge and Killian, added his son-in-law, John Warner, and converted the impressionable Dick Scaife, Alan's son.

They looked into mergers. "I was convinced it was best to have Carnegie Tech take it over," Paul says. "They were much stronger in the sciences. One of the problems with that was, the Mellon Institute always had a loose connection with the University of Pittsburgh. Weidlein and Denton were trustees over there, and they had a fit. Dick certainly wasn't happy—he just didn't like anything where the family did not have direct, tight control. That was all right until things started costing more and more. The day of the private institute was over. The backing was not going to come from the family, at least not from *my* side of the family. The Institute would have a much better future under the university, certainly that was the consensus of the new board of trustees. But Dick couldn't shake these strong family feelings, and frankly, he just didn't understand the problem."

Stoddard worked on transfer details with Dick's man, Joseph Hughes. Hughes reflected the General's terminal anxieties. The new, merged entity was slated to be called the Carnegie-Mellon University. "Why should we presume to link our name with that of Andrew Carnegie?" R.K. broke out during one aborted negotiation. "At one

Behind Carnegie-Mellon: R.K., Paul, Dr. Weidlein
PITTSBURGH *Post-Gazette*

stage Dick and I got together and had some kind of a meeting," Paul says, "and we finally set a date to make the announcement. Then, the morning before, Dick called, and he said, 'Well, I've had a long talk with Denton, and he says that this is going to upset people all over Pittsburgh.' We had to drop the whole idea, temporarily." Not that Paul rested. "When we really had it settled that the merger would go through, we had another meeting," Paul says, "and Dick said, 'What we should do now is to get Jake Warner,' who was the chairman of Carnegie Tech, 'to take over here too as head of the Institute. Then we can go on from there.'

"Well, Warner was about to retire, and he obviously couldn't do both jobs. I said, 'All right, Dick. I've done all I can. I'm through.' And I started to walk out.

"Dick said, 'I didn't know you felt so strongly about it. We'll do it as we settled.'

"This was a typical sort of thing of Dick's," Paul concludes. "He was a touchy sort of person, a little bit dictatorial. He didn't like people telling him what to do. On the whole, we were friends." By now, of course, simple relationships were harder. "The last couple years of R.K.'s life," concludes the pitiless Stoddard, "he was punishing the martinis."

The family got together a last capital gift, the institutional equivalent of the golden handshake. In July of 1967 the Institute passed over. Paul Mellon was invited to add another LL.D. and to address Carnegie Tech's last unaffiliated graduation. It was his responsibility, announced the commencement speaker, "to give free, unsolicited, high-sounding advice to the graduating victims." Paul recommended experience, firsthand. "There is immense pleasure to be had in wandering in the rich fields of archaeology, history, poetry, philosophy. And go, I beg of you, to the original sources . . . to Thucydides or Gibbon . . . to Bellini, to Titian, to Vermeer, to Turner. Read *their* words, see their own brushstrokes and colors. There is no intellectual or emotional substitute for the authentic, the original, the unique masterpiece."

Still, Mellon added, "someone quotes the sculptor Giacometti as having said, 'If a house were on fire and I could take out a Leonardo or a cat, I would rescue the cat. And then I would let it go.'

"It is life itself that counts. . . .

"Just as there is no substitute for original works of art," he proceeded, "there is no substitute for the world of direct sensual experience: the red and gold of October leaves . . . a shiny black grackle among the white blossoms of a honey locust, the brilliance of the summer stars, a child's smile . . . salt spray . . . fresh coffee in the morning, trout fresh from the stream. . . .

"And sensual feeling as well, the warm sand on your back and the warm sun in front . . . for those who ride horses, a handful of leather and the wind in your ears. And though I have left it to the end of my catalog—perhaps the most important—the thrill and mystery of touching—of love between a man and a woman. . . .

"And they are all interrelated—the experience of the senses, the flash of imagination, the act of creation, the long, intricate, delicate experiment, the poem, the symphony, the laughter of children, the snowflake. Just as man is interrelated with all other living creatures. Just as science and art and life are interrelated and inseparable, and form the whole circle."

1

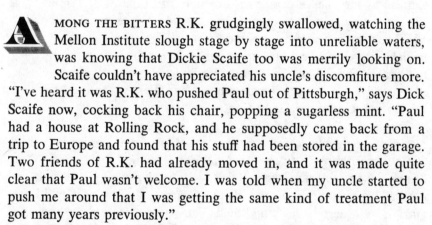

MONG THE BITTERS R.K. grudgingly swallowed, watching the Mellon Institute slough stage by stage into unreliable waters, was knowing that Dickie Scaife too was merrily looking on.

Scaife couldn't have appreciated his uncle's discomfiture more. "I've heard it was R.K. who pushed Paul out of Pittsburgh," says Dick Scaife now, cocking back his chair, popping a sugarless mint. "Paul had a house at Rolling Rock, and he supposedly came back from a trip to Europe and found that his stuff had been stored in the garage. Two friends of R.K. had already moved in, and it was made quite clear that Paul wasn't welcome. I was told when my uncle started to push me around that I was getting the same kind of treatment Paul got many years previously."

Scaife broadcasts his feelings. Nobody would deny that Dick Scaife is definitely the most unbuttoned family member around, easily the most controversial, unabashedly the most impetuous. He started circling R.K. early. Even during his adolescence he resented the run-around his father, Alan, got; he dug in young and resolved to correct the situation. "I remember one party Sarah and Alan gave at the Waldorf," Matt Mellon says. "R.K. got up and started on one of those long-winded speeches of his. It didn't take any time before Dick Scaife broke in and said, 'OK, wind it up, we've heard enough of this nonsense.' Believe me, he got called onto the carpet the next morning."

So animosities were prickling. Soon after Alan Scaife's untimely death in 1958, R.K. had assured his sister that he "did not think it wise at this time" to put young Dick upon the board of the Mellon

Institute to replace his father. As regarded T. Mellon and Sons, R.K. would shortly advise Paul, "Its head should be a Mellon if he is qualified. I do not feel that Dickie could at this time or perhaps even in the future be president of T. Mellon and Sons."

Scaife brought this partly upon himself. "He was," says Cordelia, "a funny spindly little guy, rather frail, very pretty—those lovely lovely blue eyes. I was four years older but enormous by comparison. I had to be careful not to wallop him. I don't think Dick began to grow until he was fourteen. Now he's a huge man."

Scampering around Penguin Court, he busied himself collecting newspapers. Tear sheets, historical front pages. As early as his years in Washington, while Alan was serving, Dick began to pay attention to details of government, drawbacks of the electoral system, the Capitol as the "nerve center of America." In time Scaife "made it a kind of hobby to meet as many Senators and Congressmen as I could."

When Dickie was nine he underwent the mishap everybody loves to mention. A riding horse threw him, then rolled on him and partially crushed his skull. An aluminum plate and rounds of expert plastic surgery repaired the structural damage, but Dick was tutored at home for several lonely semesters. Contact sports were out.

People used this. "He's like a bull in a china shop," R.K.'s old retainers would cluck, frowning over Scaife's latest, and next would come some reference to the time the horse mauled Dickie, or to the head-on auto collision when Dick was twenty-two. He does seem taurine—that compressed tow head, lowering, shallow ears laid back and gigantic across the mandibles. The wide-set sparkling eyes. An impression of limpid menace, solitary as a bullock in a pasture, twitching good-humoredly at flies.

And speculations, and inquiries. Data Scaife's detractors relished came out of his career at college. He'd gotten through Deerfield; Alan was quite eager to see him prosper at Yale. He started out reasonably, but one March night, as he himself tells it, he and a roommate "decided to have a Bock Beer Festival in honor of Dean Buck." At some point during the rout that developed, one of the revelers allegedly had his legs broken by a beer keg Scaife allegedly rolled down a flight of stairs. "It was an active evening," Scaife says now. "We left our trail." After a night in the New Haven lockup, Scaife was promptly expelled.

His sister was traveling in Europe just then, about to meet Sarah and Alan in Italy. "Father was like a madman," Cordy says. " 'My son! He's being thrown out of college!' A friend of mine ran into some headlines on a tabloid just then—'Enormous Explosion in Naples Harbor!' Her reaction was spontaneous: 'I thought, Oh, my God, Alan's heard about Dickie.' "

Ultimately Dick got reinstated at Yale. Then he flunked out. "Father was so incensed he told me that if I wanted to go to school it would have to be here, at Pitt, and in engineering. Meanwhile I'd have to hold a job. So I became a chemistry major, and worked at Gulf part time. I graduated in 1957, with a major in British history." Just back from a trip to Russia with Sarah, Alan Scaife had a heart attack and died in 1958, and Dick took over Alan's old desk on the thirty-ninth floor and began to represent Sarah's interests.

From then on R.K. would vacillate uncomfortably between efforts to console Sarah, who wanted her son on boards, and connivances to limit the boy. But the younger Scaife was much less susceptible to letting himself be gentled out of R.K.'s path than Alan had been. Dickie's Neanderthal politics especially sometimes exasperated the General. Mellon power still rested on the entente with Lawrence. Soreheads ranted, but Pennsylvania Republican leadership had developed, ever since the Second World War, along conciliatory lines. Politicians like Hugh Scott applauded R.K.'s reasoning. Democrats perceived Industry's needs; Republicans cultivated Labor support.

Scaife started taking exception. Reading, stirring up Scaife's temperament, convinced the excitable heir that each Republican accommodation carried bedpans for socialism. He became, young, an apocalyptic Goldwaterite. Dick Scaife had money to back his play. Early in the Sixties he began casting around.

R.K. felt repercussions. "I am told," opens U. S. Democratic Representative William Moorhead hesitantly, "that at one time Richard Scaife was going to back a Democrat to oppose me." Like Moorhead's own cousin, Joe Barr, the Representative was himself a product of Pittsburgh's endemic social cross-pollination. Moorhead's father was W. L. Mellon's attorney; another cousin was establishmentarian Jim Bovard. "David Lawrence called R. K. Mellon, I understand," Moorhead concludes, "and told him, 'I never messed in your political party, I don't want you messing in my political party.' This was around 1960 or 1962."

That stopped that, temporarily. Scaife's political mange spread. With Goldwater's emergence, the Republicans in Pennsylvania polarized outright into conservatives and Rockefeller supporters.

Scaife became a financial patsy for hungry Right-wingers. "Dick Scaife was most anxious to have some political weight locally," says Mrs. Henry (Elsie) Hillman, the Republican county chairperson who headed the Rockefeller contingent. "He was influenced by others to take some political steps which were not wise."

2

Later on Frank Denton would ask what made Scaife pick the directions he had. "You told me to select a guy likely to become a success, and back him, and thus I'd be a factor in politics," Scaife replied, possibly with a snort. Dick must have misinterpreted. "I'd told him I liked to pick myself a few State Senators and Assemblymen," Denton maintains, "and make some contributions, and that would leave me in a position to visit. . . ."

But Scaife had larger ideas. "In the middle Fifties I started to spend time with my sister's boyfriend, Robert Duggan, and after a while he urged me to run for County Committeeman in 1954." Scaife looked all right to the Republican clubhouse boss just then, Duggan's mentor, Jimmy Malone, so Scaife went on. The western Pennsylvania regulars appreciated his easy openhandedness. Scaife attended the Republican Conventions in 1956 and 1960; in 1964 he contributed $25,000 and tested his muscle promoting the Goldwater campaign. He went to San Francisco, as an alternate, courtesy of William Scranton.

By then Robert Duggan had started to provide the gut involvement Scaife craved. In 1963 Duggan ran for District Attorney of Allegheny County. Scaife functioned as treasurer; Governor Scranton helped out by sending in state police to conduct a well-publicized vice sweep just before the polling. Sixty-two arrests resulted, underlining Duggan's shrill charges that under the Democrats the county had become a "haven for criminals and deviates. . . ." Few were subsequently convicted, but that made very little difference. Duggan slid into office by thirty thousand votes. Dick Scaife was probably more excited than Duggan. "When I was a child I had always listened on the radio to 'Mister D.A.,'" Scaife says, "and that was the way I looked on Bob. His image around here was flawless, I regarded him as a person of the highest moral character." Duggan's style was convincing—he had a climber's touchy righteousness, which made it easier to shrug off

Dick Scaife
RICHARD M. SCAIFE

cuts, and considerate little gestures. He attended his widowed mother, with whom he lived.

Scaife smiles, one-sidedly. "Politics was more fun with a guy who held elective office," Dick says, ruminating on his Trident. "Remember, my sister knew Bob for thirty-one years. They traveled in Europe together, dated every Saturday night they were both in Ligonier. We were like two brothers-in-law, sharing the same interests—"

Cordelia supports all this. She is, at forty-nine, a lanky reclusive grasshopper of a woman, all crinkled outcropping elbows and a clean long flaring line of tawny hollow jawbone. Her very large eyes look powerful from getting through nights. Her voice is beautiful—compassionate, tear-softened, yet rippling at moments with the amused patois, the tender slanginess of her girlhood's America. "I went to Hollywood in 1947," say Cordy, apropos of nothing. "Fred Astaire was a friend of my parents. He arranged to get me on one of the movie production lots. I was going to be *discovered*. I went out and got my hair done, all nicely snapped, and then I made my appearance. But at that time the bond drives were still going on, and all the personalities were out of town. The only star around was Lassie." Cordelia almost smiles. "This is the story of my life."

One part, at least. A tidy woman, she lives very quietly these days in Ligonier in the unpretentious clapboard house, Cold Comfort, which belonged to Henry McEldowney. The touches are homey—the toilet seat in Cordelia's bathroom is speckled with decals of cute baby birds, their animated beaks akimbo. The Mercedes she drives is so old the sun is imparting a powdery cast to its bathtublike flanks. A bumper sticker demands: STOP THE STORK! This reflects Cordelia May's decades of contribution and committee work for International Planned Parenthood.

Two sizable studio photographs are positioned between the windows of her cozy living room. One is of Margaret Sanger, a very close friend of Cordy's grandmother Mary Scaife. "She was the one who put what fun there was into our lives," Cordy remembers. "She knew how to bleed every drop of blood out of life, raucous, a marvelous old rip." Miss Sanger first convinced Cordelia of the importance of limiting the population, a cause in which, along with land conservancy, she began to involve herself wholeheartedly soon after her divorce.

She'd divorced in 1950, months after her wedding. Why she attempted either seems hard to pinpoint. After attending the progressive local Falk School, then the more formal Ellis, "where I was one of the more contumacious students—I was not urged to return," Cordelia finished at Foxcroft. She attended Carnegie Tech and Pitt, where she intended to major in languages. "That's where I booted the whole career," she says now. Her friends were marrying. Young Herbert May, son of the butt of so many Rolling Rock jokes, asked Cordy to marry him. Her parents were opposed. May was a sociable fellow, somewhat older than Cordy, and, perhaps as much to escape the resounding solitude of Penguin Court as live with May, Cordy accepted. "I remember, at the time I was engaged to Herb, a friend came to call. The butler announced her, and I remember I flew down the stairs, thinking, What's wrong, nobody ever came *here* without an appointment before.

"Herb was a *sweet* guy," Cordelia says. "Very outgoing. I'm not much on parties. We were just unsuited." In the midst of the enormous wedding friends remember Cordy trailing up the aisle, her long neck bowed, her veiled face miserable. "Then I sprang this terrible surprise on Pittsburgh," Cordy says. "And announced Herb and I would be divorced. Here 'divorce' was a word you lowered your voice to pronounce. So Mother called Ailsa, the only renegade member of the family who had been divorced. Mother said, 'What does one do?'

"Ailsa said, 'Palm Beach.' "

So, "for publicity reasons," Cordy spent the next four years in Florida. "It was a virtual waste of four years," she says now. "I simply didn't want to come back here. This didn't hold anything."

Not anything worth facing. When she did return she started going out again with Robert Duggan, her other studio portrait. She'd known Duggan all along. Bob's father had been a Pittsburgh ice-company executive, who owned a modest summer house in Ligonier. Young Duggan turned up and tried to take Cordy out when both were barely teen-agers; Sarah stepped in brusquely. "Cordy's mother wouldn't let Duggan into the house," says Joseph Hughes. "Duggan was a little Catholic boy from down in the village."

After Cordelia came back these objections didn't matter. The estrangement between Sarah and Cordy had become so sharp Cordelia refused her mother's antique jewelry. She saw Bob frequently, and before long the arrangement had started that prompted Dick Scaife to think of Duggan as his *de facto* brother-in-law. Cordelia's admiration for Duggan gradually became her touchstone. "I think he was the

most wonderful human being I ever met, out of a fairly large acquaintance," she says now. "I find it inconceivable that he could do
anything less than honorable." It makes her pensive to review the
decades of compatibility. Occasionally Duggan, by then a member
of Rolling Rock, would "drag me to some party. He hated to dance.
I loved to dance. I'd dance with people, and he'd disappear to wherever
the men were talking. We didn't stifle each other."

The years exposed weaknesses Cordelia associates with inheritance.
"Grandmother Scaife was a merry drinker," she observes. "Many's
the time I've helped an old lady to bed." That remained mostly
convivial, but "Mother was a bad alcoholic. In her case the disgrace
was so awful she couldn't admit it. I'm an alcoholic. I can't touch
it. I spent most of 1967 and 1968 in New York. I went to a psychologist. We finally came around to the fact that if I drank a little
less my life wouldn't look so grim. Bob came out and talked to the
psychologist at his request.

"After that I flubbed it a couple of times. The disgrace was 'fess-
ing to Bob I'd muffed it. Bob was so hopeful, so positive. He'd say,
that's why pencils have erasers. He himself didn't drink enough to keep
a gnat alive. I saw him plastered twice in thirty-odd years. . . ."

In 1971 Robert Duggan was reelected the Allegheny County District Attorney for the third time. He won by very few votes, and his
Democratic opponent, Leonard Martino, accused Bob Duggan publicly
of racket affiliations. Martino cited a recent grand jury inquiry
throughout which several of Duggan's county detectives had pleaded
the Fifth Amendment. Among Pittsburgh's stolid rulers the prog-
nosis was in. "Duggan was a very likable chap," Joseph Hughes says.
"Scaife wanted to make Duggan governor of Pennsylvania. I told him
he was crazy, that kite would never fly. Duggan was not a big enough
man to be governor of Pennsylvania. I regretted this doubly because
Cordy was so devoted to him."

As he rounded forty, Duggan's bandstand mannerisms were accentuated by the withdrawal of his crinkly Irish hair around the
furrows of his forehead, and prissiness about the mouth. One visitor
to Rolling Rock Race Week remembers him as the announcer of the
lottery winners. His decade in office was punctuated by press releases
which decried moral decay, supplemented by fierce raids on dusky
little bookstores along Liberty Avenue, and a deepening feud with
the Democratic County Coroner, Cyril Wecht, who charged that the

District Attorney Duggan
PITTSBURGH *Post-Gazette*

Cordelia Scaife May
CORDELIA SCAIFE MAY

District Attorney's arrest of three doctors at Magee–Women's Hospital for performing unauthorized abortions was prompted by "an element of anti-Semitism." Throughout the entire decade Duggan himself never tried a case. His cousin and first assistant, James Dunn, effectively ran his office.

Among professionals, then widely, other rumors spread. One powerhouse, identified with the liberals, insists on having known "from within six months of the time Duggan was elected that he was no good. I happen to know some of the bad guys in town, some of the numbers people. I knew of the numbers payoffs. I tried to get word to Dickie Scaife that Duggan's purpose in castigating the liberals was not political. It was personal. I went so far as to invite one of Dick Scaife's friends in to talk to a couple of the numbers people. He heard the facts, and afterward it hit him so hard that when he was leaving he walked into the doorframe. One of Duggan's enemies even offered me X dollars to pay for certain 'pictures' of Duggan that were supposedly around, but I didn't want to stoop to that.

"I think they had information in Washington too. Dick Scaife had been a pretty heavy Nixon contributor even in 1968. But when one of our organization people took down the name of Jimmy Dunn as a possible U. S. Attorney for western Pennsylvania, even the Mitchell Justice Department wouldn't buy it. On the recommendation of Scott and Schweiker they appointed Richard Thornburgh, a Rockefeller man. Later everybody here thought that Thornburgh went in as part of a political vendetta. . . ."

Thornburgh maintains that Duggan attempted repeatedly to "derail my nomination." By that time, Thornburgh discovered, I.R.S. investigators were poking into sidelines Duggan's racket squad chief, Samuel G. Ferraro, had reputedly been nursing. The Revenue investigators needed Thornburgh's cooperation. By the summer of 1970 it was clear, Thornburgh says, "that their investigation was being obstructed." Ferraro had quietly moved on to a post as public safety director of Hampton Township, where he continued to do what he could for Duggan through country club fund-raisers, and in fact, says Thornburgh, it was the "trail of detectives in and out of Duggan's office which attached the first notoriety to the allegations of corruption. A dozen of Duggan's former associates had taken the Fifth by then. A drumfire of efforts by Duggan and Scaife to squelch the investigations was under way. We kept getting calls from Washington, from Mitchell's people. Kleindienst was their closest contact, Scaife and Duggan were talking to him."

To loosen up information, Thornburgh subpoenaed four of the detectives from Duggan's office, granted them immunity, and forced their testimony. There were enough conflicts to permit the U. S. Attorney to send up three for perjury. "The evidence was beginning to attract a lot of public attention," Thornburgh notes.

One wavering onlooker by now was Richard Scaife. In hopes of alerting the gullible heir, Government people approached Cliff Jones, an executive of the Manufacturers Association of Pennsylvania, just then the Republican state chairman and one of Scaife's closest advisers. In September of 1971 Jones presented Scaife with irrefutable specifics. "He showed me police records," says Scaife. "Suddenly it all made sense."

Awkward trivia kept compiling. That month, for example, a courier from Duggan's office turned over to Dick Scaife's secretary, Ruth Mohney, a plump brown envelope crammed full of fifty- and one-hundred-dollar bills. The cash, $9,900, totaled out to the precise amount, in the expected denominations, which local syndicate numbers boss Anthony M. ("Tony") Grosso would admit to passing along at two-month intervals to Duggan's lieutenant Sam Ferraro. Duggan accompanied this unfamiliar wad with a word of explanation for his campaign treasurer. "Dick," his memo read, "Enclosed are some of my staff members' contributions. Will forward their names to you next week. Ruth [Mohney] does not have to acknowledge these in writing as I have spoken to each of them individually." Scaife requested an itemized list before sending the money along to the campaign account in the Mellon bank. Of the twenty-nine listed contributors, a Pennsylvania Crime Commission follow-up demonstrated that only four could possibly have remitted the amounts in question. In fact, since 1964, Duggan had maintained a separate bank account, his unreported "Flower Fund," in the Potter branch of the Pittsburgh National to receive monies he methodically extracted from office employees according to a formula and in express violation of Pennsylvania macing laws.

This last surfaced later. The summer of 1971 Scaife was markedly uneasy. "By then Bob Duggan was spending money," Scaife saw, "as my grandmother used to say, like a drunken sailor. He bought a condominium, a yacht, put an addition onto his house, added a swimming pool. By 1971 he belonged to nine different clubs. He used the death of my mother to explain all this, the two hundred and fifty thousand dollars he'd gotten for legal work in helping settle her estate." But Sarah had gone in 1965, and heavy expenditures continued. "I'm saying to myself, If this guy is on the take I've got to find it out," Scaife recalls.

He repositions his meaty thighs against the shelf of his stomach and studies his remaining Tridents, frowning along the roll. "He'd been in Europe in July, and after he got back in August we went to lunch at the Duquesne Club. I got there early. After a while I see that Bob had come in. He sits down at the table, and I can see that things are not right. I went over what he'd acquired.

"He said, 'Well, I see they've finally gotten to you.'

"I said, 'If you mean the good guys, the noncorrupt politicians of the world, yes.'

"He asked me if I'd told Frannie, my wife. I said yes. Then he asked whether I'd told Cordy. I said I hadn't.

" 'Tell me that you won't tell her,' Bob said. I told him that if she didn't get involved I wouldn't tell her.

"He showed me records, the cost of his swimming pool and the rest of it. He claimed it actually didn't cost that much. I remember he said, 'My name's not Scaife, people don't hose me.'

"Then there was one other thing. The homosexual bit. People came to me and insisted that he had attacked them, drunk. I didn't believe it—when we were kids we'd often taken trips together, gone whoring around Baltimore, things like that. I remember one time in 1969, we'd both been out on a drunken evening, and when I got Bob home he was too drunk to climb the stairs, so I threw him over my shoulders and carried him up to his bedroom and laid him out on the bed. Just then his eyes came open for a second, and he put his arms around my neck and kissed me on the lips. At the time I thought the guy was just, you know, being friends. . . ."

Soon after the Duquesne Club lunch Duggan quit as a trustee of Scaife's Allegheny Foundation. In September, a matter of days after the brown envelope with all the hundred-dollar bills had passed through his office, Dick Scaife resigned as treasurer of the Duggan for D.A. Committee, purportedly overburdened with Nixon-Agnew fund-raising. Then Scaife appeared in Thornburgh's office, "very upset," Thornburgh saw, "at the way he had been used by the supreme opportunist of the twentieth century in this community."

In April of 1972 Scaife mentioned to Cordelia that investigators from the I.R.S. Criminal Division had asked him "all sorts of questions," and that there was a lot of "unsavory talk" about Bob around. The investigators were working on Scaife to talk his sister into cooperating. In November, Dick told his sister whatever he knew. "She could not believe," he says, "that Bob could do most of this." Duggan brushed off whatever was slowly becoming public about his financial affairs as owing largely to "poor bookkeeping practices." But Cordelia was disquieted, and at a Pittsburgh Athletic Association dinner early in 1973, when Duggan and Cordy were both in a "euphoric mood," she turned to Duggan and blurted, in front of Dick, "My brother has been telling me some rather shocking things about you. What do you have to say?"

Duggan's impulse was bureaucratic: "At the proper time I'll make a statement."

Shorn of Scaife's influence, Duggan became easier pickings. The federal investigation intensified. In January of 1972 the proprietor of an important East Pittsburgh numbers shop, Charles Navish, had testified in federal court that Ferraro had squeezed him repeatedly for five hundred dollars a month to assure police protection and, after the redevelopment closed Navish's store and cut his proceeds while he worked the street, sent over two county detectives to "arrest me. One said he was supposed to rough me up." By early 1973 Ferraro was under indictment for income tax fraud. He was convicted in November of 1973 for taking over $300,000, mostly from kingpin Grosso, although Navish and Donald ("Ducky") Cole had contributed their allotments.

By that time I.R.S. digging had revealed a secret Duggan bank account at the Pittsburgh National under the title "Abstracts, Incorporated." Thornburgh estimates that "approximately two hundred and fifty thousand dollars in cash payments found its way into it during Ferraro's salad days." Duggan himself was called before a grand jury. At his second appearance he took the Fifth. Meanwhile Ferraro was called up before a judge, offered formal immunity, and, when he refused to testify, sent along to jail for contempt of court— six years, thirty thousand dollars bail.

Meanwhile, in 1969, Richard Scaife had indulged his lifelong fascination with newspapering and committed almost five million dollars to acquire the *Tribune-Review* in Greensburg, a community in Westmoreland County not far from Ligonier. With Sarah's death Richard and his sister each came into control of significant fortunes—*Fortune* would peg the totals at somewhere between two and three hundred million dollars apiece. Scaife bided his time for months to scrutinize the managers of this prosperous little country newspaper as they prepared the editions. Then, obviously inspired by *Newsday*, Scaife swelled the editorial staff from eleven to forty workers, installed satellite bureaus around Westmoreland County, blew up the Sunday edition with weekend features, and imported an aging Hearst conservative to consecrate the editorial page. The new owner's tendency to redesign the news was unnerving to employees. He ostensibly combed the newspaper's photo morgue to destroy all shots of Nixon not smiling. After the Chilean coup, his editors say, he jerked an extended eyewitness Associated Press account of rightists butchering political prisoners inside a soccer stadium. The managing editor who built the paper, Tom Aikens, bore up for years, then resigned one day when Scaife arbitrarily threw out a routine story about the local poverty programs. Scaife's financial beneficiaries such as Ronald Reagan and Max Rafferty could depend on lots of space. On the other hand, Scaife laughingly concedes, "I wasn't very fond of Hugh Scott. When Hugh Scott came to town, that was a nonevent."

"We couldn't be bought, though," Scaife volunteers. "We don't kill stories because of the advertisers." Neighbors suspected deeper corruptions. In 1971 there was widespread indignation among petty local property-owners at the assessments an outside appraiser reached during a sweeping reevaluation of Westmoreland County. Minor holdings jumped, an average of 40 percent; the Mellons' rolling thousands of acres of manicured post-and-rail countryside, while masked in the public records by "plain yellow file cards bearing the cryptic reference: 'Special Set Up,'" scarcely budged from artificially low valuations. Two big Alcoa plants were revalued down by four million dollars, 52 percent.

Petitioning failed. Aroused, led by a stubborn local doctor's wife named Mrs. Dorothy Shope, a taxpayers' group was successful in electing Mrs. Shope and a Republican farmer and motel owner, Robert Shirey, to two of the three critical county commissioner slots. This should have put the reformers in place to abrogate the reassessment. Then, unexpectedly, Shirey joined the holdover commissioner in voting to retain the reappraisal. It subsequently became public that Shirey had received at least nine thousand dollars of his twelve thousand of listed campaign contributions from Mellon sources, the largest from Scaife himself.

Cut off from power, blocked in all efforts to examine county records, Mrs. Shope kept agitating. Shirey attempted to calm her down. One day she got an invitation from Robert Duggan, Shirey's "lifelong friend," with whom telephone records showed Shirey "in almost daily telephone conversation." At Duggan's request she visited the District Attorney's offices. Duggan's approach was reasoned, although he did not permit her attorney, who came in late, to attend their meeting. Duggan wanted to talk about Mrs. Shope's political activities. "Dottie, what will it take for you to work with Bob Shirey?" she remembers Duggan asking. She claims he proposed that she join him and Shirey at dinner "in a place where we won't be recognized."

She refused. "From that day on my life has become a living hell," she says. Anonymous telephone calls, repeated threats to kidnap her children. The brakes in her new car failed; the accident which resulted demolished it. Even in bucolic Ligonier strong-arm methods are reportedly in widespread use. Thornburgh told one reporter that "activities in the county are dominated by the Gabriel Kelly Mannerino family," with Pittsburgh ties to John LaRocca.

Scaife himself, wading in, authorized a six-part article in the *Tribune-Review* by his well-seasoned court reporter, Tom Wertz. Wertz called the controversy "largely a contrived tax revolt." Soon afterward, when a young *Tribune-Review* reporter named Jude Dippold, having interviewed Shirey, stopped by to see Mrs. Shope, Scaife ordered his night managing editor to let Dippold go. The night editor refused; Scaife fired him too. Wertz himself caught Scaife at the Greensburg Country Club and demanded the editor's reinstatement; Scaife countercharged: "Your resignation is accepted." Ten staffers promptly resigned to back up Wertz. The "Citizen Scaife" stories proliferated.

"One guy I fired for breach of confidence," Dick Scaife says. "Something the county commissioner told him in confidence he went next door and told another commissioner." Such things went differently then, under politically momentous skies. "These days editorial bias does not get into the news columns," Scaife says; then, ingratiatingly, every inch a cut-down Orson Welles: "Took me a couple of years to learn that."

Scaife enjoyed the exultation of purity restored. By 1973, around the dinner party circuit, Scaife was reportedly expressing in "loud— and sometimes salty—words, his dislike" for the embattled District Attorney. Richard Thornburgh was assisting the Revenue investigator with preparation of a "net worth and expenditure" case against the cornered official. This involved tracking down the sources of the funds in Duggan's recently uncovered bank accounts and demonstrating that salary and declared income couldn't explain the money. "We worried," Thornburgh says, "that at some point Cordy might step forward and testify that she gave large amounts as gifts to Duggan. In August of 1973 people from the I.R.S. had attempted to interview her to close off that possibility. They had an appointment set up in early September.

The day before, Duggan visited her counsel and told him irately that he did not want his wife interviewed. He and Cordelia had been secretly married in Nevada, days after the I.R.S. initially notified her.

Confirmation that Bobby Duggan had married the Mellon Heiress splashed into the headlines on November 7. It was a "simple ceremony," reports indicated, before a justice of the peace at Zephyr

Cove, quite different from the extravaganza with May. Duggan lambasted the newspaper stories, which alleged that "the two had been linked in a somewhat romantic way for many years," and which hinted around quite broadly about the timing, at just the moment "the heiress would be called by the grand jury to testify on Duggan's affairs." Wives, the presumption went, could not be pressured into testimony against husbands. "The story is sick," Duggan's public statement ran. "Its tastelessness represents to me the cheapest type of yellow dog journalism."

Richard Scaife, confided one source, "was intensely upset. He went into orbit."

Cordelia, musing, insists that her unexpected marriage to Duggan became inevitable just then, a gesture of confidence. "I had been determined not to become a politician's wife," she says. "He asked me to marry him I don't know how many times. I am not able to entertain, neither do I go out. But by that time efforts were being made to portray Bob as a homosexual. The deliberate attempt to get this around, the people contacted—I truly did not believe this happened in real life.

"The homosexual tag is one people in public life get when all else fails. It's a wretched stigma to put on someone. At that point I had a homosexual come up here. I knew him, but not well. We had a couple of drinks. I couldn't figure out the point of the visit. Finally he said, 'I know what agony Bob is going through. I don't know whether Bob is a crook, but I know he's not a homosexual.' After that I checked through a labor leader, a publicity guy, a reporter to try and find out who paid the people to spread the rumors.

"That infamous, scurrilous campaign!" Cordelia exclaims, stiff with new emotion. "Bob was the most decent, thoughtful person. When I think of the thousands of lives he bettered . . . People are always coming up to me, telling me what he did for them. Why did I marry Bob? I married him because it was the most overt thing I could possibly do to affirm my faith in him just then."

Dick Thornburgh, tracing evidence, cites nothing to substantiate the imputations of homosexuality. His case against Duggan on other grounds was pulling together nicely. Whatever immunities Duggan thought he acquired by marrying Cordelia fell away when a local district judge agreed with Thornburgh's brief that records of Cordy's financial transactions at T. Mellon and Sons were not interidentifiable with Mrs. Duggan herself, and so were subject to federal subpoenas.

Publicity intensified both in the Pittsburgh dailies and especially in columns of the Greensburg *Tribune-Review*, where Duggan and his unexpected wife underwent "prominent" coverage. The availability of Mrs. Duggan's checkbooks completed Thornburgh's presentation. "We were able to establish before the Grand Jury that she did not have cash available to her that could account for Duggan's unexplained cash increases.

"At the same time, Sam Ferraro got tired of jail and verified that he had paid substantial amounts of money to the D.A." On Tuesday, March 5, 1974, Robert Duggan was indicted by the federal grand jury on six counts of tax fraud. By then it really didn't matter. Hours earlier, under a mizzling rain, Duggan's body was found several feet from the rails of a fence on his Ligonier property, Lochnoch.

Three layers of clothing hadn't prevented the unfired shotgun barrel from scoring a visible ring mark in the District Attorney's chest. Duggan's handsome Parker shotgun had flung itself some distance, and perhaps the moisture explained its absence of fingerprints. The rain-soaked earth disclosed no tire marks or treads from boots.

Friends wanted to believe it was an accident, although a gun expert speculated at the time that, if it were, it must have happened while Bob was walking around with the automatic safety off, his finger on the trigger, and the weapon turned backward. Others speculated that possibly his syndicate associates had sent out experts to prevent the maneuvering District Attorney from trading evidence for immunity. Cordelia's suspicions were reportedly blackest of all.

Duggan's longtime antagonist, Allegheny County Coroner Cyril Wecht, performed the forensic examination and observed, dryly, that "In people who kill themselves with shotguns, the chest is the number one site."

Thornburgh's conclusions are similar: "Here was a guy who worked his way up from the wrong side of the tracks to riding to the hounds with the WASP elite. To have that exposed—!" There was some testimony later that Duggan had reserved the morning to clear out muskrats, and perhaps he had.

Cordelia was predictably stunned. "You don't believe these things are happening to you," she muttered when a reporter approached. She noted that she and Bob had spent their usual weekend together, walked around the farm, gone to a movie. He'd returned to Pittsburgh

The funeral—Cordy May in center

for the week; she'd called him Monday night. "We talked of the future. He was worried, but not to the point of being really depressed. . . .

"The only thing I am concerned about is how he is remembered," she said. Then, randomly, "I used to cadge rides with him from Ligonier into Pittsburgh because I didn't like to drive. I'd shop and catch a ride back with him.

"It would be a ninety-degree day and he would stop at Baskin and Robbins to buy a quart of ice cream for some little old lady in Ligonier he knew liked ice cream." How steady her voice was then isn't clear from newspaper accounts.

3

Scaife felt this differently, needless to say. He regretted the extent to which their disagreement about Bob had estranged his sister. So much was altered. When an unidentified automobile containing two unfamiliar men appeared to be parked to survey the Scaife home at Westminster Place in Shadyside, Dick sent the chauffeur to take the license number. The car moved off, but after that the house was kept under police surveillance awhile.

What could anybody trust? As the Sixties ended it seemed, if fleetingly, that people and ideas to which he'd devoted his inheritance were finally in command. Nixon was the man to stem the anarchy. In 1968 Scaife assumed the national chairmanship of the finance division of United Citizens for Nixon-Agnew. Tom Aikens, Scaife's onetime managing editor, would maintain later on that political lieutenants from family foundations went in all along as Dick's personal representatives to campaigns by extreme Right-wingers.

Early heroes proved disillusioning, however, and in the end even his venerated President subjected Richard Scaife to a powerful buffeting. As an important contributor, Scaife comments, "I was wined and dined at Camp David and White House functions. Remember, at this time Muskie was gonna give Mr. Nixon a pretty good fight." On one spirited occasion "we all sat around in the White House, and had a good dinner, and heard the 'give till it hurts' bit. We're all behind you, coach, all that. One guy said, I'll give this much. And another said, I'll give that much. So finally I said, 'Anything you guys need, I'll go along with.' "

Even the Watergate documentation doesn't suggest the merriment *that* loosed around CREEP. Little time was wasted. "In September of 1971," Scaife says, "Herb Kalmbach came along and said, 'We're counting on you for a million.' I agreed to do it." Scaife became a Nixon elector.

The resulting donation of $1,002,000 came in as three-thousand-dollar checks, 334 of them, to avoid the gift tax. Nixon returned to office, but about the time his confidence in Duggan began to erode, Scaife found himself wondering about both his President and another of his enthusiasms, Spiro Agnew. Scaife himself will deny the widely circulated story that he himself fired a reporter for observing, on spotting the confirmation of Agnew's resignation coming over the wire, "One down, one more to go." But he was edgy, bristled at the unceremonious way the Administration dumped Adolph Schmidt, a Mellon in-law and a genuinely humanitarian conservative, out of his post as Ambassador to Canada "without a word, even a note of thanks." He had himself turned down all ambassadorial overtures as earlier he rejected an offer to sit on the board of Gulf. Once Nixon fled office Scaife welcomed his leaving; by May of 1974 the Greensburg *Tribune-Review* had called for Nixon's impeachment.

There was one echo. "In December of 1974," he says, "the Friday before Christmas, my secretary came in. She said, 'You'll never believe this, but I have a telephone call from San Clemente, from President Nixon.'

"I said, 'You mean ex-President Nixon.' I wanted to get on the telephone and tell him what I thought of him, but I told her to tell him she didn't know where I was."

By that time, politically, Scaife really didn't either. He reconciled with Scott and reached the point by 1975 of "regarding myself as a middle-of-the-roader. I'm now enthusiastic about Rockefeller."

Dusty with political rubble, Scaife tried something else. Alan's death in 1958 had desolated Sarah. "While Alan was alive," Lauder Greenway reminisces, "from time to time they'd take a series of rooms in the Waldorf, and hire the best bands, wonderful entertainment, and invite all their old friends. Terribly nice parties. I always thought the people from Pittsburgh were as nice as some people were at home.

"When Alan went, that was a disaster! He died, and she just threw up her hands and sank."

Her seven remaining years Sarah divided between travel and philanthropy. She herself remained unpredictable—vinegary, given to withering asides, then swept by compassionate impulses. Frank Denton remembers a hop around Europe with Sarah and the Robert McClintics. "At one point she fell and broke her shoulder. She kept hidin' it, she didn't want to ruin the trip for everybody. We were in the sitting room of a hotel suite one day and I said, 'Goddamn it, Sarah, let me see the thing.' My wife was right there. We sent her back on Pan Am. She let us finish the trip in her Convair." The astute Denton touches on one abiding difficulty. "Her mind was exact, precise. In many ways she should have been a man." The impulses that tempted her to jeer at people and conventions kept prompting her curiosity, made her keep developing. One winter she investigated for herself what Larry Mellon was about in Haiti. She arrived in one of Port-au-Prince's battered taxis, and proceeded from the Artibonite Valley, alone with her native driver, up the coastal mule track to view the remains of the fortress at Cap-Haïtien during the worst of the rainy season.

Much sniffing around relics prepared Sarah for art. As the Fifties ended, Sarah "had a few things," Jim Bovard says. Bovard was the director of the Carnegie Institute, which offered the only public representation of paintings of consequence in Pittsburgh. The Bovards were acknowledgedly "constant companions" of the Scaifes. Sarah started collecting ceramics, and gave some money to the Carnegie to found a decorative arts collection.

"By then her cousin Ailsa had a wonderful collection of paintings," Bovard says. During earlier times, Sarah couldn't bring herself to regard her eccentric older cousin very seriously, but starting in the early Sixties Sarah started accompanying Ailsa to important Manhattan auctions. Whenever Ailsa liked something for the National Gallery, Sarah herself held back. She did buy Perugino's excellent *Saint Augustine* for the Carnegie after a while, and authorized in excess of a two-million-dollar bid for Rembrandt's *Aristotle Contemplating the Bust of Homer* because "she wanted to do something fine and wonderful for Pittsburgh." Sarah didn't get that, but she did compile a spread of durable French Impressionists, and by her death the art she'd given the Carnegie had run her $3,500,000.

"I found her to be a very shy but delightful person," says connoisseur Leon Arkus. "With a very *delicate* sense of humor, a very fabulous gal, warm, delightful. By the time I knew her I was speaking to a very, very elderly woman. There was always a concurrence. Very sharp, had a very good eye. When she died, it was quite a shock."

Dick Scaife got interested. He became the chairman of the fine arts committee of the Carnegie. After Sarah died he pondered an appropriate memorial, perhaps a setting for Sarah's paintings, and everybody involved decided to extend the sooty imperial sprawl Andrew Carnegie gave Pittsburgh by adding some sort of contemporary gallery.

"We had an architect who did the first set of plans," Scaife says, "Charles Luckman. It all looked fine to me, I guess it was terribly functional. Frannie was really tremendous." At one point, recalls Mellon cousin James Walton, who succeeded Jim Bovard as director of the Carnegie, he and Scaife's wife flew west to confer with Luckman as projections mounted wildly. "Luckman put us up in huge suites," Walton says. "Sent around a car to take us to dinner. We were afraid he was trying to snow us." At their audience with Luckman himself, surrounded by his battery of aides, Frannie opened her pocketbook—just then very much the doughty Middle Western matron —produced a scrap of notes, and presented, says Walton, "the most well-thought-out expositions of our problems and needs that I've ever heard."

They turned Luckman down. The granite-browed rectangle which subsequently went in was designed by Edward Larrabee Barnes, a Paul Mellon favorite. It came to enclose 155,000 square feet of floor space, not including the sculpture garden, and cost the family approximately twelve and a half million dollars. Arkus directs it. The collection is spotty yet. Her entire life, Sarah designated major bequests as "Sarah Mellon Scaife." Pittsburghers expected all along to find this graven upon her gallery architrave. Belatedly, just before its opening in October of 1974, there was a change so abrupt new stationery was embossed. The "Mellon" was dropped. It became the Sarah Scaife Gallery. Dick had had enough.

17 | "THE MELLONS-THEY'RE OVER"

1

" **H**OW AWFUL to put your faith in a thing like that and have it blow up on you," James Walton says, lamenting Scaife's political heartbreak, his reward for foddering the piranha of an entire generation. Critics saw other aspects. Jack Robin, Mayor Lawrence's longtime assistant, cites Scaife to demonstrate the "whimsicality" which very rich people often bring to public involvement. "This can be dangerous," Robin says, and R. K. Mellon, from beyond the grave, could almost be glimpsed conferring a weighty, justified nod.

The two had skirmished virtually to the end. They bickered over Ligonier acreage. Even when they agreed about something they reacted quite differently. "Later, when R.K. was not well," recalls Theodore Hazlett, the leonine attorney R.K. put into a series of public-service posts, "he began to feel very bitterly about the student activities, the social upheavals." Yet, always, the foundations he guided worked to support local universities; he recognized, as family correspondence elucidates, how much their companies needed continuing academic backup. Disgusted by anti-war demonstrations, Dick Scaife got off the board of Carnegie-Mellon in 1971, and after that Scaife Foundation support dried up.

The General was indeed suffering more than age. By then the director of the vestigial A. W. Mellon Educational and Charitable Trust, Ted Hazlett used office space on the thirty-ninth floor. He watched Mellon deteriorate. "He had an outer gruffness anyway," Hazlett says, "and to some extent a short fuse. I had to cool him once, I told him he was acting more like my father every day." Nate Pearson,

Wyckoff's understudy, acknowledges that he "didn't just walk in there and say, 'Mr. Mellon, you're nuts.' I approached with hat in hand."

One well-connected Pittsburgher who dealt with R.K. directly sums up the last half-decade. "There came a time when, after an important luncheon, his voice invariably thickened. The man *had* to have a certain amount to drink. It was always a big concern that R.K. *got* to big public functions. I myself remember drinking with him once, and he would comment, in his gravelly voice, about people like the Olivers, the Schoyers, the Reas, the Hillmans—people he, despite all the Mellon money, identified as *society* in Pittsburgh. He continued to think of himself as an outsider. . . .

"Toward the very end he had a kind of softness to him, not effeminate exactly, but a certain *moistness*. Moist hands. He was always surrounded by good-looking bright young men in middle positions. These he replaced every five years. They did his bidding. The governor's telephone would ring, and one of them would be on the line: 'The General asked me to call you, we gotta do something about the Squirrel Hill Tunnel. You know, it took us thirty-five minutes to get through the tunnel this morning. At least get some cops in there to wave us through.' "

Old friends were dismayed. "He really wanted satellites," Denton says. "Weak satellites. People who had fun, didn't bring up any business worries. Nobody got too close. I could give you names." A stroke had incapacitated the protean Wallace Richards late in the Fifties; R.K. replaced him with J. Stanley Purnell, a Gulf employee who doubled now as secretary of T. Mellon and Sons and R.K.'s liaison with Action-Housing, Pittsburgh's branch of Andrew Heiskell's national effort to upgrade slums. "Purnell was a nice guy, but compared with Richards, he was a pimple," observes one Mellon stalwart.

Well into the Sixties the inevitable happened. "He had some kind of seizure in the office so powerful it took three men just to hold him down during the convulsions," Adolph Schmidt remembers. Attendants rushed Dick Mellon to West Penn Hospital.

While Mellon was recuperating, J. Stanley Purnell saw fit to grant an interview to a local reporter—never a good idea, in view of R.K.'s allergy to press. "Dick really couldn't believe that he was physically like other people," Denton says. Mellon read the interview, riding in from Ligonier. The reporter had referred to R.K.'s setback and mentioned a statement by Purnell which made it clear that Mellon was withdrawing more and more from active business participation. "On arrival he walked into his office, found Purnell, and told him to pack his things and get out," Denton says. "This was exactly typical."

As the Sixties ended, it must have seemed to Mellon that armies were deserting. Paul wouldn't be swayed from his resolve that, should he or R.K. die, T. Mellon and Sons must no longer provide a sounding board for his affairs and Ailsa's. In 1968 Paul moved his accounting operations from Pittsburgh to Park Avenue—quietly decorated, as always, with paintings of thoroughbreds. Scaife was allegedly dumping Gulf. The Tax Reform Act of 1969 further weakened R.K. by prohibiting a donor from voting securities turned over to any foundation, most specifically his own. That same year, a big, shambling ex-Air Force captain and Notre Dame lawyer named Peter Flaherty went in on the Democratic ticket as mayor of Pittsburgh. Flaherty hadn't any interest in collaborating with the directorate of business leaders which had rebuilt the city. Regulars chafed, but by 1973 the tall cost-cutting maverick had become so popular that he was returned to office the nominee of both major parties.

The dominion was ending. By that time R.K.'s feelings were undoubtedly quite mixed. He remained, like all the Mellons, always in the world if never completely of it, his inherited skepticism exemplified by the slip to Robert Dietsch that if businessmen influenced voting "it would be the downfall of the nation." He *selected* company presidents, rarely identifying with one. "At the Duquesne Club all they talk to are each other," Leon Higby says. "They think there is a Republican tidal wave because they don't hear any Democratic voices." Mellon himself wasn't deceived. Along with the megalomania which produced "the General," there was a Platonic discomfort with Pittsburgh's flat-footed commerciality, a need to shape his life according to a keener discipline, a warrior's purposes. Hazlett recalls R.K., almost at the end, relaxed and ambling around the barns of Rolling Rock, pursuing his "research on deer and sheep." To youngsters he respected, Mellon gave his best. "I wonder how many people did know R. K. Mellon well," James Walton reflects. "He was the strong member on the Carnegie's board, the one who put me in here. He was always there with helpful hints, good advice. But never overbearing. I wouldn't say a heavy hand. A steady hand."

That was one side. Its converse appeared increasingly. "It was all black or white with Dick," Wyckoff says. "He'd blow a fuse if he were crossed." Cordelia ventures some explanation. "In his funny way I think Dick was uncomfortable with polish. Dick obviously felt inferior, insecure because Paul had a knowledge of broader matters. By God, this was his frog pond. You know that Pat, Adolph Schmidt's wife, is one of Thomas Alexander's granddaughters. She is terribly quiet, extremely well-read. We used to talk when things were difficult in the family. She regards A.W. and R.B. as a piratical team which put her grandfather out of business. R.K. didn't have anything to worry about as regards Thomas Alexander junior and his brother Ned, but he went out of his way to make life unbearable for them. What in hell gets into these guys that makes them so vicious?"

Schmidt's daughter, Helen Claire, backs all this up. "I was always wary of Cousin Dick," she says. "He could be really nice, then suddenly, watch out! He simply couldn't tolerate back talk. I'd see the way he would manipulate people. Who would be defeated, the whole posture would sort of change. Cousin Dick could accept that, use it to great advantage."

Alienation attacks the marrow. "This was a fault that Richard Mellon had," Cordelia says. "I remember he asked Mother once, 'What have you done about setting up trust funds? Of course, it makes sense for you, yours are not adopted.'" Then—flashing out, resigned, "'But I'm doing something like that.' Even Mother took offense at this," Cordelia notes.

R.K.'s second thoughts about the children owed something to developments. The eldest, young Dickie, obviously was not slated to replace the father. Dickie's manner appears evasive: a knack for sliding around confrontation, a tendency to swallow phrases and avoid people's eyes, a limp wet handshake. This impression of tentativeness is fortified by Dickie's wispy blondness, the play of pulses across his bulging temples. In bone-crunching Pittsburgh particularly he seems to lack much grip. Leaders write him off. "He's personable, but he'll agree with anything you want to say," one remarks. "Dickie's on the board of the Museum of Natural History," Jim Bovard says. "He comes to meetings once in a while."

Others claim there's more. Younger relatives mention Dickie's piquant down-and-under sense of humor, his "curator-level" knowledge of Early American firearms. He is plainly moved by memories of trips with his parents. The summer of his fourteenth year "we went for bear, mountain goat, moose," he says. "All four of us. Lived on a boat, moved through the Inland Passage, shooting along the river deltas . . ." After Valley Forge he did some Army time,

Dickie Mellon

attended the University of Pennsylvania, married Gertrude Adams, came home. After that he put in three years at the Carnegie Museum, mostly in the taxidermy department. "Then Pop called up one day and said, 'I think you'd better come down here and find out what's going on.' I came down, and found out."

"What was going on?"

"Don't ask me," Dickie replies, endearingly.

He bought a ranch on Maui, traveled widely for the North American Wildlife Foundation and Ducks Unlimited. Oceanography interests him. "To be perfectly truthful with you, Dickie is very much like Paul," his mother says. "In the sense that he does not like to be tied down to a desk, doing big business." After R.K. went his namesake became president of the R. K. Mellon Foundation, the survivor who "looks after the philanthropic, civic and cultural matters." Whenever he turns up. Friends regarded his marriage as ideally made, he and his wife perfectly suited, but that too dissolved. "Dickie just can't stick at anything," concludes a sympathetic relative. Another, also well disposed, reflects, "When Dickie gets a bit of booze in him, he'll tell you about the indignities visited upon him by the retainers, the feeling that he's a bit of an imposter."

"He's great with people," Prosser insists, junior to his brother by four years, subject like his siblings to a note of solemn, unconscious orphans-of-the-storm solidarity. "Dick's interested in areas I'm not interested in. Politics, he tries to keep up to date in local races. He can say, 'This guy has ideas like ours,' so we contribute to his campaign. Dick's very well informed in history." Dickie Mellon has lunch every once in a while with politically toughened Dickie Scaife.

As head of the recently formed Richard K. Mellon and Sons, Prosser has taken up the bulk of the load. His father anticipated this. "You'd better be good to Pross, because he's going to have all the money," Dr. Weidlein heard R.K. admonishing the others. Prosser was a wiry, jumpy teen-ager, a motorcycle nut, a good enough skeet shooter to make the finals of the Olympic tryouts. There were summer jobs gardening, working in the stables, trapping for the Pennsylvania Game Commission. Several classmates at Choate remember him as solitary and excessively earnest, "something of a wienie." Another came across him at a dude ranch one summer, still mostly by himself, hunkered by the hour behind patches of sagebrush, plinking prairie dogs.

His relationship with R.K. was something he yearned to define. "I remember one time that Dick was going to come to my house for dinner," Denton says. "He called to ask, could he bring Pross? Pross was about sixteen. Dick had a double-breasted dark navy-blue overcoat. Pross had the duplicate." Prosser started at Dartmouth, then switched to nearby Susquehanna University because he "wanted to be closer to home." He graduated in English.

Back home in Pittsburgh he broke in quickly as a bank trainee, moved along to the trust department, which "looked to me like the area I could learn the most." Prosser fell in love. At school he'd met a Philadelphia girl, Karen Boyd, and after a while "he brought her down," one solid retainer recalls. "Dick got Arthur Van Buskirk to check into her family." R.K. didn't like the reports he got. "Dick tried to talk Pross out of it," the retainer continues. "Told him he had this money in three or four trusts. Some he got principal, some he got interest. He told Pross none of his land, et cetera, would go to him if he married this girl. Told Pross he would be an outcast from the family. Pross would not budge." The inescapable cigar glows. "At the last minute Dick gave in. He put on a big dinner the night before the ceremony. I was assigned the job of looking after the mother. It was our impression that the family was kind of conceited that they had a Mellon, if only an adopted Mellon." Karen took the vow in an ivory peau de soie gown with long sleeves and a modified Empire waistline, in the Alumni Chapel of Saint Cornelius the Centurion at Valley Forge Military Academy, and proceeded to a reception in the student union, Mellon Hall, a gift of her father-in-law. At that point, her weight was normal.

Settling in, Prosser stuck with securities analysis a while. "One day," as he himself recalls, "I decided that Dad was in poor health, and I realized that somebody would have to carry the ball. As I sat over there and thought about it, I realized I was adopted, and that I've obviously been given the greatest break an adopted child could get. How could I pay them back?" Prosser pauses to phrase this carefully, still seeming at moments a squirrelly adolescent with strands of gray coming into his hair, his exaggerated Adam's apple moving up and down as if to prevent his voice from cracking. "I knew I'd better move up here." He adjusts the tinted pilot's glasses. "This was always a touchy subject. I sat in Mason Walch's office. I wanted to learn. I'd come in here and he would say, no, nothing to do. . . . If he had a major deal he was working on, I wasn't included. If he was worrying over a philosophical change in the direction of a company, I wasn't privy. Dad never liked doctors or hospitals. He was afraid of them. He wouldn't discuss these things. He would tell bear stories, by the thousands. . . ."

Gestures R.K. attempted met resistance. There was no protest when Prosser went in as a governor of T. Mellon and Sons and a trustee of his father's foundation. A year before he died, R.K. installed Prosser as president of T. Mellon and Sons; that induced in Paul "some feeling," Connie says, "that he was too young." There was recurrent talk about helping establish Prosser by getting him on the boards of major Mellon companies. Various explanations went around, but a veteran adviser points out, "If R.K. had wanted Prosser involved and the boards tried to keep him off, the whole town would have blown up."

One marriage R.K. reportedly liked even less than Prosser's was that of his younger daughter, Constance. He relished her especially, a tempestuous brunette with an aquiline richness about her features and a fondness for animals which matched his own. "I'm the zoo-keeper artist in the family," she would later remark, "the copout for not being in Mellonville, P.A." Her gifts are lavish—she has excellent recall and a knack for combining color and proportion rare even in a painter. She draws and photographs. In 1963 she married. "William Russell Grace Byers," her mother says, "was something else." Byers was an heir to the long-standing Pittsburgh pipe-manufacturing fortune, one of the great-grandsons of W. R. Grace, with an itch to explore public service. The household was reportedly pitched, combative; R.K. didn't like the side effects. He welcomed the divorce.

Months later, in June of 1968, "Mr. Mellon and I were presented with this cable going up in a lift in a hotel," says R.K.'s widow. "It said, 'Russell and I have remarried.'" Dick Mellon and Connie were in the midst of something very close to a state visit to the site of Thomas Mellon's birthplace, presiding over the sprawling family reunion old Matt had organized. "I saw Cousin Dick in Ireland," Helen Claire says. "One day he was fine, the next day he was beet red, sick, ranting and raving. They'd gotten a telegram from little Connie, who had remarried Byers while we were in Ireland." The timing was particularly unwelcome, in that, along with the fifty-two linear Mellons, a delegation of four hundred Northern Irish, including the Prime Minister, Captain Terence O'Neill, had arrived to sample the vast buffet of cold salmon and turkey between rain showers. The Ulstermen were eager to make the leaky hovel in which Thomas Mellon was born a tourist attraction to rival the Kennedy homesite. To reacquire the property, the family had given $24,000 to displace the former residents. Their guardian, old Mrs. Margaret Fulton, haggled until the Mellons grudgingly put up $24,000 to provide the most contemporary cement pigsties in Ulster. It took $250,000 to restore the environs on Camp Hill. Beyond that, Mrs. Fulton conceded, "It has been a great change for my pigs."

"We gave a great big party," Matt observes, "and all the Irish relatives we never heard of came and ate it all." R.K. had arrived in excellent spirits, and he and Connie looked around as the guests of the Duke of Abecorn. The logistics were cautious—because of the smoldering feud, the Thomas Alexander descendants were bivouacked in a separate hotel. Paul didn't make it. "That was just as well," Matt recognized. "He would have upstaged R.K. Dick made both his adopted sons come."

Dick began the visit exuberantly, at his raffish best. "Matt, why do you always have to dress like a Catholic priest?" he jibbed his cousin, turned out in academic black. After poking his head into the ancestral hovel, he turned to O'Neill and ventured, "It's so wonderful

I can't imagine why my ancestors ever left this place." Swept by a rainstorm, he admitted he knew. Matt dedicated a sundial. The parties went on, climaxed by a big alcoholic reception given by the Duke of Abecorn. By then the telegram had arrived and R.K. was off. "Dick was very sick," Matt says. "He had a terrible diarrhea. He had to make a speech in their Parliament. He told me, 'Matt, I don't know whether I can stand up.' "

Several months after the Mellons got back to Pennsylvania young Connie again separated from Byers, this time for good. R.K. was faltering. He left the General Motors board and, after fretting for years, gave up his seat as a director of Penn Central, too late, as litigation developed, to prevent his estate from absorbing a battery of stockholder suits. *Fortune's* widely circulated photograph of him and Connie—posed on the turnaround paving bricks before the aisles of shade trees which stripe the entrance to Huntland Downs—represents a profoundly fatigued man, the grooming as immaculate as ever but the face itself, pugged and defiant, suppressing a certain bewilderment. "About the best you can hope to do, I guess, with the new young, while they are making up their own minds, is to keep them out of trouble," he remarked just then. Weeks before his death, Carnegie-Mellon played host to a convention of radicals who reportedly "occupied most of their time denouncing his domination of the city." He voiced no comment. "I remember my last conversation with Dick Mellon," Hazlett says. "I told him how interested the E and C was getting in the dance. He literally threw up his hands. This was a few days before he died." One inveterate visitor to the Rolling Rock races recalls the elderly R.K., a bleak autumnal figure in a long dark greatcoat like a British general's, alone in the tower, putting in his appearance.

Close to the end he made the pilgrimage and visited Larry Mellon. "I was quite struck by how cyanotic his complexion was," the doctor would note. "Always a sure sign of advanced cardiac deterioration." The attack that finished him came on in Ligonier one Saturday at the end of May in 1970. He lingered in a West Penn Hospital bed until the middle of the following week. Along with a heavy ingathering of corporate dignitaries and governmental representatives, including Nixon's Secretary of the Treasury, thousands of everyday Pittsburghers paraded by his bier. Many were sharply moved—there was no doubt in anybody's mind that this man personally saved Pittsburgh. Flags flew half staff. His wife and Joseph Hughes looked after his burial, in

The General
JAMES R. MELLON II

an inconspicuous plot on the hill just behind his house. "He was a bastard but I loved him," his iconoclastic daughter Connie told one of the cousins, and hers was a summation many others secretly endorsed.

2

With R.K.'s death, the Mellons forsook even the semblance of cohesion. Taxes winnowed the holdings. "Every time there's a death everything is split five ways," Dick's widow says. "More goes to charity." He left four and a half million dollars' worth of equity stock to help endow the Rolling Rock Club; Sarah had already left a million. Half the undistributed estate, over $113 million, went to his widow; the R. K. Mellon Foundation acquired the rest after taxes. "We've cut back so," Connie says. "He was a director of the Penn Central, of course. He left money out of the estate, and it's still out, so that if a suit occurred we would have something with which to pay. It's now come down to managing on what was left."

Connie herself soon remarried. Her third husband, Peter Burrell, put in thirty years as director of The National Stud of the United Kingdom. "They were old friends," an intimate confides. "It had been a thing that was up before, although it was over as of recent years. Dick always would give his soul to avoid a divorce." Connie's friends agree on how much more relaxed she seems. This involved a price. "There was some hope that Connie would become a power within the R.K. side," observes Joseph Hughes. "When she became Mrs. Burrell these company chairmen would not call on her in the same fashion they called on R.K."

She herself is cheerful: "I didn't think it would hold together, our side of the family. It's done dashed well. Luther Holbrook is now the financial brain, and, under him, Drew Mathieson takes care of the children's foundations. Mason Walch is a great tax lawyer—sane, sensible, there's no fooling about. Prossie is coming along, although these days I don't think he can amass a fortune. . . ."

Most business people agree. "I spent the last three days with Prosser," Denton says, "he handles himself well. It's not like Dick, though. He worked his way up, he talked the language." Prosser unstintingly goes further: "I wasn't prepared for the awesome task of stepping into Dad's shoes"—words are tumbling out, augmented by monkey motions, but relieved by Prosser's overworked if genuine modesty. "Dad's two greatest assets were choosing people and foresight—the ability to look down the road ten, twenty years and say, this is the way things are going to be, and take action. I have little or no inspiration or foresight, I tried to get the right people to do the right job and get things done."

At a kind of breakfast conference interview in December of 1975 in the Mellon Suite of the Duquesne Club the R. K. Mellon and Sons brain trust will divulge at least the directions their efforts have recently been taking. A rational man, Mason Walch looks up from an outstanding spread of creamed chipped beef on waffles, and states, after swallowing, "In the old days there were the Mellon family companies. A lot of eggs in a few baskets. If somebody walked in with a million dollars, and you were a prudent banker, you would diversify."

Memory stirs. It remained A.W.'s conviction that the best thing was to put your eggs in one basket, and watch the basket. But Mathieson's characterization of the traditional companies as "older, matured companies, whose development periods have ended," is certainly borne out by stock market results. Besides, Walch remarks, "After General Mellon died this group lost influence. We have no members on Gulf, et cetera." They sold 7.25 million shares but Gulf continues to be the largest dollar holding. Between liability and disclosure requirements, directorships lately have lost a lot of allure. Mathieson serves on the boards of General Reinsurance and Koppers, although the R.K. side retained relatively little Koppers, and Prosser himself is on the board and the executive committee of the Mellon National. "We keep these directorships," he tosses off. "They allow us not to become ingrown."

Between capital gains taxes and registration fees, diversification has been costly. Each portfolio has been rebuilt—municipal bonds where taxes were a problem, a smattering of true venture capital. R.K. had encouraged each of his children to establish a relatively small foundation—around a million dollars in principal apiece—and both the bequests and capital in these need regular weeding. The enormous recreational tracts in Georgia and Nassau have turned the new generation to serious agribusiness. Limited blocks of capital now go to competitive outside managers, to see whose discretion is most worth harnessing. Computer analysis is important. There won't be any more Gulfs or General Reinsurances with everything chopped up so much, but probably this generation can ride out anything. "There's no success over at R. K. Mellon anymore," one thirty-ninth floor co-tenant concludes. "I don't have any question they're doing an adequate job." Expectations have shifted, largely. "In families like ours what life becomes is holding onto what you've got," one cousin confesses. "Spending capital is sin." R.K.'s four children each receive, reliable sources assert, the income from assets in the neighborhood of fifty million dollars.

The shake-out upset standings. When Joseph Hughes, R.K.'s confidant and lawyer through all the years since the war, charged more as executor of his estate than John Mayer, Denton's successor at the bank, felt appropriate, the recriminations drove Hughes to take his case to Prosser. Hughes seethed; Prosser ended the association. "There was a difference of opinion," Prosser states. "It was a very difficult thing to do, but it had to be done."

Community relationships remain dormant. During the middle Sixties, R.K. began acquiring property downtown, a fifteen-million-dollar parcel at the head of Grant Street, which he reportedly intended to present to the city as core of an enormous convention center and terminus for a system of contemporary mass transit, the controversial

"Skybus" proposals. "Had he lived," Hughes ventured, "Skybus would have gone ahead. R.K. had the grand concept. Let's do it again, we did it at the Point." A local business skeptic insists that the whole idea originated with planners at Westinghouse Air Brake, not a Mellon concern, and ran into entrenched opposition. "By a financial maneuver, the Mellons put the crush on the whole project, and then they developed it all over again at Westinghouse Electric, a Mellon company, and sold it on the grounds that doing it there was an act of loyalty to Pittsburgh." Technocrats at the Port Authority, still largely a creature of the Allegheny Conference, readied all the paper work. Then Pittsburgh's newly elected Mayor Flaherty resorted to the courts to block Port Authority planners from tunnels and rights-of-way. He had his own, less grandiose proposals for rapid transit. Development jammed.

Scaife cousin Edward J. Magee, who replaced Park Martin as executive director of the Allegheny Authority, publicly vented establishment frustrations: "A few months after Mayor Flaherty took office in 1970 everything was over; all progress came to a standstill. A great and powerful city came under the power of a nitwit." Mellon intentions were stymied; only adaptable Dick Scaife is believed on amiable terms with the recalcitrant populist. Scaife's purpose, his detractors claim, has been to influence the mayor to eject Magee as a director of the municipal zoo. The cousins are reportedly feuding.

An offspray of publicity in 1972 flecked R.K.'s reputation. An old-family Pittsburgher named William Rodd II recapitulated in a nonconformist local weekly the history of bickering between Mellon stand-ins and University of Pennsylvania administrators. His material, Rodd insisted, came out of the papers of embattled, dead Edward Litchfield, the versatile political scientist Leon Falk and Alan Scaife (then chairman of Pitt's board of trustees) moved in from Cornell as chancellor in 1956. Before taking the post, Litchfield explained to Rodd, he thought he'd been quite specific about what rebuilding the moldering old streetcar campus was likely to entail. "The money will be forthcoming," board members supposedly responded. Litchfield projected that "endowment would need to be increased to a total of 125 million dollars."

Between 1955 and 1965 the chancellor successfully upgraded Pitt's campus in valuation from $32,000,000 to $175,000,000, rebuilt entire disciplines, and created controversial new departments such as

GSPIA, the Graduate School of Public and International Affairs. What Litchfield was unable to generate was endowment money enough to fund this resurrection. Nobody really seemed concerned; whatever sums were involved the university could borrow from banks in the area. R.K.'s great ally Davey Lawrence was now the governor, and, presumably, under his forceful direction, the legislature would allocate new money in case a budget problem developed. Litchfield paid little attention when Westinghouse chairman Gwilym Price, who replaced Alan Scaife, made one ominous point: "Don't expect me to go to the thirty-ninth floor for you."

In 1962 the Republican William Scranton became the governor of Pennsylvania. Public money tightened. Frank Denton went conspicuously onto the university's board, and headed the finance committee. Frank would subsequently assert, before the Pennsylvania House Appropriations Committee, that after six years' effort to bail Pitt out "University finances are a mystery to me." "My job is to make [the Mellons'] money, not spend it," he reportedly snapped at one too many solicitations. A stream of university officials filed before a somber R. K. Mellon, who appeared to understand.

Litchfield's central talking point was the fact that fifty-three million of the seventy million the family turned over to the university after 1945 went directly into health facilities. There had indeed been a very early $12,500,000 Paul Mellon gift to the humanities by way of the E and C. That was long assimilated; new departments were starving.

The loan crisis intensified; Denton met with Litchfield. "In order to get out of this, we have to be partners in crime," Frank tipped the chancellor. What Denton was proposing, it developed, was that they abandon Pitt's Ivy League pretensions along with its coveted independent status. Litchfield resigned in 1966, and inside a year the institution was "state-related."

Academics charged a sellout, and faulted the Mellons. "It is known," Rodd wrote, "that on the 39th floor there was a tendency to say, 'Sarah's boys started it, let them finish it.'" Perhaps that played too; the fact was, by that time even the Mellon fortune was outstripped by expenditures. Private resources and public needs went by each other like parabolic curves in the night.

Later, under cover of foundation activity, the R.K.M. group warily looked Pitt over. There is no Mellon representation upon the university's board, but "We're intimating moral support, that's almost more important than anything just now," maintains George Taber, who coordinates overall philanthropy. A lot of emphasis remains centered upon the medical complex. They recruited Nathan Stark, and foundation money and sometimes the services of an unadvertised comptroller on loan from the thirty-ninth floor go out into projects as mundane as coordinating central laundry service. Anything, provided those wobbly academic budgets balance. But "until the political climate clears," Prosser confides, "we'll keep working quietly behind the scenes."

This sense of furtive, unpublicized involvements cloaked Prosser that December of 1975. He broke appointments suddenly, then appeared after aides sent word he wouldn't be there. Haggard, much twitchier than usual, Prosser struggled to hear.

"That's because of Prosser," one old-timer remarks when, after hours, passing across the gloomy, sweeping avocado-and-walnut foyer of the Mellon offices, the visitor must return the long, searching stare of the somnolent old fellow who doubles as porter. "Prosser's dodging a subpoena."

Wife troubles. R.K. guessed right. "That was sad," his mother says. "She was on pills. I don't know how he put up with her for seven years. He would say, 'Mother, you don't leave a sinking ship.'" Sympathetic cousins go further: "Karen was . . . way overweight, and full of profanity. . . . Prosser sure stuck that one out. He was the baby."

In 1974 the two were finally divorced. The papers went through while Karen was in a psychiatric sanitarium in Connecticut, and she insisted later on that she had agreed to Prosser's taking custody of their two little girls consequent to the Pennsylvania court award only with the understanding that he would turn both over after treatment was completed. Prosser hadn't. In December of 1975 little Constance and Catherine visited their mother at a North Carolina weight-reducing clinic. She took the children and flew to Manhattan, where she reportedly jumped in and out of fourteen different residences, under nine assumed names, until March 19, 1976. That morning a retired policeman Karen had hired, Lester Carew, was directing the girls into his station wagon in an Italian neighborhood in Brooklyn when a "late-model golden-brown Chrysler" cut Carew off. Two very serious operatives emerged. One identified himself as an F.B.I. agent, accepted Carew's .38, and took the children. Karen called Brooklyn

Karen leaving court
U.P.I.

Sandra and Prosser
PITTSBURGH *Press*

police; the manhunt wasn't organized before the father of the girls had contacted the authorities to announce that both children were "safe with me."

The abduction brought publicity to the attendant custody battle. Lawyers Karen had hired had succeeded in getting New York State Supreme Court Justice Manuel Gomez to award her custody of the girls; once back in Pennsylvania the girls were again adjudged Prosser's; later on that year a Brooklyn grand jury would pronounce the abduction itself legal in view of conflicting rulings.

"I'm scared, very upset. I'm afraid I won't see my children again," Karen told the press. "Mr. Mellon only wins." This was a plaint Nora herself might understand.

In 1975 Prosser remarried. His new wife, Sandra, is much less dramatic, solider and more maternal. She brought to Prosser a number of children by an earlier marriage and a level-headed approach to managing the reported $750,000 a year in household expenses Prosser's unitary trusts provide. The two are said especially to enjoy camping.

Karen returned to Pittsburgh, largely to take advantage of the two visits per month, under heavy guard, Prosser now permits. U.P.I. wire photos portray her as positively gaunt, avid, a severe and tragic headband giving her a wounded look. She wears enormous prop-like sunglasses. In one picture, tellingly, she clutches a deserted stuffed puppy.

3

While Prosser floundered domestically, the "Gulf Scandal" widened. Nobody ever blamed him. "We know as much about Gulf as the widow in the street," says Mason Walch, pushing away his plate. "We have the same doubts about the political giving as you do."

Walch's purity came hard. After R.K. went, Prosser's advisers moved in on then chairman Brockett. "The R.K. people went directly to the company," an insider says. "They made their case with a pretty heavy hand. Prosser wanted a directorship. And Brockett said no."

It seemed a humiliation; ultimately it spared them. The corruption dated—well back, a decade. Yet R.K. escapes. "He was a peculiar kind of a guy at a meeting," one board member explains. "He didn't want a lot of long discussion. So we'd really work things out in executive committee sessions. He kept off that."

Everybody close is sure Dick's ignorance was intact. "If he'd known, it would have been curtains," his widow says. "He'd certainly have said something to me." "Had R.K. known about the payoffs at Gulf I would have known of it," Joseph Hughes says. "I was the political man. There would have been more housecleaning than you ever read about. He was a very high-principled man in that area. . . .

"That's really what's wrong now. There's not that common table anymore where everybody could sit down and say, 'Gulf Oil is a disgrace to the city, the nation and the country. B'God, let's do something about it.' "

The corruption at Gulf deserves a volume of its own, but the chronology is simple. Watergate was churning eddies. On July 9, 1973, the director of the Watergate Special Prosecution Force, Archibald Cox, pointed up widespread violations of the Corrupt Practices Act by revealing that American Airlines had contributed $55,000 to Nixon from corporate funds. He urged other managers to disclose such infractions. Days later Common Cause procured a consent order against CREEP which compelled the Administration to release its secret contribution list—that satanic document aides in the White

House named, after its protectress, "Rose Mary's Baby." An attorney for the finance arm of the Committee to Re-Elect abruptly contacted Claude Wild, the director of Gulf's Government Relations Office in Washington and a Gulf vice-president, to ask how he expected to verify the $100,000 he'd contributed from "Employees of Gulf Oil Company" and "Mr. and Mrs. Claude C. Wild, Jr." Now Wild wouldn't confirm the source of the money. On July 16, the United States Attorney for the Southern District of New York contacted Wild while developing his case against Mitchell and Stans. Gulf brought in attorneys from the prestigious Pittsburgh law firm of Eckert, Seamans, Cherin and Mellott. Senior partner Cloyd Mellott met briefly with Wild, and on July 26 Eckert, Seamans sent a letter to Cox which informed the Special Prosecutor that Wild had decided to admit having contributed $100,000 of corporate funds to CREEP. Gulf's directors were unaware of the donation, the letter emphasized, and Gulf had already put in for the return of the money.

Gulf's spokesmen looked sheepish, but, overall, this "donation" didn't sound very different from several the investigation was surfacing just then, and quite a number afterward. It must have started with a visit by one of Nixon's familiars to Gulf executive offices. A pleasantry or two, then—hiking up his suit coat a little to settle himself companionably upon a corner of a desk—the well-worked pitch. This election was important. Oil always needed protection. The President would remember—either way. There would be fretting when he left, but payment was inescapable.

That didn't quite happen. Interviewed by the Special Prosecutor's staff in August, Wild ducked all questions except as they regarded the $100,000. But Mellott did enter a letter from Harold Hammer, Gulf's new chief financial officer, which indicated the cash itself originated in a bank account of the Bahamas Exploration Company, Limited (Bahamas Ex.), a subsidiary Gulf liquidated at the end of 1972.

The Special Prosecutor persevered. Another poke or two turned up the information that Wild had also made sizable contributions from corporate funds in 1972 to Senator Henry Jackson and to Wilbur Mills. The Prosecutor lodged charges, and before 1973 ended both Wild and Gulf pleaded guilty. They paid minor fines—Wild one thousand dollars, five thousand dollars from the oil company.

That might have allayed the worst of it, had Nixon stayed on. But Ford became President, and others in the Government felt freer to develop an interest in Wild's recent violation. People spotted loose threads. Early in October of 1974 the head of the Enforcement Division of the Securities and Exchange Commission, Stanley Sporkin, instructed members of his staff to inquire into "the use of Gulf funds for contributions, gifts, entertainment or other expenses related to political activity." Before November was over, Gulf's general counsel, Merle Minks, got together with S.E.C. representatives and attorneys from Eckert, Seamans. The Government was especially curious as to how Wild's illegal contributions got funded "within the framework of a large corporation with built-in controls such as Gulf." To get things going, the S.E.C. staffers hoped Gulf would allow its lawyers to waive all attorney–client privileges and surrender their fast-filling work sheets.

Gulf's board of directors met on December 10; at this meeting a spokesman for Eckert, Seamans was heartfelt in urging the board to ward off anything like that. He had good reasons. The summer of '73, Claude Wild had confided to Cloyd Mellott that ever since 1960 he'd passed around maybe three or four hundred thousand dollars a year, all cash. Wild's largesse wasn't partisan. John Heinz got money but Fred Harris did too, and Wild was particularly elated to reveal that he had "assisted all the Senators" on the Watergate Committee "except Senator Ervin," Senate Finance Committee Chairman Russell Long —$40,000 in one payment—Hubert Humphrey ($25,000) and the persistent Senate Minority Leader, Hugh Scott, whom Wild presented with $20,000 a year, then $10,000, finally—after the 1973 disclosures —nothing, a deprivation Scott now seemed "unable to understand."

Mellott knew that; but throughout 1974, and well into 1975, exchanges among Gulf's board of directors and the attorneys from Eckert, Seamans were still being conducted in euphemisms as guarded as whispers between teen-agers petting in a movie theater. Members' faces seemed composed, but how to explain those glows like bruises? In December of 1973 Mellott had conceded to the board that he had come upon "various other contributions in connection with federal elections since January 1, 1968," some "substantial" ones, and further corporate donations "possibly beginning in 1960." By February Mellott had spoken directly of a total since 1960 of "4.8 million," an amount which so far exceeded the several hundred thousand the Special Prosecutor uncovered that, among all these businessmen, one might have anticipated, certain . . . questions, perhaps. But nobody looked uncomfortable. When Mellott

574 / THE MELLON FAMILY

summed up by declaring "we were advised by Mr. Wild" that over the years the millions had gone into business and charitable entertaining, local candidates, delivery expenses, etc., there wasn't any objection. Wild kept no records; nobody minded that either. Gulf's auditor, Price Waterhouse, wasn't even brought in. It would surface later that Price Waterhouse kept, from 1963 to 1972, a "special confidential file" on the company.

The payoffs through Wild undoubtedly reflected in their fashion a kind of institutional morbidity, a failing of industrial tonus. Gulf retained its position, roughly, among the American megacorporations —between sixth and eighth, with sales pouring through at a fifteen-billion-dollar-a-year level. Those "offtakes" from Kuwait were regular as trust fund checks. These would be ending, someday; Gulf attempted to diversify, and as it thrashed it mounted every important wave late. Real estate seemed surest, and then regular losses accrued from investments like Reston, Virginia, and the development in Orlando, Florida. Overall results in '72 were recalculated a year later to reflect the enormous translation setbacks from German borrowings. Half of General Atomic yielded losses in the reactor business. Certain managers stood accused of "double dipping" to obscure crisis markups; not long after that the union charged management with unjustified pension-fund taps. In 1966 the company bought 2,300 City Service outlets; a number lost money, and by 1972 the board "approved the divestment of certain marginal or unprofitable operations."

Things abroad foundered continuously. As British Petroleum's ward, Anthony Sampson observes, the Pittsburghers absorbed generations of "patronizing lectures on how to deal with the Arabs"; meanwhile, little by little, the Shaikh nudged his percentage up. Libya grabbed assets. Company managers got excited about prospects in Angola; the Portuguese repressions there stirred up the activists in Congress; dissidents convulsed the 1971 meeting; dynamiters blew away a corner of the Pittsburgh headquarters. Then Portugal withdrew; by 1975 Gulf found itself depositing royalty checks which soon totaled over a hundred million dollars to unfamiliar bank accounts in Cabinda, a province effectively controlled by the Popular Movement for the Liberation of Angola—the faction the Soviets and Cubans liked, if not so extravagantly. A frustrated Henry Kissinger was unable to convince the Congress to allocate $33,000,000 to prop up rivals.

There was a tendency, afterward, to associate these eruptions with the demise of R. K. Mellon. Probably it started before. Early in the Sixties the per-share value of Gulf common had started to level off. Better-managed oil companies—the Standard firms, notably—would maintain real growth. Bundled into their oligopoly, the managers in Pittsburgh left policy leadership to sophisticated colleagues—Ken Jamieson and Monroe Rathbone of Exxon stood out—and tail-gated Robert Anderson of Atlantic-Richfield into Prudhoe Bay and the North Sea. Costs reflected all this; meanwhile, the company kept improving the dividend, borrowing outside whenever cash flow lan-guished. It would be hard to devise a strategy less congenial to A. W. Mellon. In 1963 the family disposed of nearly 3.5 million shares— that sale which outraged Gulf's chairman, Bill Whiteford. R.K. was expressing himself like any other shareholder. From then on, period-ically, the family sold stock, usually through First Boston, until their postwar percentage of the company went down from 41.3 percent in 1957 to less than half that when Wild got caught.

All this was reflected by the evolution of appointments to Gulf's own board. The total went up in 1974 from ten to fourteen. Outsiders came on, although few were outstanding, and nobody seemed inclined to boil incriminating detail out of the wastes of the balance sheets.

The Mellon participation narrowed. Only two Gulf directors would qualify by 1973 as wholly family proxies. "Dickie Scaife was smart enough to let Jim Walton represent *him*," says stony Joe Hughes. By default largely, since Prosser wasn't invited, Walton represents the R.K. side too. Walton's style is Stevensonian—dry, alternately whim-sical and curt—and, although he worked as a middle manager for Gulf for a number of years, since 1968 Walton has normally been photographed tipped elegantly against a polished marble column, inside his vaulted Carnegie. "Everyone here is sympathetic, outraged, shocked, and concerned with what is going to happen to the people involved," he stated while disclosures surfaced. Gulf Chairman Dorsey was reportedly infuriated at Walton's claim not to have had even an inkling of what was up until the newspaper barrage started. The two were old, close friends.

The other family director was Nathan Pearson. In 1968 Pearson replaced George Wyckoff. He represents Paul Mellon. Nate is a tall, grave, considerate man, a person of probity. It is quite hard to conceive of Pearson stalemating a directors' meeting by forcing a contretemps.

After these two, the Gulf board phased, individual by individual, from obvious Mellon sympathizers like James Higgins, chairman of the bank, to friends of Dorsey like Edwin Singer, a rancher from Texas. One boardroom novelty appeared in April of 1975: Sister Jane Scully, president of a local parochial college. "They put a nun on the board to try and take the heat off," says Thomas Mellon Evans, that accomplished Pittsburgh bystander. "She's going to straighten it out. Even the auditor can't figure out what Wild did with the money."

This refinement came later. That December afternoon of 1974, the day the board went along with Mellott about keeping their papers away from the S.E.C., it authorized "a good faith attempt to reconstruct historically what happened or may have happened within Gulf's corporate framework with regard to such use of corporate funds." A task force formed to prepare this document: Pearson; a board member from Toronto, Beverley Matthews; and from Manhattan, as chairman, John J. McCloy.

The surviving senior partner of Milbank, Tweed, Hadley and McCloy remained more than competent. His canniness was unapproached. He'd once been Assistant Secretary of War, High Commissioner for Germany, president of the World Bank, chairman of the Chase. Between, throughout, he'd represented the oil majors singly and collectively in wrangles with a variety of governments; on that John McCloy's *basic* reputation rested.

At first, one senses, this square-set old apologist for the cartel crouched to evidentiary scraps like an experienced tailor who intended, no matter what, to baste up *something* presentable. McCloy preferred doors open, and he was frank all along about why the oil companies retained his services: "My job is to keep 'em out of jail."

Nonetheless, in Pittsburgh managers around the headquarters grew ever more uneasy confronting McCloy's frighteningly humorous black eyes, the kind of big wry Scottish mouth that always looks about to snap a thread. He preserved his courtliness, the homey asides, the archaic literary touches. He fell to minute historical reconstruction:

The besetting difficulties appeared to commence with the ascent of Whiteford. Claude Wild personally stressed that "those in charge of Gulf—and notably Whiteford—felt that Gulf had been 'kicked around, knocked around by government' for a long time and that the time had come to do something about it." Halfway through his tenure in 1959, Bill Whiteford was distinctive for his closely razored long wax oval of a head, an air of uncommon briskness, and narrow eyes shrewd enough to score good glass. His pride was involved. One day in 1959 he summoned his administrative vice-president, Joseph Bounds, and Archie Gray, Gulf's general counsel, and told them "that he had talked to top management of some other major oil companies and learned that all of them had set up arrangements similar to that which Whiteford planned." ". . . at least some of these other corporations did not maintain any record of these arrangements," Whiteford said; "and [he] reaffirmed that he wanted no records to be kept of Gulf's political fund." Gulf woke up late, as ever; this time they wouldn't be outgutted.

That same year, Claude Wild went in to back up Kermit Roosevelt in Gulf's Washington offices. Claude Wild was bred to the job—his father had been a Humble Oil lobbyist in Texas, and managed that famous 1948 squeaker that started Johnson's Senate career as "Landslide Lyndon." A gregarious man, an able golfer and an appreciative martini drinker, Wild knew the corridors as well as anybody in the trade. Politicians enjoyed him. His approach was soft, southern—a cuddly avuncular baldy with just the mock-beseeching expression of a spaniel who knows he has probably been naughty again, but is also aware his friends are likely to indulge him one more time.

Wild's contacts went back with bagmen and administrative assistants all over the Government. One of his initial gifts, via Walter Jenkins, was fifty thousand dollars in cash to Lyndon Johnson. It was always cash, relatively small bills. Later on, when Wild started testifying, his aghast beneficiaries reacted in the usual way—they always *assumed* the money had come from individuals at Gulf. But the only effort to round up private political money around the corporation, Gulf's "Good Government Fund," was started in 1972, and issued proper checks. With time, assuming scale, Wild took on underlings to pander the hustings. Recipients still fell back on confusion about the sources, yet conditions of the transfers made clear that nobody involved was waiting for public-service awards. Cash in "plain" envelopes passed under the stall dividers in public toilets. During one nervous exchange, the payoff changed hands behind a prairie-state barn. Consultants made money easily, and certain of Gulf's own workers with political friends to market could rely on discreet finan-

William Whiteford
GULF OIL CORPORATION

Claude Wild
GULF OIL CORP.

James Dorsey
GULF OIL CORPORATION

cial extras. Word soon was around. Dick Scaife's great mentor, Cliff Jones, was miffed when company officials turned down his offer to distribute Gulf's lagniappe.

Whiteford's problem in 1959 was how to free up cash "off the books." Problematic transfers like these would unquestionably go smoother outside the federal jurisdiction. In 1944 Gulf's New York-based Exploration Division had organized a unit, Bahamas Ex., with headquarters in Nassau. The subsidiary was dormant. In July of 1959 the company sent out the assistant comptroller in the Tulsa office, William Viglia, to set up books on what would appear to be a much more ambitious program for the Bahamian appendage. Abruptly, expense accounts alone were burning up half a million dollars a year, with checks drawn regularly against an account at The Bank of Nova Scotia in Nassau.

Viglia operated the laundry. A nervous older man, Viglia disliked his part. Along with the drudgery of working up a set of fictitious ledgers to account for all these nonexistent exploration expenses, Viglia functioned as courier. Periodically, somebody from The Bank of Nova Scotia called in to tip Viglia that the casino in Nassau had just deposited cash. Viglia stopped by immediately and added this packet to whatever was already around his safe-deposit box. When that built up to $25,000 or so, Viglia visited the mainland and presented his gleanings to Wild or Bounds. Whenever Bounds took delivery, there was a punctilio. Bounds had an office safe, for which Bounds insists he himself never received the combination. It was customarily ajar. Whenever Viglia looked in, Bounds accepted the bills, quickly slid them into the safe, and slammed it shut. After hours somebody familiar with the combination—Whiteford, Bounds assumed—slipped into his office, removed the money, and left the tumblers disengaged for Viglia's next donation.

Like Whiteford and his successor at Gulf, Ernest Brockett, Joe Bounds was descended from the long-standing western oil-field tradition of the bull-bellied roustabout. Whiteford moved Bounds east to accomplish four mysterious "tasks." Bounds wasn't a fool. He realized right away that implementing this thing, although Whiteford's idea, would involve, in practice, only the company's comptroller (Crummer), its treasurer (Horace Moorhead), and Viglia and Wild and himself. Himself, most assuredly; he soon began squawking to Whiteford about "the Bahamian set-up." At an October, 1961, meeting, McCloy would report an incident, "at the Duquesne Club, where some spirits were consumed. . . . A violent argument ensued, in the course of which Bounds, according to his account of the affair, 'decked' Whiteford. The next day Whiteford told Bounds that he should fire him except for the difficulty of explaining such a move to Mr. R. K. Mellon. Instead, Whiteford 'exiled' Bounds to the West Coast. . . ." Even there, Bounds continued to process Viglia's payments until he retired in 1964, not long before Whiteford.

With Whiteford gone, a lot of romance went out of operations, although the payoffs continued. William Henry became comptroller. Frank Anderson became comptroller. Fred Deering became comptroller. At one point, the panic-stricken Viglia tore up the Bahamas Ex. records and "flushed them in a water closet." But marginalia survive. "Church," Viglia wrote one middle-level accountant in Pittsburgh, "Need letter from you per attachment. Understand via grapevine we are to amortize $400,000 for 1968." Through 1973, every few weeks, Viglia caught his airplane.

McCloy and his directors had matters reconstructed this far— many trails were cold, and gentlemen didn't pry—when Gulf Chairman Robert Dorsey put in a ritual appearance on May 16, 1975, before the U. S. Senate's Subcommittee on Multinational Corporations. Dorsey made a superior impression. Senator Percy praised him. Once Dorsey opened up, the opposite wall collapsed. While he was president, Dorsey acknowledged, he had himself authorized the payment of enormous bribes to go-betweens from President Park of South Korea, of the Democratic Republican Party. The first million went out in 1966.

To temper all this, John McCloy scuffles up as well-practiced a paragraph or two as anything in his lexicon. That moment, McCloy recalls, "American government officials" were exerting "persistent encouragement, if not pressure," on the Korean government "toward the institution of American-style elections. . . . The Gulf representatives involved viewed the 1966 contribution as supportive of the developing process in Korea, and they communicated this attitude to Pittsburgh."

Bob Dorsey's own explanation dealt less with civics: ". . . the demand was made by high party officials and was accompanied by pressure which left little to the imagination as to what would occur if the company would choose to turn its back on the request." How much Gulf's million ultimately contributed to egalitarianism in South Korea has never been quantified, but Gulf's $200,000,000 "exposure" in South Korea, including its enormous refinery at Ulsan, had started making money. In 1970 Dorsey felt the Oriental arm again, this time for three million dollars, negotiated down during several overheated sessions with one S. K. Kim, whom even McCloy will refer to as a decidedly "rough customer." Gulf soon felt comfortable with the "Korean System" of "giving," an off-the-books "gray fund" assumed its ghostly place, and between Gulf's tanker chartering splits and its fluctuating percentage of the Heung Kuk Sang Sa fuel oil distributor, it became impossible to find out who—or where—its real partners were. It seemed far easier to pay the tabs.

Korea was most expensive, but throughout the Sixties a variety of officials at Gulf were barrel-rolling cash by the auditors whenever payoffs helped. Early in the Fifties the company brought in the copious Ragusa field in Sicily. Even then their native virtuoso, Nicolo Pignatelli, blessed his uncomfortable Pittsburghers with advice on gratuities to governmental functionaries—the notorious *"omaggi"* system—the value of newspaper officials, the importance of politicians along the Socialist fringes and—by 1967—the responsible allocation of payments from the Italian subsidiary's "Black Fund" of $1.2 million to obtain a refinery license. The target community, Milan, was already excessively fouled, and both the ministry experts and environmental-ists in the area required subtle reassuring.

Gulf did its part as need arose. It took some juggling, but when, in 1966, General René Barrientos requested a $100,000 Fairchild Hiller helicopter, company managers found devices. At Barrientos' violent death in 1969 Gulf's people were funneling "an amount ex-ceeding $1 million" into numbered Zürich accounts to propitiate the caudillo. That didn't seem high compared with the anticipated profits once Gulf's capped trillions of yards of Bolivian natural gas started arriving by pipeline in Argentina.

What impressed the membership of the Multinational Subcommit-tee most about Dorsey was the readiness with which he responded with specifics. He could seem high-handed, but Bob was popular. After roughnecks like Whiteford the puckered, tweedy onetime chemical engineer looked like a manager a citizen dared enjoy a drink with.

Poking among the documents, old McCloy wasn't convinced. That testimony of his—too ingenuous, too cute, at times. To startle the nation by admitting under floodlights the sanctioning of over four million dollars in bribes, then, questioned by Mellott and Company, to deny even passing familiarity with any of the mechanics? Corrupt-ing Koreans, after all, didn't violate the law. Until 1973, Dorsey maintained, he truly knew nothing about Bahamas Ex.—although international payoffs too flushed in and out of the Nassau accounts en route to Switzerland. No clue, no interest. Could they actually assume that throughout the years he served as president of Gulf, and Brockett was chairman, he, Dorsey, saw no reason to tell his boss about what it took to placate the dictator? As for the board? "First, I didn't need the authorization of the Board to make the—to make the payments." Besides which, "the matter being rather delicate, and recognizing that any revelation of this would be both embarrassing to Gulf and embarrassing to the party to whom the payment was made, I simply decided that the better course was not to tell them." They all could read; newspapers would fill them in.

Dorsey's innocence breaks down. Around 1960, Bounds states, Whiteford himself had emphasized that knowledge of the arrangement be kept from the Mellons and the company "Boy Scouts," by whom he meant primarily Brockett and Dorsey. But early as 1963, to Claude Wild's observation, Bob Dorsey stole in and out of a meeting to decide

on the advisability of slipping forty thousand dollars to Senator Russell
Long. In 1966 and 1968 Wild met with Royce Savage, the retired
federal judge serving Gulf those years as general counsel. Wild had
been summoned to leave with Savage a rough financial accounting.
Royce confessed to Wild that "In all sincerity he didn't like it. . . .
he was trapped like—not trapped but we were involved in this merry-
go-round, and how do you get off?" Everybody knew. An October,
1973, internal memorandum of Mellott's refers to a recognition by
Dorsey, several years before that, of "a vague, general awareness that
Claude Wild did, on occasion, use funds outside his regular budget
for various purposes, including perhaps political contributions."

Dorsey's innocence was fragile; undoubtedly, in its way, R.K.'s was
too. He'd loved to generalize too much. Certainly Dick sensed something—his doubts to Paul about Whiteford's unnerving "over-activity"
suggest some intuition remained—but as he aged he too obviously
preferred not knowing. It was getting late. The company continuously
expanded, borrowed, bribed, sponsored high-minded educational television programs, distributed millions to charities. It was converting
inexorably into a giant decentralized sprawl of low-grade multinational protoplasm, as happy to traffic with Salazar as with his Marxist
successors in Luanda, as philosophical as floodwater. Shareholders
became irrelevant. "In 1970," Cordy May remembers, "there was a
stockholders' proposal that Gulf remove itself from Angola-Mozam-
bique. I did not know how evil that was. I asked the executives one
time and was rapidly told that I have no clout. I voted with management."

Afterward it would seem that Dorsey and the managers were almost
as blasé about their fourteen board members as about Cordy May,
stewing at Cold Comfort, all bothered over Mozambique. Why should
they interfere? Close to the denouement—the autumn of 1975—
Jim Walton would disclaim even the faintest hint, until earlier that
year, that the political giving went beyond the original $125,000. The
high-minded museum director had evidently been wool-gathering
whenever Cloyd Mellott spoke.

Dorsey's blitheness comes over in relations with Wild. Not long
after Wild had paid his thousand-dollar governmental fine, Gulf's compensation committee met to rubber-stamp a management recommendation that Wild receive access to 12,500 shares of common at an
option discount. This was in February of 1974, just when the board
was hearing about Wild from Mellott. Wild "had been kind of for-

given," concedes director Charles Beeghly, ex-Jones and Laughlin, "and he was included on the list that was submitted." Dorsey's inclinations were always tolerant. When Wild informed Dorsey about the $100,000 to CREEP in June of 1973, he "thinks about it, pats me on the back and says, 'Don't worry about it, and go on home.'"

In March of 1974 Claude Wild resigned. Stockholders' suits were pending. That same spring, Gulf settled an action brought against it by a public interest group called The Project on Corporate Responsibility. Wild handed over $25,000, and the corporation agreed not to rehire Wild "except on an emergency basis" unless the directors were informed and counsel for the plaintiff prenotified.

The spring of 1975, at the annual meeting, a woman stood up and asked Bob Dorsey whether Wild still worked for the company. The question seemed naïve. He didn't just then, the courtly Dorsey responded, but he had been doing some consulting with the company, on a limited contract which happened to have ended just two or three weeks previously. Forever last to hear, Gulf's directors were dumbfounded. They discovered that Claude Wild had in fact been drawing down $92,000 for eight months' work, and that he'd paid his settlement off from a $26,000 loan he'd made from the account he ran for Gulf's Good Government Fund. By this time several audit-committee directors, notably Nathan Pearson, were getting quite picky even about routine expenditures. Dorsey resented their meddling.

Between Christmas and New Year's, 1976, the McCloy Report broke. It hadn't been easy for McCloy to investigate even the clumsiest of the Sisters. McCloy's tone is venerable, and at its best his extended, sorrowful report reads like a treatise scratched up with a quill and dusted with sand. But conviction is central. "It is hard to escape the conclusion that a sort of 'shut-eye sentry' attitude prevailed upon the part of both the responsible corporate officials and the recipients," the lovely essay concludes, "as well as on the part of those charged with enforcement responsibilities."

There wasn't any choice. Throughout 1975 and into the following year details of the payoffs, their extensiveness, their blatancy, gravitated into the editions like slugs following moisture. Cash under the table had gone to assorted members of a Texas Railway Commission, an organization of anti-Zionists in Beirut, the executive director of the New Jersey Turnpike Authority, who accepted ten thousand dollars and proved "of tremendous help" in authorizing a pipeline. An I.R.S. agent was indicted for permitting the company to pick up expenses

for himself and his family at a Florida vacation resort while conducting an audit of Gulf's 1962–64 returns. Midway into the Presidential
campaign Claude Wild would insist, then deny, that Gulf had regularly poked cash at Vice-Presidential nominee Dole. The indiscretions
went on, the accounting was guesswork, and even the "final figure"
of $12.3 million looked impossible to guarantee. Gulf's operations,
McCloy conceded, were "shot through" with illegalities.

The inevitable big set-piece played out on January 12 and 13,
1976, at two "marathon session" directors' meetings. The managers
were excluded, but lawyers traipsed in and out for days from ante-
rooms. Press treatments leaked hints about an orgy of recriminations,
of philosophizings, of tiltings between the "Dorsey group" of directors,
who wanted to patch it up, and the higher-minded "Mellon group,"
who believed that "as an expression of community conscience" the
leadership must go, and recruited their "spunky nun" to swing for
decency. "If the board doesn't act," an expert remarked, "there are
going to be shareholders' suits." His board had babied Dorsey longer
than anybody could defend; with McCloy's findings in, they were
exposed as individuals to intolerable financial risk. They moved
right ahead. They "accepted" Dorsey's resignation, along with those
of Henry, Deering and Manning. Jerry McAfee of Gulf Oil of Canada
went in as chairman. McAfee had been lucky. The corporation had
paid off politicians all along up there, but that, fortunately, wasn't
against Canadian law. In Canada the government tends to organize
the cartels, sometimes with Gulf connivance.

Press treatments persevered. The grubbers lost out, overcome by
Mellon idealists. In time, hoping to calm resentments, Nathan Pearson put out a statement which indicated that in the end, once everything was public, the board was unified.

People simply wouldn't understand. "Nobody on the board tried
not to do anything about it," Nathan Pearson said afterward. "We
just didn't realize how deep this was." Partly it was scale. Even a
three-million-dollar gratuity amounted to petty cash against normal
business outlays. "People from other, smaller companies who came
onto the Gulf board used to shake their heads over the latitude our
management enjoyed. The board was rarely consulted about anything
under ten million dollars."

Certainly Paul wasn't involved. It gratifies some archaic capitalist
yen to imagine Gulf's largest shareholder, troubled beneath his sport-

ing pictures, breaking from the Brick House, bustling to his offices to initiate a purge. Nothing like this happened. "I'm not a conduit between Paul and the board," Pearson says. "To conform with S.E.C. regulations I specifically couldn't act on Paul's instructions. If I ever had to testify, that's the first thing I'd have been asked—did Paul Mellon know, did he tell you what to do, how to vote? I told him, 'I'm unhappy as hell, in time I'll tell you what is going on.' When it came out I sent him the McCloy Report."

There was no Mellon group. Only the organization survives.

4

The disturbances within Gulf affected various Mellons differently. Cousin Jay, for example, tended to step back and examine the scandal in hopes of deriving certain wider, historical perspectives. "I think this family has just about run out of commanding figures," he concluded subsequently.

Bored now with trophy hunting, his cousin Billy relates, Jay recently contacted a number of prominent taxidermists and informed them that he had now rounded out his primate collection through the addition of a Pygmy. What might he expect to pay to have this specimen competently stuffed and mounted? "Some were obviously horrified," Hitchcock observes, "and several wouldn't answer. But quite a number quoted Jay a price."

This makes Hitchcock chortle. He views the embroilments in Pittsburgh sympathetically, and avoids personal judgments. At times, as Helen Claire testifies, Billy almost seems generous to the point of being stupid. His new wife, Jane, can become quite indignant whenever she reflects that it was precisely the relatives who remained the nastiest about Billy who survived the shake-up looking negligent and inept.

Hitchcock himself moves on. Jane is a film writer, and she and Billy are collaborating on a series of educational documentaries devoted to the mysteries of aging. There was a period when Hitchcock's fascination with the extrasensory led to his interest in Israeli medium Uri Geller; finally Geller, like Leary, seemed just too commercial.

Certain promptings do abide. The Hitchcocks' big peaceable duplex apartment overlooking the East River is traditionally furnished now, filled out with polished, comfortable antiques. Upstairs, his shanks cocked up and crossed above his desk blotter, Billy himself is negotiating, in typical high spirits, an intricate commodity straddle upon the London stock exchange; one hank of hair sways loose and boyish-looking. He's still using up those awesome Paravicini losses. The room is uncluttered, except for a conversation piece behind glass —the tattered old flag, framed, Stanley bore hunting Livingstone. This Billy once received from the estate of a Hitchcock-side great-grand-father.

A fey Chinese houseman slips in and whispers unintelligibly of lunch. Out West, Hitchcock remarks, Scully's appeals are exhausted and he has begun serving time. Downstairs, dominating important walls, one passes under Billy's museum-quality collection of *thankas*, temple hangings, which memorialize the adventures of key Tibetan saints. Brocaded, serene, as depthless as contemplation, they oversee for Billy quite another—an unforgotten—universe.

5

Richard Scaife is also into his public resurrection. He directs his boisterousness these days toward his city magazine, *The Pittsburgher*, modeled unabashedly after *New York*. His political education deepens. "I don't think there is going to be a Republican Party soon if things keep on the way they are," its recent heaviest benefactor, caught on the run, decides over the telephone. But that's all right since "I'm happier with Jimmy Carter anyhow than I was with Gerald Ford."

6

It seemed to Paul the setbacks at The Gulf just didn't bear dwelling upon. "Gulf stock at twenty-one—it's disappointing, isn't it?" he asked a visitor. Sometimes events were unpredictable. The autumn of 1975 Paul nearly was killed. He and Ian Balding, his trainer in England, stood outside the paddocks after the races at Bath. "We had two runners," Balding remembers, "and after that particular race we waited there for the horses to go by. They did, but then the last one came back a step or two and kicked out and caught Mr. Mellon right in the chest. Horrifying, a most sickening sound. He sat on a bench for a bit, and then the ambulance came, and somebody got him a room at the local nursing home. He rested there. Luckily, because he'd bruised his liver." A ball-point pen Paul happened to be carrying in his vest pocket came out of his clothing bent into a V, and saved his life. The raincoat he wore that day bears the shadow of the horse's shoe, and Paul has not been able to bring himself to have it cleaned. He did not hunt any foxes that fall and winter. The ground in Virginia froze early the season after that, and Paul wasn't tempted to gamble on a fall. He did not hunt that season either. "I've gotten a lot of pleasure from the sport for forty-eight years," he remarks, "and why should I ruin all that by making a serious mistake at this point?"

Nora finally passed on. The death of Ailsa had upset her deeply, although she was scrupulous about never burdening visitors. She walked her dogs and appreciated her garden. "The last two or three years of her life she did become a little bit forgetful," Bill Wissman noticed. "But even at that stage she would always ask the watchman, 'Is there anything I can get you that would make you any more comfortable before I go to bed?' She never became despondent." While Nora lay dying in May of 1973, the indomitable George Wyckoff sometimes visited her in her room at Roosevelt Hospital. "Out in the corridor I'd tie a handkerchief on under my eyes and pretend I was breaking into the place," George Wyckoff says, "and she'd be sitting there in bed, and when she saw me I'd hear her wonderful laugh." Nora survived to ninety-four. Paul interred her bones beside A.W.'s.

After Timmy was married in 1963 Paul Mellon was given to understand that one of the newly married cousins had just become father to a boy he intended to christen Andrew. Paul telephoned the relative, and requested, very quietly, that he consider selecting another name. It would be nice if, should Tim and Sue produce a male heir, they might be free to call him Andrew without the confusion of another with the same name in the immediate family. Perhaps Paul hadn't talked this over with Timmy. Tim saw things differently: "My view of families is that they're an anachronism. The family unit is not a functioning entity anymore. It no longer serves an economic need. I suppose it's interesting as a social phenomenon." After fourteen years the Timothy Mellons remain childless. It does not look right now as if there is going to be another Andrew Mellon. Possibly this is appropriate. As Paul keeps emphasizing, the Mellons aren't dynastic. "Privately, Paul really doesn't believe in all this dough," says somebody who's known him well all along. Bunny is fully provided for, of course. But after that? "He'll do with whatever is left exactly what his sister did," his close friends agree.

They've borne enough responsibility. The Mellons are nothing if not detached.

GENEALOGICAL TABLE

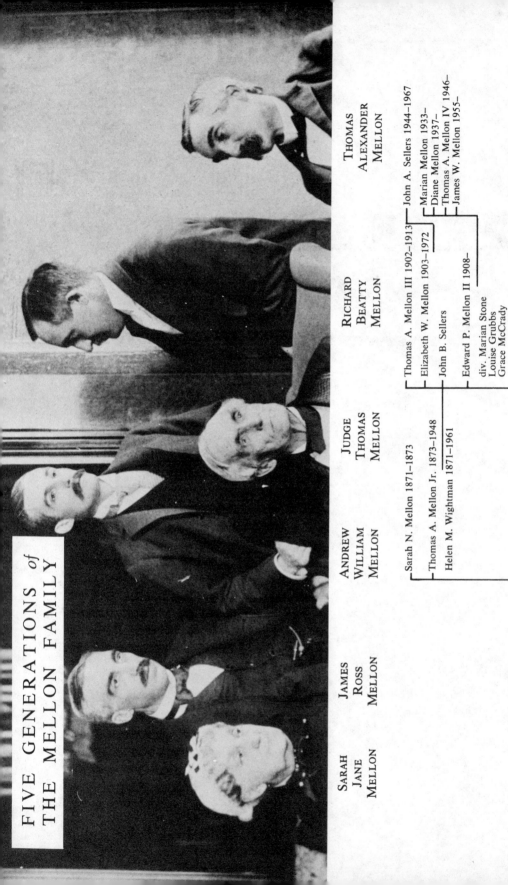

FIVE GENERATIONS *of*
THE MELLON FAMILY

SARAH
JANE
MELLON

JAMES
ROSS
MELLON

ANDREW
WILLIAM
MELLON

JUDGE
THOMAS
MELLON

RICHARD
BEATTY
MELLON

THOMAS
ALEXANDER
MELLON

Sarah N. Mellon 1871–1913

Thomas A. Mellon Jr. 1873–1948

Helen M. Wightman 1871–1961

Thomas A. Mellon III 1902–1913

Elizabeth W. Mellon 1903–1972

John B. Sellers

Edward P. Mellon II 1908–

div. Marian Stone
Louise Grubbs
Grace McCrady

John A. Sellers 1944–1967

Marian Mellon 1933–

Diane Mellon 1937–

Thomas A. Mellon IV 1946–

James W. Mellon 1955–

Helen S. Schmidt 1938–

Thomas M. Schmidt 1940–

Judge Thomas Mellon (1813–1908)

Sarah Jane Negley (1817–1909)

Thomas A. Mellon 1844–1899
Mary C. Caldwell 1841–1902

Edward P. Mellon 1875–1953
Ethel Humphrey 1880–1938

Helen S. Mellon 1914–
Adolph W. Schmidt

Jane C. Mellon 1917–
Craigh Leonard

Edward M. Leonard 1941–
Craigh Leonard Jr. 1943–
Stephanie Leonard 1947–

Mary C. Mellon 1914–
Henry Wise Jr.

Mary C. Wise 1939–
Lucy B. Wise 1942–
Eva D. Wise 1944–
Henry A. Wise III 1946–

Mary C. Mellon 1884–1974
div. John H. Kampman 1880–1957
Sam A. McClung Jr. 1880–1945

John H. Kampman Jr. 1907–1940

Mary M. Kampman 1908–
Lawrence Schwartz

Mary Schwartz 1942–
Barbara Schwartz 1945–
Sarah Schwartz 1945–

Samuel A. McClung III 1918–
Adelaide Smith

Mary C. McClung 1946–
Judith McClung 1948–
Christina McClung 1957–

Isabel McClung 1920–1967
Charles Abernethy Jr.

Charles Abernethy III 1943–
Nancy Abernethy 1946–
Christopher Abernethy 1948–
Michael Abernethy 1952–
Sam Abernethy 1958–

Cynthia McClung 1921–
Stephen Stone Jr.

Cynthia Stone 1943–
Suzanne Stone 1946–
Stephen Stone III 1948–
Ellen Stone 1954–
Martha Stone 1956–

James Ross Mellon 1846–1934
Rachel H. Larimer 1847–1919

William L. Mellon 1868–1949
Mary H. Taylor 1872–1942

Matthew N. Mellon 1897–
div. Gertrude Altegoer
Jane Bertram

Karl N. Mellon 1937–
James R. Mellon II 1942–

Sadie Mellon 1872–1876

Rachel Mellon 1873–1874

Thomas Mellon II 1880–1946

Rachel L. Mellon 1899–
John F. Walton Jr.

Anne Walton 1923–
Mary Walton 1924–
John Walton III 1926–
James Walton 1930–

Sarah L. Mellon 1887–1968
Alexander D. Grange 1876–1915
George S. Hasbrouck Jr. 1880–1942
Sidney J. Holloway 1882–1964

Margaret Mellon 1901–
Alexander Laughlin Jr.
Thomas Hitchcock Jr.

Alexander Laughlin 1925–
Louise Hitchcock 1930–

William L. Mellon Jr. 1910–
div. Ethel G. Rowley
Gwendolyn G. Rawson

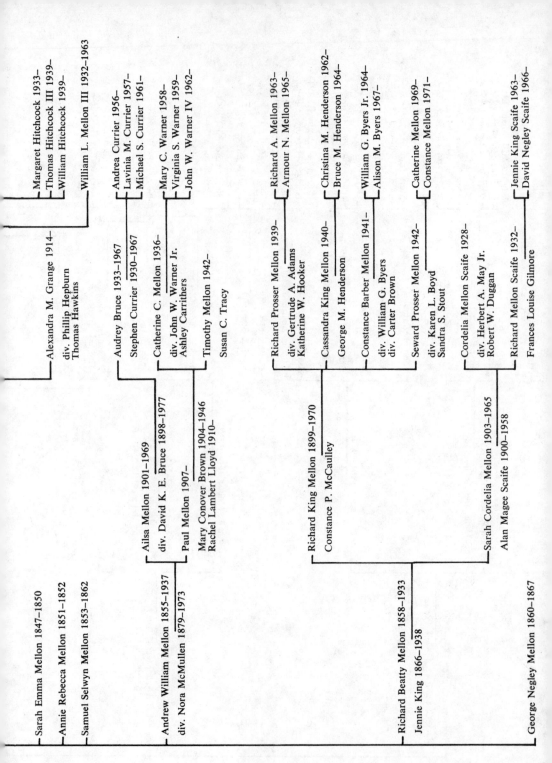

Sarah Emma Mellon 1847–1850

Annie Rebecca Mellon 1851–1852

Samuel Selwyn Mellon 1853–1862

Andrew William Mellon 1855–1937
div. Nora McMullen 1879–1973

    Ailsa Mellon 1901–1969
    div. David K. E. Bruce 1898–1977

        Alexandra M. Grange 1914–
        div. Phillip Hepburn
        Thomas Hawkins

            Margaret Hitchcock 1933–
            Thomas Hitchcock III 1939–
            William Hitchcock 1939–

        William L. Mellon III 1932–1963

    Paul Mellon 1907–
    Mary Conover Brown 1904–1946
    Rachel Lambert Lloyd 1910–

        Audrey Bruce 1933–1967
        Stephen Currier 1930–1967

            Andrea Currier 1956–
            Lavinia M. Currier 1957–
            Michael S. Currier 1961–

        Catherine C. Mellon 1936–
        div. John W. Warner Jr.
        Ashley Carrithers

            Mary C. Warner 1958–
            Virginia S. Warner 1959–
            John W. Warner IV 1962–

        Timothy Mellon 1942–
        Susan C. Tracy

Richard Beatty Mellon 1858–1933
Jennie King 1866–1938

    Richard King Mellon 1899–1970
    Constance P. McCaulley

        Richard Prosser Mellon 1939–
        div. Gertrude A. Adams
        Katherine W. Hooker

            Richard A. Mellon 1963–
            Armour N. Mellon 1965–

        Cassandra King Mellon 1940–
        George M. Henderson

            Christina M. Henderson 1962–
            Bruce M. Henderson 1964–

        Constance Barber Mellon 1941–
        div. William G. Byers
        div. Carter Brown

            William G. Byers Jr. 1964–
            Alison M. Byers 1967–

        Seward Prosser Mellon 1942–
        div. Karen L. Boyd
        Sandra S. Stout

            Catherine Mellon 1969–
            Constance Mellon 1971–

    Sarah Cordelia Mellon 1903–1965
    Alan Magee Scaife 1900–1958

        Cordelia Mellon Scaife 1928–
        div. Herbert A. May Jr.
        Robert W. Duggan

        Richard Mellon Scaife 1932–
        Frances Louise Gilmore

            Jennie King Scaife 1963–
            David Negley Scaife 1966–

George Negley Mellon 1860–1867

SOURCE NOTES

THE ADDITION of back matter involves surprising uninvited risks. I discovered this quickly after the publication of my treatment of the Kennedy family. The thing was barely into print before myriads of political reporters, anthills jarred, went after not merely my highfalutin prose; several also ran amok among those pretentious footnotes peppered around the tome. Footnotes, and about the Kennedys! Worse, I had referred the reader from time to time to one or another among my well-indexed personal notebooks. These citations seemed useful in making some distinction between material from other—public—sources and whatever I'd picked up interviewing firsthand; furthermore, since all these scaffoldings would wind up one day piled into a university repository, why not spare students of the subject their time and exasperation?

Others judged me excessive. This time—uninterested in repeating the experience, for sure, but also because a body of information as immediate and unexamined as the past of the Mellon family comes out of the soils of anonymity in quite different fashion from that of the political Kennedys—I've attempted to develop a markedly altered presentation of source notes and specific attributions. Those unsettling little numbers don't pockmark the text. Everything waits back here: corresponding to each chapter there is a paragraph or two indicating the largest, most germane sources. I have followed that up with a reasonably complete breakdown of book, periodical and documentary origins. The family's earlier history—particularly the life of Andrew Mellon—deserves decent academic foundations. The itemization follows, roughly, the material itself. By coordinating the chronology inside the text with publication dates, it should be simple to reconstruct my library.

Most bibliographies are partial; undeniably these are too: they represent a culling of major sources, the ones that came eventually to bear upon passages in the text. This presents a history of the Mellons; through them, inescapably, it turned itself into a history of our society for a century and a half, constantly glimpsed, occasionally central. I subtitled the book *A Fortune in History*. Long ago, when this got started, I construed the Mellon holdings as primarily a fortune in money.

CHAPTER 1

Inevitably, the main source for this early section remains Judge Mellon's autobiography, printed in 1885. The theological material stems from a number of sources, Durant being as solid as any and lively as most. A small cache of family papers wound up in the archives of the Western Pennsylvania Historical Society, and most of the letters indicated, particularly the ones between Thomas Mellon and James Ross Mellon, are available there. Stefan Lorant's matchless text and picture book of Pittsburgh history, *Pittsburgh, The Story of an American City*, was a regular source for the early chronicles of western Pennsylvania. The struggles between the Judge and J. B. Corey receive a lot of attention in the Judge's autobiography, and although Mellon identifies Corey only indirectly, the context makes clear who "B" really was. While privately printed, and of small distribution, the distribution was choice, and Andrew Carnegie refers to the book as the inspiration for his own famous autobiography.

BOOKS	PERIODICALS	DOCUMENTS
Thomas Mellon, *Thomas Mellon and His Times*	*Pittsburgh Dispatch* April 3, 13, 1904 June 24, 1909	Letter from Robert Graham to Judge Mellon, November 9, 1900
Will Durant, *The Reformation*	*Pittsburgh Gazette Times* January 20, 1909	James Ross Mellon papers
Benjamin Franklin, *Autobiography*	*The Home Monthly* (Pittsburgh) August, 1896	Thomas Mellon letters to James Ross Mellon March 21, 1863 October 8, 1863
Stefan Lorant, *Pittsburgh, The Story of an American City*	*Saturday Evening Post* June 27, 1931	

BOOKS	PERIODICALS	DOCUMENTS
Harvey O'Connor, *Mellon's Millions*		January 21, 1864 January 27, 1864 March 15, 1864
William Larimer Mellon, *Judge Mellon's Sons*		April 25, 1864 June 16, 1864
Rachel Mellon, *The Larimer, McMasters, and Allied Families*		July 4, 1864 July 16, 1864
J. R. Mellon, *Letters*		

CHAPTER 2

Details of Andrew Mellon's early years are harder to pinpoint than those of his father; Andrew avoided leaving evidence of any kind his entire life. Some early material has been developed from W.L.'s book, and Hendrick has been able to trace a surprising amount from Andrew Mellon's contemporaries. Hendrick is the source for early Mellon school papers and letters. The Mellon bank's own history, *One Hundred Years of Banking*, supplies some visual detail. W.L. writes of Andrew's first business ventures, and Hendrick traces the results of the panic of 1873. Andrew's own memory is documented in a *Pittsburgh Press* newsclip of March 30, 1930. The building of the Ligonier Railroad comes from the Judge's autobiography. Van Urk found among R. B. Mellon's papers much about the North Dakota years. Letters to J.R. from his father also touch on these, as do W.L.'s memoirs. Hendrick is the main source for Andrew as a young banker. W.L. breaks down the family fortune in 1890. Harvey was Henry Frick's biographer, and, though doting, had access to critical letters and reminiscences. O'Connor remains a fierce common negative source. Judge Mellon's late-developing interest in the occult is documented by both W.L. and Hendrick. Thomas Mellon's hatred of the Magee machine appears in his autobiography. Lundberg's key book *America's Sixty Families* also touches back to the politics of the period.

The source on Quay is Davenport, and Lorant is excellent on the early political rings. W.L. allows at least a peek at the early and corrupt street railroad business, and Hendrick another. He found the letter in which Andrew Mellon indicates his increasing distaste for that particular scam, and supplies some material concerning W.L.'s early years. Hendrick's extended manuscript was commissioned during the early Forties by Paul Mellon, who subsequently became apprehensive over its political as well as its literary problems, and did not permit publication. It is an important source of quotes, letters and documents throughout the early chapters of this book.

W.L. recounts his own early years as a wildcatter and the raid in Pennsylvania upon the Rockefeller interests. Newspaper accounts of the period overlap concerning the Berkman assault on Frick; and William Knox, son of Frick's attorney, supplies other memories. W.L. traces the beginnings of Union Trust, the Moore syndicate, Union Steel. O'Connor traces other aspects. Frick material also developed from Casson, Carnegie's autobiography, Holbrook and Barron. Another key book is *The History of the Carnegie Company* by James Howard Bridge, who first adored, then hated Frick. Harvey covers later infighting. The 1912 House of Representatives hearings into the phases of the organization of the United States Steel Corporation also chronicle both Mellon involvement and Carnegie evasiveness.

BOOKS	PERIODICALS	DOCUMENTS
William Larimer Mellon, *Judge Mellon's Sons*	*New York Times Magazine* December 15, 1935	House of Representatives Hearings on Formation of U. S. Steel Corporation January, 1912
Burton Hendrick, *Andrew Mellon*	*Pittsburgh Press* March 30, 1930	
Karen Horney, *Neurosis and Human Growth*	July 21, 1935 December 20, 1935 July 2, 1936	District and County Reports, Allegheny County, Pennsylvania, 1967
One Hundred Years of Banking (Mellon National Bank)	December 21, 1952 August 3–7, 1959 July 30, 1965 February 12, 1967	
J. Blan van Urk, *The Story of Rolling Rock*	*Saturday Evening Post* June 7, 1930 June 27, 1931	
O'Connor, *op. cit.*	*New York Times* July 25, 1965	
Anthony Sampson, *The Seven Sisters*	May 26, 1967 August 10, 1967	
Robert Sobel, *Money Manias*	*New Yorker* July 22, 1939	
Walter Davenport,		

BOOKS	PERIODICALS	DOCUMENTS
The Power and the Glory	*Pittsburgh Bulletin Index* December 26, 1935	
Matthew Josephson, *Robber Barons*	*Pittsburgh Post* May 7, 1899	
George Harvey, *Frick*		
Lincoln Steffens, *Autobiography, Shame of the Cities*	*New York Times Book Review* December 28, 1975	
Herbert N. Casson, *Romance of Steel*	*Pittsburgh Post Gazette* August 5, 1965	
James Howard Bridge, *Millionaires and Grub Street: The History of the Carnegie Company*		
Ferdinand Lundberg, *America's Sixty Families*		
Stewart H. Holbrook, *The Age of the Moguls*		
Andrew Carnegie, *Autobiography*		
Clarence Barron, *They Told Barron*		

CHAPTER 3

It is no accident that early Mellon business details have rotted into legend. Many can be reconstituted. The Crucible Steel history comes largely from O'Connor sources and the 1912 House hearings, as do the origins of Pittsburgh Coal. Perhaps the best account of the origins of the Aluminum Company is in Lorant, although W.L. provides some detail, and Hendrick a good deal. A.W.'s 1931 letter to Paul comes from the testimony in the 1935 tax case. W.L.'s treatment of Carborundum stands, and also forms the basis for the McClintic-Marshall and Standard Steel Car accounts. Besides W.L.'s memory of the origins of the Gulf Company, there are accounts by O'Connor and Sobel. Gulf's own account, *Since Spindletop*, represents the official version. Some detail comes from the October, 1937, *Fortune* piece on the company. Special studies authorized by Gifford Pinchot while he was governor of Pennsylvania traced the extent of Mellon ownership.

BOOKS	PERIODICALS	DOCUMENTS
Barron, *op. cit.*	*World's Work* March, 1924	Letter from A. W. Mellon to Paul Mellon, 1931
Lorant, *op. cit.*		
W. L. Mellon, *op. cit.*	*Fortune* October, 1937	
O'Connor, *Mellon's Millions* *The Empire of Oil*		
Since Spindletop (Gulf)		
Sobel, *op. cit.*		

CHAPTER 4

More personal in character, this chapter concerns Andrew Mellon's marriage to Nora McMullen. It hints at the manner in which business compulsions incinerated emotion. One very important source was Hendrick, whose access to A. W. Mellon's letter books, which have now disappeared, permitted the preservation of many of the poignant exchanges which enliven this section. W.L.'s book runs a certain amount of parallel observation; his oldest son, Matthew, was old enough to remember the years of A.W.'s marriage, and the Judge's final decade. Matthew is also a biting source of information about J.R. and Thomas Alexander. Lorant deals with Alexander King. Early Mellon bank detail is from *One Hundred Years of Banking*. Adolph Schmidt, whose wife is a Mellon, has been a ready source of early business anecdote. The *Philadelphia North American*, whose reporter Nora evidently favored with a series of outraged interviews, provided many of the quotes concerning the worst days of the estrangement. Ailsa's great friend Lauder Greenway remembers what Ailsa told him about the anxieties of her childhood. O'Connor unearthed the details of A.W.'s attempt to suppress the divorce.

BOOKS

John Walker,
  *Self-Portrait with
  Donors*
Hendrick, *op. cit.*
W. L. Mellon, *op. cit.*
Lorant, *op. cit.*
*One Hundred Years of
  Banking*
O'Connor, *op. cit.*

PERIODICALS

Fortune
December, 1967
*Philadelphia North
  American*
May 6–9, 1911
The Pittsburgh Leader
October 5, 1900

DOCUMENTS

U. S. Board of Tax
Appeals,
United States v.
Andrew Mellon,
Docket 76499 (1935)

CHAPTER 5

The years between his great organizational push and his appearance in government were unhappy for Andrew Mellon. There is some firsthand evidence of this from impressions by Matthew Mellon and John Buchanan, the elderly lawyer who worked with Frick and later managed W.L.'s affairs. Hendrick develops good material about the Rust-Koppers origins, as does W.L. A pivotal article in *Fortune* in 1937 also dredges up something of the early years. Company officials—Jack Crimmins, Paul Titus—reinforce memories of Rust. Joe Guffey's embezzlement was covered by the newspaper press of the period. Lorant is a main source of industrial history, as is O'Connor. By now Paul Mellon comes in as a regular commentator on Pittsburgh and his relatives. Details of the R. B. Mellon mansion appear in the *Pittsburgh Bulletin Index*. Van Urk remains the main authority on Rolling Rock. W.L. deals affectionately with his father's eccentricities, as does Buchanan. Thomas Mellon II, W.L.'s brother, left his *Army Y Diary* as testimony to his interests. Thomas Alexander Mellon's obituary provides high points of his life. Later magazine pieces would treat of Andrew Mellon's middle years. Matthew Mellon's own book *The Watermellons* gets at the Palatka years, and W.L.'s book rounds these out. Matt carries his chronicle further in an illustrated diary he published called *The Grand Tour, 1914*. Hendrick catches W.L. umpiring Gulf disagreements. Another Matt Mellon publication, *War Log—1918*, touches on his early years. Hendrick deals extensively with the origins of the Mellon Institute.

BOOKS	PERIODICALS	DOCUMENTS
O'Connor, *op. cit.*	*Fortune* April, 1937 October, 1967	
Lorant, *op. cit.*		
Hendrick, *op. cit.*	*Pittsburgh Bulletin Index* November 14, 1940	
Van Urk, *op. cit.*		
W. L. Mellon, *op. cit.*	*Pittsburgh Post Gazette* August 19, 1946	
Thomas Mellon II, *Army Y Diary*	*Outlook and Independent* February 4, 1931	
William Schoyer, *The Scaife Company and the Scaife Family 1802–1952*	*Current History* July, 1931	
	Country Life May, 1934	
Matthew Mellon, *The Watermellons, The Grand Tour, 1914, War Log—1918*	*Town and Country* June, 1951	
	Current Biography 1955	
	Pittsburgh Press February 5, 1934 October 20, 1934 July 13, 1946 April 22, 1957	
	Sports Illustrated March 16, 1970	
	Pittsburgh Gazette Times January 20, 1909	
	Pittsburgh Dispatch April 30, 1904 July 24, 1909	
	Pittsburgh Bulletin Index November 14, 1940	

CHAPTER 6

Andrew Mellon's entry into political life seemed unlikely to contemporaries. The Frick involvement here is clear from Harvey. Russell documents the early Harding connection. Sinclair's book also deals with Harding. Davenport is a great authority on Penrose. Lundberg's

Sixty Families deals with the power scuffle of the period in names and amounts. Harry Daugherty writes up his own version of the events, and there is a chance that some of this is true. W.L. describes the family, or bashful savior, version of A.W.'s political career. Pittsburgh old-timers like John Buchanan have supplied personal detail about W.L., as have a spate of magazine articles throughout the Twenties. O'Connor, of course, takes the "progressive" view of Mellon's Secretaryship throughout. Stephen Birmingham suggests a human side of Teapot Dome, as do Werner and Starr. Colonel Drake, A.W.'s legman throughout much of this period, is the source of many memories. The *Collier's* piece of June 13, 1925, offers the clearest explication of A.W.'s inchoate economic thinking.

Historical ransacking must begin with William Allen White's book. Again, magazine sources are important. There is some Russell overlap. Arthur Schlesinger's first volume of *The Age of Roosevelt* offers useful cultural background.

The Couzens threat is well begun by O'Connor, and Gifford Pinchot's files in the Library of Congress bear importantly on the issue, as do Couzens' own letters. Of course, the Select Committee's investigation of Mellon offers another main source.

Galbraith's spirited *Great Crash* is a good starting point for the treatment of the bust. Another useful source is Gammill and Blodgett. Holbrook supplies good insights into the mood of the aging A.W.

BOOKS	PERIODICALS	DOCUMENTS
W. L. Mellon, *op. cit.* O'Connor, *op. cit.*	*Current History* December, 1926 July, 1931	Letter from Bernard Baruch, Couzens Investigation
Harry Daugherty, *The Inside Story of the Harding Administration* Harvey, *op. cit.*	*Outlook* March 9, 1921 July 20, 1921 November 14, 1923 May 3, 1926	*Now Justice Comes to Washington,* Albert Knight (Couzens file) 68 Congress, Senate Document 87, Report 27. Investigation of the Bureau of Internal Revenue
Jeanne Lowe, *Cities in a Race With Time*	*Outlook and Independent* February 4, 1931	
Samuel Eliot Morison and Henry Steele Commager, *History of the American Republic,* Vol. II	*The Living Age* May, 1932 *The Nation* May 18, 1927 June 20, 1928	January 7, 1926 (Select Committee) Investigation of the Bureau of Internal Revenue by U. S.

BOOKS	PERIODICALS	DOCUMENTS

BOOKS

Lundberg, *op. cit.*

Francis Russell, *The Shadow of Blooming Grove*

Andrew Sinclair, *The Available Man*

Davenport, *op. cit.*

Holbrook, *op. cit.*

M. R. Werner and John Starr, *The Teapot Dome Scandal*

William Allen White, *A Puritan in Babylon*

Arthur Schlesinger, *Age of Roosevelt,* Vol. I

John Kenneth Galbraith, *The Great Crash*

Paul Gammill and Ralph Blodgett, *Current Economic Problems*

PERIODICALS

Current Opinion
April, 1921

Collier's
June 13, 1925
January 30, 1926
October 2, 1926
March 29, 1930

The American Review of Reviews
April, 1921
February, 1924
July, 1924

Literary Digest
November 24, 1923
April 5, 1924
March 21, 1925
February 2, 1929

Saturday Evening Post
October 13, 1923
January 5, 1924
May 22, 1926
May 7, 1932

Vanity Fair
December, 1926

Congressional Digest
September, 1923
October, 1931

Pittsburgh Times
April 13, 1924

Pittsburgh Post Dispatch
March 5, 1921

The Freeman
December 12, 1923

The American City Magazine
March, 1924
(address by A.W.M.)

The New Republic
October 12, 1921
November 28, 1923

DOCUMENTS

Senate Select Committee
March 19, 1924

BOOKS	PERIODICALS	DOCUMENTS

April 16, 1924
December 17, 1924
March 24, 1926
March 23, 1963

Forum
March, 1924

Independent
March 29, 1924

World's Work
May, 1921
May, 1922
November, 1922
November, 1923
March, 1924
January, 1927
February, 1928
January, 1930
March, 1932

CHAPTER 7

Occasional material about A.W.'s political sidelines shows up in Hendrick's treatment. Russell is another source. The expert on this is Lawrence Murray. Stave and W. A. White deal with the Pennsylvania face-off. The follow-up Senate hearings also pull some of the more brutal information out of characters like Grundy. O'Connor and Lorant also deal with the incidents.

The Patman attack helped cultivate new material into the public record. Most of the material comes out of Patman's hearings, some via O'Connor. Involved individuals such as Leon Higby and Paul Mellon make their contributions. Patman's hearings assembled much valuable secondary documentation—pieces from *Oil Weekly*, et cetera. Further Koppers material comes from *Fortune*, company officers, O'Connor. Drake is the best authority for his own spiraling business career, although W.L. always has something to contribute along these lines.

Gulf's development is touched on in Sampson's book and in the Epstein series in *New York*.

BOOKS

Hendrick, *op. cit.*

Russell, *op. cit.*

Bruce M. Stave,
  *The New Deal and
  the Last Hurrah*

Lorant, *op. cit.*

White, *op. cit.*

O'Connor, *op. cit.*

Barron, *op. cit.*

Lundberg, *op. cit.*

Gustavus Myers,
  *History of the Great
  American Fortunes*

Herbert Hoover,
  Memoirs

Since Spindletop

W. L. Mellon, *op. cit.*

Sampson, *op. cit.*

PERIODICALS

*Quarterly Journal of the
  Pennsylvania Histori-
  cal Association*
July, 1975

"The Mellons, Their
Money and the
Mythical Machine:
Organizational Politics
in the Republican
Twenties"

The New Republic
June 30, 1926

New York Post
February 11, 1932

*New York Herald
  Tribune*
February 4, 1932

New York Times
January 21, 1932

Washington Evening Star
January 20, 1932

*Luce's Press Clipping
  Bureau*
February 22, 1919

Fortune
April, 1937

Dallas News
December 29, 1930

New York
June 23, 1975

DOCUMENTS

Senate Resolution 324
January 11, 1927

69 Congress Senate
Report
1197, part 2

David Reed letters to
Thomas Walsh
March 19, 1927
February 7, 1929

Hearings before the
Committee on the
Judiciary, House of
Representatives
72nd Congress
1st Session on H
Res. 92
January 13, 14, 15,
18, 19, 1932

Letter from Jason
Forrester to Senator
Thomas Walsh
October 5, 1929

Special Senate
Committee
Investigation of
Campaign
Expenditures
June 9, 11, 15, 1926

Telegram from Gifford
Pinchot to A. W.
Mellon
March 17, 1925

Scratch copy letter from
Gifford Pinchot to
A. W. Mellon (related
memos)
November 28, 1931

CHAPTER 8

Hendrick is again a very good source on Andrew Mellon's art collecting, although Paul Mellon's memory is sharp about these years. David Bruce discusses his early associations with Ailsa in a long letter to the author. W.L. and Hendrick both cover the early years of the Mellon Institute, as do the Institute publications themselves and the Edward Weidlein recollections. John Buchanan remembers the Mellons' irregular church involvement. Bowman is the authority on the University of Pittsburgh. Hendrick touches on all these civilizing phases, especially the early collecting. John Walker had the advantage of knowing both the older A.W. and the younger Paul and Ailsa during their peak collecting period. John Finley's own book also contains valuable detail.

BOOKS	PERIODICALS	DOCUMENTS
Hendrick, *op. cit.*	*Current Biography* 1949 (David Bruce)	Mellon Institute, Fiftieth Annual Report, et al.
Holbrook, *op. cit.*		
John G. Bowman, *Unofficial Notes* (privately printed)	*Saturday Evening Post* March 8, 1947	
Walker, *op. cit.*	*New York Times* August 3, 1930	
David Finley, *A Standard of Excellence*	*Pittsburgh Press* March 24, 1955	

CHAPTER 9

The early section of this chapter puts together in part from important earlier sources—White, Schlesinger, Hoover. The Vare rivalry comes through the Senate investigation of 1926, Davenport and O'Connor. The 1928 nomination is best covered by White, although W.L. has observations, some accurate, and Hoover has a view of his own. Hoover is particularly pungent about the slump and A.W.'s early opinions of it. Galbraith espouses another standpoint, close to the younger Lundberg.

Most of the detail of Andrew Mellon's later financial reorganizing comes from such participants as Denton or the extensive testimony in the tax case, in which many of them were involved. R.B. testified before a Congressional committee investigating ownership brutality in the coal business, and O'Connor includes the testimony. Klein's misfortunes are chronicled in Lorant and Stave. Schlesinger is a good overall source for the period, as is Wecter. Family sources agree on the details of the Union Gulf debacle.

BOOKS	PERIODICALS	DOCUMENTS
Claude Fuess, *Calvin Coolidge*	*New Republic* June 20, 1936	
Lorant, *op. cit.*	*The Literary Digest*	
O'Connor, *op. cit.*	June 30, 1928 March 16, 30, 1929	
Davenport, *op. cit.*	February 20, 1932	
White, *op. cit.*	*The Outlook*	
W. L. Mellon, *op. cit.*	January 9, 1929 October 3, 1929	
Hoover, *op. cit.*	March 4, 1931	
Galbraith, *op. cit.*	*Saturday Evening Post*	
Lundberg, *op. cit.*	April 1, 1933	
Henry L. Stimson and McGeorge Bundy, *On Active Service*	*Fortune* October, 1937	
Martin Mayer, *The Bankers*	*Collier's* November 12, 1927	
Stave, *op. cit.*	*New York Times* February 5, 1932	
	The American Review of Reviews June, 1931	
	World's Work June, 1929	
	The Pennsylvania Magazine of History and Biography October, 1973	

CHAPTER 10

The tax investigation remains a bitter memory within the Mellon family. Hendrick attempts to deal with it, but misunderstands both technical and cultural elements and produces a rather embarrassing

defense. W.L. too avoids the obvious. Gerhart's biography is the best on Jackson's point of view.

Documents of the trial itself not only cover the charges involved but also provide a kind of oral autobiography for A. W. Mellon, with choral support from the principal Mellon lieutenants. Testimony ran to thousands of pages.

Apart from Paul's own comment there is spotty newspaper coverage of his early years after college. Relatives remember him variously.

R. K. Mellon's early manhood comes through the reminiscences of Frank Denton and other contemporaries and, sometimes, in Van Urk's book. There are occasional clips. Friends remember Ailsa's early marriage and David's search for a way of life.

BOOKS	PERIODICALS	DOCUMENTS
Hendrick, *op. cit.*	*Newsweek*	United States Board of
W. L. Mellon, *op. cit.*	March 17, 1934	Tax Appeal
	May 19, 1934	United States v. A. W.
Schlesinger, *op. cit.*	March 2, 9, 16, 30,	Mellon
Van Urk, *op. cit.*	1935	Docket 76499 (1935)
	April 6, 1935	
Gerhart, *America's Ad-vocate*	May 11, 1935	Pennsylvania State Re-ports
	Country Life	347 Eldridge 1943
	May, 1934	Letter from A. W.
	Time	Mellon to Henry Stimson
	April 12, 1937	son
	December 20, 1937	May 9, 1934
	New Republic	
	September 6, 1933	
	May 15, 1935	
	May 29, 1935	
	Pittsburgh Post Gazette	
	November 17, 1927	
	May 18, 1933	
	February 20, 1935	
	April 2, 3, 5, 1935	
	May 3, 1935	
	January 7, 1936	
	Sports Illustrated	
	March 16, 1970	
	Pittsburgh Press	
	October 21, 1930	
	January 12, 1933	

BOOKS	PERIODICALS	DOCUMENTS

December 1, 3, 6, 1933
February 5, 1934
July 8, 9, 1935
April 2, 1937
August 29, 1937
January 17, 1947

New York Times
July 15, 1933
February 21, 1935

Literary Digest
September 22, 1934

The Nation
May 15, 1935

The Cooperative Press
August 19, 1929

*International News
Service*
June 1, 1936

Pittsburgh Sun-Telegraph
July 17, 1933
August 18, 1933
December 1, 1933
April 3, 1935

Pittsburgh Bulletin Index
April 11, 1935
July 4, 1935

CHAPTER 11

The building of the National Gallery got all bound up in Mellon's tax problems, and determining his intentions became an element of the suit. Hendrick covers the gift, and Hoover and John Walker wheel in support for Mellon's philanthropic attempt. Utterances on the subject are also an important section of Hogan's emotional brief for the plaintiff.

Mellon's collecting receives extended—if somewhat apocryphal—treatment at Behrman's hand in *Duveen*. David Finley's own book covers the origins of the Gallery.

Hendrick deals with A.W.'s last months well, and there are many newspaper clips.

BOOKS	PERIODICALS	DOCUMENTS
S. N. Behrman, *Duveen*	*Pittsburgh Post Gazette*	United States Board
Finley, *op. cit.*	October 4, 1934	of Tax Appeal
Gerhart, *op. cit.*	February 28, 1935	United States v.
Hendrick, *op. cit.*	March 2, 10, 1935	A. W. Mellon
	April 5, 1935	Docket 76499
	March 16, 1937	(1935)
	August 27, 30, 1937	
	September 12, 21,	The Smithsonian
	1937	Institution, Annual
	July 22, 1938	Report, 1937

Saturday Evening Post
March 8, 1937

The Digest
September 11, 1937

Time
December 20, 1937
December 27, 1954

*Pittsburgh
Sun-Telegraph*
August 31, 1938

Pittsburgh Press
March 2, 1937
June 22, 1938

National Geographic
March, 1967

*American Magazine of
Art*
December, 1935
February, 1937

The New Yorker
November 3, 1951

Newsweek
November 24, 1934
March 2, 1935
May 18, 1935
January 9, 1937

Saturday Review
March 19, 1966

Reader's Digest
November, 1966

BOOKS	PERIODICALS	DOCUMENTS
	School and Society October 26, 1935 January 16, 1937	
	Pittsburgh Legal Journal September 23, 1937	
	The New Republic September 8, 1937	
	Pittsburgh Bulletin Index September 2, 1937	
	The Nation September 4, 1937	
	U.P.I. August 27, 1937	
	International News Service August 26, 1937	

CHAPTER 12

A lot of the material on the rebuilding of Pittsburgh comes from the quite extensive magazine coverage, supplemented by a dense pattern of interviews among people involved with the Allegheny Conference. Clips cover the early Mellon marriage. There was a series of extended magazine pieces over the years on Pittsburgh's redevelopment, and Jeanne Lowe's chapter is very good on the subject. Lawrence's piece in Lorant is probably definitive. Almost all material about T. Mellon and Sons comes from internal sources, few interested in being quoted on the point. Internal documents are especially vivid at times.

When Dick Mellon reorganized there was a lot of magazine coverage, both of the family's activities and the reshuffling in the companies. Company publications mention this, and Sampson, Middle Eastern development, especially in Iran. The December 30, 1975, S.E.C. report touches Whiteford's planning.

BOOKS

One Hundred Years of Banking

W. L. Mellon, *op. cit.*

Van Urk, *op. cit.*

Lowe, *Cities in a Race with Time*

Lorant, *op. cit.*

Sampson, *op cit.*

Harvey O'Connor, *The Empire of Oil*

Schoyer, *op. cit.*

PERIODICALS

Time
    October 13, 20, 1941
    July 22, 1946
    June 2, 1948
    October 3, 1949

Holiday
    October, 1949
    March, 1959

Pittsburgh Bulletin Index
    February 27, 1936

Business Week
    June 15, 1946
    August 28, 1948
    June 1, 1963

Natural History
    March, 1941

Fortune
    May, 1946
    February, 1947
    January, 1952
    November, 1967

Pittsburgh Press
    October 3, 1942
    September 18, 1964

New Republic
    July 26, 1975

The American City
    February, 1947

Pittsburgh Sun-Telegraph
    April 4, 1943
    June 11, 1944
    May 23, 1947

Life
    May 14, 1956

Wall Street Journal
    February 10, 1964

Town and Country
    June, 1951
    February, 1975

DOCUMENTS

Richard K. Mellon: "Management Responsibility to the Community," Wharton School of Finance November 16, 1953

Paul Mellon memorandum August 19, 1958

Report of the Special Review Committee of the Board of Directors of Gulf Oil Corporation December 30, 1975

Sarah Mellon Scaife Foundation, Annual Report, 1974 et al.

"The Pattern of Community Leadership in Urban Redevelopment: A Pittsburgh Profile" (Ph.D. thesis, University of Pittsburgh, 1960), by Arnold J. Auerbach

Richard King Mellon Foundation, Annual Report, 1973

BOOKS	PERIODICALS	DOCUMENTS
	Associated Press June 4, 1970	
	Pittsburgh Post Gazette April 24, 1936 July 9, 1946 September 24, 1946 August 14, 1950 December 20, 1952 May 20, 1953 May 21, 1957 June 4, 1957 October 28, 1957 June 4, 1970 February 14, 1973	

CHAPTER 13

Like Paul Mellon, Paul Mellon's world is personally oriented. The poet Barbara Howes knew the young Mellons in Switzerland. The recollections of friends are at the heart of these rather intimate sections. John Walker's chapters on Paul and Ailsa seem accurate and evocative. Most of the material about the Curriers comes from co-workers, friends and acquaintances, although there are clips about the tragedy. Most of the Paul Mellon impressions are mine, but there is an occasional good touch in a magazine sketch.

BOOKS	PERIODICALS	DOCUMENTS
Selected Paintings (Yale Center) April 15, 1975	*Pittsburgh Bulletin Index* February 7, 1935 July 4, 1935, et al.	Old Dominion Foundation Report 1941–1966
Gerard Lambert, *All Out of Step*	*The Blood Horse* November 17, 1975	Paul Mellon's unpublished essay about George Patton
Walker, *op. cit.*	*Pittsburgh Press* July 23, 1939 July 8, 1941 May 2, 1948	Paul Mellon's speech, dedication of Currier House November 18, 1970
Waldemar Nielsen, *The Big Foundations*		
John Oaksey, *The Story of Mill Reef*	*Sports Illustrated* March 16, 1970	Avalon Foundation Annual Report, 1968 et al.
	Pittsburgh Sun-Telegraph March 18, 1941 March 30, 1942 July 22, 1942	Potomac Institute Report, 1961–1971

BOOKS

PERIODICALS

Newsweek
March 21, 1966
December 19, 1966
October 12, 1970
December 8, 1975
August 2, 1976

Washington Post
March 5, 1967

National Geographic
March, 1967

*North American Alliance
Dispatch*
June 21, 1961

Vogue
July, 1962
December, 1965
March, 1966

The New Yorker
November 3, 1951

*New York Herald
Tribune*
October 13, 1946

Apollo
April, 1963

Parade
March 7, 1976

Fortune
December, 1967

Pittsburgh Post Gazette
February 4, 1935
June 25, 1935
July 31, 1940
December 6, 1946
March 11, 1966

New York Times
February 3, 1935
April 22, 1949
May 1, 1977

U.P.I.
April 16, 1967

DOCUMENTS

"The National Gallery
of Art: An Art Ex-
periment," Paul
Mellon's speech
April 25, 1975

"A Collector Recollects,"
Paul Mellon's speech,
The Virginia Museum
of Fine Arts
April 20, 1963

Address by Paul Mellon
at 200th annual dinner
of The York Gimcrack
Club

Letter to author from
David K. E. Bruce

Taconic Foundation Re-
ports, 1965, 1970

BOOKS	PERIODICALS	DOCUMENTS

A.P.
January 19–24, 31, 1967
February 16, 1967
April 28, 1967

International News Service
April 23, 1956

The Print Collector's News-Letter
May–June, 1977

Time
December 19, 1966
October 12, 1970
March 26, 1973
May 28, 1973

Town and Country
September 1, 1933

New York Journal American
July 29, 1965

Current Biography
1949 (David Bruce)

CHAPTER 14

"The chickabiddies" was an affectionate name W.L. had for his children and their offspring. In a way the W.L. line, undoubtedly bumped up a little by those Taylor genes, tends to more passion, more color, than the rest of the Mellons. Will himself was lively. Not only his own memories, but also those of Matt, the family's self-appointed historian, make possible the evocation of considerable mood. Larimer Mellon has, of course, become one of the family's most famous members, much written about, almost always with sanctimoniousness. Michelmore's book has touching moments.

W.L. gradually revised his notions about Tommy Hitchcock and became an intense admirer. Most of the Hitchcock material obviously comes from personal sources, some of whom had better not be identified. Billy was really helpful, as was his ex-wife, Aurora. A 1974 piece in *The Village Voice* helped inspire Hitchcock to take a chance and talk with me. The testimony and brief developed during the long trial of Scully and Sand explicate Hitchcock's drug-manufacturing period. A good deal of the information about Hitchcock's earlier business problems came out of his 1974 sentencing records.

BOOKS	PERIODICALS	DOCUMENTS
Walker, *op. cit.*	*Time* June 7, 1948 July 9, 1956 March 21, 1967	United States District Courts, Southern District of New York United States v. W. M. Hitchcock March 28, 1974
Schoyer, *op. cit.*		
Matthew Mellon, *The Watermellons*		
	Pittsburgh Press May 5, 1935 May 26, 1936 July 6, 1954 April 16, 1966	
Peter Michelmore, *Doctor Mellon of Haiti*		United States Court of Appeals for the 9th Circuit United States v. Nicholas Sand and Robert Timothy Scully
Christopher Elias, *The Dollar Barons*	*Current Biography* 1965 (W. L. Mellon, Jr.)	
Thurston Clarke and John J. Tigue, *Dirty Money*		
	Pittsburgh Sun-Telegraph March 24, 1953	Consolidated Appeals #74-2012 and #74-2328 (original case tried in San Francisco, November 8, 1973, to January 30, 1974)
Tom Wolfe, *The Electric Kool-Aid Acid Test*	*Newsweek* June 20, 1955 July 28, 1969	
	Today's Health July, 1958	
	Look October 30, 1956	
	Saturday Evening Post September 16, 1961	
	Christian Century December 29, 1954 June 27, 1956 March 20, 1957	
	The Village Voice August 22, 1974	
	Pittsburgh Post Gazette October 12, 1949	
	Carnegie Magazine November, 1949	

CHAPTER 15

R.K.'s later years were not completely gratifying. As he benefited Pittsburgh he exhausted himself. His closest friends agree as to the increasing damages. Rolling Rock too began to play a different role. R.K.'s own children are sympathetic, but honest.

The Paul Mellon story resumes as Paul attempts to order his affairs, and there is an agreement among his friends as to the role Stevens played in that.

BOOKS	PERIODICALS	DOCUMENTS
Van Urk, *op. cit.*	*Current Biography* 1965	1973–74 Report on the Activities of the Paul Mellon Centre (London Ltd.)
Lundberg, *The Rich and the Super-Rich*	*Holiday* March, 1959	
Ovid Demaris, *Dirty Business*	*Pittsburgh Sun-Telegraph* December 10, 1946 November 2, 1953	Old Dominion Reports
		Bollingen Series Princeton University Press 1975
	Pittsburgh Press December 3, 1935 November 11, 1947 June 9, 1963	Paul Mellon letter to author June 20, 1977
	Pittsburgh Point June 8, 1967	Paul Mellon draft of letter to Kingman Brewster August 20, 1976
	Sports Illustrated March 16, 1970	
	Pittsburgh Post Gazette May 25, 1957 August 8, 1957 September 12, 1966	Paul Mellon dedicatory speech, Yale April 15, 1977
	Yale Alumni Magazine and Journal April, 1977	Stoddard Stevens letter to author November 14, 1975
	Yale Daily News April 15, 1977	Paul Mellon memo January, 1957
	New York Times April 10, 1977	Paul Mellon letter to Edmund Pillsbury November 29, 1976
	McCall's January, 1977	Paul Mellon's remarks upon the opening of the Yale Center for

BOOKS	PERIODICALS	DOCUMENTS
	Time April 25, 1977	British Art April 15, 1977
	Newsweek April 18, 1977	Paul Mellon's commencement address, Carnegie Institute of Technology, June 5, 1967
		Sachem Fund Cumulative Report 1969–1973

CHAPTER 16

The story of the younger Scaifes had better speak for itself. With time both the *Pittsburgh Press* and the *Pittsburgh Forum* rode an increasingly tight herd on Duggan. The 1975 edition of Lorant's book notes the stages of Duggan's collapse.

BOOKS	PERIODICALS	DOCUMENTS
Lorant, *op. cit.*	*Holiday* March, 1959	R. K. Mellon's letter to Paul Mellon October 9, 1958
	Pittsburgh Press January 30, 1974 June 30, 1974	Scaife Gallery brochure
	Pittsburgh Forum October 29, 1971 February 4, 11, 1972 February 23, 1973 November 14, 1973 March 15, 1974	
	Pittsburgh Post Gazette June 21, 1968 October 4, 1968 September 27, 1972 October 11, 1973 November 7, 9, 11, 1973 February 1, 1974 March 7, 1974	

BOOKS	PERIODICALS	DOCUMENTS
	The Washington Monthly June, 1975	
	Concord Monitor July 1, 1974	
	Time November 13, 1972	

CHAPTER 17

R.K.'s last efforts wind down in newspaper clips and sad personal asides. Those years were difficult for Prosser. The Mellon reunion in Ireland was one of R.K.'s last exuberant moments. There has been considerable newspaper attention to the effort by the R.K. group to pick up the pieces. Karen Mellon's problems received newspaper and magazine coverage at the time her children were abducted.

The problems at Gulf also got much attention, especially following Watergate. The McCloy Report is the best source. The last reminiscent little sections come entirely from personal sources.

BOOKS	PERIODICALS	DOCUMENTS
Lorant, *op. cit.*	*Pittsburgh Post Gazette* September 12, 1966	Report of the Special Review Committee of the Board of Directors of Gulf Oil Corporation December 30, 1975
A Capsule History of the Gulf Oil Co. (Gulf)	June 4, 5, 1970 July, 1973	
Sampson, *op. cit.*	*Newsweek* July 1, 1968 March 29, 1976 October 8, 1976	Paul Mellon memo August 19, 1958
	Time June 28, 1968 June 15, 1970 January 5, 1976 January 12, 1976	
	Pittsburgh Press June 22, 1968 June 28, 1968 June 4, 5, 1970 May 31, 1973 December 1, 1975	

BOOKS   PERIODICALS   DOCUMENTS
‾‾‾‾‾   ‾‾‾‾‾‾‾‾‾‾   ‾‾‾‾‾‾‾‾‾

Fortune
November, 1967
June, 1976

Wall Street Journal
December 6, 1972
February 22, 1973
January 2, 13, 15,
1976

Pittsburgh Forum
October 29, 1971
February 18, 1972

The Pitt News
February 21, 1972

National Inquirer
March 8, 1977

Boston Globe
January 2, 1976
July 2, 1976
October 7, 1976

New York Times
June 5, 1970
May 2, 1971
June 27, 1976
May 1, 1977

SELECTIVE BIBLIOGRAPHY

Barron, Clarence. *They Told Barron*. New York: Harper and Brothers, 1930.

Behrman, S. N. *Duveen*. New York: Random House, 1952.

Birmingham, Stephen. *Real Lace*. New York: Harper and Row, 1973.

Bowman, John G. *Unofficial Notes*. (Privately printed.)

Bridge, James Howard. *The Inside History of the Carnegie Steel Company*. New York: Aldine, 1903.

————. *Millionaires and Grub Street*. New York: Brentano's, 1931.

Carnegie, Andrew. *Autobiography*. Boston and New York: Houghton Mifflin Company, 1924.

Casson, Herbert N. *The Romance of Steel*. New York: A. S. Barnes and Company, 1907.

Clarke, Thurston, and Tigue, John J. *Dirty Money*. New York: Simon and Schuster, 1975.

Collier, Peter O., and Horowitz, David. *The Rockefellers*. New York: Holt, Rinehart and Winston, 1976.

Current Biography. New York: The H. W. Wilson Company.

Daugherty, Harry, and Dixon, Thomas. *The Inside Story of the Harding Administration*. New York: Churchill, 1932.

Davenport, Walter. *The Power and the Glory—The Life of Boies Penrose*. New York: Putnam, 1931.

Demaris, Ovid. *Dirty Business*. New York: Harper's Magazine Press, 1974.

Durant, Will. *The Reformation*. New York: Simon and Schuster, 1957.

Elias, Christopher. *The Dollar Barons*. New York: Macmillan, 1973.

Finley, David. *A Standard of Excellence*. Washington, D.C.: Smithsonian Institution Press, 1973.

Franklin, Benjamin. *Autobiography*. Harvard Classics. New York: Collier, 1909.

Fuess, Claude. *Calvin Coolidge*. Boston: Little-Brown, 1940.

Galbraith, John Kenneth. *The Great Crash*. Boston: Houghton Mifflin, 1954.

Gammill, Paul, and Blodgett, Ralph. *Current Economic Problems*. New York and London: Harper and Brothers, 1947.

Gerhart, Eugene. *America's Advocate: Robert H. Jackson*. Indianapolis and New York: Bobbs-Merrill, 1958.

Gulf. *Since Spindletop*. (Also see 1953 company publication, *A Capsule History of the Gulf Oil Company*.)

Harvey, George. *Henry Clay Frick: the Man*. New York: Scribner's, 1924.

Hendrick, Burton. *Andrew William Mellon*. (Unpublished.)

Hoffman, William S. *Paul Mellon, Portrait of an Oil Baron*. Chicago: Follett, 1974.

Holbrook, Stewart Hall. *The Age of the Moguls*. Garden City, New York: Doubleday, 1953.

Hoover, Herbert. *Memoirs*. New York: Macmillan, 1952.

Horney, Karen. *Neurosis and Human Growth*. New York: Norton, 1950.

Josephson, Matthew. *The Robber Barons*. New York: Harcourt and Brace, 1934.

Lambert, Gerard. *All Out of Step*. New York: Doubleday, 1956.

Lorant, Stefan. *The Story of Pittsburgh*. New York: Doubleday, 1964, 1975.

Love, Philip H. *Andrew W. Mellon*. Baltimore: F. Heath Coggins, 1929.

Lowe, Jeanne. *Cities in a Race with Time*. New York: Random House, 1967.

Lundberg, Ferdinand. *America's Sixty Families*. New York: Vanguard Press, 1937.

————. *The Rich and the Super-Rich*. New York: Lyle Stuart, 1968.

Mayer, Martin. *The Bankers*. New York: Weybright and Talley, 1974.

Mellon, James Ross. *Letters—1862–1895*. (Privately printed, 1928.)

Mellon, Matthew. *Early American Views on Negro Slavery*. New York: New American Library; Mentor Books, 1969.

———. *The Watermellons.* (Privately printed, 1974.)

———. *The Grand Tour.* (Privately printed, 1914.)

———. *War Log.* (Privately printed, 1918.)

Mellon, Rachel. *The Larimer, McMasters and Allied Families.* Philadelphia: Lippincott, 1903.

Mellon, Thomas. *Thomas Mellon and His Times.* (Privately printed, 1885.)

Mellon, Thomas II. *Army Y Diary.* (Privately printed, 1920.)

Mellon, William Larimer. *Judge Mellon's Sons.* (Privately printed, 1948.)

Mellon Bank. *One Hundred Years of Banking.* History Mellon National Bank and Trust Company. 1970.

Michelmore, Peter. *Doctor Mellon of Haiti.* New York: Dodd Mead, 1964.

Morison, Samuel Eliot, and Commager, Henry Steele. *History of the American Republic.* New York: Oxford University Press, 1950.

Myers, Gustavus. *The History of the Great American Fortunes.* New York: The Modern Library, 1936.

Nielsen, Waldemar. *The Big Foundations.* New York: Twentieth Century Fund, Columbia University Press, 1972.

Oaksey, John. *The Story of Mill Reef.* London: Michael Joseph, 1974.

O'Connor, Harvey. *Mellon's Millions.* New York: John Day, 1933.

———. *The Empire of Oil.* New York: Monthly Review Press, 1962.

Russell, Francis. *The Shadow of Blooming Grove.* New York: McGraw-Hill, 1968.

Sampson, Anthony. *The Seven Sisters.* New York: Viking, 1975.

Schlesinger, Arthur, Jr. *The Age of Roosevelt.* Boston: Houghton Mifflin, 1957.

Schoyer, William. *The Scaife Company and the Scaife Family 1802–1952.* (Privately printed, 1952.)

Sinclair, Andrew. *The Available Man.* New York: Macmillan, 1965.

Sobel, Robert. *The Money Manias.* New York: Weybright and Talley, 1973.

Stave, Bruce M. *The New Deal and the Last Hurrah.* Pittsburgh: University of Pittsburgh Press, 1970.

Steffens, Lincoln. *Autobiography.* New York: Harcourt Brace and Company, 1931.

———. *The Shame of the Cities.* New York: McClure, Phillips and Company, 1904.

Stimson, Henry L., and Bundy, McGeorge. *On Active Service*. New York: Harper and Brothers, 1948.

van Urk, J. Blan. *The Story of Rolling Rock*. New York: Scribner's, 1950.

Virginia Museum Catalog. *Impressionist Show, 1963*. Introduction by Paul Mellon.

Walker, John. *Self-Portrait with Donors*. Boston: Atlantic-Little, Brown and Company, 1974.

Wecter, Dixon. *The Age of the Great Depression*. New York: Macmillan, 1948.

Werner, M. R., and Starr, John. *The Teapot Dome Scandal*. London: Cassell, 1961.

Whitaker, Ben. *The Philanthropoids*. New York: Morrow, 1974.

White, William Allen. *A Puritan in Babylon*. New York: Macmillan, 1938.

Wolfe, Tom. *The Electric Kool-Aid Acid Test*. New York: Farrar, Straus & Giroux, 1968.

Yale. *Selected Paintings, Drawings, and Books*. New Haven: Yale Center for British Art, 1977.

ACKNOWLEDGMENTS

EVEN THESE ACKNOWLEDGMENTS involve special problems. We lack, in America, a formal aristocracy. And this has meant that it has fallen principally upon the rich to play the role the horseback classes filled in older civilizations: the avatar of nationality, the privileged but responsible clique whose undertakings and purposes we imagine to function beyond pedestrian self-interest, above daily mongrel strivings.

To expect such motivation from individuals whose backgrounds are baldly mercantile, devoutly grasping, is perhaps a lot; still, to a certain extent, the most durable among the major fortune-bearing families have pretended, at times, to respect this mission. The remarkably low level of embittered interclass hatred in the United States is one result; this may be a consequence of extraordinary philanthropic concern by certain notable—wealthy—individuals. We elect our dictators; we blink the feudalism of riches. The experience of the Mellon family might possibly suggest why.

Such reciprocal social arrangements work much better unexamined. Why would this family—to which, for generations, unfamiliarity betokened dignity—sit still for interviews? The dangers are especially acute in that the people I talked with—and in the end I saw virtually everybody—understood well that none of them might reserve any rights of review, would see any part of this until the material was public. No quotes or transcripts were ever approved.

This put the responsibility for scrupulousness wholly upon myself. I've talked with individuals—key people, central to the narrative— who expressed the wish never to be mentioned. Most haven't been. Others, while listed, have been more forthright than perhaps they ought, and while I've used their information, I've protected their identities. Mostly, I've let the burliest among these movers and shakers talk directly for themselves. Thanks to you all:

Agnew, Sir Geoffrey
Antenucci, Dr. Arthur
Arkus, Leon
Balding, Ian
Barr, Joseph
Barrett, John
Baskett, John
Beddall, Thomas
Bovard, James
Brown, Carter
Bruce, David
Buchanan, John
Burrell, Constance
Cairns, Huntington
Carrithers, Catherine
  (Mellon)
Claire, Helen
Crimmins, John
Cunningham, James
Day, Richard
Denton, Frank
Doyle, John H.
Drake, J. F.
Eddy, Jane
Evans, Thomas M.
Finley, David
Fleming, Harold
Freeman, David
Garrison, William L.
Gotlieb, Dr. H. B.
Greenway, Lauder (G. L.)
Grove, John
Halsey, Marnie
Hazlett, Theodore
Heard, John
Henderson, George

Hennessey, Thomas
Hershey, Dale
Higby, Leon
Hillman, Mrs. Henry
Hitchcock, Aurora
Hitchcock, Jane
Hitchcock, Mrs. Thomas
Hitchcock, William
Horne, Mrs. Joseph
Howes, Barbara
Hughes, Joseph
Knox, William
Lawry, Catherine
Lawry, Robert
Lubove, Roy
Madigan, James
Mathiesen, Andrew
May, Cordelia
McGovern, John
Mellon, Constance
Mellon, Gwendolyn
Mellon, James
Mellon, Matthew
Mellon, Paul
Mellon, Rachel ("Bunny")
Mellon, Richard P.
Mellon, Seward P.
Mellon, Timothy
Mellon, Dr. William L.
Moorhead, William
O'Gara, Robert
Osborne, Ernest
Patman, Wright
Pearson, Nathan
Pease, Robert
Pemberton, Louis

Pillsbury, Edmund
Pusey, Nathan
Robin, John
Rodd, William
Rodewald, Paul
Ryskamp, Charles
Sawyer, John
Scaife, Richard
Schlesinger, Arthur, Jr.
Schmidt, Adolph
Schoyer, William
Simon, John
Smith, J. Kellum
Snelgrove, Dudley
Stevens, Stoddard
Taber, George

Taylor, Harvey
Thaw, Eugene
Thornburgh, Richard
Titus, Paul
Trice, Mrs. Harley
Walker, John
Walsh, Mason
Walton, James
Walton, Mrs. John
Warner, John
Webb, G. Arthur
Weidlein, Edward
White, Christopher
Wissman, William
Wyckoff, George

In libraries all around the East, I put in many of the months it took me to figure out what questions to ask. The archivists and researchers everywhere were competent—invaluable—and I'd like to recognize that here. Most useful were the major libraries of New Hampshire, Baker Library at Dartmouth and the State Library at Concord, the libraries at Harvard and Yale (main, legal and business), the Library of Congress (especially the wonderful photographic collection), and the New York City Public Library. In Mother Pittsburgh the archives of the major Mellon companies proved valuable, and the resources of the Hillman Library and the Darlington Collection filled many gaps. As I got into the later cross-checking and photograph-locating phases of this project, professionals in the Carnegie Library, around the morgues of the *Pittsburgh Press* and *The Pittsburgh Post Gazette*, and upstairs in the stacks of the Western Pennsylvania Historical Society all pitched in and turned over whatever they had. Individual editors and seasoned library personnel themselves occasionally put me onto a track worth pursuing.

Beyond interview subjects, I'd like to thank the people who made a special personal effort to help with the coordination of this book. I am forever grateful to Bob and Kathy Lawry, who provided me a first, shaky foothold in Pittsburgh. I would also like to thank the efficient Mrs. Gellert and the efficient Mrs. Eberhardt, secretaries respectively to Frank Denton and George Wyckoff, both of whom at various times found their lives complicated by my metronomic appearances. The same, only more so, to Dorothy Hervey of Paul Mellon's Washington office, as well as Caroline Wells and Martha Tross. I am also grateful to Messers. Spencer and Knight of the Public Files Section of the Internal Revenue Service, who repeatedly tracked down and made available to me the thousands of pages of testimony taken during the Mellon tax trial.

Closer to home, I've appreciated the clerical assistance of Marjorie Ginepra and JoAnn Ginepra Saxby and Susan Cochran and Roger Rath, and the extended typing stints, often under the pressure of deadlines, by Paula Rose, Joanne Isgett, Dorothea Baytosh and Sandra Burrows. Good friends—Charles Gaines, Peter Sylvester and George Wilson—have read this material through several drafts to suggest and encourage, as has my long-suffering editor, James Landis. And most of all, in every category, throughout, again, thanks to my durable wife, Ellen.

The continuum of photographs threaded throughout this work verges on alternative narrative, shadow to written substance. Many readers may feel I've got this backward. The pictures came in from various and unexpected sources. Numbers of the best, the freshest, were loaned by members of the Mellon family. Paul Mellon, and Matt and Jay Mellon, turned over personal archives of photographs very few of which other Mellons will see until they open this book. I used these greedily.

Three professionals at Morrow were comforting in particular during our terminal production agonies. Carl Weiss designed this book and laid it out; in certain central respects he understands it better than I ever can. Maria Guarnaschelli suffered liaison. Jean Luetzow, patient soul, mothered all the changes through revisions of revisions. Gratefully.

B.H.

INDEX